NEW FRONTIERS OF CONSUMER PROTECTION

NEW FRONTIERS OF CONSUMER PROTECTION

The Interplay Between Private and Public Enforcement

Fabrizio Cafaggi
Hans-W. Micklitz
(eds.)

intersentia
Antwerp – Oxford – Portland

Distribution for the UK:
Hart Publishing Ltd.
16C Worcester Place
Oxford OX1 2JW
UK
Tel.: +44 1865 51 75 30
Fax: +44 1865 51 07 10

Distribution for Switzerland and Germany:
Schulthess Verlag
Zwingliplatz 2
CH-8022 Zürich
Switzerland
Tel.: +41 1 251 93 36
Fax: +41 1 261 63 94

Distribution for the USA and Canada:
International Specialized Book Services
920 NE 58th Ave Suite 300
Portland, OR 97213
USA
Tel.: +1 800 944 6190 (toll free)
Tel.: +1 503 287 3093
Fax: +1 503 280 8832
Email: info@isbs.com

Distribution for other countries:
Intersentia Publishers
Groenstraat 31
BE-2640 Mortsel
Belgium
Tel.: +32 3 680 15 50
Fax: +32 3 658 71 21

New Frontiers of Consumer Protection. The Interplay Between Private and Public Enforcement
Fabrizio Cafaggi and Hans-W. Micklitz (eds.)

ISBN 978-90-5095-778-6
D/2009/7849/8
NUR 828

TABLE OF CONTENTS

PART V. CONCLUSION

INTRODUCTION

Fabrizio CAFAGGI and Hans-W. MICKLITZ*

1. THE FRAME

Consumer law is evolving rapidly under the combined pressure of increasing market integration and risk interdependency.[1] Consumer protection has become the keystone of effective market regulation. It regulates entry and exit of market products and services.[2] Enforcement of consumer laws is not only a key regulatory question when it comes to designing and implementing efficient markets but it triggers a broader set of theoretical questions concerning the relationship between states and markets and the combination of centralized and decentralized strategies.[3] It concerns public and private enforcement or, more precisely, administrative and judicial enforcement.[4] In Europe the conventional distinction between public and private enforcement, while rooted in a long-lasting tradition, does not capture the current state of affairs since judicial enforcement is sought by both public and private claimants and administrative enforcement is strongly

* This book develops out of a broader project that the two editors are carrying on in collaboration with NYU law school, in particular with Samuel Issacharoff and Geoffrey Miller. It was made possible also by the institutional support of the RSCAS and ALI which the authors gratefully acknowledge.

1 The definition and domain of consumer law differs in North America and Europe. In North America it is a combination of common and statutory law, and state or province and federal law. In Europe, it is also a combination of state judge made and statutory law (considering the UK and Ireland) but primarily a system which includes European and Member State laws.

2 At this level of generality, there seems to be higher convergence than in the past between US and Europe. Compare in this volume Issacharoff and Samuel, p. 4 ff. with Cafaggi and Micklitz, p. 357 ff.

3 We adopt a broad definition of enforcement in order to encompass the different forms in the area of judicial and administrative enforcement. While the focus is judicial dispute resolution mechanisms, we have considered different forms of alternative dispute resolution and arbitration which is ever growing in the field of consumer protection. See F. Cafaggi and H. Micklitz, Collective enforcement of consumer law: a framework for comparative assessment ERPL, 2008, p. 391 part. p. 396 ff.

4 On the relationship between public and private enforcement, see A. Ogus, Better regulation, better enforcement, in S. Weatherill (ed.) Better regulation, Hart Publishing, Oxford and Portland, 2007, p. 107 ff. Ogus, Costs and cautionary tales: economic insights for the law, Hart Publishing, Oxford and Portland, 2006, S. Shavell, Foundations of the Economic Analysis of Law, 2004, p. 445 ff. and M. Polinsky and S. Shavell, The Economic Theory of Public Enforcement of Law, J. Econ. Lit., Vol. 38, p. 45 (2000).

affected, *de jure* or *de facto*, by the role of private organisations.[5] An integrated strategy to combine remedies to deter and remedies to compensate is therefore needed. To pursue this goal, the definition of general principles including both divisible and indivisible remedies is necessary.

Consumer law's enforcement operates within a multilevel system that includes several layers: national, European and international, often diverging as to principles and practices. Multi-level systems require coordination both constitutional and institutional. They might also permit some degree of vertical and horizontal competition but within an integrated frame of rules.

Several goals lie behind enforcement strategies in consumer protection: those of private litigants may not always overlap those of public enforcers.[6] The core analysis is generally on deterrence and compensation of aggregate litigation and administrative enforcement, focusing on the institutional modes through which they can be reconciled when conflicts between the two goals arise.[7] In particular, while deterrence is a primary objective of public enforcers, it is only a secondary objective of private litigants, where claimants are primarily interested in seeking compensation. Appropriate institutional design calls for responses that ensure consistency among different enforcement strategies, maximize complementarities and minimize redundancy.

A starting point in the book is that the policy focus should not only be on the choice between administrative and judicial enforcement but also on the different components of judicial enforcement. In this framework the search for the optimal combination between injunctions and damages where size of claims and nature of losses are very important, may shift the balance between the two functions from compensation to deterrence or vice versa.[8]

A second premise is the adoption of a broad notion of enforcement including not only litigation but also negotiated agreements concerning dispute resolution.[9]

---

5 See F. Cafaggi and H. Micklitz, Collective enforcement of consumer law: a framework for comparative assessment cit., p. 391.

6 See I. Segal and M. Whinston, Public *versus* private enforcement of antitrust law: a survey, ECLR, 2007, 28(5) p. 306 ff.; C. Hodges, The reform of class and representative actions in European legal systems. A new framework for collective redress in Europe, Hart Publishing, Oxford – Portland, 2008, p. 223 *et seq.*

7 This is the key question asked by G. Miller in this volume. See G. Miller, Compensation and deterrence in consumer class actions in the United States and Europe, p. 263. See also S. Issacharoff, Group litigation of consumer claims: lessons from the US Experience, Tex. Int'l. L.J. vol. 34, p. 135 (1999).

8 See J. Coffee, Private Securities Litigation Reform Act: Reforming the Securities Class Action: An Essay on Deterrence and Its Implementation, Col.L.R., Vol. 109, p. 1534 (2006).

9 In this context Art. 4 of Directive 98/27 should be read as indicating that MS can impose/suggest prior consultation before starting litigation.

Litigation is seen not only as a means to seek remedies but also as a device to trigger negotiations among collective entities. From this perspective, litigation is aimed not only at settling the specific dispute but also at inducing behavioural changes through settlements concerning future behaviour. Settlements have become the preferred solutions in aggregate litigation but the risks of abuse at the expense of injured consumers require strong judicial review and *ex ante* regulation.[10]

In both Europe and North America, important changes are taking place. These changes pertain to the changing balance between central or federal and state level but also to the increasing importance of administrative enforcement in the US and the growing role of adjudication through aggregate litigation in Europe. The European context provides interesting additional puzzles, given the partially divergent developments of the relationship between public and private enforcement in consumer and competition law.

In competition law, the White Paper of the EC Commission endorses the institutional complementarity approach between public and private enforcement, where only damages not injunctions are considered.[11] The White Paper reflects an institutional design where deterrence is the primary goal of public enforcement while compensation should be primarily ensured by private enforcement.[12] It suggests the adoption of two complementary solutions: representative and opt-in collective actions.[13] It distinguishes between the stand-alone and follow-on relationship by recognising the binding effect of public enforcers' decisions in private litigation. The policy recommendations for MS concerning settlements and litigation costs are noteworthy.[14]

---

10 See J.R. Macey and J.P. Miller, Judicial review of class action settlements, J. Legal Analysis, vol. 1, p. 167 (2009), S. Issacharoff and R. Nagareda, Class settlements under attack, U. Pa. L. R., vol. 156, p. 1650 (2008).

11 See the White paper on damages actions for breach of EC antitrust rules, COM (2008) 165 final.

12 See W. P.J. Wils, The relationship between public antitrust enforcement and private action for damages, World competition, vol. 32,1, March 2009, p. 3, C. Hodges, The reform of class and representative actions in European legal systems. A new framework for collective redress in Europe. cit., supra at note 6, pp. 203 and 242.

13 "The Commission suggests a combination of two complementary mechanisms of collective redress ...

1. Representative actions, which are brought by qualified entities, such as consumer associations, state bodies or trade associations, on behalf of identifiable victims
2. Opt-in collective actions, in which victims expressly decide to combine their individual claims for harm they suffered into one single action"

White paper on damages actions for breach of EC antitrust rules, COM (2008) 165 final p. 3.

14 "The Commission therefore encourages member states

- to design procedural rules fostering settlements, as a way to reduce costs
- to set court fees in an appropriate manner so that they do not become a disproportionate disincentive to antitrust damages claims

In relation to collective consumer redress, legislative reforms are taking place at national level and European intervention has also been considered.[15] National reforms have introduced opt-in systems with very few exceptions.[16] The European Commission has recently published a Green Paper where different policy options are set out.[17] The Green Paper suggests the need to intervene also at EU level, encompassing both transborder and domestic litigation. In addition, legislative reform on consumer contract law has been proposed without considering the collective remedial issues.[18]

Furthermore, in the field of private international law, attention should be given to the enactment of Regulation 593/2008 (Rome I) concerning contract and Regulation 864/2007 (Rome II) related to non-contractual liability claims, which define private international law rules influencing cross-border consumer protection.[19] Regrettably, these rules are mainly conceived for individual litigation and do not specifically address issues of collective redress.[20] The selection of applicable law is not specified in Injunction Directive EC 98/27 as well, rendering the choice between the place where the infringement took place and that where the effects of the unlawful conduct occurred difficult.[21]

These legal transformations not only influence the internal institutional balance but also affect the strategic choices of claimants and defendants to choose the forum and initiate litigation in the US or in Europe - given that these two

---

– to give the national courts the possibility of issuing cost orders derogating, in certain justified cases, from the normal cost rules, preferably upfront in the proceedings." White paper on damages in antitrust, p. 10.

15 For a detailed analysis in this book see Stuyck p. 63 and Cafaggi and Micklitz, p. 357.

16 See for example Bulgaria. For a specific analysis, see A. Bakardjeva, Public and private enforcement of consumer law in the member states from CEE countries: institutional choice in the shadow of enlargement, in this volume p. 91 ff.

17 Cf. Green paper on consumer collective redress, Bruxelles, 27.11.2008, COM (2008)794 final.

18 Proposal of a directive on consumer rights 8 October 2008; see H.-W. Micklitz and N. Reich, Protection or pre-emption: the Commission Proposal for a "Directive on consumer rights", CMLR 2009 forthcoming.

19 In particular Article 6 which is not thought to be appropriate for collective disputes; see N. Reich in H.-W. Micklitz/P. Rott/N. Reich, Understanding EU Consumer Law, Intersentia, Antwerp – Oxford – Portland, 2009, 7.17 and under 5.

20 See on the potential solutions parr. 59 and 60 of the Green paper on collective consumer redress.

21 See Report from the Commission concerning the application of Directive 98/27 of the European Parliament and of the Council on injunctions for the protection of consumers, Brussels, 18.11.2008 COM (2008) 756 final par. 24 " The issue of applicable law is thus fundamental in all instances where there is a choice between two different bodies of legislation offering different degrees of protection". In one of the two cases brought by OFT "both the court of first instance and the court of appeal examined this question, and the court of first instance applied British law, whilst the court of appeal decided that Belgian law was applicable". See on the only case decided under the Directive, H.-W. Micklitz, Transborder Law Enforcement – Does it exist? in Ulf Bernitz/Stephen Weatherill (eds.), The Regulation of Unfair Commercial Practices under EC Directive, New Rules and New Techniques, Hart Publishing, Oxford – Portland, 2006, pp. 235–254 and in more detail infra, p. 29 ff.

geographical areas are increasingly interdependent as shown by the recent litigation on financial and banking issues.[22]

On closer inspection, changes relevant to consumer protection are modifying the role of traditional players, eroding national distinctions that have characterized the post-WWII landscape.

In the field of consumer protection, a distinction, within judicial enforcement, should be made between injunctions and pecuniary remedies. Injunctions are regulated at EU level through Directive 98/27, and other Directives related to specific areas such as those on unfair contract terms and commercial practices, which are included in the Annex to Directive 98/27.[23] On the other hand, collective redress concerning damages is still mainly regulated at State level by new legislation.

Administrative enforcement is mainly regulated by Consumer Protection Cooperation Regulation 2006/2004 and it includes powers to require the cessation or prohibition of any intra-community violations.[24] The focus of administrative enforcement is on infringements concerning collective interests of consumers while, at least in the current interpretation, it would not apply to individual homogeneous interests of multiple consumers.[25] While the focus of administrative enforcement is mainly on deterrence, different forms of compensation have recently been associated with public enforcement at State level. On the one hand, there is the experience of Nordic Ombudsmen, who have been given power to seek compensation. On the other hand, national public regulators formally able to impose fines have been using their enforcement power in order to 'persuade'

22 Less interchange ability has occurred in the field of product liability and safety.

23 See Article 7 Dir. 93/13 and Article 11 Dir. 2005/29. To the initial annex where 8 directives were listed, 5 additional directives have been added: 1999/44 on certain aspects of the sale of consumer goods and associated guarantees, 2000/31 on electronic commerce, 2002/65 on the distance marketing of consumer financial services, 2005/29 on unfair commercial practices and 2006/123 on services. The applicability of injunctions to consumer rights is quite diffused although there are still fields not covered.
While in most MSs the injunction directive is applied to economic losses in some countries such as Italy it has been extended to personal injury claims and product safety.

24 See Article 3 Reg. 2006/2004. It should be clarified that Injunction Directive 98/27 left MSs free to choose between administrative and judicial enforcement or both. While old MSs chose predominantly judicial enforcement new MSs often choose both. See Bakardjieva, in this volume p. 92 ff.

25 On the notion of consumer collective interest compare Recital 2 of Directive 98/27/EC: 'whereas collective interests mean interests which do not include the cumulation of interests of individuals who have been harmed by an infringement.' Article 3(k) of the Regulation 2006/2004: "'collective interests of consumers' means the interests of a number of consumers that have been harmed or are likely to be harmed by an infringement." See Green paper on consumer collective redress, cit. par. 45 proposing under option 3 the possibility that compensation be asked by public authorities which have detected infringements. In this volume, see Safjan, Gorywoda and Jańczuk, p. 171 ff.

enterprises 'spontaneously' to compensate injured consumers or to adopt restitutionary measures.[26]

The European landscape is thus characterized by a fragmented strategy that separates substantive and procedural matters and, within remedies, addresses separately injunctive relief and damages with important differences between new and old MSs.

These changes also affect other parts of the world from South America to Asia.[27] Law reforms in these countries are, to some degree, the result of legal transplants from west to east, from north to south, but to a greater extent the outcome of endogenous developments, giving rise to new forms of regulation of consumer protection in each area. These changes have also attracted the attention of institutional organisations which have put forth recommendations.[28] In this framework, differences concerning both rules (procedural and substantive) and policies (financing litigation) may provide competitive advantages to one forum over the other. World leadership in litigation may have significant impact on economic trade and location policies, given the application of conflict of law rules.[29]

It is beyond the scope of this book to engage into a comprehensive comparative analysis of different enforcement systems across the world. Such self-restraint does not imply that global factors, affecting market integration, should not be considered, even when focusing on part of the western world. The growing rate of imported consumer goods from South America and East Asia in Europe and the US, including food, are bringing about important changes in the strategies of Europe and North America, in particular with respect to striking the right balance between administrative and judicial control. But certainly, the higher level of interdependency of service provisions, especially those associated with ICT, is having a strong influence on litigation strategies across the Atlantic. On the one hand, local enforcement tends to shift from judicial to administrative calibrations, on the other hand, global enforcement primarily relies on adjudication mainly due to a lack of effective administrative global entities able to enforce the regulations.[30]

26 See for some illustrations C. Hodges, Reform of class and representative actions, supra at note 6, p. 216 ff. and 228 ff.

27 See for Argentina E. Oteiza, Procesos colectivos, Rubinzal Culzoni, Mendoza, 2006.

28 OECD Recommendations on consumer dispute resolution and redress 2007 available at www.oecd.org accessed on 27 December 2008.

29 See R. Nagareda, Aggregate litigation across the Atlantic and the future of American exceptionalism, Vanderbilt L.R. Vol. 62, p. 1 (2009).

30 A different conclusion should be drawn if the focus is on rule making, where the role of international organisations is growing at the expense of regional entities such as US and Europe. In the field of consumer protection there is a growing body of transnational law with independent enforcement bodies. See in relation to global administrative law R. Stewart, The

2. THE QUESTIONS

Laws of aggregate litigation in Europe are emerging outside a uniform path.[31] We have asked what relationship exists between this new legislation in European Member States and the US model. Which combination of deterrence and compensation will be achieved? Are tensions similar to those present in the US likely to arise in Europe, confronting courts with dilemmas pertaining to higher deterrence and greater inequality in compensation?[32]

This book focuses on the relationship between administrative and judicial collective enforcement of consumer law in Europe and North America. It addresses some strategic issues in a comparative study looking at the complementarity between administrative and judicial enforcement and the role of the institutional framework to explain differences and similarities between EU, US and Canada.[33] It reinterprets the opt-in/opt-out alternative in the light of the relationship between judicial and administrative enforcement, asking whether the choice of opt-out systems in judicial enforcement strengthens or weakens the institutional complementarity.

In particular the contributions focus on the following: (1) The different roles of lawyers and associations as main drivers of judicial enforcement but also as increasingly relevant players in administrative enforcement when it departs from command and control. (Specifically, questions of legitimacy, representation and accountability are discussed to explain the emergence of different systems within Europe and across the Atlantic.) 2) The various combinations between centralized and decentralized enforcement within multilevel systems. (3) The institutional dimension concerning the relationship between *ex ante* and *ex post* intervention

---

Global Regulatory Challenge to United States Administrative Law, N.Y.U.J. Int'l. L. & Pol., vol. 37, p. 695 (2005) and B. Kingsbury, N. Krisch, R. Stewart & J.B. Wiener, Foreward: Global Governance as Administration National and Transnational Approaches to Global Administrative Law, Law and Contemporary Problems, vol. 68, p. 1 (2005).

31 See F. Cafaggi and H. Micklitz, Collective enforcement of consumer law, supra at note 3, p. 421 ff.

32 On these questions see G. Miller, Compensation and deterrence in consumer class actions in the United States and Europe, in this volume p. 263 ff., and S. Issacharoff and G. Miller, Will aggregate litigation come to Europe?, Vanderbilt L.R., vol. 62, 179 (2009). In the European setting see R. Van den Bergh and L. Vischer, The preventive function of collective action in consumer law, Erasmus Law Review, I, 27 ff. (2008) and G. Betlem, Public and private transnational enforcement of EU consumer law, European Business L.R., vol. 18, p. 683 (2007).

33 See in relation to consumer protection F. Cafaggi, Rethinking institutional complementarities, in F. Cafaggi, The institutional framework of European private law, Oxford University Press, New York – Oxford, 2006, p. 191, in relation to insurance E. Helland and J. Klick, The tradeoffs between regulation and litigation: Evidence from insurance class actions, Journal of tort law, vol. 1, Article: 2, 2007, in relation to corporate law J. Armour, B. Black, B. Cheffins and R. Nolan, Private enforcement of corporate law: An empirical comparison of the US and UK, working paper available on www.ssrn.com.

both in judicial and administrative enforcement.[34] (In particular, the analysis concentrates on the implications coming from allowing within judicial enforcement *in abstracto* and *in concreto* control.) (4). The functional perspective, especially the combination and potential tensions between deterrence and compensation; on the one hand the use of both fines and damages and their effects on deterrence, and on the other hand the distinction between administrative and judicial injunctions. (5) The rationales for distinguishing between domestic and cross-border or diversity litigation.

This analysis is carried out by incorporating the relevant differences concerning the institutional frameworks: the strong emphasis on the private attorney general model in the US, the significant role of private associations and public entities bringing private law remedies before courts in Europe. It suggests that enacting new rules borrowed from other legal systems without adjusting the institutional framework and addressing policies concerning the modes of financing, monitoring and settling litigation is bound to fail.[35]

The project has built on some assumptions developed by the editors in earlier joint work: judicial and administrative enforcement strategies are complementary.[36] Complementarity operates across distinct domains: functional and institutional.

Functional complementarity entails not only strategies to combine deterrence and compensation but also different instruments to achieve deterrence: i.e. the combined use of injunctions and damages. It signifies a combination between *ex ante* and *ex post* strategies and the ability to vary them across time. Shifting enforcement from *ex ante* to *ex post* may permit entry liberalization, leaving pre-market authorization only for specific and riskier products or services. On the contrary, giving *ex ante* power to monitor and control by increasing the role of injunctive relief may increase deterrence and reduce the need of 'after the harm's' intervention.

Institutional complementarity means a coexistence of courts and administrative entities to enforce consumer legislation.[37] It requires coordination between agencies and courts but also control through judicial review.[38]

34 When in *abstracto* judicial control is admitted the differences with *ex ante* administrative control are smaller than contexts in which only *in concreto* judicial control is admitted.

35 Financing enforcement is a key policy question which affects both the combination of public and private enforcement but also the model of adjudication, in particular whether predominantly funded by the market or by the State.

36 See F. Cafaggi and H. Micklitz, Collective enforcement of consumer law supra at note 3, p. 393 ff. In this volume for similar considerations, see Issacharoff and Samuel, p. 5, A. Bakardjeva, p. 133 ff.

37 Complementarity permits focusing on the different functions of remedies; the relationship between injunction and damages and the role of hybrids; in particular the use of affirmative injunctions as a means to eliminate harmful effects as well as to prevent future illicit conduct.

38 See on these questions in this volume S. Issacharoff and I. Samuel, p. 47 ff., C. Sharkey, p. 139 ff., A. Bakardjeva, p. 91 ff.

Complementarity may for example imply that public enforcers may be better able to detect output standard while private litigants may perform better with input standards or that private litigants pave the way for administrative enforcement.[39] It denotes an efficient design to define the relationship between administrative and judicial ability to detect and to punish violations. The procedural sequence of enforcement is very relevant to foster the right incentives to produce information cost-effectively.[40] In some cases, the binding effects of decisions by public enforcers over private litigation may permit sequential information gathering to promote efficient monitoring over enterprises thus reducing detection costs. But the sequential model can also occur in private enforcement, where claimants seeking injunctions are moving first, and agencies, through, public enforcement are following and issuing fines. An appropriate institutional design should distinguish between simultaneous and sequential combination of public and private enforcement to ensure that the highest level of information is generated at the lowest social cost.[41]

Settlements play a very significant role in the US and a growing one in Europe. However, it is unclear whether the opt-in/opt-out alternative will affect both the ratio between settlements and trial and the function of the settlements. Settlements' regulation and its judicial oversight represent necessary parts of the legal framework in relation to judicial and, to a growing extent, even to administrative enforcement.[42] As the European competition field shows, settlements between the public authority and enterprises are becoming more common and rules concerning the settlement and its transparency are needed.[43] While the different frequency of settlements in the US and Europe is commonly acknowledged, we have assumed that one of the likely outcomes of litigation is settlement and thus considered its implications for the combination of judicial and administrative enforcement.

The complementarity is influenced by the different socio-economic structure and the set of incentives provided by the institutional multilevel framework: still mainly State-based in Europe, but more balanced between federal and State level in the US. In particular, we assume (1) the strategic relevance of the existence or absence of a competitive market for legal services and (2) the strong/weak presence of consumer associations and their level of (in)dependence from political power.

---

39 See in particular with regard to competition law in a EU-US comparison, Ch. Hodges, The reform of class and representative action, supra, note 6, p. 155 *et seq.*

40 See in this volume F. Cafaggi and H.W. Micklitz, Administrative and judicial enforcement in consumer protection, the way forward, p. 401 ff.

41 For a more detailed analysis, see F. Cafaggi, Cooperative enforcement, paper presented at NYU/ALI Conference on class actions, Firenze, June 2008.

42 The Dutch law constitutes an example of a detailed regulation concerning settlements, court's approval and opt-out provisions. On these questions see E. Hondius in this volume p. 235, www.globalclassactions.stanford.edu, The Netherlands: I. Tzankova.

43 See the Commission Communication on settlements OJC 167 2.7.2008.

In this book, the main institutional differences not only between Europe and the US but also within Europe are examined, in particular by articulating the distinctions between western and eastern countries and by addressing the new issues posed by enforcement policies to new democracies.[44] The role of the bar and that of consumer organisations has been considered a key question in the analysis of enforcement strategies, the conditions for success and failure. Consumer protection has acquired a constitutional dimension in many MSs. It is interesting to note the differences between some post-communist and some post-fascist countries.[45] The former have emphasized the obligations of the State to protect consumers, the latter have recognised powers for citizens and private organisations.

We have asked whether the changes brought by the introduction of broader forms of aggregate litigation in Europe will modify global litigation strategies. In particular, if there is reason to believe that more litigation will be initiated in Europe and then brought to the US or whether there will continue to be a strong dominance of the US as the litigation forum. Furthermore, we have asked whether deeper integration of enforcement policies between the US and Europe will empower transnational law firms and lawyer-based systems at the expense of institutional settings organized around consumer organisations to monitor compliance with consumer law.[46] In other words, will the globalisation of enforcement strategies favour the dominance of a market-oriented, litigation-based system at the expense of an administrative/corporatist system? In this respect, we ask whether the growth of group and representative actions in European MSs can be seen as a response to globalization rather than an attempt to distinguish a European model from the US.

Within the European analysis, particular attention has been paid to the specificity of new MSs in relation to enforcement policies.[47] In these countries, the implementation of the consumer *Acquis* has generated in these countries profound changes both in institutional and substantive terms.[48] Clearly, conditionality has reduced the domain of procedural autonomy and emphasized the interdependence between substantive and procedural matters.[49] Unlike

---

44 See S. Rose Ackerman, From elections to democracy. Building accountable government in Hungary and Poland, Cambridge University Press, New York, Cambridge, 2005.

45 In relation to post-communist see Poland, Latvia and Bulgaria, in relation to post-fascist see Spain and Portugal constitutional provisions.

46 For a comparison focusing on the institutional dimension, see F. Cafaggi and H. Micklitz, Collective enforcement of consumer law supra, note 3.

47 As the three contributions by Tichy and Balarin, Safjan, Gorywoda and Janczuk and Bakardjeva show, CEEC give great importance to the notion of consumer collective interest as a legal tool to differentiate between individual and collective enforcement.

48 In the view of Bakardjeva "... transposing the Acquis has implied both open and covert influence over institutional choice". See Bakardjeva in this volume p. 93.

49 See Bakardjeva in this volume p. 99 showing how the Copenhagen criteria and the White Paper on enlargement identified the institutional dimension of the consumer Acquis as a

injunctions, which were part of the consumer *Acquis*, class actions have been introduced by some eastern European countries independently from European influence. The presence of specific institutional factors related to the 'legal family' and twinning projects, influencing remedies and enforcement strategies in consumer law, has generated divergent patterns, producing further differentiation within CEEC. While the European approach after enlargement has been uniform towards CEEC, the analysis suggests that specific territorial strategies, concerning enforcement policies, might take place. We then ask if there is reason to believe that, in the near future, a more provincial approach should be considered in order to accommodate difficulties that similar countries face concerning enforcement policies. The ability to reach a more sophisticated approach to institutional differences may trigger differentiated policies aimed at improving the ability of networks of consumer associations to engage in monitoring and litigation or to promote a competitive market for legal services in a regional dimension beyond the boundaries of MSs but below those of the EU.[50]

Given the changes currently taking place in the Europe and the US we believe that a different comparative approach is needed, to analyse separately the issue of transatlantic litigation and that of consumer enforcement policies as part of the architecture of contemporary regulatory states. Introducing consideration about financing litigation, comparing the costs and benefits of judicial and administrative enforcement, considering the different path of democratic growth that consumer enforcement may bring about in new democracies, developing policies that increase human capital together with deterrence and compensation should be at the heart of policy choices that Europe and North America face in the years to come.

3. PUBLIC/PRIVATE ENFORCEMENT IN A MULTI-LEVEL STRUCTURE – THE US, CANADA AND EUROPE COMPARED

Public/private enforcement in a multi-level structure such as those operating in the EU and the US adds a further dimension to the proper choice of enforcement devices. From a political point of view, the question is how to determine the proper level of enforcement, national-state and/or European-federal. The answer is very much tied to the constitutional frame of the respective multi-level structure. The EU is neither a state nor a federation, although it bears elements of a state and

strategic pillar of implementation which was then translated into Accession Agreements and twinning projects.

50 See the Consumer Law Enforcement Forum (CLEF) co-financed by BEUC and the European Commission, www.clef.org.

although it resembles a federation. Contrary to the US, the EU has not developed a fully fledged federal structure with its own procedural rules neither at the judicial nor at the administrative level. Enforcement of EC law still lies primarily in the hands of national courts and administrations.[51] The normative dimension focuses on where to establish enforcement mechanisms at the state or the EU level. It begets a whole set of theoretical issues on the appropriate governance structure of the European Union.[52]

For our purposes emphasis shall be put on the hybrid character[53] of the current EU multi-level structure which combines elements of national and EU law both in administrative and in judicial enforcement. The hybrid character results from the fact that the EU Treaty does not provide clear-cut answers as to who is competent for what at what level in the EU, but leaves room for secondary law-making and European judicial activism. The amended Article 3a) of the Lisbon Treaty will state that 'competences not conferred upon the Union in the Treaties remain within the Member States', subject to the principle of loyalty stated in the same article.[54] Whether such a new ruling will solve the problems which result from the undetermined boundaries of where the powers of the EU end and where those of the Member States begin, remains to be seen. The purposive character of the EU, with its focus on market integration, makes such an uncoupling of national and EU enforcement strategies difficult, even more so as the Lisbon Treaty will not establish a constitutional frame for the EU. For the time being, the development is characterized by intrusive EU legislation which incrementally installs a European administrative enforcement structure, thereby introducing slowly and gradually a proper EU enforcement level to the detriment of Member States level, maybe even collective EU remedies and an active ECJ which has made its proper contribution to the hybrid character of the current EU multi-level structure.

From a historical perspective, the path-breaking function of Directive 92/59/EC on product safety as revised by Directive 2001/95/EC should not be underestimated.[55] The there-developed mechanisms on the interplay of national and EU administrative enforcement have served as a blueprint for the adoption of

---

51 See now F. Cafaggi/H.-W. Micklitz, Collective enforcement of consumer law supra, at note 3.

52 There is an overwhelming literature on this subject, which will not be discussed here. From a private law perspective, see F. Cafaggi/H. Muir-Watt (eds.) Making European Private Law, Governance Design, Elgar, Cheltenham Northampton, Mass., 2008.

53 N. Reich, Horizontal Liability in EC Law, Hybridisation of remedies for compensation of breach of EC rights, CMLRev., 2007, p. 705 ff.

54 For Temple Lang, this is the key obligation of the Member States, Article 10 EC- The Most Important General Principle of Community Law, in: U. Bernitz et al. (eds.), General Principles of EC Law in a Process of Development, Kluwer, Austin, 2008, 75.

55 H.-W. Micklitz/Th. Roethe/St. Weatherill (eds.), Federalism and Responsibility – A study on Product Safety Law and Practice in the European Community, Graham & Trotmann, London, 1994.

Regulation 765/2008[56] on market surveillance which covers (mainly technical) products outside regulated markets where more specific administrative structures have been employed.[57] The regulatory philosophy behind this reflects a common European policy: MSs are pushed to set up appropriate, competent and well-equipped national enforcement authorities.[58] The degree of federalization depends on the degree and interdependence of danger. Normally national enforcement authorities are only obliged to co-operate between themselves and with the European Commission via information exchange and in case of need via mutual administrative assistance with their national counterparts.[59] In the case of serious danger to the health and safety of consumers, however, the regulatory powers of the European Commission are considerably broader.[60] The European Commission can take regulatory measures along the line of the emergency procedure spelt out in Article 12 of Directive 2001/95/EC on consumer safety within the comitology procedure.[61] In the US, such powers are mainly vested in the Consumer Product Safety and to some extent in the FTC and the FDA Commission.[62] Transparency on the available and competent market surveillance authorities shall be guaranteed via a notification procedure under which Member States are obliged to inform the European Commission about market surveillance authorities and their competences.

The field where the US and EU regulatory schemes for the organisation of administrative enforcement most closely resemble one another is the area of regulated markets. The EU approach was certainly inspired by US experience to establish independent regulators. Whereas the US granted powers to federal agencies, the EU was bound to leave them in the hands of national agencies. The higher degree of federalization has taken place within the comitology and the Lamfalussy procedure which is gaining pace with the more recent EC proposals to create regulatory powers at the EU level independent of the European Commission.[63] Outside regulated markets, the EU does not seem to have the intention to centralize administrative enforcement in the field of consumer law.

---

56 OJ L 218, 13.8.2008, 30.

57 For a detailed analysis, see F. Cafaggi, Standard Setting in Regulation and Civil Liability, in F. Cafaggi and H. Muir Watt, The regulatory functions of European private law, Elgar, Cheltenham Northampton, Mass., 2009.

58 See Article 18 (4), Member States shall entrust market surveillance authorities with the powers, resources and knowledge, necessary for the proper performance of their tasks.

59 See Article 24(2) Reg. 765/2008.

60 See Article 20 Reg. 765/2008.

61 See Article 22(4) Reg. 765/2008.

62 Ch. Joerges, Nachmarktkontrollen im amerikanischen Recht in H.-W. Micklitz (ed.), Post Market Control of Consumer Goods, Nomos, Baden-Baden, 1990, 155.

63 See the proposals in the so-called third package on telecommunication, COM (2007) 697 and 698 final, 13.11.2007 and on energy COM (2007) 528 and 529 final, 19.9.2007.

There is no counterpart to the US Federal Trade Commission foreseen,[64] although the EU has managed to oblige Member States to establish competent administrative authorities, not necessarily in the form of an independent regulator, to strengthen conflict resolution in transborder EU consumer protection issues.[65]

The process of hybridization of remedies in the EU is even more complex. Contrary to the US, the EU managed so far only to introduce one single European collective means of redress: the action for injunction which goes back to Directive 84/450/EEC on misleading advertising before it was more prominently positioned in Directive 98/27/EC on injunctions. Its scope of application is limited. The EU product safety regulation, in particular Directive 2001/95/EC and now Regulation 765/2008 on market surveillance, does not explicitly mention the action of injunction or injunctive relief. The functional equivalent however, is to some extent the power granted to the competent authorities to ban,[66] prohibit or restrict the marketing[67] of the product and, further, to recall it from the consumer, respectively by the withdrawal of dangerous products from the market. To that extent, it might be fairly said that injunction or injunctive relief is a commonly recognised EU remedy. However, this EU remedy must be enforced by the competent national institutions, be they public bodies or in the field of unfair commercial practices and unfair terms, or consumer and/or business organisations. Only under exceptional circumstances does the regulatory power shift from the Member States to the EU Commission which can initiate EU-wide action – in case the product presents a serious risk.[68]

The presence of European legislation should not imply the existence of complete harmonization. The injunction EC Directive left many issues to MSs, which have selected different options concerning both the scope and the effect: not only with respect to the possibility to choose between administrative and judicial enforcement but also in differentiating between *in abstracto* and *in concreto* control.[69] These differences make cross-border enforcement more problematic because the same infringement by an enterprise selling to consumers located in different MSs may lead to different remedies. Two examples can

64 N. Reich, Staatliche Regulierung zwischen Marktversagen und Politikversagen – Erfahrungen mit der amerikanischen Federal Trade Commission und ihre Bedeutung für das Verbraucherschutzrecht, Müller, Heidelberg, 1984; see for an update on the US developments, by the same author, United States of America, in H.-W. Micklitz/J. Keßler (eds.), Marketing Practices Regulation and Consumer Protection in the EC Member States and the US, Band 10 der VIEW Schriftenreihe, 2002, p. 417.

65 See Regulation 2006/2004.

66 Article 21 (1) Reg. 765/2008.

67 Article 8 e) Directive 2001/95/EC.

68 Article 22 Reg. 765/2008 and Article 12 Directive 2001/95/EC.

69 *In abstracto* control occurs when regardless of any proof of harm a consumer organisation or even an individual is allowed to bring a case before a Court or an administrative agency to seek scrutiny on the unfairness of a contract or a practice. See for Poland in this volume Safjan et al., p. 171 ff.

illustrate the point: the binding nature of injunction, both temporal and spatial, including the effects of *res judicata*, and the mode of enforcement. As the Report by the EC Commission on the implementation of the directive illustrates, MSs significantly differ: some MSs limit the effects of the injunction to the litigants and deny *ultra partes* effects. Thus, the same unfair term enjoined by one court can be used by a different enterprise in the same MS and even by the same enterprise in a different state.[70] Other MSs have expanded the effect of *res judicata* in relation to injunctions to future litigation but always within the territory of the same state.[71] Proposals have been made to differentiate the effects: making it binding if the injunction is granted and allowing new lawsuits if the injunction is denied.[72] But the Commission has concluded that no legislative reform is needed.[73] Information concerning judgments in MSs is still missing despite the attempt to create a European database.[74]

In relation to the type of enforcement, Directive 98/27 left it open to both judicial and administrative solutions. The majority of MSs choose judicial

---

70 "In most Member States, a ruling on an application for an injunction has a mitigated impact. It is mandatory only with respect to the case and the parties in question, i.e. the qualified entity which brought the action and the company which is the subject of the injunction. In practice this means that if a company commits an infringement identical to that for which another company has already been convicted, a new injunction must be sought to stop the new infringement. In the same way, the annulment of an unfair term in a contract proposed by a company does not prevent the same company from continuing to use this unfair term in a similar contract." See Report from the Commission concerning the application of Directive 98/27 of the European parliament and of the Council on injunctions for the protection of consumers par. 25.

71 This has happened in relation to unfair contract terms "... in Poland, when the court in Warsaw rules that a clause in a contract is unfair, this ruling has an *erga omnes* effect. The ruling is published and applies to an identical clause in any contract proposed to consumers. In Hungary, if a court rules that a clause in a contract between a company and a consumer is unfair, it may declare this clause null and void in all contracts concluded by that company. In Austria, a clause which has been declared unfair in a contract between a company and a consumer may not be used again by the company in other contracts. In Germany and Slovenia, consumers can invoke a ruling declaring a clause unfair in order to suppress the application of an identical provision". Report on the injunctions directive cit. par. 26.
See in this book in relation to the Czech Republic, Tichy and Balarin, Efficiency of protection of collective interests, p. 167 ff.

72 See S. Chiarloni, Per la chiarezza in tema di tutela collettiva dei consumatori, Rivista di diritto processuale, 2007, p. 567 at p. 574 ff.

73 See Report from the Commission concerning the application of Directive 98/27 of the European parliament and of the Council on injunctions for the protection of consumers par. 34.

74 The European Commission had provided resources between 1995 and 2003 to build up a data file on judgments of Member State courts. The idea was that all parties concerned including courts consult the data file which was available in English and French. The project failed mainly because access to the register was much too complicated and not user friendly H.-W. Micklitz/M. Radeideh, *CLAB Europa* – Die europäische Datenbank mißbräuchlicher Klauseln in Verbraucherverträgen, ZEuP 2003, 85–113.

enforcement even if standing was given to public bodies.[75] For this reason, we shall include it within judicial and not administrative enforcement.[76] In the US, action to protect American citizens by way of regulations lies in the hands of the Consumer Product Safety Commission. As early as 1968, the United States created a modern class action procedure with the adoption of Federal Rule 23.[77] With the exception of two US States – Mississippi and Virginia – the Federal Rule 23 has either literally or substantially been introduced into the state procedural laws.[78] The recent EU initiatives from 2008 in the field of competition[79] and consumer law[80] have not (yet?) led to adoption of EU class or group action. However, the EU might take some form of co-ordinate action which brings together the diverse rulings on aggregate litigation in the MSs. Contrary to injunctions or injunctive relief, which may be taken by administrative authorities directly and by courts on the initiative of an administrative authority or a private consumer or business organisation, litigation concerning remedies generally involves courts.[81] Again, there are important differences between the US and the EU judicial system.[82] The US judiciary is based on two pillars, a coherent multi-layered federal court system with its own procedural rules and 50 different state judiciaries following their specific even though to some extent similar procedural requirements. The two systems exist largely independently from each other. If it comes down to class actions, the relatively homogeneous rules at both the federal and the state level should ideally lead to if not identical but then similar results – if we set aside that federal and state judges enjoy discretion in the interpretation of the procedural

75 See Report on the injunction directive stating that "two thirds of the Member States opted for a civil or commercial procedure, whilst only a few (Hungary, Malta, Poland and Romania, for instance) opted for a mainly administrative approach" par. 6; for a more detailed analysis see H.-W. Micklitz/ P. Rott, U. Docekal and P. Kolba, *Verbraucherschutz durch Unterlassungsklagen, Rechtliche und Praktische Umsetzung der Richtlinie Unterlassungsklagen 98/27/EG in den Mitgliedstaaten*, VIEW Schriftenreihe, Band 17, 2007.

76 It should be added that standing is granted to qualified entities including both private and public authorities that can seek injunctive relief before judges.

77 See S. Burbank, The class action fairness act of 2005 in historical context: a preliminary view, 156 U. Pa. L. R., p. 1439 (2008).

78 See.G. Miller, Punti cardine in tema di class action negli Stati Uniti ed in Italia, in AGE, Class, Action! (?), R. Lener and M. Rescigno (eds.), 1/2008, p. 211, Thomas D. Rowe, State and Foreign Class Action Rules and Statutes: Differences from – and Lessons For? – Federal Rule 23, W. St. U.L.Rev. vol. 35, 2007, p. 141. There are, however, important differences between some states' rules and the federal rule, which are outside the scope of this Introduction.

79 White Paper COM (2008) 165 final.

80 Green Paper COM (2008) 794 final.

81 On the possibility for public authorities to also seek compensation, see C. Hodges, The reform of class and representative action, supra at note 6, p. 9 ff.

82 See on this issue more generally, that is, without dealing in particular with aggregated litigation, J. Lindholm, State Procedure and Union Rights, A Comparison of the European Union and the United States, American J. of Comp. Law, vol. 57, p. 258 (2009), and the review by N. Reich, "Federalism and Effective Legal Protection" – some thoughts about a recent study by Johan Lindholm, to be published in Festschrift Gert Brüggemeier 2009.

rules. Indeed, most people think that the main difference is that state judges (and juries, if it comes to that) tend to be more sympathetic to plaintiffs than federal judges.[83] It may well be that, as a result of this, federal judges tend to apply the federal summary judgment rule (Rule 56) in such a way as to prevent cases from getting to juries more frequently, but it is often the case that state procedural rules (e.g. state rules on summary judgment) are in letter very similar to the federal rule.

The delimitation between the different levels, federal or state, follows in principle the logic that there are mass conflicts which are limited to the state territory and the affected state citizens and mass conflicts which spread over the whole country and would therefore be put in the hands of the federal courts. The reality is different and therefore there are many conflicts turning around conflicting jurisdiction when mass conflict is not limited to one state and/or in the case where the event affects citizens of more than one state. Even if there are mass conflicts that spread over the whole country, it does not necessarily follow that federal courts will adjudicate the matter. The reason is that in most consumer cases, the cause of action is common-law tort, and that is usually state law, not federal law. If, however, one of the claims for relief arises under federal law, either party (plaintiff or defendant) may bring the action to the federal court. Moreover, even when only state-law claims are alleged, the recently enacted Class Action Fairness Act (CAFA)[84] allows either party to take most consumer class action cases to the federal court.[85]

There are two different questions affecting enforcement strategies in the US and Europe: a) what is the role of state civil procedure rule and

b) have and to what extent have those rules been harmonized in the US and EU? The real difference between the US and the EU seems to be the different degree of harmonization of these rules. The high degree of semi-spontaneous

---

83 But this perception may be erroneous. Empirical studies tend to find no significant differences between state and federal judges on issues pertinent to class action litigation. See Theodore Eisenberg, Use it or Pretenders Will Abuse it: The Importance of Archival Legal Information, University of Kansas City Law Review, vol. 75, p. 15 ff. (2006) (the best available information about comparative state/federal judicial performance in class actions suggests no strong differences); Theodore Eisenberg and Geoffrey Miller, Attorney Fees in Class Action Settlements: An Empirical Study, Journal of Empirical Legal Studies, vol. 1, p. 27 (2004) (finding no significant differences in fees awarded by federal and state courts in class action settlements).

84 28 U.S.C. Sections 1332(d), 1453, 1711–1715.

85 CAFA provides for federal court jurisdiction when the total amount in controversy exceeds $5 million and any plaintiff is a citizen of a state different from any defendant, unless at least two-thirds or more of the members of all proposed plaintiff classes and the defendants are citizens of the state in which the action was filed.

harmonization in the US is far from being comparable to the current state in Europe.[86]

EU law must almost exclusively rely on Member State courts to enforce EU specific rights. Only under quite specific requirements may parties benefit from a direct application to the ECJ.[87] This means that EC specific rights are subject to 27 national procedural laws as there is no EC procedural law, either in general terms or with regard to aggregate litigation. Concrete measures are not yet in sight. Given that the differences in MSs' procedural laws are broader than in US state laws, the risk of divergent procedural standards to enforce EU law is higher. There is, however, one particularity in the EU judicial system with no counterpart in the US which allows for judicial co-operation between Member State courts and the ECJ: the preliminary reference procedure under Article 234 ET. Within this framework the ECJ has confirmed the 'procedural autonomy' of the MSs, provided the respective procedural rules guarantee effective legal protection and constitute an equivalent to comparable national claims.[88] Yet incomplete enforcement mechanisms are partly compensated for by judicial activism on "rights, remedies and procedures", to cite a seminal paper of *Walter van Gerven*.[89] The Member States' competence in private enforcement is thereby more and more restricted. This is largely because Member States' procedures quite often do not suffice to guarantee effective legal protection as required under primary[90] and secondary EC law.[91] Over time, the ECJ has linked EC rights, (national) procedural rules to the availability of appropriate remedies.[92] The principle of effectiveness and the principle of equivalence are applicable not only to procedure, but also to remedies.

---

86 On these questions, see M. Taruffo, Harmonising civil litigation in Europe? in F. Cafaggi and H. Muir-Watt (eds.), Making European private law. Governance design, *supra* at note 52, p. 46 ff.; more broadly E. Storskubb, Civil procedure and EU law, Oxford University Press, New York – Oxford, 2008.

87 See lately ECJ Case C-50/00P *Union de Pequenos agricultores v. Council* 2002 ECR I-6677 at 45. Efforts in particular of environmental organisations to stretch the rather narrow interpretation of the ECJ have been given some weight by the CFI Case T-585/93 Greenpeace Council, ECR 1995 II-2005, and in particular by AG Cosmas Case C-321/95 P at 104 *et seq.*, but were finally rejected by the ECJ C-321/95 ECR 1995 I-1651. Article 230 (4) of the Lisbon Treaty would extend standing thus allowing direct actions also against 'regulatory acts' which directly concern individuals and do not need implementing measures, http://eurlex.europa.eu/LexUriServ/LexUriServ.do?uri=OJ:C:2007:306:0042:0133:EN:PDF.

88 See Case 33/76 *Rewe Zentralfinanz et al. v Landwirtschaftskammer Saarland* [1976] ECR 1989 para 5; 45/76 *Comet v Produktschap voor Siergewassen* [1976] ECR 2043 para 13.

89 W. van Gerven, Of Rights, Remedies and Procedures, C.M.L. Rev., 2000, p. 501.

90 Private enforcement of EC law bears a strong human rights connotation, as the ECJ uses the Human Rights Convention as a reference point for strengthening individual enforceable rights.

91 See Rott, Effektivität des Verbraucherrechtsschutzes: Rahmenfestlegungen des Gemeinschaftsrechts Studie im Auftrag der Bundesanstalt für Landwirtschaft und Ernährung, 2006, available at the homepage http://www.ble.de/download/pdf/04HS033.pdf.

92 See Van Gerven, *supra* at note 89. From a consumer point of view, Micklitz/Reich/Rott, Understanding EU Law, *supra* at note 19, Chapter 8.

Whilst the ECJ made some effort to ground state liability in *Francovich*,[93] injunctive relief in *Factortame*[94], and compensation claims in *Courage*[95] and *Manfredi*[96] in the ET, one might well argue that the ECJ invented these remedies, which were not written into the Treaty and which did not exist - at least not in all Member States. However, the ECJ's jurisdiction has its limits. In *Unibet*,[97] the question before the Court was whether the principle of effectiveness demanded national law to introduce a free-standing action, which seeks primarily to dispute the compatibility of national provisions with EC law. The ECJ rejected such an obligation if it is not foreseen already in the national law, but left the door open for the introduction of appropriate remedies under exceptional circumstances.[98] The remedies may not necessarily lead to compensation claims; they may equally be tied to oblige Member States authorities to set up action plans against pollution to protect the individual rights of EU citizens like in *Janecek*.[99] So far, it seems hard to imagine that the ECJ would be prepared to oblige Member States to grant standing to a collective entity of consumers to protect their rights and to claim compensation. However, an intermediary step might, in the light of *Janecek*, be the obligation imposed on Member States to establish an action plan on how the protection of consumers in mass conflicts can best be guaranteed. It is beyond the scope of this introduction to provide a framework. One thing is for sure: the growing intervention of the ECJ in national procedural autonomy enhances the need to clarify which enforcement measures shall be taken, at what level and by whom.[100] The ECJ has been and still seems to be primarily concerned with individual rights and maybe even more with collective rights than with Member States prerogatives.[101] One possible explanation might be that national courts in the EU unlike the state courts applying national laws with at least two hundred years of experience, still have to learn that they are at the same time European

---

93 ECJ, Case combined C-5/90 and 9/90 Francovich ECR 1990 I-5337.

94 ECJ, Case C-213/89 *R v Secretary of State for Transport, ex parte Factortame* [1990] ECR I-2433.

95 ECJ, Case C-453/99, (2001) ECR I-7079.

96 ECJ, Case C-295/04 et al., (2006) ECR I-6619; thereto Bulst, ZEuP 2008, 178.

97 ECJ, Case C-432/05 *Unibet v Justiekanslern* (2009) ECR I-2271 at 32.

98 At 64 "In any event, it is clear from paragraphs 56 to 61 above that Unibet must be regarded as having available to it legal remedies which ensure effective judicial protection of its rights under Community law. If, on the contrary, as mentioned at paragraph 62 above, it was forced to be subject to administrative or criminal proceedings and to any penalties that may result as the sole form of legal remedy for disputing the compatibility of the national provision at issue with Community law, that would not be sufficient to secure for it such effective judicial protection."

99 ECJ C-237/07 *Janecek v. Freistaat Bayern*, 2008 ECR nyr.

100 See T. Craig, *EU Administrative Law*, Oxford University Press, New York - Oxford, 2006, p. 789; T. Tridimas, *General Principles of EU Law*, Oxford University Press, New York - Oxford, 2007[2], p. 418; M. Dougan, National Remedies Before the Court of Justice, Hart Publishing, Oxford and Portland, 2004.

101 See Reich in Festschrift Brüggemeier, supra at note 82.

courts at least with regard to the enforcement of EU specific rights and national courts. However, we will instead put emphasis on the key role EC specific rights have been playing and are still playing in the building of a genuine legal order, if not a European constitution.[102] The lesson to be learnt from the US multi-level structure is that judicial enforcement in aggregate litigation necessarily invokes the federal dimension of the EU and the way in which it should be handled.[103]

In sum, the European institutional framework on enforcement may still be understood as the interplay between private judicial enforcement and administrative enforcement, where Member States benefit from the leeway left to them under the doctrine of *Vollzugs-Föderalismus*.[104] The prospective policy model of EU law enforcement as promoted by the European Commission primarily seems to be guided by decentralized enforcement through national public agencies with residual competences granted to the European Commission. This model, which was established (or is still being established) in regulated markets, has now been extended to the area of consumer contract law.[105] It represents a paradigm shift away from judicial enforcement to administrative enforcement. The immediate result is a change in the choice of enforcement instruments, which finds its predecessor in comitology, as developed within the 'New Approach to Technical Standards', then extended to various fields of EC law, in particular the regulated markets and now generalized in Decision 768/2008 on the 'Common Framework on Market Surveillance'.[106] All these regulatory devices set up common enforcement structures, even largely unified remedies, but they are not aiming at the harmonization of the administrative procedural law. Here, the question remains whether and to what extent the principles of effectiveness and equivalence developed by the ECJ could and should provide further guidance in administrative enforcement at domestic level.

This does not mean that the European Commission intends – it would have no competence anyway – to substitute judicial with administrative enforcement. However, the interrelationship between the two becomes much more complex. If judicial and administrative enforcement stand side-by-side, the interface between the two, in particular with regard to private collective enforcement has to be rebalanced. This is even more so as the Member States become more active with

102 See H.-W. Micklitz, The Politics of Judicial Co-operation in the EU, Cambridge University Press, New York – Cambridge, 2005, p. 11.

103 Now J. Lindholm, State Procedure and Union Rights, *supra* at note 82, p. 258.

104 See F. Cafaggi and H.-W. Micklitz, Administrative and Judicial Collective Enforcement of Consumer Law in the US and the European Community, EUI Working Paper 2007/22.

105 See Regulation 2006/2004 on Co-operation of national authorities responsible for the enforcement of consumer law, OJ L 364, 9.12.2006, 1; thereto Kaye, Recent Developments: Regulation EC 2006/2004 on Consumer Protection Co-operation in Howells/Nordhausen/Parry/Twigg-Flesner, Yearbook of Consumer Law, vol. I, 2006, p. 417.

106 OJ L 218, 13.8.2008, 82.

regard to the establishment of collective judicial enforcement remedies.[107] Competition law might become an important testing ground for national and European legislative bodies. As a result of its decentralized enforcement strategy, the European Commission seems to foster private enforcement mechanisms, by individuals – business and consumers – and perhaps even by trade and consumer organisations.[108] Administrative enforcement via national competition agencies and the European Commission would then have to be brought into line with private individual and collective judicial enforcement.

The situation is less clear with regard to the enforcement of unfair commercial practices and unfair contract terms law where enforcement strategies still differ among Member States. Some rely on administrative enforcement via agencies, while others lay enforcement in the hands of trade and consumer organisations.[109] The recent regulatory activism of the Member States has strengthened and continues to strengthen collective redress mechanisms, not only via trade and consumer organisations, but also via public agencies. The European Commission does not seem prepared to intervene in the regulation of collective judicial enforcement at this stage, at least not beyond injunctive relief. So far, it takes a backstage role, merely announcing that it will test the feasibility of developing appropriate legal rules at the EC level.[110] For the time being, these initiatives are limited to commissioning various studies, with particular emphasis on the potential economic impact of collective compensation schemes.[111]

107 See with regard to Member States: An analysis and evaluation of alternative means of consumer redress other than redress through ordinary judicial proceedings – Final Report, Study for the European Commission, (hereinafter Stuyck Report), available at http://ec.europa.eu/consumers/redress/reports_studies/index_en.htmand as well as H.W. Micklitz/A. Stadler, Das Verbandsklagerecht in der Informations- und Dienstleistungsgesellschaft, Landwirtschaftsverlag, Münster, 2005.

108 With regard to competition law, see Green Paper, Damages action of the EC Antitrust rules, COM (2005) 19.12.2005, 672 final.

109 See references in H.-W. Micklitz/J. Keßler (eds.), Marketing Practices Regulation and Consumer Protection in the EC Member States and the US, Band 10 der VIEW Schriftenreihe, 2002.

110 COM (2007) 99 final, 13.3.2007.

111 Study commissioned by DG Sanco on the effectiveness and efficiency of collective redress http://ec.europa.eu/consumers/redress_cons/finalreportevaluationstudypart1-final 2008-11-26.pdf and study commissioned by DG Sanco on the problems faced by consumers in obtaining redress for infringements of consumer protection legislation and the economic consequences of such problems http://ec.europa.eu/consumers/redress_cons/finalreport-problemstudypart1-final.pdf.

4. THE TRANSATLANTIC SCENARIO – THE REGULATORY ROLE OF AGGREGATE LITIGATION IN NORTH AMERICA AND ITS INSTITUTIONAL PRE-CONDITIONS

Consumer law in the US paints an interesting and changing picture. It is a combination of state common law and statutory law, enacted both at federal and state level.[112] In terms of enforcement, both state and federal judiciaries are involved and a wide array of administrative agencies and governmental bodies operate, ranging from CPSA to FTC, from FDA to SEC. This implies that the analysis should not juxtapose federal governmental regulation and state common law remedies but also focus on private law remedies concerning violations of federal regulation where the interplay between courts and agencies becomes strategic.[113]

In the past, the strong emphasis on litigation as a regulatory device has been complemented by a selective yet relevant role of administrative regulation and enforcement.[114] In particular, the power of the FDA has been partly shielded from state courts' intervention in the field of tort law.[115] Aggregate litigation, however, still represents a significant means to compensate consumers and an important device to deter and regulate firms' conduct, concerning both risks associated with product safety and abuses in contractual practices.[116]

Consumer regulation has changed, moving from command and control to a more participatory and responsive model.[117] Even within consumer law, aggregate litigation plays different roles depending on the value of individual claims and the nature of the harm, whether personal injury typically associated with a tort claim or economic loss, typically associated with a contract claim. The higher value of individual claims and their relationship with personal injury may strengthen the role of compensation and influence the decision on whether and how the claims should be aggregated.[118] But aggregation has contributed to the transformation of

112 See G. Miller, in this volume part. p. 267 ff.

113 See C. Sharkey, in this volume, p. 139 ff.

114 See C. Sharkey, Product liability pre-emption: an institutional approach, George Washington L.R. vol. 76, p. 449 ff. (2008) part. p. 459 ff., where a detailed analysis of the Supreme Court jurisprudence shows the balance (or oscillation) between regulatory and compensatory functions of product liability regimes, and their relation with the pre-emption issue. She states: "The Court has oscillated between competing conceptions of tort as either primarily regulatory or compensatory, with the regulatory view justifying the pre-emptive results and the compensatory view compelling the opposite" at p. 458.

115 See C. Sharkey, An institutional perspective, in this volume, p. 145 ff.

116 See S. Issacharoff, Group litigation of consumer claims: lessons from the US Experience, Tex. Int'l. L.J., vol. 34, p. 135 (1999).

117 See for a broader perspective, Ayres and Braithwaite, Responsive regulation, Oxford University Press, New York – Oxford, 1992.

118 See in this volume, G. Miller, Compensation and deterrence, p. 263 f.

substantive law. Tort law in aggregate litigation, unlike individual proceedings, moves away from some of the core principles such as the necessity of actual harm and the rejection of probabilistic causation.[119] These institutional changes have produced transformation of substantive law both in administrative and (mass) tort.[120] Both legislative reforms and Supreme Court's decisions have started changing the legal framework. The enactment of CAFA in 2005 has brought about not only a partial federalization of class actions, rebalancing the relationship between federal and state interests, but also important indirect changes in substantive law.[121] These changes are limited and, in multi-state litigation, conflict of laws is still the main instrument for determining applicable law, often translating into the necessity to apply multiple state laws.[122]

There seems to be a robust trend towards federalization both in judicial and administrative enforcement with significant weakening of state common tort law.[123] Pre-emption has become a key factor to identify vertical but also horizontal institutional balance between legislative and executive bodies and the judiciary.[124] Often pre-emption has implied a shift from state-judicial to federal-administrative enforcement but the move towards federal level could occur within judicial enforcement by expanding federal tort law. These changes require a new interpretation of the multilevel system that has long characterized consumer protection in the US, namely an inquiry into the reasons for the predominance of litigation as a device for *ex post* regulation.[125]

---

119 The possibility to seek fluid recovery allows claimants who have not yet suffered harms to obtain recovery. Similar changes occur in relation to the so-called statutory damages. For illustrations see in this volume G. Miller, Compensation and deterrence, cit. p. 221 and 227.

120 See R. Rabin, Federalism and the tort system, Rutgers L.R. vol. 50, p. 1 ff., 1997, Id. Reassessing Regulatory compliance. Georgetown L.J., Vol. 88 (2000) Available at SRRN: http://srrn.com/abstract=201949.

121 The purposes of the Statute are stated at the outset. CAFA purports to (1) assure fair and prompt recoveries for class members with legitimate claims, (2) restore the intent of the framers of United States Constitution by providing for federal court consideration of interstate cases of national importance under diversity of jurisdiction, and (3) benefit society by encouraging innovation and lowering consumer prices". See S. Burbank, The Class Action Fairness Act of 2005 in historical context: a preliminary view, in U. Pa. L. R., vol. 156, p. 1439 (2008), J. Hazard jr., Has the Erie doctrine been repealed by Congress? in U. Pa. L. R., vol. 158, p. 1629 (2008).

122 See S. Issacharoff, Settled expectations in a world of unsettled law: choice of law after the Class Action Fairness Act, Col. L. R., vol. 106, p. 1839 ff. (2006). See also G. Miller, Compensation and deterrence in this volume, p. 232.

123 See C. Sharkey, in this volume p. 139 ff. and earlier Ead., Products liability pre-emption: an institutional approach, cit., supra at note 114, Ead., Preemption by preamble: Federal agencies and the federalization of tort law, De Paul L. R., vol. 56, p. 227 (2007).

124 See R. Epstein and M. Greeve (eds.) Federal pre-emption: States' powers, national interests, AEI Press, Washington D.C., 2007, and Issacharoff and Sharkey, Backdoor federalization, UCLA L. Rev., vol. 53, p. 1353 ff. (2006).

125 See S. Issacharoff, Regulating after the fact, De Paul L. R. vol. 56, p. 375 (2007).

Aggregate litigation performs several functions in the US.[126] Deterrence and compensation play an important role, but their balance is different from that taking place in individual litigation. Small value claims, that would not be otherwise litigated, reach courts and end in judgments or settlements due to aggregation.[127] More recently, the emphasis on the regulatory function as a complement of or an alternative to administrative regulation has been examined to show differences and similarities,[128] not only because they can both contribute to deter unlawful conduct concerning product safety but also because some of the principles applied to administrative agencies may, with some adjustments, fruitfully be transposed to aggregate litigation.[129] Aggregate litigation in North America constitutes still the exception in civil litigation whilst individual disputes concerning a single event still represent the rule.[130] However, it is an exception of growing importance whose legal regime has been revised through both legislation and adjudication.[131]

Aggregation represents an institutional response to combine an efficient use of jurisdictional resources and an effective means of granting remedies when consumer rights are violated.[132] In a recent attempt – namely, the ALI Principles on the law of aggregate litigation – three types of aggregate proceedings have been identified: aggregate lawsuits, administrative aggregation and private aggregation.[133] Similar functional distinctions concerning aggregate lawsuits and

---

126 See ALI Principles on the law of aggregate litigation, R. Nagareda, Class actions in the administrative state: Kalven and Rosenfeld Revisited, U. Chi L.R. vol. 75, p. 13 (2008).

127 Aggregate litigation is however only one institutional response to the problems presented by small value claims in consumer law. Fee-shifting, statutory damages and other devices complement aggregate litigation. See in this volume G. Miller, cit. p. 224 ff.

128 See F. Cafaggi, A Coordinated Approach to Regulation and Civil Liability in European Law: Rethinking institutional complementarities, in F. Cafaggi (ed.) The institutional framework of European private law, Oxford University Press, New York – Oxford, 2006, p. 191.

129 See R. Nagareda, Turning from tort to administration, U. Mich. L. R., vol. 94, p. 899 ff. (1996), S. Issacharoff and J.F. Witt, The inevitability of aggregate settlement: An institutional account of American tort law, Vand. L.R., vol. 57, p. 1571 (2004).

130 See B. Burbank, supra at note 77.

131 For a concise but complete description of Federal rules of civil procedure 23 see, in this volume, G. Miller, Compensation and deterrence, cit. p. 272 f.

132 Efficiency and justice are not juxtaposed in aggregate litigation although some tensions may arise and require compromise between the benefits of aggregation and the due process guarantees. See on these tensions Miller Compensation and deterrence, in this volume p. 263, and J. Coffee, Private Securities Litigation Reform Act, cit., supra note 8, Id., Law and the Market: The Impact of Enforcement 2007, Columbia Law and Economics Working Paper No. 304. Available at SRRN: http://sssrn.com/abstract=967482; Id., Accountability and Competition in Securities Class Actions. Why 'Exit' Works Better than 'Voice' (2008), Cardozo L. Rev., vol. 30, p. 407 ff. (2008).

133 See ALI Principles of the law of aggregate litigation, April 2008, §1.02, "Types of aggregate proceedings:

(a) An aggregate lawsuit is a single lawsuit that encompasses claims or defences held by multiple parties or represented persons.

administrative aggregation can be found in the new legislation enacted by Member States in Europe.

Aggregate litigation still plays a strategic role as an *ex post* regulatory device where the institutional framework, supported by the private attorney general model, constitutes a significant driver for legal innovation both in litigation strategies and in the evolution of substantive common law.[134] Funding rules are strategic to provide lawyers with correct incentives to bring meritorious legal claims.[135] The choice for an opt-out system reduces transaction costs and enhances the overall effectiveness but the costs of low monitoring by consumers may be high. Judicial enforcement concluded by settlements is broadening, and the role of ADR and arbitration is increasing. In arbitration concerning consumer matters, there is a strong attempt to move from individual to class-wide arbitration, reducing the distance with judicial enforcement.[136] However, the fact that most of the aggregate litigation is settled, poses serious questions to the modes and effects of regulation through litigation.[137]

The private attorney general model has partially shifted from the adversarial to the contractual in aggregate litigation.[138] These changes have modified the role of lawyers and the bar, forcing the redefinition of the agency relationships with represented parties. Pure market mechanisms of lawyers' selection have showed their weaknesses;[139] however, despite the relatively low level of competition, no significant antitrust action has been undertaken to promote wider competition in the provision of legal services. Conflicts of interest between both lawyers and members of the class and among the members themselves have emerged and the

(b) (b) An administrative aggregation is a collection of related lawsuits, which may or may not be aggregate lawsuits, proceeding under a common judicial supervision or control ..."

134 See Issacharoff, supra, note 125.

135 Geoffrey Miller indicates the common fund/common benefit rule as an important factor that makes consumer class actions possible. See G. Miller, in this volume p. 280 f.

136 R. Nagareda, Aggregation and its Discontents: Class Settlement Pressure, Class-Wide Arbitration, and CAFA, Col. L. Rev., Vol. 106, p. 1872 ff. (2006), available at SSRN: http://ssrn.com/abstract=920833.

137 But see S. Issacharoff and R. Nagareda, Settlements under attack, U. Pa. L. R., vol. 156, p. 1650 (2008).
On these questions see also T. Eisenberg and G. Miller, Attorneys' Fees in Class Action Settlements: An Empirical Study, J. of Empirical Legal Studies, vol. 1, p. 27 ff. (2004), W. Rubinstein, On what a Private Attorney General is and why it matters, vol. 57, p. 2129 (2004), R. Nagareda, Closure in Damage Class Settlements: The Godfather Guide to Opt-Out Rights, 2003 University of Chicago Legal Forum, 141.

138 See W. Rubenstein, supra at note 137, R. Nagareda, Administering Adequacy in Class Representation, Tex. L.R., vol. 82, p. 287, J. Resnik, Procedure as Contract, Notre Dame L. Rev. vol. 80, 593 (2005).

139 Different solutions have been used by courts among which auctions deserve great attention. See T. Eisenberg and G. Miller, Attorneys' Fees in Class Action Settlements, cit., supra at note 137.

necessity for a more effective regulation has been underlined.[140] The roles of judges and counsel in these types of litigation have changed, especially in interstate litigation and new specific rules are needed.[141]

Institutional responses have differed. On one hand, the role of judges' supervision has increased; on the other hand, conflict of interest rules have become tighter.[142] Judges have become fiduciaries of absent class-members to prevent collusive agreements among plaintiffs and defendant lawyers.[143] Differentiation with other forms of consolidation, mainly based on contractual arrangements, have emerged.[144] There is still an open issue concerning the choice of dominant players, in particular plaintiffs' lawyers, and their accountability to clients both in the choice of litigation strategies and that of settling the dispute. The differences between general class actions and securities, where the lead plaintiff is often an institutional investor, provide a good illustration of the difficulties of uniformly resolving the agency relationship between claimants and lawyers in the context of class action.[145] To support the claim that consumer litigation is a public good that deserves not only a good legislative framework but also public policies, new strategies within the private attorney general model have to be put forward.[146]

The regulatory function of aggregate litigation strongly depends on the reach of settlements and *res judicata* and its constitutional limitations. The differences concerning binding effects of settlements and judgments may strongly affect the

140 See G. Miller, Conflicts of interests in class action litigation: An inquiry into the appropriate standard, 2003 U. Chi. Legal F., p. 581 ff.

141 See A. Chayes, The role of the judge in public law litigation, Harvard L.R. 89, 1281, 1976 and S. Issacharoff, Governance and legitimacy, Supreme Court Review, 1999, p. 337 ff.

142 See G. Miller, Conflicts of interests in class action litigation, cit. supra at note 140, ALI. Principles of the law of aggregate litigation, Chapter §2.08. In the comment the rule has been rationalized in the following way: "In the context of aggregate litigation, the right of exit in subsection (a)(1) consists of the opportunity to escape the preclusive effect of the aggregate proceeding. The right to a voice in subsection (a) (2) consists of the opportunity to participate in the aggregate proceeding and, as its antecedent, notice of that proceeding. The right to loyalty in subsection (a) (3) consists of judicial review, as a precondition for aggregate treatment, to ascertain whether any structural conflicts of interest exist in the representation of claimants."

143 On the fiduciary role of judges, see S. Issacharoff and R. Nagareda, Settlements under attack, cit., supra at note 10, p. 1658 ff.

144 See ALI Principles §2.08 "Whatever the source of the structural conflict, moreover, there is room for differentiation between class actions and consolidations. The contractual nature of representation in consolidated proceedings creates at least the possibility of client consent to conflict of interest in a manner analogous to the way that multiple individual clients with conflicting interests in ordinary litigation may consent to representation by a common lawyer."

145 It is clear that the Private securities litigation reform Act (PSLRA) has not met the expectations about changes. See J. Coffee, 2006, supra at note 8, Id., 2008, supra at note 132.

146 See Issacharoff, supra, note 125.

regulatory outcome of litigation.[147] In addition, questions of fairness concerning the distribution of proceedings may have an impact on the goals of regulation through litigation.[148]

To provide a sketchy picture of current changes in aggregate litigation we must focus on the effects produced by case law, since those of CAFA are still relatively undefined.

The ability of litigation to work as a regulatory device depends on the deterrence effect of damages and the creative use of injunctions: those going beyond pure prohibition. The former has been debated; the latter exists but to a lesser extent in consumer protection than in other fields such as civil rights litigation.[149]

Rule 23 of Federal civil procedure regulates different forms of class actions, including those seeking both divisible and indivisible remedies (for example injunctive relieves and damages) – so-called hybrids.[150] When the management of indivisible remedies so requires, courts may mandate aggregation.[151] However, both principles and practices differ quite significantly if injunctions or damages are simultaneously sought. In particular, given that the binding effects and the right to opt out follow different patterns, when the two remedies are sought separately.[152] Clearly, this becomes an issue when in the same class action both remedies are needed (find a synonym) because the right to opt out is granted for

147 G.C. Hazard Jr., J.L. Gedid and S. Sowle, A Historical Analysis of the Binding Effect of Class Suits, U. Penn. L. Rev., vol. 146, 1849 (1998).

148 See R. Nagareda, supra, note 187.

149 See C. Sabel and W. Simon, Destabilization Rights: How Public Law Litigation Succeeds. Harv. L. Rev., vol. 117, p. 1015 (2004).

150 See §2.04 ALI Principles Comment "Divisible remedies are those that entail distribution to one or more claimants individually without predetermining the application of the same remedy to any other claimant in practical effect. Indivisible remedies, by contrast, are those where the distribution of the remedy to any claimant invariably affects the application of the same remedy to other claimants".

151 See subsection (c) (1) §2.08 ALI principles on the law of aggregate litigation comment h "Subsection (C) (1) recognises one of the three grounds which a court may mandate the litigation of claims on an aggregate basis: to manage indivisible remedies efficiently when multiple lawsuits are proceeding or threatened. When multiple claims exist for an indivisible remedy as against a generally applicable course of conduct on the defendant's part, unitary adjudication is desirable to avoid inconsistent results and to facilitate judicial management of the remedy … Mandatory aggregation with respect to claims for an indivisible remedy simply recognises the pre-existing interdependence of such claims. Even without an aggregate proceeding a successful lawsuit brought by an individual claimant would affect all persons subject to the generally applicable course of conduct… The mandatory nature of the proceeding advances due process in several ways. First it creates a forum in which all interested persons may voice their views concerning practice or policy. Second, it enables the court to craft an indivisible remedy that burdens the defendant and any dissenting claimants to the minimum extent needed to vindicate the rights asserted in the complaint. Third it avoids the risk of inconsistent adjudications and relief."

152 See E.F. Sherman, Segmenting Aggregate Litigation: Initiatives and Impediments for Reshaping the Trial Process, Review of Litigation, vol. 25, p. 691 (2006).

damages and not for injunctive relief. Different organisational responses are given in the US to hybrids; courts have been using different criteria when granting both remedies.[153]

Similar problems arise in the European context where very little has been said about the coordination between collective enforcement concerning injunctions and damages. In Europe, the scarcity of opt-out systems poses serious problems with respect to coordination between binding effects of injunctions for parties other than those represented in the lawsuit and binding effects of damages relevant only for those who have opted in without exercising withdrawal rights.

The relationship between divisible and indivisible remedies in aggregate litigation should be seen in the broader context of complementarity with administrative enforcement where the focus is primarily but not exclusively on injunction-like remedies.

A key difference between judicial and administrative enforcement is the selection of cases to be litigated in the judicial domain and the power to define priorities by administrative agencies in monitoring and enforcement and the choice of remedies. The level of discretion enjoyed by agencies in selecting priorities is much higher than that of Courts through class certification.[154] But the system of agency accountability is much stronger than that of courts and plaintiffs' law firms. Similar arguments can be made in the European context. That said, policies concerning administrative enforcement of consumer protection vary quite significantly despite the efforts made to increase coordination under the market surveillance policy.

One issue, which deserves more attention in comparative analysis, is coordination among courts and State administrative agencies. While Europe has developed more instruments in administrative coordination than in judicial

153 These actions, called hybrids may involve the whole class or sub-classes of plaintiffs. If class members are interested in different remedies one possible response is to create sub-classes. See N. Pace, Class actions in the United States of America an overview of the process and the empirical literature: available at http://globalclassactions.stanford.edu/PDF/USA_National_Report.pdf. *"Another hybrid situation involves instances where there are multiple subclasses in a case, each certified under a different section of Rule 23(b). One subclass might be certified as a Rule 23(b) (3) class with rights of notice and opt out while a second subclass would be a mandatory rule 23 (b) (2) claa. Mass tort class actions, for example, might seek injunctive relief ordering long-term medical monitoring of a plaintiff class certified under Rule 23(b) (3) where only monetary damages are requested. Multiple sub-classes with different legal foundations can even apply to the same type of plaintiff; a consumer class action might have a rule 23(b)(3) subclass where claims are made against a compensation fund but those very same individuals could be prohibited from making any class claim for punitive damages as part of a Rule 23b(2) subclass without any right to opt-out."*

154 R. Nagareda, Class actions in the administrative state, supra at note 126, p. 616.

cooperation, in the US the opposite, unsurprisingly, seems to be true. Judicial cooperation in the US has also been accompanied by the creation of national networks of law firms especially but not exclusively on the plaintiff side in order to promote coordinated strategies. These networks have contributed significantly to the effectiveness of the private attorney general model.[155]

The use of aggregate litigation and its interplay with administrative enforcement may change the scope of substantive law. The US experience and the recent US case law shows the attempt to replace the tort system, conceived predominantly in relation to individual litigation, with privately defined compensation schemes for mass injuries.[156] Conflict resolution in mass torts follows a different path from individual conflict if the dispute ends in judgment or settlement. This specificity enhances the regulatory function of mass tort litigation and the need to move towards the application of principles of administrative law in the field of aggregate litigation suggests that a new allocation of functions between administrative and judicial enforcement is needed. One the one hand Courts and plaintiffs' lawyers may still play the role of legal innovators for a specific class of cases, but the attribution of the overall control of compliance with standard consumer regulation can hardly be justified. Administrative control may be cheaper, more effective and have better distributional effects to ensure deterrence in relation to standard violations of consumer law.[157]

Clearly, the analysis developed here and elsewhere shows that institutional preconditions in the US to Europe differ significantly.[158] These differences make legal transplants problematic. These differences make comparison necessary in the light of the development of global class actions. The emergence of a new stream of legislation concerning group actions in Europe should thus be compared with the US and Canada internalizing the different institutional frameworks within which opt-in/opt-out options will be exercised.

---

155 On the effects of CAFA over class action lawyers see H. Erichson, CAFA's impact on class action lawyers, U. Pa. L.R., vol. 156, p. 1593, (2008).

156 References are the two famous cases *Amchem Products INC v. Windsor*, 521 US 591 (1997) and *Ortiz v. Fibreboard Corp.* 527 US 815. On the scope of the Supreme Court intervention and its effects, see S. Issacharoff and C. Sharkey, Backdoor federalization, and R. Nagareda, Class actions in the administrative state, supra at note 126, p. 607. According to Nagareda "the Court struck down as inconsistent with rule 23 ambitious efforts to use class settlements, in effect to replace the tort system prospectively with private administrative compensation schemes for asbestos-exposed industrial workers."

157 This view is advocated for Europe by Ch. Hodges, The reform of class and representative actions, supra at note 6, p. 223, see book review H.-W. Micklitz, CMLR 2009, forthcoming.

158 See F. Cafaggi and H.-W. Micklitz, Collective enforcement of consumer law, cit. supra at note 3, p. 391, S. Issacharoff and G. Miller, Will aggregate litigation come to Europe? Vanderbilt L.R., vol. 62, p. 179 (2009).

5. ADJUDICATION AND TRANSBORDER LITIGATION IN NORTH AMERICA AND THE EU

Protection of the collective interest of consumers at the same time is the objective and defines the boundaries of enforcement policies at EU level. It affects standing policies drawing the boundaries between individual and collective enforcement. The multilevel system currently operating in Europe raises several questions about the differences between domestic and transborder disputes concerning collective consumer interest protection in cases of both contractual and non-contractual liability. In Europe, infra-community infringements with a transborder dimension have been distinguished from purely domestic ones.[159] From a practical standpoint, transborder litigation concerns intra-community infringements and includes claimants and/or defendants coming from different state jurisdictions.[160] From a normative perspective, transborder litigation pertains to the desirability of devising a specific set of rules concerning these disputes and if so which combination between centralized and decentralized rules best comply with constitutional principles and policy goals.

At opposite ends of the theoretical spectrum there are two possible solutions: (1) a fully centralized legal regime enacted through European legislation; and (2) a fully decentralized system regulated by private international law. In-between, there are several combinations of centralized and decentralized rules as judicial collective enforcement shows for the combination between injunctive relief and pecuniary remedies. Currently neither have been adopted and often, specific rules are missing.

Transborder litigation poses specific questions concerning commonality of rules. While at the State level there is not a significant difference, transborder litigation may present common questions of facts but different questions of law because different state laws apply to the same facts. In order to promote transborder litigation, both substantive principles and procedural rules together with different forms of administrative aggregation are needed. Different devices have been proposed from private international law rules to subdivide claimants according to applicable state laws, which do not necessarily coincide with those of injured

159 See Article 3(b) of the Regulation 2006/2004: '"intra-Community infringement" means any act or omission contrary to the laws that protect consumers' interests, as defined in (a), that harms, or is likely to harm, the collective interests of consumers residing in a Member State or Member States other than the Member State where the act or omission originated or took place, or where the responsible seller or supplier is established, or where evidence or assets pertaining to the act or omission are to be found.'

160 How different they have to be in order to qualify as a transborder dispute is not only a practical but also a very difficult theoretical question. The example of the criteria used by CAFA is telling.

residents. Coordination may concern the whole trial or specific phases in order to save information costs related to evidence gathering. For this purpose, judicial cooperation in civil and commercial matters is a key question.[161]

At the outset, we should distinguish between judicial enforcement through injunctions and through group or class actions or, according to the American approach indivisible and divisible remedies. The former poses fewer difficulties than the latter because in litigation concerning pecuniary remedies the formation of the class or group, its composition poses highly difficult problems.

Two types of transborder conflicts may be distinguished in representative actions concerning pecuniary claims: firstly to what extent national plaintiffs, consumer organisations, self-organisations, public authorities and lead plaintiffs[162] with their lawyers in tandem may defend the rights and interests of non-nationals, *rectius* non-residents, and secondly to what extent non-nationals, *rectius* non-resident consumers might join collective actions filed in another Member State. So far, such a scenario has not yet materialized in Europe given the fact that most of the legislation on class actions/group actions is so new that there is no or very little case law, if any in a pure national context.[163] The set of legal questions which arise out of the new transborder dimension are overtly complex,[164] though scientifically fascinating.[165] Unlike Europe, where the consequences of the mismatch between 27 different approaches are not yet being discussed,[166] longstanding experience with regard to the need for co-ordinating multi-state – multi-province collective actions – exists in the US and Canada.[167]

161 See M. Taruffo, Harmonizing civil litigation in Europe? in F. Cafaggi/H. Muir-Watt (eds.) Making European Private Law, supra at note 52, p. 44 ff.; the European Commission is strengthening the co-operation and education in private law matters; see Resolution of the Council and of the Representatives of the Governments of the Member States meeting within the Council on the training of judges, prosecutors and judicial staff in the European Union OJ C 299, 22.11.2008, 1 as well as Resolution of the Council and of the Representatives of the Governments of the Member States, meeting within the Council, on the establishment of a Network for legislative cooperation between the Ministries of Justice of the European Union, OJ C 326, 20.12.2008, 1.

162 See for such a distinction Cafaggi/Micklitz in this volume p. 401 ff., 434 ff.

163 See the different country reports in www.globalclassactions.standford.edu as well as the study commissioned by DG Sanco on the effectiveness and efficiency of collective redress http://ec.europa.eu/consumers/redress_cons/finalreportevaluationstudypart1-final2008-11-26.pdf and the study commissioned by DG Sanco on the problems faced by consumers in obtaining redress for infringements of consumer protection legislation, and the economic consequences of such problems http://ec.europa.eu/consumers/redress_cons/finalreport-problemstudy-part1-final.pdf.

164 See Rott, in this volume p. 379 ff.

165 Miller in this volume p. 263 ff.

166 Some preliminary remarks are to be found in Cafaggi/Micklitz, supra at note 3, p. 418 ff. A rough account is given by Stuyck in this volume; see for a comprehensive analysis, A. Stadler, Grenzüberschreitender kollektiver Rechtsschutz in Europa, JZ 2008, forthcoming.

167 R.A. Nagareda, Aggregate Litigation across the Atlantic and the Future of American Exceptionalism, 62 Vanderbilt Law Review, p. 1 (2009); Saumier, in this volume, p. 361 ff.

This is not to say that the effects of an injunction against infringements of consumer law beyond the state pose no problems. Due to the adoption of Directive 98/27/EC, there is limited practical experience in the Member States. However, only in two cases the transborder dimension of the action of injunction has come to the fore. In *Home Shopping*, the question was whether a German consumer organisation had standing to protect French consumers against misleading advertising originating from a German mailbox address.[168] In *Duchèsne*, the UK Office of Fair Trading sued a Belgian company in order to put an end to misleading advertising directed against UK consumers. The point at stake was not so much standing, which is clarified in Directive 98/27/EC, but the decision on the applicable law – either Belgian or English.[169] Furthermore there is a far-reaching question concerning the effects of the injunctive relief: under what circumstances can, e.g. an injunction brought by an Italian consumer association before an English court, affect consumers of third States? Or even more broadly is there a relationship between standing and effects of the action for injunction?

The lack or maybe the very limited practical experience is reflected in the way courts, lawyers, claimants and defendants behave. Member State courts have not yet been faced with the transborder dimension, not at all in aggregate litigation and to a very limited extent in transborder injunctions. It seems, however, as if the overall tendency is to keep the national territory clean from foreign non-national and non-resident claims. This becomes clear in the implementation of Directive 98/27 under which Member States are obligated mutually to grant standing to so-called qualified entities. Where Member States provide for aggregate litigation beyond injunctions, EU qualified national entities are normally not granted standing.[170] Players too are still mainly State-based. This is true for claimants and to a limited extent for defendants whose lawyers are often part of international law firms. Transborder litigation taking place at State level poses several agency questions related to the ability of state players to represent the interests of non-residents.[171] From a normative perspective, transborder litigation involves at least four legal aspects:

---

168 H.-W. Micklitz, Cross-Border Consumer Conflicts – A French-German Experience, JCP Special Issue, European Consumer Policy after Maastricht, 1993, 411–434. In 2006 the German legislature clarified that German consumer organisations are entitled to protect non-German consumers independent of whether they have clarified such a mandate in their statutes and that they are entitled to reprimand foreign law before German courts; see §4a) of the German Unterlassungsklagegesetz, thereto Micklitz in Münchener Kommentar zur Zivilprozess ordnung, 3. Auflage 2008, §4 a) UKlaG at 2.

169 H.-W. Micklitz, Transborder Law Enforcement – Does it exist? in Ulf Bernitz/Stephen Weatherill (eds.), The Regulation of Unfair Commercial Practices under EC Directive, New Rules and New Techniques, Hart Publishing, Oxford and Portland, 2006, pp. 235–254.

170 Hans-W.Micklitz/Peter Rott/Ulrike Docekal/Peter Kolba, Verbraucherschutz durch Unterlassungsklagen, Rechtliche und Praktische Umsetzung der Richtlinie Unterlassungs-klagen 98/27/EG in den Mitgliedstaaten, VIEW Schriftenreihe, Band 17, 2007, p. 228–230.

171 See Cafaggi/Micklitz in this volume.

(1) jurisdictional matters – where is the litigation to take place, which courts shall have jurisdiction and under what conditions? A set of criteria to distinguish between domestic and transborder litigation, and competence to decide jurisdictional subject matters in the absence of a federal judiciary are needed.
(2) procedural law on collective actions – what is the aggregate litigation all about and who is precluded from aggregate litigation, non-residents and/or non-nationals and if yes under what conditions?
(3) applicable law – which law applies? In particular, the requirement of commonality to certify the class in transborder litigation becomes problematic when questions of law are considered in a context of no harmonized legislation. If substantive laws to be applied differ in Member States, the requirement of commonality cannot be met. Similar issues arise in the US given that the common law of torts or contracts to be applied might differ from state to state.[172] Who shall have the competence to decide which law or laws are applicable and under what criteria?
(4) transborder enforcement of judgments – are national judgments taken under a national legal regime enforceable in another Member State?

The following survey on the four different normative levels is meant to identify the major unsolved issues and to develop policy options. It does not provide a full account of the complicated doctrinal issues.[173]

The legal landscape: As early as 1968, the then six Member States of the European Community concluded an International Convention on Jurisdiction *and* Enforcement, the Brussels Convention.[174] The new Member States joined the Brussels Convention. In relation to Norway, Spain and Iceland, the Lugano Convention applies.[175] The Brussels Convention was replaced by the Brussels Regulation in 2001.[176] This was politically acceptable only under the condition that Denmark, Ireland and the UK were allowed to opt out.[177] All three protect consumers who may sue in the courts of their own jurisdiction. Again, in 1980 the Member States adopted the so-called Convention of Rome, which defined largely unified standards on contract law, with particular rules on the protection of consumers in transborder contract law litigation.[178] Unlike the Brussels

172 See on these questions G. Miller in this volume p. 268 ff.
173 See for a much more comprehensive account of the relevant issues, Rott, p. 379 ff. and Saumier, p. 361 ff. in this volume, as well as A. Stadler, Grenzüberschreitender kollektiver Rechtsschutz in Europa, JZ 2009, p. 121.
174 Http://curia.europa.eu/common/recdoc/convention/en/c-textes/brux-idx.htm.
175 Http://curia.europa.eu/common/recdoc/convention/en/c-textes/_lug-textes.htm.
176 OJ L 12, 16.1.2001.
177 See Article 1 of the Protocols on the position of Denmark, Ireland and the UK on the EU-Treaty which clearly states that chapter IV of the Treaty does not apply to these three countries.
178 See Article 5 of the Rome Convention.

Convention, the Member States could not agree on granting the ECJ jurisdiction within the preliminary reference procedure under Article 234 ET. This gap as well as the limited scope of the Rome Convention with regard to the different types of contracts covered has been closed by the 2008 Rome I Regulation.[179] The 2007 Rome II Regulation establishes International Private Law rules on tort law, with particular emphasis on product liability claims.[180]

Canada does not provide a common set of rules on jurisdictional matters, contrary to the US Multi-State District Panel under which the Panel may decide to transfer litigation pending in numerous US States with the consent of the competent judge to the best appropriate court.[181] Both however, contain procedural rules on collective actions which are aimed at solving conflicts between different jurisdictions.

In Canada, it is the Uniform Law Conference of Canada (ULCC)[182] which tries to overcome the substantial differences between the laws of the provinces on class actions by defining recommendations to handle class actions of multi-jurisdictional nature.

Unlike Europe, neither the US nor Canada have harmonized the rules on the applicable law. Conflict of law rules are in the hands of the US states.[183] The obligation to enforce interstate or provincial judgments is written down in the Constitution. One substantial difference remains between Canada and the US. Contrary to the US, in Canada the Supreme Court has no jurisdiction under a federal Rule 23 class action.

Jurisdictional matters: The Brussels Convention and the Brussels Regulation 44/2001 protect the right of the individual consumer to sue in the courts of his or her own jurisdiction. In transborder mass litigation, this is simply not possible as the transborder dimension presupposes that the consumers come from a country different from that of the defendant. Much more difficult problems arise if the consumers are domiciled in different EU Member States. There are two ways out: the parties may wish to enter a choice of court agreement, which is always possible in all jurisdictions at least after the occurrence of the event giving rise to the litigation.[184] But what if the parties cannot agree *ex post* if the shaping of the

179 Regulation 593/2008 OJ L 177, 4.7.2008, 6.

180 Regulation 864/2007 OJ L 199, 31.7.2007, 1.

181 §28 U.S.C. §1407, see Saumier in this volume.

182 See under www.ulcc.ca.

183 See in this volume G. Miller, Compensation and deterrence, p. 267 ff. On the issue of conflict of laws applied to class action, see S. Issacharoff, Settled expectations in a world of unsettled law, supra, at note 122. In general on US international private law rules (conflict of law rules), P. Hay, US-Amerikanisches Recht, 3. Auflage, 2005, p. 71 and M. Reinmann, Einführung in das US-amerikanische Privatrecht, 2. Auflage 2004, p. 349.

184 See for a full account of jurisdiction clauses under the Brussels Convention and Regulation, Micklitz §31.13–31.14 in Reich/Micklitz, Europäisches Verbraucherrecht, 4. Auflage, 2003.

collective action differs considerably - this is the case in Europe and in Canada more than in the United States?

Article 6 of the Brussels Regulation deals only with multiple defendants, but not with multiple claimants. This means that the EU ties jurisdiction to residence. If the agreement is concluded prior to litigation, a distinction must be made between jurisdiction clauses enshrined in standard contract terms and those which are concluded on an individual basis. The latter are possible if the consumer benefits from an additional advantage.[185] Standard terms are subject to control within Directive 93/13/EEC. In *Océano*,[186] the ECJ declared jurisdiction clauses to the detriment of the consumer void. With a view to mass actions, the solution under EC law is not very helpful. Jurisdiction clauses to the detriment of the consumer may be annulled in each and every country, but neither the Brussels Convention nor the Brussels Regulation tell us how to overcome the problem of conflicting jurisdictions if the injured consumers are domiciled in different EU countries. In practice, the only way out might be an *ex post* agreement to which however all affected consumers would have to give their consent.

In Canada, the courts in the province are divided over questions of jurisdiction on non-residents. Two of them in British Columbia[187] and in Ontario[188] confirmed jurisdiction in class actions over non-residents in line with the US Supreme Court in *Philips Petroleum v. Shutts*.[189] The court of Quebec,[190] however, requested appropriate jurisdictional connection between the members of the class and the place of jurisdiction. In essence, the point is whether individual rights of the non-residents, the right to be heard and due process, prevail over the 'the common issue', such as the quality of defectiveness of the product which might be common to all injured parties, residents or non-residents. In the US, such issues are solved by the Multi-district Litigation Panel which is authorized to decide conflicts over federal jurisdiction.[191] In Canada, the situation is different and in a way nearer to Europe, as the provinces are akin to independent states. The result might very well be parallel proceedings spread over the provinces just as in Europe. However, the Uniform Law Conference of Canada has laid down rules in its model law to overcome such conflicts which seem to confirm the regionalization of mass litigation.

---

185 See Article 17 Brussels Regulation.

186 ECJ Combined Cases C-40/98–244/98 ECR 2000 I-4941.

187 *Harrington v. Dow Corning Corp.* 2000 BCCA 605 (British Columbia Court of Appeal).

188 *Parsons v. Macdonald's Restaurants of Canada*, (2005) O.J. no. 506 (Ont. C.A.).

189 (1985) 472 US 797.

190 *Société Canadienne des postes v. Lépine* (2006) J.Q. No. 507 (S.C), aff'd (2007) QCCA 1092 (Qué. C.A.).

191 Manual for Complex Litigation, Federal Judicial Center, 2004 at 20.13.131, citing 28 U.S.C. Section 1407.

European procedural law: Since there are no common rules on the applicable law to collective actions, the rules on private international law suggest that the courts apply their own domestic procedural law (*lex fori*). We must clearly distinguish between actions for injunction and pecuniary damages. Directive 98/27/EC[192] sets minimum standards for the application of injunctive orders in transborder litigation. Member State courts are bound mutually to recognise the standing of the qualified entities in transborder conflicts. EC law, however, does not deal with the question of whether one national consumer organisation is entitled to protect all European citizens or whether a bilateral transborder injunction order may affect a third EU country.

Apart from injunction applications, it is for the Member States to tackle the issue of transborder litigation. They may decide to grant standing also to EU qualified entities under Directive 98/27/EC and any other potential foreign claimant. Given the large discretion available, Member States may, however, delimit the national procedural rules on aggregate litigation to all those who are resident in the respective country and/or even to their citizens alone. The different laws of the Member States on aggregate litigation show an overall tendency to 'nationalize' the scope of collective actions by limiting the enforceability of the newly established collective remedies to competent national bodies or in limiting them to the protection of nationals alone, which might run counter to Article 12 ET.[193]

In Canada, the diversity of provincial laws leads to numerous conflicts. Each court tends to protect its residents. The outcome is a regionalization of jurisdiction which could only be overcome by single federal proceedings as the one in the US under CAFA. Regionalization yields parallel procedures, maybe even with conflicting or divergent results. Lawyers may instrumentalize the large choice of jurisdictions for their own purposes.

Private international law: The subject matter of this book is consumer law enforcement. Private International Law is still organized around contract and tort with different rules. The same infringement which may consist of a breach of contract or a tort in different legal systems may thus be regulated differently from a PIL perspective. These differences may affect the litigation strategy and the choice of lawyers to bring the case according to the most favourable law before the court that can apply that law.

The European legislature has most recently undertaken a major effort to transform the Rome Convention into a Regulation and to adopt appropriate rules on transborder tort litigation. The extensive and highly conflictive debate within the Community and within the European academia focused entirely on individual

192 OJ L 166, 11.6.1998, 55.

193 See Countries report in www.globalclassactions.stanford.edu: Denmark, E. Werlauff and P. Rott in this volume.

claims and largely on the question whether and to what extent particular consumer protection rules are needed.[194] The outcome is a set of mandatory consumer protection rules whose appropriateness with regard to aggregate litigation has yet to be tested. The key to a flexible solution which is needed in aggregate litigation lies in agreements between the parties. Application of these rules to aggregate litigation may to some extent limit the fragmentation that often prevents aggregation in the US.[195]

Choice of law agreements in contractual arrangements are possible under Article 6 of the Rome I Regulation, but they shall not deprive the consumer of the mandatory protection provided by his own national law. Thus, the different claims within, e.g. a group action have to be considered under different national legal orders. The European Commission is working hard to overcome national differences in consumer protection by shifting from minimum to maximum harmonization.[196] Seen under this perspective transparency would be considerably increased if the European Commission would refer to an EU regulation instead of a directive. The current situation is somewhat more homogeneous in tort law litigation as Article 14(1) of Rome II allows for choice of law agreements even after the event giving rise to the damage occurred. This seems to be the only way out of the dilemma of different applicable laws resulting from the Rome I Regulation. However, neither Rome I nor Rome II provide any mechanism which would allow the claimants, the lawyers and the judges to come to such an arrangement. In light of the broad and deep differences in national contract and tort law despite EU harmonization, negotiations over such arrangements might face a difficult environment.

European international private law rules, just as do their counterparts in Canada and the US, where there are state laws, tend to strengthen the homeward trend. Judges might limit the group action to those members where the same legal order applies and this is in all probability the national legal order where the court is settled. CAFA has now limited forum shopping in the US.[197]

In sum, the EC legal order is deficient at nearly all four levels, due to the fact that EC policy on regulating transborder litigation has so far almost entirely focused on individual claims, setting aside the collective dimension, whereas the US and Canada have developed rules to deal with transborder litigation involving

194 See Regulation (EC) No. 864/2007, O.J. L. 199, 31 July 2007, 40 and the Commentary by A. Dickinyou, The Rome II Regulation. The Law Applicable to Non-Contractual Obligations, Oxford University Press, New York - Oxford, 2008.

195 See on these problems and the solutions, G. Miller, Compensation and Deterrence, in this volume p. 236 ff.

196 COM (2008) 614/3 8.10.2008.

197 See R. Nagareda, 'Aggregation and its Discontents, supra at note 136; C. Sharkey, 'CAFA Settlement Notice Provision: Optimal Regulatory Policy?', U. Pa. L. Rev., Vol. 156, 2008, available at http://ssrn.com/abstract=1133137; H. Erichson, 'CAFA's Impact on Class Action Lawyers', U. Pa. L. Rev., Vol. 156, 2008, available at SSRN: http://ssrn.com/abstract=1083819.

different state citizens. Europe will not be able to manage transborder litigation without taking additional regulatory steps. It might benefit from the US/Canadian experience gained over a couple of decades. Europe seems to be focused nearly completely on the opt-in opt-out debate, whereas the true problems might result from the mismatch between 27 different types of aggregate litigation each of which is designed only for national purposes completely setting aside the transborder dimension.[198] There is an urgent need for an EC policy which tackles the issues of transborder litigation.[199]

6. PURPOSE AND CONTENT OF THIS BOOK

The starting point of this collection of essays is that a combination of public and private enforcement is needed to ensure consumer protection.[200] A second premise is that this combination differs across sectors within consumer law. Thus, the complementarity of public and private enforcement varies significantly between product safety and unfair contract terms or unfair commercial practices. This variation implies that it is possible to define common variables for enforcement in consumer law but only sector-by-sector analysis can fruitfully display the relevant factors affecting the combination.

In both cases, product safety and unfair contract terms or practices, collective enforcement can be seen as a response to collective action problems in a multi-level political unit.[201] In both cases there are agency questions but they have different dimensions because information and incentives of public and private collective enforcers differ widely.

The traditional lenses through which to read this relationship are inadequate. The aim of this book is to shed some light on changes that have occurred both in the public and private domains of consumer law enforcement in Europe, Canada and the US, requiring new modalities to proceed along the lines of a European legislative reform on collective consumer redress.

The seventeen contributions from the US, Canada and the European Member States (East and West) bring the interplay of *public enforcement and private collective judicial enforcement* into perspective. This book is broken down into six

198 R.A. Nagareda, supra, note 167.

199 See the proposals in the conclusions of Cafaggi/Micklitz in this volume.

200 See Van den Bergh, Should consumer protection law be publicly enforced?, in Van Boom and Loos, Collective enforcement of consumer law: Securing Compliance in Europe Through Private Group Action and Public Authority Intervention, European Law Publishing, Groningen, 2007, p. 190, 201.

201 See for the multi-level dimension, introduction under 3.

chapters: (1) the general comparison reflects the constitutional dimension (three multi-level systems of the US, EC and Canada are compared, vertically = allocation of powers between levels and distinction between regulation and private law and administrative versus judicial control), institutional dimension (the players, regulatory and judges, private organisations and lawyers) and substantive dimension (regulation through administrative versus regulation through tort or contract law, standard setting and remedies); (2) the public/private enforcement divide analyses the choices made in the US and in Europe with regard to products and remedies; (3) the chapter on remedies focuses on the distinction between the injunctions/damages and the influence of administrative and judicial enforcement; (4) class actions/group actions clarify the features of multiple individual and collective damages, representative action, group action, model or test case action and class action as well as hybrids; (5) arbitration plays an increasing role in consumer disputes in the US and in Europe. Negotiation might aim at preventing litigation, negotiations might take place within litigation or negotiations might aim at receiving judicial approval; (6) transborder litigation and international private law break down the still very much national approach to administrative and judicial enforcement in Europe. Canada serves as an example to overcome these scattered approaches; (7) the final chapter develops policy proposals for the way ahead in Europe.

The first three essays define the main institutional variables, including the specificities of eastern European countries to which this book gives special attention.

Samuel Issacharoff and Ian Samuel focus on the relationship between enforcement strategies and institutional factors necessary to implement them. They claim that market-based systems of control such as reputation and competition have limited reach and some combination of *ex ante* and *ex post* regulation is needed especially for numerous low value claims that correspond to high aggregate gains for the defendant. Their contribution defines typologies of enforcement based on two couples of factors: agents and time. They distinguish public and private agents and *ex ante* versus *ex post* intervention. In *ex ante* regulation they compare command and control and contract in *ex post* criminal and tort law. They concentrate on private enforcement and address the negative value suit question by comparing the different institutional responses to the risk of failing to deter. They conclude by identifying the main institutional preconditions for *ex post* regulation through litigation: an independent judiciary able to aggregate claims, entrepreneurial lawyers supported by a private bar that can contribute to generate expertise in litigation and, last but not least, legal education.

Jules Stuyck sets the agenda for collective law making and enforcement in Europe. He deals with four major issues. The constitutional framework of the EC is said to allow for adopting European legislation not only cross-border but also to internal litigation. The public/private enforcement divide is understood much more as a mix of policies in the Member States that does not show a clear picture. In clear contrast to the US, the EC is considering antitrust injuries representative actions and opt-in collective actions. In the last part, Stuyck puts emphasis on the difficulties of multinational litigation of collective actions in the EC.

Antonina Bakardjieva Engelbrekt examines consumer law enforcement in Central and Eastern European countries. She first describes the impact of the Consumer *Acquis* implementation, suggesting that conditionality has produced institutional changes in CEEC far beyond the conventional reach of the procedural autonomy principle. She then examines the alternative between public and private enforcement and claims that the preference for public enforcement in CEEC can be explained by two sets of factors: one endogenous related to path dependency on public intervention, and the second exogenous and driven by enlargement European policies which favoured the establishment of public agencies as reference points for consumer protection long before the enactment of Regulation 2006/2004. Bakardjeva, focusing mainly on Bulgaria shows how the first more liberal trend of law reform which took place at the end of the last century has been replaced by a stricter one, reducing the space of judicial enforcement and in particular standing to individual consumers. She then analyses the impact of enlargement policies and illustrates how the turn towards public enforcement with Regulation 2006/2004 was partly influenced by the accession policy. She concludes by envisaging a change in European policies towards new MS: from a control system based on formal transposition to a more functionalist approach, leading towards more tailored institutional building and wider institutional pluralism.

The second section addresses the relationship between agencies and courts in consumer protection from different perspectives, developing the analysis of some eastern European countries and comparing it with the western innovative experience like that of the Dutch.

Catherine Sharkey addresses two important questions focusing on the US experience: what is the balance between government regulation and common law remedies, and at which institutional level should this balance be defined? She analyses the relationship between agencies and courts concerning violations of federal statutes and engages in a comparative institutional analysis about relative capabilities to handle consumer risks. She underlines the superiority of agencies over courts in information gathering departing from previous law and economics analysis. Sharkey designs an agency reference model where federal agencies provide information which Courts deciding pre-emption cases ought to use.

Christopher Hodges underlines those features in which the UK seems to be different from quite a number of Member States: the strong focus on ADR mechanisms to handle individual complaints speedily even in situations of mass events despite the existence of the Group Litigation Order and the ever stronger role of public administrations in collective law enforcement which is underpinned by an official governmental policy. Private judicial enforcement through consumer organisations has been enhanced in competition law, where they may launch a super-complaint to the Office of Fair Trading. Here individuals who have suffered loss may institute a claim for damages before the specialist competition court.

Marek Safjan, Lukasz Gorywoda and Agnieszka Janczuk focus on the notion of collective interest at the European level emphasizing its procedural and substantive meanings. In order to assess the effectiveness of EU policy, Safjan *et al.* distinguish between substantive and procedural open-ended terms and suggest that while the first may present social advantages, the latter can pose serious risks of too high discretion. They analyse the relationship between individual and collective interest, clarify that collective interest does not coincide with the sum of individual interests, and provide a definition of collective interest based on the number of infringements and their persistence over time, the addressees of the 'unfair' practices, and the nature of the infringed interest, i.e. whether economic or health-related. After defining collective interest, they examine its evolution in the Polish legal system during the socialist regime and after its demise, showing how the past elaboration affects the current one, mainly influenced by European legislation.

Lubos Tichy and Jan Balarin analyse judicial and administrative enforcement with regard to the Czech Republic. They describe the evolution of consumer enforcement in the Czech Republic comparing administrative and judicial enforcement. The more relevant role of administrative enforcement can be justified by institutional and normative factors. Judicial enforcement is limited to the injunctions given that no group or class actions legislation has been so far introduced. They consider factors that differentiate and factors that increase similarities. Standing requirements and remedies differ in the two modes of enforcement. However, admissibility of abstract control and expansion of *res judicata* effects reduce the differences with administrative control.

Ewoud Hondius distinguishes two levels of consumer protection: the individual level and the collective level. The adoption of a European Regulation on small claims procedures is seen as a tool to invite those countries which until then had favoured private law enforcement and out-of-court settlement of consumer complaints, to reconsider these policies. The introduction of a small claims procedure for consumer complaints is said to compensate some weak points of private complaints tribunals. On a collective level, the foundation of a Dutch Consumer Authority has sparked discussion in the Netherlands about the most desirable form of enforcement: public or private. The newly introduced settlement for mass damages shifts the balance towards private judicial enforcement.

Comparing remedies in private enforcement

The third section focuses on remedies in judicial enforcement.

Geoffrey Miller conducts a functional analysis of the interplay between compensation and deterrence, claiming that a tension between the two exists in aggregate litigation. While compensation is mainly a moral concept and concerns plaintiffs, deterrence is an economic concept and focuses on defendants. Miller demonstrates that emphasis on one or other goal implies different rule and policy choices. After identifying five different regulatory strategies including licensing, disclosure, monitoring, business practice regulation and private legal remedies, Miller focuses on the last three. He first analyses the interaction of federal and state substantive and procedural laws, emphasizing the difficulties posed by the choice of regulating an integrated market predominantly through state law, including conflict of laws. He then moves to the different devices employed in small claims cases and concludes by examining the limitations of class action remedies. In particular, he underlines the difficulties arising when injured consumers come from different jurisdictions in a framework where each state has its own law on the conflict of laws. Different solutions may depend on the way the tension between compensation and deterrence is solved. After describing the different areas where compensation and deterrence are in tension, Miller briefly overviews the European landscape, suggesting that changes are taking place without there having been sufficient consideration of accountability and funding questions.

Cristina Poncibò chooses the protection of the collective interest of consumers through consumer organisations as the starting point of her analysis. The focus therefore is on the directive on injunctions which is said to reflect the early French approach on granting standing to consumer organisations to claim compensation for violation of the '*intéret collectif*'. Poncibò elaborates on the theoretical implications of such an approach, highlights the major deficiencies being mainly the lack of a claim for compensation, but at the same time identifies the huge potential for development of the directive in line with the recent Italian reform of the Consumer Code.

Astrid Stadler concentrates on group actions as a remedy to enforce consumer interests. European type group actions are said to be different from US type class actions not only because of the opt-out model, the costs of pre-trial discovery, the American rule of costs, the jury system and punitive damages, but also because of the missing social security net. Europe is mainly favouring an opt-in model not least because of the restricted rights of group members in US type class actions. Her major concern is whether and to what extent group actions may be justified. Stadler distinguishes between mass litigation, small damages cases (skimming off-procedures, unviable claims) and test cases, each of which requires its own design, thereby using the selection of the plaintiff, the objective and basic procedural structure or the case management as the key criteria. She pleads in essence for a flexible cross over from opt-in class actions to skimming off procedures.

Geraint Howells' presentation is guided by his concern that whatever collective redress mechanism might be instituted at the UK, any other Member State or the European level shall be effective. Howells draws a rough picture of the current UK law on collective judicial enforcement as well as envisaged reforms, thereby distinguishing between a regime aiming to manage similar claims to prevent flooding of the courts and one that seeks viable claims that would not be worth bringing as individual claims. Another key issue is that of representative actions. He detects potential in developing representative actions instituted by consumer organisations provided the remedy is built on an opt-out regime combined with a *cy-près* scheme.

Norbert Reich starts from the premise that US business has found an effective "remedy" against class action litigation, namely through the introduction of "pre-dispute arbitration clauses". The US Supreme Court is allowing arbitration clauses also against mandatory state consumer protection statutes. Canadian law enforces pre-dispute arbitration clauses unless they are expressly forbidden by provincial law. The law of EU Member States regarding arbitration clauses in consumer contracts is very diverse; the ECJ so far has only intervened in enforcement procedures concerning arbitration awards against consumers, but not against arbitration clauses as such. The paper uses US and recent Canadian experiences to make some proposals on how to avoid the class action device being rendered ineffective by generously allowing pre-litigation arbitration clauses.

Transborder litigation and international private law

Genevieve Saumier considers the private international law dimensions of transborder collective private enforcement within the Canadian context to highlight the challenges posed by its federal constitution, its decentralized court structure and the co-existence of jurisdictions of the common law and civil law traditions. The way in which Canadian courts and legislatures have dealt with the transborder class action are analysed along a proposed uniform model law recently put forward to address the challenges that remain unsettled within the Canadian context. The distinct American approach is noted to underscore the significant effect of constitutional, judicial and procedural structures on the shape of responses to private international law dimensions of transborder collective private enforcement.

Peter Rott explores whether or not, or to what extent, the different collective remedies can be brought in cross-border cases. The legal situation is analysed under Brussels Regulation (EC) No. 44/2001 on jurisdiction and the recognition and enforcement of judgments and under Rome II Regulation (EC) No. 864/2007 on the law applicable to non-contractual obligations (Rome II) and Rome I Regulation (EC) No. 593/2008 on the law applicable to contractual obligations. In his final section, he considers the working around EC law by bringing or joining a class action in the US and enforcing a US judgment or in-court settlement within the EC. Rott concludes that the newly adopted instruments largely neglect the intricacies of cross-border actions on collective damages.

Administrative and judicial enforcement in consumer protection: the way forward

Fabrizio Cafaggi and Hans-W. Micklitz examine the European scenario from a comparative perspective. They first describe the relationship between administrative and judicial enforcement, then address the drawbacks of the current European multilevel system with European legislation on injunction and MSs' legislation on class and representative actions. They advocate the necessity of higher integration of consumer protection with other European policies, in particular competition and environmental ones. They then identify several policy questions to be addressed in order to design a more effective consumer enforcement system. They suggest the enactment of new rules to coordinate the simultaneous use of injunctions and damages in judicial enforcement and that of injunction when both administrative and judicial enforcement are in place in different MSs. An accountability deficit in consumer enforcement should be solved by devising new principles tailored for aggregate litigation both in relation to private organisations and to law firms. New rules are also needed to improve judicial coordination in consumer enforcement. They have to be coordinated with existing rules on private international law and mutual recognition of judgments. From the policy perspective the European Commission should promote centralized information collection, the creation of a competitive market for legal services and contribute to funding a pilot project of transboundary litigation in consumer protection.

PART I.
COMPARATIVE INSTITUTIONAL ANALYSIS

THE INSTITUTIONAL DIMENSION OF CONSUMER PROTECTION

Samuel ISSACHAROFF* and Ian SAMUEL**

INTRODUCTION

One of the central functions of the state is protecting the integrity of contracts such that markets and private ordering may thrive. This is such a well understood theme in liberal political theory as to appear to need no further exposition. Unfortunately, the classic account envisioned a single seller and a single buyer who needed the state only to make sure that cross-temporal commitments between purchase and delivery would be honoured and that disputes could be resolved without recourse to private retaliation.

As important as this account may be, it is necessarily incomplete. As the scale and scope of markets change, so too must the role of the state in providing assurances against multiple forms of market malfunction. In some markets, particularly those that are close-knit with a great deal of repeat play among the participants, reputation and other informal mechanisms may be sufficient to police against most improper conduct. There, the role of governmental supervision might well be limited to that of the final guarantor that commitments to pay and deliver are honoured. But in our increasingly global economy, with buyers and sellers interchangeable and unknown to each other, community mechanisms of enforcement are difficult and there is a corresponding push for greater governmental supervision.

We start from a simple proposition that the integrity of markets requires more than simply enforcing reciprocal terms of exchange. As the breadth of commercial activity expands and as exchange takes on forms unadorned by actual human contact, protecting consumers against harm becomes an essential prerequisite to the healthy functioning of markets. Fraud, product failure, and personal injury threaten the free exchange of goods and services by constricting the networks of

* Bonnie & Richard Reiss Professor of Constitutional Law, New York University School of Law.
** J.D., New York University School of Law 2008.

trust and exchange and sapping the vitality of markets.[1] Consumer protection is an integral part of the role of the state in mature market societies; our basic approach is to define the risk to markets as a social harm that can be managed in many ways, by many institutions.

Simply acknowledging the need to police markets and protect consumers is an important but limited first step. All reasonably developed societies do that in some fashion. What is of interest for us is how that is done and what forms of institutional arrangements follow from the array of choices that remain. In this chapter, we take up two topics: first, the typology of harm management itself. By dividing enforcement agents into "public" and "private," and the moments of enforcement into *ex ante* and *ex post*, it is possible to develop a typology. For example, the prior governmental approval of products before they may enter the market is a classic form of public *ex ante* regulation. A tort suit by an injured consumer is a corresponding private *ex post* form. Recently, American law has been dominated by disputes over how national *ex ante* regulation interacts with state-by-state *ex post* liability: if the Food and Drug Administration approves a medical device, for example, may an individual state's tort law hold the manufacturer liable for defective designs?

Our main focus, however, is not so much on identifying the forms that regulation might take, but on the institutional demands made by these different modes of regulation. It is here that the temporal dimension emerges as critical. The management of social harm can be either *ex ante* or *ex post* or, as with the public/private distinction, a mixture of both. Regulation can act prescriptively to limit the potential for injurious conduct or it can react retrospectively to provide compensation to those harmed and attempt to get private actors to condition their behaviour in anticipation of liability rules. Each of the regulatory options must have its own supporting institutions and its own societal infrastructure to make it work. The choice of how to regulate harm ought to be as sensitive to what the tool requires as it is to the shape of the harm itself. These choices are about institutional design and competence as much as alleviation of substantive harm.

Our aim here is not to revisit the debates about *ex ante* versus *ex post* regulation. These are complicated issues and there are many factors that have to be weighed in the balance, as there are trade-offs between centralized public enforcement as opposed to decentralized private enforcement. In this chapter, however, we are concerned not simply with whether markets can be made more vibrant by lifting *ex ante* forms of regulation[2] – a view that underlies most efforts at deregulation

---

1 *See generally* Karen S. Cook et al., *The Emergence of Trust Networks Under Uncertainty: The Case of Transitional Economies, in* CREATING SOCIAL TRUST IN POST-SOCIALIST TRANSITION (Janos Kornai ed. 2004).

2 There are, to be sure, complaints about every form of regulation, including those sectors of the American economy in which *ex ante* regulation has primacy. *See, e.g.*, Michael R. Ward, *Drug Approval Overregulation*, REGULATION: THE REVIEW OF BUSINESS & GOVERNMENT (1992).

– but also whether the right processes for *ex post* accountability are in place. The American experience with *ex post* regulation turns critically on the role of private enforcement to supplement more limited state responsibility for compensation and deterrence. The ability to harness private enforcement depends not only on the substantive laws governing compensation, but also on the incentives to ferret out wrongdoing, provide efficient resolution of similarly situated claims and compel the proper level of internalization of norms of proper market conduct. Our claim is not that a particular form of regulation is superior across all settings. Rather, it is that each regulatory strategy must ensure that the proper institutional actors are in place for its effective implementation.

To give but one example, the U.S. relies heavily on the incentives for private actors to unearth wrongdoing after the fact and to force future actors to discount the cost of enforcement into their primary decisions on risk and precaution. But the American approach not only allows individuals to seek compensation, but actually creates incentives for private actors to enforce substantive laws and be compensated when their efforts bear fruit – termed the private attorney general model. These private attorney generals are empowered to act on behalf of either individuals or a broad group of similarly situated individuals, bound together by the proceedings and a supervising tribunal, with incentives for the undertaking created from the proceeds of the enforcement action. Consider the civil rights statutes,[3] which permit the recovery of "a reasonable attorney's fee" upon successful litigation.[4] This represents an institutional commitment (albeit one that comes at little direct cost to the public generally) to private enforcement of individual rights. Without this commitment, the underlying prohibition against "deprivation of any rights, privileges, or immunities secured by the Constitution and laws"[5] would have little force.

If a decision is made to move to private, *ex post* enforcement of consumer protection law, then there must be corresponding institutional commitments, whether in the form of government institutions, NGOs, private aggregation mechanisms or the class action. These commitments are not without costs, of course. Private enforcement invariably turns on the incentives for private gain and there is invariably a loss of the public spiritedness represented (at least in principle) by disinterested governmental supervision. Nonetheless, the core argument is that all regulatory regimes have costs, and that if in certain circumstances a private-enforcement, after-the-fact liability regime is deemed best suited to the problems of democratised markets, then there must be corresponding provisions for the emergence of the private actors who will pursue that enforcement.

---

3 42 U.S.C. §1988.

4 Id.

5 42 U.S.C. §1983.

In Part I, we provide a spatial model of the typology of regulation. By mapping regulation on a pair of axes, one representing the moment of enforcement and the other representing the public/private divide, it is possible to classify the various schemes of enforcement fairly comprehensively. In Part II, we dig deeper and examine the institutional dimension of this enforcement: what, beyond the shape of the substantive harms at issue, ought to shape the choice of regulatory tools?

1. THE TYPOLOGY

Social harm can be managed in many ways. The term "regulation" often conjures up images of command-and-control, top-down edicts by some public agency; such edicts certainly count, but they do not exhaust the field. Regulation of social harm can also be achieved by harnessing private actors, in primary place of or in cooperation with the government. A tort system fits this model: the government provides the courts, but private actors are largely responsible for seeking redress of their own injuries.

There is another dimension as well. The management of social harm can be either *ex ante* or *ex post* or, as with the public/private distinction, a mixture of both. Broadly, this means that regulation can either try to anticipate the likely sources of harm and either prohibit certain forms of conduct or prescribe the precautionary steps necessary for avoidance of harm. Such regulatory interventions are most likely efficient where there is sufficient predictability of the sources of harm and the information necessary to ameliorate the conditions is likely ascertainable efficiently by government authorities. Thus, for example, regulators may prohibit forklifts capable of raising loads more than five metres off the ground or may require a protective cage over the head of a forklift operator. In contrast, regulators may decide that specific safety precautions are too site-specific or that optimal precautions are too variable to be suitable for direct regulatory commands. In such circumstances, tort liability – even strict liability – may better create the incentives for parties with superior access to information about risk and the cost of prevention to design a precautionary protocol.

Laying these axes out on a graph might look something like this:

Table 1

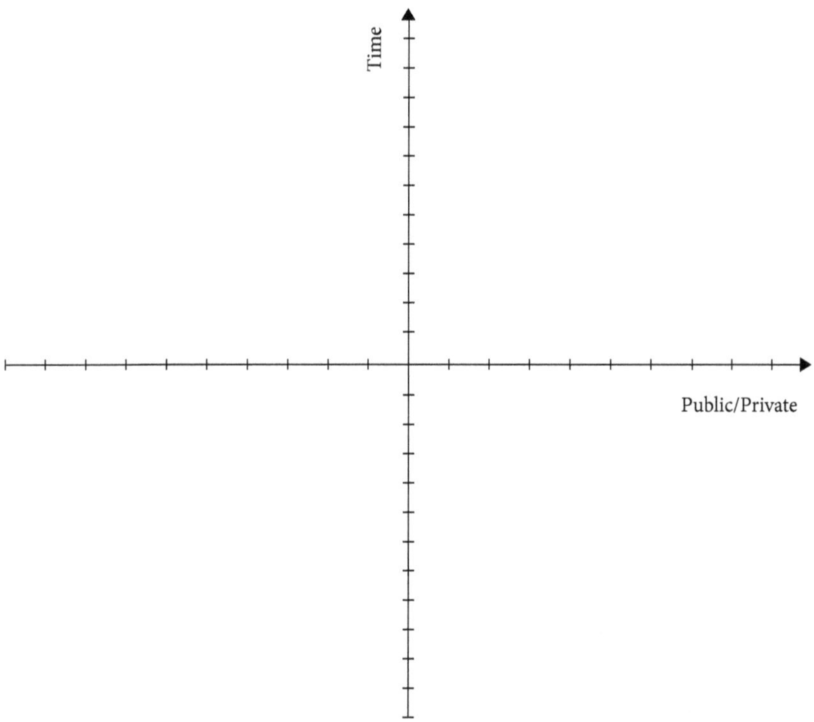

The axes of the graph, somewhat simplistically, represent two essential choices that must be made when harm is to be regulated: when and by whom. Lending itself most naturally to a spectrum is "when" is the moment of enforcement (by which we mean the moment at which coercive state power is exercised). Regulation that occurs entirely before harm ever takes place is at one end of the spectrum and regulation that begins only after the harm has been completely realized is at the other. The other axis is the public/private distinction. The further one travels along this axis, the more government is involved as a primary regulator. At some level, of course, the government must provide the instrumentalities of legal enforcement, such as court systems, positive law and the coercive ability to enforce judgments, but beyond this minimum, the limits of government regulation are (as experience demonstrates) bound only by the imagination.

These regulatory choices interact, however, and as we map several familiar forms of regulation onto these axes, we find familiar patterns. In the upper left quadrant of the graph, we find public, *ex post* enforcement: harm occurs and the government responds to it. An example is the ordinary criminal law. If a citizen is robbed, the government dispatches detectives to find facts, a public prosecutor draws up an indictment and, in fact, even if the primary victim does not wish for the case to proceed, the prosecuting authority may usually prosecute the criminal anyway, emphasising the truly public nature of the enforcement.

As regulation moves into the upper right quadrant, we find private *ex post* regulation of harm. In the American system, this is where we would situate the private law suit or its collective form, the class action.[6] In such cases, the harm has already occurred, so this mode of regulation is essentially reactive; however, the government provides the courts and the public law on which the private litigants will rely in the settlement of their dispute. In such cases, however, there must be one more form of public support if such cases are to fill a role in justifying suits where individuals may not have the level of harm that would justify seeking redress in the costly world of litigation. In such cases, it is incumbent upon the state to provide a mechanism for overcoming the collective action problem that allows diffuse harms to be visited upon a broad number of individuals, a subject to which we shall return.

In the bottom left, regulation is typified by *ex ante* government action. Regulation of speech achieved by "prior restraint" is of this sort. A more palatable example is the FDA's "Premarket Notification" program.[7] Under §510 of the Federal Food, Drug and Cosmetic Act, for example, many device and pharmaceutical manufacturers are required "to notify FDA, at least 90 days in advance, of their intent to market a medical device."[8] This allows prospective investigation and approval by the agency.[9] Regulated devices cannot be brought to market absent of compliance with regulatory requirements, and it is the government (not private parties who fear prospective harm) that enjoins the product's sale absent of such compliance.

Finally, the bottom right quadrant represents an unusual method of regulation: *ex ante* private regulation. Though a bit odd to conceive of, we believe this is the domain into which contract law best fits. In contract, private parties make advance agreements that require each to take whatever steps the other feels best to avoid harm. The simplest example can be found in liquidated damages provisions negotiated by sophisticated parties. But even in more diffuse cases, there are arguments that private parties should be incentivised to contract a set of prearranged contingencies for malfeasance or the failure of a joint venture. Thus, for example, in US bankruptcy law, there is currently a "growing schism"[10] driven by scholars who want to eliminate much public bankruptcy legislation. Their

---

6 *See generally* American Law Institute, Principles of the Law of Aggregate Litigation (2007).

7 21 U.S.C. §360 (2000).

8 U.S. Food and Drug Administration, *§510(k) Overview*, www.fda.gov/cdrh/510k.html (last visited 15 February 2008).

9 21 U.S.C. §360(k) (2000).

10 Susan Block-Lieb, *The Politics of Privatizing Business Bankruptcy Law*, 74 Am. Bankr. L.J. 77, 77 (2000).

belief is that bankruptcy is best regulated not by the government, but privately. "The notion that contract can better provide any incentive forms the theoretical divide ... between critics of and defenders of bankruptcy law."[11] Contract, on this view, may be a better regulatory tool for bankruptcy; private, *ex ante* regulation can substitute, in other words, for public, *ex post* division of spoils.

Collecting these archetypes, one might alternatively visualise them this way:

Table 2

	Public	*Private*
Ex Post	Criminal Law	Tort
Ex Ante	Command-and-Control	Contract

It should be admitted that this typology is not absolute. Contract law requires a court system to back it up should one party be in breach. The FDA's pharmaceutical regulations are routinely the source of substantive tort law, as with presumptions of negligence created by failure to conform to regulatory requirements[12] and with a reliance on the tort law to provide compensation even where federal regulatory law has pre-emptively established the terms of liability. The criminal law is meant to deter as well as punish. The threat of an *ex post* class action may induce parties to change their behaviour before the harm occurs. In this way, even "pure" examples of each regulation bleed into one another.

Moreover, some modes of regulation are explicitly designed to be hybrids.[13] For example, the government often requires a bond (public, *ex ante* regulation) before construction of a large building is undertaken; this bond could then be used to pay the judgment if a private party sues in tort after injury (private, *ex post* regulation).[14] Or consider the domain of antitrust. The Justice Department

11 Barry E. Adler, *Finance's Theoretical Divide and the Proper Role of Insolvency Rules*, 67 So. Cal. L. Rev. 1107, 1111 (1994).

12 *E.g.*, *Merrell Dow Pharm. v. Thompson*, 478 U.S. 804 (1986). In many instances, the federal regulatory issue is directly tied to after-the-fact claims in the tort system. "The violation of federal statutes and regulations is commonly given negligence per se effect in state tort proceedings." Restatement (Third) of Torts §14, Reporters' Note, p.195 Tent. Draft No.1, Mar. 28, 2001 Comment *a*. See also W. Keeton, D. Dobbs, R. Keeton, & D. Owen, Prosser and Keeton on Law of Torts, §36, p. 221, n. 9 (5th ed. 1984) ("[T]he breach of a federal statute may support a negligence per se claim as a matter of state law" (collecting authority)).

13 *See* Samuel Issacharoff, *Regulating After the Fact*, 56 DePaul L. Rev. 375 (2007).

14 For example, vendors who contract with the California government to provide health equipment are subject to a bonding requirement that ensures accountability should the equipment prove faulty. Cal. Welf. & Inst. Code §14100.75 (West 2001).

routinely prosecutes antitrust violations and secures injunctions against further anticompetitive practices. This is public, *ex post* enforcement. Equally routine, however, is the typical follow-on suit for treble damages by the competitors injured by the anticompetitive practices now enjoined; private, *ex post* enforcement. The combinations are basically endless.

Moreover, not every combination works equally well. In American law, there is an uneasy relation between the efforts to coordinate liability standards through federal regulation, yet provide for compensation through state tort law remedies.[15] The resulting battles over regulatory pre-emption of state law remedies force an uncomfortable confrontation with the adequacy of the pre-market supervision under the federal regulatory scheme. Most recently, in *Riegel v. Medtronic*,[16] the Supreme Court of the United States held that certain common law claims against medical device manufacturers (classic *ex post* tort suits) were barred by the FDA's pre-approval process. Because of the national nature of the FDA's regulations and the legislative prohibition on state-level requirements that "differ" from those regulations, the Supreme Court held that certain state remedies were barred. For the Court, the regulatory system for medical devices "is in no sense an exemption from federal safety review-it *is* federal safety review."[17] The federal regulation represented a studied cost-benefit determination of the optimal standards for particular medical devices and, accordingly, could not be second-guessed or overridden by after-the-fact jury re-evaluations of risk management for a particular device. Even here, however, injuries caused by violations of federal standards are still to be compensated through *ex post* common law litigation: "State requirements are pre-empted under the MDA [Medical Devices Act] only to the extent that they are 'different from, or in addition to' the requirements imposed by federal law ... Thus, [the MDA] does not prevent a State from providing a damages remedy for claims premised on a violation of FDA regulations; the state duties in such a case 'parallel,' rather than add to, federal requirements."[18] Though this topic is too enormous for this chapter, the interplay between different forms of regulation at different levels of government complicates the picture even further, and as *Medtronic* illustrates, those complications rage.

Further, there are difficult questions of risk trade-offs that may dictate caution in opting for an *ex post* liability regime. In many areas, such as the siting of a nuclear power plant or the development of a vaccine with known secondary effects in subsets of the population, there may be a need for society to assume the known risk of harm because of the significant benefits to be realised. *Ex post* evaluation

---

15 For an extensive discussion of this point, see Samuel Issacharoff and Catherine M. Sharkey, *Backdoor Federalization*, 53 U.C.L.A. L. Rev. 1353 (2006).

16 128 S. Ct. 999 (2008).

17 *Id.* at 1007.

18 *Id.* at 1011.

of risk, in the case of a leak of radioactive steam or a child injured by a vaccine, may lead to overdeterrence in trial settings overcome with the sense of inevitability of the realised adverse event.

A final difficulty is posed by the remedial injunction. Consider a suit brought in response to harm, seeking monetary damages but also an injunction against future conduct of the same kind or an injunction to engage in specified prospective affirmative actions. This sort of "damages plus injunction" remedy is becoming increasingly common (though more so in Europe than in North America); some have gone so far as to say that it upsets the *ex post* vs. *ex ante* distinction altogether.[19] Moreover, injunctions may be issued judicially or – increasingly – by administrative agencies.[20] When relief is both backward-looking and prospective, and includes private compensation as well as publicly administered rules of conduct, the simple view above begins to show fissures. The indirect role of litigated judgments in conditioning future behaviour becomes a direct form of regulation, one that is negotiated between private parties and is designed to have express external consequences. When the boundary line is breached, the world of private dispute resolution takes on the air of delegation of public regulation to private parties. A variation on this occurs when litigation spurs legislative attempts to regulate *ex ante* what the lawsuit challenged *ex post* – sometimes with accompanying relief from liability.[21] Legislative retroactive judgments – in much the same fashion as judicial prospective decrees – collapse many of the critical divides between the public and the private, as well as the temporal divisions between *ex ante* regulation and *ex post* accountability.

This is all true. However, this typology can be a useful starting point when thinking about regulation and, specifically, the use of the private class action as a form of private, *ex post* enforcement – especially in cases, such as consumer fraud, in which the scope of the underlying harm might not justify *ex post* private enforcement by aggrieved consumers acting alone. Critics of class actions, in other words, might use this typology to highlight alternatives, such as the extent to which command-and-control regulation (public, *ex ante* regulation, in other words) might or might not be a useful substitute. The typology is a menu for reacting to social harm. While the right menu option will depend on the harm being regulated, it is clear that in some fashion, at some point, the choices the grid

---

19 *See, e.g.* Fabrizio Caffagi & Hans Micklitz, *Collective Enforcement of Consumer Law: A Framework for Comparative Assessment*, 16 European Rev. of Private L. 391 (2008).

20 *Id.*

21 An example is provided by the dispute in the United States over the Foreign Intelligence Surveillance Act. Major telecommunications firms were accused of widespread violations of American wiretapping law and a damages action was brought in federal court for redress – a classic consumer protection suit, though one with national security overtones. The Congressional response was a legislative prohibition against conduct of the same kind, coupled with a release from civil liability for the firms being sued. Eric Lichtblau & David Stout, *House Passes Bill on Federal Wiretapping Powers*, New York Times, 21 June, 2008.

presents must be answered: who will do the enforcing? And will the aim be to avert harms or to deter future wrongs by compensating those injured when they occur? Even in the hybrid cases (such as a damages-injunction remedy), the same filaments are present: the damages represent an *ex post* private response, while the injunction will be more like *ex ante* regulation. In the advanced cases, the fit will be imperfect, but the guidelines are basically correct. And, at any rate, advanced permutations of the typology require first an understanding of the basics.

An important question lurks behind the decision of what to order from the menu. To strain the metaphor, some regulatory dishes only work if the kitchen is well equipped. The institutions present or absent in society are crucial when deciding how to regulate harm. We take this institutional dimension up in the next part.

2. INSTITUTIONS AND PRIVATE ENFORCEMENT

Let us assume, for the purposes of this chapter, that there are significant societal interests in providing means of avoiding social harms and assume further that the costs associated with a controlling regulatory regime render it a suboptimal form for either redress or prevention. In many consumer contexts, for example, the fluidity of demand requires that products be introduced and withdrawn quickly in response to market conditions. Requiring new products to undergo a necessarily dilatory process of regulatory prescreening threatens the vitality of markets and depresses the ability to meet consumer demand. In such circumstances, both producers and consumers may be better served by a system which permits liberal entry into the market and provides sufficient mechanisms of accountability such as to diminish the risk of fraud, harmful products and other forms of opportunistic misconduct.

At the same time, one cannot simply will such a system of legal accountability into being, any more than one can simply pass laws instructing all parties not to misbehave. Each of the regulatory options must have its own supporting institutions, its own societal infrastructure, to make it work. The choice of how to regulate harm ought to be as sensitive to what the tool requires as it is to the shape of the harm itself; these choices are about institutional design and competence as much as alleviation of substantive harm. When social harm is going unmanaged, the answer may be quite often that the social institutions that are needed to deploy regulatory tools do not exist yet.

Our focus here is on the institutional prerequisites for enforcement mechanisms that are both private and *ex post*. Many advanced societies disfavour both *ex post* and private methods of enforcement of laws intended to redress consumer harm. So be it. There are reasons to believe that these are both necessary and efficient. But we do not press that point here. Instead, we ask what forms of legal organisation are necessary if there is to be after-the-fact enforcement in the consumer context, a context heavily defined by a deep asymmetry between the minimal loss to the purchaser and the possibility for illicit gain realised at the expense of small harms to a broad purchasing public. Unlike the personal injury scenario represented by *Medtronic,* in the classic consumer case, the limited individual harm renders most claims for legal redress unviable what is commonly termed a negative value suit in which the costs of prosecution likely exceed the anticipated potential recovery.

Accordingly, it is incumbent for legal systems seeking to liberalise market entry and innovation to ask what institutions are required for private, *ex post* enforcement, primarily those that may be the least obvious. There is a broad body of critical commentary concerning FDA-like institutions with the power to regulate pharmaceuticals. Such regulatory bodies will be criticised for the relative delays in bringing products to market, a cost that may be justified by the unique capacity for harm represented by certain categories of medical devices or pharmaceuticals. In globalised markets, however, extensive pre-market approval processes are increasingly assumed to be intolerable restraints on necessary innovation. Wherever the line is ultimately drawn on the scope of pre-market regulatory supervision, it is clear that for an agency such as the FDA to perform its function properly, there must be certain staffing levels, administrative expertise and procedural forms that can ensure appropriate supervision.

But assuming market liberalisations such that, at least in the US, "the creation of [product standards] is still largely a private procedure,"[22] there must be a corresponding discussion of what institutions are required for effective regulation, no less than in its public counterpart. There are of course many candidates, just as there are in the public domain. The American class action, the English Group Litigation Order, the newly minted Italian use of prosecuting associations with individual rights of intervention (now termed a "class action")[23] – all represent efforts at providing an organizational vehicle for the collective enforcement of private claims for redress.

One might think that private enforcement requires the fewest social institutions. After all, in the Hayekian state of nature, all that is needed are litigants, the common law and a court of competent jurisdiction; not even

---

22 Geraint G. Howells, *The Relationship Between Product Liability and Product Safety-Understanding a Necessary Element in European Product Liability Through a Comparison with the U.S. Position*, 39 Washburn L.J. 305 (2000).

23 Legislative Decree 6 September 2005 no. 206 (in Ordinary Supplement no. 162 to the Official Journal 8 October, no. 235). – Consumer Code, pursuant to Article 7 of Law no. 229 of 29 July 2003 (collective compensation action). The most recent version went into effect on 1 July 2008.

legislatures are required to address social harm in this fashion and may even represent an unwelcome intrusion.[24] When disputes are no more complicated than one schoolboy kicking another,[25] this may be so. But as societies and their markets become more sophisticated, this utopian picture rapidly develops fissures and social institutions must grow up to respond to the challenge.

The central problem is one of incentives for opportunism as opposed to incentives for enforcement. As the scale of consumer transactions grows, there are great potential gains to be had from what may be termed "democratised theft."[26] Whenever a single actor is engaging a multitude, small-scale gains from misrepresentation, charges, quantity delivered, etc. may translate into a very substantial gain at relatively low cost to each affected consumer. So, for example, major airlines may agree not to compete on price for routes to one another's "hub" airports, raising the cost of many tickets by only a small amount but representing a major aggregated gain to the industry.[27] These schemes threaten to compromise the integrity of markets and, if unchecked, may be a drain on the ability to transact efficiently.

Such exploitation presents a dual-headed problem. For one, ordinary market incentives to treat one's customers well will probably fail in instances like these; there is every reason to believe that neither firm reputation nor market competition is sufficient to prevent this type of opportunism. These schemes are often carried out in secret and are difficult to detect, and even once detected, are conceptually difficult for many consumers to parse so that they may update the reputation of the firm. Moreover, even in those industries competing on price, the marginal cost to each consumer of such "democratised theft" is so small as to likely be overwhelmed by other factors such as materials cost or even taxes.

Equally problematic, the low level of harm to any particular consumer compromises private enforcement of consumer claims. The amount at stake for any one person does not justify the cost of seeking legal redress, even though the harm in the aggregate is potentially enormous. A legal claim that is worth less than the transaction costs of litigation is known as a "negative value suit" and such suits represent a major barrier to private enforcement, one with which institutions (if private, *ex post* enforcement is to be the tool) must grapple.

---

24 *See* Friedrich A. Hayek, The Road to Serfdom (1944).

25 *E.g. Vosburg v. Putney*, 80 Wis. 523 (1891) (in which one schoolboy kicks another to unexpectedly disastrous results).

26 By this term we mean the increased ability of concentrated providers of goods and services to engage large numbers of consumers without direct person-to-person exchange and with little direct accountability to those individuals in terms of community reputation outside the diffuse market. The term is intended to invoke the humour found in Ambrose Bierce, The Devil's Dictionary (1906) ("CORPORATION, n. An ingenious device for obtaining individual profit without individual responsibility.").

27 *See* In re Domestic Air Transportation Antitrust Litigation, 137 F.R.D. 677 (N.D. Ga. 1991) (in which essentially these facts were alleged).

Different societies deal with this in different ways. Many countries seek to minimize the cost of seeking legal redress by subsidizing the cost of private enforcement through the shifting of fees and costs in litigation. For example, the so-called "English rule" or "loser pays" model requires the losing party to pay the legal fees of the winner. [28] If liability is fairly clear, this will help reduce the transaction costs of litigation, but it cannot eliminate them: even a "free" lawsuit will be more trouble than most will endure. Even a recovery whose transactions costs are subsidised by the English rule does little to motivate a consumer to initiate proceedings when the total recovery to the consumer may amount to a relative trifle. Moreover, if liability is not clear, the English rule may worsen the problem by turning private enforcement into a high-stakes gamble. It is clear that in the "amount at stake vs. cost of legal redress" mismatch, minimising the cost of legal redress cannot work – at least not alone.

The alternative is to boost, via aggregation of claims, the "amount at stake" in any given lawsuit. Unlike providing a direct subsidy to the individual with a claim for redress, the object here is to level the playing field by creating similar incentives to litigate on both sides of the dispute. In effect, this approach assigns a portion of each consumer's claim to a litigating agent, who then has an incentive to invest in the assertion of the collective entity's potential recovery. While many European countries are now looking to forms of collective redress, there is an accompanying "folk wisdom" that the American response must be avoided.[29]

Our aim is not to take up all the arguments concerning the familiar mechanism of the class action, but rather to situate the class action within a system of private *ex post* mechanisms of providing for redress while overcoming the negative value of typical consumer claims. Once situated in a scheme or regulatory enforcement, however, it should not be surprising that class actions require supporting institutional arrangements, as do all enforcement devices. For one, a court system with the authority in positive law to aggregate private claims is required.[30] But merely the right statutory incantation is not enough. Most obviously, if any system of consumer harm is to turn so heavily on the courts, the judiciary must possess a sufficient degree of independence that rendering potentially enormous judgments against major industrial players is a realistic possibility. But far more than just "good judges" are required for this sort of enforcement to work.

---

28 For more on the English Rule and fee shifting generally, *see* John F. Vargo, *The American Rule on Attorney Fee Allocation: The Injured Person's Access to Justice*, 42 AM. U. L. REV. 1567 (1993).

29 The issue of the European distrust of American entrepreneurial agents in litigation is taken up more fully in Samuel Issacharoff & Geoffrey P. Miller, *Will Aggregate Litigation Come to Europe?*, 62 Vanderbilt L. Rev. (forthcoming 2009).

30 *See, e.g.* Fed. R. Civ. P. 23.

It has been argued by others that "the rule of law" has requirements far beyond the formal institutions of government.[31] Our claim is that effective consumer enforcement relies on some of the same non-governmental institutions. This is currently the biggest issue in the European debates over private enforcement. To date, the European efforts have shown a marked distrust of lawyer entrepreneurialism as the driving force behind collective actions. Instead, they have opted for either group consolidation orders that coordinate among litigants already in the legal system or for representative actions brought by non-governmental organisations. Even these, as in the newly minted Italian statute, have no capacity to seek damages for private harms.

What separates the European efforts from the American practices is precisely the creation of the institutional foundation for the private bar to assume the risks and rewards of representing claimants who are unable to fend for themselves. The question, therefore, is not whether Europe should or should not have American-style class actions. On that score the answer is easy: there is no obvious imperative for European legal systems to have any particular institutional actor. Europe need not have American-based forms of representation in litigation any more than Europe need reproduce the American presidential system or the Senate or the Electoral College as forms of political representation.

If, however, *ex post* private enforcement is to be a part of the legal landscape, then the question shifts once again. The issue now becomes what are the institutional mechanisms that can overcome the negative value of the typical consumer claim such as to compel accountability. If that is the object, then the private bar, for its part, must develop as an institution capable of overcoming the collective action barriers to private enforcement. This in turn requires entrepreneurs specialising in seeking out certain types of consumer harm and ones accustomed to working independently of the state. The emergence of those entrepreneurs correspondingly depends on the quality of the bar itself, which in turn depends on the mechanisms and quality of organised legal education.[32] Professions outside of the law must develop supporting institutions as well: complex, aggregated medical harms will require the existence of sophisticated medical experts to assist private attorneys generally in the development of claims.[33] Complex, aggregated accounting frauds will require sophisticated private accountants who can detect, document and testify to the existence of

31 Jeffrey Kahn, *The Search for the Rule of Law in Russia*, 37 Geo. J. Intl. L. 353 (2006).

32 This corresponds with Kahn's view that "the rule of law also requires a variety of non-state institutions: organized legal education, a professional bar, and a myriad of supporting professions." *Id.*

33 *E.g. Amchem Products, Inc. v. Windsor*, 521 U.S. 591 (1996) (in which millions of injuries from asbestos were alleged).

those frauds.[34] None of these institutions will spring into being automatically, and none of them will emerge merely by legislating into existence the formal structures of a class action. Such existence is a necessary but insufficient step for truly effective private consumer enforcement.

Thus, if social harm is going unmanaged despite the formal, first-order presence of the tort and other consumer-protection laws and courts that would otherwise enable its management, this chapter suggests the answer may lie in the absence of the necessary supporting institutions. Especially in developing or emerging nations attempting to build a system of regulation from the ground up, these institutions deserve special attention, and are not guaranteed to exist. On this level, the "one vs. the multitude" problem is recreated: those who would perpetrate a sophisticated accounting fraud on their consumers will purchase the services of skilled accountants. The public as a whole, however, has a more diffuse interest in ensuring the development of professional ethics, private monitoring organisations, sophisticated accountancy and so on. The best lawyers can be flown in from overseas to defend a class action when there is much at stake; for a nation to develop a skilled plaintiff's bar takes time and investment.

The question in the end is whether there is the capacity to harness private enforcement that will have an incentive to challenge diffuse wrongdoing, provide efficient resolution of similarly situated claims, and compel the proper level of internalisation of norms of appropriate market conduct. One such institutional response is the private attorney general who is empowered to act on behalf of a broad group of similarly situated individuals, bound together by the proceedings and a supervising tribunal, with incentives for the undertaking created from the proceeds of the enforcement action. In other words, a private class action can be an important complement to well-functioning regulatory overseeing of consumer markets. But such private enforcement will not emerge without the necessary institutions – institutions that come with costs well beyond those found in any agency relationship. The most critical institutional arrangements for the existence of class actions are the most controversial. First, there must be an incentive for private gain for the bar to assume the role of venture capitalists in prosecuting claims for individuals who cannot be relied upon to underwrite the costs of enforcement. Second, there must be a low-cost mechanism, such as the American opt-out mechanism for class actions, which allows private interests to be aggregated without overwhelming transactional barriers.

It is precisely the entrepreneurial side of class actions and the non-contractual nature of the self-volunteered private attorney generals that creates the greatest notoriety both in the US and abroad. Nonetheless, all regulatory regimes have costs and the agency costs of private enforcement are no exception. But if there is

34 *E.g.* In re Cendant Corp. Prides Litigation, 243 F.3d 722 (3d Cir. 2001) (in which the deliberate manufacture of false revenue over a multi-year period was alleged).

to be a private enforcement, after-the-fact liability regime well suited to the problems of democratised markets, there must be corresponding institutional arrangements that make such enforcement viable. The American class action is an evolutionary response to a system that values liberalised markets and *ex post* accountability. Other countries may seek to rein in some of the excesses, but there is a burden to ensure that a meaningful enforcement regime is in place, lest the desire for liberalisation lead to markets compromised not by burdensome regulation, but by fraud and consumer distrust.

PUBLIC AND PRIVATE ENFORCEMENT IN CONSUMER PROTECTION: GENERAL COMPARISON EU*–USA

Enforcement of Consumer Rights and Legal Redress for Consumers in the EU: An Institutional Model

Jules Stuyck**

INTRODUCTION

In the EU enforcement of consumer law is still mainly a matter for the Member States. The ECJ has widely recognised the procedural autonomy of the Member States and, with the notable exception of Injunctions Directive 98/27, Community legislation in this field is limited to cross-border actions. In the case of cross-border disputes, the proposed Rome I Regulation (to succeed to the Rome I Convention) favours the law of the domicile of the consumer.

In the EU there is a public law/private law enforcement divide. Regulation n° 2006/2004 on co-operation between national authorities responsible for the enforcement of consumer protection laws fails to take this divide into account but might bring more convergence in the enforcement of consumer law.

Even for Member States having a tradition of private enforcement, private litigation in consumer matters that is not initiated by (public or private) institutions (such as consumer organisations) remains difficult to accept. In Europe there seems to be a certain reticence against private enforcement in the

* The ratification process of the Treaty of Lisbon signed on 13 December 2007 (O.J. 2007, No. C 306/62) is well on its way and its entry into force at the beginning of 2009 is not unlikely. This Treaty does not only modify the existing EU Treaty and EC Treaty (the latter becoming the Treaty on the Functioning of the European Union), but it also abolishes the present three pillar structure of the EU, as a consequence of which the term European Community will disappear. Therefore I have chosen not to use "EC" anymore, except to designate the EC Treaty. On the other hand I shall use the term EU law (like many other authors already have for years) although strictly speaking the law of the first pillar (to which all the subjects discussed in this paper belong) as it stands today is not "EU law" but Community law.

** University of Leuven.

strict sense. The law favours actions for injunctive relief brought by organisations, like consumer organisations, which in some Member States are private organisations (but part of the institutional establishment and associated with the system of legislation after consultation of interest groups) and in other public bodies (like consumer ombudsmen).

This reticence is also voiced in the recent White Paper of the European Commission on Damages Claims in the Case of Infringements of EC Antitrust Rules.

The White Paper shows another feature of European law with regard to enforcement of consumer rights. Antitrust law has a constitutional foundation in the EC Treaty (Articles 81–82) including a basis of public law enforcement by the Commission and the Member States. Interestingly Article 81(2) – restrictive agreements contrary to Article 81(1) are null and void – is the only civil law sanction in the whole EC Treaty, precisely in the field of antitrust. This is the result of the fact that Articles 81–82 EC are the only provisions in the Treaty containing express obligations for private actors, i.e. businesses or "undertakings" as they are called in Community law. The treaty does not mention actions for damages in case of violations of antitrust law, but building on its *Francovich* jurisprudence (state liability for infringements of Community law) the European Court ruled that the effective application of the EC antitrust rules dictates that Member States shall grant the victims of antitrust violations a right to damages. Such horizontal liability does not exist in (other fields) of EC consumer law, although some general standards in this regard can be established.[1]

Eventually this paper will demonstrate that both at the level of the Member States and the EU, with varying degrees of private law and public law solutions, unlike the US, enforcement of consumer rights is institutionalised. Where collective private actions are possible, they are typically reserved to established representative and recognised organisations. The private lawyer model is largely rejected.

In the first section of this paper I will discuss the EU constitutional framework for the enforcement of consumer rights: the competence of the EU and its limits, the Member States' autonomy in the field of remedies and the (lack of) direct effect of consumer law directives. The second section will focus on the public/private enforcement divide and mix in the Member States concerning the enforcement of consumer law. In the last part of that section I will look more particularly at systems of collective enforcement in comparison with the US. In the third section I will try a little bit to unravel the complex interplay between the

1 Norbert Reich, "Horizontal Liability in EC Law: Hybridization of Remedies for Compensation in Case of Breaches of EC Rights", *C.M.L.Rev* 44 (2007): 705–742.

European and the national level[2] and the public/private enforcement of consumer rights by taking the example of antitrust law. In the fourth and last section I shall argue that there is a case for Community legislation in the field of collective actions for consumers due to the difficulties of multinational litigation.

1. THE EU CONSTITUTIONAL FRAMEWORK FOR ENFORCEMENT OF CONSUMER RIGHTS

1.1. EU COMPETENCE AND ITS LIMITS

Three legal bases in the EC Treaty should be considered.

First, Article 95 EC enables the EU legislature to adopt the measures for the approximation of the provisions laid down by law, regulation or administrative action in Member States which have as their object the establishment and functioning of the internal market.

In a certain number of judgments, in particular *Tobacco advertising I*,[3] the ECJ has drawn some important limits as to the use of Article 95 EC. The Court held that the measures referred to in Article 95 EC are intended to improve the conditions for the establishment and functioning of the internal market. That Article does not vest in the Community legislature a general power to regulate the internal market. This judgment has cast some doubt on the constitutionality of minimum harmonisation.[4] In *Tobacco advertising II*[5] however the Court accepted that recourse to Article 95 EC as a legal basis does not presuppose the existence of an actual link with free movement between the Member States *in every situation covered by the measure* founded on that basis. As the Court has previously pointed out, to justify recourse to Article 95 EC as the legal basis, what matters is that the measure adopted on that basis must actually be intended to improve the conditions for the establishment and functioning of the internal market.

It can certainly be argued that the harmonisation of existing national laws concerning consumer redress is intended to improve the conditions for the establishment and functioning of the internal market. Indeed consumers in several Member States may be affected while existing national laws very often do not permit a collective action to be brought on behalf of consumers from other

---

2 For a more comprehensive discussion of the frictions between European and national consumer law, see Hans.-W. Micklitz, "The Relationship Between National and European Consumer Policy – Challenges and Perspectives", in Twigg-Flessner, Parry, Howells and Nordhausen (eds.), *The Yearbook of Consumer Law 2008*, pp. 35 et seq.

3 Case C-376/98, *Germany v Parliament and Council*, [2000] ECR I-8419.

4 See Stephen Weatherill, "The Constitutional Competence of the EU to Deliver Social Justice", *European Review of Contract Law*, 2006, pp. 136 et seq.

5 Case C-380/03, *Germany v European Parliament and Council*, [2006] ECR I-11573.

Member States and, furthermore, where this is possible, disparities in the law governing such actions, are liable to deter consumers from buying certain goods in other Member States. The paradigm of the confident consumer which is underlying Community initiatives in the field of substantive consumer law[6] can in other words also justify harmonisation in the procedural field.

Directive 98/27/EC on injunctions for the protection of consumers' interests is also based on Article 95 EC.

Obviously Article 95 EC is a possible legal basis for a directive introducing rules on collective redress including the award of compensation, at least where there is a cross-border element.

A strong argument pleads for an EU competence, under Article 95 EC, to enact legislation on collective consumer redress *that is not limited to cross-border actions*. In the field of collective consumer redress actions which are *prima facie* "national" will often have a cross-border dimension (because consumers from other Member States will also have suffered damage). Therefore, in contrast to what is possible for individual consumer claims (see e.g. Article 3(1) of Regulation 861/2006 on small claims procedures: "*For the purposes of this Regulation, a cross-border case is one in which at least one of the parties is domiciled or habitually resident in a Member State other than the Member State of the court or tribunal seised*") a strict limitation to cross-border cases might prove impossible (especially in class actions where the plaintiff acts for a class of consumers) or totally inefficient (a cross-border action would be limited to consumers residing in other Member States than the Member State where the action is brought, while the majority of the victims will typically be consumers from the forum). Eventually a directive limited to cross-border situations (e.g. as defined in the small claims regulation) would not secure the useful effect of the principle of proper consumer redress as confirmed by the ECJ, in *Océano Grupo*,[7] *Mostaza Claro*[8] and *Manfredi*.[9]

Secondly, title IV of the Treaty "Visa, asylum, immigration and other policies relating to free movement of persons" relates more broadly to the progressive establishment of an area of freedom, security and justice. Article 61 provides *inter alia* for the adoption of measures in the field of judicial cooperation in civil matters as provided for in Article 65.

---

6 See Thomas Wilhelmsson, "The principle of legitimate expectations as a basic principle of Community private law", in Paasivirta and Rissanen (eds.). *Principles of Justice and the Law of the European Union*, Helsinki, 1995, p. 325 et seq.; Wulf-Henning Roth, "Berechtigde Verbrauchererwartungen im Europäischen Gemeinschafstrecht", in Hans Schute-Nölke and Reiner Schulze (eds.), *Europäische Rechtsangleichung und Nationale Privatrechte*, Baden-Baden, 1999, pp. 45 et seq.

7 Joined cases C-240/98 to C-244/98, [2000] ECR I-4941.

8 Case C-168/05, [2006] ECR I-10421.

9 Joint cases C-295/04 to 298/04, [2006] ECR I-6619.

Article 65 states that measures in the field of judicial cooperation in civil matters "*having cross-border implications*" are to be taken in accordance with Article 67 and "*in so far as is necessary for the proper functioning of the internal market*". These measures "shall include" (c) "eliminating obstacles to the good functioning of civil proceedings, if necessary by promoting the compatibility of the rules on civil procedure applicable in the Member States." Article 67 contains the rules for decision making pursuant to Article 65.

The Treaty of Lisbon, signed on 13 December 2007,[10] will replace Article 65 by a Chapter 3 Judicial Cooperation in Civil Matters and a new Article 65 (of what shall be called the Treaty on the Functioning of the European Union). According to the first paragraph of the new Article 5, the Union shall develop judicial cooperation in civil matters *having cross-border implications*, based on the principle of mutual recognition of judgments and of decisions in extrajudicial cases. Such cooperation may include the adoption of measures for the approximation of the laws and regulations of the Member States. According to the second paragraph, the European Parliament and the Council shall adopt measures, *particularly when necessary for the proper functioning of the internal market*, aimed at ensuring (...)(e) effective access to justice; (f) the elimination of the proper functioning of civil proceedings, if necessary by promoting the compatibility of the rules on civil procedure applicable in the Member States.

Article 65 post Lisbon is broader than Article 65 in its present wording in the following respects: (i) the express reference to the possibility of approximation of the laws and regulations of the Member States in the areas referred to *inter alia* in paragraph 2; (ii) the inclusion, in the list of areas in which measures can be taken, of effective access to justice. In contrast, Article 65 post Lisbon maintains the limitation to matters having cross-border implications.

It can be noted that the recently adopted Regulation 861/2007 establishing a European Small Claims Procedure,[11] which refers to Article 67 as its legal basis, is limited to cross-border cases, although the initial Commission proposal covered both cross-border and domestic small claims procedures.

It is submitted that "matters having cross-border implications" in Article 65 (present and future) shall be interpreted broadly. The aim of the Article is to ensure that citizens do not suffer any inconvenience from the fact that a civil litigation is not restricted to their Member State of residence. In that sense a cross-border case is one where there is a legal issue relating to goods or persons outside the borders of a particular Member State.[12] The reference to "in so far as is

10 O.J. 2007, N° C 306/62.

11 O.J. 2007, N° L 199/1.

12 See also C. Callies - M. Ruffert, EUV/EGV, *Das Verfassungsrecht der Europäischen Union mit Europäischer Grundrechtecharta*, 3rd ed., Beck, München, 2007, comments to Article 67, para 7 and further references.

necessary for the proper functioning of the internal market" is another limitation of the scope of Article 65 (present and future). The adjective "proper" does not appear in Article 95. However that difference should not lead to a stricter scope of application of Article 65 than Article 95. It has even been submitted that the scope of Article 65 is broader than that of Article 95, since Article 65 does not only require measures to ensure the functioning of the internal market but also the adoption of measures ensuring that the internal market functions properly. The EU would therefore be competent under Article 65 where there is an involvement of goods or persons that are present in another Member State.[13] In other words, the reference to the internal market in Article 65 does not add to the "cross-border" requirement.

With regard to the limitation of Article 65 EC to matters having cross-border implications, what has been said above concerning Article 95 applies here as well. Cross-border situations in the field of collective redress cannot be effectively isolated.

Finally Article 153(3)(b) EC should be mentioned. This article allows the European Parliament and the Council to adopt measures which support, complement and monitor the policy pursued by the Member Sates in the field of consumer protection.

This provision has hardly been used. Indeed only Directive 98/6/EC on indication of the prices of products offered to consumers has been adopted on this basis, all other consumer law directives having been adopted on the basis of Article 95 EC.

Contrary to, e.g. Article 152 on health protection that expressly excludes harmonisation, Article 153 allows Community legislation that has a substantive impact on national law, including harmonisation of laws but measures to be taken under Article 15(3)(b) do not include full harmonisation of national law. Indeed according to Article 153(5) measures adopted pursuant to paragraph 4 (i.e. 153(3)(b)) shall not prevent any Member State from maintaining of introducing more stringent protective measures, provided such measures are compatible with the Treaty.

Some authors have advocated a more intensive use of Article 153(3)(b). They argue that the condition in Article 153(3)(b) that the Community measures "support, supplement and monitor" the policy pursued by the Member States" will easily be fulfilled since all Member States have today their own body of consumer law.[14] Community legislation on collective actions would certainly

---

13 *Ibid.*

14 Norbert Reich, "A European Contract Law or an EU Contract law Regulation for Consumers," *JCP* 2005, 383; Hans-W. Micklitz, "The relationship between National and European Consumer Policy – Challenges and Perspectives", *Yearbook of Consumer Law*, 2008, 35 et seq. (at 60–61); Norbert Reich & Hans-W. Micklitz, *The Basics of European Consumer Law*, Centro de Fromaçao Jurídica e Judiciáriaria, 2007, 42.

support and supplement measures of substantive and procedural law existing in the Member States to protect consumers and therefore Article 153(3)(b) would seem to be a proper legal basis for EU legislation harmonising national laws on collective redress for consumers, but necessarily limited to minimum harmonisation.

A final word should be said on subsidiarity. In areas which do not fall within its exclusive competence – like consumer protection (see also Article 2C, TFUE, post Lisbon) – the Community shall take action, in accordance with the principle of subsidiarity, only if and insofar as the objectives of the proposed action cannot be sufficiently achieved by the Member States and can therefore, by reason of the scale or effects of the proposed action, better be achieved by the Community (Article 5(2)EC, introduced by the Treaty of Maastricht with effect in 1994). This principle has led to the withdrawal or amendment of a certain number of Commission proposals in the field of consumer protection.[15]

Legally speaking, the principle of subsidiarity does not seem to be an important limit for Community action in the field of consumer protection. The present state of European consumer law suggests very strongly that effective consumer redress cannot be sufficiently achieved by the Member States and can therefore, by reason of the scale or effects of the proposed action, better be achieved by the Community than merely at Member State level. In addition, in the field of collective consumer redress, as explained here above, cross-border and non cross-border cases cannot effectively be distinguished. As a result, if an action at the Community level is necessary for cross-border cases (which can certainly not be put into doubt) such an action will necessarily have to relate to domestic actions as well.

The analysis here above has shown that the Treaty contains three possible legal bases for an EC Directive on collective redress for consumers, including claims for damages: Article 95, Article 65 and Article 153(3)(b).

It has also been shown that since in the area of collective actions cross-border and non cross-border cases cannot be distinguished in an effective manner without putting into jeopardy the attainment of the objective of a truly internal market where consumers are confident, the EU would seem to be competent not only to enact enforcement rules for cross-border situations, but also for domestic situations.

---

15 See Hans.-W. Micklitz & Stephen Weatherill, "Consumer Policy in the European Community: Before and After Maastricht", *Journal of Consumer Policy*, 1999, pp. 285 et seq., pp. 306–307.

1.2. THE AUTONOMY OF THE MEMBER STATES IN THE FIELD OF REMEDIES AND ITS LIMITS

If the principle of subsidiarity limits (but not too much, see above) the powers of the EU legislature to the benefit of the Member States, the Court of Justice has developed another principle which is directly relevant for remedies: the principle of procedural autonomy.

According to the well established case law of the ECJ "*it is for the domestic legal system of each Member State to designate the courts having jurisdiction and to determine the procedural conditions governing actions at law intended to ensure the protection of the rights which the citizens have from the direct effect of Community law.*"[16] This principle has always been subject to two conditions, known as the condition of equivalence and the condition of effectiveness: the enforcement of Community law shall not be more difficult than the enforcement of equivalent national laws and national rules should not make it impossible in practice to exercise the rights conferred by Community law.[17]

Undoubtedly this principle of procedural autonomy only applies when there are no procedural rules at the EU level. It is obvious that Member States are, e.g. bound by the Brussels Regulation and the new Regulation on cross-border small claims.

Interestingly, EU legislation (directives, regulations), including legislation in the consumer field, goes halfway in prescribing national procedural rules for the enforcement of the substantive provisions it sets.

Three examples can be given. The first one is the so-called "Remedies" Directive in the field of public procurement, which is probably the most far-reaching set of EU rules on national procedures. The second one is Regulation 1/2003 implementing the antitrust rules of Articles 81 and 82 EC. The third and last example is the invariable formula used in EC consumer directives.[18]

The Remedies Directive

Article 1 Remedies Directive[19] provides that the Member States shall take the measures necessary to ensure that, as regards contract award procedures falling

16 Case 45/76 Comet BV v Produktschap voor Siergewassen, [1976] ECR 2043, para 13.

17 See Case C-261/95, Palmisani, [1997] ECR I-4025, para 27; Case C-295/04, Manfredi, [2006] ECR I-6619, para 62.

18 I refer only to judicial enforcement. Beyond that the Consumer Sales Directive 1999/44, e.g. harmonises substantive remedies in case of the lack of conformity in consumer sales contracts. See also Article 6(1) of the Unfair Contract Terms Directive 93/13 according to which Member States have to provide in their national law that unfair terms shall not be binding on the consumer.

19 Council Directive 89/665/EEC of 21 December 1989 on the coordination of the laws, regulations and administrative provisions relating to the application of review procedures to

within the scope of the relevant substantive directives, decisions taken by the contracting authorities may be reviewed effectively and, in particular, as rapidly as possible in accordance with the conditions set out in the following in particular on the grounds that such decisions have infringed Community law in the field of public procurement or national rules implementing that law. Article 2 states that Member States shall ensure that the measures taken concerning the review procedures specified in Article 1 include provision for powers to:

(a) take, at the earliest opportunity and by way of interlocutory procedures, interim measures with the aim of correcting the alleged infringement or preventing further damage to the interests concerned, including measures to suspend or to ensure the suspension of the procedure for the award of a public contract or the implementation of any decision taken by the contracting authority;
(b) either set aside or ensure the setting aside of decisions taken unlawfully, including the removal of discriminatory technical, economic or financial specifications in the invitation to tender, the contract documents or in any other document relating to the contract award procedure;
(c) award damages to persons harmed by an infringement.

Amending Directive 2007/66 has added a standstill provision (Article 2a): the contract shall not be concluded before the expiry of 10 calendar days (15 calendar days when surface mail is used) from the award in order to give unsuccessful tenderers a real chance to challenge the award decision before the contract is concluded.

Regulation 1/2003 implementing Articles 81–82 EC

Regulation 1/2003[20] implementing Articles 81 and 82 EC has decentralised the application of the EU antitrust rules. Not only the Commission, but also the national competition authorities (NRAs) and the national courts can and shall apply these provisions (under the old Regulation 17/62 the Commission had the exclusive power to apply Article 81(3), by granting exemptions). The Regulation details the powers of the Commission and indicates what kind of decisions the NRAs can take. The NRAs shall however apply Articles 81 and 82 according to their national procedural rules and apply sanctions provided for under national law. With regard to national courts, the Regulation merely states that they shall

the award of public supply and public works contracts, O.J. 1989, L395/33, as amended by Directive 2007/66/EC with regard to improving the effectiveness of review procedures concerning the award of public contracts, O.J. 2007, L335/31.

20 Council Regulation (EC) No. 1/2003 of 16 December 2003 on the implementation of the rules on competition laid down in Articles 81 and 82 of the Treaty, O.J. 2003, L 1/25.

have the power to apply Articles 81 and 82 (Article 6). Article 16(1) adds a rule to secure the uniform application of EU competition law by stating that when national courts rule on agreements, decisions or practices under Article 81 or Article 82 of the Treaty which are already the subject of a Commission decision, they cannot take decisions running counter to the decision adopted by the Commission. They must also avoid giving decisions that would conflict with a decision contemplated by the Commission in proceedings it has initiated. To that effect, the national court may assess whether it is necessary to stay its proceedings. This obligation is without prejudice to the rights and obligations under Article 234 of the Treaty (the possibility to refer preliminary questions to the ECJ).

Consumer law directives

As an example of the consumer law directives, the Unfair Commercial Practices Directive 2005/29[21] can be quoted. Pursuant to Article 11 (enforcement) Member States shall ensure that adequate and effective means exist to combat unfair commercial practices in order to enforce compliance with the provisions of this directive in the interest of consumers. Such means shall include legal provisions under which persons or organisations regarded under national law as having a legitimate interest in combating unfair commercial practices, including competitors, may:

(a) take legal action against such unfair commercial practices; and/or
(b) bring such unfair commercial practices before an administrative authority competent either to decide on complaints or to initiate appropriate legal proceedings.

It shall be for each Member State to decide which of these facilities shall be available and whether to enable the courts or administrative authorities to require prior recourse to other established means of dealing with complaints, including those referred to in Article 10. These facilities shall be available regardless of whether the consumers affected are in the territory of the Member State where the trader is located or in another Member State.

It shall be for each Member State to decide:

(a) whether these legal facilities may be directed separately or jointly against a number of traders from the same economic sector;
and

21 Directive 2005/29/EC of the European Parliament and of the Council of 11 May 2005 concerning unfair business-to-consumer commercial practices in the internal market ('Unfair Commercial Practices Directive') O.J. 2005, L 149/22.

(b) whether these legal facilities may be directed against a code owner where the relevant code promotes non-compliance with legal requirements.
2. Under the legal provisions referred to in paragraph 1, Member States shall confer upon the courts or administrative authorities powers enabling them, in cases where they deem such measures to be necessary, taking into account all the interests involved and in particular the public interest:
(a) to order the cessation of, or to institute appropriate legal proceedings for an order for the cessation of, unfair commercial practices; or
(b) if the unfair commercial practice has not yet been carried out but is imminent, to order the prohibition of the practice, or to institute appropriate legal proceedings for an order for the prohibition of the practice, even without proof of actual loss or damage or of intention or negligence on the part of the trader.

Member States shall also make provision for the measures referred to in the first subparagraph to be taken under an accelerated procedure:

- either with interim effect; or
- with definitive effect;

on the understanding that it is for each Member State to decide which of the two options to select.

The right of consumer organisations to bring an action for a cease and desist order in case of infringements of national rules implementing EU consumer directives has been guaranteed more widely by the so-called 'Injunctions' Directive 98/27.[22] This right of action is not limited to cross-border actions or infringements. Article 2(1) of the Directive more generally provides that Member States shall designate the courts or administrative authorities competent to rule on proceedings commenced by qualified entities from *a* Member State:

(a) an order with all due expediency, where appropriate by way of summary procedure, requiring the cessation or prohibition of any infringement;
(b) where appropriate, measures such as the publication of the decision, in full or in part, in such form as deemed adequate and/or the publication of a corrective statement with a view to eliminating the continuing effects of the infringement;
(c) insofar as the legal system of the Member State concerned so permits, an order against the losing defendant for payments into the public purse or to any

---

22 Directive 98/27/EC of the European Parliament and of the Council of 19 May 1998 on injunctions for the protection of consumers' interests, O.J. 1998, L 166/51.

beneficiary designated in or under national legislation, in the event of failure to comply with the decision within a time-limit specified by the courts or administrative authorities, of a fixed amount for each day's delay or any other amount provided for in national legislation, with a view to ensuring compliance with the decisions.

Conclusion

The different instruments mentioned show differences in respect of the procedural autonomy of the Member States. Procedures in themselves have to be defined at the national level. But in addition to the negative impact of fundamental EU principles (developed by the ECJ) on the Member State's autonomy in this respect, EU legislation increasingly defines the minimum standards of judicial remedies that must be available for the effective enforcement of rights conferred on individuals by EU law. In antitrust law the legislature has not (yet) set minimum standards, but precisely in this field the Treaty itself contains a remedy (the nullity sanction of Article 81(2) EC) which in its turn is one of the bases for the case law of the ECJ that has set minimum standards for actions for damages to the benefit of victims of antitrust violations (this will be discussed in more detail in section III). In consumer law the obligation for Member States to provide for effective ways of enforcement of consumer rights has been concretised in particular with regard to injunctions.

1.3. THE LACK OF HORIZONTAL DIRECT EFFECT OF EU (CONSUMER) DIRECTIVES

The ECJ has consistently held that a directive as such cannot impose obligations on an individual and cannot therefore be relied upon as such against an individual (no "horizontal direct effect").[23]

However, in other judgments,[24] the Court has stressed the necessity for national courts to provide legal protection which individuals derive from the rules of Community law so as to ensure that those rules are fully effective. To that effect national courts are bound to interpret national law and more in particular legal provisions that have been adopted for complying with the requirements of a

23 Case C-91/92, Paola Faccini Dori v Recreb Sr, l [1994] I-3325; see on the present state of the case law: M. Dogan, "When Worlds Collide! Competing Visions of the Relationship between Direct Effect and Supremacy", 44 CMLRev. (2007) 932 et seq.

24 See in particular Case 152/84, Marshall [1986] ECR 723, paragraph 48; Case C-91/92; Case C-91/92, Faccini Dori [1994] I-3325.

directive, so far as possible, in the light of the wording and the purpose of that directive concerned. This obligation also requires the national courts to consider national law as a whole in order to assess to what extent it may be applied so as to avoid a result that would be contrary to the results sought by directives.[25] In Berlusconi,[26] which concerned the first Company Directive, the Court confirmed this point of view, but it also ruled that in a situation where reliance on the Directive would lead to the applicability of manifestly more severe criminal penalty resulting from another provision of national law, this would be contrary to its standing case law which precludes a directive from resulting in creating or increasing the liability in criminal law.[27]

The duty to construe national law in conformity with a directive allows individuals or companies perhaps to rely on national legislation in cases where they suffer from a prejudice of a corporate decision, whereby they will emphasise that such national legislation should be interpreted in accordance with the relevant provisions of the Directive.

The ECJ also ruled that mere adverse repercussions on the right of third parties, even if the repercussions are certain, do not justify preventing an individual from invoking the provisions of a directive against the Member State concerned (a so-called triangular situation).[28]

In *CIA Security*, to which the Court refers in the judgment mentioned in the preceding note, the Court in fact recognised another type of horizontal effect of directives: an individual can use the non-conformity of a national law provision with a directive as a defence against the application of that provision. This possibility seems less relevant for consumers.[29]

Finally consumers who suffer a prejudice from the non-transposition of a directive can, under certain circumstances claim damages from the State. That happened, e.g. in Dillenkofer.[30] Germany had failed to implement correctly Directive 90/314 on package travel by not providing for a mechanism guaranteeing consumers a refund of deposits made to a tour operator in case of the latter's insolvency. The

---

25 Joined Cases C-379/01 to C-403/01, Pfeiffer [2004] ECR I-8835, paragraphs 111–118 (with many references to previous case law).

26 Joined Cases C-378/02, C-391/02 and C-403/02, Berlusconi et al. [2005] ECR I-3565, paragraphs 73–77.

27 With reference to Case 80/86, Kolpinghuis Nijmegen [1987] ECR 3969 and Case C-60/02, Rolex, [2004] ECR I-651.

28 Case C-211/02, Delena Wells, (2004) ECR I-723, paragraph 57, with reference to *inter alia* Case 103/88, Fratelli Costanzo, (1989) ECR I-1839, paragraphs 28 to 33; Case C-194/94, CIA Security, (1996) ECR I-2201, paragraphs 45 to 50.

29 See Jules Stuyck, case note Case C-192/94, El Corte Inglès, (1996) ECR I-1281; also called 'incidental direct effect', see Paul Craig – Grain De Burca, EU Law, 4th ed., Oxford University Press, 2007, 296.

30 Joined Cases C-178/94 et seq., Dillenkofer, [1996] ECR I-4845.

Court found that Germany had committed a serious breach of Community law and that this gave rise to a right of reparation for the individual consumers who had lost their money.

1.4. CONCLUSION

In the EU, the enforcement of consumer rights remains essentially a question of national law, but there are no really compelling reasons why this should have to remain the case.

First, while it is uncertain to what extent the EU legislature has the power to set procedural rules for the private enforcement of consumer rights in non-cross-border situations, such rules do exist in the field of actions for injunctions.

Second while the ECJ has recognised the procedural autonomy of the Member States, it would seem that that autonomy can be limited by EU legislation.

Thirdly, while the ECJ has until now refused to allow individuals, like consumers, to rely on directives that have not been implemented, against other individuals, like businesses, the Court has developed several doctrines, like the duty for national courts to construe national law as much as possible in conformity with the relevant directives, the possibility for individuals to rely on directives as a defence and state liability in case of infringement of Community law, which make the lack of horizontal direct effect less dramatic.

Private enforcement of antitrust law – on which the Commission has recently published a White Paper – is a good test case for the potential of an improvement of EU private enforcement of (amongst other) consumer rights. This will be discussed in section III.

2. INDIVIDUAL AND COLLECTIVE REDRESS FOR CONSUMERS IN THE MEMBER STATES: THE PUBLIC-PRIVATE ENFORCEMENT DIVIDE AND MIX

2.1. CONSUMER LAW AS PART OF PRIVATE OR PUBLIC LAW

In all Member States both public and private enforcement of consumer law exists. But the mix of private and public law remedies and procedures varies a lot. Presumably all Member States have introduced criminal sanctions to enforce basic safety rules.

On the other hand, depending on the Member State in question, the enforcement of, e.g. rules on trade practices and advertising is primarily a question of criminal enforcement (e.g. France), enforcement through administrative agencies (e.g. Consumer ombudsmen in the Nordic countries) or private enforcement (Germany and Belgium are examples).

In reality the picture is even more complex. In the Nordic countries, e.g. the law on sales methods, advertising and unfair practices is often seen as one branch of the law with its specific system of legal protection (actions by a Consumer Ombudsman or by consumer organisations and so on). In other countries, like in Germany and Belgium it is integrated into the law of unfair competition (the aim of which is historically the protection of competitors but which has been enlarged so as to include the protection of consumers and even the public at large, i.e. the general interest).[31]

2.2. PUBLIC OR PRIVATE ENFORCEMENT OR PUBLIC AND PRIVATE ENFORCEMENT?

A. *General Discussion*

There are many different opinions about the relative advantages of public and private enforcement.

It is sometimes argued that public enforcement is superior to private enforcement and that action by a public authority ensures a balanced and responsive enforcement, whereas private, especially collective private, enforcement raises issues of accountability, legitimacy and transparency, frivolous action and over deterrence.[32]

Most authors will agree that optimal enforcement of consumers rights should be based on a mix of public and private enforcement measures. Van den Bergh writes that optimal enforcement can be achieved only through a fine-tuning of four relevant parameters: i) an optimal mix of public and private enforcement, ii) the choice of an optimal sanction (injunction, administrative fine

[31] See for an interesting comparison between the German and the Swedish model: Antonina Bakardjieva-Engelbrekt, *Fair Trading Law in Flux*, thesis Stockholm, 2003, pp. 13 et seq.; see more generally on this question: Jules Stuyck, "Consumer Protection and Fair Competition – One Fight?" in *Droit de la Consommation – Konsumentenrecht – Consumer Law. Liber Amicorum Bernd Stauder* (L.Thévenoz and N. Reich (eds.), Nomos/Schultess, 2006, pp. 497–509).

[32] Willem van Boom & Marco Loos, Effective enforcement of consumer law in Europe, in W. van Boom and M. Loos (eds.), *Collective Enforcement of Consumer Law*, Europa Law Publishing, Groningen, 2007, p. 250.

or criminal fine), iii) an optimal timing of the intervention (*ex ante* monitoring and/or *ex post* enforcement) and iv) allocation of enforcement powers to the optimal government level, either centralised or decentralised. Economic analysis of enforcement shows that public enforcement is to be preferred to private enforcement if i) private parties possess insufficient information about the infringements and/or ii) the social net benefits from the enforcement exceed the private net benefits of successful claims.[33]

If it can readily be accepted that enforcement of consumer rights should probably be based on a mix of private and public enforcement measures and assuming that economic theory can teach us what the optimal mix should look like, it still remains difficult to make any pronouncements on the right mix for the entire EU. And that is at least for two reasons. The first one is cultural: the deterrent effect of public or private enforcement may be different according to the public's attitude vis-à-vis the role of the State and private organisations respectively. The second one is political: State involvement in the enforcement of consumer rights will often be bigger where there is a tradition of or a political bias against State intervention in economic life and a lesser confidence in market forces. Such difference may also exist between the US and the EU.

B. *The Injunctions Directive*

Directive 98/27/EC of the European Parliament and of the Council of 19 May 1998 on injunctions for the protection of consumers' interests[34] aims to harmonise Member States' laws on injunctions for the protection of the collective interests of consumers included in the directives listed in the annex, i.e. 13 consumer directives (unfair commercial practices, advertising, consumer credit, doorstep selling, package travel, advertising medicinal products, unfair contract terms, time sharing, distance contracts, consumer sales, e-commerce, distant marketing financial services and services in the internal market). Actions for injunctions are limited to the cessation or prohibition of an infringement. The Directive does not concern actions for damages. In the event of an infringement originating in that Member State, any qualified entity from another Member State where the interests protected by that qualified entity are affected by the infringement, may bring a case before a court or an administrative authority. It is up to the Member States to designate qualified entities, which may be private or public. It is also up to the Member States to designate the competent court *or* administrative authority

33 Roger Van den Bergh, "Should consumer protection law be publicly enforced? An economic perspective on EC Regulation 2006/2004 and its implementation in the consumer protection laws of the Member States", in W. van Boom & M. Loos (eds.), footnote 33, pp. 202–203.

34 O.J. 1998, No. L 166/51; as lastly amended by Directive 2006/123, O.J. 2006, No. L 376/36 (see consolidated text in EUR-LEX).

competent to grant injunctive relief. The courts or administrative authorities shall accept the list of entities drawn up by each Member State as proof of the legal capacity of the qualified entity without prejudice to their right to examine whether the purpose of the qualified entity justifies its taking action in a specific case.

The Directive is thus neutral as to the public or private character of the enforcement (by a court or administrative authority at the request of a qualified entity of private or public law).

C. *The Administrative Cooperation Regulation*

Regulation 2006/2004[35] organises cooperation (exchange of information, coordination of market surveillance and enforcement activities) between national consumer protection authorities (NCAs) with respect to intra-Community infringements of the laws to protect consumers that implement the 15 directives and the regulation listed in the annex to the Directive (advertising, doorstep selling, consumer credit, TV without frontiers, package holidays, unfair terms, time sharing, distance contracts, price indication, consumer sales, e-commerce, Community Code on medicines, distance selling of financial services, denied boarding in air travel and unfair commercial practices). Each Member State has to designate the competent authority. This means that Member States that did not yet have such an authority had to establish it. Sanctions (criminal, administrative or private) however remain a question of national law.

Roger van den Bergh[36] contends that the Regulation may be criticised because it seriously disrupts national legal orders by requiring public enforcement mechanisms for rules that traditionally belong to the field of private law.

D. *Conclusion*

While the Injunctions Directive does not interfere in the choice of the Member States for public or private law enforcement, the Cooperation Regulation does.

The choice for sanctions and procedural rules however remain wholly a matter of national law.

---

35 Regulation (EC) No. 2006/2004 of the European Parliament and of the Council of 27 October 2004 on cooperation between national authorities responsible for the enforcement of consumer protection laws, O.J. 2004, L 364/1; as lastly amended by Directive 2007/65/EC (see consolidated text in EUR-LEX). 11 December 200L 332 27, 18 December 2007.

36 R. Van den Bergh, footnote 34, p. 181.

2.3. COLLECTIVE ACTIONS FOR DAMAGES: COMPARISON WITH US CLASS ACTIONS

At the EU level the Injunctions Directive aims at the collective enforcement of consumer interests. In recent years both policy makers and scholars in Europe have shown an increasing interest in resolving the following question: how can consumers effectively join claims for damages that they are unable to bring in court individually, in view of the complexity or costs of proceedings. If many consumers with a small claim can act together they can share the costs.

Many Member States have recently introduced or envisaged to introduce collective actions for damages.

In view of the immense variety of forms of group litigation in Europe, many categorisations are possible.[37] The following distinction is however often made:[38] *group actions* on the one hand, i.e. actions brought by a person or entity on behalf of a group with similar claims (which feature some but not all characteristics of US-type class actions) and *joint or representative actions*, i.e. the mere bundling of several individual claims. Leaving apart real group actions, representative or joint actions can again be subdivided into representative actions in the proper sense, where an *ex ante* authorised representative body acts on behalf of a group of victims and joint actions, where individual parties join in one procedure. Variants of this type of action are test cases under German law and the joinder of claims as in the "Verbandsklage nach österreischen Recht" (based on a transfer of claims by individual consumers to a consumer organisation, VKI).[39]

Some Member States have introduced group actions, i.e. genuine collective actions for damages, but there seems to be a European consensus not to follow the US example of class actions or at least a very strong business opposition throughout Europe against class actions.[40]

Group actions as they presently exist in most of the EU Member States (like Sweden, Denmark, Finland and Italy) are based on an "opt-in". The judgment is only binding on those consumers who have expressly opted in, i.e. declared that they want to be represented and therefore to be (or can deemed to be) bound by the judgment awarding damages collectively. A recent Dutch (from 2005) law provides a real opt-out (the Dutch law has introduced a collective settlement,

---

37 See Andrea Renda et al. (Centre for European Studies – Erasmus University Rotterdam and LUISS, "Making Antitrust damages actions more effective in the EU: welfare impact and potential scenarios", Final report, 21 December 2007, Report for the European Commission, DG COMP, p. 268.

38 Jules Stuyck et al., An analysis and evaluation of alternative means of consumer redress other than redress through ordinary judicial proceedings. Final Report, 17 January 2007, DG SANCO website; F. Cafaggi and Hans Micklitz, contribution to this book; Andrea Renda et al., p. 268.

39 See Andrea Renda et al., p. 269.

40 See the contribution of Astrid Stadler to this book.

between an organisation acting on behalf of a class of potential plaintiffs, that is consecutively confirmed by a court judgment). An opt-put has also been introduced recently in Denmark, but only where a public body is the plaintiff.[41]

The main reasons for the negative attitude against the US type of class actions can be summarised as follows.

First class actions favour the pursuit of non-collective interests (clearly the private interests of plaintiff lawyers) and encourage non-meritorious claims.

Second, the (costly pre-trial) discovery procedure on which class actions is based is foreign to national procedural traditions.

Third, the system of contingency fees, explaining the success of American class actions, is contrary to public order.

Fourth, the opt-out would be at variance with the "due process" requirement of Article 6 ECHR since a person who was not heard in court could be bound by the outcome of the procedure. This is speculation. The question has not been decided by, e.g. the European Court on Human Rights and it is far from certain that an opt-out system with sufficient guarantees for individuals (like an efficient notification system) would violate the due process of law principle.

From the business side it is also said that US-type class actions are not serving the compensation of victims (which they of course should), but they are a means of punitive prosecution in order to have business disgorge profits unduly made.[42]

The private lawyer model, with a lawyer taking the risk on the basis of a contingency fee, certainly creates a financial incentive, but there may be others, including an exception to the "loser pays principle" where class actions are brought on behalf of consumers, subject to a certification system at the level of the entities authorised to bring an action and/or at the level of the concrete action (*prima facie* examination of the possibility that the action has a chance to succeed).

Still about (pre-)financing group actions, mention should be made of the system developed in Austria: the VKI concludes an agreement with a finance company that re-finances the costs of procedure. If successful the company retains 1/3 of the proceeds. This is in fact a contingency fee agreement with a non-lawyer.

---

41 See Jules Stuyck, *Class Actions in Europe? To opt in or to opt out: that is the question*, paper for NYU workshop, Fiesole 13 June, 2008.

42 Joëlle Simon, Paper for The Consumer Law Compendium: A New Era for European Consumer Law?, Leuven, 21 September 2007, forthcoming in *European Business Law Review*.

3. CLAIMS FOR DAMAGES IN THE CASE OF INFRINGEMENT OF THE EC ANTITRUST RULES

DG SANCO has liaised with DG COMP. The latter has now presented its White Paper on Damages Actions for breach of EC antitrust Rules.[43]

In antitrust law, things seem to move on more rapidly than in other fields of EU law, in particular consumer law.

This has to do with the specific constitutional basis of EU antitrust law and the importance of EU antitrust policy.

Let's recall that Articles 81 and 82 of the EC Treaty (hereafter "EC")[44] prohibit respectively restrictive agreements and practices and abuse of a dominant position. Since the entry into force (on 1 May 2004) of the new implementing (procedural) rules of Regulation 1/2003 the Commission has no monopoly anymore to grant "exemptions" on the basis of Article 81(3) for those agreements that fulfil certain conditions (in brief: agreements that do restrict competition but are efficient). National Competition Authorities (NCAs), Member State courts and the Commission can fully apply Articles 81 and 82. The objective of EU competition policy is not only to ensure effective competition and thus to raise (consumer) welfare, but also to foster market integration. State barriers to intra-Community trade have to be struck down on the basis of the internal market provisions of the Treaty (free movement of goods, persons, services and capital); barriers to trade between Member States raised by businesses are contrary to the antitrust rules.

In its famous *Courage*[45] judgment the European Court of Justice (ECJ) recognised the right of victims of antitrust infringements (violations of Articles 81 and 82 EC) to be compensated.

The Court recalls that the Treaty has created its own legal order. Community law is intended to give rise to rights to individuals. Community law has precedence over national law.[46] Furthermore Article 81 EC is a fundamental provision that is essential for the functioning of the internal market. Evidence of this can be found in Article 81(2) EC: an agreement contrary to this provision is automatically void.[47] An agreement that is null and void by virtue of Article 81(2) has no effect as between the contracting parties and cannot be set up against third parties.[48] Moreover, it is capable of having a bearing on all the effects, either past or future,

43 COM(2008)165 final.

44 Which will become the "Treaty on the Functioning of the European Union" if and when the Treaty of Lisbon (December 2007) enters into force (possibly at the beginning of 2009).

45 Case C-453/99, *Courage v Crehan* [2001] ECR I-6297.

46 See paragraph 19 of the Judgment.

47 With reference to Case C-126/97, Eco Swiss [1999] ECR I-3055, paragraph 36.

48 With reference to Case 22/71, Béguelin [1971] ECR 949, paragraph 29.

of the agreement or decision concerned.[49] Finally the ECJ recalls that it has held that Articles 81(1) and 82 EC (the prohibition of abuse of a dominant position) produce direct effects in relations between individuals and create rights for the individuals concerned which the national courts must safeguard.[50]

It follows from the foregoing considerations that any individual can rely on a breach of Article 81(1) EC before a national court even where he is a party to a contract that is liable to restrict or distort competition within the meaning of that provision.[51]

As regards the possibility of seeking compensation for the loss caused by a contract or by conduct liable to restrict competition, the Court recalls that national courts must ensure that provisions of Community law within their jurisdiction take full effect and must protect the rights which they confer on individuals[52] ("effet utile" principle). The full effectiveness of Article 81 would be put at risk if it were not open to any individual to claim damages for loss caused to him by a contract or by a conduct liable to restrict competition.[53] Actions for damages can indeed make a significant contribution to the maintenance of effective competition in the Community.

There should not therefore be any absolute bar to such an action being brought by a party to a contract or to a conduct liable to restrict competition.[54]

However the Court immediately recalls the procedural autonomy of the Member States, i.e. the right to lay down the procedural rules for bringing such actions, subject to the respect of the principles of equivalence (i.e. these rules should not be less favourable than those governing similar domestic actions) and effectiveness (i.e. these rules should not render impossible or excessively difficult the exercise of the rights conferred by Community law).[55]

In Manfredi[56] consumers claimed compensation for the damage they suffered as a result of a price fixing cartel that had been condemned by the Italian competition authority.

The Court confirms that any individual can claim compensation for the harm suffered where there is a causal relationship between that harm and an agreement or practice prohibited under Article 81 EC.

---

49 With reference to Case 48/72, Brasserie de Haecht II [1973] ECR 77, paragraph 26.

50 Case 127/73, BRT and Sabam [1974] ECR 51, paragraph 16; Case C-282/95 P, Guérin Automobiles v Commission [1977] ECR I-1503, paragraph 39.

51 Paragraph 24 of the judgment.

52 Paragraph 25 of the judgment with reference to Case 106/77, Simmentahl [1978] ECR 629, paragraph 16 and Case C-213/89, Factortame [1990] ECR I-2433, paragraph 19.

53 Paragraph 26 of the judgment.

54 Paragraphs 27 and 28 of the judgment.

55 Paragraph 29 of the judgment.

56 Joined Cases C-295/04 to C-298/04, Vincenzo Manfredi et al. v Lloyd Adriatico Assicurazioni SpA et al. [2006] ECR I-6619.

Courage gave little guidance as to the nature of the loss in case of competition infringements and the problem of causation.[57]

Manfredi clarifies that it follows from the principle of effectiveness and the right of individuals to seek compensation for loss caused by a contract or by conduct liable to restrict or distort competition that injured persons must be able to seek compensation not only for actual loss (*damnum emergens*) but also for loss of profit (*lucrum cessans*) plus interest. Confirming the principles of effectiveness and equivalence the Court also ruled that it is for the domestic legal system of each Member State to prescribe the limitation period for seeking compensation for harm caused by an agreement or practice prohibited under Article 81 EC, provided that the principles of equivalence and effectiveness are observed.

For consumers the right to damages in case of violations of Articles 81–82 EC opens important perspectives. The consumer will often be the last link in the chain of damage and will effectively suffer a prejudice without being able to pass it on to someone else.

On the other hand, the prejudice of an individual consumer will often be very low (e.g. a price cartel that has led to a small price increase) not justifying individual legal proceedings.

This raises, again the question of group actions.

In *Courage* and *Manfredi* the ECJ thus recognised the right of victims of antitrust violations to claim compensation, whether they are party to a restrictive agreement (like in *Courage*) or not (like in *Manfredi*).

The judgment in *Courage* has prompted the Commission to commission a study on damages actions for breach of EC antitrust rules and later on its Green Paper on the subject (2005).[58] Very recently (April 2008) the Commission published its White Paper and accompanying Staff Working Paper on the same subject.[59]

The Commission considers with respect to collective redress, that there is a clear need for mechanisms allowing aggregation of the individual claims of victims of antitrust infringements. Individual consumers, but also small businesses, especially those who have suffered scattered and relatively low-value damage, are often deterred from bringing an individual action for damages by the costs, delays, uncertainties, risks and burdens involved.

As a result, many of these victims currently remain uncompensated. On the rare occasions where a multitude of individual actions are brought in relation to the same infringement, procedural inefficiencies arise for claimants, defendants and the judicial system alike.

---

57 See Jules Stuyck, annotation of Courage, in *ERCL* 2005, 229, at p. 235–237.

58 COM(2005) 672 final.

59 COM (2008) 165 final and SEC(2008) 404.

The Commission therefore suggests a combination of two complementary mechanisms of collective redress to address effectively those issues in the field of antitrust:

- representative actions, which are brought by qualified entities, such as consumer associations, state bodies or trade associations, on behalf of identified or, in rather restricted cases, identifiable victims. These entities are either:

  (i) officially designated in advance; or
  (ii) certified on an *ad hoc* basis by a Member State for a particular antitrust infringement to bring an action on behalf of some or all of their members; and

- opt-in collective actions, in which victims expressly decide to combine their individual claims for harm they suffered into one single action.

The White Paper only mentions representative actions and opt-in collective actions for consumers. US-type class actions are not as such rejected, but not proposed. In the Commission Staff Working Paper accompanying the White Paper[60] the Commission mentions that excesses in US class actions have often been mentioned and that the risk of importing these excesses in Europe was raised. The Commission however notes that the overall legal context in the US, which goes well beyond the mere class action mechanism, is very different from the one in Europe. US class actions in antitrust cases are characterised by a combination of features that is very specific to the US, including the jury pre-trial, one-way shifting of costs, treble damages, wide pre-trial discovery, contingency fee agreements and an opt-out mechanism. The introduction in Europe of features similar to one or some of these features may not produce the same effects. For instance the introduction of opt-out mechanisms in Portugal and the Netherlands is not reported to have led to similar excesses.

It would thus seem that the Commission's DG Competition has not totally ruled out the possibility to introduce opt-out class actions with regard to antitrust violations to the benefit of consumers and businesses.

Difficulties also arise, on the other hand, if an indirect purchaser invokes the passing-on of overcharges as a basis to show the harm suffered. Purchasers at, or near, the end of the distribution chain (like consumers), are often those most harmed by antitrust infringements, but given their distance from the infringement they find it particularly difficult to produce sufficient proof of the existence and extent of passing-on of the illegal overcharge along the distribution chain. The

60 SEC(2008)404.

Commission proposes to lighten the victim's burden and suggests that indirect purchasers should be able to rely on the rebuttable presumption that the illegal overcharge was passed on to them in its entirety.

In the case of joint, parallel or consecutive actions brought by purchasers at different points in the distribution chain, national courts are encouraged to make full use of all mechanisms at their disposal under national, Community and international law in order to avoid under and overcompensation of the harm caused by an infringement of competition law.

Some conclusions can be drawn from this.

Antitrust law is basically public law and the discourse on private enforcement is rather new. In consumer law we have seen the opposite phenomenon. Where consumer law was traditionally a matter of private law enforcement, at least in a certain number of Member States, the Community positively promotes public enforcement (albeit – for the time being – limited to cooperation) through the adoption of Regulation 2004/2006.[61]

There is however something common in the general EU approach to enforcement of consumer rights on the one hand and private enforcement (for consumers) under EU antitrust law on the other. While collective actions are recognised as a necessity (see also Directive 98/27 on injunctions), the EU seems to distrust private lawyer actions (like US class actions). The right to bring cross-border actions for injunctive relief in the consumer interest is only given to entities designated by the Member States (i.e. public bodies or recognised representative consumer associations). Likewise in its White Paper on actions for damages, the Commission proposes to limit the possibility of collective actions for damages of consumers to entities officially designated in advance or certified on an *ad hoc* basis by a Member State (which, it must be recognised gives an opportunity for a certain flexibility) and to opt-in collective actions, in which victims expressly decide to combine their individual claims for harm they suffered into one single action. In the accompanying Staff Working Paper the Commission marks a clear preference for actions by consumer associations (and public bodies) rather than for private actions (initiated by lawyers like in the US).

---

61 See critically on this Regulation: Roger van den Bergh, footnote 33, pp. 177 et seq.

4. A CASE FOR COMMUNITY LEGISLATION? THE DIFFICULTIES OF MULTINATONAL LITIGATION OF COLLECTIVE ACTION

In the absence of EU rules on collective damages actions cross-border procedures may raise complicated questions of private international law: which courts have jurisdiction, which law(s) is (are) applicable and how can a judgment be enforced in another Member State?[62]

Cross-border litigation in itself is complex, because apart from substantive questions, questions of international jurisdiction and enforcement and the law applicable have first to be addressed.

In the case of collective actions these issues are even more complex.

I shall only briefly indicate which problems may arise in this respect for collective actions in Europe (leaving aside the problems relating to international collective litigation involving European and non-European jurisdictions such as where European victims participate in US class actions or non-European victims join a group action in an EU Member State).

The easiest question is that of jurisdiction. On territorial competence in case of multi-state litigation in the EU, the Brussels Regulation (Regulation 44/2001) provides as a basic rule that persons domiciled in a Member State shall, whatever their nationality, be sued in the courts of that Member State (Article 2(1)).

In matters relating to contracts, a person domiciled in a Member State may, in another Member State, be sued in the courts of the place of performance of the obligation in question (Article 5(1)(a)).

In matters relating to tort, delict or quasi-delict, competence is with the courts of the place where the harmful event occurred or may occur.

A person domiciled in a Member State may also be sued where he is one of a number of defendants, in the courts of the place where any one of them is domiciled, provided that the claims are so closely connected that it is expedient to hear and determine them together to avoid the risk of irreconcilable judgments resulting from separate proceedings (Article 6). This hypothesis however does not concern group actions.

The Regulation contains specific provisions for specific kinds of contracts.

For certain consumer contracts,[63] Article 16 provides the following rules: a consumer may bring proceedings against the other party to a contract either in the courts of the Member State in which that party is domiciled or in the courts of the place where the consumer is domiciled and proceedings may be brought

62 See the contributions of Peter Rott and (for Canada) of G. Saumier to this book.

63 Defined in Article 15: in short certain instalment sales and credit contracts and contracts where the consumer has shopped in another country while remaining passive.

against a consumer by the other party to the contract only in the courts of the Member State in which the consumer is domiciled.

These rules would not seem to hamper the introduction of a collective action on behalf of consumers from different Member States against a common defendant in one Member State. However if in a Member State a (public) body has standing to bring an action for damages on behalf of consumers that body will not automatically have standing in other Member States (unlike what is the case under Directive 98/27 where this right is specifically recognised in relation to bodies designated by the relevant Member State).

Where consumers of different Member States have suffered non-contractual harm (e.g. a product liability case or a claim for damages for an antitrust infringement) courts of different Member States may be competent, but the consumers will still have the possibility of suing before the courts of the residence of the defendant.

At the level of the law applicable things get more complicated.

Where consumers from different Member States are involved in a collective action for damages, the law of more than one Member State may be applicable.

This is true both for contractual and non-contractual claims.

First, with regard to contractual claims there is the Rome I Convention, to be replaced by the Rome I Regulation.[64] The principle is that parties freely choose the law applicable. For certain consumer contracts (basically where the consumer is passive) the contract is governed by the law of the country where the consumer has his habitual residence. Thus in actions involving consumers from several Member States, several national laws may be applicable.

Second, the Rome II Regulation (Regulation (EC) No 864/2007 of 11 July 2007 on the law applicable to non-contractual obligations)[65] provides basically that the law applicable is the law of the country in which the damage occurs irrespective of the country in which the event giving rise to the damage occurred and irrespective of the country or countries in which the indirect consequences of that event occur. However where it is clear from all the circumstances of the case that the tort/delict is manifestly more closely connected with another country, the law of that other country shall apply. A manifestly closer connection with another country might be based in particular on a pre-existing relationship between the parties, such as a contract, that is closely connected with the tort/delict in question.

Furthermore, still pursuant to that Regulation, in the case of product liability the law applicable to a non-contractual obligation arising out of damage caused by a product shall be the law of the country in which the person sustaining the

64 See Regulation (EC) No. 593/2008 on the law applicable to contractual obligations (Rome I), (2008) O.J. L 177/6.

65 O.J. 2007, No. L 199/40.

damage had his or her habitual residence when the damage occurred, if the product was marketed in that country, or, failing that, the law of the country in which the product was acquired, if the product was marketed in that country, or, failing that, the law of the country in which the damage occurred, if the product was marketed in that country. However, the law applicable shall be the law of the country in which the person claimed to be liable is habitually resident if he or she could not reasonably foresee the marketing of the product, or a product of the same type, in the country the law of which is applicable under the preceding rules. Where it is clear from all the circumstances of the case that the tort/delict is manifestly more closely connected with another country, the law of that other country shall apply. A manifestly closer connection with another country might be based in particular on a pre-existing relationship between the parties, such as a contract, that is closely connected with the tort/delict in question.

Finally the law applicable to a non-contractual obligation arising out of an act of unfair competition shall be the law of the country where competitive relations or the collective interests of consumers are, or are likely to be, affected.

Without going into a detailed analysis of these rules, it will be clear that in a given situation involving consumers from different Member States, law from different Member States may apply.

In its Staff Working Paper appended to its White Paper the Commission briefly discusses the possibility to apply the *lex fori*. In that case one substantive law would apply. But that may not be the most generous law for the victims. Obviously these questions merit still a lot of study.

Finally the question of enforcement may be very difficult. According to Regulation 44/2001 judgments rendered by the court of a Member State have to be recognised and enforced in other Member States, but rules on, e.g. the distribution of damages (e.g. to persons who were not party to the procedure) do not exist.

GENERAL CONCLUSION

While some Member States primarily rely on public enforcement of consumer law, others rely primarily on private enforcement.

While the ECJ has stressed – under certain conditions – the procedural autonomy of the Member States, the Community legislature has broader powers to harmonise procedures and remedies in the field of consumer protection than is often believed, in particular it would seem that legislation at the EU level is also possible with respect to intra-state enforcement.

Until now legislation at the EU level in the field of enforcement of consumer law has been limited to actions for injunctive relief. The rapid development of the law of collective actions for damages – characterised by a quasi unanimous rejection of the US type of class actions – at the national level has prompted the debate on an EU initiative in this field. The internal market dimension of the problem is particularly acute in relation to actions for damage involving consumers from different jurisdictions.

Both at the level of the Member States and the EU, with varying degrees of private law and public law solutions, unlike the US, collective enforcement of consumer rights is institutionalised, i.e. it is reserved to established representative and recognised organisations. The private lawyer model is largely rejected.

Collective actions for damages on behalf of consumers from different Member States raise difficult questions of private international law that need to be addressed at the EU level.

PUBLIC AND PRIVATE ENFORCEMENT OF CONSUMER LAW IN CENTRAL AND EASTERN EUROPE: INSTITUTIONAL CHOICE IN THE SHADOW OF EU ENLARGEMENT

Antonina Bakardjieva Engelbrekt*

1. INTRODUCTION

The Central and East European (CEE) states that recently joined the European Union (EU) constitute a particularly rewarding case for studying the choice between public and private enforcement in consumer protection. The collapse of state socialism at the end of the 1980s triggered an unprecedented process of institutionalising markets and of experimentation with institutional choice and design in these countries. Remarkably, this process unfolded 'in the shadow' of the eastward enlargement of the Union. Consequently, looking closely at the experience of the CEE states allows us to approach, in a very condensed form, both the question of the appropriate mix between public and private enforcement as well as the politically sensitive constitutional issue of competence-allocation in the European multi-level system of governance.[1]

Certainly, in the particular context of multi-faceted transformation in the CEE countries, the choice between public and private enforcement in consumer protection is one that has very specific and intricate connotations. In these newly opened and still unsettled markets the borderlines between politics, markets and the law are still in flux and a dynamic process of redefining of the social spheres takes place. There is at the same time a considerable tension between the ideology of free markets and the legacy of a pervasive state. The choice between public and private enforcement in consumer protection thus becomes part of the overarching *problematique* of defining the rights and responsibilities of the individual viz. the state and finding the point of balance between government regulation, market

* Professor of European Law, Stockholm University, Department of Law.

autonomy and civil society.[1] Still, over and beyond context specificity, it is believed that the compressed learning experience of the past decade should be of broader relevance for students of consumer law and policy.

This paper pursues three more particular objectives. The first is to provide an overview of institutional choices in consumer enforcement exercised in CEE during the period of transition. The focus of the paper is, as in the rest of this monograph, on collective enforcement where problems of diffuse interests and collective action raise dilemmas of institutional choice. The ambition is not to present an exhaustive and detailed comparative account, but rather to capture the dynamic search during the last decade for the appropriate balancing between private and public enforcement schemes in the CEE states. Administrative and collective judicial enforcement are treated separately, mapping their institutional modalities and the main actors involved. The complementary nature of such schemes is at the same time acknowledged and discussed.

The second objective is to enquire into the reasons for the institutional choices made and through the experience of CEE countries to hopefully provide a refreshing glimpse on the questions of efficiency and justifiability of government intervention viz. private enforcement. A large number of CEE countries have in the last decade introduced new public agencies with broad enforcement tasks in consumer protection. This development may seem to run contrary to deregulatory trends in Western-type market democracies, where the performance of public bodies of all kinds has increasingly come under fire, being accused of regulatory failures and inefficiency. Are the institutional choices in CEE countries misguided? Does a model relying on a regulative agency offer any advantages in the context of still unsettled markets and under what institutional modalities? Whereas the analysis proceeds and is based on the particular situation in CEE countries, the findings are, it is believed, of broader validity.

The third objective is to see in what way European Union law and policy influences national institutional choices in the new Member States from CEE countries. *Prima facie* the Community *acquis* in the area of consumer law and policy are institutionally neutral. Member States should theoretically be free to choose the way to implement Community directives into national law. A significant number of Community consumer protection directives contain provisions on enforcement and remedies but explicitly treat administrative agencies action and collective representative action on equal footing (Misleading Advertising Directive, Distance Selling Directive and more recently the Unfair Commercial Practices Directive). Likewise the Injunctions Directive does not

1 See Micklitz (ed) *Rechtseinheit oder Rechtsvielfalt in Europa? Zur Rolle und Funktion des Verbraucherrechts in den MOE-Staaten und in der EG* (Baden-Baden: Nomos, VIEW Band 1, 1996); Micklitz, 'Verbraucherschutz West versus Ost – Kompatibilizierungsmöglichkeiten in der Europäischen Gemeinschaft – Einige Vorüberlegungen' in: Heiss (ed), *Brückenschlag zwischen den Rechtskulturen des Ostseeraums* (Tübingen: Mohr Siebeck, 2001), 137–182.

give preference to any institutional arrangement, but instead applies the principle of mutual recognition of institutions to agencies and consumer organisations alike. Yet the implementation of Community acts has brought and continues to bring re-evaluation and changes of national institutional and enforcement frameworks.[2] The institutional impact is felt all the more strongly in the new Member States from CEE areas. Certainly, the dust is still settling after the mass-scale implementation of the Community *acquis* into national legislation, including the area of consumer protection. Yet it can be confidently asserted that under the sign of conditionality, transposing the *acquis* has implied both open and covert influence over institutional choice. EU enlargement can thus be studied as an extreme case of the competence reallocation taking place in the multi-level system of governance, which the Union represents.[3]

2. ANALYTICAL APPROACH

The analysis of alternative approaches to collective consumer enforcement in this paper is inspired by two theoretical strings in institutional theory, namely comparative institutional analysis and historical institutionalism.[4] The concept "institution" is used in comparative institutional analysis in a very broad sense referring to the market, the political process and the courts. Whether to leave a certain social problem or goal to the free play of market forces, to rely on private adjudication or to seek solution through the political process, including direct regulation and agency involvement, is at the heart of much political and legal decision-making. Comparative institutional analysis, as in particular developed by public policy scholar Neil Komesar,[5] insists that institutional choices should be based on careful comparison between the relative advantages and disadvantages of each institutional alternative. The costs and benefits of participation in decision-making processes are advanced as main units for the comparative evaluation. The costs of participation consist of information and organisational costs, including transaction costs, litigation costs and costs for political participation. The benefits of participation are measured by the size and distribution of the stakes. High and concentrated stakes would indicate high incentives for participation, whereas low

2 Bakardjieva Engelbrekt, *Fair Trading Law in Flux? National Legacies, Institutional Choice and the Process of Europeanisation* (Stockholm, dissertation, 2003).

3 On multi-level governance in Europe see Scharpf, 'Regieren im europäischen Mehrebenen-system – Ansätze zu einer Theorie' (2002) *Leviathan*, 65.

4 For a fully fledged elaboration of this approach see Bakardjieva Engelbrekt (2003), supra note 2.

5 Komesar, *Imperfect Alternatives. Choosing Institutions in Law, Economics and Public Policy* (Chicago, London: The University of Chicago Press, 1994).

and dispersed stakes – typically the case of consumer interests – involve a number of dilemmas of mobilising participation.[6]

In general, comparative institutional analysis stresses that the dilemmas of institutional choice begin with large numbers. This proposition is familiar from Coasean comparative system analysis. Small numbers of actors are typically associated with low transaction costs, where markets can be expected to cope endogenously with resource allocation through voluntary transactions.[7] But if there are many actors on one side of the interests involved, transaction costs increase and at least potentially, the question arises whether resorting to alternative institutions might reduce allocative inefficiencies. Yet, comparative institutional analysis demonstrates convincingly that large numbers of affected parties constitute a problem in every setting. Similar interest constellations cause analogous problems of organisation and representation. Participation malfunctions in the market setting are reproduced in the political process and in adjudication. In other words, institutions tend to 'move together'.[8] So, legislators and policy makers should seek the least imperfect alternative, rather than searching for the perfect decision-making process. Since one of the main impediments to the efficient protection of consumer interests is seen in high costs of information, organisation and litigation, the model appears highly suitable for the purposes of this analysis.

Apart from the specific constellation of interests for each law and public policy issue, comparative institutional analysis insists that institutional choice depends on characteristics inherent to each decision-making process. These characteristics have to do both with the more salient features of the market, the political process and adjudication, but also with the particular design of these complex institutions that may vary from country to country and from one issue/market to another. Such features as the accountability and transparency of the administrative process, litigation costs, openness of the judicial process to class action and to action by organisations, are all factors that influence the costs and benefits of participation and respectively the relative advantages and disadvantages of administrative and judicial enforcement. When applied to situations of reforming markets and policies the approach allows us to identify specific features of institutional design as well as obstacles to interest organisation and representation, which influence the costs and benefits of participation in decision-making processes at all levels.[9]

---

6 See the classical account of Olson, *The Logic of Collective Action. Public Goods and the Theory of the Group* (New York: Schocken Books, 1965).

7 Of course, even in small numbers of situations transaction costs can be high due to information uncertainty, strategic behaviour or other factors.

8 Komesar (1994), supra note 5, 23.

9 For an alternative application of institutional theory to studying the choice between private and public enforcement in CEE countries, see La Porta et al., 'The New Comparative Economics'

Historical institutionalism perceives institutions in a slightly different way. It highlights the role of institutions as humanly devised constraints, whose main function is to reduce uncertainty by providing a structure to everyday life.[10] Institutions thus include formal legal rules, but also informal constraints (such as ideologies and customs) and the enforcement characteristics of both.[11] North highlights institutions' propensity to persist over time. Institutional paths may be followed not because they are efficient but because their change is costly. Moreover, institutions tend to produce incentives for the creation of organisations, which then depend on the institutional framework and contribute to the latter's stability (institutional symbiosis).

Historical institutionalism gives insights into the conservative force of existing institutions, formal and informal constraints as well as the role of organisations and institutional agents as factors of continuity or change. One major contribution of historical institutionalism is the sensitisation of legal scholars to the importance of institutional culture and habits and of the existing mechanisms of enforcement. The rules in combination with mechanisms of enforcement to a large extent predetermine what agents and organisations will emerge on the institutional scene and whether they are in a position to exploit the framework and induce institutional change once preferences and prices change (to effectively signal the need for change).[12]

Merging the two perspectives appears warranted, because comparative institutional analysis alone may generate unrealistic normative advice with a touch of 'social engineering' and be in discord with the complex reality of human interaction. A historical institutional perspective demonstrates that institutional choice is contingent on a historical and institutional context that has been shaped through time and is generally resistant to change.

(2003) *Journal of Comparative Economics*, 595–619. In their article, La Porta et al. try to capture the variety of institutional choices that states face in regulating markets as a continuum between dictatorship and disorder. See also Glaeser, Johnson and Shleifer, 'Coase versus the Coasians' (2001) *Quarterly Journal of Economics*, 853–899. Cf. the analysis of Schäfer of choices between general standards and stricter directives in developing countries from the point of view of human capital, see Schäfer, 'Direktiven als Ersatz für Humankapital: Empfehlen sich für Entwicklungs- und Transformationsländer präzisere Rechtsnormen als für hochentwickelte Staaten?' (2003) *RabelsZeitschrift*, Bd. 67, 550–580; for institutional analysis in the consumer protection field, see Cafaggi, 'Recasting the Product Liability Debate', in: Cafaggi and Muir-Watt (eds) *The Making of European Private Law: Governance Design* (Cheltenham: Edward Elgar, 2008).

10 North, 'Institutions' (1991) 5 *Journal of Economic Perspectives*, 97.

11 On institutions and institutional change generally, see North, *Institutions, Institutional Change and Economic Performance* (Cambridge: Cambridge University Press, 1990).

12 Sadurski, 'Introduction: The Law and Institutions of New Member States in Year One', in: Sadurski/Ziller/Żurek, *Aprés Enlargement: Legal and Political Responses in Central and Eastern Europe* (Florence: Robert Schumann Centre for Advanced Studies, 2005).

3. THE EVOLUTION OF CONSUMER PROTECTION LAW AND POLICY IN CEE COUNTRIES

The 1989 "velvet" revolution in the CEE countries was not only a revolution for political rights and freedoms but also, in many respects, a consumer revolution. The failure of the planned economy to ensure the reasonable satisfaction of basic consumer needs constituted an important source of public discontent. One would thus expect consumer rights to be high on the political agenda of decision makers in these states in the years immediately following the collapse of state socialism. Yet in the early stage of transition the very introduction of a market economy was by many perceived as the ultimate response to consumer grievances and the end of the road for consumer rights activism. The market, despite its many imperfections and failures, was seen as the sole platform where consumers could act and express their preferences through their purchases. In the words of Poland's first Ombudsman of Citizens' Rights, Ewa Łętowska, "the paradigm of the plan was replaced by the paradigm of the "invisible hand".[13]

But while the ambition has clearly been to roll back the state and expand individual autonomy and market freedom, the result has not always been unequivocal. The transition from totalitarian rule and a command economy to democracy and free markets did not bring about the expected withering of the state.[14] In societies of mass production, complex and hazardous products and sophisticated marketing techniques, the demand for government regulation and state intervention remained high. Governments continued to be held responsible for coping with externalities, market failures, public goods and collective action problems.[15] At stake has thus been changing the role of the state from dictating to framing economic relations and reforming a rigid, secretive and politicised bureaucracy into modern public administration along principles of legality, transparency, accountability and public service.

3.1. THE CONSTITUTIONAL SETTING

The institutional choice in consumer enforcement should not be treated in isolation from its constitutional setting. For the transforming societies of CEE countries the constitutions of the early 1990s acquired the symbolic role of marking a point of no return. They represented a passionate pledge to democratic

13 Łętowska, 'Consumer Protection as Public Interest Law' (1999) (1–4) *Droit polonais contemporain*, 39–60.

14 Stiglitz, *Wither Socialism?* (Cambridge: MIT Press, 1994).

15 Rose-Ackerman, *From Elections to Democracy, Building Accountable Government in Hungary and Poland* (Cambridge: Cambridge University Press, 2005), at 7.

political values, human rights and economic liberalism. Consequently, almost all post-communist constitutions emphasise the principles of free economic enterprise. The right to freely exercise economic and professional activity ranks high in the catalogues of citizens rights solemnly proclaimed in the constitutional charters adopted at the outset of transition.[16] At the same time the constitutions seek to bridge the past through greater recognition of social and economic rights and constitutionally anchored commitment of the state to protect the week and vulnerable.[17]

Consumer protection is thus either implicitly recognised as a legitimate limitation of free economic activity or (more rarely) explicitly pronounced as part of the constitutional framework of free markets. Interestingly, the constitutions expressly addressing consumer protection (Bulgaria, Latvia and Poland) do so in terms of the obligations of the state and of public authorities to protect consumers and not in terms of private consumer right.[18] In this one can see certain constitutional predisposition for public enforcement. Nevertheless, the right to private collective enforcement through consumer organisations should also be viewed as constitutionally anchored in the general freedom of association.[19]

Yet despite the sometimes explicit constitutional commitment, the substantive law and the institutional framework of consumer protection in CEE countries evolved only slowly. The isolated consumer protection acts that were adopted in some CEE countries during the first years of economic reform were mostly of symbolic nature, lacking effective mechanisms of enforcement.[20] A real boost of consumer law and policy was experienced first with the intensification of Community accession policy in the second half of the 1990s.[21] It would thus not

---

16 See Article 26 Charter on Fundamental Rights, Czech Republic (free exercise of profession); Article 9(2) Constitution of Hungary (free enterprise and free competition); Article 74 Constitution of the Republic of Slovenia (free enterprise); Article 35 Constitution of the Slovak Republic, etc.

17 The prominent position of second generation rights in CEE Constitutions is observed by Micklitz (1996), supra note 1.

18 See Article 19(2) Constitution of the Republic of Bulgaria: "*The State* shall establish and guarantee equal legal conditions for economic activity to all citizens and legal entities by preventing any abuse of a monopoly status and unfair competition, and *by protecting the consumer.*" Article 46(5) Constitution of Latvia: "The *State* shall defend the interests of the *consumers.*" Article 76 Constitution of the Republic of Poland of 2 April 1997: "*Public authorities* shall protect *consumers*, customers, hirers or lessees against activities threatening their health, privacy and safety, as well as against dishonest market practices. The scope of such protection shall be specified by statute." (my italics).

19 See Article 70/C Constitution of the Republic of Hungary; Article 29 Constitution of the Slovak Republic; Article 35 Constitution of Lithuania, etc.

20 Alexiev et al., *Consumer Protection in Bulgaria, Czech Republic, Estonia, Hungary, Latvia, Lithuania and Romania. National Reports and Comparative Analysis* (Louvain-la-Neuve: Centre du Droit de la consommation, Université Catholique de Louvain, CICPP no. 4, 1996).

21 See Bakardjieva Engelbrekt, 'The Impact of Enlargement on Private Law Governance: The Case of Consumer Protection', in: Cafaggi and Muir-Watt (eds) (2008), supra note 9. Jacoby, *The*

be exaggerated to state that consumer protection, as a societal value and individual right, owes its constitutional legitimisation chiefly to external governance.[22]

3.2. CONSUMER PROTECTION BY CONDITIONALITY

In the first Association Agreements of 1993 with Hungary and Poland, consumer protection was only mentioned as one area where approximation of legislation should be achieved.[23] However, it acquired an ever more prominent position in parallel with the maturing and the constitutional and institutional anchoring of consumer policy at the Community level. In the Agreements of 1994 with Bulgaria, Czech and Slovak Republics and Romania, a separate article on consumer protection was included, spelling out the aim of full compatibility with the Community consumer protection policy and drawing up several particular areas of economic cooperation.[24] Finally, the last group of Agreements with the Baltic States and Slovenia signed in 1995 and 1996 singled out consumer protection among the areas where rapid progress in the approximation of laws should be made. Moreover the article on consumer protection expanded to include commitment to active consumer protection policy as well as detailed steps of technical assistance for establishing the necessary institutional infrastructure.[25]

In 1995 the Commission White Paper on the Preparation of the Associated Countries of CEE for Integration into the Internal Market of the Union exerted a catalysing effect on the harmonisation process.[26] The Community's legislative *acquis* in the area of consumer protection was outlined in *extenso* in Chapter 23 of the 1995 White Paper, dividing the substantive measures into two main

---

Enlargement of the European Union and NATO: Ordering from the Menu in Central Europe (Cambridge: Cambridge University Press, 2005).

22 On external accountability, see Rose-Ackerman, supra note 15, 37 ff. On governance by conditionality, see Schimmelfennig and Sedelmeier, 'Governance by Conditionality: EU Rule Transfer to the Candidate Countries of Central and Eastern Europe' (2004) *Journal of European Public Policy* 661; Grabbe, The EU's Transformative Power: Europeanization through Conditionality in Central and Eastern Europe (Basingstoke: Palgrave, 2006).

23 Cf. the identical texts of Article 68 of the Europe Agreement with Hungary [1993] OJ L 348/1 and Article 69 of the Europe Agreement with Poland [1993] OJ L 347/1.

24 See Article 93 of the Agreement with Bulgaria [1994] OJ L 358/1 and the almost identical texts of Article 92 of the Agreement with Czech Republic [1994] OJ L 360/1 and Slovakia [1994] OJ L 359/1; Article 93 of the Agreements with Slovenia [1999] OJ L 51/1 and Romania [1994] OJ L 357/1 respectively.

25 See Article 94 Europe Agreement with Estonia [1998] OJ L 68/1; Article 95 Europe Agreement with Latvia; Article 96 Europe Agreement with Lithuania. On this development, see Bourgoignie, 'The Approximation Process of Consumer Laws of Central and Eastern European Countries to EU Legislation: A Favourable Context but an Urgent Need for Clarification' in Micklitz (1996), supra note 1, at 91.

26 White Paper on the Preparation of the Associated Countries of CEE for Integration into the Internal Market of the Union (COM (1995) 163 final).

sections, namely: section II Quality and safety of goods and section III Protection of economic interests of consumers. Consumer policy was set as a medium priority for the CEECs and the relevant directives were enumerated and classified into stage I and stage II key measures.[27] The granting to consumers of fundamental rights as recognised by the Community's action programmes in favour of consumers since 1975 was set out as a chief condition for making the consumer *acquis* operative.

Remarkably, despite the absence of a clear institutional blueprint in EC legislation, Chapter 23 of the White Paper of 1995 laid down a surprisingly elaborate set of requirements in respect of the institutional framework necessary to operate the consumer protection *acquis*.[28] Under the title "Conditions necessary to operate the legislation" the following four components were outlined:

> (ii) … the setting-up of *an adequate institutional structure* in charge of consumer affairs, including the allocation of a general and horizontal competence on consumer affairs to *one designated authority*, who will be responsible for taking initiatives in the consumer field and for coordinating actions taken under other policies by other authorities …
> (iii) … the setting up of *consultative structures*, either general (EU Consumer Consultative Committee) or specific (in sectors such as drugs, food and cosmetics) which will represent the consumer interest and ensure the participation of consumers to the decision-making process;
> …
> (v) … the granting to consumers of *efficient redress mechanisms* enabling them to make their rights effective, some of which have been suggested in the Green Paper of the Commission on Access to Justice;
> (vi) … the promotion and aid to the development of *non-public consumer organisations*. (my italics)

This emphasis on institutional issues in the White Paper echoed the decisions of the 1993 Copenhagen European Council, which opened the prospect of full EU membership for the CEE states. At the Copenhagen Council the conditions for membership were defined not only in terms of formal legal transposition of the Community *acquis*, but importantly, in political and institutional terms. Consequently, prior to accession, candidate states had to not only transpose the substantive Community '*acquis*' in the field of consumer protection, but also to demonstrate institutional capacity to assume the obligations of membership,

---

27 As stage I measures, the White Paper lists the directives on general product safety, on misleading advertising, consumer credit, unfair terms and indication of prices. Under stage II measures, the directives on package travel, doorstep selling and time share are ordered.

28 For a similar uniform advice out of diverse experience in the area of reform of public administration, see Bugaric, 'The Europeanisation of National Administration in Central and Eastern Europe', in: Sadurski/Ziller/Żurek (eds) (2005), supra note 12.

notably by specific changes in procedural rules and institutional design.[29] Whereas the concern on the part of the Union about implementation and actual effect of transposed Community rules in the CEE countries is understandable, the process of enlargement implied a considerable shift in the constitutional equilibrium of competence sharing between Community and Member States in the areas of procedural law and institutions. The principles of procedural autonomy and institutional neutrality, widely recognised in Community law, were significantly relaxed, raising pertinent questions about the limits of Community competences and the balance between integration and national autonomy.[30]

In 1998 the Commission started to publish Regular Reports on the Progress of the Candidate Countries toward Membership of the Union (in the following referred to as RR, country and year). The Regular Reports provided a recurrent assessment of the candidate countries' efforts in legal and institutional reform and defined new targets. The reports were received with utmost attention in the candidate countries and exerted powerful impact on priority setting and the course of further substantive and institutional changes.

The association agreements, the White Paper and the Commission Regular Progress Reports represented the chief conduits of EU conditionality. However, the EU's influence was exerted under a number of more subtle and less visible forms. Already in the late 1980s the PHARE programme was set up for financial and technical assistance to Hungary and Poland.[31] In the course of accession the programme transformed into a massive project of economic and legal aid seeking to help the candidate countries to transpose the *acquis* and adapt their institutions to the EU requirements. Numerous teams of experts were deployed in the CEECs to screen national legislation and assess its compliance with the relevant *acquis*. Enforcement avenues in CEE countries were thus shaped under the real or perceived pressure of EU conditionality, rather than as a result of internally crafted legislative programmes.

---

29 See Grabbe (2006), supra note 22.

30 See Bakardjieva Engelbrekt, 'Grey Zones, Legitimacy Concerns and Boomerang Effects: On the Implications of Extending the Acquis to the Countries of Central and Eastern Europe, in: Wahl and Kramér (eds) *Swedish Yearbook of European Law* (Oxford: Hart Publishing, 2006), 1–36. On the mixed reactions of Constitutional Courts in CEE to such external governance see Sadurski (2006) supra note 12.

31 PHARE: Pologne-Hongrie, Aide a la Reconstruction Economicque, Council Regulation 3906/89. See Grabbe (2006), supra note 22.

4. INSTITUTIONAL CHOICE AND DESIGN

As a result of the above described pre-accession dynamics, upon their entry into the Union all CEE countries could boast extensive consumer protection legislation largely corresponding, and in certain cases going beyond, the Community *acquis*. The transposition of Community directives followed different techniques: from comprehensive consumer protection acts, to framework legislation, filled out by governmental regulations or special legislative acts corresponding to individual Community directives.[32] Notwithstanding these nuances in approach, however, all candidate states could report sufficient degrees of alignment with the Community consumer protection *acquis*, satisfying the rigorous screening on the part of a vigilant Commission.

Far less settled than the area of substantive law is the area of enforcement, where a process of readjustment seems to be continuing in the aftermath of EU accession. Certainly the four elements of the institutional blueprint of the White paper were put in place in all CEE countries. Yet, there appears to be a still ongoing search of the right point of balance between private and public involvement, between coercion and mediation, between regulation, private ordering and judicial enforcement.

4.1. ADMINISTRATIVE ENFORCEMENT

Public enforcement was recognised as an indispensable element of the overall institutional framework of consumer protection in all CEE countries. With the exception of the Czech and Slovak Republics, where there had been a conscious resistance against statist solutions, all CEECs established specialised public authorities for consumer protection with broad competences and powers for market supervision and administrative enforcement.[33] The White Paper's

32 On the legislative process see Bakardjieva Engelbrekt (2008), supra note 21; Jacoby (2005), supra note 21. For analysis of the Polish transposition process, see Łętowska et al., 'Implementation of Consumer Law in Poland', 15(6) (2007) *European Review of Private Law*, 873–889.

33 Bulgaria: Commission for (Trade and) Consumer Protection (CCP) (1999); Estonia: State Consumer Protection Board (CPB) (1994); Hungary: General Inspectorate for Consumer Protection (GICP) (1997); Latvia: Consumer Rights Protection Centre (CRPC) (1998); Lithuania: National Consumer Protection Board (NCPB) (2000); Poland: Office for Competition and Consumer Protection (OCCP) (1996); Romania: Office for the Protection of Consumers (1992) replaced by National Authority for Consumer Protection (NACP) (2000); Slovenia: Office for Consumer Protection (OCP) (1996). Hereinafter the consumer protection agencies will be referred to with the abbreviation CPAg when from the context it is clear which country is being discussed. On the cases of the Czech Republic and Slovakia see Jacoby (2005), supra note 21.

requirement of allocation of a "general and horizontal competence on consumer affairs to one designated authority" has thus brought a substantial degree of institutional homogeneity.

A. *Institutional Design*

Yet while demanding the creation of a consumer protection authority as an institutional condition for making the consumer protection *acquis* operational, the White Paper said little as to the institutional design of such authority. Certainly, the newly built agencies in CEE countries differ substantially in their competences, organisation and enforcement tools. There are, however, also considerable commonalities. For instance, none of the newly established CPAgs are designed as truly independent regulatory agencies of the US type. In the political science literature, different factors are advanced to measure agency independence, the most important being agency head status, the management board's status, relationship with government and parliament, financial and organisational autonomy and regulatory competences.[34] Following these criteria, the consumer protection authorities in the CEECs can at most be described as semi-independent.[35] In most CEECs the agencies fall squarely within the structure of government and are under the supervision of a Government Ministry, typically the Ministry of the Economy (Bulgaria, Latvia, Estonia, Slovenia and Hungary).[36]

One aspect that deserves closer scrutiny is the institutional interface between consumer protection and competition policy. In many CEE countries a natural link between these two policies was recognised at an early stage of economic reform. In countries like Hungary, Bulgaria and the Baltic States, competition agencies were designed to combine competences in the areas of antitrust and unfair commercial practices with clear consumer protection objectives. This design expressed a vision of a close link of competition law and policy with the consumer interest. As a whole these competition agencies were designed as strong and independent authorities, often accountable directly to Parliament. In their enforcement the agencies acquired a clear profile of consumer advocates.[37] However, the advance of consumer policy as a discrete field of regulation and the

---

34 Gilardi, 'Policy Credibility and Delegation to Independent Regulatory Agencies: A Comparative Empirical Analysis' 9 (2002) (6) *Journal of European Public Policy*, 873–893.

35 Thatcher, 'Delegation to Independent Regulatory Agencies: Pressures, Functions and Contextual Mediation', 25 (1) (2002) *West European Politics*, 125–147. Cf. Bakardjieva Engelbrekt (2008), supra, note 21.

36 In Lithuania consumer protection is located within the supervision of the Ministry of Justice.

37 Cseres, 'The Hungarian Cocktail of Competition Law and Consumer Protection: Should it be Dissolved?' (2004) *Journal of Consumer Policy*, Vol. 27, 43–74; Bakardjieva Engelbrekt (2006), supra note 30.

imperative of effective implementation of the Community *acquis* in the field of competition law raised the question whether these agencies shall be divested of their consumer protection prerogatives and should focus on antitrust enforcement. Such recommendations were formulated explicitly and followed implicitly from the Regular Reports on Progress by the Commission.[38]

As a result, whereas some competition agencies keep even today (Hungary, Latvia, Lithuania and Bulgaria) certain competences in the area of unfair commercial practices, on the whole enlargement influenced institutional choice in a direction toward greater functional differentiation and to downgrading consumer protection tasks in the priorities of competition agencies. Further divestment of functions in the field of unfair commercial practices is expected (or has already occurred) as a result of the transposition of the Unfair Commercial Practices Directive.[39] Only in Poland did the opposite development take shape. The Polish Antimonopoly Agency was reformed in the mid-1990s into a mega-agency (Office on Competition and Consumer Protection, OCCP) absorbing all consumer protection tasks and responsible for enforcement of collective consumer rights. The OCCP is under the direct subordination of the Prime Minister and enjoys a status close to that of a separate ministry.

Eventually, the institutional setup of governmental agencies in the CEECs seems to reveal conscious or involuntary bias toward hierarchical command and control governance structures. This was not counteracted but rather promoted through the Commission Regular Reports. The main factors addressed there were the staffing of government agencies and of consumer protection departments in ministries. Agency independence and status were dealt with in the Regular Reports only in respect of agencies that combine consumer protection with protection of competition.[40] Questions of accountability and transparency were only occasionally treated in the sections on consumer protection in the Regular Reports, if at all (cf. RR Bulgaria, 2000, 73/74).

B. *Ex Post v. Ex Ante*

The planned economy, as the name indicates itself, was in its very essence a system of all-pervasive *ex ante* control of economic activity. Little was to be left to the vagaries of voluntary market transactions. The whole production and marketing process was constrained and controlled through a comprehensive web of

---

38 See Bakardjieva Engelbrekt (2006), supra note 30.

39 See Bakardjieva Engelbrekt (2006), supra note 30; Bakardjieva Engelbrekt, 'An End to Fragmentation? The Unfair Commercial Practices Directive from the Perspective of the New Member States of Central and Eastern Europe" in: Weatherill/Bernitz (eds.) *The Regulation of Unfair Commercial Practices under EC Directive 2005/29: New Rules and New Techniques* (Oxford: Hart Publishing, 2007), 47–90.

40 See Regular Report Poland, 2000, 43; Regular Report Poland 2001, 50, 84.

permissions and approvals issued by a variety of public bodies. Product quality was examined in a preventive manner, whereby each product had to correspond to a national standard, set up and approved by national standardization bodies.[41]

The transition to a market economy and most of all, the imperatives of EU accession implied a dramatic conversion of the system of product control from *ex ante* to *ex post* principles. The consumer protection bodies in most CEECs are consequently entrusted with broad market monitoring and sanctioning powers, but control is carried out mainly on an *ex post* basis.[42] This is so irrespective of the area of substantive rights, be it unfair contract terms or general product safety. Still, in certain areas, such as marketing practices, the option provided by the respective Community Directives (Misleading and Comparative Advertising Directive; Unfair Commercial Practices Directive) for pre-emptive injunction has been used by a number of CEE countries.

C. *Individual v. Collective Interests*

It may seem natural that a system of public enforcement would focus on enforcement of collective consumer interests. Yet even this simple assumption does not hold in the specific institutional environment of the CEE post-communist markets. Thus, in the Baltic countries, an idiosyncratic system of mediation and enforcement of individual consumer complaints through various public institutions (Trade Inspections, Supervisory Commissions and later on Consumer Protection Agencies) was in place already at the outset of economic and institutional reforms in the early 1990s. Noting the initial striking uniformity of this procedure among the three Baltic States, Viitanen conjectures that this way of settling consumer complaints must have its roots in the Soviet system. Indeed, in an economy where all economic enterprises are owned and controlled by the state, it is only natural that public bodies take care of complaint settlement and mediation between consumers and producers.[43]

---

41 See Stiglitz, (1994), supra note 14, at 198–199: "It was hard for the central authorities to specify, in their central planning exercises, the precise nature of every commodity, including the quality of the product. … firms had no incentive to make the appropriate marginal benefit-marginal cost calculations. Rather, since they had a given target to produce, they had an incentive to get by with the lowest acceptable quality. The economic structure was such that there were strong incentives for quality deterioration."

42 See Cafaggi and Micklitz, 'Collective Enforcement of Consumer Law: A Framework for Comparative Assessment' (2008) European Review of Private Law, Vol. 16, 391–425.

43 See on consumer protection before the start of economic and political reforms Łętowski, Verbraucherschutz im Polen. Rechtslage, Wirklichkeit und Zukunft (1976) *RabelsZ*, 13–41; Banasiński 'Der verwaltungsrechtliche Konsumentenschutz in Polen an der Schwelle der Einführung der Marktwirtschaft', (1990) (4) *Zeitschrift für Lebensmittelrecht*, 459–463; Łętowska, 'Consumer Protection as Public Interest Law' (1999) *Droit polonais contemporain*, nr. 1–4, 39–60.

Interestingly the transition to a market economy did not bring about the demise of the system but resulted in gradual institutional adaptation and growing differentiation between the Baltic States. Latvia seems to have preserved the system closest to the original design. The public CPAg performs still a rather comprehensive role of mediation between individual consumers and traders and administers consumer complaints about product conformity.[44] Provided that an expert finds the product not to conform to the agreed quality, the trader is obliged to satisfy the consumer's claim. Upon failure to do so, the consumer can file a complaint before the public CPAg, which can oblige the trader to comply and impose sanctions. Thus the case is converted from a private law dispute into a public law one, whereby traders can appeal the decision of the CPAg in administrative proceedings.[45] The whole procedure is free of charge for the consumer.

In Lithuania, a similar procedure of consumer complaints before a plurality of public supervision bodies applies (Sanitary Inspections, Health Inspections, etc.) accompanied by ensuing expert assessment of safety and quality conformity (ss. 21–27 CPA). The costs for the expertise are covered in principle by the state budget or by the trader in case products prove to be of inadequate quality (s. 21 CPA). The complaint settlement is handled by the CPAg within a relatively short time frame (in principle within 20 days). It takes a quasi-judicial form following a written procedure, but in contrast to the situation in Latvia, does not lead to a binding decision. Both parties remain free to refer the dispute to courts of general jurisdiction (s. 29 CPA). Non-compliance with the decision of the CPAg does not entail sanctions. The CPAg, however, has the possibility to publicly announce the trader's non-compliance (s. 28 CPA). Apparently, such blacklisting is intended to discipline traders by soft instruments such as reputation.

Finally, in Estonia, the system of consumer complaints was in 2004 reorganised much along the lines of the Swedish Public Board of Consumer Complaints with a separate public body dealing with consumer complaints, structured into a number of panels according to the subject matter in dispute and issuing non-

---

44 See s. 25(1)(4) Latvian CPA: The Consumer Rights Protection Centre has among others the right "to examine submissions and complaints of consumers regarding violations of consumer rights, as well as to assist consumers in resolving conflicts that have arisen with respect to manufacturers, sellers or service providers, and to require compliance with the lawful claims of consumers.".

45 See Viitanen, 'Alternative Dispute Resolution Systems in the Settlement of Consumer Disputes in the Baltic States', in: Côté et al., *Access to Justice and Alternative Dispute Resolution Systems in Central and Eastern Europe* (Louvain-la-Neuve: Centre du Droit de la consommation, Université Catholique de Louvain, CICPP no. 16, 2000), 108; cf. s. 25 Latvian Consumer Rights Protection Act, in conjunction with s. 48 Cabinet Regulation No. 631 of 1 August 2006 on Procedures for the Submission and Examination of Consumer Claims Regarding the Non-conformity of Goods or Services with Contract Provisions, English translation available at: www.ttc.lv/index.php?skip=675&itid=mk_noteikumi&id=10&tid=71&l=EN.

binding recommendations for settlement of the dispute.[46] Traders are not obliged to follow the decision of the public complaint settlement body and the dispute can be taken to the courts of general jurisdiction. Yet in the event of failure to comply with a decision of the Complaints Committee, the Consumer Protection Board has the right, with the consent of the consumer and acting as his or her representative, to file an action with a county court for the same dispute to be heard, if the dispute is relevant to the application of an Act or other legislation or to the general interests of consumers.

The justifiability and viability of a system of extensive mediation by public authorities and representation of individual consumers before the courts is hard to sustain in a market economy. As the Latvian report to the Leuven study on alternative means for consumer redress indicates, such system is bound to stumble upon time and budgetary constraints and experience difficulties in settling complex consumer complaints.[47] Still, it is interesting that in the early days of screening of consumer protection institutions in the CEE candidate countries, Community experts encouraged the further preservation and expansion of the system and even its increased coupling with public sanctions and control.[48] Conversely, it is hardly surprising that in both Lithuania and Estonia, we observe a process of reshaping the role of state bodies in a direction towards less intrusive mechanisms of non-binding complaint settlement and selective intervention.

D. *Injunctions v. Penalties*

The remedies available for consumer harm to a great extent determine the incentives for addressing administrative or judicial enforcement bodies and naturally consumers' choice between the two, if both are available. Public enforcement in CEE countries was, and still to a great extent is, closely associated with the classical command and control type of sanction. In many of these countries extensive statutes on administrative law and on administrative violations and sanctions existed during the previous regime, shaped after the Soviet fashion.[49] These statutes targeted mostly the relations between administrative authorities and individuals (natural persons). With the advance of

---

46 This was certainly the effect of a twinning project with the Swedish Consumer Agency as a partner.

47 See The Study Centre for Consumer Law – Centre for European Economic Law, *An analysis and evaluation of alternative means of consumer redress other than redress through ordinary judicial proceedings. Final report* (Katholieke Universiteit Leuven, Belgium, 17 January, 2007), available at: http://ec.europa.eu/consumers/redress/reports_studies/compartaive_report_en.pdf (hereinafter Leuven Study); National Report Latvia.

48 Viitanen, 'Consumer Protection in the Baltic countries' in: Alexiev et al. (1996), supra, note 20.

49 See Galligan and Smilov, *Administrative Law in Central and Eastern Europe* (Central University Press, 1999).

the market economy, however, the possibility of penalising juridical persons (enterprises) was likewise envisaged.[50]

Consequently, officials of the CPAgs are typically empowered, upon establishing violation of the consumer protection laws, to enforce the statutes by way of fines and criminal penalties[51] and by closing down enterprises for serious cases of unfair commercial practices and violations of safety rules (Hungary, s. 47(e) CPA; Romania, RR 2002, p. 106; Bulgaria, CPA).[52] Of note is that in some countries fines on the spot may be imposed by trade inspectors not only for infringements of the rules for product quality and safety, but also of the prohibitions on misleading, indecent and comparative advertising and other rules on commercial practices where it would appear that assessment is less straightforward and requires more sophisticated judgment.[53]

Injunctions were introduced as a remedy in the sphere of consumer protection in CEE countries chiefly as a result of the implementation of the Injunctions Directive. Instead of opting for either administrative injunctive orders or court injunctions issued in civil proceedings, almost all CEE countries have introduced both possibilities, which now co-exist in a somewhat complex relationship. Thus a number of consumer agencies are furnished with the power to issue cease-and-desist orders following administrative investigation or quasi-judicial procedure. This is the usual procedure for the Polish OCCP.[54] The CPAgs in Latvia and Bulgaria are empowered to directly intervene and require change in contract conditions or termination of unfair contracts (Latvia, s. 25(4)(6) CPA) or of misleading advertising (Bulgaria, s. 34 CPA) under penalty of a fine. In addition or as an alternative scheme, the consumer agencies in Estonia, Poland, Hungary, Lithuania and Bulgaria envisage a possibility for the agency to institute injunctive

---

50 Cf. Galligan and Smilov, supra, note 49. For Bulgaria, see s. 83 Act on Administrative Violations and Sanctions.

51 Czech Republic, s 24 CPA ((1)The authorities specified in Section 23 shall impose a fine of up to CZK 50,000,000 for a breach of the duties stipulated in Sections 3, 6, 7a, 7b, Section 8, paragraphs 1, 2, 3, and 4, Section 8a, paragraph 1, and Sections 9 to 19 of this Act; when imposing such a fine, the nature of the unlawful conduct and the scope of its consequences shall be taken into consideration.); Hungary, s. 48 CPA; Bulgaria, ss. 197 ff. CPA; Slovenia, s. 77 CPA; criminal penalties Estonia, ss. 43–48 CPA.

52 See Regular Report Hungary 1998, 44.

53 Cf. Bulgaria, s. 202(1) in conjunction with s. 33(2) 2006 CPA (misleading and unfair advertising); s. 209a(1) in conjunction with s. 68j CPA (unfair commercial practices); Slovenia, s. 77(1)(2) CPA; Romania, s. 23 Advertising Act; Estonia, Chapter 5 Advertising Act).

54 To enhance efficiency, following an amendment in 2004 the President of the Polish OCCP is granted the possibility to accept – in the course of the proceedings in the matter of practices infringing collective consumer interest an obligation by the entrepreneur to undertake or to discontinue specific actions aiming at preventing these infringements. The President of the OCCP may then, by way of a decision, impose an obligation to actually exercise the undertaken commitments and to determine the final date for their realisation.

proceedings for protection of collective consumer interests before courts of general jurisdiction.[55]

On the whole, it appears that the very existence of public consumer protection authorities has made it natural to furnish them with injunctive powers. Although the Injunctions Directive in its original thrust had been viewed as a tool for empowering consumer organisations, in the CEE countries it has occasionally produced the opposite effect of concentration of enforcement powers with administrative agencies and curtailing the rights of consumer organisations. Poland is a case in point. As a result of the implementation of the Injunctions Directive, a legislative change was carried out aiming at shifting of matters for defence of collective consumer interests from the courts of general jurisdiction to the OCCP.[56] Consequently the right of consumer organisations to file an injunction on the basis of infringement of the Unfair Competition Act directly before the civil courts has been repealed and substituted by a right to lodge a petition with the OCCP. The President of the OCCP is then empowered to issue an injunctive order following a quasi-judicial procedure. The decision of the President can be appealed before the specialised Court for Competition and Consumer Protection with its seat in Warsaw (a division of a Regional Court in Warsaw). Whereas this move was defended by pointing at the advantages of a consolidated approach, critics call it the most blatant example of 'publicisation' of private rights resulting from European integration.[57]

From an individual consumer perspective neither penalties nor administrative injunctions are very efficient in compensating for consumer wrongs. It may therefore be surmised that these types of remedies would not particularly influence the incentives for consumers to report harm on collective interests. At the same time, administrative sanctions seem to lie closer to the 'habits of the heart' of public agencies in CEE countries. They are perceived as attractive due to the relatively straightforward administrative procedure compared to litigation before ordinary courts. In addition, the predisposition for administrative sanctions may be unduly enhanced by internal mechanisms for reward of enforcement officers

55 See Estonia: s.17(2)(8) CPA as amended on 11 October 2007; Poland: s. 19 Unfair Competition Act (right of the President of the OCCP to file an injunctive action before the civil courts on grounds of certain acts of unfair competition); Hungary: s. 39 CPA (upon substantial harm of consumers), cf. Hungary National Report, Leuven study, supra note 47, 15–17; Lithuania: Chapter 7, ss. 30 and 32 CPA (as amended on 12 January 2007) stipulates the general right of the CPAg to seek an injunction against infringements on collective consumer interests (previously there were separate provisions on injunctions against infringements of rules on the safety of goods, unfair contract terms, distance selling and time share).

56 See s. 24 Polish Competition and Consumer Protection Act (CCPA).

57 Mańko, 'The Culture of Private Law in Central and Eastern Europe After Enlargement: A Polish Perspective' (2005) (11) *European Law Journal*, 527–548.

or of the agency, set in proportion to the number of collected fines.[58] Public authorities will be well advised to supplant such mechanisms by carefully motivated and widely discussed long-term enforcement policies.

E. Why Public Enforcement?

Two groups of factors can be identified that explain the preference for public enforcement in CEE countries: the first group can be broadly defined as internal (domestic) legacies and the second one as external influences. If we consider first the internally generated explanatory factors, it can be safely submitted that despite ideological commitment to dismantling the state, the power of path dependence in most CEE countries accounts for a continuous reliance on public intervention for responding to social harms. As mentioned above, the planned economy presented institutionally a web of mutually connected and hierarchically structured public bodies aiming at a comprehensive *ex ante* certification of production and *ex post* product control. Quality of consumer goods and consumer safety were pursued through pervasive and largely inefficient systems of administrative control and sanction.[59]

In the early 1990s the plenitude of such regulatory bodies seemed doomed to painful dismantling or to substantial reshaping and associated cut downs of staff and resources. This probably explains the relative ease with which the need for new consumer protection entities was accepted. It was only natural for the new CPAgs to succeed, in terms of staff, structure and premises, the previous state entities that controlled the socialist economy. For instance the Bulgarian CPAg replaced the previous Commission for Prices and Trade (Regular Report Bulgaria, 1999), the Romanian NACP – the former LAREX agency for product control.[60] The Polish OCCP took over the former Trade Inspection[61]and in Hungary the GICP was set up on the basis of the professional experience of the former General Commercial Authority for Market Surveillance.[62]

---

58 In Hungary, additional income for the agency comes from fines paid by distributors and manufacturers, but this income may only be used for publications and training. In Bulgaria, more questionably, a percentage of the fines incurred goes to the enforcement officers, which may create distortion of enforcement incentives, see s. 196 CPA. An opposite trend of decline in the number of fines imposed is visible from the Annual Reports of the Estonian CPB. Annual Report, Estonian Consumer Protection Board, 2002, 2.

59 Banasiński (1990), supra note 43.

60 Consumers International, *Handbook Consumer Policy and Consumer Organisations in Central and Eastern Europe* (2000) available at: www.consumersinternational.org.

61 Meuwley, 'Consumer Policy in Poland: Institutional and Legal Features' (1998) (1) *Review of Central and East European Law*, 9–41.

62 Cseres (2004), supra note 37, 55. Cf. for Estonia Regulation No. 25 of the Minister of Economic Affairs on "Reorganisation of the Trade Inspectorate of the Republic of Estonia into the State Consumer Protection Board of Estonia (Annex of SG 1994, 36, p. 1228).

In addition, given the slow and cumbersome process of reform of the judiciary and general distrust in this institution, reforming public agencies with specific mandates and targeted competences may have appeared a more feasible task.

The second factor tilting institutional choice toward public enforcement is the process of accession to the EU.[63] This proposition appears counterintuitive and needs further substantiation. Indeed, the main essence of membership in the European Union should theoretically consist of opening markets and ensuring free flow of economic resources. The thrust of adaptation to Community law and policy would thus *prima facie* be expected to be in a de-regulative direction. Yet, not unlike the dynamics of Europeanisation in the old Member States, also the logic of enlargement implied approximation of regulative standards that preceded the opening of markets and amounted to significant re-regulation. Moreover, in the process of screening compliance with the *acquis*, public agencies have had an attraction for both accession countries and Community institutions. On the part of the accession countries the existence of an agency has been a visible way of showing compliance and commitment. On the part of the Commission an agency corresponding to discrete European policy segments has been a preferred interlocutor and partner.[64]

Likewise, as convincingly argued by Thumlets, it appears that the switch from stricter requirements for implementation of the *acquis* in the mid-1990s to Accession partnerships and twinning projects reflected the advance of the Community Open Method of Coordination (OMC) in the sphere of enlargement.[65] Indeed, twinning exhibits many features characteristic of the OMC, including emphasis on benchmarking and learning. Similar to OMC, twinning is undertaken in areas of enlargement policy, where it is no longer a question of implementation of "hard" *acquis*, but rather of institutional conditions not firmly anchored in the Treaty. Rather than simulating a common Community institutional model, twinning invites the candidate countries to an institutional 'smorgasbord'.[66] Since twinning projects were per definition designed as training programmes between national public administrations, they have most likely also enhanced the already existing affinity to public forms of governance in the area of consumer law.

---

63 See in this sense Maniokas, 'The Method of the European Union's Enlargement to the East: A Critical Approach' in: Dimitrova, *Driven to Change. The European Union's Enlargement Viewed From the East* (Manchester and New York: Manchester University Press, 2004); Bakardjieva Engelbrekt (2007), supra note 39.

64 I have elsewhere called this the 'joint interest of the rational accession seeker and the rational accession provider', see Bakardjieva Engelbrekt (2007), supra note 39.

65 Tulmets, 'The Management of New Forms of Governance by Former Accession Countries of the European Union: Institutional Twinning in Estonia and Hungary', (2005)(11)(5) *European Law Journal*, 657–674.

66 Tulmets (2005), supra note 65.

F. *What Advantages Are There With Public Enforcement? The Costs and Benefits of Participation*

In the preparatory work leading to the adoption of the Consumer Co-operation Regulation 2006/2004 the Commission summarised with surprising assuredness the advantages of public regulators in the sphere of consumer protection:

(i) sufficient investigation powers;
(ii) sufficient guarantee of confidentiality and professional secrecy;
(iii) proven efficiency and effectiveness of a public dimension to enforcement in the Member States where such exist;
(iv) impartiality and accountability.[67]

From the perspective of the CEE countries this buoyant assessment would need some tempering and the list of advantages – important qualifications.[68] Some of the defined advantages, in particular efficiency and effectiveness, but also impartiality and accountability, appear less self-evident in countries characterised by underpaid, understaffed and often incompetent public administration, moreover suffering severe problems of corruption and credibility.[69] Public enforcement may certainly offer a competitive edge in respect of information, scientific expertise and investigative powers, but only if furnished with the necessary budgetary and human resources, which are notoriously lacking in CEE countries. The consumer agencies in CEE countries have indeed been given powers to demand information from affected enterprises and can thus arguably compensate some of the information asymmetries at the heart of the under-enforcement of consumer laws. Yet the agencies are often not experienced and trained in adequately using these powers.

At the same time, an agency reveals certain advantages not mentioned in the Commission document quoted above, which are of special importance for effective consumer enforcement in CEE countries. The first is the visibility and accessibility of an agency. Arguably, by virtue of its very existence, a consumer agency raises the awareness for consumer-related problems and sensitises active consumers to such problems.[70] Given the low costs of submitting a complaint or

---

67 Commission Proposal for Consumer Protection Co-operation Regulation COM (2003) 443 final.

68 For an insight into the implementation difficulties associated with public enforcement in the area of product safety law, see Micklitz and Roethe, *Europäisches Sichercheitsrecht, European Product Safety Legislation* (Bremen: Edition Temmen, 2007).

69 Sadurski (2006), supra note 12.

70 For the Finnish experience, see Wilhelmsson, 'Administrative Procedures for the Control of Marketing Practices – Theoretical Rationale and Perspectives' in: Wilhelmsson, *Twelve Essays on Consumer Protection* (1996), 142, at 156.

announcing a perceived consumer wrong through a telephone call or by sending an e-mail, the agency can easily gather information about consumer concerns. Additionally, in a number of CEE countries, agencies can rely on already established patterns of channelling consumer discontent inherited from the time of the socialist (and soviet) economy.[71] Preserving established patterns, while adapting to the reality of free markets, may be efficient given the high costs of switching to a new system. Crucial here is, however, the building up of good administrative routines for collecting, processing and sifting out complaints. Only then can agency enforcement constitute a substantial information and efficiency advantage.

Most importantly, a decision to set up a public agency is, generally considered a long-lasting and stable commitment to a certain policy. It cuts through some of the severe problems of uncertainty and under-financing that plague the work of voluntary consumer organisations. Despite the political and financial insecurities that notoriously accompany the work of public administrations in CEE countries, an agency may still be in a position to provide a more stable platform for consumer protection enforcement.

On the negative side, the agency model typically does not give consumers possibilities of controlling agency action on the basis of consumer complaints. Essentially, the agencies possess the prerogative to pursue or drop a complaint depending on their own assessment of the public interest involved. What stands out as crucial for the efficiency of public enforcement is, consequently, the question of selection of instances for public intervention. Public agencies normally work within limited budgets and the constraints on the public purse are particularly severe in CEE countries. Priorities in enforcement should therefore be based on a careful weighing of costs of intervention (investigatory costs, information costs and procedural costs) and the benefits of intervention (prevention of harm and compensation for the harm caused). The seriousness of the interests affected, the scope and number of affected consumers, but also the potential of the market to cope endogenously with the problem, among other things, should be used as variables to evaluate the expected deterrent effects and possible skimming off effects of administrative remedies. However, under conditions of budgetary constraints and political uncertainty in CEE countries, agency discretion might be exercised to prioritise clear-cut, simple cases and shy away from complex investigations or clashes with powerful market players.

One of the major risks of economic regulation through public agencies has been identified in the economic literature as that of 'capture'. Officials of an agency regulating a sector of industry may develop professional ties and a degree of empathy with the regulated industry instead of with the large consumer community. Another form of capture is that of corruptive practices between

71 See for the Baltic countries Viitanen (2000), supra note 45.

industry and the agency. But even a benevolent agency is dependent on information for its decision-making. If repeatedly exposed to biased information originating within the regulated industry, an agency may be swayed to alter the parameters of regulation in its favour.

The risk for 'capture' in the case of broad-based consumer agencies is assumed to be less severe compared to agencies performing control over discrete industry sectors, such as banking or financing.[72] Yet in the reality of widespread corruption and underpaid public administration, this should not be taken for granted. In addition, areas such as unfair contract terms and unfair commercial practices often presuppose developing industry-specific standards and practices, often in consultation with the affected industry. In such negotiations industry may take the upper hand not necessarily because civil servants are corrupt, but because information about products and markets is complex and costly and information asymmetries work for the regulated industry.

Another risk is linked to the alleged propensity of bureaucratic bodies to seek to maximise their budgets. A model predicting such budget-maximising behaviour is advanced by Niskanen based, more generally, on the familiar principal-agent problem.[73] According to Niskanen, agencies have a monopoly over the information about the true costs of supply [of regulation], and bureaucrats may therefore use that power to secure budget and outcome levels that are higher than society's optimal.[74] Indeed, one concern should be a tendency to select clear-cut 'safe' cases of infringement in order to demonstrate high rates of enforcement at a relatively low cost.[75] In this category of 'safe' cases belong violations by perpetrators known for their willingness to comply or simply offences that do not involve high costs of investigation and evidence gathering. Komesar notes that such tendencies can in principle be effectively curbed by parliamentary control of agency action (and inaction), given that the regulated industry has its own avenues to reach political decision makers. However, parliamentary supervision in CEE countries is slow and cumbersome. Moreover, as indicated above, consumer agencies are not directly accountable to parliaments. This once again comes to stress the importance of effective accountability mechanisms to ensure that agencies act within their mandate.

---

72 Wilhelmsson (1996), supra note 69, 128.

73 Komesar (1994), supra note 5, 92, quoting Niskanen, *Bureaucracy and Representative Government* (1971).

74 Komesar (1994), supra note 5, 92.

75 On incentives for such over-enforcement see supra note 58.

4.2. JUDICIAL COLLECTIVE ENFORCEMENT

The above described tendency of expansion of public enforcement in the sphere of consumer protection in CEE countries is, however, not universal and unchallenged. Alongside agency action, the process of institutionalising consumer law and policy has opened novel avenues for private enforcement and a reverse (even if hesitant) dynamics of a growing involvement of private actors should also be acknowledged. Recent studies and interviews with consumer organisations in the new CEE Member States seem to indicate a process of gradual emergence of new entrepreneurs who enter the consumer policy sphere and demonstrate specific interest in consumer law enforcement.[76] Beyond the temporary and transitory nature of the accession process and associated benefits, these entrepreneurs find new fields of action and more stable endogenous incentives for involvement with the interest of consumers.

A. *Injunctions v. Damages*

As noted above, injunctive relief was in a number of CEE countries shaped as an administrative remedy, with competence of public consumer protection authorities to impose cease-and-desist orders following administrative investigation and establishment of infringement. However, in parallel to these purely administrative injunctions, in many (if not in all) CEE countries, the right to seek injunctions has been granted to private parties as well, notably consumer organisations or even individual consumers. The nature of these injunctive actions is not always easy to discern. They are mostly of a civil law character, where the action is to be filed before the courts of general jurisdiction.[77] But there are also hybrid forms, where private parties are granted a right of petition to public authorities and certain participatory rights in what are quasi-judicial procedures before consumer agencies and other public bodies.[78]

Reportedly, injunctive actions in some CEE countries seem to have been embraced by institutional actors such as consumer organisations, and to be

76 Interviews of the author with representatives of Bulgarian consumer organisations conducted in March and June 2008; cf. Leuven study, supra note 47, National reports on Poland and Hungary.

77 See the right of injunction action of consumer organisations in Bulgaria, s. 186(1) Bulgarian CPA, the right of action of consumer associations, consumer ombudsmen and individual consumers for declaration of the abusiveness of consumer contract terms on the basis of s. 479^{36} – 479^{45} in Poland; right of injunctive action of representative consumer associations in Estonia, s.15(4)(1) Estonian CPA.

78 See the procedure before the President of the OCCP in Poland, ss. 25 ff. CCPA. For a comprehensive analysis see Micklitz et al., *Verbraucherschutz durch Unterlassungsklagen, Rechtliche und Praktische Umsetzung der Richtlinie Unterlassungsklagen 98/27/EG in den Mitgliedstaaten*, VIEW Schriftenreihe, Band 17, 2007.

relatively widely used in practice.[79] Part of the attractiveness of these schemes is associated with advantageous rules on litigation costs. For instance, in Hungary consumer organisations are fully freed from court fees.[80] In Poland, the action for injunction for declaration of the abusiveness of contract terms in consumer contracts is likewise free of charge for consumer organisations. The picture is not uniform though, due to differences in the experience and credibility of national consumer organisations and in their procedural treatment. In many countries no litigation privileges are envisaged for consumer organisations. The organisations bear, anyway, the risk of paying the costs of the defendant, if they lose the dispute. Incentives are further undercut by the relatively limited effect of injunctions and absent compensatory effect.[81]

Against this background, collective judicial enforcement by bundling individual consumer claims in group or class action proceedings should hold particular attraction. Moreover, post-communist societies are characterised by highly concentrated economies, where privatisation and de-monopolisation have typically been slow and cumbersome.[82] Many markets in the CEEC have been tenaciously dominated by big economic actors, either controlled by the state or in the form of private entities as a result of recent privatisations. The many imperfections that plague such markets often translate into damages that are pulverised and spread among large numbers of consumers.[83] Whereas the individual losses may be miniscule, the aggregate size of the damages can be copious, given the pervasive character of such markets and the number of consumers concerned. Introducing possibilities for aggregating consumer claims in class and group actions appears at least *prima facie* to offer a tool for overcoming the inherent problems of collective action and providing an effective remedy, by combining compensatory and deterrent effects.

At the same time there are a number of institutional impediments to the effective introduction of collective judicial enforcement in the CEE countries. As demonstrated in the chapter by Issacharoff and Samuel in this book, what makes class actions possible in the US context is a complex institutional setting combining a number of institutional factors. The authors convincingly argue, that instrumental for the success of a class action system are a judiciary and a private

79 See National Reports Poland, Leuven Study, supra note 47. See ss. 479^{36} – 479^{45} k.p.c. (Civil Procedure Code), in particular the Polish account on the action for injunction for declaring the abusiveness of unfair terms in consumer contracts. Cf. National Report Hungary, Leuven Study, supra note 47.

80 National Report Hungary, Leuven Study, supra note 47.

81 For a sceptical view on the role of consumer organisations see Micklitz et al. (2007), supra note 77.

82 Montias, Review of Slay, The Polish Economy. Crisis, Reform and Transformation, Princeton, Princeton University Press, 1994, (1995) *Journal of Economic Literature*, Vol. 33, No. 3, 1390–1392.

83 Cseres (2004), supra note 37.

bar with a sufficient degree of expertise to match the information and expertise supremacy of powerful defendants and importantly, a judiciary with a sufficient degree of independence to resist the pressure that can be expected on the part of both political and economic actors in aggregated law suits. [84] Such institutional prerequisites are notoriously absent in transition societies.[85] Importantly, these institutions can hardly be created by legislative fiat. They take time to emerge, mature and to eventually be successfully harnessed to serve the consumer interest.

This is nicely illustrated by the developments in Bulgaria, one of the last countries to join the European Union. Quite remarkably, the country introduced a legislative possibility for aggregating individual consumer claims already with the 1999 Act on Consumer Protection and the Rules of Trade (1999 BulgCPA). Chapter eight of this Act entitled "Means for collective protection of consumers" set out a variety of mechanisms for collective consumer redress. Individual consumers, groups of consumers, consumer organisations and the Consumer Protection Agency were all granted the right to claim injunction of consumer law infringements under the BulgCPA or under other legal Acts that directly or indirectly protect the interests of consumers (s. 52 1999 BulgCPA).

Importantly, the same circle of actors was granted the right of action for a declaratory judgment ascertaining consumer law infringement. The law explicitly allowed the action for declaratory judgment to be lodged in a class action manner, when a number of consumers had been affected by the same violation. The action was boldly designed in an 'opt out' manner, but this stirred up little parliamentary debate.[86]

Finally, the 1999 Bulg CPA granted standing to consumer associations to claim damages inflicted on the collective interest of consumers caused by violations of the CPA or other consumer protection statutes. The plaintiff association was to notify all other consumer associations on the proceedings, the latter having a possibility to join the action. The compensation was to be awarded to all plaintiffs and to be spent exclusively for the protection of consumer interests (s. 54 1999 BulgCPA).

---

84 See Issacharoff and Samuel, 'The Institutional Dimension of Consumer Protection', in this book.

85 Needless to say, the level of competence of both lawyers and judges varies substantially throughout the CEE countries, in particular in respect to their knowledge of European law and involvement in Western theoretical debates.

86 In such proceedings the plaintiff, in a manner prescribed by the court, was to publicly announce the lodging of the action. Consumers who claimed to have been affected by the same violation were then given a possibility to join the proceedings or, alternatively, to state that they wished to pursue their defence in a separate lawsuit. The declaratory judgment of the court was binding on the defendant and on the person bringing the action, but also on the consumers who claimed to have been affected by the same violation, but who had not stated that they wish to pursue their defence individually (s. 53(4) 1999 BulgCPA).

Despite this exceptionally broad array of unconventional and daring procedural avenues for collective judicial enforcement of consumer rights, these procedures remained hardly noticed in practice. The few attempted lawsuits have been met with aversion by the courts and have not led to a breakthrough in collective consumer enforcement. With the new CPA of 2006 (2006 BulgCPA) the rights of individual consumers to lodge injunctive action and class action were curtailed, while preserving the rights of consumer associations to lodge injunctive action, representative action for damages on behalf of groups of consumers and action for damages based on the collective consumer interest (cf. ss. 186–188, Part III Means for collective protection; actions for injunctions and for compensation of consumers, 2006 BulgCPA).

Still another readjustment in the procedural framework followed with the enactment of the new Code of Civil Procedure (CCP), which introduced an independent Chapter 33, "Collective actions". This chapter is not confined to consumer-related collective actions, but can be invoked in any situation where harm to more than one person is caused stemming from the same source. The CPA has been amended accordingly and now refers to the Code of Civil Procedure for the procedural details of all types of collective actions granted by the CPA. As stressed in a letter by the Minister of the Economy to the National Assembly, the Code of Civil Procedure has introduced certain confusion as to terminology, in particular regarding the exact meaning of the term "collective action".[87] Whereas in the CPA the term is used to signify actions for injunction in defence of collective interests to be understood as something more than the sum total of individual consumer interests, in the Code of Civil Procedure the term is used both for actions of injunction as well as for typical group actions, bundling individual claims for damages.[88]

This conceptual conflation notwithstanding, it appears that for the first time group action has received detailed legislative treatment. The action can be lodged by individuals belonging to the group, organisations representing the individuals affected or individuals and organisations representing an infringed collective interest. Chapter 33 sets out a procedure for publicly announcing the filing of the action and for forming the class. The court is given broad discretion to decide on the instituting of group proceedings, and to control the formation of the class and the distribution of the awarded damages (ss. 382–383, 387 CCP). The opt-out principle applies, meaning that the decision extends to all who claim to have been

87 See Letter from the Minister of the Economy to the National Assembly, on file with the author. The letter was in turn triggered on the initiative of the Consumer Federation, see letter Nr. 432/03 by the Council of Ministers to the Federation of 15 July 2007, on file with the author.

88 On the need for clearer definition of the concept 'collective interest', see Safjan, Gorywoda and Jańczuk, 'Taking the Collective Interest of Consumers Seriously: A View from Poland', in this volume.

harmed by the same cause and who have not stated that they will pursue their defence individually (s. 386 CCP). A major difference with the previous rules is that the courts are empowered to *ex officio* check the capacity of the plaintiff to credibly and seriously represent the collective or group interest, including the ability to take on the litigation costs, etc. (s. 381 CCP). Since Chapter 33 CCP applies to all categories of collective actions, including those in the CPA, this proviso in the CCP may raise the threshold for consumer protection organisations' ability to engage in collective litigation. It has therefore been argued that the CPA shall be considered as *lex specialis* to the CCP.[89]

Time will show to what extent the new arrangements will be more viable than their predecessors and whether they will find their institutional users. The brief overview over the Bulgarian experimentations with class action, however, confirms that this institute indeed does not easily yield to legal transplantation. It requires careful legislative treatment and a high level of competence from all branches of the legal profession: legislative consultants, judiciary and the bar, an asset notoriously deficient in post-communist CEE countries. One of the few cases of attempting the bundling of consumer claims concerns damages caused by a major public utility company (central heating) from incorrect calculation of costs for central heating in condominiums and is still pending.[90] Another lawsuit for damages caused by unfair commercial practices is based on the 1999 BulgCPA. The first attempt to dismiss the case on grounds of changes in the statutory provisions has been rejected by the Appellate Court.[91] The case will in other words continue as a class action lawsuit, but it has taken two years to reach this stage.

Summing up, given the high threshold and uncertain returns from using instruments for collective consumer redress, in particular of the class action type, it is hardly surprising that the example of Bulgaria has remained isolated. It should be added that external factors, and notably Community accession policy, have in this respect neither provided any compelling procedural and institutional model, nor required specific commitment. Quite the contrary: the attitude in the old EU Member States has been markedly tepid viz. aggregate damages claims. The model that has instead received broader acceptance is enforcement through consumer associations, which pass the filter of state recognition. Unleashing uncontrolled private litigious fervour and empowering courts and lawyers are apparently viewed with certain scepticism on the Continent.

89 See letter from the Council of Ministers to the Consumer Federation, supra note 87.

90 Interview with Nezret Babuchev, Attorney, Legal consultant of the Consumer Federation, 26 March 2008.

91 See decision of Sofia City Court of 5 January 2006 in case Nr. 2444/2005, on file with the author.

B. *Institutional Actors: Consumer Organisations and Lawyers*

The scepticism to bundling individual claims in group and class action lawsuits can certainly be better understood when looking at the main actors involved in private consumer law enforcement in CEE countries. As is well-known, consumer organisations are an important institutional player in the European neo-corporatist model of consumer policy and enforcement.[92] Immediately after the system change at the end of the 1980s, the CEE countries presented an institutional conundrum given the absence or in any case the very weak presence of consumer organisations. Few of the CEE states featured any viable consumer organisations at the beginning of economic and political reforms. Certainly in the late 1980s and early 1990s consumer organisations were founded in Hungary and Bulgaria within the structures of the "Fatherland Front" – a broad-based organisation with diffuse objectives and membership closely linked with the Communist party, but these had largely nominal existence. Only in Poland the Consumer Federation set up within the government-critical Solidarity movement could rely on broad popular support.[93]

Given the mixed political legacies of these organisations, their credibility and legitimacy in the period of political and economic transformation were fragile. The existing associations were abruptly shaken by withdrawal of political and financial support. Moreover, they experienced a considerable problem of re-defining their identity, role and objectives. While the survival of the existing consumer associations was threatened, new consumer organisations were slow to emerge, partly due to a general distrust in the virtue and effect of public action inherited by the time of totalitarianism.[94]

In this unfavourable environment, the influence of Community accession policy has been aptly described as one of institutional homesteading.[95] Consumer protection did not have its strong interest groups and players in CEE countries. Therefore, with a positive interpretation, the structural and financial assistance on the part of the Community worked in a way similar to allotting land to new settlers. Consumer organizations qualified for assistance by showing willingness to take on the responsibility of representing the consumer interest. Indeed consumer organisations occupied a privileged position in the first PHARE

---

92 See Bourgoignie, 'Consumer Law and the European Community: Issues and Prospects' in: Bourgoignie, Trubek and Trubek, *Consumer Law and Federalism* (Berlin: de Gruyter, 1987).

93 See Roethe, in: Micklitz (1996), supra note 1.

94 See Roethe (1996), supra note 92. For a convincing analysis of the reasons for the unwillingness of citizens in CEE countries (and in particular Poland and Hungary) to engage in political action and to participate in voluntary or charitable activities, see Rose-Ackerman (2005), supra note 15, 24 ff.

95 Jacoby, 2005, supra note 21.

assistance programmes.[96] As a result of (in relative terms still modest) financial and technical support on the part of the Community institutions, of individual Member State governments and of national consumer organisations (notably the German AGV), the incumbent consumer associations were revived and could experience certain boost in their activity. In several other Candidate States, national associations of consumers were created, occasionally virtually from scratch, so that in 2000 Consumers International could report that only one of the Candidate (now new Member) States of the EU from CEE countries lacked a national consumer association.[97] External funding and support also brought to life a number of other smaller and more fragile consumer formations and initiatives: consumer information centres and networks, advice bureaus, etc. Structural and financial assistance on the part of the Community thus became the life-line for the consumer movement in most CEECs.

Of course apart from true "new settlers" Community funding may have also opened space for other types of actors, which we can call "fund appropriators". These are short-term players, lacking genuine commitment and quickly moving to new grounds once the source of financing has dried up. But even devoted consumer activists can eventually be forced to switch to different fields of activity in the absence of adequate resources. There is therefore considerable turbulence and concern about continuity in the post-accession period, when Community programmes are gradually being wound down. Certainly the CEE governments were strongly encouraged to ensure themselves stable funding and assistance to consumer organisations and to grant them access to decision-making procedures, consultation and litigation. Yet given the dire straits of public finances and political instability, this has not been an easy task. Whereas in the initial phase of transition the few existing consumer organisations used to receive ear-marked governmental funding, these guaranteed grants were later suspended and substituted by systems of public tenders or other distribution procedures, supervised by the CPAgs.

The heavy dependence of consumer organisations on governmental funding generates a whole array of new problems and is a source of tension between the responsible public institutions and non-governmental associations as well as of internal conflicts within the consumer movement.[98] Governments suddenly

96 See notably the CICPP series, Louvain-la-Neuve: Centre du Droit de la consommation, Université Catholique de Louvain.

97 Consumers International (2000), supra note 60. The creation of umbrella, nation-wide consumer organisations has been explicitly promoted by the Commission with a view of strengthening the organisations but also in order to facilitate the communication of these organisations with the Community institutions.

98 See on the conflicts between the Polish government and Polish consumer associations and between the various consumer organisations, Consumers International (2000), supra note 60, 72–73. Tensions are likewise reported from Bulgaria and Romania both "within the independent sector and between the Office for Protection of Consumers and some of the voluntary

acquire new tasks of controlling the reliability and accountability of private consumer organisations. Statutory instruments in a number of CEECs set requirements for representativeness, political neutrality and proof of genuine consumer protection activities as conditions for receiving funding or for grant of participatory or procedural rights. The control is often entrusted with responsible ministries and agencies.

While such accountability mechanisms may seem desirable in order to sift out less serious players, they may create the risk of what can be dubbed an 'accountability interdependence trap'. Probably more than in established social market economies in the CEE countries, consumer organisations are expected not only to monitor the market but also to act as accountability agents viz. the state – as economic actor and regulator – and its consumer protection bodies, seeing to it that these bodies stick to their legislative mandate. The relationship between governments and consumer organisations is thus not uncomplicated. The double accountability role of consumer organisations as accountability agents and accountability subjects may create conditions for 'collusive behaviour' and dual accountability failure. By placing consumer organisations under the tutelage of public authorities, the role of consumer organisations as critics and an alternative to government might be reduced. Consumer organisations may be facing a difficult choice between on the one hand, cooperating with governments and occasionally turning a blind eye to regulatory failure, and on the other hand, taking an active position and occasionally jeopardising their own existence. For governments with a still fragile democratic record, the temptation to use thresholds for ousting inconvenient and vocal consumer organisations is near at hand.

Such tensions occasionally surface in the legislative process, for instance in attempts to raise the threshold for consumer organisations' participation in consultation and policy making. Thus the 1999 Bulgarian CPA required a minimum membership of three hundred consumers in order for a consumer association to enjoy certain participatory rights and receive government support. In the Government Bill for the new 2006 CPA a higher threshold of two thousand members was proposed. Apparently this requirement was subsequently dropped. There remain, however, a number of other conditions (for instance maintaining consumer reception offices in one-third of the county cities of Bulgaria, s. 170, Bulgarian CPA), which may act as a serious barrier for young and still fragile associations.[99] In Romania a consumer organisation can qualify for participation

organisations", Consumers International, supra note 60, at 26 and 82. See more recently, decree Nr. RD-16-659 of 19 July 2008 of the Bulgarian Minister for the Economy and Energy, depriving the two most active national consumer associations from government subsidies, partly on grounds of political bias.

99 For comparison in Estonia, a minimum number of fifty members are required for an association to qualify as an association representing the collective interests of consumers, see s. 15 Estonian CPA. This gives the association the right to seek enforcement of collective consumer rights

in consultative committees on consumer policy at the national level if it can demonstrate minimum membership of three thousand members and branches in ten districts, and at the district and local level, three years of consumer protection activity.[100] Setting too strict conditions for the exercise of participatory rights and for government funding may suffocate valuable new initiatives. Small or politically inconvenient organisations may easily be ousted in favour of established and compliant actors.

The above described precarious position of consumer organisations in CEE countries and the tensions in their relations viz. regulators have immediate relevance for the role of consumer organisations as litigants. Litigation normally involves considerable costs and risks and requires competence and repeated experience. Even though consumer organisations are sometimes exempt from court fees,[101] they still face the risk of bearing the costs of the defendant if they lose the dispute. Moreover, competent legal advice is indispensable for successful litigation, in particular in complex bundling and collective interest cases. Such advice is costly and – in particular in CEE countries – difficult to find. The supply of knowledgeable lawyers is scarce and normally such lawyers are quickly drained away to more lucrative areas such as company and banking law.

Lawyers are crucial not only for their supportive function viz. consumer associations, but also in their independent position of litigation entrepreneurs provided that legislative possibilities for class and group action exist. The involvement of lawyers in consumer litigation is inevitably influenced by the status and regulation of the legal profession, which differ substantially between the individual CEE countries. The transition to the rule of law and market economy has generally implied a dramatic increase in the demand for legal services. However, this increase has provoked quite divergent responses across CEE countries. Whereas in countries like Bulgaria and the Baltic states, the Bar has been burst open by lowering thresholds for entry and ensuing tripling of the number of lawyers, in a country like Poland there has been a conservation of the status quo with extremely restrictive entry into the Bar and only slowly increasing numbers of authorised lawyers.[102] This differential regulative treatment certainly impacts on the competitive pressures within the legal profession and respectively,

through injunctive action. In other countries, the rights of consumers to form associations are laid down in the law, but no quantitative requirements for representation seem to exist: Hungary (s. 45 CPA), Latvia (see s. 22–23 CPA), Lithuania (s. 31 CPA), Poland (s. 39–41 CCPA), Slovenia (s. 63 CPA).

100 See s. 33 Ordinance 21/1992 as amended by Ordinance 58/2000.

101 See on Hungary and Poland supra note 79.

102 See Blankenburg, 'Legal Culture in Five Central European Countries' (Working Document W 111, Scientific Council for Governmental Policy, The Hague, 2000). Cf. on Poland Jagielski, 'Administrative Law', in: Frankowski (ed.) *Introduction to Polish Law* (The Hague: Kluwer Law International, 2005): "Unfortunately, many professions remain to this day tightly controlled by administrative law measures (e.g. licensing of medical doctors, lawyers and public notaries).

on the willingness of lawyers to engage in novel and uncertain legal matters such as collective litigation.

Differences exist also in the rules on litigation costs and legal fees. Bulgaria appears to be among the few CEE countries where a legal fees system close to contingency fee is allowed in the Act on the Legal Profession, still with relatively wide possibilities for the courts to adjust the size of compensation for litigation costs on equitable grounds. In contrast, in other countries, for instance Poland, there is a statutory floor and ceiling of legal fees with possibilities to define the fee as a percentage of the value of the claim within these limits.[103]

Still, it appears that lawyers are slowly beginning to specialise in consumer issues in the hope of attracting clients and reaping future litigation rewards, in particular where promises of aggregate litigation provide adequate incentives. Some lawyers have started discovering and setting in motion the so far dormant novel procedural mechanisms granted by some consumer protection acts as symbols of consumer empowerment. Alliances between lawyers and consumer organisations occasionally emerge, where incentives combine in a mutually beneficial manner.

C. *The Problem of Confused Incentives: Converting Private Vice into Public Virtue?*

Generous possibilities for aggregating individual claims in group proceedings are, however, not to be unequivocally positively assessed. They can imply risks of distorted incentives due to principal-agent problems.[104] All systems of collective interest representation inevitably rely upon intermediaries - a consumer association (union) and/or a lawyer - to mobilise and represent the collective interest. The incentives for these intermediaries may differ (and often do differ) from the interest to be represented. Both union staff and professional lawyers usually pursue their self-interest of continued activity, political or professional exposure, income or fees.[105] The system thus accepts this divergence of interests but expects, much like in the market, public virtue to flow from private vice.[106]

Problems arise, however, from the poor possibility for control over the procedural behaviour of the association on the part of the represented members.

It is doubtful whether such a heavy state interference conforms with the constitutional principle of free choice of profession." at 164.

103 Pietkiewicz and Hejmej, 'The Polish Judicial System and Legal Procedure', in: Brodecki (ed.) *Polish Business Law* (Kluwer Law International: The Hague/London/New York, 2003), 43.

104 See Olson (1965), supra note 6, 34.

105 In the case of the Bulgarian Consumer Federation mentioned above it may be interesting to mention that the President of the Federation recently stood in municipal elections, building substantially on the popularity garnered in the course of the class action lawsuit mentioned above.

106 Komesar (1994), supra note 5, 119.

The reasons are similar to those that explain the difficulties of collective action in general, namely rational disinterest in collective action and organisation. In addition, legal action is per definition a complex matter. It requires time and expertise for its proper assessment, which few are ready to invest. The principal-agent problem in a collective action through organisations may become even more severe if the chain of actors involved is longer. Schäfer provides a model capturing different constellations of dependency and control between affected group, association, lawyers and other interested groups such as political and social groups, parties and the state.[107]

Economists warn that if possibilities for collective litigation are cheap and easily accessible the right of action of the association might be used for purposes other than those originally intended by the legislator.[108] Harassing competitors through frivolous lawsuits may be one example of incentives distortion; winning political battles or voters may be another. Such principal-agent problems may be particularly severe in countries of generally low standards of living and fragile integrity of social spheres (in particular judicial and political processes).

Concerning possible opportunistic behaviour of lawyers, it should be noted that in well established Western democracies, the legal profession normally operates amidst an invisible web of soft ethical norms. The enforcement of these norms is taken care of through numerous self-regulatory and co-regulatory arrangements, but most of all reinforced by education, club-membership and peer pressure. Such norms and mechanisms are only slowly emerging and are still frail in CEE countries.

D. *The Judiciary as a Decision-Making Process*

Beyond the organisation and representation of consumer interests and related litigation incentives, the chances for effective judicial representation of consumers are heavily dependent on the characteristics of the judiciary as a decision-making process. Courts are typically a small and decentralised institution, where decisions are taken slowly and painstakingly. The costs of decision-making are high, both in terms of costs for individual litigants and in terms of societal costs, given the high remuneration of judges and expensive infrastructure.[109] At the same time courts are expected to offer a number of advantages as a decision-making institution. They are as a rule insulated from political and popular pressure, have

---

107 Schäfer, 'Die ökonomischen Grundlagen der Bündelung gleichgerichteter Interessen im Prozess' in: Basedow/Hopt/Kötz/Baetge (eds), *Die Bündelung gleichgerichteter Interessen im Prozess* (Tübingen: Mohr Siebeck, 1999), 67 ff., at 86.

108 Bebchuk, 'Suing Only to Extract Settlement Offers' (1988) 17 *Journal of Legal Studies*, 437 ff.; Rosenberg and Shavell, 'A Model in Which Suits are Brought in for their Nuisance Value' (1985) 5 *International Review of Law and Economics*, 3 ff.

109 Komesar (1994), supra note 5.

high competence and are able to devote the necessary time and effort to individual disputes.

The virtues of judicial proceedings are taken for granted in Western-type democracies. However, in many of the new Member States of the EU, judicial independence and competence are still scarce resources. To take just one example, according to European-wide surveys, only 12% of Bulgarians have confidence in the judiciary, which thus scores the lowest public trust when compared to other public institutions.[110] The strengthening of the independence and capacity of the judiciary, especially in some of the laggards in the accession process like Bulgaria and Romania has been among the burning concerns of European institutions. In addition, some of the general disadvantages of the judiciary may be exacerbated in the specific context of CEE countries. For instance decentralisation and the ensuing slow and incremental way of reaching uniform treatment of certain social problems is in CEE countries aggravated due to the lack of transparency and access to judicial decisions, in particular from lower level courts. Moreover, judicial independence is often conflated with formalistic law-interpretation and disregard for precedent-setting by higher instance courts.[111]

The recourse to specialised courts, like the Competition and Consumer Protection Court in Poland, is from this perspective an interesting innovation. The Court acts as the sole court hearing cases on grounds of infringements of collective consumer interests (either brought by the President of the OCCP or by individual consumers, consumer associations, local consumer advocates or traders).[112] Mechanisms of enhancing the transparency and the access to court decisions, e.g. through public databases and internet sites are another less radical but much needed improvement.[113] Finally, the functioning of independent administrative authorities as quasi-judicial bodies can be seen as a way of cutting across the institutional dilemmas of judicial reform in transitional societies.[114]

---

110 See 'To Sue a Trader' (2008)(4) *Potrebitel*, 10–11.

111 See Emmert, 'The Independence of Judges: A Concept often Misunderstood in Central and Eastern Europe' (2001) (3)(4) *European Journal of Law Reform*, 405–409; cf. on legal culture in CEE countries on the example of Poland Mańko, supra note 57.

112 See s. 24 CCPA.

113 For proposals in this respect see the position of the Bulgarian Social and Economic Council (2008) (4) *Potrebitel*, 11.

114 See in this respect the impressive experience of the Hungarian Office for Economic Competition and the Bulgarian Commission for Protection of Competition. For a theoretical model partly seeking to explain such preferences see La Porta et al. (2003), supra note 9.

4.3. NOVEL FORMS OF CONSUMER PARTICIPATION AND REPRESENTATION

Beyond the arsenal of conventional remedies and avenues for collective consumer enforcement, and probably as a reaction to perceived failures in these remedies and procedures, the institutional actors that have entered the consumer protection arena in CEE countries occasionally explore new and creative ways of employing remedies and procedures originally intended for different purposes. The examples below are taken mainly from the Bulgarian context which is more familiar to me. But similar stories can certainly be told for the other CEE countries as well.

A. *Abstract Control of Legality*

One example of procedural creativeness is the recourse to the very generous right that was granted to individuals and organisations in Bulgaria to exercise abstract control on legality of administrative acts of general application.[115] A broad right to abstract control was introduced already by the Constitution of 1991.[116] The constitutional provisions were interpreted as directly effective by the courts and provided the ground for a number of successful actions by individuals and economic entities.[117] The subsequently adopted Supreme Administrative Court Act continued to build on this constitutional momentum toward broad access to legality control and confirmed an extensive interpretation of the constitutional *actio popularis*. The Supreme Administrative Court in its case law not only supported such development, but also opened it for *actio popularis* by organisations on behalf of their members.

Of course one may wonder in what way legality control can benefit consumers. Yet, given the still lingering non-negligible involvement of the state in consumer markets, in particular in the sphere of public utilities, the consumer interest in such litigation becomes more apparent. Public utilities are still extensively regulated by administrative rule-making, for instance in respect to price-setting. The right to seek legality control has thus been successfully invoked by the Bulgarian Federation of Consumers to challenge the regulations of the

115 On the generous right of access to Constitutional Courts for the abstract review of legality in other CEE countries, see Arnold, 'The Constitutional Courts in Central and Eastern Europe as a Dynamic Source of New Legal Ideas' 18 (2003) *Tulane European and Civil Law Forum*.

116 Article 120 of the Constitution reads:
(1) The courts shall supervise the legality of the acts and actions of the administrative bodies.
(2) Citizens and legal entities shall be free to challenge any administrative act which affects them, except those listed expressly by the laws.

117 See Decision of the Supreme Administrative Court no. 6797 of 3 July 2003 proclaiming the invalidity of a provision in Regulation no. 4 of 12 February 1999 by the Minister of Finance on Financial Accountancy Procedures in Business Establishments.

governmental Commission for Energy laying down a methodology for price-setting of central heating in condominiums.[118]

With the entry into force of the new Act on Administrative Procedure of 2006 this generous and activist approach was seriously curtailed. The *actio popularis* was replaced by a right to challenge the legality of administrative acts, including legislative acts (secondary legislation) by those who are affected by the Act.[119] In contrast to the previous bold jurisprudence, this new right is today restrictively interpreted. The Supreme Administrative Court has for instance held that organisations cannot claim an interest in an administrative act on behalf of their members. The act must, in other words, affect the activity of the organisation, meaning that consumer organisations are prevented from claiming illegality of administrative acts that negatively affect the rights of their members.[120]

B. State Liability

Another example concerns possibilities for individuals or consumer organisations to challenge in judicial proceedings the inaction of consumer protection agencies, by claiming affirmative injunctions and damages for failure to act. The Bulgarian Consumer Federation has again been resourceful in challenging the failure of the Bulgarian Consumer Protection Agency to act in a case of unfair marketing practice employed by a major telecom operator. The claim was lodged on the basis of the Bulgarian Act for Liability of the State for Damages and is still pending.[121] In their contribution to this volume, Safjan, Gorywoda and Janćuk likewise mention a case initiated by a local consumer ombudsman (spokesman) against the inaction of the OCCP.[122] The case apparently concerns the refusal of the OCCP to take action against a practice of allegedly unfair contract terms and conditions employed by a major electricity company.

---

118 Decision of the Supreme Administrative Court no. 5901 of 23 June 2004, pronouncing the invalidity of a Regulation of the Ministry of the Economy as being issued in contravention of the Energy Act, as confirmed by decision no. 2209 of 11 March 2005 of the Supreme Administrative Court, 5-member panel.

119 See decision no. 5 of 17 April 2007 of the Bulgarian Constitutional Court, constitutional case No. 11 of 2006, finding the new Act on Administrative Procedure not to be in violation of Article 120(2) of the Constitution.

120 See decision of the Supreme Administrative Court of 25 January 2008.

121 Act on the Liability of the State and the Municipalities for Damages, State Gazette no. 60 of 5 August 1988, last amended by State Gazette no. 43 of 29 April 2008, see in particular s. 2. Interview with Nezret Babuchev, supra note 90.

122 See supra note 88.

C. Cooperative v. Bifurcated Strategies

The stories told above indicate that consumer activists are facing difficult strategic choices concerning their relationship with market actors and state institutions. Already in the mid-1990s Micklitz noted the peculiarities of consumer protection in Central and Eastern Europe as partly characterised by cooperative patterns of behaviour, where consumers instead of identifying themselves in opposition to business and actively seeking their rights, rather perceived themselves as co-players in the process of market-building, bearing their own share of responsibility.[123] In line with this conceptualisation, some of the consumer organisations that were set up during the last decade clearly seem to see their role in assisting both business and the public administration in gradually finding a mutually acceptable model of division of labour and responsibilities.

However, other consumer associations rather perceive their role as being vocal and adversarial avengers of the consumer interest viz. both market actors and public institutions. As explained by one lawyer specialising in consumer protection law, the solution to the dilemma of under-enforcement in consumer protection in CEE countries may lie in applying 'bifurcated strategies'.[124] Acknowledging the power of commercial actors and the general leniency of courts to big business, on the one hand, and the ineffectiveness of public authorities, on the other, the response is seen to lie in combining and alternating private judicial action viz. market actors with administrative law action viz. public authorities challenging their passivity and regulatory failure. To be sure, such strategies appear to attract media attention, which eventually may be an effective lever for achieving practical results. Simultaneously, increased publicity may be in line with the own interest of consumer representatives who seek broader political or professional platforms.

The described bifurcated strategies come to underscore the ambivalent perceptions of and attitudes towards both market and state in transitional economies.[125] The slow process of relaxing the grip of the state over the economy has brought about a system-specific muddling in the accountability allocation between state and market subjects. The state is still actively involved in defining the parameters of (at least some) markets and is often seen as part of the market process. Despite the seeming reorganisation on free market grounds, the failures of newly privatised enterprises are generally ascribed to the state. On the other hand, the state is equally perceived as the chief legitimate source of social

123 See Micklitz (1996), supra note 1.

124 See supra, note 90.

125 See Jung, *Consumer Lament: An Ethnographic Study on Consumption, Needs and Everyday Complaints in Post-socialist Bulgaria*, PhD Dissertation, Harvard University, Cambridge Massachusetts, September 2006.

protection. This is particularly visible in the sphere of public interest services (electricity, railway and telecommunications).

D. *Individual Consumers as Avengers of Collective Interests*

More unusually, new consumer legislation in some CEECs has empowered individual consumers far beyond what is common in the old Member States. In a couple of countries standing to seek injunctive relief against practices affecting the collective interest of consumers has been granted not only to consumer organisations and public bodies but also to individual consumers.[126] In the Czech Republic individual consumers may lodge an action for injunction of unfair competition acts as well as for violations of collective interests of consumers. In a similar manner, in Poland, individual consumers enjoy direct right of action for injunction on the basis of unfair consumer contract terms (s. 479^{45} k.p.c.). Such generous litigation rights are normally avoided by law makers in established market democracies due to fear of excessive (and possibly opportunistic) litigation. In the specific context of transition in CEE countries they are, however, only rarely used in practice, mainly due to high litigation costs and lack of adequate incentives, resources and experience. Interestingly, in the few instances where such empowerment has produced practical effects, law makers in CEE countries have often reacted by tapping the flood by simply closing these procedural opportunities or transforming them into less intrusive alternatives.

In this respect, the evolution of the *locus standi* of the individual consumer in the Bulgarian CPA is a telling example. In its 1999 version the Act granted standing to individual consumers to bring injunctive action and claim damage compensation in all cases of unfair and misleading advertising, including discriminatory advertising, provided the consumer could demonstrate a legal interest in the case (s. 30(2) CPA of 1999). The provision was for some years in a state of hibernation, attracting no visible interests on the part of consumers. Yet in 2001 a female consumer invoked the provision to challenge an allegedly offensively sexist TV advertisement for one of the most popular beer brands in Bulgaria, "Zagorka".[127] A substantial amount of approximately Euro 50,000 was claimed as compensation for harm to the dignity of the female plaintiff. The case received broad media coverage and produced a domino effect, followed by six similar lawsuits within a short period of time. Although none of the lawsuits was wholly successful, the dispute had the positive effect of triggering serious public debate, reducing the otherwise widely spread gender discriminatory

126 See National Reports, Czech Republic, Slovakia, Slovenia, Poland, Leuven Study, supra note 47. On Bulgaria, see Bakardjieva Engelbrekt (2008), supra note 21.

127 Millan and Elliot, 'Offensive Advertising, Public Policy, and the Law: The Rulings on the Zagorka Case' (2004) (27) *Journal of Consumer Policy*, 475.

advertisements and sensitising the public authorities to the issues at hand.[128] In the Bulgarian CPA of 2006 adopted shortly after the sexist advertisement saga, the Bulgarian legislator decided to rescind the individual consumer's right of injunctive action and to replace it with a right to lodge a complaint before the CPAg in cases of misleading and unfair advertising (s. 34(2) 2006 BulgCPA).

E. *European Judicial Governance: Another Forum for Consumer Voice?*

To complete the – surely non-exhaustive – list of novel forms of consumer rights enforcement, the accidental recourse to the European Court of Human Rights (ECtHR) has to be mentioned. The ECtHR has for many CEE countries opened previously unknown avenues for challenging the power of the state and for correcting what is perceived to be the failures of domestic judicial systems. Long before accession to the EU was realistically on the agenda of CEECs the ECtHR provided the only link to European institutions (in a broad sense) for individual CEE citizens. The frequent convictions of CEE governments by the Strasbourg court received wide media coverage and provided occasions for celebrating small victories of the individual citizen over the hitherto almighty state. A number of lawyers specialised early in this type of litigation ensuring constant influx of new proceedings. These lawyers in Bulgaria have even their own platform "Association of lawyers for human rights".[129] Therefore it is not surprising that in the high profile Bulgarian heating litigation saga mentioned above, the ECtHR was included as one additional forum for activism.[130]

5. THE ROLE OF ENLARGEMENT REVISITED

As indicated above, Community accession policy has had a powerful, though not always equivocal impact on institutional choices and enforcement design in consumer protection in the CEE countries. The institutional blueprint in the White Paper has clearly contributed to the building up of public consumer protection agencies with horizontal competences for the field of consumer protection. By its requirement of "one body", the White Paper has enhanced functional differentiation and led to the suppression and even abandoning of

128 In the case three public authorities had decision-making competence: the Competition Agency, the Telecommunication Agency and the CPAg.

129 The association was among the petitioners in the constitutional case No. 11 of 2006, Decision No. 5 of 17 April 2007 of the Bulgarian Constitutional Court on the *actio popularis*.

130 See on this case www.imoti.bg, 18 August 2003, challenging the mechanism of measurement and calculation of expenses for central heating as involving violations of consumers' rights to property and privacy. The case is still pending before the ECtHR.

integrated institutional solutions for consumer and competition policy.[131] The very existence of centralized consumer protection agencies has often had an absorbing effect, viz. alternative private enforcement mechanisms.

Less overtly, and unintentionally, the main features of Community enlargement policy have probably generated influence in the same direction. The conditionality approach as applied to the CEE candidate countries implied uncompromising requirements of pre-accession alignment with the Community *acquis*. The screening of legislation in view of its conformity with the *acquis* often insisted on the literal transposition of directives and looked less positively on legislative projects aiming at organic integration of EC requirements in general civil law codes.[132] As a consequence, a piecemeal approach of implementing individual Community directives through separate legislative acts or governmental decrees has been preferred by governments and law makers in many CEE countries as the one meeting less objections on the part of the Commission. It is therefore not surprising that such subject-specific laws and regulations were not easily integrated within the complex texture of civil law enforcement codes and invited instead for administrative methods of enforcement.

What can particularly be observed in the area of consumer protection is a peculiar self-generating dynamics toward public intervention over and beyond the circle of accession states. The CEE governments were urged to introduce public agencies in the area of consumer protection. Once this advice was followed, the existence of such agencies in a boomerang fashion seems to hit back at all Community Member States and is used as an argument for new Community initiatives. A noteworthy example of the importance of enlargement for the Community's demarche in the area of public enforcement provides the already mentioned European Parliament and Council Regulation on consumer protection cooperation (Regulation 2006/2004).[133] In the Explanatory Memorandum to the Commission Proposal[134] enlargement is emphatically referred to both in the opening and the closing section.

> "1. The effective functioning of the internal market calls for a significant improvement in the way laws that protect consumers economic interests are enforced in cross-border cases ... *Enlargement* further reinforces the need for action."

131 See in particular the development in Estonia and Bulgaria.

132 Łętowska et al. (2007), supra note 32.

133 Regulation (EC) No 2006/2004 of the European Parliament and of the Council of 27 October 2004 on cooperation between national authorities responsible for the enforcement of consumer protection laws (the Regulation on consumer protection cooperation), O.J. L 364/1, 9 December 2004; on the effects of the Regulation, see Micklitz, in Weatherill/Bernitz (eds) (2007), supra note 39.

134 COM (2003) 443 *final*.

> "54. The Commission considers that adoption of the proposed regulation by Council and Parliament should be undertaken as quickly as possible, in particular, given the imminent *enlargement* of the EU." (emphasis added)

The Regulation is exclusively devoted to public law enforcement of consumer protection laws. It purports to establish a network of public consumer protection authorities in the Community Member States. These authorities are to be identified, clearly listed and obliged to offer information and mutual assistance. It is interesting to note the language in the Regulation's preamble. The thesis of the indispensability of public authorities for the proper enforcement of consumer protection laws is advanced with remarkable vigour. Although the Commission underlines the "valuable role" to be played by consumer organisations in the process of enforcement, it does not appear ready to sustain the "privileged position" provided to these organisations by Community law and especially by the Injunctions Directive. Whereas public bodies are described as "both impartial and accountable in the way they operate to defend the public interest", private bodies are said to be "not so accountable."[135]

The Commission makes explicit recourse to enlargement to draw additional support for its preferred emphasis on enforcement by public authorities. The availability of public authorities for the enforcement of consumer protection in CEE countries is used to bolster the potential of the advanced Regulation to achieve a uniform and adequate enforcement across a wider Community. According to the Commission:

> 32. … A large majority of Member States and *acceding countries* nevertheless have public authorities with specific consumer protection enforcement responsibilities."
> And further:
> …
> 34. *in fine* The prospect of *enlargement* demands action to safeguard consumer interests in an *enlarged* internal market. Most of the new Member States do not have a long tradition of consumer protection enforcement, although they *have established public authorities*. The proposed regulation is therefore an opportunity to ensure that effective enforcement is in place throughout the new internal market." (emphasis added)

As argued above, however, the introduction of public enforcement in itself is hardly a panacea. What is crucial is the institutional design of enforcement bodies, and the way in which it improves interest in participation in the decision-making process. Therefore, it is to be hoped that Regulation 2004/2006 will serve as a

---

135 Commission Proposal for Consumer Protection Co-operation Regulation COM (2003) 443 final.

starting point of a debate on governance design in consumer protection and issues of accountability, transparency and access to public regulatory bodies.

What has also hopefully been confirmed by the overview above is that institutions indeed 'move together'. Those characteristics of consumer interests and consumer stakes that make them poorly represented in the market (information failures, low stakes and dispersed interests) in a similar manner create difficulties for consumer participation in alternative decision-making processes. Both public agency control and private litigation build on multiple-level representation of consumer interests where again problems of information costs and low size/dispersed nature of the stakes make consumers poor principals allowing for considerable leeway for opportunism on the part of agents. The control over diffuse interests, over their identification, formulation and representation can be described as 'loose.' The incentives for participation and representation are not always clear or at hand. Decision-making is thus a difficult and highly imperfect process irrespective of the particular decision-making process preferred. CEE consumers appear to be 'between a rock and a hard place'. Neither markets, nor political process or adjudication can offer a fully reliable solution.

According to Komesar, in such situations the question is about choosing between imperfect alternatives.[136] By emphasising choice, however, he – as well as other institutional choice theorists – may be missing an important point. As put by Stiglitz, if we pose "the problem correctly", we should not see the question as one of "markets" versus "government", but rather "the appropriate balance between markets and government, with the possibility of many intermediate forms of economic organization".[137] A similar logic of institutional diversity should apply for the case of consumer enforcement, whereby complementarity between a variety of enforcement avenues should ensure the much needed adaptive efficiency of institutions.[138]

6. CONCLUSION

The area of consumer law enforcement in Europe is indeed in flux and nowhere is the dynamics as intense as in the new Union Member States from CEE countries. The analysis of developments in CEE countries during the last decade demonstrates that EU eastern enlargement has not only caused a remarkable burst of institutional innovation in the accession countries but has also unleashed processes of institutional exchange, harmonisation and emulation in the whole of the

136 Komesar (1994), supra note 5.
137 Stiglitz (1994), supra note 14.
138 North (1990), supra note 11.

Community. Since the ambitious Leuven study on alternative means for consumer redress, a significant number of old and new Member States have introduced statutory and institutional changes in the field of enforcement. The charts on Estonia, Lithuania and Latvia, to name but a few, already need a serious update, which only underscores the fact that the area is a moving target. New institutional changes are under way as a result from the transposition of the Unfair Commercial Practices Directive.

It has been noted above that the accession process has been tainted by certain bias toward public consumer law enforcement. At the same time, in the aftermath of accession, CEE administrations, judiciaries and institutional players seem to be engaged in an active process of making sense of the transposed *acquis*, which means in the first place connecting substantive legal acquisitions with procedural rules and institutional practices. In this process, mechanical transpositions of poorly translated and poorly understood provisions of Community directives come to the fore, as do dysfunctional procedural rules for administrative enforcement, rule-making and adjudication. This institutional dynamism can probably be positively interpreted as marking the end of the accession period and a transition to genuine Union membership. In contrast to fears of post-accession shirking and non-compliance on the part of CEE governments, we may be observing a shift from formal transposition to internalisation of the Community '*acquis*'. Ideally, this new phase of making fresh consumer rules and rights truly operative would lead to increased institutional pluralism. It seems indeed that more recently, countries that have been on a trajectory of either public or private enforcement open up for new alternative enforcement avenues, adding on the catalogue of enforcement options.

In an extensive comparative analysis of collective action for enforcement of consumer law Cafaggi and Micklitz observe a greater extent of cooperative strategies between private and public institutions in the European than in the American context.[139] With the inevitable risk of generalisations, it can still be asserted that markets, administrative agencies and judiciaries function as more or less discrete decision-making processes in the US with regulatory agencies monitoring market actors and judicial entrepreneurs challenging their conduct in court. In Europe, conversely, market actors are by law bound to negotiations with agencies and civil society, whereas public agencies and publicly financed consumer organisations represent consumer interests in court. This is probably at least to a certain extent attributable to differences in constitutional ideals, where a system of division of powers and checks and balances between different institutions

139 See Cafaggi and Micklitz, supra note 42.

characterises American democracy, while a soft corporatist societal order with less distinct borders between institutional spheres is prevalent in Europe.[140]

The "accession economies" of CEE countries seem to complicate the picture. There are of course powerful centripetal forces that pull them into the influence sphere of the Union and thus closer to the European corporatist model of cooperation and tripartite negotiations between business, consumers and governments. Such tendency may be in line with the cooperative role of the consumer movement in the process of state-, nation- and civil society-building in CEE countries early noted by Micklitz.[141] At the same time, it may enhance less benevolent past legacies of conflation of social spheres and counteract attempts to boost institutional integrity through a more formal system of checks and balances with stronger roles for judicial enforcement. It may therefore prove that American institutional schemes such as independent regulatory agencies, judicial control of administrative programmes, direct participatory rights in administrative decision-making and class action resonate more successfully with the needs of CEECs than they do viz. old EU Member States.[142] And although it can appear far-fetched, it is probably not to be excluded that in the long run the new EU Member States may come to play the role of conduits for American institutional influence in Europe.

In his famous article "On Uses and Abuses of Comparative Law" written as early as 1970 Otto Kahn Freund warned against a light-hearted enthusiasm about legal borrowings, in particular of rules and institutions that are at the "organic" end of a continuum between mechanical rules (to be compared to a carburettor) and organic rules (to be compared to a kidney). He stressed more specifically that:

> [a]ll rules which organise constitutional, legislative, administrative or judicial institutions and procedures, are designed to allocate power, rule making, decision making, above all, policy making power. These are the rules which are closest to the "organic" end of our continuum, they are the ones most resistant to transplantation.

This statement is in line with institutional choice theory and with the literature on historical institutionalism emphasising institutional legacies and 'lock ins'. The experience of the CEE countries that recently became members of the EU confirms the wisdom of such analyses. Despite major societal upheaval, procedural rules and enforcement structures in these countries are characterised by institutional inertia and yield to change only slowly. Yet in this process there may

140 On the 'varieties of capitalism' literature, see Hall and Soskice, 'An Introduction to Varieties of Capitalism', in: Hall and Soskice (eds) *Varieties of Capitalism* (Oxford: Oxford University Press, 2001).

141 Micklitz (1996) and (2001), supra note 1.

142 Rose Ackerman (2005), supra note 15.

be room for occasional openings and instances of innovatory institutional design. Such developments should be carefully observed and nurtured by Community institutions, since they may be a source of inspiration for the whole of the Union.

PART II.
PUBLIC AND PRIVATE ENFORCEMENT IN CONSUMER PROTECTION

AN INSTITUTIONAL PERSPECTIVE ON THE REGULATION OF PRODUCTS IN THE UNITED STATES

Catherine M. SHARKEY*

INTRODUCTION

In the United States, there is a vibrant debate over whether consumer products, including medical devices and pharmaceuticals, are best regulated through regulations issued by the federal government or through private lawsuits commenced by plaintiffs who have been harmed by those products or, perhaps, through some combination of both.

This debate implicates two theoretical issues: first, what is the ideal balance between the level of public government regulation and the availability of common law remedies in the form of private parties' tort lawsuits? And, second, what is the level – state or federal – at which regulation or litigation should be organised?

Steven Shavell has explored the first issue in depth. He has identified four factors to help determine the optimal mix of liability (i.e. regulation through private lawsuits resulting in judgments) and regulation (i.e. public governmental legislation): (i) the different amounts of information available to private parties, on the one hand, and regulators on the other; (ii) the ability of defendants (i.e. manufacturers) to pay for the harms they cause; (iii) the likelihood that the defendant-manufacturer will actually be sued; and (iv) the relative costs of administering a liability-based system as opposed to one grounded in direct regulation.[1] Shavell concludes that two factors, differential knowledge and administrative costs, favour a liability-based regime,[2] whereas the other two

* Professor of Law, New York University School of Law.

1 See Steven Shavell, *Liability for Harm Versus Regulation of Safety*, 13 J. LEGAL STUD. 357, 358–64 (1984) [hereinafter Shavell, *Liability for Harm*]; see *also* Steven Shavell, *A Model of the Optimal Use of Liability and Safety Regulation*, 15 RAND J. ECON. 271, 271 (1984); Donald Wittman, *Prior Regulation Versus Post Liability: The Choice Between Input and Output Monitoring*, 6 J. LEGAL STUD. 193, 193 (1977).

2 See Shavell, *Liability for Harm*, *supra* note 1, at 359–60, 363–64.

factors, a defendant's potential inability to pay and its ability to escape litigation altogether, favour regulation.[3]

But Professor Shavell's analysis has limitations. His analysis does not address an important dimension of the problem of regulation: the theoretical question of whether regulation is best performed at the federal level or at the state/local level, and the related institutional choice question that might further constrain optimal regulatory solutions to the existing regulatory apparatus. In the United States, these questions boil down to whether and when the uniform centralised system that a federal-level system of regulation administered by agencies offers is preferable to the localised state regime of tort litigation commenced by individual injured consumers.

As a theoretical matter, uniform national rules may be most desirable in those circumstances characterised by significant interstate externalities, coordination problems, or economies of scale and scope. In such cases, state law claims might appropriately be deemed pre-empted by the relevant federal regulation. Conversely, state or local regulation – and, in turn, a finding against pre-emption – might be preferred on grounds of democratic accountability based upon regional differences in policy preferences, the benefits of experimentation, or the comparative advantage of inter-state competition yielding optimal policy outcomes.

Economists and legal scholars have not shied away from this debate, but their debates are both partial and indeterminate. To quote Thomas Merrill, "[o]ne person's healthy regional diversity is another's interstate externality".[4] It may well be that, at least in the products liability context, there is no general, "one size fits all" theoretical solution leading to optimal regulation.

To date, no commentator has devoted sufficient attention to what I believe to be the single most important dimension of the state/federal regulation conundrum in the United States: the question of the comparative institutional capabilities of agencies (the federal regulators) and courts (the state-level regulators, presiding over tort suits). This chapter, a synthesis of my previous work in this specific area,[5] argues that the path to the optimal regulatory solution lies in cooperation between agencies and courts. More specifically, I argue that no judicial determination of either the merits of a products liability case or the threshold question whether a

---

3 See *id.* at 360–63.

4 Thomas W. Merrill, *Preemption in Environmental Law: Formalism, Federalism Theory, and Default Rules*, *in* Federal Preemption: States' Powers, National Interests 166, 168 (Richard A. Epstein & Michael S. Greve eds., 2007).

5 See Catherine M. Sharkey, *Products Liability Preemption: An Institutional Approach*, 76 Geo. Wash. L. Rev. 449 (2008) [hereinafter, Sharkey, *Products Liability Preemption*]. See *also* Samuel Issacharoff & Catherine M. Sharkey, Backdoor Federalization, 53 UCLA L. Rev. 1353 (2006); Catherine M. Sharkey, *CAFA Settlement Notice Provision: Optimal Regulatory Policy?*," 156 U. Penn. L. Rev. 1971 (2008) [hereinafter Sharkey, *CAFA*].

plaintiff's state law claims are pre-empted can be complete without reference to the relevant agency's view on the issue before the court.

1. THEORETICAL CONSIDERATIONS

The overlapping nature of the two theoretical issues described above can best be seen on a matrix, such as that set forth in Table 1. That chart plots the two regulatory policy dimensions: namely, along the vertical axis, the relative desirability of the common law liability regime as opposed to safety regulation; and second, along the horizontal axis, the level – state or federal – at which liability or regulation should be organised.

By and large, in the United States, a decision to opt for *ex ante* regulation of products – i.e. via legislation – corresponds to a choice in favour of federal substantive law, whereas the *ex post* common law liability route is associated with state law, as most plaintiffs' claims in the products liability context take the form of alleged violations of state laws. But there are exceptions to this rule. Perhaps the most significant (and increasingly controversial) are common law negligence *per se* actions (noted in Table 1), which, while brought by private plaintiffs, are premised upon violations of federal standards and regulations.

Table 1[6]

		Federal/State Dimension	
		Federal Law	State Law
***Ex Ante/ Ex Post* Dimension**	*Ex Ante* Regulation	Federal regulations (administered by federal agencies, such as the FDA, NHTSA, CPSC)	State regulations (administered by state agencies, such as the Insurance Commissioner,[7] Gaming Commissioner[8])
	Ex Post Common law liability	Private common law negligence *per se* actions	Private common law state tort litigation

6 Taken from Sharkey, *CAFA*, *supra* note 5, at 1978 (Table 2).

7 See, *e.g.* Florida Office of Insurance Regulation, http://www.floir.com/ (last visited 12 February, 2008); Arizona Department of Insurance, http://www.id.state.az.us/ (last visited 12 February, 2008). See also Jonathan R. Macey & Geoffrey P. Miller, *The McCarran-Ferguson Act of 1945: Reconceiving the Federal Role of Insurance Regulation*, 68 N.Y.U. L. Rev. 13, 14 (1993) ("Among major financial institutions in the United States, only insurance firms are subject to plenary state regulation.").

8 See, *e.g.* Pennsylvania Gaming Control Board, http://www.pgcb.state.pa.us/ (last visited 12 February, 2008); California Gambling Control Commission, http://www.cgcc.ca.gov/ (last visited 12 February, 2008).

1.1. COMMON LAW LIABILITY VERSUS SAFETY REGULATION

The work of Professor Shavell, described above, can be understood as an in-depth exploration of the first dimension or the vertical axis in Table 1.

In his search for the optimal mix of liability and regulation, Professor Shavell reaffirms that the optimal result is, indeed, a mix: "[a] complete solution to the problem of the control of risk evidently should involve the joint use of liability and regulation, with the balance between them reflecting the importance of the determinants."[9] And he further observes that "the actual, observed use of the two methods of reducing risks may be viewed as socially desirable, or roughly so."[10]

It should come as no surprise, then, that Professor Shavell advocates against the regulatory compliance defence, which essentially constitutes a use of regulation to the exclusion of a liability regime. He asserts that, "[a]s liability will induce many of these parties [who present above-average risk of doing harm] to take beneficial precautions beyond the required ones, its use as a supplement to regulation will be advantageous."[11] As a direct corollary, he suggests that "the statutory standard ought to be regarded as a minimum."[12] But he concedes that "the fit between the theory presented here and reality is only approximate."[13]

Professor Shavell's analysis, in my view, would have more readily approximated reality had it taken into account the dual levels of regulation in our federal system and the fact that the choice between liability and regulation most often also entails a state versus federal, or localised versus centralised, dimension.

1.2. STATE VERSUS FEDERAL REGULATION

As Samuel Issacharoff and I have argued in previous work, the Rehnquist Supreme Court, in its determination of pre-emption cases arising in the products liability context, appears to have been influenced by functional considerations: the promotion of national uniformity and the resolution of coordination problems among states that tend to externalise regulatory costs to their neighbours.[14] By implicit reliance on these criteria – which, economists refer to as economies of

9 Shavell, *Liability for Harm*, *supra* note 1, at 365.

10 *Id.* at 358.

11 *Id.* at 365. Shavell includes the caveat that "just because this is true, regulatory requirements need not be as rigorous as if regulation were the sole means of controlling risks." *Id.*

12 *Id.* at 371 n.18.

13 *Id.* at 372.

14 See Issacharoff & Sharkey, *supra* note 5, at 1365–98; see *also* Samuel Issacharoff & Catherine M. Sharkey, *Supreme Court Preemption: The Contested Middle Ground of Products Liability*, *in* FEDERAL PREEMPTION: STATES' POWERS, NATIONAL INTERESTS 194, 195 (Richard A. Epstein & Michael S. Greve eds., 2007).

scope or scale and the existence of interstate externalities – the Court was, more often than not, likely to favour regulation at the national level.[15]

Scholars have also advocated national regulation in the products liability context. As the late Gary Schwartz noted in 1996, a "time arrives for more mature and experienced decision-making. After thirty years with products liability at the state level, that time has probably come."[16] Professor Schwartz and others have argued that "[t]he value associated with federalism in allowing experimentation at the state level seems undercut by the practical inability of manufacturers distributing products at the national level to respond to whatever experiments state courts might undertake."[17]

But the pro-federalisation camp is hardly unopposed. Equally vociferous are those who favour state-level or, sometimes, even more localised, regulation. These liability-regime advocates cite democratic accountability based upon regional differences in policy preferences,[18] the benefits of experimentation where there is substantial uncertainty about the correct regulatory strategy,[19] and the comparative advantage of interstate competition yielding optimal policy outcomes[20] as arguments in their favour.

But no discussion of the issue can be complete without an exploration of the institutional dimension of regulatory policy.

2. INSTITUTIONAL CONSIDERATIONS

If, at least in the products liability context, there is no "one size fits all" solution to the regulatory policy problem, what are courts, determining whether or not a state tort claim is pre-empted by a federal regulation, to do? An institutional approach may provide the best guide.

15 Issacharoff & Sharkey, *supra* note 5, at 1356 ("Our main argument is that the U.S. Supreme Court has, in preemption and forum-allocation cases, attempted to capture the considerable benefits that flow from national regulatory uniformity and to protect an increasingly unified national (and international) commercial market from the imposition of externalities by unfriendly state legislation.").

16 Gary T. Schwartz, *Considering the Proper Federal Role in American Tort Law*, 38 Ariz. L. Rev. 917, 930 (1996). *But* see Stephen D. Sugarman, *Should Congress Engage in Tort Reform?*, 1 Mich. L. & Pol'y Rev. 121, 127 (1996) ("[S]tate tort laws today are broadly the same in product injury cases.").

17 Schwartz, *supra* note 16, at 950.

18 See, *e.g.* Betsy J. Grey, *The New Federalism Jurisprudence and National Tort Reform*, 59 Wash. & Lee L. Rev. 475, 517–18 (2002); Robert Rabin, *Federalism and the Tort System*, 50 Rutgers L. Rev. 1, 29 (1997).

19 See, *e.g.* Schwartz, *supra* note 16, at 930.

20 See, *e.g.* Harvey S. Perlman, *Products Liability Reform in Congress: An Issue of Federalism*, 48 Ohio St. L.J. 503, 507 (1987).

To date, the pre-emption debate has been unduly narrow, as it has treated courts as the sole interpreters of legislation. It has, accordingly, failed to take into account the actors that are at least as important: federal agencies. By characterising agencies merely as bodies that implement a particular administrative scheme, scholars have ignored agencies' role as those who determine the administrative reach of the statutes at issue. As it turns out, federal agencies emerge as the institutional actors best equipped to provide the answer to the thorny question at the heart of the pre-emption query: whether there in fact should be a uniform federal regulatory policy.

A federal agency's determination that there is a relevant federal regulatory policy based upon uniformity or coordination demands should be the beginning – not the end – of the pre-emption analysis. Remedies and enforcement are key ingredients of integrated schemes of regulation, and any court's consideration of the comprehensiveness of a federal regulatory scheme must pay some attention to the remedial end. The Supreme Court has set a high bar to imputing a congressional intent to preempt when such an interpretation would create what I would call a remedial or enforcement "void."[21] A key question remains: does the propriety of certain remedies likewise fall within the policy expertise of agencies or, instead, do courts have a broader role to play?

This institutional angle is at the core of the "agency reference" model that I have proposed as a guide for courts deciding products liability pre-emption cases.[22] The model recognises and aims to exploit the fact that agencies have at their disposal a wealth of information that could be of vital use to courts called upon to rule on pre-emption questions and, in the process, to determine an optimal regulatory strategy.

The information that agencies possess is actually highly relevant to this determination. In the course of their own internal determinations of whether or not to enact regulations or to take other regulatory action, agencies conduct context-specific cost-benefit (or risk-risk) determinations about the product or products within their purview. Furthermore, agencies collect vital information regarding the economic consequences of various regulations and the effects of state regulation on federal regulatory schemes.

---

21 The Court has repeatedly noted that only in the clearest of cases should a court find that Congress intended wholly to remove any and all remedies for injured citizens, let alone accept an agency's view that such was the intent of Congress. See, *e.g. Bates v. Dow Agrosciences* LLC, 544 US 431, 449 (2005) ("If Congress had intended to deprive injured parties of a long available form of compensation, it surely would have expressed that intent more clearly."); *Silkwood v. Kerr-McGee Corp.*, 464 US 238, 251 (1984) ("It is difficult to believe that Congress would, without comment, remove all means of judicial recourse for those injured by illegal conduct.").

22 See Sharkey, *Products Liability Preemption*, *supra* note 5, at 477–502.

This on-point information would be indispensable to a court facing a pre-emption case. It could provide an empirical basis for a court's assessment of whether a uniform federal regulatory policy should exist in a particular area. The problem, to date, is that courts do not routinely look to this information in making their decisions in pre-emption cases. The overarching purpose of the proposed agency reference model is to systematise a court's use of this vital resource.

An agency is a rich source of information due to the multiple roles that it plays. First, as a regulator of products, it reviews and analyses products and their attendant risks on a regular basis. Additionally, an agency often weighs contemporaneous factors that may determine the pre-emptive effect of its regulatory actions.

Second, an agency may assume a distinct interpretive role as administrator of the relevant congressional legislation that embodies the federal regulation promulgated by the agency, and it can express its position on pre-emption in a variety of ways, such as official notice-and-comment rule making or less formal interpretive statements and preambles.

Finally, an agency may share its views in amicus briefs before courts (including the Supreme Court) ruling on pre-emption questions.

At present, there is no systematic way for courts to rely on agency actions, at any of the three levels described here – the level of issuance of regulations regarding pre-emptive scope, contemporaneous views interpreting regulatory action, and expressions of views in amicus briefs before courts. The question of whether, and to what extent, courts should rely on this information is hardly resolved, and is only becoming thornier, with certain agencies – the FDA most prominently – moving away from formal regulations toward less formal interpretive positions.[23]

The proposed agency reference model capitalises on two conventional rationales for judicial deference to agencies: one, the notion that agencies have great expertise, and, two, the concept that such deference makes sense because agencies can best promote coherence and uniformity of standards in areas of national law.[24]

Not surprisingly, agency expertise is the leading rationale put forward by agencies themselves. But it also finds voice in the Supreme Court, especially channelled via Justice Stephen Breyer. As he emphasised, writing for the majority in *Geier v. American Honda Motor Co.*, a case where the Court had to decide if the National Traffic and Motor Vehicle Safety Act of 1966 pre-empted a state common

23 See Catherine M. Sharkey, *Preemption by Preamble: Federal Agencies and the Federalization of Tort Law*, 56 DePaul L. Rev. 227 (2007).

24 See, *e.g.* David R. Geiger & Mark D. Rosen, *Rationalizing Product Liability for Prescription Drugs: Implied Preemption, Federal Common Law, and Other Paths to Uniform Pharmaceutical Safety Standards*, 45 DePaul L. Rev. 395, 397 (1996); Richard B. Stewart, *Regulatory Compliance Preclusion of Tort Liability: Limiting the Dual-Track System*, 88 Geo. L.J. 2167, 2173–76 (2000).

law tort action against a defendant auto manufacturer that had equipped its auto with passive restraints as required under the Act, but not air bags, an omission that plaintiffs claimed made the auto unreasonably dangerous:

> Congress has delegated to [the Department of Transportation] authority to implement the statute; the subject matter is technical; and the relevant history and background are complex and extensive. The agency is likely to have a thorough understanding of its own regulation and its objectives and is "uniquely qualified" to comprehend the likely impact of state requirements.[25]

The other rationale, the uniformity rationale, has been ably explicated by Peter Strauss. It stresses the advantage that agencies enjoy over the geographically divided federal court system in promoting a uniform standard.[26] Professor Strauss's main concern is the coherence of agreed-upon national (federal) law. The agency reference model, by contrast, aims, by formalising agency input in pre-emption cases, to bring a degree of consistency to the threshold question of whether it is optimal to regulate a product, or an aspect of a product, at the state or national level.

The model also makes explicit what appears to have been happening anyway, albeit in an almost haphazard way, in the U.S. Supreme Court pre-emption jurisprudence in the products liability context. The Court's decisions in this realm, which, at first glance, are difficult to harmonise, are, upon closer study, readily explicable: most of the time, the Court's decision as to whether a particular statute or regulation pre-empts a common law claim matches the interpretation of that statute or regulation advocated by the relevant agency.

Take, for instance, *Medtronic, Inc. v. Lohr*, a case involving common law tort claims by a plaintiff who was injured by an allegedly defectively designed pacemaker that had been granted premarket notification approval by the FDA, in a process that had been authorised by the Federal Food, Drug and Cosmetic Act (FDCA).[27] The FDA's actual regulatory review of the pacemaker consisted solely of its determination that the device was "substantially equivalent" to a device that was already on the market.[28] Moreover, the FDA indicated at the time of its regulatory action – when it issued its "substantial equivalence" letter to the manufacturer – that its premarket notification process did not amount to an endorsement of safety or efficacy.[29]

---

25 *Geier v. Am. Honda Motor Co.*, 529 US 861, 883 (2000) (quoting *Medtronic, Inc. v. Lohr*, 518 US 470, 496 (1996)).

26 See Peter Strauss, *One Hundred Fifty Cases per Year: Some Implications of the Supreme Court's Limited Resources for Judicial Review of Agency Action*, 87 Colum. L. Rev. 1093, 1121–22 (1987).

27 *Medtronic, Inc. v. Lohr*, 518 US 470 (1996).

28 See *id.* at 480.

29 *Id.*

The FDA had also issued a formal regulation, subject to notice-and-comment rule making, construing the scope of the express preemption provision of the governing statute, the Medical Devices Amendment (MDA) to the FDCA. This regulation cabins the statute's preemptive force to instances where the FDA has established "specific counterpart regulations or... other specific requirements applicable to a particular device."[30] The regulation further provides that the MDA "does not preempt State or local requirements of general applicability where the purpose of the requirement relates... to other products in addition to devices."[31]

In an amicus brief filed in the Supreme Court, the FDA adopted a narrow view of its pre-emptive power: "Neither the FDCA nor the FDA's regulations prescribe criteria for the design of devices. The design of a device originates with its manufacturer."[32] The FDA reasoned that its "substantially equivalent" determination was in no way tantamount to its more rigorous premarket approval process, which requires "a showing of reasonable assurance" that the device is safe and effective.[33] For this reason, it would not make sense to conclude that the more lax premarket notification process established a uniform, national regulatory policy – at least not one based upon anything resembling optimal standards.[34] The Supreme Court's anti-pre-emption determination in *Lohr* was far removed from the precise statutory language in the FDCA and had far more to do with the agency's explanation of its own review process and the level of rigour involved.[35]

The Court's decision in *Geier* fits this pattern as well. The relevant agency in that case was the National Highway Traffic and Safety Administration (NHTSA) and NHTSA's statement of its own federal regulatory objectives, as well as its bottom-line conclusion that state tort law would interfere with the accomplishment of those objectives, played a key role in the Court's decision. The federal regulation at issue – promulgated after nearly fifteen years of analysis, full notice-and-comment rule making, and litigation[36] – gave automobile manufacturers a range of choices among different passive restraint devices that were to be gradually introduced over time.[37] In fact, the Department of Transportation had rejected a

---

30 21 C.F.R. §808.1(d) (2007).

31 *Id.* §808.1(d)(1).

32 Brief for the United States as Amicus Curiae Supporting Respondents/Cross-Petitioners at 20, *Lohr*, 518 US 470 (1996) (Nos. 95–754, 95–886), 1996 WL 118035, at *20.

33 See *id.* at 19–20.

34 The FDA left open the issue of pre-emption following the more rigorous premarket approval process. See *id.* at 20 n.14. The agency took a pro-pre-emption position before the Court in the recent *Riegel v. Medtronic, Inc.* case, which decided that, unlike premarket notification, the premarket approval process leads to pre-emptive federal requirements under the MDA. See *Riegel v. Medtronic, Inc.*, 128 S.Ct. 999, 1004-1007 (2008).

35 See *Lohr*, 518 US at 495–96 ("Congress has given the FDA a unique role in determining the scope of §360k's pre-emptive effect.").

36 Brief for the United States as Amicus Curiae Supporting Affirmance at 3, *Geier v. Am. Honda Motor Co.*, 529 US 861 (2000) (No. 98–1811), 1999 WL 1045115, at *3.

37 *Geier*, 529 US at 874–75.

proposed regulation requiring airbags in all cars because of concerns about backlash from a public concerned about the safety of airbags, and the desire to promote a national policy whereby vehicle manufacturers would be encouraged to offer the public a choice of either automatic seatbelts or airbag passive protection systems. Given that the agency had specifically considered and rejected the airbag-only rule, plaintiffs' state-law claims arising from the manufacturer's failure to install airbags were pre-empted.[38]

But perhaps the most persuasive example of how an agency reference model might work is illustrated in *Sprietsma v. Mercury Marine*, where the Court held that the Federal Boat Safety Act of 1971 did not pre-empt the plaintiff's common law tort claims stemming from the manufacturer's failure to install propeller guards on a boat engine.[39] Concerned about a rise in the number of recreational boating accidents in which passengers were struck by propellers, the Coast Guard had asked the National Boating Safety Advisory Council to appoint a special Propeller Guard Subcommittee "to review the available data on the prevention of propeller-strike accidents and to study the various methods of shrouding propellers to prevent contact with a person in the water."[40] After an extensive eighteen-month study, the Coast Guard concluded that the data was insufficient to warrant a federal regulation.[41] But, *why* the Coast Guard chose not to regulate was key to the Court's implied preemption analysis.

The Coast Guard explained in an amicus brief to the Court that, at the time of its review, it did *not* conclude that such regulation would be economically inefficient or increase risks. Specifically, the Coast Guard stated that it never concluded either (a) that propeller guards were "technologically infeasible, economically unjustified, and likely to increase safety hazards" or (b) that manufacturers should have "unfettered discretion" to decide whether or not to install propeller guards.[42] Instead, the Coast Guard had merely determined that "[a]vailable propeller guard accident data do not support imposition of a regulation requiring propeller guards on motorboats."[43] Crucially, it had found that "[n]o simple universal [propeller guard] design suitable for all boats and motors in existence has been described or demonstrated to be technologically or economically feasible."[44] And, as the Coast Guard urged the Court, common law claims do not subvert agency policy when the agency "believe[s] that the available evidence is too inconclusive to warrant the imposition of a prescriptive standard" or "find[s]

38 See *id.* at 879–81.
39 *Sprietsma v. Mercury Marine*, 537 US 51 (2002).
40 *Id.* at 60–61.
41 *Id.* at 61.
42 See Brief for the United States as Amicus Curiae Supporting Petitioner at 26, *Sprietsma*, 537 US 51 (No. 01-706), 2002 WL 500643, at *26.
43 *Id.* at 17–18.
44 *Id.* at 5.

that … a workable prescriptive rule of general applicability cannot feasibly be adopted."[45] In this case, then, the Coast Guard concluded that state common law tort claims would in no way "subvert any federal policy reflected in the agency's decision to forgo regulation."[46]

Here was a situation where – according to the agency that studied the matter – there was no presently suitable uniform federal regulation given the diversity inherent in boat designs. Given the "thousands of hull designs" and the vast range of "hull/propulsion unit combinations,"[47] the Coast Guard decided to leave the question whether propeller guards should be required to the machinery of the tort system, where liability would be decided on a case-by-case basis at a more localised level. And the Supreme Court was persuaded that "[t]he Coast Guard's apparent focus was on the lack of any 'universally acceptable' propeller guard for 'all modes of boat operation'."[48]

The Court's reliance on the relevant agency's position in these cases might derive from the expertise rationale, the uniformity rationale, or perhaps a combination of both. The agency reference model recognises that, no matter the governing rationale, agencies are playing a key part in the Court's decision-making process, as they should be.

CONCLUSION

As we have seen, the question of regulation of products in the United States raises interesting issues, issues that the agency reference model that I have described here aims to resolve, at least in part. One issue that the model does not purport to address, and an issue that might be of particular interest when viewed from the international perspective, is the truncated role that our government appears to play in regulation. For the most part, it is a role limited to *ex ante* involvement, in the form of federal government agencies' approval processes and promulgation of statutes and other standards. To date, however, the government – both on the federal and state level – tends to shy away from significant involvement at the *ex post* stage, although there is no apparent prohibition to its doing so. On the contrary, state attorneys general (AGs) are charged with investigating and bringing actions in the public interest. Such cases are typically brought pursuant to the AGs' *parens patriae* authority under consumer protection or antitrust statutes.[49] Second, the government can participate in private litigation, as

45 *Id.* at 17.

46 *Id.* at 17–18.

47 *Id.* at 5.

48 *Sprietsma*, 537 US at 67.

49 See, *e.g.* Richard P. Ieyoub & Theodore Eisenberg, *State Attorney General Actions, the Tobacco Litigation, and the Doctrine of* Parens Patriae, 74 Tul. L. Rev. 1859, 1860–61 (2000).

intervenor, objector, or amicus.[50] It is unclear why the government has not exploited its position *ex post* more heavily, and it would be particularly interesting to explore whether this is an anomalous approach in the international regulation landscape.

---

50 See generally Arthur F. Greenbaum, *Government Participation in Private Litigation*, 21 Ariz. St. L.J. 853 (1989) (discussing myriad ways by which government can participate in private litigation, including Federal Civil Procedure Rule 19 compulsory joinder, intervention via Rule 24 or specific statutes, consolidation of a government action with a private action, and participation as an *amicus curiae*).

DEVELOPING APPROACHES TO PUBLIC AND PRIVATE ENFORCEMENT IN ENGLAND AND WALES

Christopher HODGES*

It is widely recognised that the jurisdiction of England and Wales has strong traditions in both private law on compensation and public law on regulation. For the former, the common law emphasises causes of action and rights to damages. Civil procedure, robustly modernised in 1999, emphasises speedy and effective resolution of disputes with the objective of ensuring that costs are proportionate to the amounts at stake. In addition to the traditional unitary procedures, this jurisdiction was one of the first to introduce a specific procedure to enable multiple similar claims to be managed effectively through the civil justice system, the Group Litigation Order procedure. Equally, the tradition in regulatory enforcement has strongly emphasised primary reliance on public authorities, under which a rich and diverse range of self-regulatory mechanisms flourish.

Against this background, there has been innovative experimentation with mechanisms for addressing multiple similar situations, and particularly with means that would provide a fused approach towards collective redress, that would enable both compliance and compensation issues to be addressed simultaneously. Both debate and experimentation on such mechanisms is currently continuing, so this chapter is a snapshot of work in progress, which must evolve further before it can be objectively evaluated. Even so, a number of important key policy directions are clear, if as yet incomplete.

This analysis outlines the main trends, mechanisms and debates as they currently stand. The first section describes the mechanisms for private law claims through the courts, followed by alternative dispute resolution and voluntary compensation schemes, before proceeding to mechanisms involving public authorities and consumer bodies. There follows a summary of government policy on economic competitiveness and enforcement, which is driving new approaches towards a coordinated approach to public and private enforcement and redress mechanisms.

* Head of the CMS Research Programme on Civil Justice Systems, Centre for Socio-Legal Studies, University of Oxford.

1. PRIVATE LAW CLAIMS

The dispute resolution systems that are controlled by the state courts are specified in the Civil Procedure Rules 1998 (CPR).[1] All claims brought in the public court system are subject to the 'overriding principle'[2] of providing justice through speedy, efficient and proportionate procedures. This overriding principle can be identified in various manifestations in different types of disputes or in disputes that involve different amounts.

Given that most consumer claims are comparatively small amounts, it makes sense to consider first what procedures apply to small claims. The 'small claims' procedure has a long history in England and Wales. It applies to any claim under £5,000 (£1,000 for personal injury cases). The procedure is informal, without lawyers (hence minimising cost) and, unusually, the 'loser pays' rule is disapplied. The small claims procedure presents inherent challenges for applying an aggregated approach. Instead, test cases can illuminate solutions, but do not necessarily provide binding solutions.

Claims above the small claims limit involving up to £15,000 are processed through the 'fast track' procedure. This requires parties first to exchange details of what their cases are about before starting proceedings in court so as to provide opportunities for settlement. Parties should undertake standard actions, set out in Pre-Action Protocols,[3] in advance of commencing proceedings: this facilitates verification of the facts and evidence, establishment of the nature of a case and defence, and encouragement of early settlement. Issues covered include exchange of documentary evidence, and instruction of a single expert on a joint basis. Time limits are specified. Appeal is only permissible with the court's permission.

Cases involving amounts above £15,000 are processed on a tailor-made basis by the court (in the 'multi-track' procedure) but with strong judicial case management so as to limit delay, complexity and cost.

---

1 Www.justice.gov.uk/civil/procrules_fin/index.htm.

2 CPR 1.1(2) specifies the following aspects of what this means:
"Dealing with a case justly includes, so far as is practicable –
(a) ensuring that the parties are on an equal footing;
(b) saving expense;
(c) dealing with the case in ways which are proportionate-
  i. to the amount of money involved;
  ii. to the importance of the case;
  iii. to the complexity of the issues; and
  iv. to the financial position of each party;
(d) ensuring that it is dealt with expeditiously and fairly; and
(e) allotting to it an appropriate share of the court's resources, while taking into account the need to allot resources to other cases".

3 Www.justice.gov.uk/civil/procrules_fin/contents/practice_directions/pd_protocol.htm.

The above three processes relate to individual claims. Where a number of similar claims arise, they may be managed under one of several different procedures. A 'representative action' procedure, under which a single representative party can represent all parties with the same interest,[4] has a long history but has been used very rarely.[5] The courts interpreted the requirement for 'the same interest' strictly[6] and held that this mechanism cannot apply where claimants have different personal rights or defendants have differing defences: thus, the mechanism could not be used for any damages claims.[7]

The most widely used formal procedure for aggregation of similar claims is the Group Litigation Order (GLO).[8] This was formally introduced in 1999 as part of the new procedure rules,[9] but the approach had emerged in a series of cases over the previous decade.[10]

Where a number of similar claims exist that "give rise to common or related issues of fact or law" the court makes a GLO that they be managed together.[11] The Order may be made on the application of any party or on the initiative of the court itself. A single judge will be appointed to manage the case, and will make directions at periodic case management conferences. The GLO procedure applies to all cases commenced that satisfy the description of the group: in other words, it is an opt-in approach. However, the formalities for commencement are reduced and claimants who start individual actions join a register. The court may then decide that individuals should serve general statements of their case or that generic pleadings be produced. The court may appoint lead solicitors, may control any advertising of the case, and may set a cut-off date for people to join the procedure.

The court has discretion over whether to select one or a number of lead or test cases, or adopt some other approach. Courts have been resistant to deciding

---

4 In addition to the normal techniques of joinder or consolidation of individual actions, CPR, Part 19.II specifies four different mechanisms:
- Representative parties with the same interest (Rule 19.6);
- Representation of persons who cannot be ascertained in relation to the estate of a deceased person, properly subject to a trust, or the meaning of a document or statute (Rule 19.7);
- Representation of a person who has died (Rule 19.8);
- A claim by one or more members of a company, body, or trade union for the company, body, or trade union to be given a remedy open to it (a 'derivative claim': Rule 19.9).

5 For a rare case, involving members of a football club, see *Howells and Kelly (on behalf of themselves and all other members of the Hemel Hempstead Football & Sports Club) v The Dominion Insurance Company Limited* [2005] EWHC 552.

6 *Duke of Bedford v Ellis* [1901] AC 1, HL.

7 *Markt & Co Ltd v Knight Steamship Co Ltd* [1910] 2 KB 1021, CA.

8 CPR, Part 19.III.

9 Following the fundamental review carried out by Lord Woolf, *Access to Justice: Interim Report* (1995) and *Access to Justice: Final Report* (1996). See A. A. S. Zuckerman, *Zuckerman on Civil Procedure* (Sweet & Maxwell, 2006); N. Andrews, *English Civil Procedure* (Oxford, 2003).

10 For the history, see C. J. S. Hodges, *Multi Party Actions* (Oxford, 2001).

11 CPR, Part 19.10.

preliminary issues, such as whether a medicine is defective, since that would not resolve any individual case, and the result might obscure the fact that the merits of individual cases were not strong. There is limited doctrine on the extent to which decisions in lead cases are formally binding on other individual cases, but the courts resist re-litigation of decided issues as being an abuse of process.

The GLO procedure has been used in a wide range of cases in the past decade, notably abuse in child care homes, product liability, holiday disasters, transport crashes[12] and tax disputes against the government.[13] The GLO procedure has provided the backdrop against which many of these cases have been settled,[14] sometimes only involving the court in managing specific issues and without invoking the full GLO procedure.[15] Consistent with the experience of class actions in the USA, however, cases alleging product liability for pharmaceuticals have often proved inappropriate for collective treatment, since they usually give rise to a predominance of individual rather than generic issues: many have also been unsuccessful on their merits, or have foundered because their high costs have made them unjustifiable in relation to modest potential recoveries, although a minority have been settled.[16] The major barrier to use of the GLO procedure is said by claimant lawyers to be gaining access to adequate funding. The funding of litigation is a complex subject that is fast evolving.[17]

Various features should be noted that pervade the above formal procedures. There is a strong emphasis on traditional principles, such as the need for parties to opt-in to exert their claims and the rule that the loser must pay the costs of the unnecessary litigation (except for the small claims procedure). The loser pays rule is used as a means of encouraging parties to settle claims and as a powerful means of enabling the court to control against delay and complexity. There is strong

---

12 L. Christian, 'Rail Crash Litigation – Southall and Ladbrooke Grove' [2001] J.P.I.L. 4/01, 339–355.

13 See S. Whitehead, 'Group Litigation and the European Court of Justice' [2006] *E. C. Tax J.* 8(3), 13; L. Fichardt and P. Freund, 'The UK Tax group Litigation orders – The Current Status' [2007] *E. C. Tax J.* 9(2)2.

14 Information provided by participants at the conference on Group Actions held at the Centre for Socio-Legal Studies, Oxford on 14 December 2006.

15 An example is claims arising out of the major fire at an aviation fuel facility in 2006 (Buncefield) were progressed some way by the lawyers without the need to invoke the court's assistance or the GLO procedure; once various aspects had clarified, the GLO procedure was invoked in order to manage specific disputes.

16 Notably Myodil contrast medium, Opren, haemophiliacs with HIV, Gamagard, human growth hormone.

17 Legal aid, previously extensive, was deconstructed during the 1990s and replaced by conditional fee agreements (CFAs) linked to insurance policies for costs. Significant teething problems have been encountered with the CFA and insurance systems, both technical aspects and in the marketing activities of some intermediaries, and also with the front-loading of costs required by the CPR. Recently, third party investors have been fast emerging as investors in litigation, and the landscape may undergo considerable change.

court control of processes through case management and judicial discretion. Some of these issues are not without sometimes vigorous debate.[18]

2. COMPENSATION SCHEMES

The CPR emphasises its encouragement for parties to settle their disputes through direct negotiation, if necessary assisted by informal and professional structures of alternative dispute resolution (ADR), notably mediation. A rich range and variety of dispute resolution schemes exist[19] operated by business organisations. These often involve codes of conduct, which may be formally approved by the OFT,[20] under a Consumer Codes Approval Scheme.[21] Under recent legislation, suppliers in the energy and postal services sectors are required to belong to redress schemes that provide for complaint resolution and awards of compensation when warranted, and estate agents are required to belong to an independent approved ombudsman scheme.[22]

Various schemes exist in relation to health claims. Two very large personal injury compensation schemes were created by the government in the 1990s after test cases established liability, one for lung diseases due to inhaling coal dust and the second for hand injuries due to operating vibrating machinery. England is shortly to introduce a medical injury compensation scheme.[23]

A range of ombudsmen exists.[24] The Financial Ombudsman Service (FOS) has been very active in resolving disputes between consumers and financial

18 R. Mulheron, *The Class Action in Common Law Legal Systems: A Comparative Perspective* (Hart Publishing, 2004).

19 *United Kingdom, Challenges at the Cutting Edge*, (OECD, Paris, 2002). J. Stuyck and others, *Commission Study on alternative means of consumer redress other than redress through ordinary judicial proceedings* (Catholic University of Leuven, 17 January, 2007, issued April 2007).

20 Enterprise Act 2002, s. 8.

21 *Consumer Codes Approval Scheme: Core Criteria and Guidance* (OFT, 2004). The British Association of Removers is a recent example of an approved code, which includes financial protection such as money back guarantees of up to 150% if a member cancels a removal at short notice or ceases to trade, plus an obligation on all members to use fair terms and conditions, and formal procedures for dealing with consumer complaints and a conciliation service: see www.oft.gov.uk/news/press/2008/26-08. Other approved codes are those of the Society for Motor Manufacturers and Traders, the Vehicle Builders and Repairers Association Ltd., the Direct Selling Association and the Carpet Foundation.

22 The Consumers, Estate Agents and Redress Act, 2007.

23 NHS Redress Act 2005.

24 A recent list included 24 UK Ombudsmen, 30 other public complaint handling bodies and 50 public sector tribunals. The leading public sector ombudsmen are the Financial Services Ombudsman, the Parliamentary and Health Service Ombudsman, and the Local Government Ombudsman.

institutions, since its commencement in 2001.[25] It receives around 600,000 enquiries annually, which turn into some 94,000 cases. Many cases are settled through mediation, failing which an Ombudsman makes a finding, which may be up to an award of £100,000 and is binding on institutions, although it may be appealed (only 8% of cases are). The system handles more contested cases than County Courts, excluding family cases, and is notably successful in resolving cases swiftly and at no cost to claimants. The costs are paid by financial institutions through levies and case fees.

The FOS has developed a series of techniques to deal with mass problems, notably the lead case, test case and the 'Wider Implications' procedure. If the FOS identifies that there exists a group of cases that involve a common principle, which usually involves claims against an individual provider, such as over standard terms, it will identify an individual case that will be dispositive of the issue and decide that. Even though the result of the lead case would not be formally binding on any other case, the experience has been that it is swiftly followed by resolution of all other similar cases, either through offers of payment or being dropped by consumers.

Secondly, if the FOS identifies that one or more cases turn purely on a point of law, and the provider agrees to pay the consumer's costs, a test case can be referred to the High Court for authoritative, binding determination.

Finally, if there is a new issue with significant implications for consumers in general, or for industry, or even for one business, and the implications involve the Financial Services Authority, FOS or the Office of Fair Trading (OFT), these bodies may invoke the Wider Implications procedure, and decide informally whether one of them should take official action or whether the FOS should instigate a special procedure.[26] The latter has been designed to parallel how issues would be dealt with in court, involving an open due process involving written briefs and assistance from experts.[27]

These mechanisms provide powerful routes to resolve mass issues. Emphasis on ADR is consistent with policy on the promotion of self-regulation by business.[28] British regimes follow the policy that self-regulation will be most effective when subject to public oversight based on systems control, transparency and

---

25 The FOS was created as an umbrella organisation at the same time as the FSA, and combined various sectoral bodies, stretching back to the Insurance Ombudsman scheme of 1981, the Banking Ombudsman of 1985 and the Personal Investment Authority Ombudsman after 1988.

26 See www.wider-implications.info.

27 As at December 2007 there were about 10 such case studies, and 12 refused.

28 I. Bartle and P. Vass, *Self-Regulation and the Regulatory State – A Survey of Policy and Practice* (Centre for the Study of Regulated Industries, University of Bath School of Management, 2005). The government's Better Regulation Task Force published a sequence of reports pressing the advantages of self-regulation between 1999 and 2005.

accountability.[29] In other words, an appropriate 'big stick' will encourage compliance but need not require frequent use under the right conditions and is preferable to 'punitive' approaches to regulation.[30]

3. POWERS OF PUBLIC AUTHORITIES AND CONSUMER BODIES

Enforcement of consumer protection law and of competition law reveals a sophisticated and evolving matrix of mechanisms. There is a clear emphasis on enforcement by public bodies. Although private consumer bodies can possess certain enforcement powers, the number of organisations, the subject matter of substantive provisions which they may enforce, and their powers and mode of operation are all strictly limited and controlled. Governmental policy documents may include rhetoric on empowerment of consumers and consumer bodies, but the reality of enforcement rests firmly on public structures. Indeed, given the general effectiveness of the public authorities, of which there are now quite a number at both national and local level, there is little enthusiasm on the part of consumer associations for assuming wider or significant enforcement roles.

3.1. COMPENSATION ORDERS IN CRIMINAL PROCEEDINGS

Any public authority has power to seek a compensation order from the courts as part of the criminal enforcement process. Criminal courts possess a general power to order a person convicted of an offence to pay compensation for any personal injury, loss or damage resulting from that offence, or any other offence that is taken into consideration by the court in determining sentence.[31] Such compensation shall be such amount as the court considers appropriate, having regard to any evidence and representations made.[32] If a person in whose favour a compensation order is made also claims damages in civil proceedings, such damages shall be assessed without regard to the compensation order, but the claimant may only recover an amount equal to the aggregate of any amount by

29 A. I. Ogus, 'Rethinking Self-Regulation' 15 *Oxford J. Legal Stud.* 97–108 (1995); J Black, 'Constitutionalising Self-regulation', 59 *Mod. L. Rev.* 24–55 (1996); I Bartle, above.

30 R. Baldwin, 'The New Punitive Regulation' (2004) 67(3) *Modern Law Review* 351–383.

31 Powers of Criminal Courts (Sentencing) Act 2000, s. 130. The power originated in the Powers of Criminal Courts Act 1973, before which it was used in serious crime and damage to property: see P. S. Atiyah, J. N. Adams and H. L. MacQueen, *The Sale of Goods* (Pearson Education, 11th ed., 2005).

32 Ibid, s. 130(4). Compensation ordered by a magistrates' court may not exceed £5,000, but higher courts are not subject to a limit.

which the award of damages exceeds the compensation order or a sum equal to any portion of the compensation which he fails to recover.[33] The compensation order mechanism has not been widely used but is currently receiving renewed attention.

3.2. SPECIFIC POWERS ON RESTITUTION

The Financial Services Authority has a significant armoury of combined criminal, administrative and civil enforcement powers, including the power to request the court to order restitution to firms and individuals.[34] This power is not often used and an important reason for this is the existence of the FOS, discussed above.

3.3. ENFORCEMENT OF EU CONSUMER PROTECTION LAW

Various measures of Community law provide enforcement mechanisms. As Regulation 2006/2004 on consumer protection cooperation (the CPCR) recognises, Member States have different traditions in respect of whether primary (or sole) responsibility for enforcement rests with public authorities or with private consumer representative bodies.[35] Although a number of measures have included requirements that certain enforcement functions are to be undertaken by consumer associations, the most significant recent policy development has been a mandatory requirement for all Member States to have public authorities in order to operate a mutual recognition cross-border enforcement system.

As mentioned above, the UK approach rests firmly on the public authority model. Thus, the Office of Fair Trading (OFT) is designated as the Single Liaison Office for the CPCR. The OFT occupies a pivotal position in relation to enforcement of both consumer protection and competition law, assisted by local authorities' Trading Standards Departments and sectoral regulators. The authorities possess extensive powers, expertise and resources. It may be notable that for some years the only cross-border injunction sought or obtained under the Injunctions Directive was instituted by the UK regulator rather than by a consumer organisation.[36]

---

33 Ibid, s. 134.

34 Financial Services and Markets Act 2000, ss. 382 and 383.

35 J. Stuyck and others, *Commission Study on alternative means of consumer redress other than redress through ordinary judicial proceedings* (Catholic University of Leuven, 17 January, 2007, issued April 2007). This important study includes reports from every EU Member State plus the USA, Canada and Australia on the range of existing mechanisms.

36 The case was brought by the Office of Fair Trading against a Belgian company that was sending unsolicited mail order catalogues to UK residents together with notifications of a prize win,

All enforcers of consumer protection law are given powers to apply to the courts for enforcement orders against businesses infringing any of a wide range of consumer protection laws.[37] Importantly, consultation with the business is required unless action is urgent and consultation should normally last for at least 14 days. There is a distinction between general enforcers (the OFT and local authorities),[38] enforcers designated by the Secretary of State[39] and Community enforcers.[40] The OFT has been given the coordinating role of ensuring that action is taken by the most appropriate body. Some of the designated enforcers have general designation (can bring cases in all matters) whilst others have limited designation (can bring cases within the scope of this designation). The OFT may direct that if an application to the court in respect of a particular infringement is to be made, it must be made only by the OFT or such other enforcer as the OFT directs,[41] although this does not prevent an application for an enforcement order being made by a Community enforcer.[42] Breach of an enforcement order is a contempt of court and can incur a fine or imprisonment. An enforcer or the court has power to accept an undertaking from a person to comply.[43]

Thus, there is a strong emphasis on public enforcement, with the OFT retaining overall control and a right of veto save in cross-border Community action and only one consumer association having been designated so far. UK implementation of the various EU consumer protection provisions is summarised in the following table.

---

usually £10,000. The Belgian court issued an order banning the practice as constituting a breach of the Misleading Advertising Directive, on the basis that consumers believed that they had only to make a purchase in order to secure a prize, whereas winners were pre-selected and few recipients would receive a prize. The company was reported to have received about 4,000 orders per day from its catalogues, and many consumers complained: press release at www.oft.gov.uk/News/Press+releases/2004/208-04.htm, and see *Report from the Commission: First Annual Progress Report on European Contract Law and the Acquis Review*, COM (2005) 456, 23 September 2005. *OFT v. D Duchesne SA* referred to in *TS Today* February 2006, 4.

37 The principal statute is the Enterprise Act 2002, Part 8, which implements the Injunctions Directive and the CPCR.

38 Enterprise Act 2002, s. 213(1).

39 Ibid, s. 213(2). The Secretary of State may designate bodies that have protection of the collective interests of consumers as one of their purposes. As at 2007 the following had been designated: The Civil Aviation Authority; The Director General of Electricity Supply for Northern Ireland; The Director General of Gas for Northern Ireland; Ofcom; The Water Services Regulation Authority; The Gas and Electricity Markets Authority; The Information Commissioner; The Office of Rail Regulation; The Financial Services Authority; Consumers' Association (Which?). A public body will only be granted designated enforcement powers if it is independent: DTI guidance at www.dti.gov.uk/files/file11976.pdf.

40 Enterprise Act 2002, s. 213(5). Community enforcers are qualified entities for the purposes of the Injunctions Directive (based in other EEA states) and specified in the list published in the Official Journal of the European Communities.

41 Enterprise Act 2002, s. 216.

42 Ibid, s. 216(6).

43 Enterprise Act 2002, s. 219 and 217(9).

EU legislation	UK legislation
Directive 84/450/EEC on misleading advertising[44]	Control of Misleading Advertisements Regulations 1988, SI 1988 No 915[45]
Directive 93/13/EEC on unfair contract terms[46]	The Unfair Terms in Consumer Contracts Regulations 1999, SI 1999 No 2083, Schedule 1, Part Two.[47]
Directive 98/27/EC on cross-border injunctions for breach of specified consumer protection[48]	Enterprise Act 2002, Part 8, especially ss. 212 and 221: Enforcement Order[49]
Regulation 2006/2004 on consumer protection cooperation[50]	Enterprise Act 2002, Part 8, especially ss. 212 and 221: Enforcement Order
Directive 2005/29/EC on unfair business-to-consumer commercial practices (UCP), article 4[51]	Consumer Protection from Unfair Trading Regulations 2008[52]

Only the consumers' association, Which?, has been granted approval as a designated body in relation to taking action against infringements under the Unfair Terms in Consumer Contracts legislation.[53] The OFT has been

44 Replaced as of 12 December 2007 by Directive 2006/114 on misleading and comparative advertising. (OJ L 250, 19 September 1984, p. 17–20), amended by Directive 97/55/EC of the European Parliament and of the Council of 6 October 1997 amending Directive 84/450/EEC concerning misleading advertising so as to include comparative advertising (OJ L 290, 23 October 1997, p. 18–23); web link to consolidated version: http://eur-lex.europa.eu/LexUriServ/LexUriServ.do?uri=CELEX:31984L0450:EN:NOT.

45 web link: www.opsi.gov.uk/SI/si1988/Uksi_19880915_en_1.htm.

46 OJ L 95, 21 April 1993, p.29–34, web link: http://eur-lex.europa.eu/LexUriServ/LexUriServ.do?uri=CELEX:31993L0013:EN:NOT.

47 web link: www.opsi.gov.uk/si/si1999/19992083.htm.

48 OJ L 166, 11 June 1998, p. 51–55, web link: http://eur-lex.europa.eu/LexUriServ/LexUriServ.do?uri=CELEX:31998L0027:EN:NOT.

49 web link: www.opsi.gov.uk/acts/acts2002/20020040.htm.

50 OJ L 364, 9 December 2004, p. 1–11, web link: http://eur-lex.europa.eu/LexUriServ/LexUriServ.do?uri=CELEX:32004R2006:EN:NOT.

51 OJ L 149, 11 June 2005, p. 22–39, web link: http://eur-lex.europa.eu/LexUriServ/LexUriServ.do?uri=CELEX:32005L0029:EN:NOT.

52 I. 2008 No. 1277, www.opsi.gov.uk/si/si2008/draft/pdf/ukdsi_9780110811574_en.pdf. Consultation paper at www.oft.gov.uk/shared_oft/reports/consumer_protection/oft931con.pdf.

53 The Unfair Terms in Consumer Contracts Regulations 1999, SI 1999 No 2083, Schedule 1, Part Two. This was after the Consumers' Association brought a judicial review against the government for failure to implement the Directive correctly, and the government caved in: see Case C-82/96 *R v Secretary of State for Trade and Industry ex parte Consumers' Association and Which? Limited.*

particularly active in attacking unfair contract terms[54] and Which? has referred cases to the OFT but not taken enforcement proceedings itself.[55]

3.4. COMPETITION LAW MECHANISMS

Two innovative mechanisms were introduced in UK competition law in 2002.[56] First, a designated consumer body may make a "super-complaint" to the regulator, the OFT, that any feature, or combination of features, of a market in the UK for goods or services is or appears to be significantly harming the interests of consumers.[57] It is the relevant public authority,[58] rather than the consumer body, which is empowered to take any subsequent action, so the private body acts as a watchdog, but the OFT must publish a response explaining its position.[59] The power to designate a consumer body for these purposes rests with the Secretary of State, who may do so only if it appears to him to represent the interests of consumers of any description and only subject to any other criteria which he has published.[60]

---

54 See Bulletins on many enforcement actions taken and Guidance issued at www.oft.gov.uk/advice_and_resources/resource_base/consumer-regulations/443727/446883/443845/445427. A recent leading example is a test case between the OFT and the consumer banks over whether charges for unauthorised overdrafts are subject to the Unfair Terms in Consumer Contract Regulations, and hence unfair: OFT press release, 31 August 2007.

55 See for example estate agents in 2007, www.which.co.uk/reports_and_campaigns/house_and_home/Reports/utilities_and_services/Estate_agents_contracts_news_article_557_89603.jsp.

56 Www.ukincorp.co.uk/s-BM-9-enterprise-act-2002.html.

57 Enterprise Act 2002, s. 11.

58 The authorities that have a duty to respond to super-complaints are: OFT (general authority), the Civil Aviation Authority (responsibility for traffic services under the Transport Act 2000), the Office of Gas and Electricity Markets (OFGEM, responsibility for gas and electricity services under the Gas Act 1986 and Electricity Act 1989 amended by the Utilities Act 2000), the Office of Telecommunications (OFTEL, responsibility for telecommunications industry under the Telecommunications Act 1984 – a role now taken over by the Office of Communications (OFCOM)), the Northern Ireland Authority for Energy Regulation (OFREG-NI), the Office of Water Services (OFWAT) and the Office of the Rail Regulator (ORR).

59 The response must be published within 90 days of the super-complaint being received. Possible consequences include enforcement action, a market study or a market investigation by the authorities, or a finding that the complaint requires no action, it is unfounded or frivolous.

60 Enterprise Act 2002, s. 11. Guidance for bodies wishing to apply for such designated status is at www.oft.gov.uk/NR/rdonlyres/98D1E0AD-11C1-4997-BA27-26C9D93F7487/0/oft514.pdf. So far the organisations designated are The Consumers' Association, National Consumer Council and Citizens Advice (designated in July 2004), Energywatch and Watervoice (both designated in January 2005), Postwatch, CAMRA and the General Consumer Council of Northern Ireland (all designated in October 2005).

A super-complaint must be accompanied by facts and evidence.[61] Super-complaints have been made in relation to private dentistry, doorstep selling, consolidation of postal services, care homes, home collected credit and payment protection insurance.[62]

Secondly, any person who has suffered loss as a result of an infringement may institute a claim for damages before the specialist competition court, the Competition Appeal Tribunal (CAT).[63] Multiple individual claims that all relate to the same infringement may be brought in a representative capacity by a "specified body".[64] The mechanism is a typical 'follow on' type – it must have been established by either the OFT or the European Commission that an infringement of competition law has occurred.[65] Each individual must also consent to the claim being brought.

An award is normally to be paid to individual consumers, although there is a possibility for CAT to arrange for the award to be paid to the specified body that will then enforce the award (the latter is possible if all individual consumers and the specified body are in agreement). Any award of costs or expenses against a specified body in these proceedings may not be enforced against any individual on whose behalf a claim was made or continued in those proceedings.[66]

The Consumers' Association has so far brought one collective damages claim, which has highlighted various issues with the procedure. The case followed a finding that various companies were involved in a cartel to fix the prices of replica football T-shirts.[67] The level of individual loss was small (perhaps £15) and some consumers obtained payments under offers made by the company; very few signed up to bring individual claims. The case was settled in 2008.[68]

---

61 OFT Guidance *Super-complaints: Guidance for designated consumer bodies* specifies. The facts and evidence do not need to be comprehensive enough for the regulators to immediately start proceedings. They are only to help the OFT or other regulator decide whether and what action is appropriate. They must, however, provide a reasoned case – frivolous complaints will be rejected. An annex to the guidance provides an indicative list of evidence to be considered.

62 Www.oft.gov.uk/Business/Super-complaints/cases.htm.

63 Competition Act 1998, s. 47A & B.

64 As with the other mechanisms discussed above, specification is made by the Secretary of State on the basis of published criteria, for which guidance is at www.dti.gov.uk/files/file11957.pdf.

65 This is known as a 'follow on' claim, as opposed to a 'stand alone' claim.

66 Enterprise Act 2002, Schedule 4, cl. 7.

67 See www.which.co.uk/reports_and_campaigns/consumer_rights/campaigns/Football%20 shirts/index.jsp.

68 Details at www.which.co.uk/reports_and_campaigns/consumer_rights/campaigns/ Football%20shirts/index.jsp.

4. DEVELOPING LINKAGES BETWEEN CONSUMER, COMPETITION AND ECONOMIC POLICY

In the early years of the new millennium, the UK government made a strong link between, on the one hand, enforcement of consumer protection and competition regulation, and, on the other hand, competitive markets. In the 2005 Consumer White Paper, the government set out "a strategy to empower consumers and support business success" for the next 5–10 years:[69]

> "We have rejected the old-fashioned idea that businesses need to be routinely regulated and inspected to keep them in line. The vast majority of businesses want to act responsibly. The pressure to attract and retain customers is a far more powerful and effective incentive on business to act with integrity and responsibility than anything Central or Local Government can do."[70]
>
> "Our consumer regime will be based on the principle of proportionate, risk-assessed and evidence-based intervention. Instead of regulating and inspecting on a routine all-inclusive basis, we want to see more effort targeted on rogue traders, and a lighter touch for mainstream responsible businesses."[71]

An international comparison carried out by the UK had found that the UK consumer policy regime was amongst the best in several areas, but behind other countries in having a more fragmented enforcement framework that led to inconsistent enforcement.[72]

It was said that where brand reputation plays little role, settlement by traders may depend on the ease of access by consumers to advice on remedies and use of "small claims" courts and any mechanism for alternative dispute resolution (ADR) which is available to consumers. Important innovations stemming from the Consumer White Paper were the establishment of a national first point of contact for consumers, called Consumer Direct, which refers consumers to high quality specialist advice and redress services,[73] and a proposal aimed at slimming

---

69 *A Fair Deal for All. Extending Competitive Markets: Empowered Consumers, Successful Business* (Department of Trade and Industry, 2005). See also Consultation Document *Extending Competitive Markets: Empowered Consumers, Successful Business* (Department of Trade and Industry, 2004); *Empowering Consumers in the Enterprise economy: The Enterprise Bill Consumer Measures* (Department of Trade and Industry, 2002).

70 *A Fair Deal for All. Extending Competitive Markets: Empowered Consumers, Successful Business* (Department of Trade and Industry, 2005), para. 1.2.

71 *A Fair Deal for All. Extending Competitive Markets: Empowered Consumers, Successful Business* (Department of Trade and Industry, 2005), para. 1.9.

72 *Comparative Report on Consumer Policy Regimes*, (Department of Trade and Industry, October 2003).

73 Www.consumerdirect.gov.uk.

down seven consumer bodies into a single body, Consumer Voice.[74] Significant effort has been put into consumer education, particularly access to information on rights, responsibilities and options on redress.[75] However, wide variations were identified in accessibility, standards and performance of dispute resolution mechanisms.[76]

5. A REVOLUTIONARY POLICY LINKING ENFORCEMENT AND REDRESS POLICIES

The UK government has recently established policies on enforcement that have profound implications, not merely for enforcement but also for compensation. The primary policy is that of encouraging economic health and competitiveness. Amongst various ways in which this primary policy is encouraged[77] are reducing administrative burdens,[78] adopting a risk-based and impact-assessment[79] approach towards regulation and enforcement,[80] which is aligned to the government's view of a contemporary world in which competition is fierce, consumers are better informed, and resources are scarce.[81]

---

74 *Strengthen and Streamline Consumer Advocacy: Consultation on consumer representation and redress* (Department of Trade and Industry, (2006). This estimated that expenditure of £29.9 million on the seven bodies could be reduced by £18.0 million.

75 *Consumer education: A strategy and framework*, (Office of Fair Trading, 2004).

76 *Seeking Resolution* (National Consumer Council, 2004).

77 See C.J.S. Hodges, 'Encouraging Enterprise and Rebalancing Risk: Implications of Economic Policy for Regulation, Enforcement and Compensation' [2007] *European Business Law Review* 1231.

78 It has been estimated that UK small businesses spend 9.5% of their total working time ensuring compliance with regulations, excluding regulations on tax, employment relations, health and safety, and environmental issues: F. Chittenden, S. Kauser & P. Poutziouris, *Regulatory Burdens of Small Business: A Literature Review* (Small Business Research Trust). That study also found that in businesses with less than 20 employees, the compliance costs were at least 35% higher than for firms with more than 500 staff. It further found that governments had yet to discover how to reduce this relatively higher burden, which led to the small business sector and the economies of the countries studied being smaller than they otherwise would be: see also G. Bannock and A. Peacock, *Governments and Small Businesses* (Paul Chapman Publishing, London, 1989), p 17.

79 *Better Policy Making: A Guide to Regulatory Impact Assessment* (Cabinet Office, 2003); *The Tools to Deliver Better Regulation: Revising the Regulatory Impact Assessment: A Consultation* (Cabinet Office, Better Regulation Executive, July 2006).

80 P. Hampton, *Reducing administrative burdens: effective inspection and enforcement* (H M Treasury, 2005). See also *Less is More: Reducing Burdens, Improving Outcomes* (Better Regulation Task Force, 2006). *Moving Towards The Local Better Regulation Office: The way ahead* (Department for Trade and Industry, 2005).

81 HM Treasury, Better Regulation Executive, and Cabinet Office, *Implementing Hampton: from enforcement to compliance*, November 2006.

'It is no longer true that most businesses, if unregulated, will act irresponsibly. Well-informed consumers, corporate social responsibility, organised labour, pressure and interest groups have all encouraged businesses to take measures to reduce risk to society.'

> 'Underpinning the review's recommendations on advice was the principle that regulators should also support economic progress by only intervening where there was a clear case for protection, as well as taking action to encourage economic growth where possible. Therefore it is important that regulators take responsibility for any costs that they bring to businesses and work to minimise them. Regulators should also be held accountable for their effectiveness.'[82]

The Legal and Regulatory Reform Act 2006 imposes a duty on specified regulators[83] to exercise their regulatory functions in accordance with five principles of good regulation (the Hampton principles), namely that activities must be carried out in a way that is transparent, accountable, proportionate and consistent.[84] Regulatory activities should be targeted only at cases in which action is needed.[85] That Act contains powers to enable the Hampton principles to be established in UK law through a Statutory Code of Practice for Regulators.[86]

This approach is based on the philosophy that risk assessment should comprehensively underpin regulatory and enforcement policy. This seeks ways in which the administrative burden of regulation on business can be reduced, while maintaining or improving regulatory outcomes. An important finding by Hampton was that regulators lack effective tools to punish persistent offenders and reward compliant behaviour by business.[87]

The risk assessment policy is expressly based on the 'responsive regulation' theory.[88] In propounding this theory, Ayres and Braithwaite defined an 'enforcement pyramid', with a peak sanction of removal from society (removal of liberty or licence to operate) and a broad base of simple, low key discussions, up to which regulators would progress depending on the seriousness of the regulatory risk and the non-compliance of the regulated business. They argued that regulatory compliance was best secured by persuasion in the first instance, with inspection,

---

82 HM Treasury, Better Regulation Executive, and Cabinet Office *Implementing Hampton: from enforcement to compliance*, November 2006, p. 32.

83 See The Legislative and Regulatory Reform (Regulatory Functions) Order 2007, SI 2007/3544.

84 S. 21.

85 Ibid.

86 Published by the Department for Business, Enterprise and Regulatory Reform on 17 December 2007, www.berr.gov.uk/files/file45019.pdf. This Code replaces the previous Enforcement Concordat.

87 Hampton, above, para 7.

88 I. Ayres and J. Braithwaite, *Responsive Regulation: Transcending the Deregulation Debate* (Oxford, 1992). J. Braithwaite, *Restorative Justice and Responsive Regulation* (Oxford, 2002).

enforcement notices and penalties being used for more risky businesses further up the pyramid.

This new thinking led to a review of policy on penalties, leading in two directions. First, there has been support for positive incentive schemes and for further self-regulation through the OFT's Consumer Codes Approval Scheme.[89] Secondly, a new approach is being introduced in relation to the sanctions used by public authorities.[90]

Most breaches will face penalties that are quicker and easier to apply while there will be tougher penalties for rogue businesses that persistently break the rules. Greater flexibility will be introduced so as to provide regulators with better deterrence options and therefore encourage compliance from business. Crucially, a link is also made between penalties and civil compensation: by removing any financial gain from failure to comply, a level playing field will be ensured for all businesses. Regulators are to be given access to civil sanctioning powers as well as criminal enforcement powers, which include the wider ability to apply to a court for a compensation order, referred to above, as part of their extended range of civil sanctions.[91]

Six Penalties Principles were identified in the Report by Macrory:

1. Aim to change the behaviour of the offender;
2. Aim to eliminate any financial gain or benefit from non-compliance;
3. Be responsive and consider what is appropriate for the particular offender and regulatory issue, which can include punishment and the public stigma that should be associated with a criminal conviction;
4. Be proportionate to the nature of the offence and the harm caused;
5. Aim to restore the harm caused by regulatory non-compliance, where appropriate; and
6. Aim to deter future non-compliance.

Principles 2 and 5 have clear links with private compensation law. In adopting a 'restorative justice' approach he focuses on a holistic process that addresses the repercussions and obligations created by harm with a view to putting things right.[92] The emphasis is on a *process* 'whereby those most directly affected by a wrongdoing come together to determine what needs to be done to repair the harm

---

89 See the government's Consumer Strategy: *Extending Competitive Markets: Empowered Consumers, Successful Business*, Department of Trade and Industry, 2004 at www.dti.gov.uk/ccp/topics1/consumer_strategy.htm.

90 Adopting the Report by R. Macrory, *Regulatory Justice: making sanctions effective* (2006).

91 Regulatory Enforcement and Sanctions Act 2008.

92 Para 4.32.

and prevent a reoccurrence'.[93] Even though Macrory's approach was focused on sanctioning from the regulatory and compliance perspective[94] and not from the perspective of compensation, it is likely that the implications in relation to compensation will lead to further developments in government policy. A large number of public authorities have now been given power to make civil restitution orders, which can include compensation, under s 42 of the Regulatory Enforcement and Sanctions Act. Government has recently recognised that progress can be made in the area of collective redress, and the queue for legislation and its associated delays can be avoided, merely by amending general enforcement policy and guidelines.

A recent example of the new approach is the imposition of a lower fine by the broadcasting regulator, Ofcom, on a company in breach of various provisions of the Broadcasting Code and ITC Programme Code arising out of phone-in competitions. Ofcom stated that the fine of £2,000,000 would have been higher if the company had not taken a series of remedial steps, including the resignation of responsible officers, strengthening of compliance systems and offering refunds to individuals in relation to a potential 25 million entries, plus making a £250,000 donation to a children's charity. This combination of the use of regulatory muscle in achieving compliance, responsive sanctioning and provision of compensation to individuals can be seen to provide effective, comprehensive redress speedily and at low cost without running the risk of incurring transactional costs of intermediaries and burdening the court system. As analysed above, 'redress' in this context comprises both regulatory control and provision of compensation, and the mechanism adopted delivers both.

6. AN UNFINISHED STORY: SCOPE FOR A UNIFIED APPROACH?

There has been considerable discussion about collective redress in the past three years. Some have argued exclusively for extension and greater facilitation of court-based collective damages actions.[95] This approach has coincided with promotion

---

93 *Restorative Justice and Practices* – presented at 'Restorative Justice in Action ... into the Mainstream', The 3rd International Winchester Restorative Justice Group Conference, 29th and 30th March 2006, London: quoted in Macrory, above, para 4.33.

94 Macrory recommended wider use of Profit Orders to address the level of illicit gain by an offender, Confiscation Orders under the Proceeds of Crime Act 2002, and the introduction of Corporate Rehabilitation Orders, designed to address a company's poor practices and prevent future non-compliance, such as through commitment to a plan of action to remedy a matter.

95 Proposals of the Civil Justice Council of England and Wales on reform of funding systems, February 2006. M. Napier and others, *Improved Access to Justice – Funding Options & Proportionate Costs*, (Civil Justice Council, 2007). See www.civiljusticecouncil.gov.uk/publications/publications.htm.

by the competition authorities in the European Commission[96] and the UK[97] of the enlistment of damages actions as an additional regulatory enforcement tool on the assumptions that compliance with competition law is insufficient, and that the appropriate response is to increase deterrence through increasing financial burdens, thereby forcing greater costs to be internalised. Some have criticised an absence of empirical evidence that would establish these assumptions.[98] Others have argued that there is a need for court-based opt-out class actions.[99]

The government may take steps to improve certain of the collective mechanisms that currently exist, but it is strongly mindful of the political imperative of avoiding a charge of fuelling a litigation culture. For example, it might appear initially attractive to devise a collective approach towards small claims, whether under the small claims mechanism or the fast track mechanism. But such a course would encounter the problem that the amounts at stake are so low in comparison to the costs of coordinated action that costs would be disproportionate and hence lawyers would benefit rather than consumers. That conclusion underpins a policy that providing individual restitution and access to justice is less important than ensuring that the market operates effectively: in other words, it should be more of a priority to remove 'skimmed off' profits than to provide private actions for recovery of compensation. Accordingly, the logic would follow that regulatory responses are of greater importance than providing compensation for small sums, especially where anti-competitive behaviour (as opposed to breach of other consumer protection provisions) is involved.

However, the Hampton and Macrory policies offer the opportunity of a holistic approach to both encouragement of compliance, responsive regulation, risk-based action, and provision of restitution and compensation, as illustrated by the Ofcom example above. Instead of viewing collective redress in terms solely of private court actions and damages, the latest thinking points towards development of an integrated matrix of public and private actors and procedures. More detailed analysis is being undertaken but there is a genuinely exciting possibility of providing increased behavioural compliance, increased access to justice, increased restitution, and lower costs for regulators, business, consumers and courts.

---

96 Green Paper: damages actions for breach of the EC antitrust rules, COM (2005) 672, 19 December 2005; Commission Staff Working Paper: Annex to the Green Paper 'Damages actions for breach of the EC antitrust rules', SEC(2005) 1732, 19 December 2005.

97 *Private actions in competition law: effective redress for consumers and business. Recommendations*, Office of Fair Trading, November 2007. www.oft.gov.uk/shared_oft/reports/comp_policy/oft916resp.pdf.

98 C. J. S. Hodges, 'Competition enforcement, regulation and civil justice: what is the case?' *Common Market Law Review* 43: 1381–1407, 2006.

99 R. Mulheron, *The Class Action in Common Law Legal Systems: A Comparative Perspective* (Hart Publishing, 2004). R. Mulheron, *Reform of Collective Redress in England and Wales: A Perspective of Need*, 2008, available at www.civiljusticecouncil.gov.uk/files/collective_redress.pdf.

The vision would place enforcement by public authorities in a primary position, albeit not on an exclusive or comprehensive basis. Self-regulation and voluntary schemes of dispute resolution would also be encouraged by ombudsmen (akin to the FOS), and business codes of conduct or schemes. Court-based private collective actions would have their place, but would be regarded as long-stops and not encouraged, partly in order to avoid adverse consequences of high transactional costs and abuse. Voluntary adoption of virtuous behaviour would be encouraged by the existence of adequate, but flexible 'big sticks'. Unlike the USA, the 'big stick' would not be that of private class litigation, but would primarily be that of public authorities, which would operate on a far more immediate, flexible and responsive basis, involving incentives for restitution rather than delayed weighty financial penalties. Thus, there would be a shift from *ex post* towards what would be largely *ex ante* behavioural control. This approach ticks most of the boxes. It is sophisticated and encouraging of virtuous behaviour and of the economy.

In evaluating how a sensible balance should be set between public and private mechanisms, more discussion is becoming based on academic thinking and an evidence-based approach. The position is still developing, but the future looks interesting.

TAKING THE COLLECTIVE INTEREST OF CONSUMERS SERIOUSLY: A VIEW FROM POLAND

Marek SAFJAN*, Łukasz GORYWODA** and Agnieszka JAŃCZUK***

1. INTRODUCTION

Over the last decades markets have been developing rapidly. On the one hand, market developments have provided consumers with immense welfare gains; on the other, they have also brought about new types of harm, mainly related to mass production and novel types of market practices. Among those new types of negative externalities generated by market transactions, 'collective harm' is of particular importance because of its strong adverse effects on the functioning of consumer markets.

Collective harm refers to situations where multiple consumers suffer harm caused by the same or similar detrimental behaviour of a trader or service provider. In situations of collective harm, consumers who have small or scattered claims often refrain from bringing an individual court action because the cost is likely to outweigh the amount of damages claimed. As a policy response to collective harm resulting in under-enforcement of consumer rights, various mechanisms of collective redress have been developed in the Member States (hereinafter: for Member State 'MSs').

At the European Union (hereinafter: the 'EU') level, collective redress has been on the agenda for some time.[1] Recently, it has received increased interest

---

* Professor of Civil Law, Warsaw University; Former President of the Constitutional Tribunal of Poland. This paper was written during Professor Marek Safjan's Fernand Braudel Senior Fellowship at the European University Institute, Law Department (1 April 2007 – 31 January 2008).

** PhD Candidate, European University Institute.

*** PhD Candidate, European University Institute.

1 As early as 1984 it was stressed that '[o]ne aspect of the Community's concern for its citizens is its interest in access to justice, in particular the right to obtain a just and fair settlement of disputes arising out of ordinary consumer transactions.' European Commission, 'Discussion paper: Consumer redress. Memorandum from the Commission' COM(84) 629 final, 12 December 1984, I. In 1998 the European Commission acknowledged that access to justice for consumers in pursuing their complaints is imperfect and it might be useful to consider whether measures are needed to make it easier for consumers to take legal action collectively

from policy makers, academics and the public at large due to the fact that the European Commission (hereinafter: the 'Commission') has intensified its work on designing a strategy concerning collective redress.[2] Collective redress, as part of a more general programme of improving the consumer access to justice, has become one of the priorities of EU consumer policy. This also marks a shift from the substance-oriented to enforcement-oriented perspective of consumer policy.[3]

It has been recognised that substantial input is needed for any subsequent decision on possible policy action in order to help steer the future work of the Commission in this field.[4] It is beyond doubt that some part of this input should come from the analysis of the existing schemes of collective redress already present at the MSs level. This follows from the assumption that disregarding national experiences related to collective redress may undermine the effectiveness of future EU strategy.

Various forms of collective redress already exist in a number of MSs and others are currently considering the options of introducing them. Collective redress systems at the MSs level are all rather different.[5] In particular, the balance between public and private enforcement has changed over time in each MS and varies between them.[6] Another characteristic of the current state of play is that in the EU actions for injunctive relief are widespread but collective actions for

when they have suffered similar damage; see European Commission, 'Consumer Policy Action Plan 1999–2001' (Communication) COM(98) 696 final, 1 December 1998, 18.

2 In the Consumer Policy Strategy 2007–2013 the Commission announced that it would consider action on collective redress; see European Commission, 'EU Consumer Policy Strategy 2007–2013 'Empowering consumers, enhancing their welfare, effectively protecting them'' (Communication) COM(2007) 99 final, 13 March 2007, [5.3], 11. Consultation on the consumer collective redress benchmarks was organised by the Directorate General for Health and Consumer Protection ('DG SANCO') in the first quarter of 2008. On 18 November 2008 the Commission published a report on the application of Directive 98/27/EC of the European Parliament and of the Council on injunctions for the protection of consumers' interest, COM(2008) 756 final. On 27 November 2008 the Commission adopted the Green Paper on Consumer Collective Redress, COM(2008) 794 final.

3 It goes without saying that ineffective enforcement of consumer rights would undermine the objectives of EU consumer policy. This principle was already contained in the latin maxim *ubi ius ibi remedium*.

4 See (Director General for DG SANCO) R Madelin, 'Collective Redress (Remarks)' (Conference on Collective Redress in Lisbon, 9 November 2007) http://ec.europa.eu/consumers/redress_cons/docs/rm_cr_lLisbon_speak_09-%2011-07.pdf, accessed 15 March 2008.

5 See The Study Centre for Consumer Law – Centre for European Economic Law, 'An analysis and evaluation of alternative means of consumer redress other than redress through ordinary judicial proceedings. Final report' (Katholieke Universiteit Leuven, Belgium 17 January, 2007) http://ec.europa.eu/consumers/redress/reports_studies/comparative_report_en.pdf, accessed 15 March 2008. The Commission has also launched a study evaluating the effectiveness and efficiency of existing collective redress mechanisms.

6 It has been observed at the EU level that this balance should be respected as much as possible; see Madelin, 'Collective Redress (Remarks)' (n 4). More on possible constellations between civil and administrative measures see F. Cafaggi and H.-W. Micklitz, 'Collective Enforcement

damages are in a state of infancy.[7] Many of the differences between MSs stem also from their different administrative capacities.[8]

Relatively slow developments in the field of collective redress in Europe are partly due to a marked reluctance to and considerable critique of the US model of class action.[9] The core of this critique boils down to the collective pursuit of non-collective interests which characterises the US-type class action.[10] In contrast to this, the Commission's intention is to develop a form of collective redress which would pursue collective rather than individual interests of consumers.[11]

It seems surprising that despite the Commission's interest in the scheme of collective redress aimed at protecting the 'collective interest(s)' of consumers, no debate on the concept of collective interest, as an essential element of such a scheme, has developed. Moreover, the existing EU instruments aimed at facilitating consumer redress in cross-border situations, Directive 98/27 and

---

of Consumer Law: A Framework for Comparative Assessment' (2008) 16 *European Review of Private Law* 391.

7 J. Stuyck (Conference on Collective Redress in Leuven, 29 June 2007). Http://ec.europa.eu/consumers/redress_cons/docs/leuven_event_JSpresentation.pdf, accessed 15 March 2008. For an overview of the various models of consumer collective redress see Cafaggi and Micklitz ibid.

8 See, for example, C. Knill, 'European Policies: The Impact of National Administrative Traditions' (1998) 18 *Journal of Public Policy* 1.

9 In this paper we do not take a stance on the merits of this critique. Another reason for the slow developments concerning collective redress might be the principle of procedural autonomy, as articulated by the European Court of Justice (ECJ) since the 1976 *Rewe* case; see Case 33/76 *Rewe-Zentralfinanz eG et Rewe-Zentral AG v Landwirtschaftskammer für das Saarland* [1976] ECR 1989 and Case 45/76 *Comet v Produktschap* [1976] ECR 2043. However, some EU measures dealing with procedural law have already been adopted, see European Parliament and Council Directive (EC) 98/27 of 19 May 1998 on Injunctions for the Protection of Consumers' Interests, [1998] OJ L 166/51; European Parliament and Council Regulation (EC) 2006/2004 of 27 October 2004 on cooperation between national authorities responsible for the enforcement of consumer protection laws, [2004] OJ L 364/1; European Parliament and Council Directive (EC) 2004/48 of 29 April 2004 on the enforcement of intellectual property rights [2004] OJ L 157/45. On the procedural autonomy and consumer redress see G. Betlem, 'Public and Private Transnational Enforcement of EU Consumer Law', (2007) 18 *European Business Law Review* 683.

10 See Stuyck (n 7).

11 See Madelin, 'Collective Redress (Remarks)' (n 4) and M. Kuneva, 'Healthy markets need effective redress' (Speech at Conference on Collective Redress in Lisbon, 9 November 2007) http://ec.europa.eu/consumers/redress_cons/docs/mku_cr_lisbon_final.pdf, accessed 15 March 2008. The Economic & Social Committee adopted in 1979 a report requesting the Commission to take action by, *inter alia*, proposing a directive giving consumer associations the right to bring general interest actions (that is to say, to defend the interests of consumers collectively), even where no direct loss has been suffered. See European Commission, 'Memorandum from the Commission on Consumer Redress 1984' (n 1) VI. Already in 1993 the Commission clarified that '[t]he legal defence of collective interests is not to be confounded with the collective defence of individual interests – hence "class actions" are considered as a separate category'. European Commission, 'Access of Consumers to Justice and the Settlement of Consumer Disputes in the Single Market' (Green Paper) COM(93) 576 final, 16 November 1993, 15.

Regulation 2006/2004,[12] also employ the concept of collective interest of consumers.[13] However, so far no comprehensive strategy towards this concept at the EU level has been elaborated.[14] We argue that the lack of strategy concerning the collective interest, in particular its definition, makes it difficult to designate instruments that would effectively protect it. We also argue that an imprecise notion of collective interest, which does not go further than stating that it is not a mere sum of individual interests is problematic to be applied by the enforcers and consequently may lead to under-enforcement of consumer rights.[15]

A comprehensive strategy towards the collective interest is necessary both from the harmonisation and the accountability viewpoint. As to the former, clarification of the meaning of the concept of 'collective interest of consumers' might contribute to the harmonisation of enforcement practices and cooperation between enforcement bodies governed by Directive 98/27 and Regulation 2006/2004.[16] As to the latter, a clear notion of consumer collective interest could

---

12 Both n 9.

13 Recital 2 of Directive 98/27/EC: 'whereas collective interests mean interests which do not include the cumulation of interests of individuals who have been harmed by an infringement.' Article 3(k) of the Regulation 2006/2004: "'collective interests of consumers' means the interests of a number of consumers that have been harmed or are likely to be harmed by an infringement". Article 3(b) of the Regulation 2006/2004: '"intra-Community infringement" means any act or omission contrary to the laws that protect consumers' interests, as defined in (a), that harms, or is likely to harm, the collective interests of consumers residing in a Member State or Member States other than the Member State where the act or omission originated or took place, or where the responsible seller or supplier is established, or where evidence or assets pertaining to the act or omission are to be found.'

14 It could have been deliberately left for the European Court of Justice (hereinafter: the 'ECJ') to fill in the content of the concept. The Polish legislator, for example, intentionally copied out the vague definition from the Directive expecting that the ECJ might decide on the matter (cf. text accompanying n 82). So far, however, the ECJ has not delivered any ruling clarifying the meaning of the concept of collective interest of consumers.

15 In fact, it has been argued that the difficulty in applying the vague concept of collective interest of consumers in practice has led French jurisprudence to award only very limited compensation in consumers' collective interest cases; G. Howells and S. Weatherill, *Consumer Protection Law* (2nd edn, Markets and the Law, Ashgate, Aldershot 2005) 593–594.

16 It is worth mentioning that understanding of the concept of collective interest of consumers has already proved to be relevant in the first cross-border case under Directive 98/27, *Duchesne*. In this case, the Office of Fair Trading took action against a Belgian company that allegedly harmed British consumers. While assessing admissibility of the case, the Brussels Court of Appeal had to decide whether the collective interest of consumers was infringed. It held that because the challenged practice could harm the interests of one or more consumers, the criterion of damaging the collective interests of consumers was met; Cour d'appel de Bruxelles, 8 December 2005, *Duchesne v L'Office of Fair Trading*, unreported, RG: 2005/KR/38, see M. Haley, 'Stop Now – Injunction: Protecting the Interests of European Consumers' (Conference on Effective Legal Redress – The Consumer Protection Instruments of Actions for Injunction and Group Damages Actions in Vienna, 24 February 2006), www.bmsk.gv.at/cms/site/attachments/0/8/3/CH0036/CMS1141717684789/eu-studie_teil_i.pdf, accessed 15 March 2008.

serve as a benchmark for the accountability of bodies vested with appropriate enforcement functions.

Thus, any EU-based reflection on collective redress should include, *inter alia*, a closer look at the concept of consumer collective interest and its application at the MSs level.[17] A comprehensive analysis of this concept would require a thorough comparative exercise. Given the limits of this paper, we restrict our analysis only to Poland. As Poland represents a new MSs and has experienced transformation from a centrally planned to free market economy, our case study is particularly important for understanding how political and economic conditions shape the concept of collective interest. Accordingly, we show how the notions of public and collective interest pertaining to consumer protection developed and were applied in Poland before and after the transformation in 1989. We also show how Poland's historical legacy has influenced the present practice of application of the collective interest in consumer matters.

This paper is structured as follows. In the next section (2), the procedural functions of the concept of collective interest of consumers will be introduced and possible approaches to building a definition of the concept will be sketched out. An historical overview of the relationship between the public interest and consumer protection in Poland will be provided and the current state of play concerning protection of the consumers' collective interest in this MS will be described (3). Some preliminary conclusions will follow (4).

2. COLLECTIVE INTEREST OF CONSUMERS AND ITS FUNCTIONS

The concept of collective interest of consumers performs an important procedural role in the functioning of Directive 98/27 and Regulation 2006/2004. It might also be relevant for ensuring the effectiveness of the future EU collective redress mechanism, if the decision to adopt it were taken. Because of its central functions, a clear definition of the concept of collective interest is necessary.

17 Actions in the collective interest of consumers are available in the following countries: Austria (for cases relating to unlawful or unconscionable terms in standard form contracts and business terms and conditions); Belgium; France (for cases relating to illegal clauses in standard form non-negotiable consumer contracts); Germany (for cases relating to unfair competition or to prevent a breach of certain consumer protection laws); Hungary; Ireland (for cases relating to unfair contract terms); Italy; the Netherlands; Norway; Poland; Switzerland (for cases relating to unfair and deceptive commercial practices); Turkey. See OECD, 'Background Report' (OECD Workshop on Consumer Dispute Resolution and Redress in the Global Marketplace in Washington, 19–20 April 2005), www.oecd.org/dataoecd/59/21/34699496.pdf, accessed 15 March 2008. In Poland a draft law on group claims is currently being discussed at the governmental level. See http://www.ms.gov.pl/kkpc/kkpc.php, accessed 15 December 2008.

2.1. COLLECTIVE INTEREST OF CONSUMERS AS A PROCEDURAL INSTRUMENT

The debate on the EU scheme of collective redress is characterised by a relative neglect of a preliminary, and – given the Commission's stance – fundamental issue, i.e. the concept of consumer collective interest. This concept performs the role of a procedural instrument to decide on the admissibility of a legal action. We will therefore approach the collective interest as a procedural instrument to sort out consumer claims which on the basis of a normative point of reference (existence of the collective interest) deserve legal protection in the form of a special procedure (accompanied by special enforcement instruments) from those which are deemed unnecessary to receive such a special treatment.

The individual/collective divide is far from being perfect but it is clear that collective interest is the interest which grasps the attention of a group or public at large. Recognition of the collective interest has pushed legal systems to relax various doctrines, including standing, that were designed to address issues involving individual interest which once dominated the legal setting.

As introduced above, the policy approach at the EU level seems to move in the direction that any form of European collective redress scheme should aim at protecting the collective interest of consumers.[18] Identification of the collective interest would therefore be a precondition for the availability and initiation of legal proceedings in any future collective redress mechanism. In other words, the collective interest would be a requirement for standing and would define the procedural situations of particular consumers or their representatives, either before the court or in relationships with administrative bodies and social organisations. From this perspective, the central claim of this paper is that a procedural notion which is vague, meaning its construction being functionally similar to a general clause, is undesirable as ineffective for the purposes of protecting consumers. Moreover, imprecise formulations of procedural requirements might also be challenged from a constitutional viewpoint.

A procedural precondition for admissibility of a legal action formulated in vague terms is undesirable for two reasons. First, if competences of the bodies representing consumer interests are defined in very general terms, these bodies (the decision whether to intervene) as well as courts (the assessment whether intervention or non-intervention was justified) are given a wide discretion. This implies a risk of misuse of such discretion in various ways, one of them being an arbitrary practice of consumer protection bodies to dismiss consumers' requests for instituting legal proceedings on their behalf with a justification that no

[18] As mentioned above, this policy approach constitutes one of the grounds for discarding the idea of transplanting the US-style class action because of its focus on the protection of an aggregate of individual interests.

collective interest of consumers could be identified in a given case.[19] This evidently runs counter to the primary function of these enforcement institutions which is to facilitate consumer redress. As a result of such practice and given procedural obstacles related to court proceedings, consumers remain powerless in those situations.

Second, excessive discretion concerning admissibility of a legal action might effectively preclude consumers' access to justice and as such may give rise to constitutional concerns. This was the case in Poland where the Constitutional Tribunal held that although, as a general rule the Constitution does not grant a right to cassation, the fact that it is provided for by the Code of Civil Procedure (hereinafter: the 'CCP') means that its construction must meet constitutional requirements of the rule of law and procedural justice. According to the Tribunal, if the conditions for admissibility of a claim (preliminary assessment of a cassation claim) are formulated in imprecise terms, the right to court cannot be exercised effectively because of the risk of arbitrariness of the assessing body.[20]

An important caveat is in order. There is a marked difference between procedural and substantive general clauses, the latter being, for example, traditional concepts of good faith or good morals. The use of substantive open-ended concepts may create net gains, mainly due to the contextualisation of a dispute allowing the incorporation of a broader evidence base into the decision and, as a result, making it better tailored to the circumstances at hand.[21] At the same time, in the case of traditional substantive general clauses it is possible to refer to the previous case law to operationalise their meaning which is not the case for the collective interest understood as a procedural instrument. As far as procedural general clauses are concerned, the advantages of contextualisation are dubious and the case law providing guidance on their application is almost non-existent. Thus, it seems fair to assume that the necessity of having a general clause in a procedural situation requires at least a stronger justification than in the substantive law.

---

19 It is also possible to frame the problem of the degree of precision of the content given to the law at the promulgation stage as the problem of how the legislator gathers and disseminates information, see L. Kaplow, "Rules versus Standards: An Economic Analysis' (1992) 42 Duke Law Journal 557, 585-586. Framing this issue in terms of the uncertainty of the content of the law, a more precise definition of the collective interest of consumers would provide consumer protection bodies with superior guidance as to when they should take action since the procedural preconditions can be more readily ascertained.

20 Judgment of the Polish Constitutional Tribunal of 31 March 2005 – SK 26/02, [2004] 11A OTK ZU Item 120.

21 Of course, contextualisation bears a risk of uncertainty but taking a stance on this issue is outside of the scope of this paper. On the role of general clauses in contract law see S. Grundmann and D. Mazeaud (eds.), *General Clauses and Standards in European Contract Law: Comparative Law, EC Law and Contract Law Codification* (Kluwer Law International, *Private Law in European Context Series*, The Hague 2006) with a review of F. Cafaggi in (2007) 4 *European Review of Contract Law* 491.

The distinction between substantive and procedural general clauses may be derived, for example, from the jurisprudence of the Polish Constitutional Tribunal. In addition to the aforementioned decision concerning the constitutionality of the indeterminate conditions for admissibility of a cassation, formulated in vague terms, the Tribunal was also asked to decide whether an open-ended criterion underlying the institution of abuse of right – a general clause of the 'principles of community life'[22] – violates the right to court.[23] The Tribunal held that this general clause is a provision of substantive law and as such cannot contravene the right to court granted by the Constitution.[24] Thus, reading these two cases of the Polish Constitutional Tribunal together, the difference between the two concepts is clear-cut: whereas in the case of preliminary assessment of a cassation a general clause it was related to the procedural situation of an individual, in the case of abuse of right the assessment concerned the substantive right itself. The first situation was said to violate the constitutional right of access to court, but the second not.[25]

Another reason for our scepticism towards procedural general clauses is the accountability concern. It seems plausible to assume that the way the concept of collective interest – as a precondition for action by bodies representing consumer interests – is defined, i.e. whether in precise or vague terms, has implications for the accountability of these bodies. A precise definition would allow the public to have a clear benchmark for the assessment of their activities, i.e. it would make it possible to check whether on the one hand they reject or take up claims in an arbitrary way and whether they reject or take up cases with doubtful consumer collective interest on the other. A vague concept obviously cannot serve as an accountability benchmark because it does not provide any criteria for evaluation.

All of the above considerations prove that a vague concept of collective interest may run counter to the policy of ensuring effective means of consumer collective redress. In order to remedy this situation we provide a proposal of how to make the concept of consumer collective interest a workable tool.

---

22 Article 5 of the Polish Civil Code (hereinafter: the 'CC'). The term 'principles of community life' (*zasady współżycia społecznego*), which may also be referred to as the 'principles of social co-existence', has been adopted from the Soviet Constitution and is a basic general clause commonly found in the Polish law.

23 Article 45(1) of the Polish Constitution.

24 Judgment of the Polish Constitutional Tribunal of 17 October 2000 – SK 5/99, [2000] 7 OTK ZU Item 254.

25 Accordingly, we do not claim that all general clauses are undesirable because of their vagueness and for that reason should be defined more precisely, but we draw a line between the functions performed by substantive general clauses and the consumer collective interest being employed as a procedural requirement.

2.2. POSSIBLE APPROACHES TO BUILDING A DEFINITION OF THE COLLECTIVE INTEREST OF CONSUMERS

It is possible to approach the concept of consumers' collective interest in various ways. Given that its construction is similar to a general clause, the first step of our analysis concerns the feasibility of its definition. One may adopt either of the two approaches to this issue. The first approach argues futility of defining a general clause, the collective interest in our case, because of the inherent vagueness of the concept precluding its clear and comprehensible description. According to this approach, it is not possible to push the analysis further than a general statement that the consumers' collective interest means any social or public interest related to consumers as a group. It is clear that such a statement leaves the definition open.

The second approach seems to suggest that the only possible way of defining this general clause is to adopt a negative definition. Accordingly, collective interest is deemed not to be a sum of individual interests. This approach was developed by the French jurisprudence[26] and subsequently was adopted by the Community legislator;[27] it was followed also by the Polish implementing legislation.[28] However, in our opinion, this negative definition does not provide adjudicators with much guidance on how to apply the concept in practice. Given the lack of guidance and impossibility of verifying *ex post* the merits of a decision on the admissibility, such an imprecise definition may undermine the effectiveness of the enforcement system based on the concept of collective interest.

2.3. AN ATTEMPT TO BUILD A DEFINITION

A definition of the collective interest limited to a statement that it is not a sum of individual interests is unlikely to perform its role of improving the procedural position of consumers. However, this negative statement can serve as a starting point for building a positive definition.

A. *Compensation and Deterrence Perspective*

At first, a statement that collective interest is not a sum of individual interests might make us look at the collective interest through the lens of the compensation/deterrence divide. This perspective would mean that the collective interest does not refer to an amount or a sum of individual harms and corresponding

26 See, for example, Cass Crim, 20 May 1985, *Bull Crim* 485.
27 Recital 2 of Directive 98/27/EC (n 9).
28 Article 24(3) APCC (n 81).

compensation claimed. Because the collective interest pertains to a group as a whole, the instruments employed to protect it should focus primarily on deterrence and prevention rather than on compensation.[29] From the perspective of the definition of the consumers' collective interest it implies that one would identify the collective interest whenever the deterrence of particular market behaviour or practice is desired according to an external normative standard.[30]

Such a functional approach to the collective interest determines the choice of instruments for its protection. This does not imply, however, that recourse to administrative measures or development of new private law tools is absolutely necessary. Traditional private law instruments like unenforceability and invalidity of contracts, information duties or injunctions, might also be used to protect the collective interest. Invalidity and unenforceability are traditional instruments aimed at preventing contracts detrimental to the public interest. They conventionally concern contracts which, depending on the legal system, violate good morals, are contrary to good faith, and are unfair or unconscionable.[31] Invalid are also contracts violating the provisions of competition law. Invalidity and unenforceability of such contracts is intended to discourage parties from entering into certain types of contractual relationships and thus to protect the public interest. Information duties, in turn, are supposed to enable parties to the contract to make an informed choice. In this way, proper functioning of the market and consumer satisfaction should be ensured. Finally, injunctions aim at discontinuation of a practice which adversely affects an individual or the collective interest as well.

It might also be advisable to examine national civil codes and other private law legislations in order to search for other dormant instruments which could be used to protect the collective interest. For example, Article 439 of the Polish Civil Code provides that a person who is threatened by a direct damage resulting from conduct of another person may demand that person to take measures necessary to prevent the imminent danger and, if needed, to provide appropriate security.

---

29 Of course, compensation might also have a deterrence value (see n 33 and 34). What we want to stress is that we focus on deterring wrongdoing and not on a personal right of an individual to have the harm suffered compensated. See also *Office of Fair Trading v MB Designs (Scotland) Ltd and others* 2005 CSOH 85 (Court of Session) [14]. The difficulty of determining damages in collective interest litigation and thus its deterrence value has been underlined also in the French literature; see S. Carval, *La responsabilité civile dans sa fonction de peine privée* (Bibliothèque de droit privé, LGDJ, Paris 1995). See G. Howells and R. James, 'Litigation in the Consumer Interest' (2002) 9 *ILSA Journal of International & Comparative Law* 1, 43.

30 Market confidence can, for example, be such a standard; cf Howells and James, 'Litigation in the Consumer Interest' ibid 44.

31 For a comparative overview see, e.g. K. Zweigert and H. Kötz, *Introduction to Comparative Law*, translated by T. Weir (3rd edn OUP, Oxford 1998) 380–387.

Although particularly well suited to protect the collective interest of consumers, this provision has been rarely used by the Polish judiciary.[32]

All the instruments mentioned above are not directed at awarding compensation, thus their main objective is not to protect the individual interest. As already stated, however, it should not be overlooked that compensation might also have a deterrent value, especially if it is set at a high, for instance, punitive level.[33] In particular, the regime of product liability employs compensation as a tool of prevention.

Still, despite being apt to protect public and collective interest, the procedural and institutional aspects undermine the effectiveness of the traditional private law instruments in deterring a harmful conduct.[34]

B. *The Role of Individual Interest*

To acknowledge that the purpose of introducing the concept of collective interest is to focus on deterring rogue market practices (a forward-looking approach) rather than compensating losses suffered by consumers (a backward-looking approach) is informative, but still does not provide much guidance on its content and consequently does not remove the uncertainty related to its application. Having stated that the collective interest is not a sum of individual interests, the next step should be to examine the relationship between the collective and individual interest in more detail. Such examination will enable us to answer the question whether consumer protection bodies should be entitled to act also in the absence of or divergence from the individual interest. In other words, the policy question is to determine whether evidence of the individual interest involved

---

32 On the possible use of Article 439 CC for the sake of consumer protection see B. Lewaszkiewicz-Petrykowska, 'Bezpieczeństwo konsumentów w prawie polskim' in G. Rokicka (ed.), *"Model Prawnej Ochrony Konsumenta" Harmonizacja Polskiego Prawa Konsumenckiego z Regułami Unii Europejskiej* (Stowarzyszenie Konsumentów Polskich, Warszawa 1996), www.skp.pl, accessed 15 March 2008.

33 In Poland the deterrent and preventive function of compensation has already been underlined by W. Warkałło, *Odpowiedzialność odszkodowawcza: Funkcje, rodzaje, granice* (Państwowe Wydawnictwo Naukowe, Warszawa 1972). More general on the role of market transactions in producing aggregate or social outcomes see N.K. Komesar, *Imperfect Alternatives: Choosing Institutions in Law, Economics, and Public Policy* (Chicago University Press, Chicago 1994) Chapter 4.

34 See, for example, H. Collins, *Regulating Contracts* (Oxford University Press, Oxford 1999), discussing regulatory functions of private law; A. Ogus, *Regulation: Legal Form and Economic Theory* (Clarendon Press, Oxford 1994) Chapter 12; F. Cafaggi, 'The making of European private law: governance design' in: F. Cafaggi and H. Muir-Watt, *Making of European Private Law: Governance Design* (Edward Elgar Publishing, Cheltenham 2008). Vagueness of the concept of collective interest of consumers might also undermine the deterrent value of enforcement mechanisms based on it; see J. Calais-Auloy and F. Steinmetz, *Droit de la consommation* (4th edn, Dalloz-Sirey, Paris 1996) cited in Howells and James, 'Litigation in the Consumer Interest' (n 29) 43.

should be a prerequisite for the activity of consumer protection bodies. For this purpose, three sets of relationships between the collective and individual interest can be identified: the collective and individual interest can (1) overlap; (2) conflict; or (3) be detached from each other, meaning situations in which the individual interest is irrelevant from the collective viewpoint and *vice versa*.

First, one needs to assess whether the existence of individual interest should be a necessary requirement for bringing a legal action in the collective interest of consumers. Although the negative definition analysed in this paper might suggest that these two concepts are detached from each other, it seems that such interpretation would not be desirable from an institutional and accountability viewpoints. As to the former, a possibility to legitimise action in the collective interest also in the absence of any individual consumer interest might lead to an overlap in terms of allocation of competences between the judicial and regulatory bodies. Traditionally, whereas litigation has been concerned with satisfaction of the claimants' private interests, administrative regulation has been used to foster the public interest.[35] While extending the scope of litigation by also including actions in the public interest may ensure that the law can regulate market failures where individuals lack adequate incentives to act against harmful trading practices,[36] litigation exclusively in the public interest may lead to an overlap with the activities of the regulatory bodies. Such an overlap is not desirable because due to institutional factors regulatory authorities seem to be better placed to perform activities in the public, including the collective, interest than the judiciary.[37] As to the accountability point, a possibility to act without an underlying individual interest would provide consumer protection bodies with an excessive amount of discretion in instituting legal proceedings. Thus, in order to act in the collective interest of consumers the competent bodies should be required to show an infringement of at least one individual consumer interest.[38]

35 However, litigation, via enforcement of private interests, can also pursue the public interest.

36 Cf Howells and James, 'Litigation in the Consumer Interest' (n 29) 31.

37 These factors include expertise, market monitoring capacities, enforcement powers, etc. For example, because of these constraints it is more efficient to delegate the task of market surveillance to regulatory authorities than to the judiciary. On the limitations of the judiciary in adjudicating in the public interest, see Ogus, *Regulation* (n 34).

38 Too much discretion may lead to over-activity of social organisations and they might be instrumentalised for the purpose of rent-seeking. It is worth noticing that the ECJ denied *locus standi* to challenge a Community act by an association formed for the protection of the collective interests of a category of persons if its members could not do so individually, i.e. were not directly and individually concerned by the act in question. See Case C-321/95 P *Stichting Greenpeace Council (Greenpeace International) and Others v Commission* [1998] ECR 1651. See also R. Van den Bergh and L. Vischer, 'The Preventive Function of Collective Actions for Damages in Consumer Law' (2008) 1 *Erasmus Law Review* 1, 27. In the Italian literature one may find an interesting view that the consumer interest is the combination of an individual and a group interest: an individual interest in the protection of specific interests relating to given situations (health, hygiene, economic benefits, etc.) and a group interest to the extent

This should ensure that there is no overlap with other regulatory policies allocated to sector-specific bodies and improve the accountability of the consumer protection bodies.

Second, one needs to examine whether it is possible to identify situations where exercise of an individual interest of a consumer would violate the collective interest of the group and *vice versa*. One possible example concerns a situation where an individual consumer has an interest in a particular abusive contract clause because of the lower price he or she can obtain in return. From the point of view of consumers as a group, such a clause should be struck down because in general consumers are not in a position to defend themselves from abusive clauses, especially in the case of transactions concluded through standard form contracts.[39] Thus, although the use of abusive clauses may incidentally benefit a particular consumer, it violates the collective interest of the group. Accordingly, this case requires an individual interest of a consumer to be sacrificed in order to protect the collective interest of the group.[40] It has been noted in French jurisprudence that the collective interest goes beyond the individual interest, the community having higher expectations than individuals.[41] It follows that it would also be possible to identify the collective interest of consumers as a procedural requirement if it is in conflict with some individual interests. It is precisely the possibility of conflict between the two which implies that the collective interest is not a sum of individual interests.

The fact that the collective interest is not a sum of individual interests also follows from the third possible relationship between the two, i.e. when the individual consumer interest is irrelevant from the collective viewpoint. In such

that it belongs in an identical manner to everybody. Even if the threats to that interest are normally felt at the individual level, in actual fact they affect the group as a whole; see G. Ghidini, *Per i consumatori* (Zanichelli, Bologna 1977) cited in 'Memorandum from the Commission on Consumer Redress 1984' (n 1) 33–34.

39 See, for example, R. Korobkin, 'Bounded Rationality, Standard Form Contracts, and Unconscionability' (2003) 70 *University of Chicago Law Review* 1203. On the other hand, taking a paternalistic approach one would deny that a consumer might have an interest in abusive clauses at all. Paternalists are sceptical about the ability of some groups of people to make decisions in their best interest and are in favour of intervention into their private autonomy when the conditions of full rationality do not hold. See, for instance, D. Kennedy, 'Distributive and Paternalist Motives in Contract and Tort Law, with Special Reference to Compulsory Terms and Unequal Bargaining Power' (1982) 41 *Maryland Law Review* 563.

40 Further examples may be provided. For instance, situations where a consumer is denied an award of credit because of the lack of collateral, should be treated in a similar way. See E.A. Posner, 'Contract Law in the Welfare State: A Defense of the Unconscionability Doctrine, Usury Laws, and Related Limitations on the Freedom of Contract' (1995) 24 *Journal of Legal Studies* 283. The issue of rebates may also be approached similarly. Moreover, credit reporting illustrates a situation where the collective interest overrides the interests of an individual. See P. Blume, 'The Citizens' Data Protection' (1998) 1 *Journal of Information, Law and Technology*, www2.warwick.ac.uk/fac/soc/law/elj/jilt/1998_1/blume, accessed 15 March 2008.

41 Cass Crim, 10 October 1996, *Bull Crim* 358.

situation, members of the public, other than the parties directly concerned, do not receive any benefits or suffer any negative consequences of the transaction. As an example, it is hard to imagine any collective interest in a private purchase of a pre-ordered painting or any other customised item.

In particular situations individual interest may foster the public interest. The procedure of a 'constitutional complaint', contained in Article 79 of the Polish Constitution, is a particular tool for initiating the specific review of legal provisions. A natural or legal person, whose case has been finally settled by a court judgment or a decision of an administrative body, may challenge before the Constitutional Tribunal the conformity of the legal provisions forming the basis of this decision with constitutionally guaranteed rights and freedoms. The Constitutional Tribunal's judgment in such cases has universally binding force (Article 190 of the Constitution), meaning that it will also be applicable in cases other than the one involving the current appellant. In this regard, the review of legal provisions initiated in accordance with the procedure of constitutional complaint does not differ from the abstract review of norms or the review of norms following the referral of questions of law by courts.

A similar *actio popularis* is provided for by the CCP for the abstract control of fairness of clauses in standard form contracts.[42] The control can be initiated by any person that might potentially enter into a contract on the basis of the standard form contract.[43] The abstract examination is performed by the Court for Protection of Competition and Consumers which evaluates a particular clause *in abstracto*, regardless of any circumstances underlying a particular contractual relationship.[44] If the court declares a clause abusive, it is published in the public register of abusive clauses and becomes illegal (Article 479^{42}(1) CCP). Such a judgment is effective *erga omnes* (Article 479^{43} CCP). It implies that further use of a listed clause in standard form contracts will be regarded as infringing the collective interest of consumers (Article 24(2)(1) APCC). It was long controversial whether the prohibition concerned only the entrepreneur who participated in the court proceedings declaring a clause abusive or all entrepreneurs. The matter was

42 The abstract control of abusive clauses was introduced into the CC in 2000 in the course of implementation of Directive 93/13 (*Ustawa z dnia 2 marca 2000 r. o ochronie niektórych praw konsumentów oraz o odpowiedzialności za szkodę wyrządzoną przez produkt niebezpieczny*, DzU 2000, No 22, Item 271).

43 In addition, the control can be requested also by a consumer organisation, including a qualified organisation in the meaning of Directive 98/27, a regional consumers' spokesman or the President of the Office for Protection of Competition and Consumers (Article 479^{38} CCP).

44 Judgment of the Polish Supreme Court of 19 December 2003 – III CZP 95/2003, (2003) 12 Biuletyn Sądu Najwyższego 11; judgment of the Polish Supreme Court of 13 July 2006 – III SZP 3/2006, (2007) 1–2 OSNP Item 34. In contrast, in the case of individual control of contract clauses the court takes into consideration the content of the contract, circumstances underlying the closing of the contract and other contracts related to the contract under examination (Article 385^2 CC).

decided recently by the Supreme Court in favour of the latter approach.[45] As a result, within the institution of the abstract control of unfair contract clauses, an individual interest may foster the collective interest of consumers.

An interesting question concerns the relationship between the collective interest and the public (general) interest. On the one hand it has been claimed that consumers' collective interests are distinct from the general public interests.[46] The report on collective redress prepared by the French Inter-Ministerial Working Group explicitly states that the collective interest should not be confused with the public interest.[47] On the other, in some MSs the collective interest is identified with the public interest. Article 3:305a of the Dutch Civil Code, introduced by the Law on Claims by Interest Organisations of 1994 (*Wet vorderingsrecht belangenorganisaties*) grants associations or foundations with full legal capacity the right to sue in courts to protect collective interests which are defined as 'interests similar in kind which are held by other persons'. The preparatory work of the Law of 1994 states explicitly that it does not distinguish between the collective interests of a group of individuals, such as inhabitants of an apartment building or employees, and the general interest, shared by an indefinite number of persons.[48] Polish courts, in turn, consider the collective interest of consumers to be a variant or a part of the public interest.[49] Finally, according to the Commission's examination of the selected legal systems provided in the Green Paper of 1993 the scope of the category of collective interests is wider than that of individual interests (which are defended through the right of individual action) but more limited than that of the general interest (whose defence lies with the Ministry of Public Order).[50]

In general, a more comprehensive study of the possible relationships between the collective interest of consumers on the one hand and an individual and the public interest on the other, is needed. As a preliminary conclusion, however, it seems reasonable to demand that in order to pursue the collective interest of consumers competent bodies should be required to provide evidence that individual interest of at least one consumer is also present. At the same time,

---

45 III SZP 3/2006 ibid.

46 See, for example, T. Bourgoignie, 'Characteristics of consumer law' (1992) 14 *Journal of Consumer Policy* 293.

47 Groupe de travail présidé par G. Cerutti and M. Guillaume, 'Rapport sur l'Action de Groupe', 16 December 2005) www.minefi.gouv.fr/directions_services/sircom/protection_conso/protection_eco/rapport.pdf, accessed 15 March 2008.

48 See W. van Gerven, J. Lever and P. Larouche, *Cases, Materials and Text on National, Supranational and International Tort Law* (Ius Commune Casebooks, Hart Publishing, Oxford 2000) 270/7.

49 Judgment of the Polish Supreme Court of 26 February 2004 – III SK 2/2004, (2004) 19 OSNP Item 343; Judgment of the Court of Appeal in Warsaw of 14 February 2007 – VI ACa 980/2006, LexPolonica No 1625352.

50 Commission, 'Green Paper on Access of Consumers to Justice' 64.

designing institutions where an individual interest would foster the collective interest of consumers might be a valuable additional tool for improving the effectiveness of consumer protection mechanisms.

C. *Towards a Positive Definition*

As stated above, despite not being comprehensive, a negative definition might serve as a starting point for identifying positive elements guiding the application of the concept of collective interest. As regards the collective interest of consumers, we believe that the following factors should be taken into account when building a more precise definition: (1) the number of infringements and persistence of a harmful practice; (2) the addressee of a practice; and (3) nature of the interest infringed.

First, a large number of infringements and the persistence of certain detrimental practices will, in our opinion, usually be present in cases where the collective interest of consumers might be involved. In its consultation document the UK Department of Trade and Industry (hereinafter: the 'DTI') indicated that a one-off act that harms an individual consumer and which is unlikely to be repeated cannot be viewed as harming the collective interests of consumers.[51] On the other hand, as noted by the DTI in the same document, 'a one-off single breach capable of affecting a large number of consumers (e.g. a misleading advertisement) or which is likely to be repeated would harm the collective interests of consumers because consumers generally would be put at risk'.[52] According to the Polish Office for Protection of Competition and Consumers (hereinafter: the 'OPCC'), a one-off infringement may sometimes be a sign of a large-scale harmful practice.[53] It would therefore be sensible to introduce a rebuttable presumption of the existence of the collective interest if the number of infringements is large or harmful practice persists over time. At the same time, however, evidence for either a large number of infringements or persistence of the breach should not be a necessary requirement and it should be clear that also small-scale infringements are likely to affect the collective interest of consumers.[54]

---

51 DTI, 'Consultation on implementing the EU Directive on Unfair Commercial Practices and Amending Existing Consumer Legislation' (December 2005, 42), www.berr.gov.uk/files/file15311.pdf, accessed 15 March 2008.

52 Ibid 42.

53 See Section 3.3.

54 In Germany, the former version of the Law Against Unfair Competition required an intentional persistent breach of consumer protection provisions which rendered the possibility of consumer associations to take actions against unfair traders very difficult. For this reason, Germany abolished this requirement. See P. Rott, 'The Protection of Consumers' Interests After the Implementation of the EC Injunctions Directive Into German and English Law' (2001) 24 *Journal of Consumer Policy* 401, 425. See also Howells and Weatherill, *Consumer Protection Law* (n 15) 594.

Second, the collective interest should be presumed whenever a particular practice might potentially harm every consumer finding him or herself in a given situation. In other words, the collective interest is likely to be involved when a practice is directed not at a particular consumer but at every potential consumer. For example, an unfair clause inserted into a contract drafted by business especially for the needs of a particular consumer would not imply an infringement of the collective interest. On the contrary, if the same unfair clause was inserted into a standard form contract to be used in dealings with any consumer willing to enter into a relationship, such a practice would be likely to endanger the collective interest of consumers.

Third, although Directive 98/27 and Regulation 2006/2004 concern 'economic interests' of consumers, it might be worth asking whether the type of the interest being infringed might be decisive for identifying the collective interest in a given case. From this perspective it would be possible to argue that an infringement of goods that are under special protection of the legal system, for example the life or health of a person, would imply an infringement of the collective interest of consumers. Such an approach could ensure a coherent regulatory strategy towards the economic and non-economic interests of consumers.

The function of the above presumptions would be to simplify a procedural situation of a claimant. The presumptions would also add more predictability for both consumers and businesses as to the requirements of instituting legal proceedings in the collective interest of consumers.

D. A Proposal for the Definition

Given the above considerations, we propose the following preliminary definition of the consumers' collective interest:

1. Collective interest of consumers is not a sum of individual interests.

2.1. Existence of the collective interest of consumers shall be presumed when:

- *a. A large number of consumers are affected by a particular practice or the breach is persistent; however, a small number of infringements or discontinuation of a practice shall not in itself preclude the existence of the collective interest of consumers; and/or*
- *b. A particular practice affects every potential consumer in a given situation; and/or*
- *c. A particular practice affects interests which are of special importance for consumers, in particular life and health.*

2.2. If one of the aforementioned conditions is met, rejecting a claim for protection of the collective interest of consumers requires appropriate justification.

3. *In order to demonstrate the existence of the collective interest of consumers, example(s) of individual consumer interest involved shall be provided as evidence.*

Such a preliminary definition, inserted, for instance, in a soft law EU measure, could guide the application of the concept of collective interest and ensure the achievement of a consistent approach towards the admissibility test of the actions in the collective interest of consumers.

3. PUBLIC INTEREST AND CONSUMER PROTECTION IN POLAND

In the first part of this section we will examine how the concept of public interest was construed by the Polish judiciary during the socialist regime. In the second part we will investigate whether transformation from the centrally planned to free market economy in 1989 had any impact on the attitude of the Polish judiciary to consumer protection and whether it affected the notion of consumers' collective interest. In subsection three we will show that the way the public interest was conceptualised in the past political and legal system – in particular its relationship with individual interest – has had an influence on the present understanding of the consumers' collective interest.

3.1. THE PERIOD OF SOCIALISM

The relationship between the public and the individual interest in private law and potential frictions between the two were particularly clearly observable in Poland during the socialist regime. First, the concept of public interest was distorted as every interest of the State tended to be regarded as the public interest. Second, there was a clear hierarchy of interests and in the case of conflict the public interest prevailed.[55] As an example, in 1950[56] the Polish Supreme Court rejected a claim for eviction of a state-owned company from a private building as it would have

55 In particular, the general clause of the socio-economic purpose of right introduced into the Polish Civil Code of 1964 aimed at promoting decisions free 'from the subjective understanding of fairness' and preventing decisions 'extensively or exclusively highlighting an individual interest without taking into account the general interest', Codification Commission in the explanatory memorandum to the project of new Civil Code (Komisja Kodyfikacyjna, *Projekt kodeksu cywilnego* (Warszawa 1962)); see M Safjan, 'Klauzule generalne w prawie cywilnym (przyczynek do dyskusji)' (1990) (11) *Państwo i Prawo* 48, 50. It should be clarified that the Civil Code of 1964 is still in force in Poland, though it has been amended many times.

56 Judgment of the Polish Supreme Court of 9 May 1950 – Ł C 495/50, (1951) 3 OSN Item 67.

infringed the interest of that company. In this judgment the Supreme Court explicitly held that (1) the interest of a state-owned company was equal to the public interest of the State and society; and (2) private (individual) interest must rank after the interest of the State and society.

Furthermore, judges tended to link individual interest with the public interest by stating that protection of the latter was indispensable for protection of the former. This practice might be explained in two ways. First, there was an apparent hostility towards the consumers' individual interests viewed as 'exaggerated, egoistic claims' and juxtaposed with the consumers' interests deserving protection (public interest).[57] For that reason, consumers' interests tended to be enforceable only when underlying public interest could be identified.[58] On the other hand, even if somewhat artificial, associating an individual interest with the public interest allowed for the development of consumer protection mechanisms which were not provided for by the statutes.[59] In this way, by means of creative

57 This approach was pointed out and criticised by E Łętowska, 'Ochrona konsumenta z punktu widzenia polityki prawa' (1978) (4) *Państwo i Prawo* 16, 20–21.

58 It should be noted, however, that the concept of consumer was not normatively defined and it was referred to by the judiciary rather freely and interchangeably with the concept of purchasers.

59 It would, however, be false to say that there were no instruments of consumer protection in the CC. For example, Article 384 CC empowered the Council of Ministers and other administrative bodies to issue general terms of contracts and model contracts to be used by 'units of socialized economy' ('USE'). In 1968 and 1971 the first general terms of contracts for relationships between the USEs and consumers (population) were issued. Later on, great use was made of this provision which led to the prevalence of numerous sectoral model contracts. Although the introduction of Article 384 CC was justified in terms of consumer protection, this objective was not achieved, mainly due to lack of any control over the model contracts issued. For a general overview see E. Łętowska, *Wzorce umowne: ogólne warunki, wzory, regulaminy* (Zakład Narodowy im. Ossolińskich, Wrocław 1975). There were also many legal acts providing for the administrative and criminal protection of the economic interests of consumers (or purchasers) and many administrative agencies entrusted with the protection of these interests were established. It goes without saying that the protection effectively awarded was illusory. Given the specific characteristics of social economy (price regulation, regulation of production, etc) as well as a (resulting) general shortage of supply, the main concerns of the policy of consumer protection were related to the observance of the price regulation and to the quality of products and variances of the two, i.e. (1) sale of products of lower quality or quantity than required for a given price, (2) collecting higher prices than the regulated prices, (3) improper designation of products. Accordingly, the tasks of the competent agencies amounted mainly to monitoring whether price, quantity and quality of goods as prescribed by detailed regulations were observed. A key concern was the fight against 'speculation'. Quite often the agencies also had power to enforce particular regulations by means of imposing fines and other penalties. In addition to agencies, there was also a sign of social society organisations empowered with protection of consumer interests: 'Social Committees for Price Control' (so-called 'control trios'). They were supposed to monitor prices, quantities and qualities of products at commercial sites. However, due to organisational and human resources problems, their role was very limited and they were resolved very quickly. See B. Piasna, 'Powstanie i rozwój instytucjonalnych form ochrony interesów konsumentów w Polsce Ludowej' (1971) 4 *Ruch Prawniczy, Ekonomiczny i Socjologiczny* 135, 142. The focus of the consumer protection as described above

interpretation, Polish judges often managed to circumvent the official 'commandment' of supremacy of the public interest in private relationships.

As an example, in 1959[60] the Polish Supreme Court ruled that any ambiguities in general terms and conditions applying to an insurance contract should be interpreted *contra proferentem*. According to the Supreme Court, any interpretation imposing negative effects of confusing provisions on the party with no influence on their formulation would violate the principles of community life. It was emphasised that especially when offers are directed at an indefinite number of persons (*ad incertas personas*), the offeror has a duty to declare his or her intent in a way which is understandable and not misleading for the addressees and the effects of the breach of this duty must lie with the offeror. Thus, the Supreme Court effectively granted legal protection to an individual consumer but at the same time indirectly referred to the public interest. Namely, the Supreme Court reasoned that a practice employed by the offeror was likely to harm an indefinite number of persons and as such should be ceased and deterred *pro futuro* by means of civil liability.

Another example of the tendency to associate individual interest with the public interest dates back to 1978[61] when the Polish Supreme Court rendered a decision according to which a court should be allowed to disregard a one-year prescription period for a statutory warranty claim if rejecting a late claim would manifestly harm the purchaser.[62] In the reasoning behind this decision the Supreme Court argued that departure from the rigour of one-year prescription period is justified not only by the individual interest of a purchaser but also by the 'general socio-economic interest' involving the protection of consumers as well as the protection of production, both industrial and agrarian (the claimant purchaser was a farmer). The Supreme Court also referred to the general shortage of supply in Poland and argued that the institution of statutory warranty aims at disciplining producers to ensure proper quality of goods. It further emphasised that a considerable loss suffered by a farmer might have had negative economic implications for his farm and thus for the general level of agrarian production. As a result, in this case as well the Supreme Court awarded protection to an individual

---

was primarily on deterrence and the various legal acts were setting an enormous amount of technical, production and organisational standards backed by administrative or even criminal penalties. The role of agencies was to monitor and enforce administrative rules. As can be seen, consumer protection measures were aimed at interventionist market regulation rather than ensuring consumer satisfaction; see M. Skory, *Klauzule abuzywne w polskim prawie ochrony konsumenta* (Zakamycze, Kraków 2005) 60. No special legal protection of individual interests of consumers was provided for.

60 Judgment of the Polish Supreme Court of 24 July 1959 – 4 CR 1027/58, (1961) 2 OSPiKA Item 32.

61 Resolution of the Civil Chamber of the Supreme Court of 20 May 1978 – III CZP 39/77, (1979) 3 OSNCP Item 40.

62 In this case defects of the goods materialized more than one year after the sale took place.

consumer but simultaneously considered it to be an instrument of protecting the public interest.

The link between an individual interest and the public interest is also illustrated by a judgment of 1983.[63] In this judgment the Polish Supreme Court held that a commission agent cannot exclude his or her liability for hidden defects of goods by way of posting on the wall a general note containing an exclusion clause. In order for the exclusion of liability to be effective it should be communicated directly to a respective buyer. The Supreme Court argued that such an interpretation is justified for social reasons. Economic positions as well as the possibility to detect hidden defects of goods by a professional on the one hand and by a consumer on the other are considerably different. Hence imposing the risk of acquiring defective goods on a consumer can be justified only if the consumer knowingly assumes that risk and this can only be the case if the consumer is warned *ex ante* about the factual possibility of buying defective goods. Only such an interpretation meets the requirements of justified consumer protection. As it can be seen, in this case as well the Supreme Court implicitly referred to the protection of the collective interests of consumers.

Another judgment linking protection of an individual consumer interest with the collective interest of consumers was delivered in 1986.[64] The case concerned a sale agreement of a washing machine. Having concluded a contract of sale for a fixed administrative price, the parties had to wait for the washing machine to be delivered to the seller. In the meantime the fixed price had increased. The seller argued that the initial agreement was only a preliminary one and required the buyer to make up the difference in prices. The buyer paid the additional charge and, having received the washing machine, claimed it back. The lower courts dismissed the claim and the buyer decided to go up to the Supreme Court. As the revision was filed after the prescribed period, the Supreme Court was to consider whether the decision of the lower court had violated the interest of Poland. Accordingly, it argued that boosting consumers' confidence in undertakings (producers or sellers) is in the interest of Poland. The State and society are interested in the protection of legitimate interests of citizens and other persons as consumers. The priority of the public (general) over an individual interest does not imply that the former as a rule excludes the protection of legitimate individual interests. In particular, protection of an individual interest may be indispensable for the protection of the social interest. In sum, according to the Supreme Court, protection of an individual interest may be a function of the social interest.

---

63 Judgment of the Polish Supreme Court of 18 November 1983 – I CR 336/83, OSNCP 1984, No. 9, Item 159.

64 Judgment of the Polish Supreme Court of 20 February 1986 – III CRN 443/85, OSNCP 1986, No. 12, Item 211.

Finally, a regime of product liability was also developed by Polish jurisprudence with references being made to the need to protect human life and health as well as to warrant the appropriate quality of production. In numerous judgments gradually developing this institution[65] up to the Guidelines of the Supreme Court of 1988,[66] the Supreme Court referred to the interest of society and of the State in protecting justified interests of purchasers. The Supreme Court argued that an individual interest was part of the general interest and that awarding protection to purchasers might have influenced the general quality of products.[67]

The case law discussed above shows that the practice of linking individual interest with the public interest enabled the Polish judiciary to develop various forms of consumer protection which at that time were not provided for by the statutes.[68] The question which arises is why civil courts in the socialist regime, notwithstanding the official ideology of the supremacy of the public interest, had a propensity to implant the individual interest of consumers into the concept of public interest. This judicial approach followed from two factors. First, a centrally planned economy lacked any regulatory mechanisms ordinarily built into the market system, in particular a price mechanism, which would ensure a proper balance of interests between the supply and demand sides of the market. As a result, the only possible way to steer the behaviour of market participants in order to ensure at least some level of consumer satisfaction was through an external corrective action. Given that administrative provisions were ineffective and focused more on heavy-handed market regulation than on consumer protection, only civil law litigation could serve this function. Second, Polish civil courts were relatively independent from the executive branch (which was, by the way, a peculiarity in the 'socialist camp') and remained strongly influenced by the

65 Judgment of the Polish Supreme Court of 6 February 1963 – 2 CR 96/62; Judgment of the Polish Supreme Court of 28 April 1964 – II CR 540/63, (1965) 2 OSNCP Item 32; Judgment of the Polish Supreme Court of 28 June 1972 – II CR 218/72, (1972) 12 OSNC Item 228.

66 Judgment of the Polish Supreme Court of 30 December 1988 – III CZP 48/88, (1989) 3 OSNCP Item 36.

67 Ibid.

68 Ewa Łętowska identified five trends in Polish 'pro-consumer' jurisprudence: (1) prevention of the abuse of dominance by undertakings (not to be confused with the concepts used in European competition law); (2) prevention of undesirable conduct by undertakings; (3) intensification of professionals' duties; (4) objectivisation of liability for hazardous products; and (5) preference for specific performance. Given the characteristics of the socialist economy and in particular a general shortage of goods, specific performance was of great importance for consumer protection as a tool allowing consumers to stay in possession of the goods. This was in marked contrast to the modern approach to consumer protection in the EC where the tendency has been rather to allow an unsatisfied consumer to get out of a contract as easily as possible so that he or she could obtain alternative goods or services on the market. Cf. E Łętowska in S Pawela and K Piasecki, 'Sesja Sądu Najwyższego PRL – Sprawozdania' (1985) (5) *Nowe Prawo* 63, 77–79.

traditional concepts of private law. Influenced by the private law tradition, Polish judges pushed for a more balanced approach towards the individual and public interest than the official socialist ideology would require.

As a conclusion, the tendency to associate an individual interest with the public interest during the socialist time might render the operationalisation of the collective interest in Poland easier. In particular, Polish jurisprudence has already recognised that a single case might have a deterrence value and thus in certain circumstances evidence of a single infringement will suffice to establish the collective interest of consumers. As it will be demonstrated further, this approach is still present among the Polish judiciary. On the other hand, prevalence of the public interest in conjunction with the absence of an underlying individual interest led to pathology, namely a situation where the interest of the State could prevail over the interest of an individual. As the enforcement of consumers' rights necessarily involves an infringement of the conflicting interest of business(es), a possibility that an unclear concept of the collective interest of consumers would override an individual interest of an entrepreneur (or even some consumers) should be prevented. For this reason, the concept of collective interest of consumers should be specified in more detail. In addition, as it was claimed above, in order to take a legal action endorsing the collective interest of consumers, consumer protection bodies should be required to provide evidence for the existence of an individual interest of consumer(s).[69] Finally, the developments in Poland show also the potential conflict between the public interest in general and the collective interest of a class. The implications of such a clash should be studied in more detail.

3.2. AFTER THE TRANSFORMATION

Transformation from a centrally planned to a free market economy in 1989 marked itself extensively in the field of private law. As regards contract law, private autonomy and freedom of contract came to the foreground. The introduction of Article 353[1] expressly guaranteeing the freedom of contract into the CC had a somewhat symbolic value.[70] In the legal doctrine, a claim that undistorted market

69 For other justifications for this requirement see Part 2.3.2.

70 An express provision providing for the freedom of contract was actually brought back into Polish civil law as the former Polish Code of Obligations of 1933 contained it (Article 55). It shall also be recognised that even though absent of an express provision guaranteeing the freedom of contract, the legal doctrine derived it from other provisions of the CC. Also courts, though with hesitance, tended to acknowledge it. See, for instance, C Żuławska, 'Wokół zasady wolności umów (art. 353[1] k.c. i wykładnia zwyczaju)' (1994) 1690 *Acta Universitatis Wratislaviensis* 173. See also M Safjan, 'Zasada swobody umów. (Uwagi wstępne na tle wykładni Article 353[1] k.c.)' (1993) (4) *Państwo i Prawo* 12.

competition is the best way to achieve a high level of consumer satisfaction emerged. Accordingly, any arguments justifying the need to protect the 'weaker' contractual party tended to be rejected and associated with the former socialist system.[71] At the same time, individual and not public (or collective) interest turned to be emphasised as an overriding value in contractual relationships. However, as far as the jurisprudence is concerned, its approach to consumer protection remained ambiguous. On the one hand, one could observe judgments denying any protection and promoting formalistic understanding of the freedom of contract; on the other there were many judicial decisions acknowledging the need to protect the 'weaker' party.

As an example of the *laissez-faire* approach, one can quote decisions concerning the control of unfair clauses in standard form contracts. The amendment of the CC of 1990[72] introduced Article 385^2 which specified that if standard form contracts conferred grossly unjustified benefits on the drafting party, the counterparty was entitled to require a court to declare their unenforceability. This entitlement was vested only with a party who entered into a contract outside his or her economic activity, thus essentially with a consumer. This provision shows that the legislation adopted after 1989 awarded some form of protection from unfair clauses to consumers, but required them to actively enforce their rights, and in particular to bear the burden of proof (Article 6 CC). The Polish judiciary approached this provision in a very formalistic way, or even went further by saying that the entitlement awarded by Article 385^2 is exceptional and as such cannot be taken into consideration by a court of its motion.[73] This judgment clearly reveals an anti-consumer stance and is in stark contrast to a subsequent judgment of the ECJ in *Océano* which required an *ex officio* control of unfair clauses in consumer standard form contracts.[74]

---

71 It was pointed out and criticised by, for example, E Łętowska, *Prawo umów konsumenckich* (CH Beck, Warszawa 2002) 3. Those voices ignored the fact that certain forms of protection, and in particular 'protection by information', aim at safeguarding and enabling the private autonomy of both sides of the contractual relationship.

72 Act of 28 July 1990 (*Ustawa z dnia 28 lipca 1990 r. o zmianie ustawy – Kodeks cywilny*), DzU 1990, No. 55, Item 321.

73 Judgment of the Polish Supreme Court of 16 April 1996 – II CRN 48/96, (1996) 6 Radca Prawny 32. In the Explanatory Memorandum to the Amendment of the CC of 2000 implementing Directive 93/13 and entirely modifying the model of control of unfair clauses it was argued that Article 385^2 had remained dormant since the courts tended to require that in order for a clause in a standard form contract to be declared unfair and thus unenforceable, it had to contravene an express provision of law. In addition, long court proceedings (more than three years) had rendered any protection fictitious; *Uzasadnienie rządowego projektu ustawy o umowach zawieranych poza lokalem przedsiębiorstwa lub na odległość oraz o zmianie ustaw: Kodeks cywilny, Kodeks postępowania cywilnego i Kodeks wykroczeń (druk sejmowy nr 945)*, available at www.sejm.gov.pl.

74 Joined cases C-240/98 to C-244/98 *Océano Grupo Editorial SA v Roció Murciano Quintero and others* [2000] ECR I-4941.

In contrast, an example of the protective approach might be drawn from the line of cases regulating the use of general terms and conditions by banks. In general, banks were prohibited from unilaterally changing the interest rates[75] and required to notify any change of general terms and conditions to a consumer and to allow him or her to withdraw from the contract in case of such modifications.[76]

There was also a line of cases concerning liability of commercial agents for the legal defects of products. After the transformation, many persons found themselves buying a second-hand 'western' car from a commercial agent where afterwards the car appeared to be stolen. The unfortunate buyers claimed compensation from the agents arguing that it was their responsibility to properly verify the origin of the car. In numerous judgments, the Polish Supreme Court expressed an opinion that persons who run an agency professionally are bound to adopt a higher measure of diligence[77] and should be conscious of the common phenomenon of placing stolen cars on the market. Although a commercial agent was not obliged to perform a specialist technical examination in order to verify the origin of a car, he or she should, however, make a general inspection of the car and examine its documentation in a way that an experienced driver would be expected to do. If, as a result, a commercial agent became suspicious that the car might have been stolen, he or she should notify this suspicion to a potential buyer in due time.[78] Thus, the line of cases could be described as favouring consumers. At the same time, however, cases concerning liability of agents selling cars which turned out to be stolen, confirm the thesis about judges' ambivalent approach to consumer (or rather purchaser) protection after the transformation. Based on a similar factual situation, the Supreme Court rejected in 1996[79] a claim of a buyer who demanded that an agent repay her the price paid for a car which turned out to be stolen. The Court held that a commercial agent may effectively exclude his or her liability by a unilateral statement made prior to the conclusion of the contract.

As a conclusion, a radical change of the approach to consumer protection after the transformation might also have implications for the understanding of the concept of the collective interest of consumers. However, although some authors

75 Judgment of the Polish Supreme Court of 3 July 1991 – III CZP 59/91, (1992) 3 OSNCP Item 41; Judgment of the Supreme Court of 19 May 1992 – III CZP 50/92, (1993) 6 OSP Item 119.

76 Judgment of the Polish Supreme Court of 22 May 1991 – III CZP 15/91, (1992) 1 OSNCP Item 1.

77 Diligence generally required in the relationships of a given kind is prescribed by Article 355(1) CC. Article 355(2), inserted into CC in 1990, further specifies that diligence of a debtor within the scope of his or her economic activity shall be assessed in view of the professional character of this activity.

78 Judgment of the Polish Supreme Court of 18 December 1990 – III CZP 67/90, (1991) 5–6 OSNCP Item 65; judgment of the Polish Supreme Court of 24 June 1997 – II CKN 224/97, (1998) 1OSNC Item 8.

79 Judgment of the Polish Supreme Court of 30 May 1996 – III CZP 42/96, (1996) 10 OSNC Item 128.

argue that the Polish judiciary has never been 'consumer-friendly' and after the transformation even turned back from the pro-consumer track which started to emerge in the 1980s,[80] it seems that the situation after the transformation was not so clear and as such makes it impossible to arrive at any clear-cut conclusion. In addition, since as of the 2000s the case law has been gradually becoming more consumer and EU-oriented, it seems fair to assume that the 'after the transformation' period has not had any significant implications for the current understanding of the concept of collective interest of consumers in Poland.

3.3. THE CURRENT STATE OF PLAY

The concept of the consumers' collective interests was introduced into Polish law – the Act for Protection of Competition and Consumers[81] (hereinafter: the 'APCC') – in 2002 as an implementation of Directive 98/27.[82] The Polish legislator consciously copied out the definition from Directive 98/27 expecting that it could be decoded from the future case law of the ECJ. That is why there was no attempt to introduce a statutory definition of the collective interest of consumers as it could have become inconsistent with the interpretation of the ECJ expected to be provided in the future.[83]

The APCC stipulates a general prohibition of unlawful practices infringing the collective interests of consumers (Article 24(1)). The APCC provides an indicative list of such unlawful practices: (1) the use of general terms and condition listed in the public register of abusive clauses;[84] (2) breach of the duty to provide reliable, true and full information to consumers; and (3) unfair commercial practices and acts of unfair competition (Article 24(2)).

A practice can be declared to be infringing the collective interest of consumers in the administrative proceedings before the OPCC. Decisions of the OPCC are

80 See Łętowska, *Prawo umów konsumenckich* (n 71); Skory, *Klauzule abuzywne* (n 59).

81 *Ustawa z dnia 15 grudnia 2000 o ochronie konkurencji i konsumentów*, DzU 2000, Issue 122, Item 1319. The new draft of the APCC was adopted on 16 February 2007, *Ustawa z dnia 16 lutego 2007 o ochronie konkurencji i konsumentów*, DzU 2007, Issue 50, Item 331 as amended. Its Article 24(3) states that the collective interest of consumers is not a mere sum of individual interests.

82 Amendment of the APCC introducing the concept of collective interests of consumers of 5 July 2002 (*Ustawa z dnia 5 lipca 2002 o zmianie ustawy o ochronie konkurencji i konsumentów, ustawy – Kodeks postępowania cywilnego oraz ustawy o zwalczaniu nieuczciwej konkurencji*, DzU 2002, Issue 129, Item 1102). It came into force on 15 December 2002.

83 See Explanatory Memorandum to the Amendment of the APCC introducing the concept of collective interests of consumers (*Uzasadnienie rządowego projektu ustawy o zmianie ustawy o ochronie konkurencji i konsumentów, ustawy o zwalczaniu nieuczciwej konkurencji oraz ustawy – Kodeks postępowania cywilnego (Druk Sejmowy No 366)*) www.sejm.gov.pl, accessed 15 March 2008.

84 See Part 2.3.3.

subject to judicial review. A claim to start proceedings by the OPCC can be filed by (1) the Ombudsman; (2) the spokesman of the insurance policyholders; (3) a consumers' spokesman; (4) a consumer organisation; (5) the Financial Supervisory Committee (Article 100a(1) APCC); and (6) a qualified consumer organisation in the meaning of Directive 98/27 (Article 100a(2)). Consumers themselves are not given this power.

In the following we will provide an overview of how the collective interest of consumers is interpreted by Polish courts and administrative bodies. We will show that there is a link between the present understanding of the public interest and its conceptualisation in the past. At the same time, we will show that even within one MS the content of the concept of collective interest of consumers can be unclear. We will also demonstrate that the lack of a precise definition of the concept of consumers' collective interest might lead to ambiguities as regards the competence of consumer protection bodies to take action. This supports our claim that a comprehensive strategy towards the concept of collective interest of consumers at the EU level is needed.[85]

In 2004 the Polish Supreme Court decided a case initiated by a regional consumers' spokesman against the OPCC.[86] The case dealt with a dispute between the two authorities concerning the competence of the OPCC to take actions aimed at the protection of consumers' collective interests.

In 2001 the OPCC refused to start proceedings against an energy company 'Energetyka' upon the motion of the regional consumers' spokesman. The OPCC believed that there was no public interest at stake.[87] The spokesman filed a complaint against Energetyka arguing that it was imposing unfavourable terms and conditions upon consumers. In the justification for its motion, the spokesman referred to the example of an individual consumer. The OPCC refused to take action claiming that the spokesman did not provide evidence that a wider group of consumers was affected by the objectionable practices of Energetyka. Accordingly, the dispute pertained only to an individual and not public interest. The Antimonopoly Court[88] upheld the OPCC's reasoning and argued that the APCC protects the interests of consumers as an institutional phenomenon. According to the Antimonopoly Court, particular practices should be regarded as infringing the interests of consumers only if they affect a wider group of market

85 Of course if we move beyond Poland the differences are likely to be even more apparent.

86 Judgment of the Polish Supreme Court of 26 February 2004 – III SK 1/2004; (2004) 18 OSNP Item 18.

87 The facts of the case had taken place before the notion of collective interests of consumers was introduced into the APCC. Still, the APCC specified in Article 1 that protection of consumers was to be undertaken in the public interest.

88 Now: Court for Protection of Competition and Consumers; it is a District Court in Warsaw; Article 32(2)(2) APCC.

participants, thus do not concern an individual entrepreneur or consumer but rather market distortions.

The Supreme Court quashed the ruling of the Antimonopoly Court and held that in order for the OPCC to take action there is no need to demonstrate that an undesired practice is of repetitious character and has affected many consumers. The APCC empowers and at the same time obligates competent bodies to take also preventive actions. It follows that a prerequisite for the start of administrative proceedings is also met in the case concerning only an individual consumer if the circumstances of this case demonstrate that undesired business practices might potentially distort the functioning of the market by infringing the interests of consumers (public interest). A reverse interpretation would preclude effective protection of consumers by means of preventive actions. In view of this, the Supreme Court held that although the regional consumers' spokesman referred to a single infringement, the circumstances of the case demonstrated that the challenged practices could be followed on a wider scale and thus infringe the public interest. Accordingly, starting the administrative procedure by the OPCC was justified.[89]

The case concerned the notion of the public interest and not the collective interests of consumers as the facts of the case had taken place before the latter was introduced into the APCC. Nevertheless, it seems arguable that the conclusions of the decision remain valid also for the concept of collective interest of consumers, especially as both courts and the OPCC consider the collective interest of consumers to be a variant or a part of the public interest.[90]

The case shows that a linkage between the individual and public interest utilised in the socialist Poland might have implications for the present understanding of the concept of public and consumers' collective interest. In the case under consideration, the regional consumers' spokesman explicitly quoted the Polish Supreme Court judgment of 1988[91] to justify its claim that a decision delivered in the individual case might have preventive effects beneficial for the general interest and thus there might be a general interest identified even if a case concerns individual interest only. Although the Supreme Court did not refer to the case quoted by the consumers' spokesman, it followed its argumentation.

The case further illustrates a possible discrepancy between the interpretation of the concept of collective interest of consumers by the OPCC and lower courts on the one hand and the Polish Supreme Court on the other. The OPCC and lower courts read the collective interest of consumers as meaning a situation in which

89 The cassation of the regional consumers' spokesman was dismissed on other grounds, however.

90 III SK 2/2004 (n 49); VI ACa 980/2006 (n 49). Moreover, in the case under discussion the Polish Supreme Court referred also to the collective interest of consumers.

91 III CZP 48/88 (n 66).

interests of an indefinite group of consumers are affected.[92] The APCC is said to protect consumers as a class and as an institutional phenomenon: in order to establish a breach concerning the collective interest of consumers, it must not be possible to identify all the individual breaches.[93] Accordingly, even if there is a large but closed group of affected consumers, the existence of the collective interest of consumers is precluded. In contrast, the position of the Supreme Court seems to be somewhat different. The Supreme Court holds that infringement of an individual consumer interest does not preclude existence of the collective interest of consumers if the individual infringement might in any way lead to the rise or preservation of monopolistic practices or disturb the market in another way.[94] For this reason, the Supreme Court does not focus on the indefinite number of consumers harmed, but on the potential for market distortions. As demonstrated by the case analysed above, the two approaches might be conflicting.

To conclude, on the basis of the Polish example, we demonstrated that the lack of a clear definition of the collective interest of consumers might lead to ambiguities concerning the competences of the consumer protection bodies to take action and thus undermine the effectiveness of consumer protection.

4. CONCLUSIONS

The existing EU instruments aimed at facilitating consumer redress in cross-border situations. Directive 98/27 and Regulation 2006/2004 employ the concept of collective interest of consumers. Given the Commission's focus on the protection of the collective interest, it will probably also underlie any European mechanism for collective redress elaborated in the future. Despite these developments, no comprehensive strategy towards the concept of consumers' collective interest at the EU level has so far been elaborated. We have argued that the lack of a precise definition of the collective interest may lead to under-enforcement of consumer rights due to an unclear situation concerning the competence of consumer protection bodies to institute legal proceedings. In order to remedy this situation we have put forward a proposal on how to make the concept of consumer collective interest a workable tool.

A definition of the collective interest limited to a statement that it is not a sum of individual interests is unlikely to perform its role of improving the procedural

92 Recently, VI ACa 980/2006 (n 48); Judgment of the Court of Appeal in Warsaw of 21 December 2006 – VI ACa 543/2006, LexPolonica nr 1428369; Decision of the OPCC of 29 September 2006 *w sprawie stosowania praktyk naruszających zbiorowe interesy konsumentów przez Rossmann Supermarkety Drogeryjne Polska Sp. z o.o. w Łodzi* ((Nr RLU-28/2006), DzUrzUOKiK 2006 No 4 Item 56.

93 Ibid.

94 III SK 2/2004 (n 49).

position of consumers. This negative statement can, however, serve as a starting point for building a positive definition. The following factors should be taken into account when building a more precise definition: (1) the number of infringements and persistence of a harmful practice; (2) the addressee of a practice; and (3) the nature of the interest infringed. We have proposed to introduce a rebuttable presumption of the existence of the collective interest if the requirements related to any of these factors are met in a given case. The function of such presumption could be to simplify the procedural situation of a claimant.

We have also examined how the concept of public interest was construed by the Polish judiciary during the socialist regime and shown that the way the public interest was conceptualised in the past political and legal system – in particular its relationship with individual interest – has an influence on the present understanding of the consumers' collective interest.

Finally, the *Duchesne* case[95] and the Polish case of 2004[96] show that interpretation of the concept of the collective interest of consumers might in fact be relevant for the effectiveness of collective redress schemes. Clear understanding of the notion, which currently varies from one MS to another, is thus essential for the creation of the internal market in the collective redress.

REFERENCES

CASES

European Cases

Case 45/76 *Comet v Produktschap* [1976] ECR 2043

Joined cases C-240/98 to C-244/98 *Océano Grupo Editorial SA v Roció Murciano Quintero and others* [2000] ECR I-4941

Case 33/76 *Rewe-Zentralfinanz eG et Rewe-Zentral AG v Landwirtschaftskammer für das Saarland* [1976] ECR 1989

Case C-321/95 P *Stichting Greenpeace Council (Greenpeace International) and Others v Commission* [1998] ECR 1651

Belgian Cases

Cour d'appel de Bruxelles, 8 December 2005, Duchesne v L'Office of Fair Trading, unreported, RG: 2005/KR/38

French Cases

Cass Crim, 20 May 1985, Bull Crim 485

Cass Crim, 10 October 1996, Bull Crim 358

---

95 N 16.

96 III SK 1/2004 (n 86).

Polish Cases

Judgment of the Polish Constitutional Tribunal of 17 October 2000 – SK 5/99, [2000] 7 OTK ZU Item 254

Judgment of the Polish Constitutional Tribunal of 31 March 2005 – SK 26/02, [2004] 11A OTK ZU Item 120

Judgment of the Polish Supreme Court of 9 May 1950 – Ł C 495/50, (1951) 3 OSN Item 67

Judgment of the Polish Supreme Court of 24 July 1959 – 4 CR 1027/58, (1961) 2 OSPiKA Item 32

Judgment of the Polish Supreme Court of 6 February 1963 – 2 CR 96/62;

Judgment of the Polish Supreme Court of 28 April 1964 – II CR 540/63, (1965) 2 OSNCP Item 32

Judgment of the Polish Supreme Court of 28 June 1972 – II CR 218/72, (1972) 12 OSNC Item 228

Resolution of the Civil Chamber of the Supreme Court of 20 May 1978 – III CZP 39/77, (1979) 3 OSNCP Item 40

Judgment of the Polish Supreme Court of 18 November 1983 – I CR 336/83, OSNCP 1984, No. 9, Item 159

Judgment of the Polish Supreme Court of 20 February 1986 – III CRN 443/85, OSNCP 1986, No. 12, Item 211

Judgment of the Polish Supreme Court of 30 December 1988 – III CZP 48/88, (1989) 3 OSNCP Item 36

Judgment of the Polish Supreme Court of 18 December 1990 – III CZP 67/90, (1991) 5–6 OSNCP Item 65

Judgment of the Polish Supreme Court of 22 May 1991 – III CZP 15/91, (1992) 1 OSNCP Item 1

Judgment of the Polish Supreme Court of 3 July 1991 – III CZP 59/91; (1992) 3 OSNCP Item 41

Judgment of the Supreme Court of 19 May 1992 – III CZP 50/92, (1993) 6 OSP Item 119

Judgment of the Polish Supreme Court of 16 April 1996 – II CRN 48/96, (1996) 6 Radca Prawny 32

Judgment of the Polish Supreme Court of 30 May 1996 – III CZP 42/96, (1996) 10 OSNC Item 128

Judgment of the Polish Supreme Court of 24 June 1997 – II CKN 224/97, (1998) 1OSNC Item 8

Polish Supreme Court of 19 December 2003 – III CZP 95/2003, (2003) 12 Biuletyn Sądu Najwyższego 11

Judgment of the Polish Supreme Court of 26 February 2004 – III SK 1/2004, (2004) 18 OSNP Item 18

Judgment of the Polish Supreme Court of 26 February 2004 – III SK 2/2004, (2004) 19 OSNP Item 343

Judgment of the Polish Supreme Court of 13 July 2006 – III SZP 3/2006, (2007) 1–2 OSNP Item 34

Judgment of the Court of Appeal in Warsaw of 21 Decemeber 2006 – VI ACa 543/2006, LexPolonica nr 1428369

Judgment of the Court of Appeal in Warsaw of 14 February 2007 – VI ACa 980/2006, LexPolonica No 1625352

Decision of the OPCC of 29 September 2006 *w sprawie stosowania praktyk naruszających zbiorowe interesy konsumentów przez Rossmann Supermarkety Drogeryjne Polska Sp. z o.o. w Łodzi* ((Nr RLU-28/2006), DzUrzUOKiK 2006 No 4 Item 56

Scottish Cases

Office of Fair Trading v MB Designs (Scotland) Ltd and others 2005 CSOH 85 (Court of Session)

LEGISLATIVE AND OTHER DOCUMENTS

European Documents

European Parliament and Council Regulation (EC) 2006/2004 of 27 October 2004 on cooperation between national authorities responsible for the enforcement of consumer protection laws, [2004] OJ L 364/1

European Parliament and Council Directive (EC) 98/27 of 19 May 1998 on Injunctions for the Protection of Consumers' Interests, [1998] OJ L 166/51

European Parliament and Council Directive (EC) 2004/48 of 29 April 2004 on the enforcement of intellectual property rights [2004] OJ L 157/45

Commission (EC), 'Discussion paper: Consumer redress. Memorandum from the Commission' COM(84) 629 final, 12 December 1984

Commission (EC), 'Access of Consumers to Justice and the Settlement of Consumer Disputes in the Single Market' (Green Paper) COM(93) 576 final, 16 November 1993

Commission (EC), 'Consumer Policy Action Plan 1999–2001' (Communication) COM(98) 696 final, 1 December 1998

Commission (EC), 'EU Consumer Policy Strategy 2007–2013 'Empowering consumers, enhancing their welfare, effectively protecting them'' (Communication) COM(2007) 99 final, 13 March 2007

Commission (EC), 'Report from the Commission concerning the application of Directive 98/27/EC of the European Parliament and of the Council on injunctions for the protection of consumers' interest', COM(2008) 756 final, 18 November 2008

Commission (EC), 'Green Paper on Consumer Collective Redress' (Green Paper) COM(2008) 794 final, 27 November 2008

French Documents

Groupe de travail présidé par Guillaume Cerutti and Marc Guillaume, 'Rapport sur l'Action de Groupe' (16 December 2005) www.minefi.gouv.fr/directions_services/sircom/protection_conso/protection_eco/rapport.pdf accessed 15 March 2008

Polish Documents

Polish Code of Obligations of 1933

Civil Code of 1964 as amended

Act of 28 July 1990 (*Ustawa z dnia 28 lipca 1990 r. o zmianie ustawy – Kodeks cywilny*), DzU 1990, No 55, Item 321

Uzasadnienie rządowego projektu ustawy o umowach zawieranych poza lokalem przedsiębiorstwa lub na odległość oraz o zmianie ustaw: Kodeks cywilny, Kodeks postępowania cywilnego i Kodeks wykroczeń (druk sejmowy nr 945), available at www.sejm.gov.pl accessed 15 March 2008

Ustawa z dnia 2 marca 2000 r. o ochronie niektórych praw konsumentów oraz o odpowiedzialności za szkodę wyrządzoną przez produkt niebezpieczny, DzU 2000, No 22, Item 271

Ustawa z dnia 15 grudnia 2000 o ochronie konkurencji i konsumentów, DzU 2000, Issue 122, Item 1319

Ustawa z dnia 5 lipca 2002 o zmianie ustawy o ochronie konkurencji i konsumentów, ustawy – Kodeks postępowania cywilnego oraz ustawy o zwalczaniu nieuczciwej konkurencji, DzU 2002, Issue 129, Item 1102

Uzasadnienie rządowego projektu ustawy o zmianie ustawy o ochronie konkurencji i konsumentów, ustawy o zwalczaniu nieuczciwej konkurencji oraz ustawy – Kodeks postępowania cywilnego (Druk Sejmowy No 366)), available at www.sejm.gov.pl, accessed 15 March 2008

Ustawa z dnia 16 lutego 2007 o ochronie konkurencji i konsumentów, DzU 2007, Issue 50, Item 331 as amended

UK Documents

DTI, 'Consultation on implementing the EU Directive on Unfair Commercial Practices and Amending Existing Consumer Legislation' (December 2005, 42) www.berr.gov.uk/files/file15311.pdf, accessed 15 March 2008

BIBLIOGRAPHIC RESOURCES

Gerrit Betlem, 'Public and Private Transnational Enforcement of EU Consumer Law' (2007) 18 *European Business Law Review* 683

Peter Blume, 'The Citizens' Data Protection' (1998) 1 Journal of Information, Law and Technology, www2.warwick.ac.uk/fac/soc/law/elj/jilt/1998_1/blume/, accessed 15 March 2008

Thierry Bourgoignie, 'Characteristics of consumer law' (1992) 14 *Journal of Consumer Policy* 293

Fabrizio Cafaggi, 'Review of Stefan Grundmann and Denis Mazeaud (eds), *General Clauses and Standards in European Contract Law: Comparative Law, EC Law and Contract Law Codification (Kluwer Law International 2006)*' (2007) 4 *European Review of Contract Law* 491

Fabrizio Cafaggi and Horatia Muir-Watt, *Making of European Private Law: Governance Design* (Edward Elgar Publishing, Cheltenham 2008)

Fabrizio Cafaggi and Hans-W. Micklitz, 'Collective Enforcement of Consumer Law: A Framework for Comparative Assessment' (2008) 16 *European Review of Private Law* 391

Jean Calais-Auloy and Frank Steinmetz, *Droit de la consommation* (4th edn, Dalloz-Sirey, Paris 1996)

Suzanne Carval, *La responsabilité civile dans sa fonction de peine privée* (Bibliothèque de droit privé, LGDJ, Paris 1995)

Hugh Collins, *Regulating Contracts* (Oxford University Press, Oxford 1999)

Gustavo Ghidini, *Per i consumatori* (Zanichelli, Bologna 1977)

Louis Kaplow, 'Rules versus Standards: An Economic Analysis' (1992) 42 *Duke Law Journal* 557

Michael Haley, 'Stop Now – Injunction: Protecting the Interests of European Consumers' (Conference on Effective Legal Redress – The Consumer Protection Instruments of Actions for Injunction and Group Damages Actions in Vienna, 24 February 2006) www.bmsk.gv.at/cms/site/attachments/0/8/3/CH0036/CMS1141717684789/eu-studie_teil_i.pdf, accessed 15 March 2008

Geraint Howells and Rhoda James, 'Litigation in the Consumer Interest' (2002) 9 ILSA *Journal of International & Comparative Law* 1

Geraint Howells and Stephen Weatherill, *Consumer Protection Law* (2nd edn, Markets and the Law, Ashgate, Aldershot 2005)

Duncan Kennedy, 'Distributive and Paternalist Motives in Contract and Tort Law, with Special Reference to Compulsory Terms and Unequal Bargaining Power' (1982) 41 *Maryland Law Review* 563

Christoph Knill, 'European Policies: The Impact of National Administrative Traditions' (1998) 18 *Journal of Public Policy* 1

Komisja Kodyfikacyjna, *Projekt kodeksu cywilnego* (Warszawa 1962)

Neil K. Komesar, *Imperfect Alternatives: Choosing Institutions in Law, Economics, and Public Policy* (Chicago University Press, Chicago 1994)

Russell Korobkin, 'Bounded Rationality, Standard Form Contracts, and Unconscionability' (2003) 70 *University of Chicago Law Review* 1203

Meglena Kuneva, 'Healthy markets need effective redress' (Speech at Conference on Collective Redress in Lisbon, 9 November 2007) http://ec.europa.eu/consumers/redress_cons/docs/mku_cr_lisbon_final.pdf, accessed 15 March 2008

Biruta Lewaszkiewicz-Petrykowska, 'Bezpieczeństwo konsumentów w prawie polskim' in Grażyna Rokicka (ed.) *"Model Prawnej Ochrony Konsumenta" Harmonizacja Polskiego Prawa Konsumenckiego z Regułami Unii Europejskiej* (Stowarzyszenie Konsumentów Polskich, Warszawa 1996), www.skp.pl, accessed 15 March 2008

Ewa Łętowska, *Wzorce umowne: ogólne warunki, wzory, regulaminy* (Zakład Narodowy im Ossolińskich, Wrocław 1975)

Ewa Łętowska, 'Ochrona konsumenta z punktu widzenia polityki prawa' (1978) (4) *Państwo i Prawo* 16

Ewa Łętowska in Stanisław Pawela and Kazimierz Piasecki, 'Sesja Sądu Najwyższego PRL - Sprawozdania' (1985) (5) *Nowe Prawo* 63

Ewa Łętowska, *Prawo umów konsumenckich* (CH Beck, Warszawa 2002)

Robert Madelin, 'Collective Redress (Remarks)' (Conference on Collective Redress in Lisbon, 9 November 2007) http://ec.europa.eu/consumers/redress_cons/docs/rm_cr_lLisbon_speak_ 09-%20 11-07.pdf, accessed 15 March 2008

OECD, 'Background Report' (OECD Workshop on Consumer Dispute Resolution and Redress in the Global Marketplace in Washington, 19–20 April 2005) www.oecd.org/dataoecd/59/21/34699496.pdf, accessed 15 March 2008

Anthony Ogus, *Regulation: Legal Form and Economic Theory* (Clarendon Press, Oxford 1994)

Barbara Piasna, 'Powstanie i rozwój instytucjonalnych form ochrony interesów konsumentów w Polsce Ludowej' (1971) 4 *Ruch Prawniczy, Ekonomiczny i Socjologiczny* 135

Eric A. Posner, 'Contract Law in the Welfare State: A Defense of the Unconscionability Doctrine, Usury Laws, and Related Limitations on the Freedom of Contract' (1995) 24 *Journal of Legal Studies* 283

Peter Rott, 'The Protection of Consumers' Interests After the Implementation of the EC Injunctions Directive Into German and English Law' (2001) 24 *Journal of Consumer Policy* 401

Marek Safjan, 'Klauzule generalne w prawie cywilnym (przyczynek do dyskusji)' (1990) (11) *Państwo i Prawo* 48

Marek Safjan, 'Zasada swobody umów. (Uwagi wstępne na tle wykładni art. 353[1] k.c.)' (1993) (4) *Państwo i Prawo* 12

Maciej Skory, *Klauzule abuzywne w polskim prawie ochrony konsumenta* (Zakamycze, Kraków 2005)

The Study Centre for Consumer Law - Centre for European Economic Law, 'An analysis and evaluation of alternative means of consumer redress other than redress through ordinary judicial proceedings. Final report' (Katholieke Universiteit Leuven, Belgium January 17, 2007) http://ec.europa.eu/consumers/redress/reports_studies/comparative_report_en.pdf accessed 15 March 2008

Jules Stuyck (Conference on Collective Redress in Leuven, 29 June 2007) http://ec.europa.eu/consumers/redress_cons/docs/leuven_event_JSpresentation.pdf accessed 15 March 2008

Roger Van den Bergh and Louis Vischer, 'The Preventive Function of Collective Actions for Damages in Consumer Law' (2008) 1 *Erasmus Law Review* 1

Walter van Gerven, Jeremy Lever and Pierre Larouche, *Cases, Materials and Text on National, Supranational and International Tort Law* (Ius Commune Casebooks, Hart Publishing, Oxford 2000)

Witold Warkałło, *Odpowiedzialność odszkodowawcza: Funkcje, rodzaje, granice* (Państwowe Wydawnictwo Naukowe, Warszawa 1972)

Konrad Zweigert and Hein Kötz, *Introduction to Comparative Law*, translated by Tony Weir (3rd edn OUP, Oxford 1998)
Czesława Żuławska, 'Wokół zasady wolności umów (art. 353[1] k.c. i wykładnia zwyczaju)' (1994) 1690 *Acta Universitatis Wratislaviensis* 173

ABBREVIATIONS

Bull Crim	Bulletin des arrêts de la chambre criminelle de la Cour de cassation
Cass Crim	Cour de Cassation, Chambre Criminelle
CSOH	Court of Session Other House
DzU	Dziennik Ustaw
DzUrzUOKiK	Dziennik Urzędowy Urzędu Ochrony Konkurencji I Konsumentów
ECR	European Court Reports
OJ	Official Journal
OSN	Orzecznictwo Sądu Najwyższego
OSNC	Orzecznictwo Sądu Najwyższego (Izba Cywilna)
OSNCP	Orzecznictwo Sądu Najwyższego (Izba Cywilna, Pracy i Ubezpieczeń Społecznych)
OSNP	Orzecznictwo Sądu Najwyższego (Izba Pracy)
OSP	Orzecznictwo Sądów Polskich
OSPiKA	Orzecznictwo Sądów Polskich i Komisji Arbitrażowych
OTK ZU	Orzecznictwo Trybunału Konstytucyjnego Zbiór Urzędowy

EFFICIENCY OF THE PROTECTION OF COLLECTIVE INTERESTS: JUDICIAL AND ADMINISTRATIVE ENFORCEMENT IN THE CZECH REPUBLIC

Luboš Tichý and Jan Balarin*

1. INTRODUCTION

1.1. TOPIC AND PURPOSE

The purpose of this short study is to show the readers the specific conception of protection of consumer interests in the Czech Republic and to try to find out if any useful guidance can be drawn from this experience.

Using empirical data from our research among Czech consumer organisations, we concentrate in particular on collective judicial enforcement of consumer interests (sections 2, 3); we analyse the current fragment regulation of collective remedies in Czech procedural law (Civil Procedure Code[1]); we comment on it from the critical perspective and, as a contrast, we show the practice of enforcement of consumer rights (section 4), which has found its own ways how to streamline protection. Section 4, in addition, centres on some of the types of collective-interest actions, which have developed under these conditions and analyses their subject. We also discuss the basic principles of judicial collective protection and examine them through the optics of the doctrine of human rights (section 5). On the other hand, we test the common presupposition that the instant effect of administrative supervision of consumer rights is less intensive than judicial overview (section 6). In the conclusion we ask the question whether a materially unconfined collective element in the judicial proceedings, as it currently results from Czech law, may be somehow inspirational for Europe (section 7).

* Luboš Tichý is Professor at Charles University Prague and chair of the European Law Department of Faculty of Law, Jan Balarin is Ph.D. candidate at this Faculty of Law.

1 Act No. 99/1963 Coll., Civil Procedure Code.

We build on a hypothesis that, compared with other EU countries, even the new ones,[2] enforcement of consumer interests is neglected in the Czech Republic. This observation follows not only from the underdevelopment of written law but especially from the practical experience of consumer organisations. And what is true for consumer law generally, applies *a forteriori* to collective redress.

This basically unfavourable situation has, surprisingly, some upsides – the collective interest regulation stands on the starting line and the collective remedies can be rethought in their model form (whether deduced from the positive law or considered *de lege ferenda*). From this point of view we raise three questions:

a) To what extent are specific procedural mechanisms for the protection of consumers needed or, in other words, does a demand for a collective consumer procedure really exist?
b) What is the place of the group interest in a post-communist country and how is the group interest protected? May a consumer group interest qualify as the public interest?[3]
c) How effectively is the collective protection implemented and what efforts[4] should be made to achieve effectiveness?[5]

1.2. METHODOLOGY. DEFINITIONS AND NOTIONS

Generally, we analyse the topic from the perspective of (i) the access of consumers and competent institutions to the mechanisms of protection, especially to judicial and administrative organs, (ii) the extent of rights, which may be heard in judicial and administrative proceedings, and (iii) the efficiency of enforcement (i.e. if the result of a protection mechanism is able directly to affect subjective consumer rights).

At the very beginning, we should clear up two important aspects, namely the concept of rights, which we are going to discuss, and the characteristics of their enforcement.

The "consumer rights" are to be understood as subjective private rights, which take the form of a claim or might take this form in the near future, and are based

---

2 See the assessment of the situation prior to the accession: H.-W. Micklitz (ed.), *Rechtseinheit oder Rechtsvielfalt in Europa? Zur Rolle des Verbraucherrechts in der MOE-Staaten und in der EG*, Baden-Baden, 1996.

3 See, e.g. E. Letowska, *Consumer Protection as Public Interest Law, Droit polonais contemporain*, 1999, 39f.

4 See H. B. Schäfer, Anreizwirkungen bei der Class Action und der Verbandsklage, in: J. Basedow et al. (eds.), *Die Bündelung gleichgerichteter Interessen im Prozess*, Tübingen, Washinton D.C., 1999, 67f.

5 For the importance of the class action as a regulatory means, see D. Rosenberg, The Regulatory Advantage of Class Action, in: W. K. Viscusi (ed.), *Regulation through Litigation*, 2002, 244f.

on the law or on a contract with a supplier. However, the rights may be enforced only by specific means, which have been developed in theory and instituted by the law; from these means, only the cease and desist remedy (injunctions), restitution remedy and damages remedy are of interest here.

"Enforcement" is the means for benefiting the drawing of a benefit from consumer rights. Assertion of violated or endangered rights can proceed in various ways: from negotiations, through mediation and arbitration, to judicial and administrative procedures. Since Czech law does not yet provide for preliminary remedies (mediation), we centre on judicial and administrative proceedings.

Another major terminological question in the context of collective judicial protection is the concept of "collective action". It is important to bear in mind that the collective action, as a means of procedural enforcement of rights, does not necessarily represent a public interest.

In this study, we take into account the situation in EU Member States[6] where, on principle, two forms of collective legal protection of consumers exist.[7]

The first, which we designate as the "community action", means assertion of rights by a body representing the public interest. This action does not primarily accumulate individual claims,[8] but embodies a common interest that abstracts from particular aggrieved persons. In this sense, it functions as *ex ante* protection (prevention).[9] Community actions are the domain of consumer organisations advocating, not their own, but consumer interests.[10] The consumer interest thus gets promoted to the level of a public interest.[11] The key incentive for this kind of remedy is usually extreme diffusion and diminutiveness of individual elements of the cover claim, which require, besides the class enforcement (as described below), also a higher attention manifested in the consumer organisations' specific litigation powers.

In contrast, class actions are typically filed by a class member in his own interest and, potentially, in the interest of the entire class. It is only here that the

---

6 See *inter alia* H. Beuchler, A. Mom, Rechtvergleichendes Fazit, in: H.-W. Micklitz, A. Stadler, *Das Verbandsklagerecht in der Informations- und Dienstleistungsgesellschaft*, Münster, 2005, 1129f., but especially H. Koch, Die Verbandsklage in Europa, *ZZP*, 2000, 413f.

7 However, we depart from the conception to some extent, especially as concerns the position and significance of the so-called Musterklage (cf. infra in this section).

8 See one of the first and most influential works: N. Reich, *Europäisches Verbraucherschutzrecht*, 2nd ed., Baden-Baden, 1993, and later in the Czech literature: L. Tichý, La notion du consommateur en tant que partie contractante en droit tchéque et européen, in: Cefres – Prague, *Le droit communautaire de la consommation et sa transposition dans les Etats membres et dans les pays candidats*, Prague 2001.

9 See infra 2.7.

10 If individuals are allowed to file this action, then only upon certain given conditions (see, e.g. Federal Rules of Civil Procedure Rule 23), which are, however, absent in Czech law (see section 5).

11 See, e.g. H. Koch, *Prozessführung im öffentlichen Interesse*, 1983.

question of aggregation of claims and claimants gains relevance. The class action does not *prima facie* concern a common claim,[12] but consists of a number of claims of particular individuals (a group of individuals who pertain to a wider class[13]). This collective mechanism may also be regarded as a temporary summation of individual interests, which will be diversified again on the occasion of adjudication of the class suit, whether the action is upheld or dismissed.

Both community and class actions may lead to a model proceeding and a model judgment.[14] The question of our interest is how to interpret provisions of Czech Civil Procedure Code which underlie the judicial collective procedure. Do they found a community action, a class action or a combination of both? Unfortunately, Czech authors do not sufficiently recognise the above-described concept[15] and the same is true for the legislature, which has done no more so far than mechanically transpose Directive 98/27/EC without a real in-depth understanding of the collective enforcement.

2. PROCEDURAL PROTECTION OF COLLECTIVE INTERESTS

2.1. DEVELOPMENTS OF COLLECTIVE LITIGATION[16]

A. *Beginning*

First, opportunities for the protection of collective interests appeared in the Czech Republic at the beginning of the nineties. The Economic Competition Protection

12 Very convincingly clarified in J. Calais-Auloy, Les actions en justice des associations des consommateurs, *D.* 1988, Chron. 193.

13 See H.-W. Micklitz, A. Stadler, Allgemeine Fragen zur prozessualen Ausgestaltung von Verbands-, Muster- und Gruppenklagen, in: H.-W. Micklitz, A. Stadler, *Das Verbandsklagerecht in der Informations- und Dienstleistungsgesellschaft*, Münster 2005, 1185, and especially 1188–1190, from the material law point of view; see also, e.g. E. Schmidt, In diffusis submerses – oder aber: diffusitas non nocet, in: L. Krämer et al. (eds.), *Law and Diffuse Interests in the European Legal Order*, Baden-Baden 1997, 81f, and Th. Roethe, Der Konsument – autonom. Seine Interessen – spezifisch, in: L. Krämer et al. (eds.), *Law and Diffuse Interests in the European Legal Order*, Baden-Baden 1997, 93f.

14 See P. Gottwald, Zum Ausbau des kollektiven Rechtsschutzes in Deutschland, in: L. Tichý (ed.), *Schutz der kollektiven Interessen im Zivilprozessrecht*, Prague 2008, 40 – 42, for Austria see W. H. Rechberger, Verbandsklagen, Musterprozesse und "Sammelklagen", in: *Festschrift R. Welser*, Vienna 2006, 871f.

15 See P. Smolík, Hromadné žaloby (Collective Actions), in: *Pocta (Liber amicorum) Marta Knappová*, Prague 2005, A. Winterová, Právní důsledky skupinové žaloby v českém právu (legal consequences of a collective action in the Czech law), in: *Pocta (Liber amicorum) Jiří Švestka*, Prague 2004, 349, and especially L. Drápal in: Bureš et al. (ed.), *Občanský soudní řád – Komentář*, 7. ed., Prague 2006, I. vol.

16 For a concise outline see L. Tichý, Prozessrechtlicher Schutz der Verbraucherinteressen in der Tschechischen Republik, in: Bundesministerium für Ernährung, Landwirtschaft und

Act from 1991 instituted a collective action in its model form,[17] but any empirical data on if and how the action has been used are missing. This early stage was concluded by a new antitrust law enacted in 2001, which no longer provides for collective judicial redress. The Consumer Protection Act from 1992 has set some basic terms of consumer protection and facilitated the administrative protection of collective interests, which is the pillar of the regulation. The Act unfortunately did not make any room for judicial enforcement initially.

B. *Civil Procedural Law*

The trigger for judicial collective proceedings in consumer matters was the Directive 98/27/EC, which brought about an amendment of the Civil Procedure Code (§83[18] and §159a[19]),[20] but a somewhat peculiar one: the only the change consisted of loosening the binding effect (legal force) of judgments so that not only parties are bound by the judgment, but all persons in the same position as the parties. Thus, the gates for litigating in collective interest have been opened. However the novelty meant an insensitive breakthrough in the traditionally run-in concept of individual judicial protection.[21]

2.2. ADMINISTRATIVE PROTECTION

Various branches of law enable parallel judicial and administrative protection. In some cases, the parallel is exact, in other, where the subject of the proceedings is dictated by the method of adjudication, the parallel is rather blurred and may be spotted especially by the analysis of the goals of protection. The common feature of both the mentioned types of procedure consists of the injunctive relief against unlawful interference (or its consequences), but the procedures differ with respect to other remedies, e.g. only the administrative bodies have the authority to impose

Verbraucherschutz, *Kollektive Rechtsdurchsetzung – Chancen und Risiken*, 2006, 213f.

17 Act No. 63/1991 Coll., on the Protection of Economic Competition; cf. §17(2): once the proceedings have been initiated or finally ended, no law suits based on the same legal grounds are permitted.

18 §83(2) reads: "Commencement of a proceeding [...] to cease and desist from an unlawful conduct in the matters of protection of consumer rights [...] shall, in relation to the same defendant, bar any other judicial proceedings on actions of other plaintiffs asserting the same claims following from the same conduct or state.".

19 §159a(2) reads: "A ruling in an effective judgment awarded in the matters specified in §83(2) shall be binding upon not only the parties to the proceeding, but also other persons entitled against the defendant to the same claims following from the same conduct or state [...].".

20 See Act No. 151/2002 Coll. that refers to §25 of Consumer Protection Act (Act No. 634/1992 Coll.) – the legal basis of a collective action for protection of consumer interests which can be filed by a consumer organisation.

21 Cf. the critique of this six-year-old and unaltered regulation in sections 3 and 5.

fines and other sanctions. Unfortunately, enforcement of collective interests in administrative proceedings does not go beyond filing motions by consumer organisations, which might, at the highest, signal an infringement; a motion does not launch proceedings, but can (and should) only induce authorities to check the alleged wrongdoing and, eventually, institute the proceedings *ex officio*.

Although even administrative proceedings may involve highly individual subject matter,[22] the essential finding, in our view, is that administrative decision-making in itself proves an "abstract" or "mass" impact, for the large part. We address an effect of administrative measures, which can be described as relative finality.[23]

2.3. ADHESION PROCEDURE WITHIN ADMINISTRATIVE AND CRIMINAL PROCEDURE

The Czech Republic has a relatively long history of adhesion procedures.[24] Since a recent Criminal Code amendment, which has introduced a special consumer-related crime ("actions to the detriment of consumers") into law, the question of adhesion procedure against a violator of consumer rights has become even more real. It can be supposed that not only individual consumers but also consumer organisations may take part in criminal proceedings in consumer-rights related crimes.[25]

Similarly, adhesion claims can be raised also in the minor offences procedure tried before administrative bodies, which might, in consumer cases be more useful than the criminal adhesion procedure. Consumer organisations can participate in the administrative adhesion procedure, we assume, to the same extent as they can in the criminal procedure.[26]

2.4. DIFFERENCES WITHIN THE PROCEDURAL MODES OF PROTECTION

Administrative and judicial procedures differ in a substantial way. Whereas the administrative procedure is governed by the principle of officiality, the judicial

---

22 P. Lakkis, *Der kollektive Rechtschutz der Verbraucher in der Europäischen Union*, Bielefeld 1997, 23f.

23 See the overview in F. Cafaggi, H.-W. Micklitz, Collective Enforcement of Consumer Law: A Framework for Comparative Assessment, *European Review of Private Law*, 2008, 397 f. In the Czech Republic, Directive 98/27/EC has not been transposed directly into the administrative enforcement rules (see further infra in section 6).

24 P. Smolík, *op. cit.* in footnote 15, 381.

25 Cf. §121 of the Criminal Code (Act No. 140/1961 Coll.).

26 Cf. §43f. of the Criminal Procedure Code (Act No. 141/1961 Coll.).

procedure is an adversarial mechanism and the position of the "collective petitioner" varies accordingly. It is therefore important to ask if and to what extent the consumer organisations should be granted the standard procedural rights and the party status in the administrative procedure.[27]

Everybody may file administrative motions of any cause and that is (supposedly) why consumer organisations and individual consumers acting in the interests of a group of consumers do not hold any special procedural position, even in cases where they need to prove first that they act in collective interests.[28] Except for the above mentioned adhesion procedure, claims are enforced indirectly (indirect claims) in administrative procedure, so the "collectiveness" does not play any role with respect to the manner in wich the competent authority handles the motion. As a rule, there are no remedial instruments if the motion is mismanaged by the authority.[29]

2.5. INSTITUTIONAL BACKGROUND

One of the important aspects of the collective consumer protection is its institutional background. Disregarding the group actions filed by one consumer on behalf of a group of consumers, collective enforcement requires institutions that perform specific tasks in the enforcement process.

To categorise such institutions, we need to use certain criteria, the most important of which is the relation to the consumer and the public sector (state). From this perspective we can distinguish several types of institutions, which, depending on their status, are or are not equipped with public law competence in the collective protection procedure. We can primarily differentiate between consumer organisations and public (governmental) bodies.

A. *Consumer Organisations*

The consumer organisations may be either established or supported by the government or be entirely independent of the State.[30]

Czech law, in principle, does not distinguish between these two kinds of consumer organisations. Despite that fact, consumer organisations are quite numerous, which is probably a consequence of consumer "self-help" in the

27 This part of public law enforcement was developed without any influence from the Community law.

28 Cf. §26 of the Consumer Protection Act.

29 E.g. J. Stuyck et al., *An Analysis and Evaluation of Alternative Means of Consumer Redress other than Redress through Ordinary Juridical Proceedings*, Louvain 2007, 72f.

30 Main consumer organisations are financed fully or at least partly by the public sector, predominantly by the state.

situation where the legislator still does not care enough to adapt the standard judicial and administrative remedies to the needs and capabilities of individual consumers (see below).

B. Public Bodies

aa) Courts. In the Czech Republic, there are neither specialised courts[31] to deal with consumer collective interests, nor an advantage of territorial jurisdiction in favour of consumers, e.g. an opportunity to file the actions in the place of their residence.[32] In almost all consumer matters, the lowest level of courts (district courts) is competent. It is obvious that the judicial system still does not deem enforcement of collective interests desirable.

bb) Administrative agencies. We talk about governmental administrative bodies, which deal with consumer motions. As in the judiciary, no agencies focused on consumer complaints are at work. Powers of administrative agencies are of course closely interrelated with the administrative procedure;[33] a procedure may be initiated on the basis of a motion or proposal of a consumer or consumer organisation. Administrative procedure does not fit within the traditional system of remedies (as developed in the judicial process), but rather functions as a specific administrative intervention against wrongful consequences of trade, vocational or other similar activities.

cc) Ombudsman. The Czech ombudsman[34] does not primarily deal with consumer matters; his competence is mostly limited to disclose failures within the framework of public administration. So, the Ombudsman is able to provide only a kind of mediated protection to consumers through control of administrative supervisory bodies competent in consumer matters.

As already mentioned, no specialised mediation or arbitration proceedings exist and neither do corresponding institutions or legal aid (the function is partially assumed by consumer organisations). Consumer claims of a collective nature relating to certain professions may be, in addition, brought before public chambers associating practitioners of that profession (e.g. lawyers, notaries and architects).[35]

---

31 See A. Winterová, *op. cit.* in footnote 15.

32 A law suit has to be filed in the court of the defendant (Civil Procedure Code §85).

33 See the Administrative Procedure Act No. 500/2004 Coll.

34 Cf. Act No. 349/1999 Coll., on Public Defender of Rights. The status of the Czech Ombudsman differs from other EU countries (see A. Edling, The Consumer Ombudsman Scheme and Group Actions, in: T. Bourgoignie (ed.), *Group Actions and Consumer Protection*, Brussels, 1992, 51f).

35 E.g. L. Tichý, Procesní ochrana skupinových zájmů – přehled a řešení (Collective Actions – A Solution), in: L. Tichý, *Procesní ochrana kolektivních zájmů (Protection of Collective Interests in Civil Procedural Law)*, AUC iuridica, 4/2005, 51f.

2.6. EFFICIENCY OF PROTECTION

The efficiency of protection is one of the crucial parameters to be taken into account.[36] The efficiency can be reviewed from various angles. For our purpose, the relevant criteria are the scope of applicability as to time, persons and subject matter, and the cost aspect.

a) In both the judicial and administrative procedures, collective claims may be raised by individual consumers as well as consumer organisations (although in judicial procedure consumer organisations are limited to injunctive actions), so this issue does not create a problem.
b) As for the subject matter of claims, we would like to underscore beforehand that collective consumer interests include, in our view, also claims of administrative nature (e.g. administrative prohibition to exercise a profession), but we do not further discuss the issue. Consumer claims capable of remedy in court may be distinguished into injunctive claims. Injunctive claims are to be understood as claims to desist from certain acts, i.e. a ban on certain activity.
   The only private consumer claims, which may be remedied in administrative procedure, are damages. Other benefits resulting from administrative measures are mediated effects attained indirectly.
c) Claims are enforced either directly or indirectly. Direct enforcement means that the plaintiff's cause of action (a right following from the substantive law) is addressed immediately. Direct enforcement must always be the primary means of protection, as it best embodies the private essence of consumer rights. If the action is dismissed, especially in the case of an injunction, the result is transmitted indirectly to the entire collective interest, because all separate claims pertaining to the class are estopped from litigating in the future.[37] The extensive *res judicata* effect prevents the matter from being relitigated by different parties, so even a dismissing judgment strongly influences the factual position of every person afflicted by the defendant's conduct.
   In administrative procedure, upholding a motion may impress the collective interest merely indirectly. Administrative decision serves in this sense especially as a precondition to assertion of a claim in course of negotiation or a judicial proceeding. Not even the dismissal of a motion radiates directly throughout the collective interest because its significance is strictly limited to the individually reviewed case.

36 See J. Calais-Auloy, *op. cit.* in footnote 12 or H. B. Schäfer, *op. cit.* in footnote 4.
37 Cf. Civil Procedure Code §159a.

d) Of crucial importance is also the question of time. Effects of timely protection are obviously multiplied and are a source of transaction cost savings. This requirement is mostly translated into the issue of time limits of procedural mechanisms. Judicial proceedings generally resist any time limitation for resolution of cases (except for drawing up the judgment). On the other hand, administrative procedure, although (or because) only an indirect way of enforcement, is usually clearly time-scheduled.
e) Despite all that, the dominant practical issue is the costs (and not only proceedings costs, such as court fees, but also preparatory and other costs which merely indirectly relate to the enforcement procedure). Costs are a substantial distinctive factor between the judicial and administrative enforcement, as the administrative procedure usually means to the motioning party no or relatively minor costs.

2.7. PROTECTION *EX POST, EX ANTE*

The judicial and administrative protection may be further discriminated whether provided *ex post* or *ex ante*. Any redress, such as injunction, restitution or damages award, has the *ex post* effect.[38] A judgment may also operate *ex ante* as a deterrent, because it may be (and usually is) of importance for other similar cases heard in courts. The question grows more complex in the administrative procedure. A positive decision delivered on the basis of a consumer motion is undoubtedly an *ex post* remedy, and the deterring effect is regularly reduced to the present case. With regard to the widespread fractionalisation of public administration, any *ex ante* effect usually follows from other than legal instruments, such as media publicity.

3. ANALYSIS OF THE REGULATION OF JUDICIAL ENFORCEMENT

3.1. COMMUNITY ACTION

The party who represents the consumer interest, i.e. who acts on behalf of a group of consumers not identified on an individual basis, may primarily be a consumer protection organisation (see Czech Consumer Protection Act §25(1) speaking

[38] See Fr. Zoulík, Problematika hromadných žalob se zřetelem k českému právu (Collective Actions in Czech Legal System), in: L. Tichý, *Procesní ochrana kolektivních zájmů (Protection of Collective Interests in Civil Procedural Law)*, AUC iuridica, 4/2005, 16. The preventive (*ex ante*) effect is inherent to the community action.

about organisations and other entities established for the protection of consumers). The organisation must possess legal personality and be recognised by the law as such (however, there are no special requirements to qualify for the protection of consumers).

Besides consumer organisations, consumer interests may be judicially enforced also by entities included in the list maintained by the European Commission according to Directive 98/27/EC. Nevertheless, there is a difference between these two categories of plaintiffs. Whereas the former one cannot be reviewed by the court whether entitled to represent consumers, assuming that the "consumer protection" is recorded in the organisation's articles as a subject of its activity, (Consumer Protection Act §25(1)(2)(a)) the latter may be required to prove that it is a qualified entity under Directive 98/27/EC (Consumer Protection Act §25(2)(b)).

It is important to note that only actions brought by consumer organisations for injunctions may qualify as community actions. So, Czech consumer collective litigation does not include actions for removal of a wrongful state of affairs, such as restitution or award of damages. Actions filed by a consumer on behalf of other consumers or by a consumer organisation for protection of consumer interests, which claim restitution or damages, do not acquire the effect of collective remedy and cannot have any consequences beyond the circle of the actual parties to the proceedings.

3.2. CLASS ACTION

The Civil Procedure Code does not expressly entitle individual consumers to bring a class action on behalf of other consumers (class), or, more precisely, does not specifically connect the class effect with individual actions. The nature of litigation initiated by individual consumers may be disputed, because the wording of Civil Procedure Code §83(2), which constitutes the class action procedure, is in the relevant part the same as the Consumer Protection Act §25(2), which gives the right to act exclusively to consumer organisations. Although this view would mean that an individual's action would not entail *lis pedens* and *res judicata* for persons in the same position as the plaintiff, we hold another opinion: that a class action may be instituted by any individual, who falls within the group of aggrieved consumers, and who therefore acts at the trial on behalf of the entire group.

As can be seen, Czech class action regulation is strictly minimalist. Only the very core of Directive 98/27/EC has been transposed into Czech law.[39] This situation collides especially at the point of contact with third parties' rights, whose

[39] One can doubt whether – with regard to Article 2 of the Directive – the Czech Republic even met all requirements when transposing this provision.

procedural specifics remained not reflected by the law. The problem is further multiplied by the fact that the concepts of "disputed case" and "procedural identity of the subject matter" are still not sufficiently clarified. For instance an authoritative commentary on Civil Procedure Code declares the "claim" to be not only a part of the "case" but also of the "subject matter" of the proceedings.[40]

3.3. NEGATIVE CONSEQUENCES OF CLASS ACTION

A legislatively problematic situation is which article of the law is being cited. This arises when the litigation is pursued by the wrong plaintiff (a person not affected by the unlawful practice, an organisation not qualified to protect consumer interests, etc.) and the action is dismissed for that reason. According to the Civil Procedure Act wording, each new proceeding initiated in the same matter by anybody else would be inadmissible. However, this would not be an acceptable conclusion. Some legal writers therefore assume that proceedings with collective effect (i.e. extended binding effect of the judgment) may be initiated only by an "entitled person", which designates a person who is materially qualified to bring the action.[41] More generally, it can be supposed that if the result of a controversy should be binding on persons in the same position as the plaintiff, the controversy must be heard on the merits at least. Could an example be given? Has it ever been tried or is it academic debate?

The judgment is binding on all members of the class, even those who indirectly took part in the proceedings, although the fact that it has entered into force is materially incorrect. The same holds true for a judgment which (incorrectly) dismisses the action for procedural reasons, e.g. because of the missing qualification to pursue the claim.

As indicated, the shortcomings of the Czech collective procedure regulation manifest themselves most in the question how other members of the aggrieved class of consumers take part in the proceedings. At this point, Czech law does not much respect the principle that everybody who should be bound by a decision must be given an opportunity to participate at the trial. No special regard is paid to procedural rights of persons who should be bound by the judgment, but who are not parties to the proceedings. It is not even required that the class members receive notice of the proceedings.[42]

---

40 L. Drápal in: Bureš et al. (ed.), *op. cit.* in footnote 15, I. vol., 625.

41 L. Drápal in: Bureš et al. (ed.), *op. cit.* in footnote 15, I. vol., 373.

42 Contradiction between admitting this type of protection and hypertrophy of statutory prerequisites is obvious; a solution of this complicated situation based on private initiative is difficult and controversial.

If a class member becomes aware of the litigation, he may access it solely by the help of standard procedural means: either as another plaintiff (Civil Procedure Act §92(1)) or as an enjoined party (Civil Procedure Act §93). But neither may happen contrary to the will of the original plaintiff. Further, the position of a class member who learns about the proceedings after the judgment has come into force is even more compelling. Such fall-out is indeed conceivable considering that the judgment is not served on the class members who are not parties; neither is it necessarily published. The consumer should be *ipso jure* bound by a judgment, whether approving or dismissing, and this unfavourable result cannot always be attributed to his fault. The disparity between the extent of effects of the judgment and the scope of participants in the proceedings influences numerous other issues: a review of the judgment may be requested exclusively by the parties to the proceedings, i.e. not by every class member, and, similarly, enforcement of the judgment may not be instituted by anybody other than the original party or its direct successor.

4. PRACTICAL EXPERIENCE

4.1. ACTIONS OF CONSUMER ORGANISATIONS

The Czech Consumer Protection Act §25(2) qualifies consumer organisations to file actions for the protection of consumer interests. Material reasons for the actions follow from the substantive law and encompass injunctions of all possible infringements of consumer rights which exceed a purely individual scale. The provision is invoked infrequently and serves the redress of blatant cases. Approximately ten actions have been filed so far, but it must be admitted that the filing has accelerated. A similar option is the action for unfair competition according to the Commercial Code §54(1) which may be employed not only by competitors but also by consumers (consumer organisations) injured by unfair practices. However, these actions are an even rarer appearance than those based on the Consumer Protection Act. In both cases only injunctive relief may be sought.[43]

The second type of litigation with a tinge of collectiveness to be met in Czech law are actions filed by a select consumer on the initiative and with the financial support of a consumer organisation (test claims). This instrument is of course not limited to injunctions and is, as a matter of fact, the only collective instrument in Czech law which steps over the passive cease-and-desist relief. Unfortunately, as the test-claim procedure is mostly a makeshift aid of consumer organisations, the

[43] According to the information (data) of the most important consumer organisation – Sdružení obrany spotřebitelů (Association of Consumer Defense), www.responsibility.cz.

law does not distinguish between the test-action and other ordinary cases (for instance with regard to suspension of prescription period), which does not facilitate consumers' position much. This unfavourable situation is multiplied by the fact that the existing collective proceedings regulation does not apply to the test-claim procedure and thus the result of the proceedings is not *per se* binding upon the class.

The test-actions are in practice used for contesting bank charges. The cases are usually advanced on the basis of a public invitation of the interested consumer organisation to the aggrieved consumers to participate in the pursuit of the case.

The present experience shows that a substantial portion of cases are being finished by a withdrawal of the action after the case has been settled or after the defendant has voluntarily desisted from the contested practice (sometimes with an apology to the public).[44] On the other hand, if the case progresses to judgment, the defendant's chances for success materially enhance. Although only few cases have been definitively adjudicated, the interim score does not count in favour of the consumers: the actions have been mostly dismissed and the matter appealed.

4.2. MOTIONS TO ADMINISTRATIVE BODIES

Of five Czech consumer organisations listed as qualified entities under Directive 98/27/EC, only three are engaged in the field of administrative protection of consumer rights, each of which yearly files dozens of motions to administrative bodies (as a rule to the Czech Trade Inspection, but also to the Czech Agriculture and Food Inspection Authority, Trade Licensing Offices, etc.). Consumer organisations file either on the basis of consumers' complaints (in dependence on the seriousness and frequency of occurrence of a particular interference) or according to their own supervisory activities.

Usually 50 to 70 percent of motions are upheld after the examination.[45] However, the ratio is influenced by the fact that the delinquent is often called to desist from the wrongful conduct together with filing the motion and the redress is reached before the authority orders the adoption of any measures.

Nevertheless, consumer organisations are unhappy with the value of imposed sanctions (fines), which usually does not exceed a few thousand Czech Crowns, regardless of the seriousness of the case. It is repeatedly felt that administrative authorities are overly cautious, being afraid that their conclusion will be challenged and vacated in the administrative or judicial remedial procedure.

44 See footnote 43.
45 See footnote 43.

4.3. CONCLUSION

Although the conception of class action reveals serious problems and invites understandable critique in the literature,[46] it does not yet seem to have translated into greater difficulties in practice. The cease-and-desist actions of a wider reach are, according to the available data, quite rare and are mostly filed by selected consumers under the auspices of a consumer organisation (test cases). With respect to the expensiveness of judicial proceedings, separate consumers prefer the administrative line instead (motions for sanctions, etc.), negotiations through and by the help of consumer organisations (mediation), and other similar out-of-court solutions. Furthermore, it is not yet known whether the strict extent of the binding effect of judgments in collective proceedings have been misused (e.g. through a dummy plaintiff).

It can be concluded that although Czech law of judicial collective enforcement of consumer rights represents an extreme, the emphasised time and place concentration of litigation corresponds to the practice. Rather, the statutory requirements of collective enforcement support (and reflect) the consumer organisations' activity in community actions than that of consumers themselves in class actions. Czech procedural law is not equipped with tools which would enable the coordination of diffuse interests of a numerous group of persons, and thus, the class action may keep up with its function only if the plaintiff already in himself sufficiently represents (and consolidates) the interests of the affected consumers.

5. OVERCOMING THE INDIVIDUAL PROTECTION PATTERN, CRITIQUE OF POSITIVE LAW AND THE COLLECTIVE ACTION *DE LEGE LATA*

5.1. IMPORTANCE OF THE CIVIL PROCEDURE CODE PROVISIONS

However, inadequate the Czech regulation of collective proceeding may be, it breaks the individual protection monopoly: the provisions in the Civil Procedure Code[47] enable protection of collective interests in the widest sense. The difference

---

46 Cf. footnote 1.

47 Relevant is a qualified legal interest of clarification of the existence of the legal relationship. Without this clarification the position of the plaintiff would become unsecured or could be threatened (see A. Winterová et al. (eds.), *Civilní právo procesní (Civil procedural law)*, 3rd. ed., Prague 2004, p. 150). This regulation (fulfilment of this condition) prevents abuse of the action on ascertainment in cases where one can (and must) file an action on performance.

is displayed by the new definition of legal force of judgment and particularly its "block effect". The requirement of identity of parties drops out from the notions of the "merits of proceedings" and the "binding force of judgments". The litigation on protection of collective interests is being transformed into a specific "model" or "exemplary" proceedings, while the binding effect of judgments delivered in this litigation are discharged from any interpersonal limitation and prevent all new proceedings on the matter.

On the other hand, the drawbacks of the protection of collective interests stem exactly from the image of boundlessness. The plaintiff's position in both class and community actions is unclear. All technical questions such as service of notices and summons, and participation in the proceedings are left aside. The same is true for discovery proceedings which will have to be developed step-by-step in case law. The fundamental change brought about by the establishment of the class litigation is all the less reflected in other branches of law, such as the bar regulations and legal fees.

5.2. COLLECTIVE ACTIONS AND PUBLIC INTEREST

One of the basic questions which apply to every kind of enforcement of collective interest, is that of the legitimacy or essence of the enforcement. In other words, to what extent is this means of protection needed along with the individual protection of a particular interest.

From the point of view of civil procedural law, the problem is manifested in the rules on who can bring the action (active procedural legitimisation resulting from the substantive law) and the question arises if and on what conditions a "public" collective action is legitimate. Do these conditions differ from the legitimisation to file a private action?

To solve this problem the following issues are of relevance:

a) Interests. When examining the collective action in the context of consumer protection, we should look at the following matters: aa) what should be understood under the concept of "consumer interest" and to what extent is the consumer interest (interest on consumer protection) a public interest? bb) Can consumer interest be evaluated as public interest, e.g. as provided by Directive 98/27/EC preamble point 2? cc) What is the relationship between consumer interest and collective interest?

Consumer interest can be defined (see section 1 above) as a set of values inherent to a certain group of persons of common attributes. In our case we consider values, which pertain to the "weaker" party in legal relationships of certain type, and therefore their interest is that of an unlimited number of persons, who are, in principle, in a "disadvantageous" position in relation to the supplier. Knowledge and experience of these persons is incomparable with the same factors on the supplier's side. Abstractly expressed, everyone is a consumer. Thus, if public interest corresponds with the entire of society's interest then the consumer interest must fall within the scope of public interest. In short, consumer interest is the public interest.

Consumer interest is in this sense undoubtedly the collective interest pursuant to Directive 98/27/EC. The Directive's qualified entities thus represent the consumer, collective and simultaneously, even the public interest.

However, the collective interest may encompass a substantially narrower aggregation of persons and have a substantially more limited significance. So, it can be assumed that not every collective interest is a public interest at the same time (but the consumer collective interest as expressed in Directive 98/27/EC is certainly to be regarded as public in any case).

b) Necessity of collective actions and their regulation. This is a question as to what extent remedies in representation of a certain interest may be invoked by someone, who is not the bearer of that interest, or who is not – by standard criteria – sufficiently qualified to advocate the collective (group) interest. At this point we cross over to the problem of structure of the concepts of "claim" and the "right to bring an action" in case of community actions on one side and class actions on the other. In the former case the power to act is given to a third person who is able to appropriately represent the common interest and in the latter the power belongs to persons who are primarily privately interested and who are not necessarily qualified to proceed in the public interest.

The question is obvious. Admitting these actions reflects in the procedural and material position of third persons. It is the first criterion for their regulation. The second criterion is the problem of the right to act as a public law entitlement to protection granted by the State, whose duty is to ensure the procedural protection. Generally, to what extent is it possible to utilise this right or, more specifically, use (or burden) the State's judiciary? That is why even in the sphere of individual protection certain limits exist, as, e.g. the necessity to prove an "urgent legal interest" in the case of declaratory judgments.

The need for some regulation (filter) of admissibility of collective protection mechanisms is evidenced in some examples. The case in point is the oldest and probably best elaborated system of US class action, which requires four well-known conditions to be met in addition to individual protection requisites.[48]

---

48 Cf. Section 32 of the Civil Procedure Code until its repeal in 1992: "If a national committee (local authority) believes that the interest of society so requires, it may file an action or may enter the proceedings at any time. However, it may not file an action if purely personal right of

c) Solution *de lege lata*. The question of public interest appears neither in Czech procedural law nor in Czech legal literature – at least not expressly. However, as mentioned, a kind of regulation of admissibility of collective procedure compared with the private individual approach is necessary.

The Czech legislator, having transposed the European Directive on collective protection, entrusts the plaintiff's standing in collective proceedings to select entities only. In a sense, this attitude in itself means an admissibility regulation, but yet it can be assumed that the court has to submit the case to a more detailed control, even if it is not expressly required by procedural rules (especially to reduce the risk of abuse of the collective procedure).

The public collective consumer interest, as a condition of procedural legitimisation, is thus a parallel of the concept of "urgent legal interest" postulated for the declaratory actions (actions for determination whether a relation exists or not including a declaration of a contract as void).[49]

If the necessity of a regulation of admissibility is beyond doubt in case of community action, there is no reason why it should not be the same in the case of class actions brought by one class member (consumer). Also here the court should examine if the class action prerequisites have been fulfilled and, if they are not, the consumer action should be handled as an individual means of protection.

Apart from this, one interesting feature could have been viewed in Czech law in the recent past. During the communist government the concept of actions filed by public prosecutors and local authorities[50] was an approach which recalls the contemporary methods of protection of collective interest, especially the community action. However, there can be no talk about a public asset as we understand it nowadays because the interest asserted by the public prosecutor (and actually also the interest asserted by other social entities) was in fact a

---

an individual is involved". The same wording finds itself in Section 35 par. 1 of the Code of Civil Procedure in the case of a prosecutor.

49 The purpose of the participation of local authority and prosecutor in the proceedings is the promotion of the interest of the society in respecting rules of the socialist cohabitation as well as protection of civil rights, focus on ascertaining of the facts and increasing of the educative influence of the proceedings (motives of the sections 32–35 of the Civil Procedure Code). The basis of the conception of "public interest" (interest of the society) of that time follows clearly from this: it is the surveillance of the court's activity in the civil proceedings as a instrument of the totalitarian state regime (O. Plundr, in: Hándl, Rubeš (eds.), *Občanský soudní řád, Komentář Praha 1985, I. vol (Civil Procedure Code, Commentary)*, p. 194, Comment on Section 32, which states, that the core of the notion of the "interest of society" is based on "political, ideological directives" and that it can be derived from the class substance and orientation of actual laws.").

50 On the notion of "interest of society", see Fr. Štajgr, Zájmy společnosti (Interest of the society), *AUC* 3/1967, p. 209 f. and J. Pauly, Odkaz na zájmy společnosti (On the reference to interests of society), *Socialistická zákonnost*, 1981, p. 262–268.

domain of the totalitarian state.[51] After the collapse of the communist regime, the public powers to act on behalf of third persons have been dramatically cut back. This trend of minimising the influence of public interest in procedural law is quite obviously a consequence of the distrust in the concept of public assets or values, which were until recently an expression of superiority of collective interest over individual or private interest.

d) Normative effects of the protection. The collective consumer interest may be often assumed and asserted only by an independent third person (entity), which represents the consumer interest in its abstraction. It is the result of "normative effects" of some juridical acts, as, e.g. standard contract terms. A preventative protection may not be invoked by a separate consumer, who frequently has no legal relationship with the supplier yet and has neither procedural nor material title to demand, e.g. a declaration of invalidity of a juridical act. So, the abstract right to bring an action in public interest may be asserted only by an entity, which enjoys the right, as a consumer organisation.

5.3. ABSTRACT CONTROL, PUBLIC INTEREST AND CONSUMER RIGHTS

Abstract control is review of juridical acts that embodies a normative effect, i.e. consequences for an unlimited generically defined group of persons. It is typically the case of standard contract terms or standard form contracts, which may be prohibited from usage or declared invalid. The review activity necessarily entails a quasi-normative effect and thus is an example of *ex ante* protection. This applies especially with regard to practices of particular suppliers or in particular fields of business. Such a preventive (*ex ante*) protection may not be invoked by a consumer who has not entered into a legal relation with a supplier using standard contract terms yet, and has neither procedural nor material title to demand, e.g. a declaration of invalidity of a juridical act. So, the abstract right to bring an action in the public interest may be asserted only by an entity, which enjoys the right, as a consumer organisation.

51 See Fr. Zoulík, Hromadné žaloby a současnost (Collective Actions at Present Time), *Pocta (Liber amicorum) Marta Knappová*, Prague 2005, 269f.

5.4. DUTIES OF PUBLIC BODIES AND THEIR RELATION TO THE PARTIES

Different status of courts on the one hand and administrative authorities on the other presupposes differences in judicial and administrative procedures. The basic question is represented by the officiality principle in the administrative procedure and the adversary principle in the judicial proceedings. The Civil Procedure Code constitutes no special duty of court to instruct the parties and other participants in course of the collective proceedings. Maybe it should be understood by itself that the instruction is of special significance here; it is quite notorious that participants in collective proceedings tend to be procedurally passive far more often than in other cases.[52] It is probably useless to emphasise that the judge in collective proceedings must assume the active role of procedural manager, which demonstrates itself especially in the instruction activity.

5.5. PRINCIPLE OF PARTY PRESENTATION AND OFFICIALITY PRINCIPLE[53]

The rules on commencement of court proceedings are clear: exclusively the parties may initiate a collective procedure, which is an understandable consequence following from the dispositive substance of rights dealt with in courts. By contrast, the administrative procedure is designed to cope with more varied situations and thus must offer more plastic mechanisms, such as institution of proceedings also on the authority's own motion. This is a feature of the officiality principle predominantly governing the administrative activity.

As for the rules of evidence, Czech law unfortunately misses any special evidence provisions, which would facilitate assertion of collective interests in the civil judicial procedure. There is no arrangement similar to the US discovery procedure[54] and the court is only exceptionally allowed to hear evidence on its own motion, so the onus of proof may pose a significant obstacle to collective protection. It is especially obvious in contrast with assertion of antitrust claims in continental law compared with the US practice. The administrative procedure on

---

52 For the situation in England see N. Andrews, Multi-Party Proceedings in England: Representative and Group Actions, *ZZP Int.* 2000, 3f.

53 Cf. the amendment of Federal Rules of Civil Procedure Rule 23 (taken effect on 1 December, 2003), which encourages judges to decide "as soon as practicable" and enables to conduct limited discovery proceedings (Rule 23(c)(1)).

54 For a more liberal *res judicata* approach see L. S. Mullenix, New Trends in Standing and Res Iudicata in Collective Suits, in: *Paper on XIII World Congress of Procedural Law*, Rio de Janeiro 2007.

the contrary does not struggle with this problem as it does not consider the parties' responsibility of proof.

5.6. HUMAN RIGHTS ASPECTS: IS IT AN ACADEMIC OR A POLITICAL DEBATE OR BOTH?

A. *Opt-In, Opt-Out*

The first question concerns the principles of opt-in and opt-out. As already indicated, one of the basic shortcomings of the Czech civil judicial procedure, but also of the administrative procedure, is the absence of a clear definition of persons included in the collective proceedings and in the outcome thereof. The current Czech regulation may result in two scenarios. Either, as a consequence of an objection of deprivation of the right to due process, the court will not respect the Civil Procedure Code *lis pedens* and *res judicata* provisions (§83(2)(b) and §159a) and will accept an action on the already adjudicated subject matter, this time brought by another plaintiff. Or, the court may adopt a "liberal" position, which would be based on the exact language of the mentioned Civil Procedure Code rules. However, that would (and should) incite criticism of the infringement of the basic right to due process. A solution probably lies in the maximised efforts of the plaintiff and the court in the first process to inform all class members of the initiation and course of the litigation, which can save its class-wide effect.

B. *Informing the Aggrieved Consumers*

The next problem is about the way of informing the class of aggrieved consumers. Even the opt-in system, which is probably the Czech case, has its pitfalls. Using this practice under current Czech conditions would mean that the potential plaintiffs waive their procedural rights. That is why it is needed to inform the class members not only about the existence of the action, but especially about its contents, in order they can make a qualified decision if to transfer the procedural rights. Nevertheless, advantages of opt-in look to be evident in comparison with opt-out mechanisms. Automatism of inclusion, which is the basic feature of opt-out, is much more demanding and endangering for the potential plaintiffs than opt-in.

C. *Res Judicata*

The key point in this context is the *res judicata* effect[55] in injunction cases after an earlier action filed by another plaintiff has been dismissed based not on the merits (e.g. for formal or other mistakes of the action). The problem becomes compelling in several aspects. The definition of procedural subject matter that omits any personal linkage induces a special situation: after delivery of a dismissing judgment, the whole group of persons, affected by the wrongful conduct in the same way as the plaintiff, is deprived of the right to be heard in court. This consequence concerns especially the injunctive protection but materially has a wider range (see above). The question is what is the damage to the right to due process, which must be of course be observed also in collective procedural mechanisms of any kind.

D. *Participation in Proceedings*

Similar conclusions apply to every aspect of the theory of party presentation and in fact to all other due process principles because the "collective plaintiff" finds himself in a situation where his (seemingly petrified) procedural rights suddenly get limited for a large part. These can even be discussed if the class member who approves the role of collective plaintiff does not evoke his own mandatory rights.[56]

5.7. SOLUTION *DE LEGE LATA*

The fragment regulation enables and requires a wide creativity in the class suit preparation phase. The basic question is how to define a collective (class or group) action and how to distinguish it from an individual one, which may involve also a large number of persons, who have to be individually identified though. This is the main distinctive factor between the individual and collective protection. It can be supposed that in order to reach the quality of collective proceedings, the plaintiff and the court are required to adopt certain steps, which are to be deduced from procedural cover principles. The plaintiff must make a maximum effort in order for all the potential claimants (or persons injured by the same wrongful conduct) to have a real opportunity to learn about the proceedings. It is especially up to the consumer organisations to publish an announcement about the ongoing collective suit to an appropriate extent and comprehensibleness. The context of the regulation prompts the announcement to take the form of an opt-in call. The

55 See *inter alia* A. Winterová, *op. cit.* in footnote 15.
56 Cf. footnote 20.

due course of the proceedings further certainly requires that the plaintiff advise the court about his informational activity and propose to publish the fact of initiation of the litigation on the court's bulletin board in hard and electronic form. Under these maximum and good-faith efforts towards publicity it can be concluded that the action may invoke the *lis pedens* effect of collective proceeding foreseen by the Civil Procedure Code §83(2).[57]

The plaintiff should also demand in the action to be granted a right to publish the result of the proceedings at the defendant's expense. The published information should include at least the information that the proceedings are of a collective nature and involve a generically defined group of participants, who are not parties to the proceedings. Only in this way can the extension of the *res judicata* effect be conceivable.

6. ADMINISTRATIVE ENFORCEMENT

6.1. STATUS OF CONSUMER ORGANISATIONS AT THE REGULATORY AUTHORITIES

The administrative procedure on protection of collective interests is made to measure for consumer organisations, so not every qualified entity from the list of the European Commission according to Directive 98/27/EC is entitled to initiate the process. Similarly as in the judicial procedure, the status of consumer organisations may not be reviewed on the quality of the protection activity.

Consumer organisations may file motions to initiate administrative proceedings according to the Consumer Protection Act §26 and Administrative Procedure Act §42. In the former case the consumer organisation can file actions with consumer protection supervisory authorities (without defining which authorities are to be regarded as such), but in the latter the filing right extends to every authority (so the question is not so pressing).

In both cases a specific procedure follows, which is finished by the processing of the motion and its course is unfortunately almost unregulated. "Processing" means refusal of the motion or its acceptance and initiation of administrative proceedings *ex officio* (such as the minor offences procedure, etc.). It is quite obvious that a consumer organisation is neither party to the subsequent proceedings nor an affected person in the proceedings, which is a weaker participation status according to the Administrative Procedure Act §2(3). The

57 Cf. Act No. 200/1990 Coll.

statutory period for processing a motion is 30 days (Administrative Procedure Act) or two months (Consumer Protection Act).

So, as can be deduced, a consumer organisation may not itself initiate administrative proceedings on imposition of injunctions or sanctions, but only a preliminary phase which can lead to the proceedings. Collective damages compensation in the administrative adhesion procedure within the framework of the Minor Offences Act (§70)[58] is probably only a theoretical consideration. The expression "a person who suffered damage" used in the Minor Offences Act is presumably to be construed restrictively as the person who (individually) suffered the damage and not to include consumer organisations acting on behalf of injured consumers.

6.2. INDIRECT AND DIRECT ENFORCEMENT, ABSTRACT AND CONCRETE CONTROL

Administrative procedure has direct as well as indirect effect. In the abstract form of prohibitions, sanctions, etc., it immediately benefits consumers. Futher, pursuing wrongdoing functions preventively in relation to suppliers' behaviour deterring the suppliers from objectionable activities (and inflicting damage) in the future. And, in addition, the direct enforcement in itself also has indirect effects, e.g. in relation to consumer damages claims.

6.3. REGULATORY AUTHORITIES AND FURTHER PERSPECTIVES

Administrative enforcement of consumer rights is especially the domain of regulatory authorities, but the competence is partially assumed also by authorities of general competence (municipal and other). A Czech specialty is the administrative proceedings in which private consumer claims are adjudicated, such as the procedure on telephone charges at the Czech Telecommunication Office.[59]

The phenomenon of collectiveness could typically here, as well as in the subsequent judicial review, gain influence. The rules of administrative procedure are by default designed to cope with much more diverse situations than the judicial procedure and multi-party administrative proceedings have always been well-known, although usually in other than consumer-related matters. As we

58 Cf. Act No. 127/2005 Coll.

59 It is a paradox that the administrative procedure is, as a matter of fact, the only statutorily anticipated opportunity for collective compensation for damage (although a debatable one).

have already mentioned, we believe that administrative mechanisms are one of the workable options how to procedurally manage mass consumer participation (see point 5.2).

7. UNLIMITED PROTECTION OF COLLECTIVE INTERESTS – A MODEL FOR EUROPE? CONCLUSION

7.1. STATE OF JUDICIAL ENFORCEMENT

a) Due to its rudimentary nature, Czech regulation of private protection of collective interests, especially as concerns the class actions, is largely imperfect. The main defects consist of the following:

   aa) Limited and undervalued extent of protection. The existing rules suffer from the limitation to injunctive relief. The law does not offer any space for collective restitution or award of damages.
   bb) Lack of efficiency. As mentioned above, Czech law does not provide for some of the basic procedural and institutional requisites so that collective proceedings can become an effective means of protection. Appropriate provisions are missing even in the phase of enforcement of judgments – it is unclear how consumers, not parties to the proceedings, may benefit from the judgment.
   cc) Insufficient personal jurisdiction. Any instruments to ensure homogeneity of potential plaintiffs are missing. The law does not enable the constitution of a class of defendants, similarly as for the plaintiff side, (e.g. all businesses participating in the challenged practices). There is probably no reason why the "collectiveness" should not apply to both sides of the litigation.

b) Under certain requirements, though not explicitly stipulated by the law, the effects of class, group or model action can though be achieved. Nevertheless, the quality of the result is questionable, especially because uncertainty about the qualification to initiate the proceedings (who can file the action) persists.
c) Pursuant to the new (fragment) *lis pendens* and *res judicata* provisions as the sole statutory instruments of judicial collective protection, an unacceptable intervention into the constitutional right to due process looms on the horizon.

7.2. NEGLECT OF PUBLIC INTEREST AND IMPORTANCE OF PRIVATE INITIATIVE

The austere regulation of civil collective procedure is therefore an interesting phenomenon, which probably lacks analogy in the legal history of Continental Europe. The plaintiff is required to shape, under the court's supervision, the course of proceedings independently in each particular case, whereas his field of operation is set by the classic procedural rules serving the individual protection. Thus, it is the plaintiff's responsibility to navigate through the proceedings to attain the collective protection effect (without offending third parties' rights at the same time).

7.3. COLLECTIVE ACTION SOLUTION *DE LEGE LATA*

This is an extraordinary situation. The autonomy of parties' will penetrate the procedural law, which generally belongs to the volume of public law. The plaintiff must necessarily "prescribe" to the court how to deal with questions, which remain unstipulated by the law and which are of special importance in the collective context. The plaintiff should offer the court solutions of some technical issues, such as serving of the process, and the publication of judgments and orders. Otherwise it can be assumed that the effect of collective protection would be foiled or at least disputed: either the wide-ranging *res judicata* effect will be ignored and other plaintiffs will be able to sue individually, or the collective judgment will be exposed to the danger of vacation for violation of the right to due process.

7.4. ADMINISTRATIVE PROTECTION – A GUARANTEE?

In contrast, recent developments in administrative law have brought an opportunity to raise collective damages claims in minor offences procedure[60]

[60] But it would be incorrect to compare the situation with the attitudes of communist governments, which, allegedly, ensured the consumer protection better. There can be no discussion about consumer protection in a totalitarian state, because the "care" for consumers has another purpose than the consumer protection in free-market conditions (see L. Tichý, Verbrauchervertragsrecht im tschechischen Recht, in: S. Grundmann, M. Schauer (eds.), *The Architecture of European Codes and Contract Law*, 2006, The Hague, 242, 243). It is more suitable to describe the situation as limiting (in the sense of omitting or pushing back) the state and public sector, and thus neglecting the public interest (including the opposition against mandatory provisions in contract law as an expression of the publicisation of private law). This is a consequence of refuting the past, which reminds one of vulgar paternalism and collectivism.

and the right of consumer organisations to file motions with regulatory authorities supervising supplier practice. But besides these situations, consumer organisations' powers in the administrative process do not go beyond the indirect enforcement of rights.

Generally concluded, despite serious deficiencies in the regulation of collective judicial procedure and disputable efficiency of administrative procedure, it seems in practice, that consumers and consumer organisations have come to terms with the situation and, within its framework, try to find suitable solutions on their own. This is clear evidence that the current consumer protection regulations are quite small in size compared with the needs of the contemporary consumer.

7.5. POST-COMMUNIST REVIVAL OF PUBLIC INTEREST

Answering the questions raised in the introduction, we endorse the critique. Especially the law on judicial protection of consumer interests proved its essential drawbacks; basic attributes of collective enforcement through class action suits remain unregulated. It seems that the legislature entirely omitted considering the public interest question while implementing mechanisms of judicial collective protection[61] (even the Ombudsman is out of play) and thus inadvertently passed the initiative to private parties. The care for the course of proceedings occurs to be up to the litigants.

Although also the administrative sphere yields helpful remedies and interesting results (as, e.g. in the fields of health protection or safety of products), it is not able to duplicate or replace judicial procedure.[62] However, the regard for public interest in consumer matters cannot be limited to the administrative sphere. Whether we like it or not, the consumer community is so significant in number and influence that consumers' concerns infiltrate the public interest in the widest sense. And what is needed now is the corresponding public feedback into consumer (collective) remedies. In other words, the responsible weighing of the public aspect of consumer interest should be, in our view, the beacon of further developments of collective mechanisms of consumer protection.

---

61 Nevertheless, no major pressure to improve consumers' procedural position has been recorded so far, at least from the consumer organisations. The passivity of consumer organisations is probably a toll, which the western countries had to pay already long ago.

62 Nevertheless, no major pressure to improve consumers' procedural position has been recorded so far, at least from the consumer organisations. The passivity of consumer organisations is probably a toll, which the western countries had to pay already long ago.

PUBLIC AND PRIVATE ENFORCEMENT IN CONSUMER PROTECTION – A DUTCH PERSPECTIVE*

Ewoud HONDIUS**

SUMMARY

This paper distinguishes two levels of consumer protection: the individual level and the collective level. The adoption of a European Regulation on small claims procedures has invited those countries which until then had favoured private law enforcement and out-of-court settlement of consumer complaints, to reconsider these policies. The introduction of a small claims procedure for consumer complaints may compensate some weak points of private complaints tribunals. A small claims procedure should not replace existing consumer complaints tribunals. Some competition between the two systems can even be desirable. On a collective level, the foundation of a Dutch Consumer Authority has sparkled discussion in the Netherlands about the most desirable form of enforcement: public or private. Group actions are a well established phenomenon in Dutch law, but they are not often used in consumer matters. In such matters, the newly introduced settlement for mass damages proves an interesting instrument.

1. INTRODUCTION

Being *entitled* to something does not necessarily mean that one will get it. This maxim is particularly true for consumer matters, where the advantage of having a claim adjudged in court is usually outweighed by the risk of having to pay the other party's costs in case of loss of the ensuing litigation.[1] In many, if not most

* This paper is partially based on Ewoud Hondius, Towards a European small claims procedure, in: Luc Thévenoz and Norbert Reich (eds.), *Droit de la consommation/Liber amicorum Stauder*, Genève: Schulthess, 2006, p. 131–146.

** Professor of European Private Law, University of Utrecht.

1 In Germany this interest is indicated by the notion of 'Streuschäden'. Ianika N. Tzankova has tried to introduce this terminology into the Netherlands – see her *Strooischade/Een verkennend onderzoek naar een nieuw rechtsfenomeen*, The Hague: SDU, 2005, 165 p.

cases, this risk is one of the main elements which prevent consumers from trying to enforce their claim in court. That is why they increasingly make use of private consumer complaint schemes, which do not pose such a risk. In the Netherlands, the only financial risk which consumers face when they lose a case before such a tribunal – apart from the amount which is in dispute itself – is a small fee of some EURO 50 for introducing their claim.

An alternative to the private schemes before consumer complaints tribunals is a special procedure under the umbrella of the courts: the small claims procedure, to be found in some common law jurisdictions. Ideally this procedure has a similar risk structure as that before consumer complaints tribunals: there is no possibility for the adjudicator to make the consumer pay for the legal costs of the other party, even when the consumer loses the case. Unfortunately, the European small claims procedure is currently being established do empower the adjudicator to charge the other party's costs of legal representation to the private consumer who filed the claim.

An alternative to these individual schemes – the private consumer complaints boards and the small claims tribunals – is collective redress. There is now a widespread movement for better possibilities to obtain compensation for costs in Europe.[2] In the Netherlands, a recent statute which is based on a wholly different legal notion – that of the specific contract of 'transaction' – now appears to serve the same interests as collective actions. Group actions are a well-known phenomenon in the Netherlands, but not particularly in consumer matters.

This paper aims at giving a broad overview of the existing situation in the Netherlands. It will first present some data as to Dutch consumer complaints and their access to justice (No. 2). It will then focus on complaints boards (No. 3), small claims (No. 4), collective action (No. 5) and mass damage transactions (No. 6). The paper was originally conceived to focus on the dilemma of public v. private enforcement mechanisms which at present are faced by the Dutch Consumer Authority. But due to the fact that recent data on this point only became available when this paper went to press, this issue will only be briefly touched upon (No. 7). This lack of data is in contradistinction with the earlier paragraphs, where abundant – Dutch language – materials are available, which where necessary have been supplemented by the author's personal knowledge of the Dutch situation.[3]

---

2 See the Advice of 14 February 2008 of the European Economic and Social Committee on *Group actions in European consumer law/Defining the collective actions system and its role in the context of Community consumer law*, CESE 258/08.

3 He is a Judge in the Court of Appeal in Amsterdam, President of a number of consumer complaints tribunals and member of the Dutch consumer council (*Commissie voor consumentenaangelegenheden*) of the Social and Economic Council.

This paper will not address specific cross-border issues,[4] such as those relating to the European Extra-Judicial Network (EEJ-Net),[5] cross-border injunctions by groups[6] and order for payment procedure,[7] nor will it deal with cross-border collective actions in other areas,[8] with legal aid[9] or conciliation and mediation.[10]

2. CONSUMER COMPLAINTS AND ACCESS TO JUSTICE

A first question to be raised concerns the number of consumer complaints. What is their – relative – number? How do consumers with a complaint react? Taking court cases as a yardstick provides us with a false picture: precisely because so few consumer claims result in court litigation, the number of consumer cases heard in court is relatively small. Real data as to the number of complaints of Dutch consumers are presented in *Geschilbeslechtingsdelta 2003.*[11] This report covers all kinds of complaints of a legal nature. The report is based on the idea that any citizen of a *Rechtsstaat* with problems should have access to the law. According to the report, two out of every three Dutch citizens have had at least one legal

4 According to the *Annual report 2007* of 'De geschillencommissie' (p. 13), in 2007 the European Consumer Centre in the Netherlands received 220 claims from consumers domiciled outside the Netherlands. Of these, 57 concerned package travel, 24 recreation, 18 retail banking, 17 lawyers, 17 interior decorating, 15 telecommunications, 13 energy and water and 10 water recreation. Most complaints came from Germany (77), Belgium (69), France (13), Spain (9), England (6), Italy (6) and Andorra (6).

5 SEC (2000) 405. See the SANCO-website as to the merger with the European Consumer Centres or 'Euroguichets'.

6 See Urs M. Weber-Stecher, Unterlassungsklagen von Konsumentenorganisationen unter besonderer Berücksichtigung der EG-Richtlinie über Unterlassungsklagen zum Schutz der Verbraucherinteressen, in: A. Brunner, M. Rehbinder, B. Stauder (eds.), *Jahrbuch des Schweizerischen Konsumentenrechts*, Bern: Staempfli, 2000, p. 155–177.

7 Regulation 805/2004/EC creating a European enforcement order for uncontested claims, *OJ* L143. See Xandra Kramer, *Eenvormige Europese procedures voor de inning van vorderingen/De Europese betalingsbevelprocedure en de Europese procedure voor geringe vorderingen*, Deventer: Kluwer, 2007, 102 p. and the forthcoming publication of the Utrecht PhD thesis by Bartosz Sujecki on the subject.

8 As for labour law see Filip Dorssemont, Teun Jaspers and Aukje van Hoek (eds.), *Cross-border collective actions in Europe: a legal challenge/A study of the legal aspects of transnational collective actions from a labour law and private international law perspective*, Antwerp: Intersentia, 2007, 481 p.

9 See Green Paper from the Commission *Legal aid in civil matters: the problems confronting the cross-border litigant*, COM(2000) 51 final.

10 *Communication from the Commission on widening consumer access to alternative dispute resolution*, COM(2001) 161 final; *Green paper on alternative dispute resolution in civil and commercial law*, COM(2002) 196 final and Proposal for a directive October 2004.

11 B.C.J. van Velthoven, M.J. ter Voert, M. van Gammeren-Zoeteweij, *Geschilbeslechtingsdelta 2003/Over verloop en afloop van (potentieel) juridische problemen van burgers*, The Hague: Boom/WODC, 2004 (www.wodc.nl), 241 p.

problem over the past five years. Consumer problems come up on top: most problems have to do with the delivery of goods and supply of services (32%) and with work (30%). Then come the problems of the poor and the rich: financial problems (22%) and its opposite for the rich: problems of real estate (20%), followed by distance by rent of dwellings (12%) and relational and family problems (10%).[12] A remarkable finding is that Dutch citizens complain more often than the British,[13] although the researchers do warn that the questionnaires in the two countries were not exactly the same. In both countries complaints as to goods and services are relatively often solved by citizens themselves.[14] The report shows what most readers will know already: that the percentage of those who are unable to come to grips with their complaint rises with a lower income and less schooling.[15]

Lawyers do not score high in this report. Only 18% of respondents consider them honest and trustworthy, 23% find the contrary, while 59% 'could not tell' or hold the belief that it is 'neither true nor untrue'. A total of 68% feel that they charge too much. Judges score worse than one might have expected: 49% find them honest and trustworthy, but 8% do not and 43% do not know or hold the belief that it is neither true nor untrue.[16] The report concludes that citizens are better off when they are able to come to partial agreement with the other party than when their complaint ends with an official procedure.[17] That is why the authors are warm partisans of mediation.[18] They finally concede that a lack of 'social capital' – help by third parties – may contribute to the juridification of relations.[19]

This is not the only research of consumer complaints. Other research projects, conducted by EIM,[20] NIPO,[21] Twijnstra Gudde[22] and the Ministry of Economic Affairs[23], point in the same direction: from a quantitative point of view consumer affairs are an important, if not the most important source of complaints. Consumers are able to solve a large number of these complaints themselves.

One weak point in the statistics given above is that the seriousness of the complaint is not measured. It has been suggested, correctly, that a complaint

12 *Geschilbeslechtingsdelta 2003*, p. 68.
13 *Geschilbeslechtingsdelta 2003*, p. 135.
14 *Geschilbeslechtingsdelta 2003*, p. 136.
15 *Geschilbeslechtingsdelta 2003*, p. 140.
16 *Geschilbeslechtingsdelta 2003*, p. 173.
17 *Geschilbeslechtingsdelta 2003*, p. 190–191.
18 *Geschilbeslechtingsdelta 2003*, p. 193.
19 *Geschilbeslechtingsdelta 2003*, p. 195.
20 EIM, *Afhandeling van collectieve consumentenklachten*, April 2004.
21 NIPO, *Klachtenafhandeling in de detailhandel en autobranche*, April 2004.
22 Twijnstra Gudde, *Onderzoek naar afhandeling van individuele consumentenklachten*, April 2004.
23 Ministry of Economic Affairs, *Strategisch Actie Programma*, June 2004.

about a malfunctioning car, irritating as it can be, is less serious than a complaint about a malfunctioning marital relationship or safety in the city. In other words, the measuring of the seriousness of the subject of the complaint may lead to a list which is different from the one suggested above.[24]

Access to justice has also been the subject of a publication by Barendrecht and Kamminga.[25] Under what circumstances do citizens require such access? What are the alternatives? How is the quest for justice met? How can access to justice be ameliorated? The authors conclude that information as to substantive law is very important. Information as to procedures to be followed in general appears to be easily obtainable. The information should better adapt to the needs of the citizen.

3. COMPLAINTS BOARDS

Access to the law does not seem guaranteed in the case of consumer complaints. The judicial procedure allegedly is slow, expensive and formal. That is why a number of jurisdictions such as the Netherlands have increasingly sought alternatives in out-of-court settlement. A visiting card for the Netherlands and its *poldermodel* of sorting out differences of opinion by deliberation rather than litigation is constituted by the consumer complaints tribunals. Most of these tribunals operate under the wings of the *Stichting geschillencommissies voor consumentenzaken* (Foundation for complaints tribunals for consumers) in The Hague.[26] The foundation is subsidised by trade and industry as well as by the State. The subsidy by the latter is based on the assumption that the consumer complaints tribunals take cases from government courts.[27] It is doubtful whether this assumption is correct: from studying the reported cases one rather obtains the impression that many of the cases submitted to the complaints tribunals would never have been submitted to a government court.[28]

The complaints boards adhere to the requirements set out in Commission Recommendation 98/257/EC on the principles applicable to the bodies responsible

24 M. Barendrecht, Y.P. Kamminga and J.H. Verdonschot, *Priorities for the justice system: responding to the most urgent legal problems of individuals*, Tisco working paper 001–2008, http://ssrn.com/abstract=1090885.

25 J.M. Barendrecht, Y.P. Kamminga, *Toegang tot het recht/De lasten van een uitweg*, The Hague: Boom, 2005, 95 p.

26 See C.H.M. Last, J. Nijgh, The Dutch system of alternative dispute resolution schemes relating to consumer disputes in the European Union, *Consumer Law Journal* 1999, p. 417–441.

27 *Actieprogramma een versterkte consumentaliteit* (2004).

28 In this sense also E. Bauw, R. Hartendorp, Consumentenzaken: kantonrechter of geschillencommissie?, *Nederlands Juristenblad* 2005, p. 2304, 2305.

for out-of-court settlement of consumer disputes.[29] The number of complaints submitted to the boards has been rising over the years, as has the number of tribunals – at present some forty tribunals.

The year 2000 brought a new consumer complaints tribunal for computers[30] and in 2001 a tribunal for general consumer affairs. In that year, the number of complaints rose from 9,100 to 10,000. Complaints regarding telecommunications especially (+415) rose in a spectacular way. The length of dealing with complaints also rose: from 5.8 to 6.7 months.[31] In 2002, a further increase of complaints was reported: the number of incoming complaints rose by 8% to 11,372.[32] package travel (3,200) led the group, followed by interior decorating (1,903), retail banking (1,200) and telecommunications (1,100). The length of the period for dealing with complaints did slightly recede: from 6.9 to 6.5 months. In 2004, a further increase of cases was reported.[33] With nearly 2,500 cases, public utilities almost doubled its case-load. Package travel, with more than 4,000 complaints, led the group as usual, followed by interior decorating (2,000), retail banking (1,800) and telecommunications (1,100). In 2005, 20% more complaints were filed. This was mainly due to an increase in complaints about the supply of energy and water. The length of the period for dealing with complaints diminished from 6.1 to 5.1 months. As of 1 September 2005 there is a complaints tribunal for childcare and in 2006 a complaints tribunal for brokerage in real estate was established.

In 2008 there were negotiations over the establishment of some more new tribunals, with the aim being 50 trade and industry organisations affiliated by the end of 2008.[34] By the end of 2007, 39 complaints boards were in operation. The number of complaints and awards however diminished for the first time in a number of years. This has been attributed to the fact that two popular complaints boards – for retail banking and mortgages – were transferred to an independent financial complaints board, and because the digital intake of complaints immediately makes complainants aware of their chances of winning their case, resulting in a considerable number being dropped. Also because of the time constraints of digitalisation, the length of handling a claim rose to 4.6 months.

An interesting development in the newly independent financial complaints board – which combines previous complaints boards as to banking, insurance and investment – is that it combines the classical court-like procedure of the

---

29 *OJ* L/115.

30 Stichting Geschillencommissies voor Consumentenzaken, *Annual report 2000,* The Hague, 2001, 136 p.

31 This compares unfavourably with the length of procedures before the *kantongerecht*, the court for cases below EURO 5,000 – see Bauw/Hartendorp (2005), p. 2306.

32 Stichting geschillencommissies consumentenzaken, *Jaarverslag 2002*, The Hague, 2003, 120 p.

33 Stichting Geschillencommissies voor Consumentenzaken, *Jaarverslag 2004*, The Hague, 2005, 144 p.

34 De geschillencommissie, *Jaarverslag 2007*, Den Haag: SGC, 2008, 152 p.

complaints boards with modern mediation techniques. This new approach apparently works, because the number of financial claims which have to be adjudged by a full commission has dropped considerably.

The number of awards of the consumer complaints tribunals is approximately four times the number of arbitral awards in commercial cases.[35]

Out-of-court settlement is also growing more popular in other jurisdictions, such as France,[36] Italy,[37] Portugal,[38] Spain[39] and Switzerland.[40] In Germany, the point of departure is still quite the opposite of that in other jurisdictions, witness a study which seeks to find how consumers may oppose arbitration clauses in general contract terms.[41] Of some interest are the Nordic complaints tribunals.[42] In 2003, Denmark introduced a new Act on consumer complaints.[43] The Danish procedure is quite similar to the Dutch one, especially with regard to the composition of the tribunal (par. 12/13). A strong point of the Danish Act is that the relation with the courts is regulated (par. 3). A weak point is the lack of a guarantee by trade and industry that awards will be enforced (par. 4 (2): 'In the event of failure to comply with decisions or compromises reached in conjunction with processing a complaint, the Danish Consumer Agency may, at the request of the consumer, bring the case before the courts on behalf of the consumer.'

Although the complaints tribunals do function well, especially in the Netherlands,[44] there are also some disadvantages. A disadvantage which is only

---

35 Alex Brenninkmeijer, Michael van Ewijk, Cornelis van der Werf, *Aard en omvang van arbitrage en bindend advies in Nederland*, Leiden: Meijers Institute, 2002.

36 E. Camous, *Règlements non-juridictionnels des litiges de la consommation*, Paris: Librairie générale, 2002.

37 Guido Alpa, *Il diritto dei consumatori*, Bari: Laterza, 2002, p. 427–454.

38 Isabel Mendes Cabecadas, The Lisbon Arbitration Centre for Consumer conflicts: the Portuguese approach, *Consumer Law Journal* 1999, p. 493–510.

39 See Blanca Garrido Courel, El acceso de los consumidores a la justicia, *La Ley* 19 augustus 2002, p. 1–16; L.J.H. Mölenberg, El sistema arbitral de consumo, *TvC* 2004, p. 84–99. In the book edited by María Reyes López (ed.), *Derecho de consumo*, second ed., Valencia: Tirant lo Blanch, 2002, Aballán Tolosa deals with consumer arbitration on p. 366–440.

40 Xavier Favre-Bulle, Arbitrage et règlement alternatif des litiges (ADR): une autre justice pour les consommateurs?, in: Luc Thévenoz and Norbert Reich (eds.), *Liber amicorum Bernd Stauder, Droit de la consommation/Konsumentenrecht/Consumer law*, Genève: Schulthess, 2006, p. 95–121.

41 Lars Weihe, *Der Schutz der Verbraucher im Recht der Schiedsgerichtsbarkeit*, PhD Konstanz 2004, Frankfurt: Lang, 2005, 352 p.

42 See Jens M. Scherpe, *Außergerichtliche Streitbeilegung in Verbrauchersachen*, Tübingen: Mohr, 2002, 328 p.

43 See the English translation – Consumer complaints act 2003 (Denmark), [2004] *Commercial Laws of Europe* 1–8).

44 The handling of consumer complaints by the various consumer complaints tribunals administered by the *Stichting Geschillencommissie voor Consumentenzaken* is well considered by consumers, according to two surveys: SWOKA, 'Het maatschappelijk belang van geschillencommissies' and Legal Vision, *Evaluatie geschilbeslechting consumentenzaken*, Rotterdam, 2002, 95 p. As to complaints boards for hospitals, see: N. Doornbos, P.P.M. van Reijsen, *De Geschillencommissie Ziekenhuizen*, The Hague: Vermande, 2000.

theoretical is the following. In the Netherlands, the tribunals issue their award in the form of a 'binding advice'. This means that the award cannot be enforced against an unwilling debtor. However, because trade and industry guarantee the enforcement, the practice is quite different. A more important inconvenience is that not all trades and industries are well organised and that enterprises therefore do not take part in the complaints tribunal system.[45] The increasing awareness of the competition authorities of intra-trade co-operation also is a negative element[46] – more so than before.[47] The entry on the market of foreign traders who probably are less prone to seek membership of traditional Dutch trade organisations may also be such an element.

4. SMALL CLAIMS PROCEDURES

A different approach to the problem of consumer access to justice is the establishment of a specific consumer procedure within the judiciary. The English small claims procedure has been in operation for more than thirty years and according to Baldwin has proven its usefulness: over 87% of all cases are now dealt with in this way.[48] It is this procedure, which the British presidency propagated in 2005 for the EU. A good – albeit slightly out of date – analysis of the small claims procedures in a number of common law countries, Germany and Japan, has been published by Whelan.[49] In a more recent essay, Baldwin criticises a number of inconsistencies in the British system. The upper limit of small claims procedures has increased fivefold without any increase in the number of complaints. The author also criticises judges in small claims procedures for becoming too pro-active. Finally, small claims procedures have a major disadvantage in that only a minority of traders comply with the judgments issued against them.[50]

In 1993, the European Commission produced a Greenbook on access of consumers to justice.[51] In 2002 there followed a Greenbook on order for payment proce-

---

45 In some instances this can be taken care of, when upon payment of a fee the complaints tribunal takes on a case against a non-member.

46 See I.S.J. Houben, *Contractdwang*, PhD Leiden, Deventer: Kluwer, 2005, 384 p.

47 Katalin Judit Cseres, *Competition law and consumer protection*, PhD Utrecht 2004, The Hague: Kluwer, 2005, 450 p.

48 John Baldwin, 'Is there a limit to the expansion of small claims?' in: M.D.A. Freeman (ed.), *Current legal problems*, vol. 56, Oxford: Oxford University Press, 2004, p. 313–343.

49 Christopher J. Whelan (ed.), *Small claims courts/A comparative study*, Oxford: Clarendon, 1990, 253 p.

50 Baldwin (2004), *ibidem*.

51 COM(93) 576 def. See B. Stauder, Konsumentenverfahren in Europa (EU-Grünbuch Zugang zum Recht im Binnenmarkt, in: A. Brunner, M. Rehbinder, B. Stauder (eds.), *Jahrbuch des Schweizerischen Konsumentenrechts*, Bern: Staempfli, 2000, p. 179–195.

dures and on small claims procedures.[52] Having first come up with a proposal for an order for payments procedure, the European Commission on 15 March 2005 introduced a draft regulation on a European *small claims* procedure, which should apply next to each national procedure.[53] The procedure would apply to both internal and cross-border complaints (Article 1) below EUR 2,000 (Article 2). The main asset for the consumer would have been that in case of loss of the procedure, he would not have to bear the legal costs of the other party (Article 14 paragraph 2). The draft provided for the use of pre-established forms (Article 3). The procedure would begin with a registered letter (Article 11) and be in writing, unless the court or arbitrators deemed an oral hearing expedient (Article 4). Within six months, a final award should be made (Article 10), which should lead to an enforcement order (Article 13). The EU has accepted the draft with some modifications.[54] What was kept was the limitation to claims under EUR 2,000 (Article 2) – which from a Dutch perspective is a very low amount.[55] Maintained was also the focus on a written procedure – which once again from a Dutch point of view is not a good thing: in the Netherlands, oral procedures do much better serve the goal of making it possible for complainants to get a grief off their chest, whereas travelling distances are not a major problem.[56] The limitation to cross-border complaints is understandable from a constitutional point of view. Positive are the limitation of the recoverability of translation costs (Article 6) and the obligation for the court to act swiftly (Article 7). What really is to be deplored is that the final text, which is bound to enter into force on 1 January 2009, has introduced the possibility to order an unsuccessful complainant to pay the costs of the procedure (Article 16).

Whether or not a European regulation of *national* procedural law is really necessary, had already been doubted. It appeared to be an infringement of the principle of subsidiarity.[57] On the other hand, one may raise the question whether a small claims procedure only for transborder claims is really necessary.[58] If it were to be introduced, should it not also be made available for domestic disputes? The introduction of the regulation has raised a number of technical questions,

52 *Greenbook for a European payments procedure and small claims*, COM(2002) 746def.

53 *Proposal for a Regulation of the European Parliament and the Council establishing a European Small Claims Procedure*, SEC(2005) 351/352.

54 See Paulien N.M. van der Grinten, kroniek Europese ontwikkelingen, *Tijdschrift voor Civiele Rechtspleging* 2005, p. 79, 86–88.

55 For the Netherlands, the limitation to EUR 5,000 to EUR 10,000 would have been more appropriate.

56 A procedure in writing may be advisable for geographically large countries such as France, Spain and Sweden, but for a spaciously limited country such as the Netherlands an oral hearing is much more advisable.

57 For that reason, the Council of Ministers on 1 December 2005 decided to restrict the payments directive to cross-border transactions.

58 ECC-network.

which will not be dealt with in this paper. This paper will rather address the policy question whether or not the regulation should serve as a catalyst on the national level. Access to ordinary justice allegedly has three disadvantages, as we saw. Two of these seem to be met by the Regulation. The financial risk involved in bringing a claim before a government court is taken away and legal aid no longer is necessary – at least not in simple cases. Second, the regulation provides for a maximum period of six months. In a jurisdiction such as the Netherlands, this length is already receding at present[59] through a number of measures.[60] Against this the length of dealing with complaints before the private complaints tribunals has been around six months for the past few years. This leaves us with the informal character of out-of-court settlement, but is that is all there is? The idea of reconsidering the present government policy towards financing out-of-court settlement of consumer complaints has also occurred to a Dutch government commission on a fundamental reconsideration of civil procedure (*Fundamentele herbezinning Nederlands burgerlijk procesrecht*). In her intermediary report, the Commission raises the question whether a small claims procedure should be introduced[61] or whether such cases should be left to the care of legal aid insurance companies.[62]

It should not necessarily be either/or: a measure of competition between a governmental small claims procedure and out-of-court settlement by private complaints tribunals is not inconceivable, as is integration of the existing complaints tribunals in the judiciary after the Nordic model.

Once a small claims procedure is instituted, its scope of application raises some problems. In the first place there is the question whether what is good for consumers, is good for citizens in general. A positive response to this question at first instance appears reasonable, until one appreciates that this would also mean that in B2B transactions the winning party will no longer be entitled to compensation for legal aid. Extension of the scope of small claims procedures would also give rise to the question whether there should lie appeal to an appellate

59 Roland Eshuis, Sneller procederen: empirisch onderzoek naar de afdoening van civiele bodemprocedures, *Rechtstreeks* 2005/2, p. 7–68; A.D. Reiling, Rechtspraak in de digitale delta, *Nederlands Juristenblad* 2003, p. 2286–2291.

60 M.B. Beekhoven van den Boezem en anderen, Geschillenbeslechting door een niet-overheidsrechter: een gewenste ontwikkeling?, in: L.C. Winkel and others (eds.), *Privatisering van veiligheid*, The Hague: Boom, 2005, p. 195–213; A.W. Jongbloed (ed.), *Beschouwingen over het nieuwe procesrecht*, The Hague: Boom, 2001, 107 p.

61 W.D.H. Asser, H.A. Groen, J.B.M. Vranken, I.N. Tzankova, *Een nieuwe balans/Interimrapport Fundamentele herbezinning Nederlands burgerlijk procesrecht*, The Hague: Boom, 2003, p. 263–268.

62 This suggestion met with much criticism and was not retained in the Commission's final report.

court, something which would once again raise problems of cost and time.[63] A second question is whether or not the procedure should only be open to consumers or also to their counterparts. In case of the latter, the small claims procedure may in fact become a *de facto* payments procedure.

5. COLLECTIVE ACTION

There is another alternative for – individual – small claims litigation. That is the collectivisation through group actions and class actions. Most EU Member States do already possess a group action.[64] In the Netherlands this has been codified in Articles 3:305a/b *Burgerlijk Wetboek* (Civil code); the group action for unfair terms in consumer contracts is to be found in Article 6:240 *Burgerlijk Wetboek* (Civil code). Although both provisions seem to enable consumer organisations a widespread use of such actions, the contrary is the case. Two reasons may be put forward by way of explanation: one legal, the other financial. The *financial* reason lies in the cost of litigation. When the Hobby Computer Club (HCC) won an unfair contract terms case against Dell Computers,[65] the court's award left some issues unanswered or answered in an unsatisfactory way according to the HCC. But revision in cassation simply proved to be financially impossible.[66] A *legal* inconvenience is that the Dutch group action does not provide for compensation in damages.[67]

The class action is a phenomenon which perhaps is best known for its occurrence in the United States of America, but it also exists in other common law jurisdictions – witness the excellent analysis of the federal class actions in Australia and the US and the Canadian provincial class action of Ontario and British Columbia by Rachael Mulheron.[68] This book consists of three parts. In an

---

63 In favour of a specific consumer civil procedure in Germany is Harald Koch, Brauchen wir ein eigenes Verbraucherprozessrecht?, in: Hans W. Micklitz (ed.), *Verbraucherrecht in Deutschland – Stand und Perspektiven*, Baden-Baden: Nomos, 2005, p. 345–353.

64 See the *Comparative tables of collective redress in consumer law litigation, by country* prepared by Mrs Gaëlle Patetta, Appendix to the working document *Defining the collective actions system and its role in the context of Community consumer law* of the European Economic and Social Committee (February 2008).

65 Gerechtshof (Court of Appeal) The Hague 22 March 2005, *Tijdschrift voor Consumentenrecht* 2005, p. 150 (Notes M.Y. Schaub and M.B.M. Loos).

66 The only option left in such cases is 'cassatie in het belang der wet', which may lead to revision of the court of appeal's award, but only on principle, without changing the existing rights and duties of the parties – and this is what the HCC requested – but the problem here is that only between 1–2% of all requests are taken into consideration and this one was not among these.

67 Niels Frenk, *Kollektieve akties in het privaatrecht*, PhD Utrecht, Deventer: Kluwer, 1994, 383 p.

68 Rachael Mulheron, *The class action/in common law legal systems – A comparative perspective*, Oxford: Hart, 2004, 535 p.

introductory part, the author analyses the characteristics of modern class actions[69] and the aims of legislation.[70] Part II is devoted to the introduction of a class action.[71] Part III deals with the question how to conduct a class action.[72] What strikes the reader of this book is the large number of points where something may go wrong: the number of class members for instance is too small,[73] the class representative is unauthorised[74] or the statute of limitations bars a suit.[75]

Outside the common law jurisdictions, there is an increasing interest in class actions. Finland and Sweden have been the first two continental countries to introduce a class action. In Sweden, Per Henrik Lindblom, who pioneered this type of legislation, has analysed the experience with two years of grupptalan as the Swedes call this model.[76] No more than five cases have so far been brought, so the floodgates argument does not appear well-founded. In Finland, the Consumer Ombudsman has published a file on the internet. And in France, class actions are already being prepared, as we may read on *le site français des actions collectives*.[77] This is in accordance with a universal tendency, witness the OECD Report on *consumer dispute resolution and redress in the global marketplace*.[78] A comparative survey, with proposals for the future, was published by Micklitz and Stadler.[79]

69 Mulheron (2004), p. 23–45.

70 Mulheron (2004), p. 47–111.

71 Mulheron (2004), p. 115–318: which cases are suitable (p. 115–164), the requisite commonality (p. 165–217) and the requisite superiority (p. 219–273) and assessing the class representative (p. 275–318).

72 Mulheron (2004), p. 321–479: shaping the class membership (p. 321–366), potential impediments to ongoing conduct (p. 367–388), monetary relief (p. 389–434) and costs and funding of class actions (p. 435–479).

73 Mulheron (2004), p. 115–130.

74 Mulheron (2004), p. 275–318.

75 Mulheron (2004), p. 373–385.

76 Per Henrik Lindblom, Lagen om grupprättegang – bakgrund och frantid, *Svensk Juristtidning* 2005, p. 129–191.

77 *Le site français des actions collectives*, www.classaction.fr/.

78 OECD, *Workshop on consumer dispute resolution and redress in the global marketplace*, www.oecd.org/dataoecd/59/21/34699496.pdf.

79 Hans W. Micklitz, Astrid Stadler (eds.), *Das Verbandsklagerecht in der Informations- und Dienstleistungsgesellschaft*, Schriftenreihe des Bundesministeriums für Verbraucherschutz, Ernährung und Landwirtschaft, Münster: Landwirtschaftsverlag, 2005, 1488 p. The report not only describes the situation in Germany: it also entails national reports by Holger Beuchler (France, p. 57–157, Greece, p. 169–236, the United Kingdom, p. 795–938, the United States, p. 941–1125), Andreas Mom (Netherlands, p. 343–496, Spain, p. 655–793 and Sweden, p. 497–654) and Julia Müller (Italy, p. 237–342), as well as a comparative report (p. 1127–1437). See also Astrid Stadler, Individueller und kollektiver Rechtsschutz im Verbraucherrecht – Wege zu einem ausgewongenen Verhältnis, in: Hans W. Micklitz (ed.), *Verbraucherrecht in Deutschland – Stand und Perspektiven*, Baden-Baden: Nomos, 2005, p. 319–343, and Caroline Meller-Hannich (ed.), *Kollektiver Rechtsschutz im Zivilprozess/Hallesches Symposium zum Zivilverfahrensrecht am 6. Oktober 2007 -Tagungsband*, Baden-Baden: Nomos, 2008, 127 p.

6. MASS DAMAGE TRANSACTIONS

How to cope with mass damages is something which most Europeans still have to learn. In the Netherlands, when in the past companies were confronted with mass damages, they used to appoint a (three-member) commission to deal with all the complaints. Thus the *Planta*-case which affected some 300,000 Dutch citizens in the 1960s was solved by the suppliers of Planta margarine, Unilever. Not a single complainant went to court. When the authorities sought to solve the *Legiolease* case in a similar way, it did not work this time. And when at a later stage the former President of the European Bank, the late Wim Duisenberg, came up with a compromise proposal, this was on the one hand applauded, but there have also been critics.[80]

The regulation of mass damages brings us close to the class action.

The Dutch act on mass damages does enable compensation for damages. This Act was inspired by the *DES* case.[81] It was also used in the *Dexia* case,[82] which left some 700,000 Dutch investors with sometimes severe losses.[83] One of the advantages of the Act is its opt-out character. This sets it apart from the American settlement class action, which has developed without any specific legal basis.[84]

6.1. THE DES CASE

From 1953–1967 a drug called 'diethylstilbestrol', better known as 'DES', was prescribed as a sedative in the Netherlands, as it was in other countries. DES was supposed to prevent miscarriages, but instead happened to cause grave side-effects. Daughters of the women who used the drug developed a specific form of cancer in the uro-genital system. Not only did the victims suffer a medical plight, their legal plight has also come to the fore. May the manufacturers of the drug be

80 N.J.H. Huls, Is de Duisenberg-regeling royaal genoeg voor alle legitieme Dexiaclaims?, *Nederlands Juristenblad* 2005, p. 1386–1390. See also Erica Verdegaal, Leasebelegger slijpt messen/Alternatief om 'magere' Duisenberg-regeling aan te vechten, *NRC Handelsblad* 18 September 2005.

81 See P.N. van Regteren Altena, 'De collectieve afwikkeling van de DES-zaak in Nederland', in: A.I.M. van Mierlo and others, *Het wetsvoorstel collectieve afwikkeling massaschade*, The Hague: Boom, 2005, p. 27–35.

82 See Hans W. Micklitz and Astrid Stadler, in: Gabriel/Pirker-Hörmann, *Massenverfahren/ Reformbedarf für die ZPO?* (2005), p. 139–140.

83 N. Frenk, De wet collectieve afwikkeling massaschade en de aandelenlease-affaire, *Weekblad voor Privaatrecht, Notariaat en Registratie* 2005, nr. 6630; the same, Vie d'Or, aandelenlease en de reikwijdte van het collectief actierecht, *Nederlands Tijdschrift voor Burgerlijk Recht* 2005, p. 296–300.

84 Martin H. Redish and Andrianna D. Kastnek, Settlement class actions, the case-or-controversy requirement, and the nature of the adjudicatory process, 73 *University of Chicago Law Review* 545–614 (2006).

held liable? This question raises a number of issues: did the manufacturers commit a tort? Are the victims time-barred from instituting proceedings? How can one sue a manufacturer when one cannot prove who brought the drug into circulation? It is especially the latter issue which has come to be associated with *DES* cases. DES being a generic drug, was marketed by a large number of manufacturers. Twenty-five years later it was all but impossible to prove which manufacturer produced the particular drug which was used by the mother of any victim. Does this mean that victims cannot be compensated? Not necessarily.

In order to find an equitable solution, American courts introduced the notion of market share liability.[85] This idea attracted much attention in Europe, but generally has not been applied by European courts. Would it be adopted by the Dutch courts which were called upon to decide a *DES* case?

On 28 April 1986, six DES daughters sued ten pharmaceutical companies before the Amsterdam (District) Court. The case was dismissed, as it was on appeal, basically on the ground that none of the victims could prove which of the defendant manufacturers had brought the particular drug into circulation. In cassation, however, the Advocate-General Hartkamp concluded that the decision be annulled on the ground that it did not follow the market share liability theory. The *Hoge Raad* (Dutch Supreme Court) went one step further. The court first dismissed the Appellate Court's rejection of Article 99 Book 6 of the Dutch Civil Code as an obstacle to the daughters' case.[86] 'When constructing this Article', said the court, 'the text, the purpose and the parliamentary history of the law should be taken into consideration' (section 3.7.1 of the decision, as numbered by the Court).

According to the *Hoge Raad*, 'the situation occurring in the present case is covered by this text: it must be assumed by way of supposition that the companies which marketed Des in the relevant period are each liable therefore on account of fault on their part, that the entire damage of each injured party may have resulted from each of these "events" – the marketing – and that at any rate the damage was the result of one of these "events". If the Court of Appeal (...) imposes the requirement that the alleged facts must include a "specific act", it makes a requirement which does not find support in the text of Article 99' (3.7.1).

85 In the landmark case *Sindell v Abbott Laboratories*, 607 P2d 924, the California Supreme Court, ever since followed by a number of courts in some other American states, held that if the manufacturer cannot be traced, all manufacturers are liable for their share in the market.

86 The text of Article 6:99 reads:
'Where the damage may have resulted from two or more events for each of which a different person is liable, and where it has been determined that the damage has arisen from at least one of these events, the obligation to repair the damage rests upon each of these persons, unless he proves that the damage is not the result of the event for which he himself is liable' (translation Haanappel, Deventer 1990).

As to the purpose, the High Court continued: 'The application of the Article in a situation like the one involved in the present case is also in keeping with its purpose. The Article aims at removing the unreasonableness that the injured party would have to bear the damage himself because he is unable to prove whose act was the cause of his damage. This is the difficulty of providing evidence with which the injured parties are confronted in the present case' (3.7.1).

Then came a difficult point: how to explain away the absence of any reference to this kind of case in the Parliamentary proceedings.[87] But the *Hoge Raad* found a way to counter this argument.[88] Another important point, said the *Hoge Raad*, 'is that the system accepted by the Court of Appeal leads to an unacceptable result. Even though in the present case it must be assumed by way of supposition that each of the Pharmaceutical Companies was at fault by marketing Des and that the Des-Daughters sustained serious injuries as a result of the use of Des by their mothers, in this system the Des-daughters will nevertheless be denied any claim for damages merely because they are unable to state from which producer the Des tablets taken by their mothers originated' (3.7.2). The Court did not accept the American market share liability, as advocated by its Advocate-General.[89]

The Appellate Court had not applied Article 6:99, because the Des-daughters had not stated who belonged to the circle of persons who had marketed Des. The Appellate Court had not required that all such persons be summoned in the procedure, correctly so, according to the Hoge Raad, since it sufficed for an injured party to summon one of the persons liable.[90]

---

87 It should be mentioned that unlike in the United Kingdom, where only since the end of 1992 consultation of Hansard's, when constructing legislation, has been allowed (*Pepper v Hart*, [1993] 1 *All ER* 42), on the Continent this construction method has a long-standing tradition.

88 'It is true that in the "Toelichting Meijers" and in the parliamentary documents there is no mention of a situation like the one occurring in the present case in connection with the Des product, but it is likely that at the time this type lay beyond the range of conceivable situations. Therefore it may not be concluded from the fact that this situation was not discussed, that the Article does not apply in such situation' (3.7.1).

89 It observed: '(…) it is unsatisfactory that this system lays the risk of insolvency of one of the producers and also the risk that a producer has ceased to exist or can no longer be traced, with the victims and not with the producers. It is also burdensome that the victims will have to bring claims against as many producers as possible and that the market share of each of the producers will have to be established in the litigation between the victims and the producers. From the standpoint of victim protection, moreover, there is no need for market share liability in a situation like the one occurring in the present case, since each of the producers is in principle liable for the entire damage, as has been ruled above' (3.8).

90 The Court continued: 'Likewise, it is not a requirement that the injured party allege – and prove – which persons belong to the circle of persons liable. Even in the traditional situation falling within the scope of Article 6:99, where several persons fire a rifle or throw stones in the same direction, such a requirement would already lead to an unreasonable result: if it is impossible to identify all riflemen or stone throwers, the injured party would have to bear his damage himself. In a situation like the one under review a requirement like the one just referred to would all the more lead to an unreasonable result: the injured party would have to bear her own damage if she is unable to identify all the producers which marketed Des in the

The Court also dealt with the burden of proof.[91] The defence that Des was also marketed by producers who were not liable, was rejected.[92] As for recourse between the various manufacturers, the Court was curt.[93]

This case was not decided on the basis of the EC Directive on Product Liability and its implementation in the Dutch Civil Code.[94] The DES decision has met with a positive reception in the Netherlands. The majority of writers are happy with the result.[95] The decision has also met with criticism by some commentators.[96]

relevant period, even though in fact such identification of producers will be virtually impossible' (3.7.4).

91 'Each of the Des-daughters will have alleged sufficient facts by alleging with respect to each of the Pharmaceutical Companies, as in fact each of them did in the present proceedings:
(i) that the Pharmaceutical Company in question marketed Des in the relevant period and is liable therefore on account of a fault committed by such company;
(ii) that there are also one or more other producers – whether or not joined as defendants – who also marketed Des in the relevant period and who is/are also liable therefore on account of fault; and
(iii) that she has suffered damage and that the damage is the result of the use of Des, but that it is no longer possible to establish from which producer the Des that was taken originated.
In principle the burden of proof of the above rests with the Des-daughter in question.
The concluding words of Article 6:99 entail that as a rebuttal of his liability, each of the Pharmaceutical Companies may allege and if necessary prove in relation to each of the Des-daughters that the damage of the Des-daughter in question is not the result of the use of any Des marketed by him' (3.7.5).

92 This is what the Court has to say on this point: 'it is conceivable that it will be established that in the relevant period Des was also marketed by one or more producers who are not liable therefore because there is no question of fault and that the damage of the Des-daughter in question may also have been caused by such Des. This will not release the other producers from their liability for the entire damage unless in the given circumstances which include the degree of risk that the damage of the Des-daughter in question was caused by Des originating from a producer who is not liable, such liability would be unacceptable according to criteria of reasonableness and equity' (3.7.6).

93 It said 'that the producers, who are jointly and severally liable to the injured parties for the entire damage, have mutual recourse, so that in principle they will not have to bear more damages, eventually, than their share in the total damage. Anyway, since recourse is not a point of discussion in the present proceedings, it need not be decided here in which proportion each of the producers will have to contribute to the damages' (3.7.3). And a little further: 'It need not be decided here whether the market share of each of the producers may be a relevant factor in the determination of the proportional contribution to be made by each of the producers' (3.8).

94 As the *Hoge Raad* stated, this is 'already for the mere reason that this is a case about liability for products which were marketed before 1985 while Article 17 in conjunction with article 19 shows that the Directive does not apply to these in any case' (3.5).

95 Jac Hijma, *Ars Aequi* 1993, p. 123, P. Ingelse, *Nederlands Juristenblad* 1992, p. 1403, J. Knottenbelt, *Nemesis* 1993/5, p. 23, G.J. Rijken and J.G.J. Rinkes, *Tijdschrift voor Consumentenrecht* 1992, p. 325 and A.J.O. van Wassenaer van Catwijck, *Verkeersrecht* 1993, nr. 19 and myself, *Tijdschrift voor Gezondheidsrecht* 1993, p. 382.

96 L. Dommering-van Rongen, *Weekblad voor Privaatrecht en Notariaat* 6089, A.S. Hartkamp, in: Kabaal in Holland/Asscher-bundel, Arnhem 1993, p. 76–78 and J. Spier, *Nederlands Tijdschrift voor Burgerlijk Recht* 1992, p. 193.

The importance of the Des case may be summarised in three points: (i) it is a major boost for the many victims of Des, although the liability of the manufacturers is yet to be assessed. It may also serve as an argument in other European countries to compensate the victims. (ii) The practical consequences of the decision should not be overestimated. Environmentalists have, incorrectly in my opinion, assumed that the case could immediately be applied to environmental claims. This cannot be read in the Court's decision. Even, liability under the EC Directive, being constructed as a strict liability, may not be affected by the Des-decision, being based on fault liability. (iii) On the other hand, the importance of this case for the Dutch law-finding process should not be underestimated. Indeed, few Dutch lawyers would have predicted the outcome of this procedure, their type of argument still being based on Civil Code-related arguments. Since the present Civil Code is of such recent origin (it entered into force on 1 January 1992), it was generally presumed that the Court would stick to these arguments. Instead, the *Hoge Raad* uses policy arguments, just as an American court would. Since such arguments always must play some role, it is better to bring them out into the open, in order that a decision can be judged on its real arguments. This is the major gain which the 1992 decision has brought.

Now this is a long introduction to the question which is at hand in this paper: how were the DES victims compensated. This proved to be a time-consuming exercise which was only brought to an end with the decision of the Amsterdam Court of Appeal to declare an agreement between producers and representatives of consumers generally binding under the new Act.

6.2. THE DEXIA CASE

A second case which has sparked interest in the new Act has been the Dexia affair. In the late 1990s some 700,000 Dutch consumers invested part of their savings in high-risk investment products marketed by Bank Labouchere, which before the scandal broke out was bought by the Belgian Dexia Bank. The product itself had not been invented by Bank Labouchere but by private citizens who initially wanted to obtain a higher share in the continually rising share markets without banks creaming off their commissioner's share.

The product itself consisted of a scheme whereby a bank would use the consumer's investment as a security to obtain a loan which would triple the investment. The product was market as a 'winstverdriedubbelaar': a device to obtain treble profits. What the bank would not disclose is that when the stock market goes down, losses would also treble. After the fall of the stock exchange on 9/11, many consumers were for the first time confronted with the conditions under which they had invested. This resulted in thousands of cases being brought before Dutch courts. Because the cases were very similar, one of the results was that Dutch courts started to cooperate more than ever before in arriving at model decisions. Some specific cases were handled in a specific way. For instance, married investors who had not consulted their partner suddenly found an Article in the Civil Code which aims to protect family life by among others requiring the partner's consent to hire-purchase contracts. The question then arose whether the treble profit scheme could qualify as hire-purchase. This question has presumably come to a close with a decision of the *Hoge Raad* that held indeed that this may qualify as hire-purchase.[97] But the most interesting decision from the point of view of this paragraph, was the decision of the Amsterdam Court of Appeal to declare the Duisenburg agreement generally binding, with an opt-out possibility.[98] The court did so by using the newly introduced statute on settlement of mass damages.

6.3. SHELL HYDROCARBON RESERVES

Early 2004, the Anglo-Dutch Shell company reassessed its proved oil reserves downward. Shareholders reported losses, which resulted in various class actions and settlements. Agreement was reached and the Amsterdam Court of Appeal is expected to announce its agreement in early 2009. The settlement, together with that in the US, amounts to some $ 600 million, according to Christopher Hodges (see the Bibliography).

6.4. DOCTRINAL COMMENTS

The new Act has attracted considerable attention from Dutch authors, not in the least because of the two spectacular starting cases. Leiden University's Mordenate College[99] devoted one of its conferences to the subject.[100] Because the language of the volume is Dutch and the Publishers have no distribution channels outside the Netherlands, a little more will be told of the contents. In Part I, Alexandra Timmer provides us with a survey of the historical development.[101] On the occasion of the preparation of the bill, the Netherlands Association of Judges expressed its

97 HR 28 March 2008, *LJN* BC2837.

98 Court of Appeal Amsterdam 25 January 2007, LJN AZ 7033.

99 The foundation of this fraternity goes back to the late Henri Schermers, who gave students an opportunity to participate in an honours class, provided their marks were eight or higher – 'More than eight' – out of ten.

100 Nienke van den Berg, Rens Henkemans and Alexandra Timmer (eds.), *Massaclaims, class actions op z'n Nederlands*, Nijmegen: Ars Aequi, 2007, 213 p.

101 P. 13–27.

concern over the manifold tasks which the bill entrusted to judges. Rens Henkemans utters his surprise over the lack of response to this alarming news.[102]

When a foundation has the statutory aim of promoting the interests of those who suffer damages as a consequence of a specific activity, the question may be raised whether a causal link and damages can be established. The Amsterdam lawyer D.F. Lunsingh Scheurleer analyses this question in the light of American and Canadian case law.[103]

Part II is about Dutch legal practice. Tamara Buruma analyses on the basis of two cases whether or not the *Staatkundig Gereformeerde Partij*, a political party which considers women should stay home and look after the children, should be subsidised by the government.[104] F. Kroes of the Amsterdam bar analyses the opt-out rules of the Act on the basis of the Dexia case.[105] His colleague A.R.J. Croiset van Uchelen, who appeared for the 11,000 insured victims in the *Vie d'Or* case[106], proposes a number of amendments to the present regulation of collective actions.[107] Article 3:305a/b should allow an *opt-out* or *opt-in* system and the curator's possibilities to claim mass damages by way of redress should be broadened.

Part III is devoted to international perspective. In his paper, which was earlier published in a law review,[108] Martijn Polak analyses litispendency and connexitity.[109] Nienke van den Berg raises the question whether or not mass claims are available in arbitration.[110] Ianika Tzankova is interested in learning from the English about financing mass claims (p. 171–204).

It is interesting to note that in other European countries, investors' problems have also led to new legislation. In Austria, a case of 3,000 investors against a credit institute in Salzburg – and other affairs – have led to an outcry for new legislation.[111] In Germany, several thousand investors filed a claim against Deutsche Telekom on the basis of prospectus liability, leading to the adoption of the *Gesetz zur Bewältigung von Musterverfahren im Kapitalanlegerrecht*, which entered into force on 1 November 2005.[112] The German Act has a sunset clause – it was enacted for a period of five years – and owing to the high requirements

102 P. 29–58.

103 P. 59–64.

104 P. 67–86.

105 P. 87–103.

106 *Jurisprudentie Onderneming Recht* 2006, 295/297.

107 P. 105–128.

108 M.V. Polak, Iedereen en overal? Internationaal privaatrecht rond 'massaclaims', *Nederlands Juristenblad* 2006, p. 2346–2355.

109 P. 131–146.

110 P. 147–169.

111 See Tamara Gabriel, Beate Pirker-Hörmann, *Massenverfahren/Reformbedarf für die ZPO?*, Wien: Verlag Österreich, 2005, 452 p.

112 See Peter Gundermann, Philip Härle, Das Kapitalanleger-Musterverfahrensgesetz – eine Momentaufnahme zum Jahresende 2006, *Verbraucher und Recht* 2006, p. 457–461, and Hans

which it imposes as to the cases where the procedure is available, as to the minimum number of participants and as to the absence of an opt-out it remains to be seen whether it will be continued.[113][115] Abroad, the Dutch act – most probably due to problems of a linguistic nature – has so far elicited not much comment, apart from the statement that it is highly interesting but 'speziell auf die holländische Rechtskultur zugeschnitten und – jedenfalls derzeit – schwer übertragbar'.[114]

7. PUBLIC ENFORCEMENT

When the Netherlands finally got a public Consumer Protection Agency, this Agency (*Consumentenautoriteit*) was entrusted with both private and public enforcement competences. Private law enforcement will take place in case of infringement of the law on misleading advertising and unfair contract terms (with the exception of the black list). The Hague Court of Appeal may issue an injunction. No such injunction has so far been applied for by the Consumer Authority. Public law enforcement will take place in case of infringements of door to door sales and the black list of unfair contract terms legislation. The maximum fine to be applied by the Consumer Authority is EURO 74,000. The fine shall be in accordance with the principle of proportionality. In practice, a warning or an invitation to discuss matters is often sufficient to bring an end to the bad practice. The Consumer Authority may also make use of private complaints tribunals to submit requests; it has used this option in the case of the *Reclame Code Commissie* (Advertising Standards Authority).[115]

Whether the combination of private and public enforcement was a wise choice, has recently being debated in Parliament in the light of the transposition of the Directive on B2C trade practices. The Consumer Protection Agency feels restrained because public and private enforcement impose a different internal organisation. It may therefore be expected that the dual enforcement system will be changed into a single public enforcement system. Against this most probable change, it has been argued that the public enforcement officers are not familiar

W. Micklitz and Astrid Stadler, in: Gabriel/Pirker-Hörmann, *Massenverfahren/Reformbedarf für die ZPO?* (2005), p. 111 ff.

113 Astrid Stadler is critical: 'Für eine endgültige Bewertung des KapMuG ist es vielleicht noch zu früh. Jedenfalls kann man aber feststellen, dass die Regelungen des KapMuG von einer Reihe prozessualer Ungereimtheiten gekennzeichnet sind und "einer klaren dogmatischen Konzeption [entbehren]"' – in: Caroline Meller-Hannich (ed.), *Kollektiver Rechtsschutz im Zivilprozess/Hallesche Symposium zum Zivilverhahrensrecht*, Baden-Baden: Nomos, 2008, p. 99.

114 Stadler, *o.c.*, at p. 102.

115 L.B. Melcherts and E.L.M. Vos, De Consumentenautoriteit: het duale stelsel, een overzicht van de handhavingspraktijk, *TvC* 2008 (forthcoming).

with the mostly private law nature of trade practices, which therefore may better be entrusted to private law courts.[116] On the other hand, there is an active interaction between private law and administrative law in the Netherlands,[117] which is perhaps encouraged by the fact that first-instance cases are dealt with by the same courts.

8. CONCLUSIONS

On the individual level, a small claims procedure should not replace the consumer complaints tribunals. A small claims procedure should not replace existing consumer complaints tribunals. A competition between the two systems can even be desirable. On a collective level, the foundation of a Dutch Consumer Authority has sparked discussion in the Netherlands about the most desirable form of enforcement: public or private. There now seems to be a tendency to replace the dual enforcement system by single, public law machinery. Such development should be deplored. Group actions are a well established phenomenon in Dutch law, but they are not often used in consumer matters. In such matters, the newly introduced settlement for mass damages proves a very interesting instrument.

SELECTED BIBLIOGRAPHY

G. Alpa, *Il diritto dei consumatori*, Bari: Laterza, 2002, p. 427–454.

W.D.H. Asser, H.A. Groen, J.B.M. Vranken and I.N. Tzankova, *Een nieuwe balans/ Interimrapport Fundamentele herbezinning Nederlands burgerlijk procesrecht*, The Hague: Boom, 2003, 306 p.

J.M. Barendrecht and Y.P. Kamminga, *Toegang tot het recht/De lasten van een uitweg*, The Hague: Boom, 2005, 95 p.

J. Baldwin, 'Is there a limit to the expansion of small claims?' in: M.D.A. Freeman (eds.), *Current legal problems*, vol. 56, Oxford: University Press, 2004, p. 313–343.

M. Barendrecht, Y.P. Kamminga and J.H. Verdonschot, *Priorities for the justice system: responding to the most urgent legal problems of individuals*, Tisco working paper 001–2008, http://ssrn.com/abstract=1090885.

E. Bauw and N. Frenk, Het verhaal van schade ten behoeve van grote groepen slachtoffers, in: A. Akkermans and E. Brans (eds.), *Aansprakelijkheid en schadeverhaal bij rampen*, Nijmegen: Ars Aequi, 2002, p. 86–94.

[116] M. van Campen, in: W.H. van Boom, S.D. Lindenbergh, S.B. Pape (eds.), *Privaatrecht ondersteund/Doelen, baten, kosten en effecten van bijzondere ondersteuning door de overheid van privaatrechtelijke handhaving*, The Hague: Boom, 2007, p. 35–60.

[117] See R.J.P. Kottenhagen and P.A. Kottenhagen-Dezes, Tort and regulatory law in the Netherlands, in: W.H. van Boom, M. Lukas, Chr. Kissling (eds.), *Tort and Regulatory Law*, Vienna: Springer, 2007, p. 187-204.

E. Bauw and R. Hartendorp, Consumentenzaken: kantonrechter of geschillencommissie?, *Nederlands Juristenblad* 2005, p. 2304–2308.

M.B. Beekhoven van den Boezem and others, Geschillenbeslechting door een niet-overheidsrechter: een gewenste ontwikkeling?, in: L.C. Winkel and others (eds.), *Privatisering van veiligheid*, The Hague: Boom, 2005, p. 195–213.

N. van den Berg, R. Henkemans and A. Timmer (eds.), *Massaclaims, class actions op z'n Nederlands*, Nijmegen: Ars Aequi, 2007, 213 p.

C.B.E. van Bladel, *Arbitrage in de praktijk/Een empirisch onderzoek naar institutionele arbiyrage, met name bij de Raad van Arbitrage voor de Bouw*, PhD Utrecht, The Hague: Boom, 2002, 144 p.

W. van Boom and M. Loos (eds.), *Collective enforcement of consumer law/Securing compliance in Europe through private group action and public authority intervention*, Groningen: Europa Law Publishing, 2007, 254 p.

J.R. Branbergen, De rechter in eerste aanleg in de aandelenleaseprocedures, *Nederlands Juristenblad* 2008, p. 498–502.

A. Brenninkmeijer, M. van Ewijk and C. van der Werf, *Aard en omvang van arbitrage en bindend advies in Nederland*, Leiden: Meijers Instituut, 2002, 53 p.

A. Brunner, M. Rehbinder and B. Stauder (eds.), *Jahrbuch des Schweizerischen Konsumentenrechts*, Bern: Staempfli, 2000, 506 p.

E. Camous, *Règlements non-juridictionnels des litiges de la consommation*, Paris: Librairie générale, 2002.

M. van Campen, in: W.H. van Boom, S.D. Lindenbergh and S.B. Pape (eds.), *Privaatrecht ondersteund/Doelen, baten, kosten en effecten van bijzondere ondersteuning door de overheid van privaatrechtelijke handhaving*, The Hague: Boom, 2007, p. 35–60.

A.R.J. Croiset van Uchelen, De verbindendverklaring volgens de WCAM als procesvorm, *Aansprakelijkheid Verzekering en Schade* 2007, p. 222–227.

E. De Baere, Massaschade, *Tijdschrift voor Privaatrecht* 2007, p. 1–58.

C.J.M. van Doorn, De 'Amsterdamse' oplossing: het einde van de Dexia-affaire in zicht?, *Tijdschrift voor Consumentenrecht* 2007, p. 141–147.

C.J.M. van Doorn, De tweede WCAM-beschikking is een feit: tijd voor een terugblik en een blik vooruit, *AV&S* 2007, p. 105–114.

N. Doornbos and P.P.M. van Reijsen, *De Geschillencommissie Ziekenhuizen*, The Hague: Vermande, 2000.

F. Dorssemont, T. Jaspers and A. van Hoek (eds.), *Cross-border collective actions in Europe: a legal challenge/A study of the legal aspects of transnational collective actions from a labour law and private international law perspective*, Antwerp: Intersentia, 2007, 481 p.

EIM, *Afhandeling van collectieve consumentenklachten*, April 2004.

C. Ervine, The importance of small claims courts in the resolution of consumer disputes in the United Kingdom, *Consumer Law Journal* 1995, p. 24–28.

R. Eshuis, Sneller procederen: empirisch onderzoek naar de afdoening van civiele bodemprocedures, *Rechtstreeks* 2005/2, p. 7–68.

N. Frenk, *Kollektieve akties in het privaatrecht*, PhD Utrecht, Deventer: Kluwer, 1994, 383 p.

N. Frenk, De wet collectieve afwikkeling massaschade en de aandelenlease-affaire, *Weekblad voor Privaatrecht, Notariaat en Registratie* 2005, nr. 6630.

N. Frenk, Vie d'Or, aandelenlease en de reikwijdte van het collectief actierecht, *Nederlands Tijdschrift voor Burgerlijk Recht* 2005, p. 296–300.

N. Frenk, Massaschade: de Nederlandse benadering, *Aansprakelijkheid Verzekering en Schade* 2007, p. 214–221.

M. Freudenthal, Europese betalingsbevelprocedure: op weg naar een Europees burgerlijk procesrecht, *Tijdschrift voor Procesrecht en Bewijsrecht* 2004, p. 225–237,

T. Gabriel and B. Pirker-Hörmann, *Massenverfahren/Reformbedarf für die ZPO?*, Wien: Verlag Österreich, 2005, 452 p.

B. Garrido Courel, El acceso de los consumidores a la justicia, *La Ley* 19 August 2002, p. 1–16.

P.N.M. van der Grinten, Kroniek Europese ontwikkelingen, *Tijdschrift voor Civiele Rechtspleging* 2005, p. 79–88.

Chr. Hodges, The reform of class and representative actions in European legal systems/A new framework for collective redress in Europe, Oxford: Hart, 2008, 319 p.

E.H. Hondius, Rechter en bindend adviseur, *Tijdschrift voor Arbitrage* 2003, p. 43–54.

E.H. Hondius and G.J. Rijken (eds.), *Handboek consumentenrecht*, second ed., Zutphen: Paris, 2006, 516 p.

E. Hondius, Towards a European small claims procedure, in: L. Thévenoz and N. Reich (eds.), *Droit de la consommation/Liber amicorum Stauder*, Genève: Schulthess, 2006, p. 131–146.

E. Hondius, Andreas Mom, Die Durchsetzung von Verbraucherrechten in den Niederlanden/Zwischen alternativer Konfliktlösung, Verbandsklage und "Polder-class action", in: Bundesministerium für Ernährung, Landwirtschaft und Verbraucherschuts, *Kollektive Rechtsdurchsetzung – Chancen und Risiken/Internationales Symposium Bamberg 20. bis 21. Februar 2006*, 2006, p. 157–176.

D. von Hoyningen-Huene, *Außergerichtliche Konfliktbehandlung in den Niederlanden und Deutschland*, PhD Vrije Universiteit Amsterdam, 2000, 300 p.

N.J.H. Huls, Is de Duisenberg-regeling royaal genoeg voor alle legitieme Dexiaclaims?, *Nederlands Juristenblad* 2005, p. 1386–1390.

N.J.H. Huls and C.J.M. van Doorn, De constructie van een massaclaim/Een rechtssociologische analyse van de eerste fase van de Dexia-affaire, *Rechtsgeleerd Magazijn Themis* 2007, p. 51–60.

W.A. Jacobs, *ADR en consument*, PhD Utrecht, Deventer: Kluwer, 1998.

A.W. Jongbloed (ed.), *Beschouwingen over het nieuwe procesrecht*, The Hague: Boom, 2001, 107 p.

R.J.P. Kottenhagen and P.A. Kottenhagen-Dezes, Tort and regulatory law in the Netherlands, in: W.H. van Boom, M. Lukas and Chr. Kissling (eds.), *Tort and regulatory law*, Vienna: Springer, 2007, p. 187–204.

X. Kramer, *Eenvormige Europese procedures voor de inning van vorderingen/De Europese betalingsbevelprocedure en de europese procedure voor geringe vorderingen*, Deventer: Kluwer, 2007, 102 p.

C.H.M. Last and J. Nijgh, The Dutch system of alternative dispute resolution schemes relating to consumer disputes in the European Union, *Consumer Law Journal* 1999, p. 417–441.

Legal Vision, *Evaluatie geschilbeslechting consumentenzaken*, Rotterdam, 2002, 95 p.

P.H. Lindblom, Lagen om grupprättegang – bakgrund och frantid, *Svensk Juristtidning* 2005, p. 129–191.

R.H. Maatman, A.F.A. Coemans, Class actions made easy, *Tijdschrift voor ondernemingsbestuur* 2007/2, p. 43.

L.B. Melcherts and E.L.M. Vos, De Consumentenautoriteit: het duale stelsel, een overzicht van de handhavingspraktijk, *TvC* 2008 (forthcoming).

C. Meller-Hannich (ed.), *Kollektiver Rechtsschutz im Zivilprozess/Hallesche Symposium zum Zivilverhahrensrecht*, Baden-Baden: Nomos, 2008, 127 p.

I. Mendes Cabecadas, The Lisbon Arbitration Centre for Consumer conflicts: the Portuguese approach, *Consumer Law Journal* 1999, p. 493–510.

H.W. Micklitz (ed.), *Verbraucherrecht in Deutschland – Stand und Perspektiven*, Baden-Baden: Nomos, 2005, 458 p.

H.W. Micklitz and A. Stadler, *Das Verbandsklagerecht in der Informations- und Dienstleistungsgesellschaft*, Münster: Landwirtschaftsverlag, 2005, 1488 p.

A.I.M. van Mierlo and J.H. van Dam-Lely, *Procederen bij dagvaarding in eerste aanleg*, Deventer: Kluwer, 2003.

Ministerie van Economische Zaken, *Strategisch Actie Programma*, June 2004.

L.J.H. Mölenberg, El sistema arbitral de consumo, *Tijdschrift voor Consumentenrecht* 2004, p. 84–99.

R. Mulheron, *The class action/in common law legal systems – A comparative perspective*, Oxford: Hart, 2004, 535 p.

NIPO, *Klachtenafhandeling in de detailhandel en autobranche*, April 2004.

OECD, *Workshop on consumer dispute resolution and redress in the global marketspace*, www.oecd.org/dataoecd/59/21/34699496.pdf.

M.V. Polak, Iedereen en overal? Internationaal privaatrecht rond 'massaclaims', *Nederlands Juristenblad* 2006, p. 2346–2355.

M.F. Poot, Internationale afwikkeling van massaschade met de Wet Collectieve afwikkeling massaschade, in: M. Holtzer, A.J.F.A. Leijten en D.J. Oranje (red.), *Geschriften vanwege de Vereniging corporate litigation 2005–2006*, 2006, p. 169–202.

M.H. Redish and A.D. Kastnek, Settlement class actions, the case-or-controversy requirement, and the nature of the adjudicatory process, 73 *University of Chicago Law Review* 545–614 (2006).

P.N. van Regteren Altena, 'De collectieve afwikkeling van de DES-zaak in Nederland', in: A.I.M. van Mierlo en anderen, *Het wetsvoorstel collectieve afwikkeling massaschade*, The Hague: Boom, 2005, p. 27–35.

A.D. Reiling, Rechtspraak in de digitale delta, *Nederlands Juristenblad* 2003, p. 2286–2291.

J.M. Scherpe, *Außergerichtliche Streitbeilegung in Verbrauchersachen*, Tübingen: Mohr, 2002, 328 p.

Stichting geschillencommissies voor consumentenzaken, *Informatiebulletin* September 2005.

A. Tolosa, in: M.J. Reyes López (ed.), *Derecho de consumo*, tweede druk, Valencia: Tirant lo Blanch, 2002, p. 366–440.

T. Gudde, *Onderzoek naar afhandeling van individuele consumentenklachten*, April 2004.

I.N. Tzankova, *Strooischade/Een verkennend onderzoek naar een nieuw rechtsfenomeen*, The Hague: SDU, 2005, 165 p.

I.N. Tzankova, *Toegang tot het recht bij massaschade*, PhD Tilburg, Deventer: Kluwer, 2007, 235 p.

I.N. Tzankova, Financiering en kosten van massaclaims: legal realism/Ofwel: wat kunnen we leren van de Engelsen (en van andere common law landen)?, in: N. van den Berg, R. Henkemans and A. Timmer (eds.), *Massaclaims, class actions op z'n Nederlands*, Nijmegen: Ars Aequi, 2007, p. 171–204.

D.C. Umbach and D. Dettling (ed.), *Vom individuellen zum kollektiven Verbraucherschutz*, Frankfurt: Lang, 2005, 135 p.

B.C.J. van Velthoven, M.J. ter Voert and M. van Gammeren-Zoeteweij, *Geschilbeslechtingsdelta 2003/Over verloop en afloop van (potentieel) juridische problemen van burgers*, Den Haag: Boom/WODC, 2004 (www.wodc.nl), 241 p.

E. Verdegaal, Leasebelegger slijpt messen/Alternatief om 'magere' Duisenberg-regeling aan te vechten, *NRC Handelsblad* 18 September 2005.

K. Viitanen, Consumer redress, *Consumer Law Journal* 1995, p. 6–15.

L. Weihe, *Der Schutz der Verbraucher im Recht der Schiedsgerichtsbarkeit*, PhD Konstanz 2004, Frankfurt: Lang, 2005, 352 p.

Chr. J. Whelan (ed.), *Small claims courts/A comparative study*, Oxford: Clarendon, 1990, 253 p.

L. Woolf, *Access to justice/Final report to the Lord Chancellor on the civil justice system in England and Wales*, London, July 1996.

PART III.
COMPARING REMEDIES IN PRIVATE ENFORCEMENT

COMPENSATION AND DETERRENCE IN CONSUMER CLASS ACTIONS IN THE UNITED STATES AND EUROPE

Geoffrey P. MILLER*

One of the ironies of market-based economic systems is that consumers are simultaneously more powerful than ever and also more vulnerable. Consumers are more powerful because systems of trade, production, distribution, and inventory management make available a vast array of goods and services displaying an enormous range of quality, functionality and design. Consumers are more vulnerable because these systems cause a separation between consumer and provider and thus limit the available sanctions for poor quality, and because consumers sometimes lack the ability to assess the quality or performance of the products they acquire. A challenge for any modern legal and economic system is to promote the advantages of mass production and distribution while compensating consumers and deterring abusive practices.

All developed countries use a mix of regulatory strategies in pursuit of these twin goals of compensation and deterrence. These strategies include:

(1) licensing (permitting only qualified firms to do the particular business);
(2) disclosure (requiring providers to supply information about their products backed by sanctions for false statements);
(3) monitoring (assessments of product quality by the government or by independent evaluators);
(4) business-practice regulation (setting minimum standards or directly mandating production or distribution activities); and
(5) private legal remedies.

This paper examines the availability in the United States and Europe of the last of these strategies, private legal remedies. This chapter considers how the goals of compensation and deterrence come into tension with one another in the class action context. The paper then describes the privately enforceable substantive remedies available to consumers in the United States under federal and state law

* Stuyvesant Comfort Professor, New York University Law School.

and examines problems with achieving compensation and deterrence under those theories. The final part of the chapter considers recent class action legislation in Europe and evaluates how these procedures serve the goals of compensation and deterrence.

1. THE GOALS OF COMPENSATION AND DETERRENCE IN CONSUMER LAW

I start with some general observations about compensation and deterrence in consumer law.

These twin goals express different values. Compensation focuses on the plaintiff and is largely a moral concept. The restorative principle of corrective justice suggests that people should be able to return items which are not what they bargained for, and if return is not possible, that they should receive compensation for the difference in value between what they bargained for and what they received. Compensation has, at best, an ambiguous economic rationale. To the extent it represents a post-hoc payment by the defendant to the plaintiff, it appears to represent a mere transfer payment with no efficiency consequences (aside from the transactions costs associated with the payment itself). The economic rationale for compensating the plaintiff independently of any effect on the defendant thus appears problematic (consider whether it would be efficient for the state simply to pay people for harms they suffer from invasions of their legal rights, without seeking to deter the wrongdoing).

Deterrence, in contrast, focuses on the defendant. Its goal is to induce people to behave in good rather than bad ways. The moral basis for deterrence is not clear-cut. Morality has to do with obligation based on principles of right or justice. Deterrence is not about such things, but rather is concerned with power, incentives and self-interest – fundamentally economic rather than moral concepts. On the other hand, the economic case for deterrence is straightforward: by imposing a price on socially costly behaviors, the legal system discourages such behaviors from occuring in the first place. Optimal deterrence is achieved when, after accounting for enforcement effects, the penalty for a violation equals its social cost.

Compensation and deterrence play out differently in consumer cases than in other types of litigation. In an ordinary business-to-business case, compensation and deterrence are closely linked. There are typically only two parties to the transaction and to the litigation. If the plaintiff proves in court that the defendant has acted wrongfully and caused damage, the restorative principle of corrective justice calls for the defendant to pay compensation for the harm. Considerations of deterrence dictate the same result. Payment of compensation measured by the plaintiff's harm generally also creates efficient incentives for others to avoid similar misconduct in the future.

The special features of consumer cases, however, tend to drive a wedge between compensation and deterrence. The deterrence concern is greater in a consumer case than in an ordinary business-to-business dispute. In a transaction between equals, the chances are reasonably high that the counterparty will detect the problem and exercise his or her legal rights. This is not so for consumer cases, where only a fraction of the people who have been damaged are likely (absent a class action procedure) to enforce their rights. Also in the business-to-business setting, firms producing shoddy products face extra-legal sanctions, such as loss of reputation in the industry or termination of valuable relational contracts, which are not present in consumer contracts.

On the other hand, while the deterrence rationale is stronger in consumer cases, the compensation rationale tends to be problematic. First, compared with business-to-business cases, the harm suffered by consumers is usually small both in absolute terms and relative to the value of the transaction. In ordinary life we ask people to overlook petty offences as the cost of living in proximity to one another. People don't usually demand payment for the dry cleaning bill when someone spills coffee on their suit. If a friend borrows a few dollars and neglects to repay it, most people will not pursue the debtor. The intuition is that negligible harms do not require compensation.

This idea has consequences for consumer law. If a product costing three thousand dollars is only one dollar less valuable as a result of some defect, the harm appears minor – less than one tenth of one percent of the value of the item. We do not sense that buyers have a compelling moral claim to reimbursement in such a case. Those who file lawsuits seeking compensation for such harms appear to be complainers who like to stir up litigation. Worse yet, perhaps they have been inflamed by greedy lawyers scavenging for a fee. The suggestion is that defects in consumer products are simply part of life and we should put up with them rather than create problems where none exist.

A second distinctive feature of the compensation rationale in consumer cases arises from the fact that corrective justice requires that only people who have actually suffered harm receive a remedy. It does not serve the restorative principle to give compensation to someone who has not been hurt. In consumer cases, however, especially when framed as class actions, the court may be hard-pressed to direct the remedy to people who have actually suffered an invasion of their legal rights. In fact, many American consumer class actions do not even pretend to do so. "Fluid recovery" relief allows people who have experienced no harm at all to obtain benefits from the settlement. "Cy pres" settlements do the same, allocating some or even all of the relief from the litigation to charitable activities which may have a tangential relationship, at best, with the alleged wrongdoing. In these and other cases, the compensatory principle is abandoned in favour of the need to achieve deterrence.

A third feature of the compensation rationale in consumer cases concerns a principle of equality. In contrast to business-to-business cases where the harm is unique to the transaction, most consumer cases involve many people who have suffered identical harms. This fact of mass consumer harm becomes problematic when the relief distinguishes among class members, giving more to some than to others. It is even more problematic when – as is often the case in actions transcending jurisdictional boundaries – some class members receive compensation while others who purchased the identical product receive nothing at all. If the purpose of compensation is to restore that which has been wrongfully taken, it seems particularly unfair that some should receive compensation and others not.

Consumer cases, therefore, present a conflict between the goals of compensation and those of deterrence. As will be seen in the pages that follow, this conflict has important implications, especially for the conduct of class action litigation. Courts that focus on compensation tend to be suspicious of class actions. Since the individual harm to individual class members is often minor, these courts tend to see little cost in denying class relief, even if the result is that the defendant incurs no sanction for its misconduct. To the extent compensatory remedies are needed, moreover, courts that focus on compensation principles tend to view the class action procedure with suspicion because it imperfectly achieves the goal of corrective justice, namely restoring to victims that which has been improperly taken from them.

On the other hand, courts that perceive deterrence as the most important goal are favourably disposed towards class actions. These courts do not focus on the small damage suffered by individual plaintiffs. They look instead to the overall harm caused by the defendant, which is typically large. These courts perceive a significant cost in denying a remedy because the defendant would then be allowed to escape without sanction even though it has inflicted substantial harm on society in general. Courts concerned with deterrence are also less troubled about matters such as conflicts of interest among class members or the failure of the remedy to direct relief accurately to those who have suffered harm. As long as the aggregate relief is of sufficient magnitude, the goals of deterrence are met, regardless of who receives the benefits.

In the pages that follow, we will see this dialectical tension between compensation and deterrence being explored in the context of important doctrinal disputes under US and European class action law.

2. COMPENSATION AND DETERRENCE UNDER US LAW

2.1. SUBSTANTIVE REMEDIES

In the case of the United States, the inherently interstate nature of mass consumer goods and services suggests that private legal remedies for consumer harm ought to be provided by federal law, in order to make the scope of the remedy coextensive with the scope of the harm. The United States has not, in general, followed this prescription.

A. *Federal Law*

Significant private enforcement under federal law is available in some areas – antitrust law, pension law and securities law, for example. But coverage is not complete: under federal antitrust law, for example, direct purchasers have standing to sue for damages stemming from anticompetitive practices, but indirect purchasers do not;[1] and in the securities area, private rights of action do not reach parties who facilitated fraudulent conduct but who were not primary violators.[2]

In other areas federal law is even more limited, targeting only specific forms of conduct. A private right of action is available to consumers of financial services under the Truth in Lending Act[3] (requiring accurate disclosure of essential terms of financing contracts), to debtors under statutes like the Fair Debt Collection Practices Act[4] (regulating debt-collection practices), the Fair Credit Reporting Act[5] (protecting consumers in connection with the collection, dissemination and use of credit-related information) and the Credit Repair Organizations Act[6] (protecting consumers against abusive practices by credit repair organizations) to purchasers of goods under warranty under the Magnuson-Moss Warranty Act[7] (regulating disclosure of the terms of warranties for consumer products), to recipients of unwanted marketing under the Telephone Consumer Protection Act[8] (prohibiting certain advertisements by facsimile or by telephone), to home buyers under the Real Estate Settlement Procedures Act[9] (prohibiting kickbacks

1 See *Illinois Brick Co. v. Illinois*, 431 U.S. 720 (1977).
2 See *Stoneridge Investment Partners, LLC v. Scientific-Atlanta, Inc. and Motorola, Inc.*, 552 U.S. ___ (2008); *Central Bank, N.A. v. First Interstate Bank*, N.A., 511 U.S. 164 (1994).
3 15 U.S.C. §1601 et seq.
4 15 U.S.C. §§1692–1692p.
5 15 U.S.C. §1681 et seq.
6 15 U.S.C. §1679 et seq.
7 15 U.S.C. §2301 et seq.
8 47 U.S.C. §227.
9 12 U.S.C. §2601 et seq.

and unearned fees in home sale transactions), to borrowers from national banks under federal usury law,[10] and to consumers of various services and goods under other federal statutes.

In still other areas, private rights of action under federal law are essentially absent: insurance marketing practices, for example, are regulated by the states pursuant to the McCarran-Ferguson Act.[11] Federal law provides no general protections for consumers claiming breaches of contract. Nor does federal law provide private rights of action for fraudulent, unfair or deceptive trade practices.[12]

B. *State Law*

The spotty availability of private rights of action for consumers at the federal level does not necessarily mean that no private remedy is available. The states are generally free to provide more generous protections and have done so in many areas.

Contract law, administered by the states rather than the national government, provides the most fundamental protection for consumer interests. Consumer transactions are contracts and if the provider of goods or a service has not supplied a product meeting the conditions of the contract (including any express or implied warranties), then the consumer has a remedy under state law. Contract law, however, has pitfalls for consumer suits. Companies providing goods and services to the mass market control the terms of their consumer contracts. Thus they have the ability to include "fine print" disclaimers or limitations that effectively curtail rights consumers might otherwise enjoy. US law recognises that contracts may be rejected as unconscionable, but usually courts are unwilling to alter the terms of a written contract unless the unfairness is shown to be egregious.[13] Some contract remedies are also hedged in by limitations that reduce their effectiveness as consumer protection measures. For example, about half of US states require "privity" as an element of a claim of breach of implied warranty of merchantability; the effect is to preclude implied warranty suits against manufacturers of defective products if – as is typically the case – the consumer purchased the item from another party (e.g. an unaffiliated retailer). A few states also recognise that the

---

10 12 U.S.C. §85.

11 15 U.S.C. §§1011–1015.

12 The Federal Trade Commission Act does prohibit such conduct: section 5 of the Federal Trade Commission Act prohibits unfair methods of competition and unfair or deceptive acts or practices in or affecting commerce. But this section is enforceable only by the FTC; private lawsuits for violations are not permitted.

13 States in the United States vary in their willingness to reject consumer contracts as unconscionable. California, for example, is quite receptive to these arguments, whereas New York generally rejects them. See Geoffrey P. Miller, *Bargains on the Red-eye: New Light on Contract Theory* (NYU Law School Law & Economics Working Paper, 2008).

consumer's negligence may provide a partial or complete defence to claims for breach of implied warranty.

Consumer transactions may also implicate principles of tort law. If a company induces a consumer to purchase a product by means of false representations, this fact may give rise to a private lawsuit for negligent misrepresentation or fraud and if a product is shown to be defective, the defendant may be liable on theories of negligence or strict products liability. Again, however, consumer claims sounding in tort are subject to significant limitations. For fault-based tort theories, contributory negligence or comparative fault may limit or preclude recovery. Consumers may also find it difficult to establish which of several firms caused the defect. Even more serious problems afflict tort claims for un-manifested harm. Defendants argue that under the law of many states, if you purchase a car with a 30% chance of engine failure within five years, you have no right to recover for the defect until it becomes manifest in the form of a breakdown, even if the present market value of the car is depressed because the problems have become known to the auto-buying public.

States have struggled with the fact that tort and contract principles overlap in consumer cases: a claim of breach of contract could easily be reframed as an action for misrepresentation by the simple device of claiming that the promise allegedly breached by the defendant was a false statement on which the plaintiff relied. The issue is important because the remedies available under tort law are more extensive than those available under contract law: under the latter the plaintiff's recovery is usually limited to lost profits, whereas tort law may provide a recovery for items such as mental or emotional distress, punitive damages and consequential damages. Limitations on the admissibility of evidence, applicable in contract claims, are also relaxed when the claim is framed as a tort suit. Although tort law thus offers a promising avenue for consumer relief, many states resist the alchemy of transmuting contract base metal into tort gold. Typically, US states require that the lawsuit must be framed as one for breach of contract if the only harm at issue is a pure economic loss.

Equitable principles may also provide grounds of relief that do not fit neatly within the categories of tort or contract: unjust enrichment, for example, allows a plaintiff to recover the value of items unfairly received and held by the defendant. Unjust enrichment is an appealing consumer remedy. But this remedy is also subject to limitations, including affirmative defences of unclean hands, waiver and estoppel, as well as requirement, in some states, that the defendant have privity of contract with the plaintiff.

Supplementing these baseline consumer remedies is a rich tapestry of state statutes. All states have enacted "Blue Sky" securities laws, which provide a backdrop to the federal securities laws and which typically authorise private rights of action. Because federal law is so extensive in the securities area, however, the Blue Sky laws do not add many significant protections beyond what is available under the national statutes. All states also have laws prohibiting anticompetitive practices. These overlap federal antitrust laws in many respects, but in one important respect they can be broader: a number of states permit indirect purchasers to sue for violations of state antitrust laws. States regulate the insurance industry and may provide policyholders with rights to sue for false or deceptive marketing of insurance contracts. All states, moreover, provide what the federal government does not: privately enforceable consumer protection statutes (called "deceptive trade practice" or "unfair trade practice" laws or words to that effect). These statutes, in different ways and to different extents, provide consumers with private remedies for practices deemed to be unfair, deceptive or abusive.

Overall, US substantive law provides substantial consumer remedies, but fails to achieve either full compensation or full deterrence for consumer harms. There is no general federal remedy in consumer cases, and states offer varied and inconsistent protections. The consequence for compensation is that some consumers have effective rights to reimbursement and other consumers who suffer the identical harm do not. As for deterrence, the result is that unscrupulous companies ordinarily do not face a sufficient penalty for placing defective products in the stream of commerce. Even if they are sued and forced to pay compensation in some states, the chances are that they will avoid liability in others, making it advantageous for them to stay in the market so long as their anticipated legal costs do not exceed the profits they expect to earn from selling poor quality products.

2.2. SMALL CLAIMS CASES

Even if US law provided adequate protections at the national level, which it does not, the goals of compensation and deterrence would not be served if consumers were required to bring individual actions for relief. Individual consumer actions are ineffective because the typical amount at issue is so small that it is simply not worthwhile to the consumer to pursue his rights. This small-claims problem is a fundamental problem for consumer law.

The US legal system had adopted several strategies to deal with the small-claims problem. One approach is to relieve the consumer of the need to pay the costs of litigation in the event the claim turns out to be justified. Many consumer statutes include "fee-shifting" provisions under which a successful plaintiff is entitled to have the defendant pay his reasonable legal fees as well as any damages (these statutes differ from the Continental "loser pays" approach in that they are one-way shifts: the defendant is not entitled to have the plaintiff pay the defendant's fees if the plaintiff loses).

Fee-shifting statutes hold some promise to overcome the small-claims problem: winning plaintiffs wind up being made whole for the harm they have suffered and do not have their recoveries eaten up by the litigation costs. But these statutes are not a complete response to the problem. Fees shift only if the consumer wins; thus if there is a possibility that the lawsuit will be unsuccessful (as there usually is), the consumer must weigh up this cost. Suppose that the consumer will recover ten dollars if the case is successful and zero if not; the legal fees will be twenty dollars in both cases and the chance of success is 50%. Even with a fee-shifting statute in place, this case would not be economical for the consumer to bring: the benefit to the consumer if the case succeeds is ten dollars (because the defendant will pay his legal fees), but the cost to the consumer if the case fails is twenty dollars. Since there is a 50% chance of success, the expected value of the lawsuit to the consumer is minus five dollars.

To deal with these problems, consumer protection statutes sometimes provide for "statutory" damages. These damages are payable even if the consumer proves no harm at all. Merely establishing a violation of the statute is sufficient to trigger a right to relief.[14] An evident purpose behind these statutes is to make it worthwhile for consumers to bring individual lawsuits notwithstanding the chance of non-success.

We may doubt, however, that these statutory damages provisions effectively serve their purpose. Given the amounts of legal fees required to bring even a simple case, a one-thousand dollar recovery may not be enough to overcome the risk of having to pay one's lawyer if the case does not succeed. Even if an individual suit is brought by a plaintiff committed to enforcing his rights, the defendant can simply offer a full settlement; if only a few cases are brought, this is a trivial expense relative to the overall revenues associated with the product.

All this leads to the solution of aggregate litigation and in particular the US-style class action. As is well-known in Europe, the class action is an important feature of the American litigation landscape. The procedure – embodied in Rule 23 of the Federal Rules and its counterparts among the states – provides a mechanism for joining a large number of claims in a single proceeding under the representation of a single lawyer (or group of lawyers). Absent class members – those who have not affirmatively entered the litigation – are made subject to the ultimate judgment or settlement even if they take no role in the case. If the relief sought is injunctive – an order that the defendant must do or not do something – absent class members are automatically bound to the judgment. If the relief sought is monetary damages, the class member enjoys the technical right to "opt

14 Statutory damages are typically set at one thousand dollars, at least under federal law (so for example, in the Fair Credit Reporting Act, the Telephone Consumer Protection Act and the Fair Debt Collection Practices Act).

out" of the case (although almost no one does so). If they do not opt out, they are also bound by the judgment.

As might be expected, the class action procedure is hedged by a number of important restrictions and limitations. The class must be so numerous that joining class members in individual actions would be impracticable.[15] There must be questions of law or fact common to the class.[16] The "named plaintiff" – the class member who ostensibly brings the case on behalf of others similarly situated – must have claims that are typical of those of the class[17] and must (together with class counsel) be an adequate representative of the absent parties.[18] In the case of "opt-out" damages class actions, the court must conclude that a class action would be superior to other available means to resolve the controversy, and also that the common issues "predominate" over issues that vary across class members.[19] The decision on whether to certify a class[20] and also whether to approve a proposed class action settlement,[21] are vested in a judge who must examine the proposals with a view to protecting the interests of absent class members.

The great benefit of the class action device is that it offers a means to overcome the small-claims problem. If a given class member's claim is only one hundred dollars, the case will not be viable as an individual action, but if there are one million plaintiffs joined in a class action, the potential damages are one hundred million dollars. Such a case is likely to be economically viable to prosecute. All that is necessary is that the aggregate claims of the class be large enough to justify the litigation.

But the aggregation created by the class action creates another problem: who pays the lawyer? The named plaintiff is not going to pay because to do so would re-create, in exacerbated form, the small-claims problem: out of an expected hundred dollar recovery, the named plaintiff would have to pay legal fees for litigating on behalf of an entire class. Nor, for the same reason, is the lawyer going to take the case on a contingent fee basis if the fee is to come only out of the named plaintiff's recovery, since then the attorney could expect a fee of only about thirty dollars for representing a class of a million people.

The US has adopted two solutions to this problem of compensating counsel in class action cases. One solution is to require the defendant to pay the fees of the plaintiffs' counsel when the case is brought under a fee-shifting statute. This solution has the potential to avoid the problems mentioned above with respect to fee-shifting statutes in individual litigation. The problem of consumers not

15 Federal Rule of Civil Procedure 23(a)(1).
16 Federal Rule of Civil Procedure 23(a)(2).
17 Federal Rule of Civil Procedure 23(a)(3).
18 Federal Rule of Civil Procedure 23(a)(4).
19 Federal Rule of Civil Procedure 23(b)(3).
20 Federal Rule of Civil Procedure 23(c)(1).
21 Federal Rule of Civil Procedure 23(e).

knowing of their harm or their legal rights is overcome because, in a class action, it is necessary that only *one* member of the class know of the harm and the legal right. Indeed, even this is not required because consumer class action litigation is driven by lawyers who identify the claim and locate a client willing to lend his or her name to the litigation. The problem of the risk of non-success can be addressed if the class attorney is given sufficient compensation, in the event the case is successful, to compensate for the risk of non-success if it is not. This can be done by awarding the attorney a contingency enhancement over the fee the lawyer would charge for working on an hourly basis.

The viability of paying counsel in a class case under fee-shifting statutes has been undermined, however, by the decision by the United States Supreme Court in *City of Burlington v. Dague*,[22] which declared that counsel seeking fees under a fee-shifting statute could not receive a contingency enhancement. It requires little imagination to see that if contingency enhancements are not permitted, a fee shifting statute will not adequately compensate counsel for bringing class action cases, since lawyers will always prefer a normal hourly-rate case, with a certain payment regardless of outcome, to a class case where they will receive a fee of the same amount, but only if the case succeeds. Although not all courts have applied the *Dague* case to class actions brought under fee-shifting statutes, the risk that counsel will be limited to an hourly fee with no contingency enhancement is enough to deter many cases.

Given the *Dague* case, the preferred solution to the problem of compensating class counsel is the "common fund" doctrine, a marriage of the equitable idea of *quantum meruit* and the contingent fee. This common fund doctrine holds that when a lawyer litigates on behalf of a class of people, and through the litigation generates a common fund, the lawyer is entitled to be paid a fee out of the fund so created. Courts have expanded the common fund rule into an idea of "common benefit": if the lawyer's action confers a benefit on the class, he may be entitled to a fee in compensation for the benefit conferred even if no fund is created. The difference between the common fund and the common benefit is that the latter does not involve the creation of any fund, and therefore does not offer the court a convenient pot of money to draw on in rewarding the lawyer. Thus, in common benefit cases, the attorney is typically paid by the defendant as part of a settlement of the controversy. Many but not all consumer cases involve common-benefit theories for compensating the lawyer.

The US rules on litigation funding serve both deterrence and compensation goals. Class members would not be compensated at all if no lawyer was willing to come forward to represent the class. Likewise potential wrongdoers would not be deterred if they expected that they would not be sued. The various devices

22 505 U.S. 557 (1992).

developed by US courts to ensure legal representation for consumer interests thus serve both compensatory and deterrent purposes.

2.3. LIMITATIONS ON THE CLASS ACTION REMEDY

The combination of the common fund/common benefit rule and the class action device makes consumer class action litigation possible in the United States. But despite the promise of this approach, it is no panacea. This section will focus on some of the important impediments to consumer class actions.

1. One problem lies in the requirement that the class receive "adequate" representation. In *Amchem Products, Inc. v. Windsor*[23] the Supreme Court imposed limits on class counsel representing competing interests within the class in a mass tort class action. The *Amchem* case involved two groups of claimants seeking compensation for exposure to asbestos: people who were presently ill with asbestos-related health problems and others who were not ill but might become ill. The Court held that a single lawyer could not represent both groups because of the fundamental conflict between them: the currently ill members of the class wanted lots of money paid upfront, whereas the exposure-only group wanted a fund sufficient to pay for anticipated future harm.

Many consumer cases involve the same sort of conflict as those found fatal to class treatment in *Amchem*. Suppose that the class consists of people who have purchased a washing machine with a normal useful life of twenty years that has a 5% statistical probability of failing each year due to a design defect. At the time the class action is filed 10% of the washing machines have already failed and 90% are at risk of failure. Can counsel represent both parts of the class? Such consumer class actions have been certified, but the lurking *Amchem* problem persists: the class in the washing machine example consists of two groups with conflicting interests: people whose machines have already failed, who want money now to compensate them for their harm and people whose machines might fail, who want compensation for possible future harm.

The fact that the *Amchem* case has not generally been applied to consumer cases may relate to the implicit tension between deterrence and compensation discussed above. The settlement proposed in *Amchem*, while not perfect as a means for distributing the settlement proceeds equitably among class members, nevertheless would have extracted a large amount of money from the defendants. Arguably the Supreme Court's decision was based on the perceived importance of achieving equity in compensation, regardless of whether the deterrence goals of the class procedure were met. This idea may provide a means for distinguishing

23 521 U.S. 591 (1997).

the problem of future claims in the mass tort setting, which was fatal to class certification in *Amchem*, from the analogous problem in the case of consumer products. Where the claims are large in size, as was the case in *Amchem*, the concerns about equitable distribution among claimants plays a more important role than it does in the ordinary consumer case where average claims represent only a tiny fraction of the average class member's assets. The goal of compensation is implicitly viewed as less important in consumer cases and therefore inequalities of distribution that would not be tolerated in a mass tort case are generally allowed.

2. Some statutes impose specific limitations on class litigation. The Fair Debt Collection Practices Act, for example, imposes limits on the amount of statutory damages that can be recovered in a class action: $500,000 or one percent of the defendant's net worth.[24] Since defendants in FDCPA actions are usually thinly capitalised collection agencies, the net worth limitation typically precludes recovery of significant damages; these cases generally result in minimal cash recoveries for absent class members, statutory damages of $1,000 to the named plaintiff and an award of legal fees to the lawyer.

These FDCPA procedures arguably serve the goals of compensation to a reasonable extent. It is nearly impossible to ascertain how much a class member is damaged by a violation of a statute like the FDCPA. Thus corrective justice does not strongly demand that class members receive any particular amount in compensation. On the other hand, the restriction of damages to one percent of the defendant's net worth is very poorly designed as a deterrence mechanism. The impact of the statute is to encourage unscrupulous debt collectors to operate with thin capital, which appears antithetical to the statutory goal of deterring irresponsible practices. In this statute, in other words, the legislature has focused on compensation rather than deterrence, with deleterious effects for the enforcement of the legal norm.

3. Claims of fraud generally require that the plaintiff plead and prove that he relied on the defendant's misleading statements. The problem for consumer cases is that if each plaintiff must prove that he heard and relied on the representation, the individual issues would swamp the common issues, thus making class certification inappropriate. Thus, even if a defendant has made false statements to thousands or millions of customers, a class action for fraud might be impossible to certify.

Securities fraud cases also confront the problem of reliance, but here the courts have developed the "fraud on the market" theory as a way around the problem. This doctrine recognises that in an efficient securities market, many

24 15 U.S.C. 1692k(a)(2)(B)(ii).

traders rely on the market price as reflecting all publicly available information about share value.[25] Because most traders "rely" on the market price, proof of reliance can be made on a class-wide basis. But the fraud on the market presumption only applies if the transactions in question occurred on an efficient market (such as the New York Stock Exchange). This requirement can be fatal for trades in other settings – as lawyers found out recently when an important class action claiming fraud in the initial public offering market came to grief for failure to establish an efficient market as a predicate for the fraud on the market presumption.[26]

The requirement of reliance, in fraud cases, can also be analysed along the compensation/deterrence divide. Cases that reject class treatment because of the need to show reliance implicitly privilege the compensation goal over the deterrence goal. Where reliance is absent, compensatory relief is not warranted because the individual class member has suffered no damage from the defendant's wrongful conduct. Requiring reliance ensures that compensation is paid only to those who deserve to get it. On the other hand, if requiring proof of reliance defeats class certification, deterrence is severely undermined, since without a class action few consumer fraud cases would be brought at all. The fraud-on-the-market presumption in US securities law reflects the Supreme Court's implicit judgment that the goal of truthful communications in securities markets outweighs the concern that compensation be awarded only to people who are actually harmed by the defendant's misconduct.

4. The applicability of the laws of multiple states can be a serious threat to class certification. The natural scope of consumer class actions is the United States as a whole. If a product is marketed to all fifty states, it hardly makes sense to force plaintiffs to bring fifty separate lawsuits. But, as we have seen, the principal basis for relief in a consumer class action is state law. A nationwide, state-law class action thus requires the court to determine (a) which law applies to the claims of the individual class members and (b) if multiple state laws apply, whether the case is suitable for class treatment.

On the first issue – which law applies – US law is notoriously murky. The applicable law is determined by the conflict-of-laws rules of the court where the action is brought (if the case involves state law but is brought in a federal court, the federal court would apply the conflict-of-laws rules of the state where the federal court is located). Conflicts of law rules vary from state to state. Even within a state, the applicable law may be difficult to determine because of uncertainties as to the individual class member's contacts with the forum and the transaction.

---

25 See *Basic, Inc. v. Levinson*, 485 U. S. 224 (1988).

26 In re: Initial Public Offering Securities Litigation, 471 F.3d 24 (2d Cir. 2006). The author acted as a consultant to plaintiff's counsel in this case.

In the worst-case scenario the court may find itself facing the need to apply the law of fifty different jurisdictions.

One approach to this problem, advocated by my colleague Samuel Issacharoff, is to apply the law of the *defendant's* domicile. Defendants would have a hard time objecting that it would be unfair to subject them to the law of their home state and if a single law applies, the problem of identifying the applicable law for each class member disappears. This proposal would pass constitutional muster because the defendant's home state certainly would have enough contacts with the litigation to justify application of its law. The difficulty with the proposal is that it does not, at present, describe what most states actually do when applying their conflicts of laws rules to class action litigation.

We are left, in many cases, in the uncomfortable position of applying the law of many states. But this threatens to make the litigation unmanageable, particularly if there is a trial by jury. In an important federal appeals court decision, *In re Bridgestone/Firestone, Inc. Tire Products Liability Litigation*,[27] the appeals court held that the laws of several states applied to the claims of different members of the class and then concluded that the need to apply the laws of multiple states prevented class certification. While not all courts have agreed that the need to apply multiple state laws defeats class certification, many multi-state consumer class actions today face a daunting obstacle on certification.

A possible solution to the preceding problem is to group the different state laws into a manageable number of categories. It turns out that it is possible to *generally* group state laws into a few categories. Even so, it sometimes remains the case that potential, arguable or subtle variations remain. The plaintiffs' counsel and defendant then argue as to the importance of these in-category differences: defendants saying that the variation is so great as to preclude class treatment – plaintiffs arguing that the differences are insignificant, ephemeral or imaginary. As yet there are few rulings as to how much commonality there needs to be among state laws before they can be grouped into categories for class certification purposes or how many categories a court will tolerate before concluding that a case becomes unmanageable.

This problem of multi-state, state law class actions again implicates the distinction between compensation and deterrence. Focus on the law applicable to a particular class member's claim implicitly draws on the compensation rationale, namely that relief should be given to those who have actually suffered a legal wrong and that the amount of relief should be tailored to the individual circumstances of each class member. Courts that are willing to overlook interstate differences and allow nationwide class actions to proceed are implicitly serving the deterrence goal. They are willing to tolerate significant inaccuracies in the

27 288 F.3d 1012 (7th Cir. 2002).

allocation of relief in order to achieve greater efficiency in the deterrence of misconduct.

5. Another threat to the viability of consumer class actions is the presence of class action waivers and mandatory arbitration clauses. These are found in many consumer contracts in financial services, telecommunications and other industries where services are provided on a mass market basis. The class action waiver, if effective, precludes aggregate treatment, thus remitting the consumer to the empty promise of private remedies. The mandatory arbitration clause purports to define the forum for consumer complaints as a private arbitration, thus also ruling out class treatment. A related clause, increasingly found in consumer contracts, purports to preclude class-wide arbitration. These clauses have been challenged as unconscionable and such challenges are occasionally successful. However, in the case of arbitration clauses, the challenges must overcome a longstanding judicial approval of arbitration and also the argument that arbitration benefits consumers by offering a convenient forum for resolving complaints. At present there is a dispute among the states over the enforceability of class action waivers and related clauses. In New York they are presumptively valid and regularly enforced against claims that they are unconscionable or violate public policy.[28] California, in contrast, generally invalidates such clauses.[29] The US Supreme Court has yet to rule on this question.[30]

---

28 See *Ranieri v. Bell Atlantic Mobile*, 304 A.D.2d 353, 354, 759 N.Y.S.2d 448, 449 (1st Dept. 2003) ("given the strong public policy favoring arbitration, and the absence of a commensurate policy favoring class actions, we are in accord with authorities holding that a contractual proscription against class actions, such as contained in the Agreements, is neither unconscionable nor violative of public policy") (citations omitted); *Flynn v. Labor Ready, Inc.*, 193 Misc. 2d 721, 751 N.Y.S.2d 722 (N.Y. Sup. 2002) ("[t]he fact that a class action lawsuit, as plaintiffs contemplate, may be a less costly alternative to arbitration (which is generally less costly than litigation) does not alter the binding effect of the valid arbitration clause"); *Brower v. Gateway 2000, Inc.*, 246 A.D.2d 246, 676 N.Y.S.2d 569 (1st Dept. 1998).

29 See *Discover Bank v. Superior Court*, 36 Cal.4th 148, 113 P.3d 1100 (Cal. 2005) (class action waiver unenforceable under California law); *Gentry v. Superior Court*, 42 Cal.4th 443, 165 P.3d 556 (Cal. 2007) (class arbitration waivers in employment agreements could not be enforced if class arbitration would be significantly more effective way of vindicating rights); *America Online, Inc. v. Superior Court*, 90 Cal.App.4th 1, 108 Cal. Rptr. 2d 699 (1st Dist. 2001) (rejecting choice-of-law and forum selection clauses that would have precluded class action treatment under California consumer protection law); *Aral v. Earthlink, Inc.*, 134 Cal.App.4th 544, 36 Cal.Rptr.3d 229 (2nd Dist. 2005) (class action waiver invalidated as unconscionable); *Lee v. AT & T Wireless Services, Inc.*, 2006 WL 1452936 (2nd Dist 2006) (the same); *Klussman v. Cross Country Bank*, 134 Cal.App.4th 1283, 36 Cal.Rptr.3d 728 (1st Dist. 2005) (the same); *Gatton v. T-Mobile USA, Inc.*, 152 Cal.App.4th 571, 61 Cal. Rptr.3d 344 (1st Dist. 2007) (the same).

30 A related issue reached the Court in *Green Tree Financial Corp. v. Bazzle*, 539 U.S. 444 (2003), but the ultimate decision left the basic question unresolved.

A research by Eisenberg, Miller and Sherwin suggests that the reason why companies require mandatory arbitration in consumer contracts is simply to preclude class action treatment.[31] These authors studied consumer and non-consumer contracts executed by the same companies, and found that the rate of arbitration clauses was much higher in consumer than in consumer contracts. This finding raises doubts about whether the arbitration clauses are really, as business interests claim, inserted for the purpose of offering a cheaper and more convenient dispute resolution forum to customers.

The dispute over the enforceability of class action waivers also relates to the compensation/deterrence distinction. Courts that reject such waivers implicitly focus on the need to deter misconduct by companies doing business with consumers. The fact that a consumer may have signed a contract that contained a mandatory arbitration clause or a waiver of aggregate dispute resolution is, for these courts, largely beside the point. Even if the consumers had executed a contract legal in form, these courts seek to force large companies to comply with legal requirements. Courts that enforce class action waivers and related agreements, in contrast, are implicitly relying on compensation ideas. These courts seek to do justice in the individual case. Since the consumers signed contracts agreeing to waive their rights, corrective justice does not, in the view of these courts, require that they receive compensation for the harm that ensued.

3. COMPENSATION AND DETERRENCE IN EUROPEAN CLASS ACTION LAW

I now turn to a brief discussion of European class action law. As an outside observer I can only offer general observations on this topic, limiting myself to cross-cutting trends I perceive in the various statutes and proposals for reform. It should be acknowledged that these developments represent a profound and important step forward in the protection of consumer rights in Europe. They are also, in many cases, quite explicitly advanced as experiments – and for that reason, are sometimes hedged in by limitations and qualifications designed to prevent a too-rapid, too-radical alteration of traditional practices. Over the coming years, class action practice in Europe will evolve as courts and legislatures evaluate the new regimes.

One common feature in European practice is that standing to sue on behalf of consumers is often restricted to organised groups. The possible benefits of

31 See Theodore Eisenberg, Geoffrey P. Miller, and Emily L. Sherwin, *Arbitration's Summer Soldiers: An Empirical Study of Arbitration Clauses in Consumer and Nonconsumer Contracts* (working paper, 2008), available at http://papers.ssrn.com/sol3/papers.cfm?abstract_id=1076968#PaperDownload.

consumer organisation standing appear to include the capacity of these organisations to underwrite the costs of class action litigation and also the idea that they can be relied on to faithfully serve consumer interests. The possible lack of accountability is an obvious problem, however.[32] It would be worrisome if consumer organisations, in the name of protecting class members, actually used their positions to advance other agendas not directly related to consumer protection. Like all institutions, moreover, consumer organisations face agency costs of management. The managers of these organisations experience the usual temptations to shirk the performance of their duties, to award themselves excessive compensation and to engage in personally beneficial self-dealing transactions. The power to allocate lucrative legal work is also a concern, since this creates opportunities for referral fees that may not result in an efficient selection of class counsel. Presumably the courts will exercise discretion to vet the candidates for lead counsel rights and to monitor their conduct of the litigation on behalf of the class. But judicial supervision is hindered by the fact that the courts have only a partial and obstructed view of the day-to-day conduct of litigation. These issues of accountability will need to be worked through carefully in the coming years.

Another common feature of European class actions is that they employ an "opt-in" rather than an "opt-out" methodology for determining membership in the class. The opt-in approach offers two advantages: it ensures that people who participate in the litigation are actually interested in the outcome; and it addresses the jurisprudential perception that litigation is not legitimate if a party who has committed no actionable wrong is subjected to a preclusive judgment without voluntarily agreeing to participate. The opt-in approach also has disadvantages as compared with the opt-out system, however. Most importantly, American experience suggests that consumers in class action cases usually do nothing. In an opt-out system doing nothing includes them in the case, whereas in an opt-in system if they do nothing they get no remedy. Thus, participation rates may turn out to be distressingly low in cases where the consumer organisation acts on behalf of consumers in general. Rates may be higher in systems where the organisation brings litigation only on behalf of its own members, since membership in the organisation signals a willingness to join in its activities, but even here it may be difficult to obtain high levels of opt-ins, especially if members perceive any risk from joining in the lawsuit.

Litigation funding is another key element of European class action practice. This is a complex subject the detailed analysis of which depends on the unique circumstances of each country. A few general observations may be in order, however. It is a truth universally acknowledged that no class action system can

32 See Fabrizio Cafaggi & Hans-W. Micklitz, *Collective enforcement of consumer law: a framework for comparative assessment (identifying and analyzing accountability problems with consumer organization standing)*.

function effectively if the lawyers are not adequately compensated.[33] No matter how excellent a country's class action law may be in fundamental design, it will be nothing but a Potemkin village if lawyers cannot be induced to come forward to represent class interests. European class action laws face significant challenges in adapting traditional litigation funding rules to the new procedures. It is difficult to work within these rules so as to give lawyers sufficient compensation for representing consumer interests. Adjustments to the traditional rules have been observed already,[34] but more experimentation may be required.

Overall it is fair to say that the European approach thus far has tended to favour the goal of compensation over that of deterrence. A focus on compensation, for example, seems to underlie the preference for opt-in regimes. An opt-in regime serves the corrective goal of corrective justice by ensuring that the party seeking relief genuinely feels an involvement in the controversy. On the other hand, an opt-in regime, because of anticipated low participation rates, is likely to be much less effective than an opt-out regime at deterring misconduct in future cases.

Similarly, the restriction of standing to consumer organisations appears to serve compensatory rather than deterrence goals. Especially if the consumer organisation can only sue on behalf of its own members, the rule tends to ensure that the relief generated by the litigation will be accurately directed to people who have actually suffered harm. Broad conferrals of representational standing, such as observed in most US class action cases, are less closely aligned with compensation goals but better adapted, overall, to serve the goal of deterrence.

CONCLUSION

This chapter has explored the nature and limits of private litigation as a remedy for consumer harm, with a view to assessing the impact of different arrangements on the twin goals of compensation and deterrence.

The chapter has suggested that those goals are in tension when the legal rights of consumers are at stake. Courts that focus on compensation tend to be suspicious of class actions, both because these courts assign a relatively low value to the need to reimburse class members for consumer harms and because they see class actions as very imperfect devices for distributing compensation to people who

33 See Fabrizio Cafaggi & Hans-W. Micklitz, *Collective enforcement of consumer law: a framework for comparative assessment* ("Pecuniary and non pecuniary incentives need to be provided for plaintiffs' lawyers. These may not be only market driven but also public policy oriented thus affecting the selection of claims to be litigated.").

34 The German Constitutional Court has ruled, for example, that a legislative prohibition on contingent fees violated fundamental rights to legal representation and to practice a profession. BVerfG, 1 BvR 2576/04 vom 12 December 2006, Absatz-Nr. (1–115), www.bverfg.de/entscheidungen/rs20061212_1bvr257604.html.

have actually been harmed. Courts that focus on deterrence, in contrast, consider the aggregate harm caused by the defendant's conduct, which is likely to be substantial, and thus perceive strong reasons of public policy to encourage class action litigation. For these courts, the fact that class actions often inaccurately allocate the benefits of the litigation among class members is unimportant. What matters is that the defendant be made to pay for the total harm caused.

A class action litigation in the United States is lately based on concepts of deterrence – hence the existence of devices such as opt-out actions, fluid and cy-pres recoveries, and the conferral of standing on all class members. As yet, the general approach in Europe focuses on compensatory rather than deterrent goals, but the early state of play in European class action procedures suggests that necessary adjustments may need to be made as these new regimes mature.

THE REFORM OF DIRECTIVE 98/27/EC

Cristina Poncibò*

1. SETTING THE SCENE

All the Member States provide for an injunction procedure to protect the collective interests of consumers as a result of the implementation in their national laws of Directive 98/27/EC of the Council and Parliament, governing injunctions for the protection of collective interests of consumers ("Injunctions Directive").[1]

The major concern which led to the enactment of the Injunctions Directive was that the consumer rights laid down by means of the Community legislation during the last thirty years, needed to be efficiently enforced. The purpose of the Injunctions Directive has been made clear in the preamble:

> "Whereas current mechanisms available both at national and at Community level for ensuring compliance with (...) Directives do not always allow infringements harmful to the collective interests of consumers to be terminated in good time" (Recital 2).

The Injunctions Directive was indeed introduced to address what was perceived to be a gap in the enforcement of existing consumer protection regulations. The lack of speedy remedies and relief for consumers meant that a new approach was required.

Without mechanisms to bring about swift, certain and adequate enforcement of consumer law, those laws would not be respected.

In the light of its objective, the Injunctions Directive indeed provides for injunctions against businesses that infringe the collective interests of consumers,[2]

---

* Researcher, Comparative Private Law, Faculty of Law, University of Turin (Italy), Email: cristina.poncibo@unito.it.

1 Council Directive (EC) 98/27 of the European Parliament and of the Council of 19 May 1998 on injunctions for the protection of consumers' interests, [1998] OJ L 166/51–5.
On the implementation of the Injunction Directive: J. Stuyck, E. Terryn, T. Van Dyck, V. Colaert, N. Peretz and P. Tereszkiewicz, *Study on alternative means of consumer redress other than redress through ordinary judicial proceedings (for the EU-25, Australia, Canada and the US*, 17.01. at 324.

2 Additional remedies are the publication of the decision, where appropriate and/or the publication of a corrective statement with a view to eliminating the continuing effects of the infringement (cf. Article 2(b) of the Injunctions Directive); insofar as the legal system of the Member State concerned so permits, an order against the losing defendant for payments into

without the need to show any actual harm to individual consumers: it was regarded as an important mechanism to correct market failures, where the collective harm that is caused by the defendant's action is more than the sum of the individual losses involved.[3] In this respect, an important development was that the Injunctions Directive allows "qualified entities" to bring such actions before the competent court or administrative bodies *in other Member States*. This means that "qualified entities" have standing before the competent courts or other public bodies in all Member States to seek an injunction. In other words, Member States are obliged to accept the legal standing of foreign "qualified entities" that fulfil the requirements established by their national laws in order to take action, in case an infringement of the collective interests of consumers has a cross-border dimension.

After ten years since its adoption, there is a growing consensus within the European legal scholarship about the need to rethink the system of consumer protection designed by the Injunctions Directive.[4]

This issue is deeply related to the ongoing reform of the Consumer Law Acquis: in the last year, the European Commission adopted a Green Paper and launched a consultation on some key issues on the future developments of EC consumer law. Recently, the European institution has issued a staff working document which summarises the outcome of the consultation and briefly indicates the debate about the revision of the Injunctions Directive.[5]

Empirical evidence recently gathered has shown that this action is scarcely used before national courts: for example, the data available from the "EC Consumer Law Compendium" reports only sixteen cases of application of national laws implementing the Injunctions Directive.[6]

---

the public purse or to any beneficiary designated in or under national legislation, in the event of failure to comply with the decision within a time limit specified by the courts or administrative authorities, of a fixed amount for each day's delay or any other amount provided for in national legislation, with a view to ensuring compliance with the decisions (Article 2(c) of the Injunctions Directive).

3 The scope of application of the Injunctions Directive is restricted. It does not apply to infringements of consumer protection legislation in general, but only to infringements of provisions of the directives listed in the Annex, as they are incorporated in the internal legal order (see at paragraph 1.3).

4 F. Cafaggi and H.-W. Micklitz, 'Collective Enforcement of Consumer Law: A Framework for Comparative Assessment', (2008) 16 *ERPL* 391, 425; W. H. Van Boom and M.B.M. Loos, 'Effective Enforcement of Consumer Law in Europe: Synchronizing Private, Public, and Collective Mechanisms' [2008], http://ssrn.com/abstract=1082913, accessed 26 June 2008.

5 Commission (EC), DG Health and Consumer Protection, 'Preparatory Work for the Impact Assessment on the Review of the Consumer Acquis, Analytical Report on the Green Paper on the Review of the Consumer Acquis' submitted by the Consumer Policy Evaluation Consortium, http://ec.europa.eu/consumers/rights/cons_acquis_en.htm, accessed 26 June 2008.

6 H. Schulte-Nölke (ed.) in co-operation with C. Twigg-Flesner and M. Ebers, 'EC Consumer Law Compendium, Comparative Analysis', [2007], http://ec.europa.eu/consumers/cons_int/safe_shop/acquis/comp_analysis_en.pdf, accessed 26 June 2008.

Some criticism also comes from the study of the University of Leuven that, *inter alia*, underlines the various inconsistencies in the ways in which the Community measure has been implemented at national level.[7] The study notes that the lack of uniformity makes it difficult for a foreign "qualified entity" to act against a trader in another Member State.

Given that this instrument suffers a series of shortcomings both at theoretical and practical level, national initiatives concerning consumer collective redress have emerged in the last years. Experiments in the Member States may be considered to follow three main solutions: the test case (England and Wales[8] and Germany[9]); the model of action provided by the Injunctions Directive with some improvements (Italy,[10] Spain[11] and France[12]); and the model offered by the class actions with some modifications (Sweden[13]).

In consideration of the proliferation of various mechanisms at national level, a common European core regarding the collective judicial enforcement of consumer law is needed to assure the "same" level of protection to the European consumers. Urged by the mushrooming of national initiatives, the European Commission recognised the importance of effective mechanisms for seeking redress in its Consumer Policy Strategy for 2007–2012 and it announced it would consider action on collective redress mechanisms necessary for consumers: "If consumers are to have sufficient confidence in shopping outside their own Member State and take advantage of the internal market, they need assurance that if things go wrong they have effective mechanisms to seek redress. Consumer disputes require tailored mechanisms that do not impose costs and delays disproportionate to the value at stake."[14]

---

7 Stuyck and others, *Study on alternative means of consumer redress other than redress through ordinary judicial proceedings*, Catholic University of Leuven, January 17, 2007, published by DG SANCO, April 2007.

8 R. Mulheron, 'Justice Enhanced: Framing an Opt-Out Class Action for England', (2007) 70:4, *Modern Law Review* 550–580; 'Some difficulties with Group Litigation Orders – and Why a Class Action is Superior', (2004) 24 *CJQ* 40,68 and *The class action in common law legal systems: a comparative perspective* (Hart Publishing, Oxford 2004).
CJS Hodges, *The Reform of Class and Representive Actions in European Legal Systems. A New Framework for Collective Redress in Europe* (Hart, Oxford, 2008).

9 M. Sturner, 'Model Case Proceedings in the Capital Markets – Tentative Steps Towards Group Litigation in Germany', (2007) 26 *CJQ* 250–267.

10 Article 140-bis Legislative Decree September 6, 2005, No. 206 ("Consumer Code" "Azione collettiva risarcitoria").
For an introduction to Article 140-bis, C. Poncibò, 'Consumer Collective Redress in the European Union: The 'Italian Case', in G. Howells, A. Nordhausen, D. Parry and C. Twigg-Flesner (eds.), *The Yearbook of Consumer Law*, (Ashgate, London).

11 Artículo 11. Legitimación para la defensa de derechos e intereses de consumidores y usuarios, Ley 1/2000, de 7 de enero, de Enjuiciamiento Civil.

12 L. Boré', 'L'action en représentation conjointe: class action française ou action mort-née?', (2005) *Dalloz*, III, chr., 267.

13 The Swedish Group Proceedings Act entered into force on 1 January, 2003.

14 Commission (EC), 'Communication from the Commission to the Council, the European Parliament and the European Economic and Social Committee, EU Consumer Policy strategy

In consideration of the above, the European Commission launched, in March 2007, two studies on collective redress. The first of these studies will evaluate the effectiveness and efficiency of the national collective redress systems that currently exist in the Member States, assess whether consumers suffer a detriment in those Member States where collective redress mechanisms are not available, and examine the existence of negative effects for the Single Market and distortions of competition. The second study will analyse in detail the problems faced by consumers in obtaining redress for mass claims, as well as the economic consequences of such problems for consumers, enterprises and the market. After receiving the results of these studies, the Commission will consider a Communication on consumer collective redress in December 2008.

Developments about collective redress also arise from the White Paper "Damages actions for breach of the EC antitrust rules" issued on 2 April, 2008 (the "White Paper") that I will introduce at paragraph 2.1.[15]

On such basis, the Commission has recently launched the Green Paper on Consumer Collective Redress[16] to consider whether, and if so, to which extent an initiative on consumer collective redress is necessary at European level. In particular, these efforts are directed to evaluate a possible new measure and/or to improve the existing framework provided by the Injunctions Directive. This article, by taking into consideration the proposals indicated in the Green Paper, discusses the possibility to enlarge the standing of the consumer associations. under the Injunctions Directive.

1.1. THE COLLECTIVE INTERESTS OF THE CONSUMERS

The Injunctions Directive protects the collective interests of the consumers that can be distinguished from the accumulated interests and rights of the single consumer.[17]

2007–2012, Empowering consumers, enhancing their welfare, effectively protecting them', COM (99), 13 March, 2007, at 11.

15 Commission (EC), 'White Paper on Damages actions for breach of the EC antitrust rules', COM (165) 2 April 2000, at 4; and 'Staff Working Paper accompanying the White Paper on Damages actions for breach of the EC antitrust rules', Brussels, 2 April, 2008, SEC (404), 2 April 2008.

16 Commission (EC), 'Green Paper on Consumer Collective Redress', COM (794) 27 November 2008.

17 Whereas 2 of the Injunctions Directive: "*Whereas current mechanisms ... for ensuring compliance with [consumer protection] Directives do not always allow infringements harmful to the collective interests of consumers to be terminated in good time; whereas collective interests mean interests which do not include the cumulation of interests of individuals who have been harmed by an infringement; whereas this is without prejudice to individual actions brought by individuals who have been harmed by an infringement; Parliament and Council have adopted this Directive.*".

In doing so, it assumes that a group of consumers provides an identity distinct from that of its individual members, an identity that makes sense only in the context of the consumers' relationship to one another and to other actors in the social world. In few words, consumers share in an identity separate from and irreducible to their identities as isolated individuals.[18]

The collective interest of consumers is a collective good, so that an injury to that good cannot damage a single consumer's rights.

Many years ago, the Cour de Cassation clarified this point by openly stating that: "(...) *le préjudice direct ou indirect qui est cause par une infraction à l'intérêts collectif des consommateurs ne se confond pas avec le préjudice subi personnellement par les victimes directes de l'infraction qui seules peuvent en demander réparation*".[19]

Because a collective good consists in being shared among people, those individuals also share the harm of any impediment to its achievement: thus, no single consumer can claim the injury as one to him alone and the possibility to recover the "collective damage" is discussed in the literature (see paragraph 1.2).

An immediate objection to the construction adopted in the Injunctions Directive is that there is no strong commonality of interest among consumers.[20]

Consumers' identity is composed of a wide range of different characteristics such as: religion, class, profession, ethnic origin and sex. Actually, consumers do not construct their identity as members of the social group of "consumers" simply by acquiring goods: the said attributes tend to be stronger than our consumer attribute and thus it is not possible to establish a distinctive consumer identity.[21] Further complexity to this picture has been added by the proliferation of the consumer identities in the social sciences.[22]

In consideration of the multiple – but uncertain – dimensions of the identity of the consumers, it is really problematic to say what their collective interests are and who may represent them. Thus, it is possible to question "what right or ability

---

18 M. Cappelletti, '*Vindicating the Public Interest Through the Courts: A Comparativist's Contribution*', in M. Cappelletti and B. Garth (eds.), III *Access to justice: Emerging issues and perspectives*, (Alphen aan den Rijn, Netherlands and Milan: Sijthoff/Giuffre, 1979). 513, 564.

19 Cour de Cassation, crim., 20 mai 1985, *Bull. crim.*, 1985, 485.

20 Before the adoption of the Community measure, the same concept was present in the Verbandsklage. H. Koch, 'Class and Public Interest Actions in German Law', (1986) 4 *CJQ* 66, 79.

21 R. Keat, N. Whiteley, N. Abercrombie (eds.), *Introduction, The Authority of the Consumer*, (Routledge, London, 1994) at 8.

22 W.H. Van Boom, 'Introduction: Collective Interests, 'Prêt À Porter' Justice?' (2008) 1:2 Erasmus Law Review, http://papers.ssrn.com/sol3/papers.cfm?abstract_id=1101427#PaperDownload, accessed 26 June 2008.
K. Soper, 'Re-thinking the "Good Life"', (2007) 7:2 *Journal of Consumer Culture*, 205, 229. (2007); R. Harrison, T. Newholm, D. Shaw (eds.), *The Ethical Consumer*, (Sage, London, 2005).

a body staffed by professional consumer advisers has to claim to be able to determine what is in the consumer interest".[23]

1.2. THE "COLLECTIVE DAMAGE"

The adoption of the notion of "collective interests" in the Injunctions Directive implies a major question: the possibility for the associations to claim the 'collective damage' for the infringement of the collective interests of the consumers: a damage that is not the simple accumulation of numerous individual claims, but rather a nominal or a non-material, lump sum that cannot be exactly calculated and proved.[24] The "collective damage" represents damage to the collectivity of the consumers, i.e. all citizens in the act of consumption. Given that this is different from the damage individually suffered by the consumers, it may also be considered within the shadow of the "punitive or exemplary damages", that have recently been admitted, only in principle, by the European Commission in cases of infringement of EC competition law.[25]

The difficulty in admitting the collective damage is mainly a consequence of the unsatisfactory conceptualisation of the collective interest of the consumers. In any case, I believe that the collective – as opposed to individual – interests of consumers should be vindicated by damages only under certain circumstances and, particularly, in the case below described.

When associations have to claim damages on behalf of a group of consumers, this does not pose any particular problem (the "named consumers"). In such case, the group of injured play an active role in the suit and is highly interested in the action (e.g. for example in the case of severe health injuries caused by chemicals or pharmaceutical products). The compensation claimed will often be high enough to provide incentives to the injured consumers to notify their individual losses to the association. The suing association submits a list of all the injured parties and the judge should be able to substantiate the individual damage suffered by each injured.

This is not actually possible in the case of truly widespread damage and where it is difficult to substantiate the individual damage because it may be very small and diffused over a large number of consumers (the "unnamed consumers"). Here, it is conceivable to award the "collective damage" for the benefit of the consumers, in general. In such case, the damages would be awarded to the

23 G. Howells, 'Opinion: Consumer Representation' (1993) 17 *Consum. LJ*, 18.

24 H. Koch, 'Non-class group litigation under EU and German Law', (2001) 11 *Duke J. of Comp. & Int'l L.* 355, 361.

25 Commission (EC), 'Staff Working Paper accompanying the White Paper on Damages actions for breach of the EC antitrust rules', *SEC* (404), 2 April 2008, at 59.

organisation and the amount recovered, instead of being directed to the individual plaintiffs harmed in a particular case, could be directed to a specific fund designed to offset the type of harm at issue in the case or more generally to promote *specific* consumer initiatives.

In this regard, French courts have developed a set of criteria to allocate the "dommage collectif", to include, for example, the legal costs sustained by the organisation-claimants.[26] The proposed solution aims to avoid the risk of the juxtaposition of the individual and the collective damages, which results in an over-compensation of the damage occurring in the case in issue.

The critiques to the notion of collective interests are relevant also in this respect and I have serious concerns about the manageability of such damage.

1.3. THE LIMITS OF THE INJUNCTIONS DIRECTIVE

Apart from the theoretical shortcoming arising from the adoption of the concept of consumers' collective interests, the Injunctions Directive also presents practical limitations.

The first limit of this measure is the constraint on the number of claimants who may bring an action.[27] The "qualified entities" of the Community measure vary greatly in number and power in the Member States,[28] while this article focuses on the consumer organisations (i.e. private institutions that are created on a voluntary basis or established by the national governments, with the aim of pursuing collective purposes on behalf of large groups of consumers).

In most cases, organisations are allowed to sue for the protection of collective interests only when they have particular characteristics defined by the law and concerning the number of members, the presence in the territory, the internal organisation and so forth. The existence of these conditions is normally checked by an official entity (i.e. a Ministry) and then the approved association is included in an official list. On the basis of the strict bureaucratic control exercised by the government, only a few officially authorised associations may actually have a role in consumer litigation. Unfortunately, the accreditation system before the government lacks flexibility in granting access to justice to newly established groups of consumers.

---

26 J. Frank, 'Pour une véritable réparation du préjudice causé à l'intérêt collectif des consommateurs', in C. Albigès, J.F. Artz, J.M. Badenas Carpio, J. Beauchard (eds.), *Etudes de droit de la consommation. Liber amicorum Jean Calais-Auloy*, (Dalloz-Sirey, Paris, 2004) 409–419.

27 R.B. Cappalli, C. Consolo, 'Class Actions for a Continental Europe? A Preliminary Inquiry', (1992) 6 *Temp. Int'l & Comp. L.J.* 217, 220.

28 Note 7 at 14.

This mechanism does not accommodate the inherent tensions about how to represent consumers. In theory, consumers do not participate to a large extent in organisations because, as individuals, they are self-interested in their own welfare and therefore will not make any sacrifices to help the group to attain its political objectives. This is so because once the public good is achieved it is available to everyone regardless of who contributed to its provision. Accordingly, some consumers will try to free ride on the efforts of others and will have no incentive to contribute to the provision of the public good, hoping that others will shoulder the burden. Such problem becomes acute once everyone attempts to free ride and no one is left to take any action.[29] In practice, there are sociological studies confirming the relatively small public support for national consumer organisations in the Member States.[30]

The second limit concerns the domain in the Injunctions Directive, which applies only to the matters indicated in the Annex (e.g. misleading advertising, consumer credit practices, television broadcasting, package holidays, advertising of medicines and unfair terms in consumer contracts)[31] and the lack of action for damages to complement injunctions. The European Commission explained this solution by stating that this measure has been designed to prevent damages: "as distinct from actions for damages which are designed to 'make good' the consequences" and that "clearly an action for an injunction can play a preventative role only provided it is part of an effective and rapid procedure".[32]

On such basis, this action has been considered as a policy-oriented remedy based on the fact that it does not vindicate individual rights but it pursues the policy-goal of consumer protection.[33] This policy-oriented action has therefore proven to be quite ineffective in preventing the wrongful behaviour of the businesses in the Single Market.[34]

1.4. A LACK OF COURAGE: THE ISSUE OF STANDING

In light of the above, one may conclude that the failure of the model of action introduced by the Community measure is primarily the result of the lack of understanding of the notion of the collective interest of consumers.

---

29 M. Olson, *The Logic of Collective Action Public Goods and the Theory of Groups* (HUP, Cambridge 1965), at 126.

30 V. Kendall, *EC Consumer Law* (Wiley Chancery, London, 1996) at 19.

31 Annex to Directive 98/27/EC, List of Directives covered by Article 1.

32 Commission (EC), 'Proposal for a European Parliament and Council Directive on Injunctions for the Protection of Consumers' Interest', COM 712() 712, 1995, 3.

33 M. Taruffo, 'Some Remarks on Group Litigation in Comparative Perspective', (2001) 11 *Duke J. Comp. & Int'l L.* 405.

34 Note 7 at 347.

The Injunctions Directive has expressly introduced such concept, but it has failed to go further in adopting a "communitarian" vision of such problems and, particularly, in providing an adequate protection of such interests in terms of access to justice.[35]

Usually, an individual claimant must have suffered a legally cognisable injury to bring an action before national courts. When the claimant is an association, rather than a single individual, the doctrine has always had serious problems in reducing the interests that the association seeks to protect to an interest that can be construed individualistically.

Despite the acknowledged importance of such concerns in the Consumers Law Acquis, the current standing doctrine before the courts in the Member States – and particularly before the European Court of Justice[36] – grants a very limited judicial protection to associations and other groups.

This prevents courts from redressing an injury to any interest best modelled as a collective one. Often, such interests take shape just because a group of people form an association to share a joint concern: alone, no one member embodies the interest at stake, but in banding together, all of the members create a vehicle that does possess a distinct, potentially vulnerable interest. The association serves as such a vehicle not because the organisation is like any single individual, but specifically because it is unlike an individual.

The tension in the judicial system between acknowledging these benefits and sticking to an individualistic model of interest manifests itself in inconsistent grants of associational standing. And consequently, real collective interests worthy of judicial protection fall by the wayside for want of a framework to accommodate them.

If European institutions intend to maintain the idea of the collective interest of consumers and to make the Injunctions Directive really work for consumers, it is necessary to "take courage" in order to re-conceptualise the doctrine of standing in cases involving the collective interests of consumers, investors and employees.[37]

A new conceptualisation is possible and may ground on the recognition of the identity of a collective. When collectives seek to solve problems regarding shared goods, they face concerns pertinent exclusively to themselves, rather than to any single individual. The collective possesses its own identity that may grow from members' relationships with one another and the members' relationships with

35 M. Cappelletti, 'Formazioni sociali e interessi di gruppo davanti alla giustizia civile', (1975), *Riv. dir. proc.*, 361.

36 O. De Schutter, 'Public Interest Litigation Before the European Court of Justice', (2006) 13:1 *Maastricht Journal of European and Comparative Law*, 9–34.

37 C. Stone, 'Should Trees Have Standing? Toward Legal Rights for Natural Objects', (1972) 45 S. *Cal. L. Rev.* 450.

non-members, but it is distinct from members' individual identities and singular concerns.

In the words of Teubner: "If (…) a systems-theory approach is chosen, the very distinction between individualism and collectivism becomes questionable. Systems theory neither reduces collective action to individual action nor vice versa, but interprets both as different forms of social attribution of action. [W]e would suggest that the social reality of a legal person is a 'collective': the socially binding self-description of an organized action system as a cyclical linkage of identity and action".[38] Concrete, corporate law recognises this by defining a corporation as a legal person, apart from its directors, shareholders and employees. Labour law also acknowledges distinctive collective identity by institutionalising the status of unions. The law in these areas has responded to the reality of contemporary social life: business and labour require definitively collective identities to pursue their goals. In fact, courts already recognise interests other than those unique to individual persons, allowing corporations and associations to argue their claims, even at the expense of a particular individual's interest.

If we agree to give a central role in our society to consumer organisations, we may consider them as the main bearers of standing for the protection of the collective interests of the consumer. This means to assign to the courts the technical (and political) task to recognise these organisations as representatives of particular collective interests according to the association's degree of formal organisation and demonstrated commitment to the claimed interest.[39]

2. THE REFORM OF THE INJUNCTIONS DIRECTIVE: ENLARGING ASSOCIATIONAL STANDING?

A possibility to reform the current European framework consists of enlarging the standing of the "national consumer bodies" and, particularly, the consumer organisations to recover damages on behalf of consumers.

Clearly, in this case, it is not the collective interests as in the Injunctions Directive that is vindicated by the organisation, but the rights of a certain group of consumers collected together for purposes of procedural economy. This idea is present in the work by Cappelletti and Garth who drew a distinction

38 G. Teubner, 'Enterprise Corporatism: New Industrial Policy and the "Essence of the Legal Person" (1988) 36 *American Journal of Comparative Law*, 130.

39 M. Shapiro and A. Stone Sweet, *On law, politics, and judicialization* (OUP, 2002); A. Stone Sweet, *Governing with Judges* (OUP, 2000).

between the mechanisms designed to protect the collective aspects of certain rights and those designed to protect the individual ones.[40]

The model of action here considered represents a case of representative litigation – a tool that plays an important role in modern civil adjudication, being used in a number of different procedural settings to justify imposing the effects of a lawsuit on a person who had no opportunity to participate personally in the litigation and sometimes no knowledge that the suit was even pending.

In the last years this device has been largely discussed both in the United States (where the class actions are generally conceived by the literature as representative lawsuits[41]) and in the European Union (e.g. LDC Consultation Paper on Representative Claims[42]).

My point is that, nowadays, the success of the representative litigation is not the expression of a corporatist vision of society as it was in the past,[43] but it finds an explanation due to efficiency reasons, especially in mass tort cases, involving a large number of individual suits and raising many common issues: in such case, as the number of consumers involved grows, this device has proven to be more efficient than voluntary joinder of parties and consolidation.

2.1. DEVELOPMENTS IN EC COMPETITION LAW

The White Paper mentioned at paragraph 1 before expressly considers a representative action brought by consumer organisations.[44] In particular, it clearly states the necessity to introduce a mechanism allowing the aggregation of the individual claims of victims of antitrust infringements: consumers, especially those who have suffered a relatively low-value damage, are often deterred from bringing an individual action for damages by the costs, delays, uncertainties, risks and burdens involved. As a result, many of these they currently remain uncompensated.

Thus, the White Paper suggests a combination of two complementary mechanisms of collective redress to address effectively those issues in the field of antitrust. A representative action for damages brought by entities with certain

40 M. Cappelletti at note 17.

41 R. Mulheron, at note 9. J. Bronsteen and O. Fiss, 'The Class Action Rule', (2003) 78 *Notre Dame L. Rev.* 1419, 1420.

42 LDC, *Representative Claims: Proposed New Procedures*: Consultation Papers, February 2001 quoted by R. Mulheron, 'From representative rule to class action: steps rather than leaps', (2005) 24 *CJQ*, 425.

43 S.C.Yeazell 'Group Litigation and Social Context', (1977) 77 *Colum. L. Rev.* 866, 867, 877.

44 Commission (EC), 'White Paper on Damages actions for breach of the EC antitrust rules', COM (165) 2 April 2000, at 4.

characteristics[45] – such as consumer organisations, trade associations and State bodies – on behalf of identified or, in rather restricted cases, identifiable victims (not necessarily their members) and an opt-in collective action where the claims from individuals or businesses are combined in one single action. In such model of action, as opposed to representative actions as defined above, the claimant himself has suffered harm. Moreover, the opt-in collective action system envisaged by the European institution is a system where the victims have to express their intention to be included in the action.

According to the European Commission these two types of action complement each other for two main reasons: first, the qualified entities will not be able or willing to pursue every claim; second, it is important that consumers are not deprived of their right to bring an individual action for damages if they so wish.

This proposal is therefore not fully convincing in consideration of the risk that the duplication of the actions will produce an over-compensation of the antitrust damages. It is evident that the proposed solution implies the putting in place of safeguards to avoid the same harm being compensated more than once.[46]

Anyway, these suggestions on damages actions in the field of antitrust are part of the European Commission's wider initiative to strengthen collective redress mechanisms and may develop further within this context.

2.2. NATIONAL EXPERIMENTATION: ARTICLE 140-*BIS* OF THE CONSUMER CODE

Among the cases of national experimentation it is interesting to comment on the action provided for by the new Article 140-bis of the Italian Consumer Code ("azione collettiva risarcitoria") granting associations the standing to recover damages or to bring an action for restitution on behalf of consumers.[47]

The new action would enter into force, subject to integrations and/or amendments, on July 1, 2009.[48]

---

45 Qualified entities should include (i) entities designated in advance by the Member States according to national procedures, representing legitimate and defined interests; and (ii) other existing entities whose primary task would be to protect the defined interests of their members, other than by pursuing damages claims, which would be certified on an *ad hoc* basis in relation to a particular infringement according to national procedures.

46 Commission (EC), 'Staff Working Paper accompanying the White Paper on Damages actions for breach of the EC antitrust rules', *SEC* (404) 2 April 2008 at 18–20.

47 Similar solutions are present, for example, in France (see at paragraph 2.3) and Spain (see at paragraph 1).

48 Article 140-bis Legislative Decree 6 September, 2005, no. 206 ('Consumer Code'). The Article was introduced by Article 1, sections 445–9 of the Law on 24 December, 2007 No. 244 ('*Disposizioni per la formazione del bilancio annuale e pluriennale dello Stato. Legge finanziaria 2008*') [2007] OJ No 300, Supplement No. 285.

This action relies on a bureaucratic accreditation,[49] but leaves to Italian judges the possibility to grant standing to other organisations and committees that are sufficiently representative of the collective interests in issue; it is clear that this solution aims not to exclude valuable voices from consumer litigation: consumers, who believe they have interests in common with others are likely to establish *ad hoc* organisations with the aim of bringing collective actions seeking compensation for damages.

The model of action of Article 140-bis provides an opt-in mechanism: those consumers and users who intend to benefit from the protection afforded by this Article must notify the association in writing of their intention to join the collective action. Consumers may join the action even during the appeal and up until the hearing scheduled in order for the parties to specify their conclusions.[50]

The claimant may act in order to request (i) the ascertainment of the right to be compensated for damage, (ii) an order to return any due amounts to the individual consumers or users within a legal relationship relating to standard agreements. The action may also arise as a consequence of tort liability, unfair trade practice or anti-competition behaviour, providing that such unlawful acts damage the rights of a plurality of consumers and users.

The Article introduces a sort of "filter": at the first hearing the court shall declare the admissibility or inadmissibility of the claim by way of an order that may be challenged before the Court of Appeal, which shall rule in Chambers. The claim is declared inadmissible when it is clearly groundless, when there is a conflict of interest or whenever the judge does not ascertain the existence of any collective interest deserving protection pursuant to this Article.[51]

Should the judge accept the claim, he or she shall also set the criteria to be used in order to calculate the amount to be paid to the individual consumers and users who have joined the collective action or who have intervened in the

The Italian government has recently postponed the entering into force of this provision to July 1, 2008.

49 The associations of consumers and users registered on the list pursuant to Article 137 of the Consumer Code are entitled to act before the courts under Article 140-bis of the Consumer Code. Such list is kept by the government and, precisely, by the Ministry of Productive Activities.

50 The commencement of the collective action or the fact of joining it afterwards shall interrupt the statute of limitations pursuant to Article 2945 of the Italian Civil Code.

51 The judge is entitled to postpone the assessment of the admissibility of the claim when preliminary investigations concerning the same subject matter are underway before an independent authority (primarily the Italian Antitrust Authority). Moreover, should the judge declare the admissibility of the claim, then the party who has initiated the collective action is ordered to duly advertise the content of the claim and actions are also taken for the continuation of the proceedings.

proceedings.[52] Within 60 days of the service of judgment, the company shall make its offer for payment by way of a written deed to be served upon any entitled party and to be filed with the clerk's office.[53]

When the company fails to make its offer within the period indicated or should its offer remain unaccepted after 60 days of its service, the chief judge of the court shall appoint a sole Camera di Conciliazione (that is, conciliation committee) in order to set the amounts to be paid to consumers and users who have joined the collective action and who so request.[54] The decision that brings the proceedings to an end also has legal effects for those consumers and users who have joined the collective action. Those individual consumers or users who have not joined the collective action shall continue to have their right to bring individual actions. The judgement is binding only for the consumers, who have opted-in by conferring the mandates to the organisations.

2.3. CONSUMER ASSOCIATIONS AND LAWYERS

In the model of action considered in the previous paragraphs, the consumer associations are "intermediaries" in the provision of access to justice for individuals. The relationship between the consumer and the association poses a principal-agent problem:[55]

In cases of legal actions taken by associations, the agency chain between the consumers and the lawyer(s) is lengthened: the client is the association, whose members are known and whose standing is based on the consent of its members, and this may decrease the ability of an 'otherwise self-interested' lawyer to act contrary to the interests of the consumers he or she purports to represent.

The intermediation of the organisations may therefore create a series of specific shortcomings to the action.

In particular, the associations represent their own interests, which may diverge from those of the injured consumers they seek to represent. In the Green Paper "Damages Actions for the breach of EC antitrust rules" the European Commission highlighted these concerns and stressed that collective actions in antitrust law may be abused by consumer associations in order to advance their own interests, which might be different from those of the individuals who have suffered from an

52 The judge shall also establish the minimum amount to be paid to each consumer or user should this be possible on the basis of the documents at his or her disposal.

53 Any form of proposal accepted by the consumer or user shall be enforceable.

54 The conciliation committee is composed of a lawyer indicated by the claimant and by a lawyer indicated by the defendant, and it is chaired by a lawyer appointed by the chief judge of the court, chosen from among those entered in the special register for higher jurisdictions.

55 H.B. Schaefer, 'The Bundling of Similar Interests in Litigation. The Incentives for Class Action and Legal Actions taken by Associations', (2000) 9:3 *European Journal of Law and Economics*, 183, 213.

infringement of the competition rules.[56] For instance, if consumer associations are awarded damages for their own benefit, consumer associations might have an incentive to settle the dispute, although this would not necessarily be in the best interest of the consumers, since they may gain more benefit should the procedure proceed. The Green Paper urged the necessity to ensure that damages awarded by the courts are not used for the personal benefit of the representatives, but are rather designated to a particular project that will benefit consumers as a whole.

In addition, the consumers whom the association seeks to represent may have internal conflicts which make it impossible to represent the group: some individuals who purchased a product already have suffered an injury while others may be concerned that their ingestion of the product will cause them to develop an injury in the future. Moreover, some may have serious or life threatening injuries or may have only minor complaints and some may have been warned by their doctors of potential side-effects, while others may have received no warnings. Evidently, it is difficult to represent a large group of consumers who are in different situations.

Moreover, in comparing lawyers and organisations as litigation intermediaries, it is necessary to consider the key issue of funding of the action.

Lawyers, as entrepreneurs, are obviously incentivised to act before the court by the prospective of obtaining remuneration and thus they are available to initially fund the costs of litigation. Consumer associations are, therefore, reluctant to initiate judicial proceedings due to the high costs involved in such proceedings and the risk that they will incur substantial costs should they lose the case.

The funding may be provided by the victims launching the action themselves or by the entity representing the latter by legal aid mechanisms or other publicly or privately administered funds, by insurance companies or other players on the market, or by the claimants' lawyers working under a contingency fees agreement. Another possibility is to create a special fund which will assist in financing the costs of the proceedings.[57]

Moreover, the organisations are exposed to liabilities in terms of claims by consumers if they do not exercise their mandate properly and by producers if they damage their reputations unfairly. Under certain circumstances, they may also be held liable for the defendant's legal costs of the action. The way to overcome this reluctance is by limiting the potential costs and liability that consumer associations could incur in legal proceedings. In light of the above, it has been proposed that

---

56 Commission (EC), Green Paper 'Damages actions for breach of the EC antitrust rules', COM (672) 19 December 2005.

57 O. Dayagi-Epstein, 'Representation of Consumer Interest By Consumer Associations – Salvation for the Masses?', (2006) 3:2 *Competition Law Review*, 209, 249, 224–225 also quoting S. Smismans, *Law, Legitimacy and European Governance Functional Participation in Social Regulation* (OUP, Oxford 2004).

the consumer associations should not be liable for the other parties' costs where their claim was unsuccessful, unless it was proved that they had acted unreasonably.[58]

In the Member States there are already examples of the practical and financial difficulties incurred by these organisations. In France, since 1992, a non-profit, government-authorised consumer organisation may seek compensation for damages that must have been caused by the same person and have a common origin, suffered on behalf of consumers ("action en représentation conjointe" – Article L. 422–1 of the French Consumer Code).[59] However, very few actions of this kind have been brought (that is, 3 cases in about twenty years). The reason is that this mechanism suffers serious shortcomings: the difficulty in collecting the mandates without adequate instruments of advertising, the costs of running the collective actions, the complexity in managing a large group of consumers and the risk of liability. In 2005 the French President asked the government to propose legislation on collective actions and a working group of ministers, consumer organisations, companies and lawyers was formed to prepare draft legislation for collective consumer actions ('actions de groupe').[60] The aim of the proposed new law was to introduce a 'French-style' collective action for consumers by reforming the action en representation conjointe or by introducing a new instrument.[61]

A more recent example comes from the Netherlands,[62] where any incorporated interest group, even if it has been founded on an *ad hoc* basis, has standing to sue in the interest of their members and may file for injunction to stop and desist from orders. Notwithstanding the above, the organisations hardly ever appear in civil courts and one of the main reasons for this absence of consumer organisations in civil procedures is the lack of funds to pursue civil litigation.

---

58 BEUC, (BEUC/190/2006), 'Damages Actions for breach of EC antitrust rules BEUC position on the Commission's Green Paper', 21 April 2006, http://ec.europa.eu/comm/ competition/antitrust/others/actions_for_damages/129.pdf, accessed 26 June 2008.

59 L. Bore at note 12.

60 A lively debate took place on such reform. In April 2006 two bills were submitted to the Parliament – Sénat and Assemblée Nationale – one by socialist Members of Parliament and the other by a Member of Parliament from the current majority right-wing party ('UMP'), to incorporate a system of collective action into the French legal system. However, the new bill on consumer rights, which comprised some provisions on collective consumer actions, was withdrawn from Parliament's agenda at the end of January 2007. The debate on the introduction of class actions in France is still open.

61 The parallelism with Article 140-bis of the Italian Consumer Code is evident.

62 W.H. Van Boom and M.B.M. Loos, *Collective enforcement of consumer law in Europe. Securing compliance in Europe through private group action and public authority intervention'* (Europa Law Publishing, Groningen 2007).

3. AN IMPACT ASSESSMENT OF THE REFORM

The proposal to enlarge the standing of consumer associations under the Injunctions Directive will have an impact on European society.

In particular, there are at least two wider questions, deeply related to the aims of European consumerism,[63] lying behind the reform of such instrument and/or the introduction of mechanisms for consumer collective redress in the European Union.

The first regards the role that the consumer-citizen may play in the de-centralised enforcement of EC Consumer Law, while the second concerns the evolution of the consumer organisations in European society: do we agree to grant a central position to these organisations in consumer litigation? Are they to be seen as quasi-public organisations funded by (and part of) the European institutions and the Member States as in the Nordic countries or as private watchdogs funded by their members? The answer evidently has practical consequences: a solution to the resources problem is for the State to fund consumer associations, but an excessive proximity to the government could create an undesirable degree of dependency by consumer associations on the governments and the need to please those sponsors. This could in turn lead to loss of support from their constituents and the loss of their social role.

3.1. EMPOWERING THE CONSUMER-CITIZEN

The possible expansion of the scope of liability for widespread damages under the Injunctions Directive (or under the national mechanisms mentioned at paragraph 1) contributes to empower the consumer, who is viewed as an important agent of consumer policy, contributing to achieving a high quality and competitive business climate in the Single Market: this conceives of the consumer as an active player in the market rather than a victim who needs to be protected. More importantly, the effects of a new instrument will not be limited to the domain of EC consumer law and this is due to the recent convergence in the social sciences of the notions of consumer and citizen.[64]

Traditionally citizenship and consumption have been considered to belong to separate areas of study: whether their consumption choices have been theorised as authentic expressions of selfhood or as socially constructed, individuals qua consumers have most often been presented as obedient to forms of self-interest

---

63 J.Q. Whitman, 'Consumerism Versus Producerism: A Study in Comparative Law', (2007) 117 *Yale L.J.*, 340.

64 F. Trentmann, 'Citizenship and consumption', (2007) 7:2 *Journal of Consumer Culture*, Vol. 7, No 2, 147–158.

that either limit or altogether preclude the capacity for the reflexivity, social accountability and cultural community associated with citizenship. Only in their role as citizens do they supposedly look above the parapet of private needs and desires or could be said to aim for the public good.[65]

This perception is further reinforced in the theoretical division between a public domain of citizenship – and its concerns with rights, duties, participation and equality – and the private domain of the supposedly purely self-interested consumer.

This picture, however, relies on the implausibly abstract and egoistic homo economicus of neo-classical and rational choice theory that has been roundly criticised by economists.[66]

These developments should be taken into consideration in the legal construction of the consumer.[67] This notion is important in sensible economic legislation where it is common to insist on the relevance of consumer welfare: "[T]he only legitimate goal of American antitrust law is the maximization of consumer welfare."[68] But, the idea of the citizen-consumer is not limited to pure economic law because it also deals and intersects with many other areas of law and policy, including the social and health policies.[69] For example, the interplay between consumer law and the protection of the environment has emerged in the legal scholarship where – in contradiction to those who see the goals of these disciplines as being totally incompatible – an author has underlined the necessity to transcend the traditional boundaries. He suggested replacing the consumer by the citizen, who is interested not only in his own consumption but in all aspects of social life and supported the idea that the development of certain consumer law measures can be used to raise the awareness of consumers regarding environmental issues.[70]

Evidently, the evolution of the consumer into a master category of collective and individual identity is relevant for consumer litigation: the consumer-citizen will bring cases before the Courts not only to advance the fairness of the contractual terms and the safety of the products but also to pursue their social rights and the goals of environmental protection and fair trade. As the historian of the book "A Consumers' Republic" confirms, in the United States consumerism

---

65 F. Trentmann (ed.), *The Making of the Consumer: Knowledge, Power and Identity in the Modern World* (Berg, Oxford and New York 2006).

66 A. Sen, 'Beyond Self-Interest, in '*Rational Fools*', J.J. Mansbridge (Chicago University Press, Chicago 1990) 25–43.

67 See note 65 before.

68 R. Bork, *The Antitrust Paradox: A Policy at War with Itself* (Basic Books, New York 1978), 51.

69 M. Everson and C. Joerges, 'Consumer Citizenship in Postnational Constellations?' European University Institute Working Paper LAW No. 2006/47, http://ssrn.com/abstract=964187, accessed 26 June 2008.

70 T. Wilhelmsson, 'Consumer Law and the Environment: From Consumer to Citizen', (1998) 21 *JCP*, 45–70.

has opened up political possibilities for women and racial minorities: "Citizen consumers are people who are ready to make vigorous demands for rights."[71]

3.2. THE EVOLUTION OF THE CONSUMER MOVEMENT

The enlargement of associational standing under the Injunctions Directive will grant the consumer associations the role of principal intermediaries between the consumers and the courts and, consequently, it will definitively assign them a central role in European society.

Social scientists underline that the consumer movement has gained influence within the European Community's headquarters in Brussels (i.e. the Bureau Européen des Unions des Consommateurs and the European Association for the Coordination of Consumer Representation in Standardisation), while the status of organisations at national level is very different in the Member States in size, background and capacity, according to each country's history.[72]

Recently, the "European Consumer Policy Strategy 2007–2012" has demonstrated an overarching concern with guaranteeing a more powerful voice for the consumer, even though that voice is already far from going unheard (in particular, at Community level).[73] The document also compels the national governments to provide support for their consumer organisations and it takes the lead in creating such organisations in the new Member States.

What is surprising is that the empowerment of the consumer movement is occurring as a top-down approach rather than bottom-up process in the sense that it is driven from the European institutions more than consumers.

Actually, the construction and the promotion of the economic interests of the consumers have often been dependent on wider national and international interests and ideologies.

An author quotes historical studies suggesting that many of the postwar measures protecting the consumers' interests in the United Kingdom were introduced because they served the goals of the government players who wished to break down trade restrictions and that consumer protection laws essentially "piggy-backed" on the achievement of this scope.[74]

---

71 L. Cohen, *A Consumers' Republic: The Politics of Mass Consumption in Post-war America* (Vintage Books, New York 2003), 18–51.

72 More details from Consumer Law Enforcement Forum at www.clef-project.eu/cms/project.php.

73 Commission (EC) Communication to the Council, the European Parliament and the European Economic and Social Committee, "EU Consumer Policy Strategy 2007–2012, Empowering consumers, enhancing their welfare, effectively protecting them", COM (99) 13 March 2007, 99.

74 I. Ramsay, *Consumer Law and Policy, Text and Materials on Regulating Consumer Markets'* (Hart, Oxford 2007) 25.

Focusing on the last years, sociological studies confirm that: "But more careful examination of the dynamics behind the new consumer culture suggests that it cannot simply be understood as driven from below by an 'empowered' consuming public."[75]

This may be explained by the fact that the development of EC Consumer Law has been driven by the process of market integration. In constructing a single market, the European institutions have restricted the extent to which States can insist upon regulations that limit imports from other Members States and, at the same time, they have made many efforts to avoid the risk that the ending of all indirect national trade restrictions may undermine the level of consumer protection. Within these efforts there is the political and economical support granted to consumer organisations at both European and national level.

The point here made is how much proximity with European and Member States institutions and bureaucracies is desirable?

While historically most consumer groups in the United States have been privately financed, government funding has been commonplace in Europe where – in Scandinavian countries, France and Germany – consumer groups were created and funded by the governments confirming that the potential role of such organisations is to manage consumer matters.[76]

Nowadays, it is still not clear if European consumer organisations are developing as private watchdogs, pressuring the governments and European institutions into action from below or as "government officials" appointed from these institutions and expressing their views.

Some issues proper of consumer litigation – I think those concerning the funding of actions and the standing requirements in consumer litigation – will be fundamental to determine the very nature of the consumer movement.[77]

4. CONCLUSIONS

For a long time, the private enforcement of EC Consumer Law has been undeveloped in the Single Market and this has been so primarily because the model of action designed by the Injunctions Directive failed to assure an adequate level of consumer protection.

I argue that this is mainly due to the lack of understanding of the notion of the collective interests of the consumers and to the practical consequences of this

75 A. Burgess, 'Flattering Consumption: Creating a Europe of the consumer', (2007) 1 *Journal of Consumer Culture*, 93–117.

76 A. Burgess at note before.

77 Some improvements to the state of the art have been recently proposed by Dayagi-Epstein at note 56.

unmanageable concept on the issues of associational standing and remedies (I think, for example, of the notion of "collective damage").

According to the model of action described in the White Paper, a reform of the Injunctions Directive may consist of granting consumer associations standing to recover damages on behalf of consumers (some Member States have adopted such instrument (France and Spain) while other countries, such as Italy, are seriously considering this mechanism).

The current system needs to be reformed, but I believe that this solution presents serious shortcomings: in particular, having an association as the named plaintiff will not automatically eliminate the difficulties proper of the relationship between the principal and the agent, but will introduce some specific problems (see paragraph 2.3 before).

The "centrality" of the consumer associations in the model of action here examined grounds on what remains, nowadays, of the "communitarian idea of justice":[78] an ideology that has been maintained – to the limited extent that I have discussed before – in Commission Directive (EC) 98/27.

Anyway, if we are aiming to develop the Injunctions Directive by considering the consumer associations as the intermediaries between consumers and lawyers, we should ensure that these organisations have *not only* the opportunities, but *also* the ability to adequately represent the consumer interest. Some practical issues – e.g. funding, liabilities and incentives – are crucial to assure effective consumer protection. In the lack of these conditions, the solution here discussed and envisaged in the Green Paper on Consumer Collective Redress[79] will not have the results hoped for by the European institutions.

---

78 M.J. Sandel, *Liberalism and the Limits of Justice* (CUP, Cambridge, second edition 1998, first edition 1988).

79 Commission (EC), 'Green Paper on Consumer Collective Redress', COM (794) 27 November 2008, at p. 13 point no. 53.

GROUP ACTIONS AS A REMEDY TO ENFORCE CONSUMER INTERESTS

Prof. Dr. Astrid STADLER
University of Konstanz - Germany

1. INTRODUCTION

Group actions have become a popular topic of political and legal debate in the EU Member States as well as on the European level. The European Commission takes class actions or group actions – a term which is sometimes preferred in order to prevent bringing up negative connotations to US-style class actions – into consideration as a means of enhancing private enforcement in antitrust and consumer law.[1] The Commission first raised the issue of class actions for the enforcement of consumer interests in the early 1980s but at that time refrained from any proposals for harmonisation due to the complexity and diversity amongst the national systems of collective redress.[2] Today, the class action debate is embedded into the larger context of whether means of private enforcement should prevail over or at least complement public enforcement of consumer rights. The diversity amongst the Member States has even grown since the 1980s. There are different concepts of private or public enforcement in consumer law as well as different types of collective redress. In some Member States the protection of consumer interests was entrusted to a public prosecutor's office – such as the UK Office of Fair Trading – or to an authorised public body like the ombudsman in the Nordic states. In a great number of Member States, responsibility for the defence of collective interests of consumers was put on consumer associations. However, the conditions and criteria organisations have to satisfy in order to take enforcement action under consumer protection provisions vary considerably

1 For EC consumer policy, cf. Green Paper on Consumer Collective Redress COM (2008) 794, 27.11.2008. For competition and antitrust law, the Ashurst study prepared the EC's Green Paper on damages actions for breach of the EC antitrust rules, and is available at: http://ec.europa.eu/comm /competition/ antitrust/others/actions_for_damages/study.html. The Green Paper and the White Paper are available at the website of the Commission, DG Competition.

2 Memorandum of the Commission: Consumer Redress COM (84) 692, Dec. 12, 1984; Hodges, *Global Class Actions Project, Summary of European Union Developments*, www.law.stanford.edu/calendar/details/1066/, p. 1.

between Member States. The same is true with regard to the financial strength and human resources of these associations. This heterogeneity of systems has to be taken into account when discussing the enforcement of collective consumer interests.

In terms of strengthening collective actions, Community measures in the past have advanced primarily injunctive relief[3] which has remained the most prominent device of collective enforcement for many decades. Since the turn of the millennium however, there has been an increasing debate in the Member States on the improvement of collective actions in consumer law. Irrespective of the considerations on the EU level, which are still in its initial stages, a number of Member States implemented reforms, sometimes quite hastily and regardless of the multilevel dimension of the problem.

Thus, today we can observe within the European Union a rag rug of different instruments. The scope of procedural devices ranges from the traditional representative action for an injunction to representative actions which require the transfer of consumer rights to a consumer organisation or state agency in order to bring an action for damages to different types of test case litigation and group actions. The European Community has not even agreed on a common terminology of the different procedural tools. The fact that a kind of competition emerged among Member States for the most effective enforcement of consumer interests may help the European legislator to select the appropriate solution on the Community level in a bottom-up approach. However, different levels of collective enforcement of consumer rights in the Member States may as well imbalance competitive conditions for businesses and call for some basic regulations on behalf of the Community that apply not only to cross-border but also for domestic cases. This touches upon the tricky question of the Community's competence to harmonise rules of civil procedure. At any rate, the Commission should attend to the cross-border cases, as they require a Community-wide solution and tend to be disregarded by national legislators.

The legal and political debate on the European level as well as in many Member States still concentrates on the question whether to expand collective enforcement in the first place. The outcome of this debate will, nevertheless, be strongly influenced by the various types of collective redress which can be taken into account. In particular any proposal for a kind of group or class action evokes the fear that this will be the first step on the slippery slope towards an "American state of law". This paper will, therefore, discuss the justification of group actions, their scope of application and some vertices of the proceedings. Political acceptance of group actions and their effectiveness will depend on several key issues such as the question of who has legal standing to initiate group actions. Selection of the group

3 Directive 98/27, for details of its implementation cf. Docekal/Kolba/Micklitz, *The Implementation of Directive 98/27/EC in the Member States*, Bamberg/Vienna 2005.

plaintiff, the court's supervision of his way to conduct the case, and the option of an "opt-out" or "opt-in" model are highly controversial issues as well.

2. MASS LITIGATION AND SMALL DAMAGE CASES

Collective actions irrespective of their type aim at a consolidation of numerous individual claims which share common factual or legal questions. A review of the case material in the Member States reveals that two completely different situations have to be taken into consideration. First, courts struggle with the phenomenon of mass litigation – complex lawsuits involving sometimes hundreds or thousands of plaintiffs claiming damages.[4] These situations are a special challenge for any civil justice system and the answers given by national legislators focus more or less on group actions and test or sample proceedings. Representative actions play a minor role in this context.[5] Second, debates on collective actions have to take into consideration not only challenges arising from mass claims. Violation of consumer laws, misleading advertising and the infringement of antitrust rules often cause only small individual damage. Nevertheless, the illegal profits gained by businesses are immense. Despite the clear unlawfulness of these strategies, due to the small amounts of individual damage, hardly any consumers assert their claims. Thus, we face a gap in the enforcement of law and an access-to-court problem. At least at first sight it is very likely that these two very different problems – mass litigation and small damage cases – call for different legal solutions in terms of private or public enforcement.

For small damages cases the question is how to compensate the individual's apathy. Opt-out group proceedings following the historical idea of US class actions are one option to allow adjudication of small claims.[6] Skimming-off procedures as implemented recently in the German Unfair Competition Act and the German Antitrust Act are another possibility. Actions for skimming-off ill-gotten gains are a new type of representative action which can be filed by associations that

4 In many Member States these were capital market investment cases or actions brought against insurance companies. Large numbers of small investors claimed damages based on allegedly false stock market information or other fraudulent strategies; cf. for example the German case of the "Deutsche Telekom", the Dutch and Belgian "Dexia" case and the Swedish "Skandia" case.

5 However, in Austria the "Verein für Konsumenteninformation (VKI)", the most important consumer organisation, was quite successful in the past in claiming damages on behalf of a large number of consumers who had transferred their claims to the VKI for enforcement.

6 Group action regulations in Denmark and Norway, which are in principle based on an opt-in mechanism, leave it to the discretion of the court where the action is pending to allow opt-out proceedings if the claims involve amounts that are so small that it must be assumed that a considerable majority of them would not be brought as individual actions or that consumers will not opt-in, cf. Sec. 35–7 Norway Dispute Act; §254e (3) Danish Code of Civil Procedure.

satisfy certain criteria.[7] Such a procedure neither compensates individual damage nor collective damage. The legislator instead favoured deterrence as a primary objective. There is no widespread consensus on the legitimacy of this approach and the success of the whole idea depends on the efficiency of the skimming-off mechanism and its strict enforcement by (consumer) associations.

It takes a general discussion whether deficits in private individual enforcement should be counterbalanced by public enforcement through public bodies and agencies or by private group proceedings and/or representative actions. This is not the place to discuss at length the advantages and disadvantages of the different approaches. However, group actions might have a market regulatory function by filling a gap where public agencies or bodies either do not exist or are not able to guarantee a sufficient control of markets.[8] In this respect the situation may be different from Member State to Member State and even among different fields of law such as antitrust or consumer law. Group actions may even be one option to deal with the rather heterogeneous systems in the Member States. The Nordic states, which turned out to be protagonists in implementing group litigation in recent years,[9] found a compromise between the traditional role of the Ombudsman, which is an authorised public body, and a turning to more private enforcement. Group actions in Denmark, Sweden and Norway can be brought either by private individuals who suffered damage or by organisations, associations or public bodies charged with promoting specific interests. With the juxtaposition of the two strategies, these states established a mixture of representative action and group action.

3. COLLECTIVE REDRESS FOR DAMAGES: HOW TO COPE WITH MASS LITIGATION

3.1. MASS CLAIM SITUATIONS IN EUROPE

The phenomenon of mass litigation has been something unknown to courts in Europe for many years, whereas in the United States the 1970s and 80s was the era

---

7 According to German regulations, consumer organisations have legal standing to file a skimming-off action only under the Unfair Competition Act, Sec. 10. They have been denied that right in case of violations of antitrust rules. In the US the Federal Trade Commission has legal standing to consumer redress under Sec. 19(b) Federal Trade Commission Act (FTCA) and to a disgorgement of illegally gained profits under Sec. 13(b) FICA.

8 This position is, among others, strongly opposed by Säcker, *Die Einordnung der Verbandsklage in das System des Privatrechts*, 2006.

9 Sweden was the first European country to implement a group action following to a large extent the example of US class actions in 2003: Group Proceedings Act (Lag om grupprättegang, SFS 2002-599). Denmark (Act no. 181/2/2007, Sec. 254a-k Code of Civil Procedure), Finland (Class Action Act 444/2007) and Norway (Dispute Act, January, 2008) followed. The Finish model gets out of line insofar as only the Consumer Ombudsman has legal standing to bring a group action; §4 Class Action Act 444/2007.

of mass personal injury litigation. At that time it provoked a debate in the US as to whether class actions, originally implemented as an instrument to grant access to justice for small claims, should also be used to handle complex tort litigation such as product liability cases or mass accidents. Product liability cases, for some time, amounted to almost 25% of all class actions in the US; however, since the 1990s this type of class action has been on the demise.[10] A number of Circuit Courts in the US declined to certify mass tort class actions because issues of causation and damages require individual adjudication of each claim and a class action is therefore not superior to individual litigation.[11] Nevertheless, over the years, experience in the United States proved that almost all certified class action cases result in a – court approved[12] – settlement and that courts are not required to decide on each of the individual claims. This should be kept in mind when discussing the concept of group actions in Europe. A European type of group actions should not assume that – as a rule – the court has to adjudicate on every detail of the individual claims. It should, first of all, offer the parties a procedural frame to obtain a solid legal basis to settle the case.

Moreover, there are significant differences in the type of mass litigation in the United States and Europe. Product liability, mass toxic cases and mass accidents play a prominent role in the US system where the social insurance system provides only rudimentary protection and great parts of the population have no health insurance at all.[13] Personal injury mass tort litigation in the US typically involves as well, future claimants who have not yet suffered an injury or illness, but rather share a statistically enhanced risk of future illness or injury. Such a broad concept of class members entails serious conflicts of interest and makes it almost impossible

---

10 Some commentators even assert that mass tort class action "is as dead as a doornail", cf. Gilles, Opting out of liability: the forthcoming, near-total demise of the modern class action, 104 *Michigan Law Review* 373, 388 (2005); Coffee, Class action accountability: reconciling exit, voice, and loyalty in representative litigation, 100 *Columbia Law Rev.* 370, 372–374 (2000); *Gibson*, A response to Professor Resnick: Will this vehicle pass inspection?, 148 *Pennsylvania Law Review* 2095, 2097–98 (2000). There are, however, still a considerable number of personal injury class actions. For an overview of the range of class actions in recent years cf. Willging/Lee III, *The impact of Class Action Fairness Act of 2005 on the Federal Courts, 3rd Interim Report to the Judicial Conference Advisory Committee on Civil Rules*, April 2007: http://pubcit.typepad.com/clpblog/files/cafa_preliminary_reportiiifinal.pdf.

11 For details cf. Gilles, 104 *Michigan Law Rev.* 373 et seq. (2005). Some District Courts in the US certified tort class actions solely to try one or two issues common to all claims being aware that at a later stage, individualised issues such as injury-causation and damages would require decertification. Gilles labels these court decisions as certifying to try issues, as opposed to cases, ibid p. 384. However, a number of Circuit Courts rejected this approach. In many cases this was based on a strong concern of the rights of defendants in mass tort class actions, where class certification creates insurmountable pressure on defendants to settle the case. Cf. for example Judge Posner's position in the Rhone-Poulenc case, 51 F. 3d, 1298 et seq.

12 Rule 23 Federal Rules of Civil Procedure.

13 Coffee, 95 *Columbia L. Rev.* 1343, 1355 (1995).

to find a fair settlement.[14] In Europe, with its well established system of compulsory health insurance almost everywhere, personal injury mass claims are absorbed by the social security system and have not reached the courts in the past. Nevertheless, with the trim back of public insurance benefits and lower standards of social security in some of the new Member States, the situation may change in Europe as well.

Up to the present, mass litigation in Europe involving a great number of plaintiffs included predominantly suits filed by investors claiming damages for failed capital investment and some sporadic antitrust and product liability cases.[15] In other cases such as overpriced consumer credits or the German "Heininger" cases – a well-known synonym for a series of marketing "junk real estate" – consumers had to fight in individual law suits as there was no effective procedural device to pool the interests into the same proceedings. Such parallel proceedings do not only burden the judiciary and increase the potential of conflicting decisions. Only those consumers accepting to run a high procedural risk in view of rather difficult fact finding and demanding legal issues can obtain compensation.

3.2. US-STYLE CLASS ACTIONS AS A ROLE MODEL FOR EUROPE?

The European debate on class actions is strongly influenced by the business sector which tends to describe them as a worst case scenario. Consumers, by contrast, set much hope on the introduction of group actions, but it is still a rather broad category which has not yet gained a particular profile in Europe. As companies, having been defendants in US class actions, emphasise the misuse and dangers of US class actions, this resulted in a predominantly negative attitude against collective redress. US-style class actions are associated – and deservedly so – with a high potential for abuse, blackmail or the potential to ruin entire companied. The US legislator had to make several efforts to restrict the misuse of class action proceedings – take for example the Class Action Fairness Acts of 2003 and 2005.

This negative attitude deserves particular attention, although, it must be pointed out very clearly that the potential for misuse in the US does not result from the fact that class actions are an effective instrument of pooling the interests of plaintiffs. The immense pressure put on the defendant in a certified class action is rather due to other circumstances such as the high cost of pre-trial discovery

---

14 Defendants tend to reach a global settlement of the case before the estimates of future claims may grow, cf. Coffee, 95 *Columbia L. Rev.* 1343, 1350, for detail see as well footnote 29 below.

15 Cf. the English antitrust case "*The Consumers Association v. JJB Sports plc.*" (case no. 1078/7/07). For further details on examples of Group litigation orders cf. the 2008 research paper of Rachel Mulheron, available on the Civil Justice Council's website: www.civiljusticecouncil.gov.uk.

proceedings, the American rule of cost, the jury system, the availability of punitive damages and the fact that the whole system encourages even non-meritorious claims to be taken to court against "deep pocket" defendants. It is only the combination of these factors which puts the defendant in a situation where he might be well-advised to seek an early settlement of the case even if the plaintiff's case might be weak. Contingency fee arrangements and the usually high amounts involved in class actions make them an attractive source of income for lawyers and turned the procedural system upside down: many class actions are not instigated by the victims, but are "lawyer driven". Lawyers play a key role in initiating, organising and financing the litigation, whereas the compensation of the victims takes a back seat.[16]

Despite the fact that the procedural systems in Europe are completely different from the US and that there is an overall consensus that any type of group action in Europe must avoid the negative effects observed in the US, political resistance remains. Business points out that the implementation of group actions along with other reforms may finally lead to a situation like the one in the US. They emphasise that recent reforms tend to integrate more and more US elements into the European system of civil procedure. For example, contingency fee arrangements with lawyers have been implemented to some extent. The ECJ decided in 2006 that a strict regulation enjoining (Italian) lawyers from charging more than legally fixed fees violates Article 49 of the EC treaty.[17] In Germany, the Federal Constitutional Court forced Parliament as well to lift the ban on contingency fee arrangements in 2006.[18] Therefore, today the situation in Europe is very heterogeneous. However, roughly speaking, contingency fees are still subject to a number of restrictions and are not allowed to the large extent that they are in the United States.[19]

---

16 In particular in securities class actions, lawyers were obviously tempted to "buy" a plaintiff for a class action. The 1995 reform of securities class actions (Private Securities Litigation Reform Act) amended Sec. 27 of the Securities Act to prevent misuse. The reform included as well restrictions on legal fees and costs and the obligation to full disclosure of settlement terms including legal fees and costs, Sec. 27 (7) Securities Act.

17 ECJ 5 December 2006 (C-94/04 and C-202/04); meanwhile Italian legislature has reacted to the decisions and allowed contingency fee arrangement to some extent, see Rodolfo Dolce, *BRAK-Mitt.* 2006, 203.

18 BVerfG 1 BvR 2576/04, 12.12.2006, NJW 2007, 979; French Courts meanwhile accept such arrangements as well, cf. Cour de cassation, Cass. 2e civ., 4 juill. 2007, no 05–18.774, P+B; Cass. 2e civ., 4 juill. 2007, no 06–14.555, P+B; Cass. 2e civ., 4 juill. 2007, no 06–14.633, P+B. The Swedish group action law permits a "risk agreement" with the group plaintiff's lawyer (Sec. 38). In Spain the ban of "pactum de quota litis" is subject to debate, cf. Gutiérrez de Cabiedes Hidalgo, *National Report "Globalization of Class Actions"*. (www.law.stanford.edu/display/images/dynamic/events_media/spain_national_report.pdf), sub. 12.

19 For a survey cf. Mirco Ros, *Fédération des Barreaux d'Europe: Der Erfolg und das Honorar des Anwalts – Entwicklungen zu erfolgsorientierter Vergütung des Rechtsanwalts*, Conference report 2006: www.bgfa.ch/scripts/getfile?id=1107.

Some Member States allow exceptions to the "loser pays" principle, even though the rule prevails as a basic principle.[20] Procedural reforms in some Member States have strengthened as well the parties' rights to obtain evidence from the other party or third parties but this is not in the least comparable to the scope and costs of US pre-trial discovery proceedings.[21] Even taken together, these developments are a far cry from the US system and its litigation culture. In any case, European group actions must be aware of carefully balancing the interests of plaintiffs and defendants and they must avoid creating false incentives to bring actions based on weak claims. The "loser pays" principle, for example, is a well established filter which should not be given up for group actions. However, group plaintiffs should have the chance to alleviate their procedural risk by way of risk insurance[22] or support by public funds in appropriate cases.

3.3. TEST CASE PROCEEDINGS

There are several procedural options to prevent mass claim situations. Group actions are only one of them, though in terms of procedural economy probably the best. Due to the "long shadow" of US class actions, the German legislator is the only one in Europe to resort exclusively[23] to test case proceedings in order to handle mass litigation. This concept should be discussed briefly in order to

---

20 The EC Commission's White Paper on Damages Actions for Breach of the EC antitrust rules COM(2008) 165, 2 April 2008 proposes as well to allow exceptions to the "loser pays rule" in order to alleviate access to justice in some cases. However, national legislatures should be careful and reluctant to drop the rule as it has proved to work extremely well as a vehicle to prevent weak cases being taken to court.

21 This argument refers basically to a recent reform of German civil procedural rules. However, even with the new regulations in Sec. 142–144 of the German Code of Civil Procedure, the German system is gradually catching up with other European systems and is still rather reluctant to require any cooperation in the presentation of evidence by the party who is not carrying the burden of proof. Even the Civil Procedure Rules of England and Wales which are probably the most far-reaching rules regarding the production of documents and other evidence by parties are restrictive compared to US pre-trial discovery and require a cost-efficient handling of the taking of evidence. In contrast to the US system, the taking of evidence in European systems is strictly limited to facts that are directly relevant to the outcome of the litigation.

22 In Austria, the VKI cooperated several times with private insurance companies ("Prozessfinanzierer") that cover the procedural risk of lawsuits. These companies normally work on a *quota litis* basis. As they carefully examine the case before providing insurance coverage, this filters out weak cases as well.

23 The Austrian legislator put forward a draft bill according to which plaintiffs have a choice between group actions for damages and test case litigation. According to the English Civil Procedure Rules the managing judge within a GLO may direct that some claims proceed as test claims, Practice Direction Group Litigation, 12.3., CPR Part 19.15. For practical examples of the test case approach, cf. Mulheron, *Reform of Collective Redress in England and Wales, A Research Paper* 2008, p. 26: www.civiljusticecouncil.gov.uk.

straighten out its particular legal difficulties and the difference to group actions. It will be shown that each form of collective action must balance the rights of the parties and procedural efficiency.

The main characteristic of test cases is that one case serves as a model for equal or similar cases. Many European jurisdictions do not have explicit rules on test case proceedings.[24] It is then generally up to the defendant and to a group of prospective claimants to enter into an agreement, to select one typical claim for test case proceedings and to suspend the other cases until a judgment in the test case has been rendered. Without statutory regulation and due to traditional *res judicata* rules, a judgment in a test case then has no binding effect upon other claimants not formally a party to the test case.[25] In such a situation, test case litigation can disburden courts from a multitude of actions only if all parties involved settle the dispute out of court on the basis of the test case judgment. However, in practice, defendants are generally not interested in such agreements. They hope, instead, that a series of scattered individual trials entails tactical advantages. In order to solve the problem of mass tort litigation it is necessary to create procedural rules that give claimants the ability to force test case proceedings to take place.[26]

In Germany the so-called Capital Markets Model Case Act (KapMuG)[27] came into force in 2005. As a pilot project it is expressly limited to securities litigation and according to its "sunset clause" is set to expire in November 2010. The basic concept is that proceedings in cases with a large number of claimants who sue the same defendant on the same legal and factual basis are put "on ice" while one representative case is chosen by the court and allowed to proceed to the High Court in a kind of intermediate proceedings. The High Court is not to adjudicate upon the test case as a whole but is required to rule only upon legal or factual

24 For Germany cf. Article 1 Sec. 3 No. 8 Legal Advice Act and the Capital Markets Model Case Act of 2005 (since 2008: Sec 79 para 3 Civil Procedure Code).

25 However, the parties may agree that the outcome of the test litigation shall be binding upon them and be the basis for an out-of-court settlement. For a discussion on such agreements in Germany before recent reform, cf. Wagner, *Prozessverträge*, 1998, p. 425 et seq., 727 f; Haß, *Die Gruppenklage*, 1996, p. 64 et seq.; Schlosser, *Einverständliches Handeln im Zivilprozess*, Tübingen 1968, p. 33 et seq.; von Bar, *Gutachten* 62. Deutscher Juristentag Bremen (1998), p. A 81 et seq.

26 In the past, in some mass events plaintiffs finally succeeded to obtain an out-of-court settlement with the wrongdoer's insurance company. However, this type of compensation often lacks transparency and control and must sometimes be seen as a second best solution which is accepted by the victims only due to the lack of efficient procedural vehicles to enforce the claims, Koch, *Juristenzeitung (JZ)* 1998, 801, 805 et seq.; Koch/Willingmann, in: Koch/Willingmann (ed), *Großschäden – Complex Damages*, 1998, 40 et seq.

27 For a general debate on the Act cf. Hess, *Wertpapiermitteilungen (WM)* 2004, 2329; v. Hein, *Recht der internationalen Wirtschaft (RIW)* 2004, 602; Hess/Michailidou, *ZIP* 2004, 1381; Reuschle, *Wertpapiermitteilungen (WM)* 2004, 2334; Wagner, *Gutachten* 66. Deutscher Juristentag, Stuttgart 2006, p. A 120-A 126; Maier-Reimer/Wilsing, *Zeitschrift für Gesellschaftsrecht*, 2006, 79 et seq.

issues that are common to all cases pending. This mechanism is limited to those parties who have already filed actions. Their claims are bundled only for this intermediate stage of the litigation. Once the judgment on the selected issues has been released, the individual lawsuits which have, in the meantime, been suspended are to be continued and each individual claim is adjudicated upon by the court of first instance. The parties and the courts are – roughly speaking – legally bound by the "test case decision".

Extending the legal effect of the intermediate proceeding to all plaintiffs involves a major problem of the legal construction of test cases.[28] If the High Court's decision is to be binding for all claimants even if they were not party to the intermediate test procedure, this violates their constitutionally guaranteed right to be heard. According to the prevailing opinion not only in Germany, the outcome of litigation, as a general rule, can only have a binding effect upon those parties and persons who were entitled to participate in the litigation. The "KapMuG" formally restricts the intermediate test case procedure to the court-selected representative plaintiff and the defendant in order to reduce the complexity to a two-party scheme. Then, however, there is no way to justify a binding effect of the High Court's decision on the remaining claimants. The legislator is in a catch-22 situation as he cannot fully guarantee the right to be heard of those claimants who are not a party to the test proceedings *and* provide rules for the effective handling of mass litigation at the same time. In attempting to balance these conflicting interests, the "KapMuG" had to give priority to the claimants' constitutional rights by entitling all claimants to participate to some extent in the intermediate proceedings. They may raise their own objections, allege their own reasons, and, of course, attend the trial and participate in the taking of evidence. In the end, this is no way out of the dilemma as there is no real relief for the judiciary. The intermediate proceedings as well as the whole litigation remain complex and time-consuming due to the large number of parties involved.

The only way to solve the problem are group actions based on a clear concept of representation. Procedural economy requires the bundling of cases based on the same legal and factual issues. This can be done only by reducing the number of parties involved. If the outcome of the litigation should nevertheless be legally binding for all parties, they must waive their procedural rights of participation by authorising one of them to represent the whole group. Due to constitutional guarantees which are more or less the same all over Europe and are part of Article 6 of the European Convention on Human Rights, this waiver must meet strict requirements.

---

28 For a detailed review cf. Micklitz/Stadler, The development of collective legal actions in Europe, especially in German Civil Procedure, 17 *European Business Law Review* 1473, 1487 et seq. (2006).

4. GROUP ACTIONS

4.1. JUSTIFICATION OF GROUP ACTIONS

A. *Procedural Economy and Justice*

Theoretically, there are different reasons for implementing group actions. In the US, the major reason was to grant access to justice for small claims. Without the pooling of claims which in the aggregation make a contingency arrangement attractive for lawyers, victims would not have a chance to go to court. In order to make the action profitable, it requires a large sum to be in dispute which explains why the US system relies on the opt-out mechanism in order to include as many claims as possible. If we leave aside the problem of very small claims which is closely related to the opt-in or opt-out alternative, a European concept of group actions should be implemented primarily for reasons of procedural economy.

The traditional European two-party system of civil procedure is not able to cope with mass litigation. Several cases in recent years proved that lawsuits with hundreds of plaintiffs or even more do paralyse whole courts for years. Using judicial resources efficiently by avoiding time-consuming parallel proceedings is not only in the interest of the individual plaintiff but is of public interest. Closely related to this is the question whether group actions can bring more justice to the victims than individual litigation. This may be doubted from the point of view of the individual interest. In a group action, each group member will have less influence on the litigation and probably some particularities of his/her case will not be attended to as much as in an individual lawsuit. However, the due process right includes a time factor as well. If the number of claimants is too large, they cannot prevail on the basis of individual actions as courts will not be able to deal with all the cases in due time. Plaintiffs cannot develop a joint strategy and defendants tend to play out and take tactical advantages from the series of scattered individual lawsuits. They will be very reluctant to settle the individual case as this might be a precedent to others and there is no chance for them to settle all claims at one time. Thus, it cannot be doubted that the bundling of claims into a group action attracts more attention on the part of the defendant than any individual claim and enhances the chance for an overall settlement.

This is exactly the point where it takes a careful balancing of interests: group actions should certainly exert some pressure on the defendant to offer a fair settlement for all plaintiffs once liability cannot be denied seriously, but they should not have any blackmailing effect if the defendant's liability is doubtful. From the US experience we can also learn that a settlement of the case is not always a success in itself.[29] The more the plaintiff's lawyers have an economic interest of their own in the outcome of the case, the more courts have to scrutinise a proposed settlement before confirming it. In the US, the failure of courts to do so in many cases[30] and the difficulty to fully take account of the group members' interests led to a 2003 legal reform offering group members the chance for a second opt-out if they do not agree with the proposed settlement (Rule 23 [e] [3]). The 2005 Class Actions Fairness Act additionally implemented several amendments to prevent misuse class action settlements.[31] We will have to discuss this issue for European group actions as well.

B. *Access to Court and Market Regulatory Function of Group Actions*

Even where the amount of individual damage exceeds the threshold of small damage, group actions can improve access to justice. Enforcement of individual interests and rights is a matter of time, costs and risk. Taking of evidence such as expert opinions is expensive in many cases and involves a high risk for the individual plaintiff if he loses the case. Sharing the risk with a group of claimants will offer the chance to go to court even though the outcome of the lawsuit depends on controversial facts or difficult points of law and cannot be predicted easily.[32] The market regulatory function of group actions has been mentioned already. The mere availability of an effective procedural device to enforce claims will act as a "stick behind the door" and will provide an incentive for businesses to change marketing strategies and stand to the rules.

---

29 In the US, mass tort class actions (in particular with respect to defective products and pharmaceuticals) appear to have changed from a sword of the plaintiffs to a shield for defendants, Coffee, 95 *Columbia L. Rev.* 1343, 1350 et seq. (1995). This is due to the fact that a class may include class members who have not yet experienced illness or disease, but rather share a statistically enhanced risk of future illness or injury. There interests tend to be neglected in class action settlements and defendants have an obvious incentive to "buy" a cheap settlement of the case at a very early stage of the litigation. Later on it may turn out that the established fund is far too small to compensate all victims. According to Coffee, p. 1350 "unsuspecting future claimants suffer the extinction of their claims even before they learn of their injury".

30 Coffee, 95 *Columbia L. Rev.* 1343, 1366 et seq., 1376 et seq. (1995); cf. Beuchler, in: Micklitz/Stadler, *Das Verbandsklagrecht in der Informations- und Dienstleistungsgesellschaft*, 2005, p. 1077 et seq.

31 For details cf. Rubenstein, *Understanding the Class Action Fairness Act* 2005, p. 10–15, available on the internet: www.classactionprofessor.com/cafa-analysis.pdf.

32 There are only few procedural regulations which allow the use of evidence such as expert opinions again which have been heard in a previous or parallel lawsuit. Cf. the new Sec. 411a of the German Code of Civil Procedure which gives the court the option to use an expert opinion which has been obtained in another case if it refers to the same facts which have to be decided upon in a case pending. However, if one of the parties objects to the use of such an expert opinion good cause must be shown to refrain from getting a new opinion or one from a different (court-appointed) expert.

4.2. CONSTITUTIONAL RIGHTS OF GROUP MEMBERS: OPT-IN OR OPT-OUT?

Group actions have the advantage of being based on a clear model of representation: one plaintiff (so-called lead or group plaintiff) represents the whole class of persons suffering from the same alleged unlawful act by the defendant. The court has to deal with two parties only and, the decision is nevertheless binding for all class members. As this representation takes the approval of the group members, the debates on European group actions concentrate more or less on the same critical issues. The most import questions are 1) how to justify the representation of a whole class of victims by one claimant, and 2) how to select the appropriate lead plaintiff. Whereas the US class action (Rule 23 [b] [3] Federal Rules of Civil Procedure) relies on an opt-out mechanism, most European jurisdictions reject the opt-out principle due to constitutional reasons. The passivity of group members who do not opt-out is taken as their approval of being represented by the lead plaintiff. However, for those group members who despite considerable efforts did not receive any information about the group action – and no notice system is perfect – this is not even a tacit or implied consent because they are completely unconcerned about any reaction. This may violate the class members' constitutional right to be heard, as well as their right to decide for themselves whether to sue the defendant or not.[33] This position is strongly supported in German doctrine and it was the main reason why the 2003 group action legislation in Sweden switched from an opt-out to an opt-in model at the last minute.[34] Almost all drafts and proposals for group actions in Europe rely on an opt-in mechanism which requires an explicit consent of each group member to participate in the proceedings.[35] In the UK, the *Woolf* report discussed both options pointing out however, that opt-in proceedings are more in line with the traditional English system. The report recommended leaving it to the discretion of the court to choose

33 Haß, *Die Gruppenklage*, 1996, p. 326 et seq.; Lüke, *Die Beteiligung Dritter im Zivilprozess*, 1993, 94 et seq.; Koch, *Alternativen zum Zivilprozess, KritV*, 1989, p. 323, 337; Stadler, in: Brönneke (ed.), *Kollektiver Rechtsschutz im Zivilprozessrecht*, 2001, p. 1 et seq. with further reference. In the Austrian reform discussion, Kodek (in: Gabriel/Pirker-Hörmann, *Massenverfahren – Reformbedarf für die ZPO*, Wien 2005, p. 311 et seq., 394–396) argued in favour of an opt-out system referring to the case law of the European Court of Human Rights, which held that a mandatory representation of a group of persons may be acceptable, if those persons in turn benefit from the collective enforcement, ECHR, 8 July 1986 (*Lithow v. United Kingdom*), *EuGRZ* 1988, 361, 365.

34 The draft bills prepared by Lindblom and Nordh (March 2000) suggested an opt-out principle; cf. Lindblom, Group actions and the role of the courts – a European perspective, *Forum Internationale*, No. 23, p. 16; Nordh, 11 *Duke J. of Comparative and International Law*, 381, 399 et seq. (2001).

35 Cf. the drafts and enacted legislation in Austria (§624 ZPO-E), France (Art L. 422–4 proposition Luc Chatel); Sweden (Sec. 14 Group Proceedings Act), Denmark (§254e subsec. 6 Civil Procedure Code), Finland (§6 Class Action Act 444/2007); Norway (Sec. 35–6 Dispute Act).

the appropriate mechanism depending on the individual case.[36] Part 19.11 of the 1999 Civil Procedure Rules, however, did not seize that suggestion and decided in favour of an opt-in procedure for Group Litigation Orders requiring registration of the group members.[37] The *Woolf* concept has been resumed since by legislators in Denmark and Norway.[38] According to their recently enacted rules, the court may allow an exception from the opt-in principle in the case of small individual damage.

If the representation of the group members is based on their explicit consent to accept the out-come of the group action, legislators may refrain from granting them any right to actively participate in the proceedings. Of course they should have the right to obtain information. This can be provided quite easily via electronically operated registers on the internet. In addition to that, the court will have the obligation to see that the group plaintiff adequately represents the interests of the group members in conducting the case. Opt-in proceedings have as well the clear advantage that the group members can be identified easily at any stage of the litigation. The US opt-out system calls for a detailed description of the class, but in many cases the class can be characterised only by very broad and general terms. This entails difficulties once a judgment against the defendant or a settlement has been obtained and it must be decided who should be entitled to benefit from it.

4.3. SELECTION OF THE APPROPRIATE GROUP PLAINTIFF

Group members will only opt-in, if they have the feeling that they can rely on the group plaintiff and his attorneys to conduct the case effectively.[39] The more group members that participate in the lawsuit, the better the group action can achieve its objective to attain an overall solution of the case.

---

36 Lord Woolf, *Access to justice, Final Report to the Lord Chancellor on the civil justice system in England and Wales*, 1996, Chapter 17 para 43–46.

37 For details on the GLO and its difference from class actions, cf. Mulheron, Some Difficulties with Group Litigation Orders – and Why a Class Action is Superior, 24 *Civil Justice Quarterly*, 50–68 (2005) and Justice Enhanced: Framing an Opt-out Class Action for England, 70 *Modern Law Review* 550–580 (2007).

38 Sec. 35–7 Norway Dispute Act; §254e (8) Danish Code of Civil Procedure.

39 Until now, there is little experience why claimants do opt into collective actions. The comprehensive study of Mulheron (footnote 23) covers only Group Litigation Orders in England and Wales, which have a somewhat different concept than class actions or group actions. Critics point out, for example, that the approach of the Group Litigation Order, which requires that claimants must commence their proceedings as if they were unitary claimants, might create a very high threshold for participation, cf. Mulheron, p. 29, for other reasons for not opting-in cf. p. 32 et seq.

A. *Group Plaintiff Assigned by the Group Members*

The best solution to find the appropriate group plaintiff would undoubtedly be an appointment by the group members themselves. Despite the high legitimacy the group plaintiff derives from such a democratic process, it requires a high degree of organisation. The group plaintiff can be chosen by the group either before the group action is filed or in a formal court organised meeting of the group members during the first stage of the litigation. The first option – a self-organisation of the group – can be realised only with a limited number of victims which are easily to be identified and, with somebody who takes the initiative to build up an organisational structure. Representative actions organised by consumer associations such as the Austrian VKI in recent years are good examples of this mechanism, even though these lawsuits were not group actions, but actions filed by the VKI based on a transfer of consumer claims. In Germany, such efforts have failed for many years due to the strict legal rules granting lawyers a monopoly for the representation of parties. *Ad hoc* associations founded by victims of mass accidents or defective products as well as in securities cases were denied the right to represent the victims in court.[40] These restrictions have been gradually eased and consumer organisations are now allowed to sue a defendant based on the assignment of consumer claims which have been transferred to them for the purpose of enforcement. In a famous "cement cartel" case, German courts accepted on a preliminary basis that a private corporation in Belgium acts on behalf of those who have transferred their alleged claims for damages against the participants of the cartel to the corporation.[41]

If the group members are able to organise their representation in court before the group action is filed, their decision should be accepted as a start. Claimants who consider an opt-in to such a group action may decide for themselves whether they accept the group plaintiff or not. Nevertheless, even though the group representative has been chosen by the group, the judge should be given the right and the obligation to monitor the appropriate handling of the case by the representative including the right to substitute him if necessary.

However, self-organisation of the group should not be taken for granted and cannot be the general concept of group actions. From insolvency proceedings we

40 OLG Düsseldorf ZIP 1991, 932; BGH ZIP 1993, 1708; LG Hannover, Urt. v. 10 July 1991, 6 O 371/90; Haß, *Die Gruppenklage*, 1996, p. 106 et seq.

41 LG Düsseldorf BB 2007, 847. OLG Düsseldorf WuW/E DE-R2311. Both courts, however, decided only on the admissibility of the damage action. They left it to the decision on the merits whether the assignment of claims to CDC violates the law. The Belgian corporation "Cartel Damage Claim" (CDC) sued leading German producers of cement for 114 Mio. Euros damages in a follow-on action to a 2003 decision of the German Cartel Office imposing a 661 Million Euro fine on the participants of the cartel. Meanwhile CDC is very active in enforcing claims for damages in antitrust cases all over Europe. For private enforcement of claims by a private partnership cf. Koch, *NJW* 2006, 1469.

are all familiar with the institution of creditors' meetings organised by the court or the insolvency administrator. This can also be taken into consideration for group actions.[42] Once a group action has been filed and the period for opt-in declarations has expired, the group members may come together and elect one of them or even a third party to act as a group plaintiff. However, such proceedings require considerable administrative efforts. At least with a very large group, probably scattered to several Member States, such meetings are too expensive and too complex to organise as long as video conference techniques have not become a standard procedure for courts. Apart from practical obstacles, this concept implicates a number of legal questions: what kind of majority is necessary to elect the lead plaintiff (absolute/simple; majority in numbers or weighted by the amount of the alleged claim?).[43] Does the right to elect the representative imply the right to withdraw his mandate during the litigation if the group members are not satisfied with his way of conducting the case? Should those creditors who did not succeed in voting through "their" candidate have another chance to opt-out of the lawsuit? Once established as part of the group action, regular meetings might be held more or less on a regular basis or on demand to supervise the group plaintiff and to let group members participate in important decisions like a proposed settlement of the case. The list can be continued almost *ad infinitum*. Nevertheless, it should be self-evident that giving the group members too much of a say undermines the principle of representation and will probably result in a number of controversies which call for a court decision in the end anyway. Thus, the advantage of a democratically legitimated lead plaintiff must be balanced against the loss of efficiency of the proceedings. Therefore, meetings of the group should be taken into account only for the election of a representative and even then, for very large groups this does not seem appropriate. This leaves two options: the group plaintiff may be appointed by the court or may be identified on a "first come, first serve" basis.

B. *"First Come, First Serve" Principle or Appointment of the Group Plaintiff by the Court*

Originally the US class action system applied the "first come, first serve" principle in order to identify the class representative. The member of the class who first filed an action automatically became the class representative. This turned out to be inadequate as the predominant role of lawyers and their own financial interest in a group action often lead to a "race to the courtroom" among law firms. Since a 2003 amendment of Rule 23 (g) Federal Rules of Civil Procedure the class counsel is appointed by the court. With respect to securities class actions the Private

---

42 For such proposal cf. already Stadler, *62. Deutscher Juristentag*, Bremen 1998, I-35, I-50.

43 For an example cf. § 627 of the Austrian group action draft bill.

Securities Litigation Reform of 1995 introduced the court appointed lead plaintiff (Sec. 27 [a] [3] [B] Securities Act). In Europe, the situation seems to be different from the US. Law firms do not pre-finance the lawsuit and there is little incentive for a "race to the courtroom". On the contrary, the reputation of a law firm will be seriously damaged and they will face professional liability if they file a not well prepared complaint which is going to be dismissed by the court.

Current concepts in Europe to identify a group representative differ considerably. In England, the group litigation order (GLO) may include a court order appointing the solicitor of one or more parties to be the lead solicitor (Part 19.13 [c] CPR). The Practice Direction however recommends that claimants' solicitors choose one of them to act as a lead solicitor.[44] Under the German "KapMuG", the representative plaintiff for the test case procedure is chosen by the court.[45] The Swedish legislator decided in favour of the "first come, first serve-principle". A group action will be admitted only if the plaintiff has the financial capacity to bring a group action and is appropriate to represent the members of the group.[46] If it turns out during the litigation that the plaintiff is no longer considered appropriate to represent the members of the group in the case, the court may substitute him.[47] In Norway and Denmark the class representative is appointed by the court at the outset of the litigation.[48] In the case of an opt-out group action,[49] Danish law permits only the Danish Ombudsman to be appointed as a group representative.[50] The Austrian draft bill for a group action submitted to Parliament in 2006, leaves it to the group to appoint a representative who must be named in the complaint, otherwise the person commencing the litigation represents the whole group.[51]

Until now, there is only very limited practical experience with these different approaches. If the responsibility for appointing the group representative is completely placed on the court, the legislator must provide guidelines for the selection. They will be rather abstract and cannot be related in any way to the conduct of the plaintiff or his counsel in the particular case. In Germany, the

44 Practice Direction – Group Litigation Order, 2.2.

45 § 8 II KapMuG.

46 Sec. 8 no. 5 Group Proceedings Act.

47 Sec. 21 Group Proceedings Act.

48 Sec. 35–9 (2) Norway Dispute Act; §254c Danish Code of Civil Procedure. In his national report Werlauff, p.4 (www.law.stanford.edu/display/images/dynamic/events_media/Demark_Legislation.pdf) points out, that the court can subsequently appoint a new class representative if at least half of the class members who opted in so request.

49 Sec. 254e (8), opt-out group proceedings apply only for claims below 2000 DK (approx. 270 Euros).

50 According to Sec. 254c subsec. 2 in opt-out proceedings only a public authority who is authorised to so by law may be appointed as group representative. For the time being this is only the Consumer Ombudsman.

51 § 626 of the Draft bill. There is no provision giving the court the right to substitute the representative of the group.

experience with the courts' discretion to appoint insolvency administrators shows that courts tend to resort to the same persons again and again and that it is extremely difficult to establish fair competition for those appointments.

In terms of procedural efficiency the "first come, first serve" principle combined with the court's continuous control whether the group plaintiff adequately represents the group members and acts in their best interest seems to be the best solution. As an *ultima ratio* the court must have the right to substitute the group plaintiff and his counsel. The opt-in mechanism will have an additional regulatory function in this respect: claimants will only decide to participate in a group action instead of bringing an individual action if they have the feeling that they can rely on the group plaintiff or more precisely on his counsel. Therefore, it will be inevitable and necessary that some law firms specialise in group actions and can come up with a special experience in this field. In the US and in England, it is already self-evident that requirements as to the suitability of the group plaintiff focus on the plaintiff's counsel rather the plaintiff himself. His abilities are critically important to the successful handling of a group action. In some European systems an increased awareness of that fact remains to be developed.[52]

4.4. OBJECTIVE AND BASIC PROCEDURAL STRUCTURE OF GROUP ACTIONS

Group actions must be designed to allow the enforcement of claims for damages or any other performance on the part of the defendant. Notwithstanding this overall objective, it is clear that only very few cases of mass damages can be resolved through full judicial trial and decision in a group action. Particularly in tort cases the claims pooled in the group action are uniform claims only insofar as they are based on the same accident or tortious act by the defendant. Questions of causation, contributory negligence or damages, however, must be adjudicated upon on an individual basis. It has been mentioned already that in the US this caused a debate on whether a class action is superior to individual lawsuits in these cases. A European concept should be more liberal and permit group actions whenever the claims give rise to common, or related issues of fact or law of the defendant's liability. Courts should be given broad discretion to admit group actions whenever they offer a better chance for the victims to enforce their claims in due time or to obtain a settlement with the defendant. Even though the victims

52 Take for example § 8 II of the German KapMuG. This section offers the court some guidelines on how to select the representative plaintiff for the test case proceedings. The selection should take into consideration the amount of the plaintiff's claim and an understanding of the plaintiffs to choose one of them as a representative. The qualification of the representative's counsel is not even mentioned in this section, cf. Vorwerk/Wolff/Lange, *KapMuG*, Kommentar 2007, § 8 Annot. 20.

should get fair compensation for their damage, lump sum compensation and a quick payment by the defendant is sometimes much better than any lengthy proceedings in order to exactly define the amount of individual damages. This is particularly true in mass events that threaten the economic survival of the defendant. The longer it takes for the individual to obtain a final judgment, the greater the risk that the defendant has become insolvent in between.

In fact, it may be appropriate and the most efficient way to handle a case, if the court decides only on the controversial legal and/or factual issues which are common to all claims by way of a declaratory judgment or assesses only the defendant's liability on the merits.[53] The whole case might be settled then on the basis of the legally binding declaratory judgment. For this purpose the group of claimants might be divided into sub-groups. This stage of the proceedings requires a close cooperation of the judge and the parties' counsel. Nevertheless, the court should have the authority to select those issues which will be subject to an intermediary declaratory court decision.[54]

If negotiations with the defendant following a declaratory court decision fail, the court will proceed with the individual claims or can split up the group action into individual lawsuits if appropriate. It is assumed that the vast majority of group actions, at least those with large groups, will not proceed to an individual adjudication of claims. This is not only the experience in the US,[55] but as well with mass events in Europe, depending however on the pressure emanating from existing mechanisms of collective compensation in societies. Group actions seem to be an appropriate device to get controversial issues concerning the defendant's liability out of the way before entering into negotiations.

4.5. CASE MANAGEMENT AND PARTICIPATION OF GROUP MEMBERS

If we take a look at existing group action regulations it comes as a surprise that most of them do not provide detailed rules for case management by the court, even though there seems to be widespread consensus that group actions require a more active and managing judge than other lawsuits. The English Civil Procedure Rules are the only ones explicitly emphasising the managing role of the judge and give him wide discretion to handle a case.[56] If the scope of application of group actions is wide-ranging, this is in fact essential as the courts will face very different

53 This is the concept of the Austrian group action, cf. § 630 of the draft bill.

54 See for example § 625 of the Austrian group action draft bill.

55 In particular securities class actions almost never get to trial, Coffee, 95 *Columbia L. Rev.* 1343, 1369 (1995).

56 CRP Part 19.11 (2) (c), 19.13; Practice Directions – Group Litigation Order 9.1, 12.1–12.4.

situations and cases. Group action rules in Sweden and in the Austrian draft bill mention explicitly only some of the court's rights. They can, however, rely on a long procedural tradition of active judges whereas the English system in this respect still passes through a paradigm shift released by the 1999 Civil Procedure Rules. All in all, legislators should be aware that complex proceedings such as group actions ask for giving leeway to judges to manage the case. This requires considerable confidence in the ability of judges who must on their part be given the chance to gather experience with complex litigation. Jurisdiction for group actions should, therefore, be restricted to a few courts in order to allow them to build up special competences.

At any rate it should be set forth clearly that the court is responsible for seeing that the group plaintiff adequately represents the interests of the group members and has the right to substitute the group plaintiff. Both, any abandonment of action by the group plaintiff and the settlement of the case must be given the court's approval or confirmation. With respect to these key issues of the litigation a participation of the group members can be discussed again. The principle of representation based on an opt-in declaration can be applied in a rather strict sense in order to guarantee rather speedy proceedings. Therefore, as a rule, group members should not interfere with the conduct of the case. It must be admitted, however, that in some situations it might be very difficult for the court to decide whether a proposed settlement is in the interest of the group. In order to provide more information and an additional control mechanism, group members may be permitted to comment on a proposed settlement of the case. Following the reform of US class action, they may instead be given a second chance to opt-out of the lawsuit if they don't want to accept the settlement and prefer to enforce their claim on an individual basis instead. Thus, the parties, in particular the defendant who wants to settle the whole case, have a strong interest to find a fair settlement to avoid opt-outs at the last minute.[57]

As group action cases may vary considerably in terms of the size of the group, the uniformity of claims and the extent of individual damage, the best solution might be to leave it to the discretion of the court to fix the way or degree of participation of the group members regarding a settlement. With a small group, the judge might

57 In the US, some defendants tried to "freeze" the group members into the class action and a proposed settlement by filing a bankruptcy petition. As this automatically stays litigation against the defendant opting-out of the class, this gains a class member little because they cannot start an individual lawsuit against the defendant, for example, cf. Coffee, 95 *Columbia L. Rev.* 1343, 1409 (1995). Such a strategy should be taken into account by the court when the parties apply for a confirmation of the settlement. If the defendant is in fact insolvent, there is of course little the court can do for the group members. However, European bankruptcy laws do not encourage precautionary bankruptcy petitions as much as Chapter 11 of the US Bankruptcy Code.

invite them to comment on the proposed settlement. If the group includes several hundred claimants, he will probably not be able to take a large number of statements into consideration and prefer to permit a "second opt-out".

5. GROUP ACTIONS AND SMALL DAMAGE CASES

Although details of group action proceedings cannot be fully discussed in this paper, there is one key issue with respect to the scope of application that we should come back to. It is the question whether group actions are a suitable procedural tool to enforce small claims. This refers not only to the scope of application of group actions but has an important influence on the above-mentioned role of the group plaintiff, the judge and even the objective of the litigation. Pooling large claims into a group action helps to enforce individual, but plural rights. A public or common interest comes into play only with respect to a preferably efficient use of scarce judicial resources. Compensation of individual damage is the overriding objective of this type of action and, therefore, group members are assumed to weigh the pros and cons of a group action against individual litigation, to take interest in the conduct and in the outcome of the case.

If, however, a large number of consumers have suffered only small damage due to an unlawful act, taking action against the defendant is of a supra-individual or common interest and fulfils primarily a market regulatory function. Traditionally those interests are represented by associations or public bodies such as a consumer ombudsman. So, if small damage cases are to be integrated into group actions, these institutions should be given standing to sue at any rate. This has consistently been done by legislators in the Nordic states. As the group of consumers can be assumed to stay passive, an opt-out mechanism must be chosen to cover as many claims as possible. Constitutional concern against the opt-out principle does not weigh too heavily for very small claims as individual lawsuits are no real alternative for consumers and the common interest to react to the unlawful act of the defendant may prevail over the individual's right to decide for him or herself whether to sue the wrongdoer or not.

Nevertheless, I still have doubts whether group actions are the appropriate means to cope with small damage cases. Group actions aim at a compensation of the group members. If the amount of the individual damage is below a certain threshold – which still has to be defined – it is simply not manageable and not efficient to hand out the small amounts to each consumer. In the US, small claim class actions normally result in the establishment of a fund in favour of the victims. But only very few of them will come forward to claim compensation and if they do so, the group plaintiff, his counsel or the court – whoever is responsible for the distribution – may face considerable difficulties to decide who is entitled to benefit from the fund.

In order to cope with the problem of distribution and the question of what to do with the residuum of a fund, courts in the US have created several options under the *cy près*-doctrine. The remains of the fund may be used to indirectly compensate consumer interests by financing or taking measures that come as close as possible to direct compensation. A famous example is the Yellow Cab case[58] where a taxi company was ordered to pay compensation for the illegal manipulations of their taxi meters by offering lower taxi prices for a fixed period of time. Only by mere accident would a consumer who had become the victim of the previous overpriced rates benefit from such a measure.[59] In fact, the main purpose of the idea was to take away the ill-gotten gains from the defendant as a deterrence and punishment. This becomes even more evident if the residuum will be forfeited to the state for a general benefit (general escheat) or on the condition of it being used for a special purpose closely related to the cause of action (earmarked escheat).

It is of course highly respectable to make at least an effort to compensate consumers for the small damage they suffered. From an economic point of view, however, it is not efficient to conduct a rather complex group action only to find out in the end that it is either not possible to identify the vast majority of the group members or they are not interested in receiving a few cents or euros. Balance must be struck between idealism and pragmatism. The legal objective of deterrence can be achieved as well by simply skimming-off the ill-gotten gains from the defendant. Standing to sue can be granted to associations or public bodies representing general consumer interests, depending on the tradition of each Member State. As the procedure does not aim at the compensation of individual consumers from the outset, it takes less precaution to safeguard the interests of "group members". In order to work as a deterrent, skimming-off procedures must, as a matter of course, be effective and the representatives with standing to sue must have the financial strength to bear the procedural risk involved in such proceedings. Practical experience with the already existing skimming-off procedures in Germany will allow conclusions to be drawn as to how to optimise these actions in the near future.

If different procedural devices apply for large claims and small claims it becomes necessary to define the threshold between them. In Denmark, where the new group action law leaves it to the court to decide whether an opt-out mechanism

---

58 *Daar v. Yellow Cab Co.*, 33 P.ed. 732, 745 (Cal. 1967).

59 *In re Matzo Food Prod.* Litigation, 156 *F.R.D.* 600 (D.N.J. 1994), the defendant convicted under the Sherman Act of fixing prices of groceries, agreed to create a "Food Products Fund" to be distributed to specific charities for a period of 4 years in order to settle a class action brought by grocery stores and retail sellers.

should apply due to the small individual damages involved in the case, there seems to be a consensus that small damages are those beyond 2,000 DK (approx. 270 Euros). A 2003 survey of the Eurobarometer[60] revealed that 18% of the consumers will not take legal action if the amount at stake is below 500 Euros and the same percentage will refrain from legal action for any amount below 1,000 Euros, which seems surprisingly high.[61] However, almost 40% of the consumers said that they would more likely go to court if they had the chance to ally themselves with other consumers. Any amount to be legally fixed for an opt-in group action might be attacked as being arbitrary. However, one should not be too pessimistic to overcome the passivity of consumers. One way out of the dilemma to render an abstract definition of small claims might be to start a group action on the opt-in basis either on the initiative of a consumer organisation, a public authority, an ombudsman or an individual consumer. If the fixed period for opt-in declarations has expired without a considerable number of consumers exercising this option, the court may offer the ombudsman, public authority or consumer organisation the option to proceed with a skimming-off action instead of a group action.

6. CONCLUSION

Group actions are necessary in Europe to disburden the judiciary from mass litigation and to give consumers a better chance to enforce their claims by way of a joint strategy or to obtain at least a settlement with the defendant once his liability is no longer disputable.[62] Group actions will be embedded in a different procedural framework than in the US and, therefore, they will not develop a similar potential for misuse. A European type of group action should be based on an opt-in mechanism and a rather strictly realised principle of representation. The group representative is responsible for the conduct of the case, even though

60 Eurobarometer 60.0 (Access to Justice), European Opinion Research Group, October 2004.

61 The survey referred to domestic cases only. 16% of the consumers indicated that they would not take any legal action against the supplier of a defective product or service, irrespective of the amount involved. Probably the percentage of consumers who are reluctant to go to court will be higher in cross-border cases.

62 I have always taken the position, that the legislator should offer claimants the choice between group actions and test cases (without a legally binding effect of the judgment due to the reasons mentioned in the text sub III 3). In some cases it might be more appropriate under a cost-benefit analysis to have the simpler form of test case litigation instead of a group action (in the same sense, Mulheron, footnote 23, p. 27). Group actions as a "stick behind the door" might encourage defendants to enter into a test case agreement with the claimants and concede to settle the case on the basis of the test case judgment. For details of this approach cf. Micklitz/Stadler, footnote 30, p. 1281 et seq.; Micklitz/Stadler, 17 *European Business L. Rev.* 1473, 1498 (2006); Stadler, in: Meller-Hannich (Hrsg.), *Kollektiver Rechtsschutz im Zivilprozess*, Tagungsband Symposium Halle 2007 (in print).

supervised to some extent by the court. Judges must be given wide discretion to manage the case. In small damages cases, compensation of a large number of consumers is not manageable. Nevertheless, there is a strong supra-individual interest to deter business from engaging in unlawful, but rather profitable marketing strategies. Skimming-off procedures seem to be more appropriate and more effective to achieve that objective than opt-out group actions. Due to the difficulty to define the amount of individual damage below which consumers tend to stay passive, legislators should allow a flexible cross-over from opt-in class action for the recovery of individual damages to skimming-off actions.

COLLECTIVE CONSUMER REDRESS REFORM – WILL IT BE A PAPER TIGER?

Geraint HOWELLS
Manchester Law School

1. INTRODUCTION

Class actions are on the political agenda both in the United Kingdom and at the European level like never before. It is important that those who favour class actions in the consumer context are clear about their objectives in the current debate and argue cogently for a class action procedure that delivers what they desire. To be frank, my concern is that an opt-out class action will be adopted, but it will be ineffective because it will focus on the need for consumer organisations to be the engine powering the system without providing them with sufficient incentives and even more importantly the rationale will be premised on the comforting basis that the objective will be to return to individual consumers' damage they have suffered as the result of a wrongdoing. It will be argued that for small losses it is unrealistic for consumers to opt-in to even very simple procedures and that the true motive should be to skim off the profits both as a deterrent and to ensure there is no unfair competition.

The next section discusses the various forms of class action currently known in legal systems and notes that they are different beasts often addressing different concerns. The current case for an opt-out class action in consumer cases focuses on the problem of small individual losses being inflicted on a mass of consumers. It is suggested that it is better to develop such collective procedures within particular contexts and so a specific regime for consumers is the way forward. The following section notes that there is no such procedure in either United Kingdom or European law. The reform discussions are commented on before some of the key features of any new procedure are discussed: namely its scope, whether it is opt-in or opt-out, who can bring the action and how incentives can be built into the system in order to ensure the actions are actually brought and the procedure does not become merely a paper tiger.

2. CLASS ACTION, GROUP ACTIONS AND REPRESENTATIVE PROCEDURES

The distinction between the different civil procedure rules for dealing with mass claims is too well-known for me to dwell long on the subject. Indeed I will not even attempt to discuss the different labels used or to draw distinctions depending upon whether certification stages are included or not. Instead I will seek to draw some broad functional distinctions.

Foremost is the basic difference between a regime aiming to manage similar claims so that the court does not become overwhelmed and one that seeks to make viable claims that would not be worth bringing as individual claims. The former rationale is well illustrated by the German law passed in direct response to thousands of investors claiming in the Frankfurt court.[1] The English group litigation also fits into this format. Admittedly, the amalgamation of claims may make some claims viable that might not otherwise succeed in reaching the courts as the parties are able to share costs, particularly of expert witnesses. Nevertheless, these are primarily procedures concerned with substantial viable cases that are simply being managed efficiently.

The big political question is whether such procedures should operate on an opt-out or opt-in basis. Where claims are substantial, the arguments are more finely balanced, but in low level consumer claims the only way in which such claims can be viable is if they can be run on an opt-out basis. Whether this is desirable is a question returned to below.

Another key issue is whether a representative can take control of the litigation. In an opt-out regime, of course a representative is needed and the question then becomes who can that be and should it be limited to various formally approved consumer organisations that meet key criteria. The rationale for this is that it ensures that litigation does not become dominated by profit motivated lawyers and financiers. In the United Kingdom context it will be argued that the costs of litigation are such that this is in some ways a false argument as even consumer organisations are going to have to invoke novel funding arrangements to support such litigation.

1 See 2005 German Capital Markets Model Proceedings Act.

3. CURRENT LAW

England and Wales[2] know of two relevant procedures, namely the representative action and the Group Litigation Order.[3] The representative procedure has a long heritage and was first used for determining feudal land rights. In truth it is still best suited to dealing with collective rights in property, be they tenancy agreements or shares. Its utility in the consumer context was always limited because of court decisions holding that it was inappropriate where there were individual damage claims, separate contracts or the possibility of separate defences and causation issues. Following on from the case of *Prudential Assurance v Newman Industries*[4] Jolowicz foresaw a way forward for a uniquely English approach to class actions whereby the representative procedure could determine generic issues with individual actions then being brought to prove individual claims.[5] In recent times two commentators in particular have picked up on some more flexible court interpretations to argue that the representative action has the potential to be used more widely.[6] However, in its current form, the representative procedure is certainly not fit for the purpose and even if some courts might be prepared to be flexible, many consumer claims could still not be brought on that basis and the inherent ambiguity as to the scope of the procedure and how flexible the courts will be is a severe disadvantage. Moreover, if developments in this area are to be based on using ideological claimants like consumer associations then the decision in *Chocosuisse Union des Fabricants Suisse de Chocolat v Cadbury Ltd.*[7] that an association cannot itself be a representative unless it also suffered the harm is unhelpful.

---

2 Scotland knows no such procedures, but there have been proposals for reform: see Scottish Consumer Council, Class Actions in the Scottish Courts: a new way for consumers to obtain redress? (1982) and *A class of their own – why Scotland needs a class actions procedure*, (2003) and Scottish Law Commission, Multi-Party Actions: Report by Working Party (1993) and Multi-Party Actions: Court Proceedings and Funding (1994).

3 See generally N. Andrews, "Multi-party Proceedings in England: Representative and Group Actions" (2001) 11 *Duke J of Comp and Int Law* 249; C. Hodges, *Multi-Party Actions* (Oxford, 2001) and C. Hodges "Global Class Actions Project Country Report: England and Wales" available at www.law.stanford.edu/display/images/dynamic/events_media/England_Legislation.pdf (2007) M. Mildred, 'Group Actions', in G.Howells, *The Law of Product Liability* (Butterworths Lexis-Nexis, 2007).

4 [1980] 2 WLR 339.

5 J. Jolowicz, "Representative Actions and Damages – A Compromise Solution?" (1980) 39 *Cambridge Law Journal* 237.

6 See the excellent works of R. Mulheron, 'From Representative Rule to Class Action: Steps Rather Than Leaps' (2005) 24 *Civil Justice Quarterly* 424–449; J. Seymour, "Representative Proceedings and the Future of Multi-Party Actions" (1999) 62 *MLR* 564–584 and J. Seymour, "Justice and the Representative Parties Rule; An Overriding Interest?" (2005) 25 *Legal Studies* 668.

7 [1998] E.T.M.R. 205.

The representative action might have some potential to be amended to suit the context of mass small consumer claims, but it will be argued a specific regime is to be preferred. In contrast, the Group Litigation Order is not even a contender. It is premised on individual claimants issuing their claims and joining the register. It is an opt-in system and in truth merely offers extra case management tools to the judge.

However, the United Kingdom does have one more procedure of particular interest which is the collective redress procedure in s. 47 B Competition Act 1998.[8] This is a collective redress follow-on action for consumers once an infringement of competition law has been established by the regulatory authorities or the courts. In that sense it is a fairly straightforward action, with the only issue being to determine the extent of any damage caused by the wrongdoing to the claimants.

To bring a collective consumer competition law case the body must meet the following criteria established by the Secretary of State:

> '1. The body is so constituted, managed and controlled as to be expected to act independently, impartially and with complete integrity;
> 2. The body is able to demonstrate that it represents and/or protects the interests of consumers. This may be the interest of consumers generally or specific groups of consumers.
> 3. The body has the capability to take forward a claim on behalf of consumers.
> 4. The fact that a body has a trading arm will not disqualify it from bringing consumer group claims, provided that the trading arm does not control the body, and any profits of the trading body are only used to further the stated objectives of the body.'

Which? The main consumer organisation is the only body so far recognised.[9] To bring an action, consumers need to give their consent. The main principle is recovery of individual damages. As s. 47B(6) Competition Act 1988 states:

> "Any damages or other sum (not being costs or expenses) awarded in respect of a consumer claim included in proceedings under this section must be awarded to the individual concerned; but the Tribunal may, with the consent of the specified body and the individual, order that the sum awarded must be paid to the specified body (acting on behalf of the individual)."

As we shall see it has proven hard to make consumers enthusiastic about signing up to such actions. To sign up and then sign away one's right to damages – as is

8 See O. Dayagi-Epstein, "Representation of Consumer Interest by Consumer Associations – Salvation for the Masses?" (2007) 3 *Competition Law Review* 209.

9 The Specified Body (Consumer Claims) Order 2005, SI. 2005/2365.

required if the consumer organisation is to obtain any financial reward itself – is likely to be even less appealing.

Which? has only brought one action to date and that involved price fixing of football shirts.[10] This has now been settled. In addition to paying Which?'s legal costs, 500 consumers, apparently accounting for a total of 900 replica shirts, joined the group and will be eligible for compensation of £20 per shirt. The defendants, JJB, have put aside a sum of money that should enable anyone able to prove they bought a replica shirt from the sports retailer between the 2000–01 and 2001–02 seasons to claim £10 in compensation from any branch until 2009.[11] At one stage it was widely reported that Which? had only 144 consumers signed up and even if the final total reached 500 this was only a small proportion of the consumers affected. But is this any surprise? With only £20 on offer, how many people would be expected to sign up, especially as proof of purchase was needed many years after the purchase? It is tempting to argue that if potential claimants do not want to sue then why should there be any concern and litigation like this only imposes a further layer or regulatory costs on industry. However, class actions have traditionally had at least both compensatory and deterrent functions with deterrence being a key feature of such non-viable claims.[12] My assessment of both the theory and the practice as evidenced by the *Which?* case is that it is a false argument to use the language of restorative justice to support such procedures if by that it is meant returning damages to specified individuals. There may be occasions when this is practical, where for example a mass supplier has wrongly levied a fee that can be easily calculated and returned. In many cases the consumers cannot be motivated and indeed the costs of providing individual assessment of losses may simply not be cost justified. Either one therefore relies upon a broader concept of restorative justice (where the restoration is to the consumer community) or one sees collective redress as an example of private regulation of markets supplementing traditional public law controls.

Europe has to date no collective redress procedures. It does of course have a collective injunction procedure,[13] which is now implemented in the United Kingdom by the Enterprise Act 2002. It will be argued at the end that adding flexible powers to award compensation to skim off profits to that Directive, which already in addition to the injunctive powers allows for additional remedies such as publishing the judgment or a corrective statement, is perhaps the easiest and least controversial way forward at the European level.

---

10 See notice of claim at www.catribunal.org.uk/documents/Note1078Consumers050307.pdf.

11 See report at www.legalweek.com/Articles/1084376/Clydes+wins+for+Which+in+replica+kit+claim.html.

12 'Developments in the Law – Class Actions' (1975–76) 89 *Harv L Rev* 1319.

13 Directive 98/27/EC of the European Parliament and of the Council of 19 May 1998 on injunctions for the protection of consumers' interests: OJ 1998 L166/51.

4. REFORM

In 2002 the Lord Chancellor's Department (as it was then called) published a report on *Representative Claims: Proposed New Procedures* report which favoured introducing a representative action. The successor Department for Constitutional Affairs concluded that whilst there was general support for representative claims they should be taken forward in specific legislation for particular types of cases where there is evidence to support the introduction of such provisions. There is much to be said for this approach. The collective dimension takes on different forms in different contexts and whilst there may be much common ground there is also a need to gear the regime to the particular context. For instance, the availability and nature of representative bodies will vary from sector to sector.

In *A Fair Deal For All*[14] the Department of Trade and Industry (DTI)[15] committed itself to introducing representative actions for consumers, although it noted only certain organisations may be allowed to bring such actions and the permission of the court may be required. This policy is developed further in *Representative Actions in Consumer Protection Legislation*[16] where it recognises that there is a role for representative actions. It would prefer the representative action to cover all consumer-to-business infringements without the need to list specific rules or separate areas of consumer law. However, it is also conscious of the need to prevent inadvertently promoting a compensation culture. Therefore it proposes claims should only be brought by representative associations (that are of good reputation, have the ability to handle the case and have the well-being of consumers rather than profit at the centre of their ethos). Furthermore such actions should only be brought on behalf of named consumers.

The National Consumer Council and Scottish Consumer Council[17] responded positively to the DTI consultation on representative actions, but were disappointed that consideration had not been given to individually led representative actions. Likewise the Office of Fair Trading (OFT)[18] also supported representative actions but felt that the DTI had proposed too many safeguards. Under its alternative model for instance, claims could be brought by a designated body or if not there would be a permission stage, but it considered having both filters was not necessary. It also considered that it would not address the problem of unidentified

14 (2005).

15 Now known as the Department for Business, Enterprise and Regulatory Reform (BERR).

16 (2006). See also for parallel developments in other sectors the Patent Office, Representative Actions for the Enforcement of Intellectual Property Rights, (2006).

17 Representative actions in consumer protection legislation, (2006).

18 Representative actions in consumer protection legislation – A consultation response by the Office of Fair Trading, (2006).

victims or where individual detriment was too small. The question of representative actions is also being taken up by the Civil Justice Council.[19]

Domestic interest in law reform has been harnessed by European developments. Europe has no collective redress procedures. However, its interest has been awakened in using collective redress in order to make competition law enforcement more effective.[20] In turn this prompted DG SANCO to include consideration of collective redress mechanisms for consumers in its *Consumer Policy Strategy for 2007–2013*.[21] It is currently consulting on the following benchmarks for consumer redress:[22]

1. The mechanism should enable consumers to obtain satisfactory redress in cases which they could not otherwise adequately pursue on an individual basis.
2. It should be possible to finance the actions in a way that allows either the consumers themselves to proceed with a collective action or to be effectively represented by a third party. Plaintiffs' costs for bringing an action should not be disproportionate to the amount in dispute.
3. The costs of proceedings for defendants should not be disproportionate to the amount in dispute. On the one hand, this would ensure that defendants will not be unreasonably burdened. On the other hand, defendants should not for instance artificially and unreasonably increase their legal costs. Consumers would therefore not be deterred from bringing an action in Member States which apply the "loser pays" principle.
4. The compensation to be provided by traders/service providers against whom actions have been successfully brought should be at least equal to the harm caused by the incriminated conduct, but should not be excessive as for instance to amount to punitive damages.
5. One outcome should be the reduction of future harm to all consumers. Therefore a preventive effect for potential future wrongful conduct by traders or service providers concerned is desirable – for instance by skimming off the profit gained from the incriminated conduct.
6. The introduction of unmeritorious claims should be discouraged.
7. Sufficient opportunity for adequate out-of-court settlement should be foreseen.
8. The information networking preparing and managing possible collective redress actions should allow for effective "bundling" of individual actions.
9. The length of proceedings leading to the solution of the problem in question should be reasonable for the parties.

---

19 R. Mulheron, *Reform of Collective Redress in England and Wales – A Perspective on Need*, Research Paper for Civil Justice Council (2008). See also, *Improving Access to Justice through Collective Actions*, Recommendations to the Lord Chancellor of the Civil Justice Council (2008). This important report was published too late to be considered, but is an important contribution to the debate.

20 *Green Paper – Damages actions for breach of the EC antitrust rules* COM(2005) 672 final.

21 COM(2007) 99 final.

22 See http://ec.europa.eu/consumers/redress_cons/collective_redress_en.htm.

10. Collective redress actions should aim at distributing the proceeds in an appropriate manner amongst plaintiffs, their representatives and possibly other related entities.

These benchmarks contain laudable and sensible, if somewhat anodyne, principles. The practical issues come to the fore when one starts to operationalise them and has to determine how best to strike the right balance between competing objectives. For instance, to take one example, Benchmark 10 talks about the crucial issue of distribution of proceeds. It seems implicitly to accept that returning money to the consumer's pocket is not the only answer. But how do you decide how much claimants, representatives and other related entities should obtain and in what circumstances? Can representatives act with a profit motive or is that merely a fall back position if consumers cannot be identified or motivated to sue? These questions will be explored when the contours of a new regime are addressed in the next section.

Before moving on to that topic it is worthwhile commenting on the excitement the EC's involvement in these topics has caused in legal and business circles. The US class action phenomenon casts its long shadow as far as Europe and industry and their advisers are vigilant in trying to ensure they are not exposed to such risks in Europe. Those who fear that this might give rise to more product liability litigation probably have little to fear from the latest initiatives of DG SANCO. DG SANCO is more interested in the problems of misleading advertising and unfair contract terms and their interest is in how to permit recovery for small amounts of harm inflicted widely on many consumers. Indeed taken into account the possible legal base and the general political context, it is hard to see the Commission wanting to engage in reform of national civil procedure law. Interestingly, in the few areas where this has been undertaken in the consumer context it has been limited to cross-border contexts: namely with respect to legal aid[23] and small claims procedures.[24] Nevertheless, enhanced enforcement is a key issue for DG SANCO and one can expect there to be some developments in this area.[25] This fits in with the domestic policy agenda of several Member States. In the next section some of the key policy choices are addressed.

---

23 Council Directive 2003/8/EC of 27 January 2003 to improve access to justice in cross-border disputes by establishing minimum common rules relating to legal aid for such disputes: 2003 *OJ L 26/41*.

24 Regulation (EC) No 861/2007 of the European Parliament and of the Council of 11 July 2007 establishing a European Small Claims Procedure: *OJ 2007 L 199/1*.

25 As this paper went to press, the EU published the *Green Paper on Collective Consumer Redress*, COM (2008) 794 final.

5. KEY FEATURES OF THE NEW REGIME

5.1. SCOPE

There are many areas of law where collective procedures may be desirable. For instance, labour law is another area in which the utility of such a procedure is evident in the United Kingdom at the moment.[26] However, the United Kingdom government's policy is to develop such procedures in specific areas. This also fits in with the EC approach which is linked to initiatives by specific Directorate-Generals. In the consumer context it can be argued that any European initiative should be a development out of the Injunctions Directive. This limits protection to those measures of European law aimed at the protection of the collective interests of consumers and these are listed in the Directive's Annex. Using this route to introduce a European measure seems quite astute as it limits the impact to those areas where Europe has a legitimate interest in ensuring the effective protection of its legislation and where the collective interest is evident. It may help assuage the fears that US-style litigation will take over if the procedure develops out of the existing *acquis*. In national law it might be possible to simply adopt the scope of the European legislation. The government has signalled that it favours it applying to any breach of consumer law. One approach might be to build on existing domestic law. S. 211 of the Enterprise Act 2002 provides a definition of a domestic infringement to complement the scope of the Community infringements regulated by the Injunctions Directive. Although rather inelegant this seems to have a sufficiently broad scope, admittedly limited by the requirement that the infringement harms the collective interest of consumers in the United Kingdom, but otherwise covering most conceivable situations when a representative action would be brought.[27]

An important issue in practice is whether this procedure applies to all consumer claims or only those which are non-viable. The approach of Denmark and Norway to only allow opt-out for non-viable small claims is interesting as it attacks the mischief of the need to provide an incentive to litigate in these classes of cases. The more that is at stake, the more one might expect individuals to be responsible for bringing their own claims and for there to be the presumption that they should control the litigation. There is however a complex debate to be had, if this approach is adopted as to what level the threshold figure should be pitched, combined with the need to ensure that the justice system makes it possible to

---

26 Mulheron (2008), *op cit.*, Ch 18.

27 That section however requires that the Secretary of State has made an order as to which acts or omissions within those categories can be subject to injunction proceedings. Such a pre-requisite would be against the government's preferred approach. It may seem strange that the scope for collective redress is broader than for injunctions, but the broader approach does have much to commend it.

sensibly bring cases above such a threshold. Rather than fix an arbitrary figure it might be better to have a procedure where the court of its own motion or at the request of the defendant or one of the claimants can find an opt-out procedure inappropriate. In any event it is obvious that where mass small claims are being pursued collectively it is not appropriate for such claims to be required to be pursued under small claims procedures. They are in effect important large-scale litigation.

One suspects the real debate will be on opt-out opt-in, who can bring the action and the incentives for litigation.

5.2. OPT-IN OR OPT-OUT

If litigants cannot be bothered to claim for their harm is there any sense in burdening industry with such claims? The football shirts case might be taken as a good example. Consumers may make a rational choice that it is not worth exerting themselves to find the evidence of purchase and register for the sake of £10–20; especially for a loss that they may not have perceived they had suffered (as they freely paid the asking price) and in any event had long written off. The lawyers may well be viewed as the only real winners in such litigation and there is the risk of such claims with low take-ups bringing consumer law into disrepute. This is the criticism levelled at the US legal system where so-called 'coupon settlements' seem in some instances to give little tangible compensation to the victims and act as a settlement trigger for a pay-off for the lawyers who took the initiative to bring the claim.

The reason why the football shirts litigation appears to have been ineffective in leading to large-scale compensation is that the legislation is premised on an individual compensation model. To be blunt, this will never work if one is really interested in using private law as a mechanism for providing justice in these situations. In some cases restorative justice might be possible direct to individuals, for example where a charge has been wrongly applied to account customers and this can simply be repaid. However, in other cases, restorative justice will need to be indirect by some form of cy-près scheme.[28] In some cases this will be necessary because individual losses cannot be calculated because they simply cannot be identified, as in the famous instance of taxi fares in the US where overcharging was remedied by undercharging for a similar period.[29] In other cases the economics of individual calculation may make individual compensation unrealistic.

Whether legal action is justified where individual compensation is not possible depends upon one's view of the purpose of such actions. Such actions are clearly

28 R. Mulheron, *The Modern Cy-pres Doctrine*, (Cavendish 2007).

29 *Daar v Yellow Cab Co*, (1967) 63 CA R 724.

concerned with skimming off profits made by wrongdoing. This could be achieved by a strong regime of administrative penalties. Such an approach has much to commend it, but in practice at various times regulators have shown themselves unable or unwilling to prosecute malpractices and punish to the extent that the wrongdoing was not profitable and regulation imposed an effective deterrent. Indeed some might argue that regulatory sanctions should be a deterrent over and above any claim to skim off profits; for what is the threat in a sanction that merely makes you give back that which you tried to obtain illegally. Well-known problems of increasing demands on stretched enforcement resources and agency capture make some sceptical of the state's ability to control the market so that they at least want the fall-back option of a private remedy. Moreover some are not happy that any penalties flow directly to the state and want the victims to benefit, if not directly then at least through some form of cy-près scheme. However, it does seem that what this model is really concerned with is making sure that wrongdoers do not benefit. The hope is to produce better functioning markets by taking the incentive away from those who think to chance their arm with sharp practices. Without such a collective redress measure some businesses may well conclude that it is worth taking the risk of some regulatory sanction for they may well end up in profit even after the sanction, assuming they are even caught. At least ensuring those caught gain no profit is desirable for efficient healthy markets. Importantly this is vital not only for consumers, but also for competitors who are not then made to feel the need to engage in the same sharp practices in order to stay competitive.

5.3. WHO CAN BRING AN ACTION?

The fear of US litigation runs even to the highest levels in the English legal system. As Lord Steyn stated at the Duke/Geneva conference, "we do not want a litigation-driven society."[30] Mulheron also quotes him as saying "There is also an unarticulated but nevertheless real conviction among judges that we must not allow our social welfare state to become a society bent on litigation."[31] Similar comments are found around Europe and have been expressed from within the Commission. American commentators (and no doubt even within this collection of essays) will debate the plusses and minuses of their system. The horror stories may be exaggerated; US-style class actions may bring real benefits, but to package something up as a US-style class action will kill it politically in the European context. This may not be rational, but it is politics. Europe still likes to believe that

30 Quoted in Andrews, *op. cit.*

31 Mulheron *The Class Action in Common Law Legal Systems* (2004) at 72.

the regulatory approach is the main means of protecting its consumers.[32] This is one reason for favouring the development of a collective redress mechanism that builds on the Injunctions Directive.

When France tried to address the collective redress problem it sought a French approach that differentiated it from the US class action and adopted a representative organisational model.[33] This model is now well-known in Europe thanks to the Injunctions Directive. However, the diversity of enforcement approaches in Europe means that the Directive leaves it to Member States to decide whether the enforcement role is placed in the hands of public bodies or consumer organisations or both. It is likely that consumer organisations will be a vehicle for introducing the collective redress action. The United Kingdom's approach of requiring such representative associations to have the well-being of consumers rather than profit at the centre of their ethos is a good counter to the fear of litigation being hijacked by profit driven lawyers. However, as a European wide policy there needs to be taken into account the reality that there are a wide variety of consumer organisations. Some simply would not have the resources to litigate (especially in the new Member States). Some may be well funded by government as in Germany and have a lot of experience of going to court. Others may litigate but only in specific circumstances where they see this satisfies a strategic need. In the United Kingdom Which? threatened to go to the European Court of Justice to obtain the right to seek injunctions against unfair terms. It has not used that right, partly because the Office of Fair Trading has been active. It took on the football shirts case, but it will be interesting to see how keen it is to take on such cases in the future. Consumer organisations need incentives to bring such actions as we shall discuss below. For now the question is simply whether consumer organisations are best placed to filter such claims.

An alternative to consumer organisations might be public agencies, but it is not really feasible to envisage that public agencies would consistently use limited resources to obtain damages for consumers. It is more likely that they will focus on enforcing existing administrative sanctions. The Nordic ombudsmen are the most likely candidates to bring collective redress actions, but one suspects even they may prefer other means to deliver consumer justice. Under the United Kingdom's Enterprise Act 2002 the OFT has a role in monitoring the use of injunction powers and can even decide who should bring the matter to court. Although ousting the consumer organisation may seem draconian, in practice the consumer organisation is more likely to be grateful that the OFT is willing to

32 This preference for negotiation is one of the themes of C. Hodges, *The Reform of Class and Representative Action in European Legal Systems* (2008).

33 See J. Calais-Auloy, 'Settlement of Disputes by Judicial Means: Situation in France', in *III European Conference on Consumer Access to Justice* (Instituto do Consumidor, 1992) and report by Magnier for Global Class Actions Project available at www.law.stanford.edu/display/images/dynamic/events_media/France_National_Report.pdf.

take on the burden. The position may be different in other states where there is a different relationship between the public agencies and consumer organisations. Certainly unless willing to bring the cases themselves, public agencies should not prevent representative bodies from bringing actions. A useful power that public bodies do often have is to require evidence to be produced and again in the Enterprise Act 2002 this can be used to help other enforcers decide whether to bring actions. This co-operative approach is something that could usefully be encouraged.

The legitimacy of consumer groups is sometimes questioned. How can they claim to speak for the entire consumer population? There is moreover a great difference between the motivations of different types of consumer organisation. A membership-based consumer organisation like Which? survives from selling its magazine and hence needs to be in tune with the aspirations of its largely middle class membership. In contrast the United Kingdom's National Consumer Council has a specific brief to speak up for vulnerable consumers – not that the National Consumer Council (now Consumer Focus) is a likely target to bring collective redress actions. The position is different again where, as in Germany, consumer organisations are funded by the state and have a central role in market regulation. Each consumer organisation is often able to justify its role and if it is only a question of putting matters before the court, little harm can be done. The problem comes when consumers cannot persuade the consumer organisation to take on their case. Consumer organisations may take collective redress actions for a mixture of motives (see below). But equally important is the need to remember that they may also decide not to act. This may be less of a problem in a state where there are a plethora of consumer organisations for consumers to approach, but in the United Kingdom it could be a problem if as is likely Which? is the only recognised consumer organisation. In such circumstances it may be important for *ad hoc* consumer groups to emerge to deal with specific problems, perhaps related to a particular trader. If such groups are to be permitted they have the advantage of being motivated and focused on the matter at hand, but they may also need to be vetted by the courts to ensure their motivations are the promotion of consumer interests (and not a medium for private gain – assuming such a model is not favoured). Such vetting is probably not desirable nor necessary if the organisation itself has been pre-vetted.

5.4. INCENTIVES

Using the consumer organisation as an ideological representative seeks to reassure the business community that the collective redress mechanism will be genuinely aimed at promoting the consumer interest and not become a means for lawyers to seek out profit. Indeed consumer organisations may be useful in fulfilling this task as long as they are vetted so that they truly have the consumer interest and not profit as their raison d'être. However, one must not be naive either about the need to motivate consumers or the likelihood that lawyers will, at least in the United Kingdom context, play a central role.

My work with the Consumer Law Enforcement Forum has demonstrated to me that consumer organisations in many countries are already doing much good work litigating cases on behalf of consumers.[34] The motivations for bringing such actions are doubtless mixed, but may include tackling consumer grievances and highlighting particular concerns as well as more market orientated concerns such as delivering tangible benefits to members and promoting the organisation. However, their resources are limited and if such litigation is to become a systematic feature of their work, greater incentives are needed. It is telling that Which? had originally sought to claim:

> "exemplary or restitutionary damages in the sum of 25 per cent of the relevant turnover of the defendant net of VAT, or such other sum as the Tribunal considers appropriate, to be distributed in accordance with the direction of the Tribunal."[35]

In truth some incentive like this is needed. However, punitive damages sound equally American and are unlikely to be adopted easily within Europe. That is why making use of an opt-out procedure combined with a cy-près doctrine could be the key. Where consumers do not want to come forward or monies cannot economically be returned to the individual consumers, paying it over to a consumer body ensures that the profits are skimmed off the wrongdoer (but he only pays a sum equal to the illegal profit he has made) and consumers and consumer organisations benefit from receiving the money. What incentive is there for consumer organizations to act where monies can be returned to consumers? It must be hoped that in such circumstances consumer organisations may feel the benefits to their members and their mission justifies taking such actions, but equally this explains why formally approved consumer organisations should not have the monopoly of initiating such actions.

Few consumer organizations will have the resources internally to bring such collective consumer redress mechanisms. They will have to outsource them to lawyers. So at the end of the day the consumer representative model cannot avoid the need to ensure lawyers have incentives to become involved. In part this may lead to the need to reform costs rules and funding arrangements. It is unlikely that a scheme of no costs or protective costs will be introduced immediately as the risk of having to pay costs is seen as a major constraint on consumer organisations

---

34 See www.clef-project.eu/cms/project.php.

35 See notice to Competition Appeal Tribunal at www.catribunal.org.uk/documents/Note1078Consumers050307.pdf.

that reduces the threat of them bringing speculative actions. However, unless lawyers are going to take a share of the damages generated they will have to work on contingent fees that allow for success rates. There may also be a need to combine enforcement with collective redress so that, as in the competition field, the redress procedure can follow on a finding that the law has been breached and hence reduce the costs and risk faced by a consumer organisation bringing an action. However, if this route is the way forward one can expect more and more novel means of funding litigation – witness the advent of third party funding in the United Kingdom. These developments raise major ethical issues as funders with no interest other than profit emerge on the scene and major practical questions about where their payment should come from. Where risks are beyond those acceptable to even lawyers working on a contingent fee with a success fee, such external funders may be needed if all but the safest actions are to be litigated but in all likelihood their payment will have to be out of the damages recovered. This prospect is being faced in high risk litigation in the United Kingdom.[36] It seems that rather than denying justice the modern preference is to allow the market to deliver it at a price to the victim. That said, many consumer collective redress claims should be fairly unproblematic, especially if the regulatory authorities have established the fact of a breach of consumer law.

6. CONCLUSION

One can readily appreciate the fears that collective consumer redress may change the character of consumer law and place its development in the hands of lawyers and financiers. To restrain these developments consumer organisations are probably going to be given a major role in policing access to the legal system for such claims. However, one must appreciate the need to incentivise consumer organisations to bring such actions, unless one wants this procedure to remain a novel but unused addition to civil procedure rules. An opt-out regime combined with a cy-près scheme seems an essential feature if such a collective redress scheme is to work. There is nothing worse than consumer laws passed for popular appeal that deliver very little to consumers. The reforming spirit of the moment must be captured so that an effective procedure is adopted. Reformers should not settle for an opt-in regime if they believe small mass consumer claims represent a real problem that the legal system has to address. The new procedure must be more than a paper tiger. In the coming months the task will be to convince legislators that this is a serious concern that needs to be addressed.[37]

36 Civil Justice Council, *Improved Access to Justice – Future Funding of Litigation Costs*, (2007).

37 A good start has been given by Mulheron (2008).

NEGOTIATION AND ADJUDICATION

Class Actions and Arbitration Clauses in Consumer Contracts

Prof. Dr. Dr. H.C. Norbert Reich*

1. A NEW INTEREST IN THE CLASS-ACTION DEVICE IN MEMBER COUNTRIES AND THE EU

In its Consumer Policy Strategy 2007–2013[1] the Commission wrote that it will consider action on "collective redress mechanisms for consumers both for infringements of consumer protection rules and for breaches of EC antitrust rules in line with the 2005 Green paper on private damages actions". To date no concrete proposal has been put forward. But two important and interesting documents are worth mentioning without giving an in-depth analysis. Prior to that, two major studies had been delivered, one for the German Consumer Ministry by *Micklitz* and *Stadler*,[2] the other by *Stuyck* and collaborators[3] for the EC Commission.

On 13/14 February 2008, the European Economic and Social Committee delivered an own-initiative opinion on "Defining the collective actions system and its role in the context of Community consumer law".[4] The opinion discusses a number of issues without making concrete proposals. It clearly rejects the American system of class actions[5] which is said to serve more the interest of lawyers in legal fees rather than consumers in effective legal protection. The

* Emeritus professor, University of Bremen; Visiting professor (extraordinarius), University of Tartu (Estonia) till 30 June 2008.

1 COM (2007) 99 final of 13 March 2007, 11. See now: EC Commission, Green Paper on Consumer Collective Redress of 27 November 2008, COM (2008) 7694 final containing four options, but non discussing problems of arbitration clauses.

2 H.-W. Micklitz/A. Stadler (Endbericht), *Das Verbandsklagerecht in der Informations- und Dienstleistungsgesellschaft*, Münster-Hiltrup 2005 (in the following: Micklitz/Stader).

3 J. Stuyck et al., *An analysis and evaluation of alternative means of consumer redress other than redress through ordinary judicial proceedings*, The Study Centre for Consumer Law, available at http://ec.europa.eu/consumers/redress/reports_studies/comparative_report_en.pdf, 2007 (in the following: Stuyck).

4 CESE 258/2008 of 13/14 April 2008.

5 For an overview see the excellent study by H. Beuchler, *Class Actions und Securities Class Actions in den USA*, Berlin, 2008.

procedural "environment" towards class actions is much more restrictive in EU Member countries than in the US. On the other hand, "class" or rather collective actions (Sammelklagen) must be regarded as an effective means of consumer redress and access to justice. Whether an *opt-in* (all plaintiffs must agree beforehand to join in the action) or *opt-out*-scheme (the lawyer of one plaintiff takes the action on behalf of a "named plaintiff" and the other injured consumers who may later however decide not to join if they do no want to share the risks and costs of the proceedings) is chosen to determine the group of plaintiffs depends on the nature of the claim: small claims can only be effectively enforced under a system of opt-out; larger claims (e.g. those arising out of product liability) will require an opt-in scheme. The EC law instrument can either be a Regulation under its competence for judicial proceedings in civil matters or a directive under Article 153 EC specifically serving the consumer interest. So far the Commission has not yet taken up this initiative.

As a second step in a similar direction, the Commission White Paper on "Damages actions for breach of the EC antitrust rules",[6] accompanied by a more detailed Staff Working paper,[7] puts forward suggestions for alternatively:

- representative actions brought by qualified entities, e.g. consumer associations, state bodies or trade associations, on behalf of identified or, in rather restricted cases, identifiable victims; or
- opt-in collective actions in which victims expressly decide to combine their individual claims for harm they suffered into one single action.

However, the White Paper is not accompanied by a legislative proposal. It does not discuss the legislative basis of EC action in this field.[8]

The aim of this paper is not to discuss the different policy options which are still rather vague and imprecise on the EU level. It seems to be more interesting to pay attention to a phenomenon which has not yet provoked debate in the EU but which has raised much controversy in the US and to a lesser extent in Canada. The problem concerns how far arbitration clauses "negotiated" between business and consumers can not only be set against individual judicial dispute procedures,[9]

6 COM (2008) 165 final of 2 April 2008.

7 SEC (2008) 404 of 2 April 2008.

8 See the different evaluation by Th. Eilmannsberger, The Green Paper on Damages Actions for Breach of the EC Antitrust Rules and Beyond: Reflections on the Utility and Feasibility of Stimulating Private Enforcement Through Legislative Action, *CMLRev* 2007, 431 at 2.4; Reich, Horizontal liability in EC Law – "Hybridisation" of remedies for compensation in case of breaches of EC rights, *CMLRev* 2007, 705 at 742. W.-H. Roth, Rechtssetzungskompetenzen für das Privatrecht in der EU, *EWS* 2008, 401 at 406.

9 See my paper: More clarity after "Claro", *ERCL* 2007, 41.

but also against more recent types of "collective", "group" or "class action" devices. Since class actions as a means of collective redress are well-known yet controversial instruments in the US and, to a lesser extent, Canadian jurisdictions, it is useful to give a view on the practice in these "more advanced jurisdictions" (II, III), before making some tentative suggestions and drawing conclusions referring to the upcoming EU debate (IV/V).

2. US EXPERIENCES

In the words of the Supreme Court in Southland Corp. v. Keating,[10] the Federal Arbitration Act (FAA – 9 U.S.C. Sections 1–16) "declared a national policy favoring arbitration and withdrew the power of the states to require a judicial forum for the resolution of claims which the contracting parties agreed to resolve by arbitration". Therefore, US law usually takes a very liberal view towards mandatory arbitration clauses agreed "in commerce" without making a distinction between commercial and consumer arbitration, including class actions.[11] This was confirmed by a controversial decision of the Supreme Court in Green Tree Fin. Corp.-Ala. v. Randolph[12] in a consumer case, including the defence of statutory rights under state law. Consumers bear the burden to prove that the arbitral forum is financially inaccessible to them. This opinion was challenged by a strong dissent of Justice Ginsburg, in which Justices Stevens, Souter and Breyer (in part) concurred, insisting that "as a repeat player, Green Tree has superior information about the costs to consumers of pursuing arbitration".[13] This rigid approach by the majority of the Supreme Court means that legal redress mechanisms to consumers can easily be avoided by arbitration clauses entered into by standard form contracts with consumers which was later confirmed in Green Tree v. Bazzle.[14] Arbitration could be conducted as "class arbitration" unless the clause forbids it; its interpretation is a matter for the arbitrator.

There have been however some cases from state courts which show a more nuanced approach towards arbitration clauses. Comb v. Paypal Inc.[15] concerned a class action against an electronic disbursement service alleging illegal removal of funds. This was opposed by an arbitration clause inserted in the contracts of

10 465 U.S. 1, 10 = 104 S.Ct. 852, 858 (1984).

11 A critique from a consumer policy point of view has been voiced by L. Weihe, Der Schutz der Verbraucher im Recht der Schiedsgerichtsbarkeit, Frankfurt, 2005 at 116; with regard to "informed consent" see the references at 205–206; see also Beuchler, supra note 5, at 39–40; F. Cafaggi/H.-W. Micklitz, Administrative and Judicial Enforcement of Consumer Law in the US and the EC, *EUI Working papers Law* 2007/22, at 11–12.

12 531 U.S. 79 = 121 S.Ct. 513, 521 (2000).

13 121 S.Ct. at 524.

14 539 U.S. 444 at 453 (2003) (per Justice Breyer).

15 218 F.Supp.2d 1165 (N.D.Cal. 2002).

the supplier. The District Court, Fogel J., held that the arbitration clause, despite its wide use and recognition in the relevant law of California, was both procedurally and substantively unconscionable. Substantive unconscionability was derived from a number of factors, namely a lack of mutuality whereby arbitration is imposed on the weaker party while choice of forum is permitted for the stronger party, prohibition against consolidation of claims, costs of arbitration and venue because the "place or manner" in which arbitration is to occur unreasonably does not take into account "the respective circumstances of the parties".[16]

Cruz v. Pacific Health Systems, INC[17] concerned an action on behalf of the general public for false advertising and deceptive business practices inducing persons to subscribe to health plans. This was opposed by an arbitration clause of the defendant. The California Supreme Court distinguished this case from the above mentioned Supreme Court decisions at least insofar as injunctive relief is concerned, but not with regard to restitution and unjust enrichment. Therefore, claims for unjust enrichment are arbitrable, while injunctions against deceptive advertising are not because they are undertaken "in the public benefit".

With regard to the unconscionability of an arbitration clause against class actions,[18] state courts have been divided in their opinion. The California Supreme Court, in Discover Bank v. Superior Court of Los Angeles,[19] said:

> "We do not hold that all class action waivers are necessarily unconscionable. But when the waiver is found in a consumer contract of adhesion in a setting in which disputes between the contracting parties predictably involve small amounts of damages, and when it is alleged that the party with the superior bargaining power has carried out a scheme to deliberately cheat large numbers of consumers out of individually small sums of money, then, at least to the extent the obligation at issue is governed by California law, the waiver becomes in practice the exemption of the party from 'responsibility for (its) own fraud, or willful injuries to the person or property from another'. Under these circumstances, such waivers are unconscionable under California law and should not be enforced."

The recent Supreme Court decision of 21 February 2006, Buckleye Check Cashing Corp. v. John Cardegna[20] seemed unconcerned by attempts to limit the effects of arbitration clauses in consumer contracts. The litigation concerned a class action suit brought against usurious terms in a consumer credit agreement which

16 See also the unconscionability cases mentioned by R. Alderman, Consumer Arbitration: The Destruction of the Common Law, *The Journal of American Arbitration 2003*, 1 at supra note 40.

17 66 P.3rd 1157 (Cal. 2003).

18 See J. Sternlight, As Mandatory Binding Arbitration Meet the Class Action, Will the Class Action Survive? 42 *Wm. & Mary L. Rev.* 2000.

19 113 P.3d 1100, 110 (2005); similar *Shroyer v New Cingula Wireless Serv.*, 498 F.3d 976 (9th Cir. 2007); a different view has been taken by the Supreme Court of North Dakota in *Strand v U.S. Bank Nat'l Assoc.* 693 N.W.2d 918 (2005).

20 546 U.S. 440 (2006) = 126 S. Ct. 1204.

contained a broad arbitration clause. The Florida Supreme Court[21] set aside the arbitration clause reasoning that to enforce an agreement to arbitrate in a contract challenged as unlawful "could breathe life into a contract that not only violates state law, but is criminal in nature ..."

The Supreme Court, per Justice Scalia, squashed the judgment, distinguishing two cases only where arbitration clauses could be challenged before courts of law, namely:

- the arbitration clause is unlawful as such;
- the entire contract is invalid from which the arbitration clause cannot be severed which was not the case in a usurious credit agreement.

As a consequence, Justice Scalia held:

> "We reaffirm today that, regardless of whether the challenge is brought in a federal or state court, a challenge to the validity of the contract as a whole, and not specifically to the arbitration clause, must go to the arbitrator."

Consumer protection therefore depends on the willingness of arbitrators to apply and enforce consumer protection provisions in particular of state law and eventually to take class action litigation; their awards are not subject to critical public and academic debate. It seems that there is no remedy under US law against an arbitration award disregarding mandatory consumer protection provisions. Arbitration clauses thereby have become a prominent and "popular" instrument to avoid the application of consumer protection provisions at least in contract litigation between business and consumers, in particular against class action suits. Their importance concerns mostly cases of recovery of smaller sums in litigation against telecommunication, health and financial service providers. If a claim is not amenable to arbitration, e.g. for public policy reasons relating to product or environmental liability, actions based on fraud in securities transactions, the pre-trial arbitration clause would not be valid anyhow, or an award could not be enforced.[22] However, the borderlines are not easy to ascertain, especially where both contract and tort law principles apply in parallel.

In public opinion, critique has been voiced against the "excessive use" of mandatory arbitration clauses in consumer contracts.[23] Their disadvantages seem to be greater then the frequently invoked advantages of arbitration, namely:

- no possibility of a rational decision for or against arbitration before the dispute arises;

21 894 So.2nd 860, 862 (2005).

22 A. Loewenfeld, *International Litigation and Arbitration*, 3rd ed. 2005, at 352, 422–424.

23 For details see Weihe note 11 at 43–45; R. Alderman, Consumer Arbitration: The Destruction of the Common Law, *The Journal of American Arbitration* 2002, 1; same, *The Future of*

- the trader can always amend the arbitration clause unilaterally;
- no legal representation, no class actions, limited possibilities for bringing evidence, no legal dispute insurance;
- arbitrators cannot be formally obliged to apply state consumer protection legislation;[24]
- only limited access to documents which are usually in the hands of the trader, no pre-trial discovery procedure;
- no jury; only limited appeal possibilities;
- frequently excessive costs, compared with existing small claims procedures;
- the place of arbitration may be far away from the residence of the consumer.

3. CANADIAN EXPERIENCES

A lively discussion existed in Canada on whether pre-trial arbitration clauses could be enforced in consumer contracts, and whether they could eventually be used to avoid class actions similar to the US discussion. The debate in legal theory was divided.[25]

In a recent decision of 13 July, 2007 the majority of the Justices of the Canadian Supreme Court[26] held arbitration clauses in an electronic consumer contract (concerning the purchase of computers from a US company by a citizen of Quebec) to be enforceable, also against a class action brought by the Quebec "*Union des consommateurs*". The Court was satisfied that the consumer had access to the arbitration clause via a hyperlink on the website of the company and that he had agreed to it by clicking on the link. The Court went on to say:

> "... the clause was no more difficult for the consumer to access than would have been the case had he or she been given a paper copy of the entire contract on which the terms and conditions on the back of the first page"

Consumer Law in the US – Hello Arbitration, Bye-bye Courts, so-long Consumer Protection, University of Houston Public law and Legal Theory Series 2008-A-09; with regard to then existing small claims procedures see N. Reich, *Staatliche Regulierung zwischen Marktversagen und Politikversagen*, 1988, at 129: A critical view (without citing the harsh case law of the US Supreme Court) has also been voiced by G.-P. Callies, *Grenzüberschreitende Verbraucherverträge*, 2006, at 308–314.

24 The AAA Consumer Due Process Protocol contains such an obligation, while the rules of the ABA and the ICC are silent on that point, Callies at 359.

25 Against the use: Sh. McGill, The Conflict between Consumer Class Actions and Contractual Arbitration Clauses, *Canadian Business Law Journal* 2006, 359; J. Hamilton, Pre-Dispute Consumer Arbitration Clauses: Denying Access to Justice? *McGill Law Journal* 2006, 693; in favour of their use according to the US model which is said to strike the "right balance": D. Neave/J. Spencer, Class proceedings: The New Way to Trump Mandatory Arbitration Clauses, *The Advocate* 2005, 495.

26 *Dell Computer Corp. v. Union des consommateurs*, 2007 SCC 34.

Any challenge to the arbitration agreement must be resolved first by the arbitrator who has competence-competence under International Agreements and Canadian law. The fact that the class action is of public interest does not affect the admissibility of the action:

> "it is a procedure and its purpose is not to create a new right".

However, the Canadian case law does not lead to a complete preemption of federal law against consumer protection legislation by provinces like in US consumer arbitration cases. The Supreme Court explicitly held that:

> "(s)ince the facts triggering the application of the arbitration clause occurred before the coming into force of s. 11.1 of the Consumer Protection Act, which prohibits any stipulation that obliges a consumer to refer a dispute to arbitration, that provision does not apply to the facts of this case."

It depends mostly on provincial law how they regulate mandatory arbitration clauses in standard form contracts with consumers. Once they are forbidden and provincial law is applicable under conflict-of-law rules, they prevent the case being taking to mandatory arbitration. If not, then the general law on standard contract terms would apply, including cross-border transactions via the internet, as pointed out in the above mentioned Supreme Court decision. There is an intense policy discussion in Canada about the pros and cons of mandatory arbitration clauses in consumer contracts which cannot be taken up here.[27]

4. APPLICABLE EU AND MEMBER STATE LAW

4.1. CLARO REVISITED: ORDRE PUBLIC ALSO AGAINST AN "ARBITRATION DEFENCE CLAUSE"?

Those Member States that have recently introduced group action devices so far have not seemed to encounter pre-dispute arbitration clauses which would run counter to the very purpose of the legislation. If we follow the information available in the above mentioned reports by *Micklitz/Stadler* and *Stuyck* and without trying to be in any way exhaustive, countries like Sweden,[28] France (action en représentation conjointe),[29] Spain (group action),[30] the UK (multi-

27 See Public Interest Advocacy Centre, *Mandatory Arbitration and Consumer Contracts*, Ottawa 2004.

28 Mom in: Micklitz/Stadler at 562.

29 Beuchler in: Micklitz/Stadler at 133.

30 Mom, in: Micklitz/Stadler at 722 ff.

party actions),[31] Germany (representative actions of consumer associations and model claims for capital market injuries)[32] have introduced new devices allowing groups of persons injured by identical or similar acts stemming from the same business to join together for compensation. All these devices have followed the "opt-in", not the American "opt-out" model. Thereby it would in theory be possible for the defendant to plead the arbitration defence if an arbitration clause has been inserted in a contract with a potentially injured consumer.

It is a matter of national law whether such an arbitration clause in a consumer contract will be regarded as unfair like in France[33] and the Scandinavian countries, restricted like in Spain or the UK,[34] or merely submitted to some formal requirements as in Germany.[35] EU law comes only indirectly in place. In the recent judgment in the *Claro*-case[36] the European Court of Justice (ECJ) had to decide whether the national court, in an action for annulment of an arbitration award against a consumer based on a violation of the national "*ordre public*", can on its own motion determine the unfairness of the arbitration clause. The Court answered positively, while at the same time expressly excluding the question of whether the clause as such was violating Directive 93/13/EC on Unfair Contract Terms[37] which it left to the national court. Once this court is convinced of the unfairness of the clause, overriding concerns of consumer protection according to Article 3(1) t) EC as implemented by Directive 93/13, namely:

> "... as measure which is essential to the accomplishment of the tasks entrusted to the Community and, in particular, to raising the standard of living and the quality of life in its territory ..." (require the court) "to assess of its own motion whether a contractual term is unfair, compensating in this way for the imbalance which exists between the consumer and the seller or supplier" (para 37).

The opinion of AG Tizzano argued not so much with consumer protection but with reference to the right of the consumer to a fair hearing and the right to be heard which was seriously impaired if the national court could not raise the unfairness of the arbitration clause on its own motion in the secondary enforcement proceedings (paras 56–59). Therefore it is most remarkable that the Court insisted on consumer protection as one of the basic tasks of the EC.

---

31 Beuchler, in: Micklitz/Stadler at 858 ff.

32 For an overview Beuchler, supra note 5 at 23–24; also Micklitz/Stadler at 1187 ff. with detailed proposals referring to existing German law.

33 See Reich, supra note. 9 at 47.

34 Reich at 48.

35 Reich at 45–47; exceptions apply to securities transactions; see also infra note 41.

36 ECJ, 26 October 2006, case C-168/05 *Elisa Maria Mostaza Claro v Centro Movil Milenium* SL [2006] ECR I-10421.

37 OJ L 95, 21 April 1993, 29.

But the limits of the approach of the Court are easily perceptible. The Court was only concerned with the enforcement proceedings where the "*ordre public*" defence may be raised, not with the inverse situation where a consumer takes his claim before a court of law, and the trader raises as a defence the existence of an arbitration clause ("Einredesituation") which seemingly cannot as such be challenged under "*ordre public*" arguments.[38] According to Article II(3) of the New York Convention of 1958, this defence is only possible in cases "that the agreement is null and void, inoperative or incapable of being performed". It is not clear whether this defence can be raised only on the motion of the defendant[39] or also *ex officio* by the trial court. In a recent comment on *Claro*, Loos[40] was of the opinion that the New York Convention does not say anything on whether the judge can on its own motion regard the arbitration clause as unfair and thereby reject the defence of the defendant, thus rejecting the "competence-competence" of the arbitrator. Such opinion seems to be particularly justified where national law allows a group action in order to improve the legal situation of the consumer which should not be frustrated by taking the case to arbitration. The "*ordre public*" argument of *Claro* would certainly also be valid in this situation.

Finally, it should also be remembered that the Court expressly refused to review the arbitration clause as such, even though para 1q) of the "indicative list" of the Annex to Directive 93/13 condemns such clauses if they:

> "exclude(e) or hinder (...) the consumer's right to take legal action or exercise any other legal remedy, particularly by requiring the consumer to take disputes exclusively to arbitration not covered by legal provisions ..."

This is a matter of Member State courts. In a recent controversial decision of 1 March 2007, the German Federal Court (Bundesgerichtshof – BGH)[41] refused to review an arbitration clause as unfair either under German or (not mentioned) EU legislation. If the consumer's right to name an arbitrator is unduly restricted, he can ask a state court to take care of the fair balancing of the arbitration panel. The clause as such is not void, quite contrary to the transparency principle of Article 4(2) EC-Directive 93/13 and §307 (1) of the German Civil Code (BGB) relating to standard contract terms.

---

38 Weihe, supra note 11, 2005, 248–251. H.-W. Micklitz, Rechtsprechung zum Europäischen Verbraucherrecht: Vertrags- und Deliktsrecht, *EWS* 2008, 353 discussing the question of "Präklusion" (loss of a defence if it has not been raised in due time in the arbitration proceedings).

39 This is the case of German law, K.-H. Schwab/G. Walter, *Schiedsgerichtsbarkeit Kommentar*, 7th ed. 2005 Kap. 7 para 1.

40 ERCL 2007, 439 at 44.

41 BGH JZ 2008, 359 with a critical comment of G. Mäsch.

4.2. THE IMPORTANCE OF BRUSSELS REGULATION 44/2001 FOR CONSUMER ARBITRATION

If the arbitration clause concerns a cross-border consumer contract and is raised against a plaintiff in a group action based on an opt-in scheme, so-called Brussels Regulation (EC) 44/2001[42] which is a follow up to the earlier Brussels Convention of 1980 [43] will apply. In cross-border litigation with the EFTA-countries, the Lugano Convention is applicable.[44]

There is however a certain ambiguity in the interpretation of these instruments with regard to mandatory arbitration clauses in consumer contracts which has not yet been settled by the case law of the ECJ. On the one hand, Article 1(2) lit d) expressly excludes arbitration from the applicability of the Brussels Convention/ Regulation. In its Rich case[45] the Court has given this exclusion a broad interpretation since it also refers to the validity of an arbitration clause and therefore the competence and composition of the arbitration tribunal. In the later Van Uden case[46] it took a somewhat narrower approach by allowing provisional measures despite an arbitration clause.

With regard to consumer protection, the Regulation, in following the Convention contains rather strict rules on protecting the consumer's right to take the case to his home jurisdiction according to the criteria set out in Article 15 of Reg. 44/2001.[47] Therefore, jurisdiction clauses are possible only under the very limited circumstances described in Article 17. Most of all, they can normally be concluded only after the dispute has arisen.[48] Shouldn't these principles be applied

42 OJ L 12, 1 January 2000, 1; with regard to Denmark see Council Decision 2006/325/EC, OJ L 120/22.

43 Consolidated text OJ C 27, 26 January 1998, 1.

44 With regard to competence concerning the conclusion of an agreement between the EU and the EFTA-states see ECJ, 7 February 2006, *opinion* 1/03, [2006] ECR I-1145.

45 ECJ, 25 July 1991, C-190/89 *Marc Rich v Società Italiana Impianti*, [1991] ECR I-3855 which concerns only commercial arbitration; for a comment see P. Rogerson, in: U. Magnus/P. Mankowski (eds.), *Brussels Regulation*, 2007, Article 1 note 38.

46 ECJ, 17 November 1998, C-391/95, *Van Uden maritime BV v KG in Firma Deco Line* [1998] ECR I-7091.

47 With regard to the changes that Article 15 of Reg. 44/2001 introduced compared with the former Article 13 of the Brussels Convention see N. Reich/A. Gambogi, Gerichtstand bei internationalen Verbrauchervertragsstreitigkeiten im Internet, VuR 2001, 269; K. Vasileva, 1968 Brussels Convention and the EU Council Regulation 44/2001: Jurisdiction in Consumer Contracts concluded online, *ELJ* 2004, 121; P. Mankowski, Zum Begriff des "Ausrichtens" auf den Wohnsitzstaat des Verbrauchers, *VuR* 2006, 289; P.A. Nielsen in: Magnus/Mankowski, note 44 at Article 15 note 34–36.

48 The relationship between Directive 93/13 and the Brussels Convention with regard to jurisdiction clauses has been discussed by Th. Pfeiffer, Gerichtsstandsklauseln und EG-Klauselrichtlinie, in *FS Schütze*, 1999, 671, insisting on a uniform interpretation which however has not been taken up by the ECJ in *Océano*, ECJ, 27 June 2000, cases 240–244/98, [2000] ECR 4941 at para 24.

per analogiam to arbitration clauses which may have a similar effect on the consumer's right to have his case heard in his home jurisdiction if the conditions of Article 15 are met? I have defended this argument in a different context,[49] which has been criticised by other authors who insist on the complete exclusion of arbitration from the Brussels Convention/Regulation[50] without paying attention to the protective ambit of the rules on jurisdiction in consumer matters which have even been increased by Regulation 44/2001 compared to the Convention of 1980. There is however no reason to argue against such analogy because for the consumer it does not make any difference whether the denial of his home jurisdiction is effected through a jurisdiction or an arbitration clause before litigation.[51] The exemption of arbitration from the scope of application of the Brussels instruments wants to privilege commercial arbitration, but not deprive the consumer of his right to defence and a fair hearing.

A similar argument can be derived from Article 1(2)(e) of the new Rome I Regulation 593/2008[52] which excludes both jurisdiction and arbitration clauses from its scope of application. This parallel treatment suggests that arbitration clauses should be interpreted and applied by analogy to jurisdiction clauses, at least as they impose upon the consumer non-judicial proceedings and deny access to his home jurisdiction under conditions contrary to Article 17 of Regulation 44/2001.

4.3. COLLECTIVE ACTIONS BASED IN TORT

Article II(1) of the New York Convention of 1968 allows arbitration agreements for contractual and non-contractual claims. Arbitration practice has tended to broadly interpret this provision and will therefore extend the arbitration clause in a contract to both contractual and related non-contractual (tort) claims.[53] On the other hand, arbitration may be excluded by public policy reasons. This may especially apply, in my opinion, e.g. on tort actions based on product or environmental liability or fraud in securities. Hence by their very nature they cannot be subjected to pre-trial arbitration clauses; the exemption of arbitration from the Brussels Regulation does not seem to be applicable here. With regard to

49 N. Reich, Zur Wirksamkeit von Schiedsklauseln in grenzüberschreitenden Börsentermingeschäften, *ZEuP* 1998, 981–994; ibid, Replik zu Samtleben, *ZEuP* 1999, 982; see also Weihe, supra note 11, at 94–96.

50 J. Samtleben, *ZEuP* 1999, 974; K.P. Berger, Schiedsgerichtsbarkeit und Finanztermingeschäfte – Der "Schutz" der Anleger vor der Schiedsgerichtsbarkeit durch §37h WpHG, *ZBB* 2003, 77 at 79; H. Schmidt, in: Ulmer/Brandner/Hensen, AGB-Recht, 10th ed. 2006, Anh. §305 para 20.

51 In this sense Weihe, note 11 at 104, 116.

52 Regulation (EC) No. 593/2008 of the EP and the Council of 17 June 2008 on the law applicable to contractual obligations ("*Rome I*"), OJ L 176, 4.7.2008, 6.

53 Schwab/Walter supra note 33 at Kap. 3 para 19, referring to German and US cases.

antitrust injuries one must with *Basedow*[54] distinguish between transactional and non-transactional situations: in a transactional situation involving antitrust matters it can be enforced, but the execution of an arbitral award can be challenged under *ordre public* reasons.[55] Tort-related claims are not arbitrable.[56]

Jurisdiction in tort cases is determined by the mandatory rules of the Brussels Regulation in cross-border situations. Article 5(3) contains a specific provision "in matters relating to tort, delict or quasi-delict", where "the courts for the place where the harmful event occurred" have jurisdiction, parallel to the courts at the domicile or business seat of the defendant under Article 2. The concepts of "tort, delict or quasi-delict" have to be interpreted autonomously by Community law. They include all actions which seek to establish the liability of a defendant and which are not related to a contract in the sense of Article 5(1).[57] This is the case for instance with:

- compensation based on pre-contractual obligations such as *culpa in contrahendo*;[58]
- the French *action directe* which extends contractual liability for defective products to third parties in the line of distribution;[59]
- however, mere consequential damages arising out of a tort towards another person are not covered by Article 5(3);[60]
- in the *Kronhofer* case,[61] the Court insisted on a narrow interpretation of Article 5(3) as an exception to the general rule of Article 2 Brussels Convention. In tort actions regarding the marketing of financial services, the mere fact that the claimant had its business seat or assets in one Member State is not sufficient to constitute the "place where the harmful event occurred".

54 J. Basedow, Jurisdiction and Choice of Law in the private Enforcement of EC Competition Law, in: J. Basedow (ed.), *Private Enforcement of EC Competition Law*, 2007, at 231–234.

55 ECJ, 1 June 1999, case C-126/97, *ECO SWISS v. Benetton*, [1999] ECR I-3055 para 36–39.

56 Against the earlier decision *American Safety Equipment Corporation v J.P. Maguie & Co*, 391 F.2d 821 at 827 (2d Circ. 1968) the Supreme Court was more friendly to arbitration even in antitrust claims: *Mitsubishi Motors Corp. v. Soler Chrylser-Plymouth, Inc.*, 473 U:S. 614 (1985); *Gilmer v. Interstate/Johnso Lane Corp.* 500 U.S. 20 (1991) see the discussion by P. Greene/P.S. Julian/J. Bidard, Arbitrability of Antitrust Claims in the US, *EBLRev* 2008, 43 at 48 relating to class action suits.

57 ECJ, 27 September 1988, 189/87, *Kalfelis*, [1988] ECR 5565, para 16 and later cases.

58 ECJ, 17 September 2002, C-334/00, *Fonderie Officine Meccaniche Tacconi SpA/Heinrich Wagner Sinto Maschinenfabrik (HWS)*, [2002] ECR I-7357.

59 ECJ, 17 July 1992, C-26/91, *Handte*, [1992] ECR I-3967.

60 ECJ, 11 January 1990, C-220/88, *Dumez-France/Helaba*, [1990] ECR I-49.

61 ECJ, 10 June 2004, C-168/02, *Rudolf Kronhofer/Marianne Maier et al.*, [2004] ECR, I-6009.

Under Article 5(3), the plaintiff is allowed to profit from *forum shopping*, namely to take the action:

- in the country of the domicile of the defendant, per Article 2;
- in the country where the harmful event occurred, that is where the legally protected interests (life, limb and property) have been injured, usually the domicile of the plaintiff.

This forum shopping which the ECJ allowed in cross-border environmental and product liability in the *Mines-de Potasse* case[62] is particularly important where access to jurisdiction and applicable law differ between Member countries. It puts the producer at a specific risk in the case of multi-state product-related risks. However, Article 5 (3) of Regulation 44/2001 has maintained the existing state of the law and extended it to preventive injunctions. It may not be excluded by pre-trial arbitration clauses.

5. CONCLUSION

If EU or national legislation introduces (or already has introduced) collective remedies in favour of the consumer interest, it should pay attention that the effects are not frustrated by standard business terms opposing individual or collective consumer claims by mandatory arbitration clauses. As a US critic, R. Alderman, has said:

> "Arbitration is not about relocating or simplifying consumer dispute resolution; it is about eliminating consumer disputes and controlling their resolution."[63]

It would certainly be paradoxical if the increase in consumer protection via collective redress mechanisms whatever their nature could be counteracted by mandatory pre-trial arbitration clauses in consumer contracts. The American experience need not be repeated in the EU where the protection of consumers' effective access to justice must be seen as a fundamental right under Article 6 of the ECHR, confirmed recently by Article 47 of the Charter of Fundamental Right in the EU which has become part of the Lisbon Reform Treaty of 13 December 2007.[64] Therefore, reference to arbitration – whether in individual or in group

---

62 ECJ, 30 November 1976, case 21/76, *Handelskwekerij G.J. Bier v. minds de Potasse d'Alsace*, [1976] ECR I-1735.

63 Alderman, The Future, supra note 23 at 11.

64 See Micklitz/Reich/Rott, *Understanding EU Consumer law*, Antwerp, 2008, §8.2–8.3; for a recent reference to Article 47 see case C-42/05 *Unibet v Justiekanslern*, [2007] ECRI-2271 para 37.

action proceedings – should only be allowed as an option for the consumer like in Denmark,[65] but not as a mandatory clause unilaterally imposed on him or her.

65 See Reich, supra note 9 at 48.

PART IV.
TRANSBORDER LIGITATION AND INTERNATIONAL PRIVATE LAW

TRANSBORDER LITIGATION AND PRIVATE INTERNATIONAL LAW: THE VIEW FROM CANADA

Geneviève SAUMIER*

The collective action as a private mechanism for consumer protection faces challenges in the transborder context because of the added complexity brought by private international law. While the benefits of collective private enforcement are seen to be connected to the aggregation of common claims, rules regarding jurisdiction, choice of law and recognition of foreign judgments can act as obstacles to aggregation that reach across markets and legal borders. Most regimes of private international law, whether in Europe or North America, are ill-suited to cope with collective private enforcement, whether existing or contemplated. Yet with the prevalence of settlement of class actions in the North American context, the private international law dimensions tend to be muted. As Europe considers the adoption of a North American-style class action, it becomes critical to take account of these private international law issues, to examine if and how they have been addressed and finally to determine whether those responses would be appropriate or workable elsewhere.[1] While the particular constitutional and

* Associate Professor and Member of the Institute of Comparative Law, McGill University. I gratefully acknowledge the research assistance of Andrew Mason, BCL/LLB 2008 as well as the support from McGill University's travel grant fund that allowed me to participate in the original workshop in Fiesole in May 2007.

1 The North American experience is a useful comparator for several reasons: (i) in western legal systems, only Canada and the USA have had significant experience with an opt-out damages class action mechanism for private consumer enforcement; (ii) the Canadian province of Quebec has had such a mechanism for over 25 years and has been able to integrate it into a civil law tradition, with codified substantive and procedural law; (iii) both Canada and the USA have a common approach to jurisdiction and recognition in international cases similar to the European model (Brussels Regulation) but do not have formally harmonised choice of law rules, unlike Europe (Rome I and II); (iv) there is little jurisprudence in Canada on transborder injunctions, which have been specifically enabled in the European model; (v) the approach to transborder or multi-jurisdiction class actions in Canada differs considerably from that in the USA, suggesting a diversity of options with a varying degree of constitutional or institutional contingencies. For a useful overview of the Canadian class action landscape, see W.A. Bogart, Jasminka Kalajdzic and Ian Matthews "Class Actions in Canada: A National Procedure in a Multi-Jurisdictional Society? A report prepared for The Globalization of Class Actions Conference", Oxford University, December 2007, available online at www.law.stanford.edu/calendar/details/1066.

institutional frameworks for European private international law should allow for different approaches and instruments to be deployed, the underlying challenges posed to jurisdiction, choice of law and recognition in transborder group litigation remain largely similar, given the common origins of private international law in both regions.

This article will consider the private international law dimensions of transborder collective private enforcement within the Canadian context to highlight the challenges posed by its federal constitution, its decentralised court structure and the co-existence of jurisdictions of the common law and civil law traditions. The way in which Canadian courts and legislatures have dealt with the transborder class action will be considered along with a proposed uniform model law recently put forward to address the challenges that remain unsettled within the Canadian context. The distinct American approach will also be noted to underscore the significant effect of constitutional, judicial and procedural structures on the shape of responses to private international law dimensions of transborder collective private enforcement.

1. INTRODUCTION TO THE PRIVATE INTERNATIONAL LAW CHALLENGES TO THE TRANSBORDER CONSUMER CLASS ACTION

The private international law challenges facing transborder consumer class actions are acute in North America given the design of their class action procedures. Under this model, all consumers covered by the definition of the "class" will be bound by the outcome of the action, whether it favours the plaintiff or the defendant. On the positive side, this means that a non-resident class member will be entitled to benefit from any order or settlement approved by the court; on the other hand, it also means that the non-resident class member will be precluded in principle from bringing a claim in any other jurisdiction covered by the class definition, including his home jurisdiction. Courts in Canada and in the US have confirmed this state of affairs even in cases where the non-resident class member's claim had no connection to the jurisdiction where the action was instituted.[2] Where the types of class action allows for individual class members to "opt out" of the class, however, they reserve their right to pursue their own claim but lose any benefits otherwise accruing to remaining class members. While I will concentrate mainly on the opt-out model that is representative of the Canadian

2 *Phillips Petroleum Co. v. Shutts*, 472 US 797 (1985); *Harrington v. Dow Corning Corp.*, 2000 BCCA 605 (British Columbia Court of Appeal), (leave to appeal to the Supreme Court of Canada refused [2001] S.C.C.A. No. 21); for a recent application of that reasoning see *Ring v. The Queen #2*, 2007 NLTD 213 (Newfoundland Supreme Court).

system, other class action mechanisms exist in the USA which have the same preclusive effect on claimants without the opportunity to opt out.[3] Given the very low rate of opt-outs,[4] however, the significance of this option should not be overstated.

The group action models that have so far developed outside the North American context have followed an opt-in system,[5] whereby the express consent of the group members is required in largely modernised versions of the traditional common law representative action or of a large-scale system of joinder. The problems concerning jurisdiction over class members and the resultant claim preclusion do not arise where the members of the collective are actual parties to the action. In such cases, the private international law questions facing the transborder group action are no different in nature than those facing individual actions though they may be more complex as a result of the multiplicity of parties and claims.

The private international law challenges posed by the typical North American class action are threefold. The first is jurisdictional and relates to the authority of the forum state over the non-resident class members. The second is also jurisdictional and is the corollary of the first in that it deals with the effect of the decision(s) of the forum (whether on certification, on the merits or on settlement approval) outside the jurisdiction, specifically in the jurisdiction of the non-resident class member who did not opt out. This is usually referred to as the preclusive effect of the forum's decision(s). Finally, the third challenge relates to the law applicable to the aggregated claims which are, potentially, subject to different substantive legal regimes depending on connections to the underlying individual claims. These three challenges are raised against the backdrop of federal constitutional structures, according to which both in the USA and Canada, legislative competence over private international law is decentralised but subject to constitutional constraints against extra-territoriality. Unlike in Europe, there

---

3 The so-called mandatory class action and limited-fund class action of Federal Rule 23(b)(1) and (b)(2), in contrast to the opt-out model of Rule 23(b)(3), as amended by the *Class Action Fairness Act* (CAFA) 28 U.S.C. sec. 1332 (d), 1453, 1711–15. For a full discussion, see, e.g. Edward F. Sherman, "Class Actions after the Class Action Fairness Act of 2005" (2006) 90 *Tul. L. Rev.* 1593.

4 Empirical research has found that opt-out rates are very low, calculated at less than one percent: Theodore Eisenberg & Geoffrey P. Miller, "The Role of Opt-Outs and Objectors in Class Action Litigation: Theoretical and Empirical Issues" (2004) 57 *Vand. L. Rev.* 1529 at 1534. See also Thomas E. Willging et al., *Empirical Study of Class Actions in Four Federal District Courts: Final Report to the Advisory Committee on Civil Rules 45–54* (1996), cited in Eisenberg & Miller at note 49.

5 See for example Antonio Gidi, *Class Actions in Brazil – A Model for Civil Law Countries,* 51 Am. J. Comp. L. 311 (2003); Per Henrik Lindblom, *Group Litigation in Sweden*, available along with 27 other national reports on the state of collective action in individual countries at www.law.stanford.edu/calendar/details/1066/. But see new trends in Europe discussed in Cafaggi/Micklitz.

has been no formal uniformisation of the jurisdictional or choice-of-law rules within each country, let alone within the NAFTA legal space, although informal harmonisation is noticeable in many areas.[6] I now turn to each challenge in turn.

2. JURISDICTIONAL ISSUES FOR TRANSBORDER CONSUMER CLASS ACTIONS

In the North American context, it is useful to distinguish the "national" class action and the "international" or "transnational" class action. Both types can be described as "transborder" because within each federal state, the units are likely to be considered distinct jurisdictions for the purposes of consumer class actions.[7] Where the identified class remains within each country, however, constitutional concerns may play out differently than if the class straddles the border.[8] For example, under current Canadian and American constitutional law, judgments from sister-provinces or sister-states are entitled to recognition with few limitations.[9] While recognition of judgments between the two countries is also likely given the generous regime in place in both, this recognition is not constitutionally mandated such that different standards could apply.[10] This

---

6 See Symeon C. Symeonides, "Choice of Law in the American Courts in 2006: Twentieth Annual Survey" (2007) 54 *American Journal of Comparative Law* 697; H. Patrick Glenn, "The Morris Lecture: Conflicting Laws in a Common Market? The Nafta Experiment" (2001) 76 *Chi.-Kent. L. Rev.* 1789.

7 In Canada, for example, class actions are largely governed by provincial statutes and claims in contract or tort/delict which will be determined in accordance with the applicable provincial substantive law. While there is a federal class action procedure, it applies only to the Federal Court with jurisdiction over areas of federal law which in Canada are unlikely to be relevant to consumer claims. See in general W. Branch, *Class Actions in Canada* (Aurora, Ont.: Canada Law Book, looseleaf edition). The US situation is largely similar despite a different court structure and the importance of the federal class action regime. For a useful review of the state/federal dimension of the US system, see Thomas D. Rowe, "State and Foreign Class-Action Rules and Statutes: Differences from – and Lessons for? – Federal Rule 23" (2007) 35 *Western State University Law Review* 101.

8 Classes that include non-residents from outside Canada or the US are also caught by this "international label" although the absence of an equivalent class action regime in other countries accentuates the private international law challenges. I note that the landmark American case in *Shutts* included class members from Europe and elsewhere but the US Supreme Court dealt with the issues as if it were a "national" US transborder case, without ever mentioning the international character of the class. For a critique of this dimension of the case, see Debra Lyn Bassett, "US Class Actions Go Global: Transnational Class Actions and Personal Jurisdiction" (2003) 72 *Fordham L. Rev.* 41.

9 In the USA, as a result of the Full-Faith and Credit Clause of Article IV of the US Constitution; in Canada, as a result of the Supreme Court of Canada decisions in *Morguard Investments Ltd. v. De Savoye*, [1990] 3 S.C.R. 1077 and *Hunt v. T&N plc*, [1993] 4 S.C.R. 289.

10 In fact, since the Supreme Court of Canada's decision in *Beals v Saldanha*, [2003] 3 S.C.R. 416, any remaining gap in treatment appears to have disappeared except perhaps in terms of

situation mirrors the European context where the regime of the Brussels Regulation ensures enforcement within the EU, leaving the treatment of non-EU judgments to each Member State's national rules on recognition and enforcement.[11] The main difference is the presence of uniform rules of jurisdiction in the EU, which does not have its counterpart within the US or Canada.

Still, despite the diversity of rules within the relevant North American jurisdictions, the principal challenges regarding jurisdiction in transborder class actions, whether "national" or truly international, remain largely convergent and involve considerations of procedural justice for the class members. Existing private international rules on jurisdiction do not address this issue because those rules are essentially directed at protecting foreign defendants against illegitimate or excessive exercises of jurisdiction by local courts (so-called "long-arm" jurisdiction).[12] Concerns about fairness to the plaintiff in non-class actions seem misplaced since the very status of plaintiff implies consent to jurisdiction and formal intention to be bound by the outcome of the action where the plaintiff instituted it and elsewhere.[13]

It may be useful to approach the jurisdictional issue according to two different scenarios. The first scenario involves the case where the defendant is being sued in its home jurisdiction, in the sense of its domicile, residence or head office.[14] For

evaluating the "fairness of the process" which is excluded within the federation. While that decision is binding only in the common law provinces, not being a constitutional imperative, it is worth noting that the rules on recognition in the Civil Code of Québec treat all non-Quebec decisions on the same footing, thereby approximating the Beals effect. For commentary, see Joy Goodman & Jeffrey Talpis, "*Beals v. Saldanha* and the Enforcement of Foreign Judgments in Canada", (2004) 40 *Canadian Business Law Journal* 227 (Quebec perspective); Stephen Pitel, "Enforcement of Foreign Judgments: Where *Morguard* Stands after *Beals*", (2004) 40 *Canadian Business Law Journal* 189 (common law provinces perspective). In the USA, it has been remarked that US courts seems to give little consideration to the potential distinction to be drawn between sister-state and truly foreign judgments. See generally Eugene Scoles et al., *Conflict of Laws* 1139 and ff (3rd ed. 2000) at 1190–93, on the impact of Erie for international recognition and the corresponding waning relevance of the Hilton doctrine. The authors also note that the Uniform Foreign Money-Judgments Recognition Act (1962) in force in a large number of US states endorses equal treatment of foreign judgments (*id.* at 1192). But see the recently adopted American Law Institute statute on *Recognition and Enforcement of Foreign Judgments* available for a fee at www.ali.org.

11 *Council Regulation (EC) No. 44/2001 on jurisdiction and the recognition and enforcement of judgments in civil and commercial disputes* (that replaced and modified the 1968 Brussels Convention of the same name).

12 Even rules directed at foreign plaintiffs such as standing rules and rules on security for costs are meant to protect local defendants or local courts, not the plaintiffs.

13 The foreign plaintiff may not have had any choice of forum but this does not negate the fact that by instituting the action, the plaintiff is at the very least submitting voluntarily to the jurisdiction of the forum. If the plaintiff loses and thereafter attempts to sue in another forum, a defence of *res judicata* by the defendant is unlikely to fail on any jurisdictional argument relating to fairness to the plaintiff in the original forum.

14 This is the primary basis for jurisdiction under the Civil Code of Québec (Article 3134) and the Brussels Regulation and is routinely accepted in Canadian common law jurisdiction (see the

such a case to take on a transborder dimension either the plaintiff has to be "foreign" or the cause of action has to have arisen outside the jurisdiction. In a class action, the "foreignness" of the plaintiff may be apparent only from a reading of the proposed class, since it is usually the case that the actual party, i.e. the representative plaintiff, is a resident of the forum. In such a case, it is likely that for at least some of the class members, the only link between their claim and the chosen jurisdiction is the defendant's link to that jurisdiction. Insofar as these non-resident class members could have instituted an action against the defendant in that forum, the exercise of jurisdiction by that forum may arguably not be considered exorbitant in and of itself, except for the fact that the class member has not expressly indicated his or her assent to the jurisdiction.

A different case altogether arises where the forum for instituting the action is selected on the basis of connections to the cause of action as opposed to objective links with the defendant. In such cases, the legitimacy of the forum's exercise of jurisdiction is based not on a formal "presence" of the defendant within the jurisdiction but on the conclusion that there are nevertheless sufficient "minimal contacts"[15] to amount to a "real and substantial connection"[16] with the forum. The establishment of the jurisdictional basis is typically derived from the relational aspect of the contract or tort/delict claim in the sense that the links are the ones that connect the plaintiff to the defendant. So in a contracts case, if the forum is the place where the contract was to be performed, regardless of the "foreign" status of plaintiff or defendant, the forum is considered a legitimate place to determine the rights and obligations of those parties. For a torts claim, if the defendant's allegedly defective product was purchased in the forum or the non-resident victim was injured in the forum, the foreignness of either party will not be sufficient to deny the *prima facie* legitimacy of the forum's exercise of jurisdiction over the action.[17] In a transborder class action, however, this binary relationship between the plaintiff and defendant will likely be connected to different jurisdictions through the diversity of the class, putting into question the

landmark Supreme Court of Canada case of *Morguard Investments Ltd. v. De Savoye*, [1990] 3 S.C.R. 1077.) It has been recognised as legitimate in the US ever since the landmark case of *Pennoyer v. Neff*, 95 US 714 (1877).

15 This is the consecrated American standard for personal jurisdiction since *International Shoe Co. v. Washington*, 326 US 310 (1945).

16 This is the consecrated Canadian standard for jurisdiction following *Morguard, supra* note 14.

17 Admittedly, in both cases the links may be stronger with another jurisdiction in which case it may be possible for the forum to stay its proceedings under a *forum non conveniens* doctrine or its equivalent. For Quebec, see Article 3135 Civil Code of Québec; for the Canadian common law provinces, see *Amchem Products Inc. v. B.C.*, [1993] 1 S.C.R. 897 (S.C.C.); moreover, US courts have tended to be less hospitable to truly foreign claimants, see Donna Solen, "*Forum Non Conveniens* and The International Plaintiff" (1994) 9 *Fla. J. Int'l L.* 343.

very legitimacy of the chosen forum for some claims and bringing to the fore arguments of invalid extra-territorial exercises of jurisdiction.

This problem was addressed indirectly in a breast implant class action launched in British Columbia, in the early days of that province's class action experience.[18] The defendant Dow Corning, a foreign defendant, was sued in BC and the class included, among others, women with implants who resided in BC, women who had received implants in BC and women who resided in other Canadian provinces. The defendant challenged the BC court's jurisdiction over claims by members of the class who had no connection to BC. Indeed, since the jurisdictional basis of the BC court was based only on its connection to the product or the injury and not to the defendant *per se*, the defendant argued that for claims by non-residents who had neither been implanted in BC nor suffered any alleged injury in BC, there was no connection with the province to found its jurisdiction.

In an unprecedented move, the court decided that the nature of the class action was such as to effect a modification of the rules of jurisdiction as they applied to the defendant. The court focused on the "common issue", which was the quality or defectiveness of the product, and which was common to both resident and non-resident women in the class. The court concluded that the nature of the action was such as to justify its exercise of jurisdiction over the foreign defendant even in relation to the claims that had no connection to the province. In other words, the common issue had the effect of extending the jurisdiction of the court, by assimilating the non-resident members to the resident members, which it said was justified by the statutory scheme of the class action and the policy objective underlying the procedural mechanism.[19]

This apparent modification of the jurisdictional rule in an inter-provincial case was considered and approved by the Ontario Court of Appeal in its 2005 decision in the international case of *Currie v. Macdonald's Restaurants of Canada*.[20] The Quebec courts have not followed suit, however, holding on two

---

18 *Harrington v. Dow Corning*, *supra* note 2.

19 It must be noted that the BC class action system requires that non-resident plaintiffs "opt in" to the class in an express manner (*Class Proceedings Act, R.S.B.C.* 1996, c. 50 s. 6(1)). This means that these women would be estopped from later seeking to sue in their home province at least on jurisdictional grounds.

20 [2005] O.J. no. 506 (Ont.C.A.), discussed in detail in G. Saumier "USA-Canada Class Actions: Trading in Procedural Fairness" (2005) Global Jurist Advances: Vol. 5: Iss. 2, Article 1, available at www.bepress.com/gj/advances/vol5/iss2/art1. This case involved the recognition of a settlement class action involving a Canada/USA class, approved by an Illinois court. The Ontario court admitted the possibility of recognition in principle but refused it on the facts of the case, holding that the Canadian class members had received insufficient notice of the American proceedings. It must be noted that in *Currie*, the defendant was being sued at its domicile (McDonald's being headquartered in Illinois). For approval of the jurisdictional holding in a subsequent class action certification involving non-resident members with no connection to Ontario, see *McCutcheon v. Cash Store*, (2006), 80 *O.R.* (3d) 644 (Ont. Superior Court).

occasions that an appropriate jurisdictional connection must exist between every member of the proposed class and Quebec,[21] leading to the possibility that transborder class actions can only be brought against defendants domiciled in Quebec or where the links to the action are established with Quebec for every putative class member. The Supreme Court has recently agreed to hear an appeal in one of these cases, opening the possibility of a reversal on that question, with perhaps an attempt to harmonise the diverse judicial responses to this question throughout the country.

Any attempt to apply to non-resident class members jurisdictional rules designed to protect foreign defendants is unlikely to succeed because it is based on a consent theory of international jurisdiction[22] that is at odds with the opt-out class action model.[23] This may explain why the Canadian decisions that appear to extend traditional jurisdictional rules are more accurately understood as seeking proxies for consent in the class action model that will serve to safeguard the procedural justice rights of the persons eventually meant to be bound by the outcome of the proceedings. This is exactly what the Ontario Court of Appeal did in its reasons in *Currie*, by focusing on the opt-out and notice requirements imposed in the class action legislation as the means for providing procedural justice protection for absent class members, including non-residents.[24] In so doing, it was following the lead of the US Supreme Court in the landmark *Phillips Petroleum v. Shutts* case,[25] which had held that the due process rights of absent class members were not equivalent to those of defendants and were instead guaranteed by the procedural safeguards prescribed by the class action regime, namely notice, opt-out and adequate representation as opposed to any limits based on connections to the adjudicating forum. While this rationalisation has

---

21 See *Société canadienne des postes v. Lépine*, [2006] *J.Q.* No. 507 (S.C.), aff'd [2007] QCCA 1092 (Qué. C.A.), *HSBC Bank Canada v. Hocking*, [2006] *J.Q.* no 507 (S.C.), aff'd 2008 QCCA 800 and from Saskatchewan, *Englund v. Pfizer Canada Inc.*, [2006] *S.J.* No. 9 (Q.B.). The inconsistency across Canada was discussed at length in *McCutcheon*, *ibid*. The Quebec Court of Appeal's recent judgment in *Hocking* includes a surprising obiter to the effect that the Ontario court's exercise of jurisdiction over Quebec class members was unconstitutional. While only one of the three judges put forward that view, it was the first time that it had been expressed by any court in Canada. The Supreme Court of Canada may well feel compelled to comment on it when it hears the *Lépine* appeal given that no further appeal of *Hocking* is anticipated.

22 I use this term in the civil law sense of jurisdiction in "international" cases which I find less pejorative than the expression "long-arm jurisdiction".

23 See Owen Fiss, "The Political Theory of The Class Action" (1995) 53 *Wash. & Lee L. Rev.* 21 (arguing that the preclusionary effect of the class action cannot be justified on a theory of substituted consent or representation since the class action representative is self-appointed).

24 See Saumier, *supra* note 20. For a practitioner's view of the case, see Ward Branch and Christopher A. Rhone, "The Bond between Class Members – the Wedge between Counsel: Trans-National Class Actions in the Wake of Parsons v. McDonald's Restaurants" available online at www.branmac.com/about/branch.htm.

25 (1985) 472 US 797.

been criticised by American scholars,[26] these views do not appear to have been considered by the Ontario court in 2005.

Such an interpretation of the role of the opt-out and notice provisions may serve to extend international jurisdiction over a regional, national or international class even in the absence of any connections between those class members and the jurisdiction seized of the action or of the request for settlement approval, so long as the international jurisdiction of that court is established with respect to the defendant and the representative plaintiff's claim.[27] Despite this apparently generous landscape for transborder class actions in the Canadian context, it is interesting that the three cases involving the recognition of class action judgments have resulted in three refusals to give effect to those judgments, on the basis of insufficient or unsatisfactory notice to the non-resident class members.[28] As mentioned above, however, the latest case is heading to the Canadian Supreme Court which might signal an upcoming change either in the articulation of the conditions for recognition or in the strictness of their application by Canadian judges.

It is here that the particular constitutional imperatives for interprovincial recognition might be expected to give rise to a distinction between the national or internal action and the truly international class action. Indeed, when the Canadian Supreme Court first discussed the notion of mutual recognition of judgments within the federation, it noted that objections to recognition based on breaches of procedural justice could not be raised given the presumption of natural justice in judicial proceedings within the Canadian legal system.[29] In later cases dealing with the recognition of American judgments, the Canadian Supreme Court seemed to extend this courtesy to its southern neighbour, referring to due process safeguards enshrined in the law and policy of the US.[30] In essence, the Canadian Supreme Court was putting the onus on parties to raise procedural justice claims in the originating forum as opposed to the recognising forum. But because class

---

26 See Linda S. Mullenix, "Class Actions, Personal Jurisdiction, and Plaintiffs' Due Process: Implications for Mass Tort Litigation" (1995) 28 *U.C. Davis L. Rev.* 871 and Bassett, *supra* note 8. For a more recent assessment of *Shutts* see Stephen C. Yeazell, "Overhearing Part of a Conversation: Shutts as a Moment in a Long Dialogue" (2006) 74 *Univ. Missouri-Kansas City L. Rev.* 779.

27 The British Columbia decision in the *Harrington* case is not instructive here because the non-resident class members there were required to opt in, as provided for in the applicable B.C. class proceedings statute, *supra* note 20. The requirement that non-residents opt into the class is also prescribed by legislation in Saskatchewan, Newfoundland, Alberta and New Brunswick, following the ULCC model, as does the B.C. statute. This is not the case in the Manitoba statute; the Ontario and Quebec schemes are silent but have been interpreted to allow for opt-out transborder classes. See Branch, *supra* note 7.

28 *Currie*, *supra* note 20, *Hocking* and *Lépine*, *supra* note 21.

29 See *Morguard*, *supra* note 14 at 1100 and 1107.

30 See *Amchem Products Inc. v. B.C.*, [1993] 1 S.C.R. 897 and *Beals*, *supra* note 10 (but see contra in the dissent in that case).

members are not parties to the class action, and have only limited rights to intervene in the originating proceedings, the exclusion of procedural justice objections at the recognition stage cannot hold. Indeed, on the three occasions where Canadian courts considered this question, they refused to give effect to "foreign judgments", two from sister provinces and one from a US state, on the basis of violations of procedural justice. In hearing the appeal in the *Lépine* case, the Canadian Supreme Court will have to face this challenge and may be forced to draw a distinction between the "national" transborder action within Canada and the "international" North American action. It is likely that the Supreme Court of Canada will want to avoid maintaining a system that allows for meaningful objections only at the recognition stage, given the inefficiency and incongruity of such a mechanism within a federal state. This may indeed dictate the adoption of a specific mechanism for allocating jurisdiction in inter-provincial actions, an objective that has so far eluded courts and law-makers and to which I now turn.

3. MULTIPLE COMPETENT COURTS, *FORUM NON CONVENIENS* AND CONSOLIDATION: THE CANADIAN EXPERIENCE

The history of class actions in Canada highlights the distinct advantage of a uniform approach to the issue of private collective enforcement in a transborder context. Indeed, the diversity of class action regimes in the Canadian provinces, coupled with its decentralised judicial structure,[31] has magnified the challenges posed by transborder class actions. When there were only two provinces with class action regimes,[32] options were limited and there was a clear incentive for courts to accept non-resident class members for reasons of justice, the argument being that to refuse their membership could be equivalent to denying them a remedy since they did not have the option of commencing class proceedings in their home province. Reference to the substantive legislative objective of access to justice was readily available to justify the expansive interpretation of jurisdiction in otherwise silent legislative provisions.

The subsequent provincial schemes were all drafted and implemented in the wake of a proposed uniform Act put forward in 1996 by the Uniform Law

31 See generally G. Gall, *The Canadian Legal System*, 5th ed. (Scarborough, Ont.: Thomson, 2004) at 265ff.

32 Quebec and Ontario were the original two, but at a fifteen year interval; for dates of enactment see note Branch, *supra* note 7.

Conference of Canada.[33] That uniform Act severely limited the likelihood of national classes because it required non-resident class members to opt into the class, unlike in Ontario and Quebec where courts interpreted the silent legislation as permitting the constitution of an opt-out class that could include non-residents.[34] Based on the theory that aggregation is of the essence of a class action, maximum aggregation of non-economically viable consumer contract claims is not compatible with the opt-in model in a transborder context. The ensuing provincial schemes did not all follow the model Act, such that there now exists a patchwork of regimes across Canada, making all too predictable the ensuing multiplication of overlapping class actions.

The challenge in the Canadian context is the absence of a judicial structure that could accommodate a consolidated class action or that could make decisions on the allocation of jurisdiction to one or more provinces using a doctrine such as *forum non conveniens*. There is no structure analogous to the US Multi-district Litigation Panel[35] which can act to consolidate multiple proceedings, whether class actions or otherwise. Nor does Canada have a federal court institution analogous to the American one, where class actions can be brought under the aegis of the uniform class action procedure of Federal Rule 23.[36] When it comes to private collective enforcement in consumer cases, the Canadian provinces are akin to independent states with separate class action procedures.[37] This has led to

33 The Uniform Law Conference of Canada is a governmental advisory; for details on its projects and uniforms acts, see www.ulcc.ca.

34 For a review of the early case law see Stephen Lamont, "The Problem of the National Class: Extra-Territorial Class Definitions and the Jurisdiction of the Court" (2001) 24 *Advocates' Soc. J.* 252.

35 The federal Judicial Panel on Multidistrict Litigation is "authorized to transfer civil actions pending in more than one [federal] district involving one or more common questions of fact to any district for coordinated or consolidated pre-trial proceedings upon the Panel's determination that transfer 'will be for the convenience of the parties and witnesses and will promote the just and efficient conduct of such actions.'" (*Manual for Complex Litigation, Fourth – Federal Judicial Center*, 2004 at 20.13.131, citing 28 U.S.C. Section 1407).

36 The Canadian Federal Court has adopted a class action procedure to deal with its limited areas of federal jurisdiction that include admiralty, tax and intellectual property in addition to cases brought by or against the Crown, which can include collective claims against the Federal government alleging some regulatory failure in an area of federal jurisdiction (health products, for example). So far, these types of cases have been brought in the superior courts in the provinces rather than in the Federal Court (see, e.g. the breast implant litigation against Health Canada, brought in B.C. *(Harrington v. Dow Corning Corp.* (2002), 3 *B.C.L.R.* (4th) 51 (S.C.)), Ontario, (*Attis v. Canada (Minister of Health),* [2007] O.J. No. 1744) Quebec (*Doyer v. Canada (Ministre de la Santé)*, [2001] Q.J. No. 1300 (Que. S.C.) and Saskatchewan (*Chapman v. Canada (Health and Welfare Canada)*, 2007 *SKQB* 151 (CanLII); in that case, the first claim was brought to the Federal Court but that action was stayed when the Crown sought to implead the manufacturers, putting the case beyond the Federal Court's jurisdiction: *Aussant v. Canada(Minister of Health and Welfare)* (2002), 226 *F.T.R.* 25 (T.D.); for a recent discussion see also *Dobbie v. Canada (Attorney General)*, 2006 FC 552 (CanLII).

37 Although, as noted earlier, the provinces remain constitutionally bound to recognise each other's judgments.

serious jurisdictional conundrums resulting from the multiplication of proceedings across the country and the absence of any formal mechanism to allocate jurisdiction among them. Two examples are illustrative.

In the first case, a number of class proceedings were begun across the country against drug manufacturer Bayer in relation to the cholesterol-lowering drug known as Baycol, after its withdrawal from the Canadian market in the summer of 2001. By 2004 proceedings had been instituted in British Columbia, Saskatchewan, Ontario, Quebec, Newfoundland and Manitoba.[38] By that same point, settlements had been reached in the B.C., Ontario and Quebec cases, with regard to the most serious injury linked to the drug.[39] Certification had been granted in Newfoundland in relation to a broader scope of injuries but was on appeal when Manitoba was seized of similar proceedings in its courts. Eventually, the proceedings in Manitoba were certified as an opt-out national class (excluding Quebec), with sub-classes for Saskatchewan and Newfoundland residents,[40] where the local actions were eventually discontinued voluntarily. In the early moments of the Manitoba certification proceedings, the judge specifically referred to the complications arising from the lack of any procedural mechanism available to resolve multiple jurisdictional claims within the country in relation to the same cause of action or variations of such claims.[41]

The second illustration is provided by a series of claims brought against the Government of Canada in relation to the spraying of Agent Orange on a military training base in the province of New Brunswick. According to the recent judgment of the Newfoundland court, nine proceedings have been filed across the country, mainly headed by the same counsel or lead counsel.[42] The Newfoundland judge was asked to stay the proceedings that he had certified in his province, on the basis of parallel proceedings underway in New Brunswick, under its newly adopted class action legislation.[43] He refused to do so, rejecting the defendant's *forum non conveniens* argument. The same result was obtained in Manitoba, where the Court of Appeal refused to stay that action in favour of the New

38 See the review provided by the Manitoba court in *Walls v. Bayer Inc.* (2005) 189 *Man.R.* (2d) 262.

39 [2004] *B.C.J.* 2101, [2004] O.J. No. 2775, [2004] *QJ* 11125.

40 Actually, the Newfoundland sub-class is entitled the "Atlantic sub-class" and includes residents from the four Atlantic provinces. See the final version of the class definition in *Walls v. Bayer Inc.* (2007), 217 *Man. R.* (2d) 66 at para. 4.

41 *Walls*, *supra* note 38 at para. 81: "Regrettably, there is no legislation that would take control of a class proceeding for all of Canada."

42 *Ring v. The Queen #2*, 2007 *NLTD* 213. A claim was also filed in Federal Court in 2005; that court had jurisdiction because the claim was against the Crown, but the action was stayed when the Crown sought to implead the manufacturers, which put the action beyond the court's jurisdiction: see *Dobbie v. Canada (Attorney General)*, 2006 *FC* 552.

43 *Ibid.*

Brunswick one.[44] In discussing the *forum non conveniens* point, the former court referred to its "opt-in" model for non-residents as an element favouring maintenance of the proceedings in Newfoundland whereas in Manitoba, the court considered that the opt-out model in place in that province favoured retaining its jurisdiction over the claim. In both cases, the courts noted the advantageous costs provisions in their respective class action legislation compared to the available structure under the New Brunswick scheme. Even without any further consideration of the claims in the six other provinces, it is evident that this case against a defendant amenable to suit in every Canadian jurisdiction would be more efficiently pursued in a single proceeding but that the courts seized of the matter are not prepared to deny access to their local residents or to cede jurisdiction to another province's court without a formal structure in place.

This challenge of competing class actions in Canada has been considered by the Uniform Law Conference of Canada in the context of suggesting an amendment to its model law. Having determined early on that extending the jurisdiction of the Federal Court was a political non-starter, the ULCC relied on the discretionary doctrine of *forum non conveniens* to invite judges to exercise their jurisdiction in light of the "multi-jurisdictional" nature of a class and the existence of competing or anticipated proceedings elsewhere. Among other things, the amendment allows for modification to the composition of the class, the creation of sub-classes and the appointment of separate representatives, all to take explicit account of the interest of non-resident class members, particularly those who might be involved in similar proceedings in their home province.[45] The ULCC also accepted the recommendation that a national registry of class actions be created to support the exercise of the *forum non conveniens* discretion set up in the amendment.[46] Since then, courts in several major centres have issued practice directives requiring parties to send notices of class action proceedings instituted in those courts.[47]

It is still early to gauge the effect of these initiatives on the landscape for consumer class actions in Canada. A look at the database in March 2008 shows that there are seven actions pending in seven different provinces in relation to the identical claim in competition law against Hershey and that in each case the class is limited to residents of that province. At first glance, one may surmise that the availability of a class action procedure in most provinces and in the absence of a

---

44 *Ward v. Canada (Attorney General) et al.*, [2007] 11 *W.W.R.* 410 (Man. C.A.).

45 See sections 4(2) and (3) and s. 4.1 of the *Uniform Class Proceedings Act (Consolidated 2006)* available online at www.ulcc.ca.

46 It is run by the Canadian Bar Association and has records from 1996 to the present in a free searchable database: www.cba.org/ClassActions. For a detailed description of this database, see Ward Branch and Christopher Rhone, "Solving the National Class Problem", 4th Annual Symposium on Class Actions (Toronto: Osgoode Hall Law School of York University, 2007) available online at www.branmac.com.

47 This includes courts in Quebec, Ontario, British Columbia and Alberta as well as the Federal Court. See "Information and Practice Directives" on the CBA website, *ibid.*

uniform mechanism or supervision mechanism regarding jurisdiction, the default position is a return to the local action, with all of the potential negative implications for maximum aggregation and judicial economy. On the other hand, six of the seven claims list the same legal counsel, either acting as lead counsel (in the original British Columbia claim) or as co-counsel in the other provinces. This suggests that the multiplicity of proceedings does not reflect the actual underlying aggregation of claims that may well be largely equivalent to the defendant's transborder market. The question becomes whether judicial economy and efficiency can be achieved indirectly through the consolidation of the legal work as opposed to directly through the consolidation of the legal proceedings. Admittedly, judicial economy may also be enhanced by the elimination of jurisdictional challenges either at the outset or at the recognition stage through the elimination of the transborder dimension of the claims and therefore the private international law challenges.

This response by legal practice to the jurisdictional challenges of the transborder Canadian class action may be specific to this country as a result of the growing number of national law firms, the small market and the limited number of plaintiff-side class action boutique firms in a few large urban centres. Coupled with the absence of a uniform class action mechanism and a decentralised judicial system, it may well be that the Canadian experience holds lessons only for itself. Still, this experience points to the possibility that in the case of private collective enforcement in a transborder context, we might consider a reassessment of the presumed utility of maximum aggregation in favour of coordinated diversity throughout a regional, national or international market.

4. CHOICE OF LAW, DIVERSE LEGAL TRADITIONS AND TRANSBORDER CLASS ACTIONS

The jurisdictional challenges posed by the transborder class actions tend to hide another significant obstacle facing this type of claim, namely possible conflicts relating to the substantive law ultimately applicable to resolve the legal claims between the parties.[48] While the "common issue" at the heart of the action may well be seen as justifying a modification of the traditional jurisdictional rules, that should not easily extend to the choice of law issue. This is particularly obvious where there is a potential conflict between the laws that would be applicable to the individual claims. The formal difference in the legal regime governing liability for

48 For a general discussion from an American perspective, see Ryan Patrick Phair, "Resolving the 'Choice-of-Law Problem' in Rule 23(b)(3) Nationwide Class Actions" (2000) 67 *U. Chi. L. Rev.* 835.

defective products in Quebec and the Canadian common law provinces[49] as well as the distinct consumer protection legislation in the various provinces provide ample illustration. Beyond these divergences in substantive law, a second obstacle to the transborder action is the diversity of choice-of-law rules. Indeed, while the Civil Code of Québec contains a comprehensive codification of private international law,[50] the common law provinces continue to rely largely on rules emanating from decided cases, few of which provide any distinct rules for consumer claims, whether in contract or tort.[51] Unlike in the European Union, there are no instruments providing for the harmonisation of substantive or choice-of-law rules relating to consumer claims.[52] One can see how prejudicial this may be to the non-resident class member with no connection to the forum seized of the transborder action, regardless of the availability of an opt-out. Indeed, the framing of the case before the forum seized of the action may well depend on the law designated by that court's choice-of-law rules which may present a claim altogether different from the one availing the non-resident class member should he opt out and begin a claim in his home jurisdiction or commence the group action in his home province.[53]

The diversity of substantive applicable law may also be circumvented as a result of the proliferation of the settlement class action, where the court is asked to certify the claim as a class action and approve the settlement already negotiated by the parties in the same proceedings. Settlements will often exclude any conclusions on liability and the necessary compromise on compensation implied by settlement will deflect arguments about what could have been obtained under different substantive laws.

---

49 Quebec follows the European Union, having adopted a strict liability model based on a consumer expectation test (see Articles 1468 and ff. of the Civil Code of Québec) while the common law provinces continue to rely on the tort of negligence (See generally S.M. Waddams, *Products Liability* (4th ed., Carswell, 2001).).

50 The choice-of-law provisions are largely inspired by European codifications, particularly that of Switzerland. See H.P. Glenn, "Codification of Private International Law in Quebec" (1996) 60 *RabelsZ* 231.

51 For a brief general overview of the Canadian common law, see Chapter 5 of M. Baer et al., *Private International Law in Common Law Canada*, 2nd ed (Toronto: Edmond Montgomery, 2004). For Quebec, see the treatise by G. Goldstein & E. Groffier, *Droit international privé québécois* in two volumes, (Cowansville, Qc.: Yvon Blais). For an English text, see H.P. Glenn, *supra* note 50.

52 See especially the *1980 Rome Convention on the law applicable to contractual obligations* (to be replaced by a broadly similar Regulation *(EC) No. 593/2008* of the same name in December 2009, see OJ no. L 177, p. 6 ff.). On the impact of this different approach to the conflict of laws, see Symeon Symeonides, "The American Revolution and the European Evolution in Choice of Law: Reciprocal Lessons" (2008) 82 *Tulane Law Review* (forthcoming).

53 There is little chance that the notice to non-resident class members will raise this issue given its complexity.

Where the potential diversity of substantive applicable law is raised, it may lead the court to exclude from the class those members whose claim would be subject to the different law or to refuse certification on the grounds that the case would be unmanageable.[54] The US option of consolidating actions from across the country through the MDL panel mechanism may bring to light any implications relating to the diversity of applicable law and allow these to be addressed at earlier stages of the process. The option of separating the class into sub-classes is also available in both countries and can arguably serve to respect the diversity of underlying substantive laws. Whether such an approach is preferable to separate class actions coupled with national legal counsel and judicial cooperation is not obvious. Finally, it is worth noting that both the ULCC amendment to the Uniform Class Proceedings Act and the 2005 American *Class Action Fairness Act*[55] make specific reference to the applicable law as a criterion in the certification process.

5. CONCLUSION

The challenges posed by transborder private collective enforcement are multiple and raise concerns about procedural justice that go beyond those usually raised by the opt-out class action model typical of the Canadian and American procedures. For consumer redress, where the typical case will involve a very large class whose membership is distributed across a regional or international market, the transborder action may appear attractive as aggregation creates significant economies of scale for litigation purposes and can be transformed into meaningful bargaining power in settlement negotiations. In contractual cases, particularly those where individual claims based on standard-form contracts would not be economically viable, safeguarding individual consumer's rights, both substantive and procedural, is more theoretical than practical. In those cases, the difficulties associated with establishing jurisdiction over non-resident class members and the risks associated with a failure to properly ascertain the applicable substantive law are minimal. And yet, recent experience in Canada suggests that its courts will treat procedural justice concerns seriously to the point of refusing to recognise settlements approved by sister provinces. In non-contractual cases, particularly those involving significant individual variances in terms of assessment of injury and damages (for example in pharmaceutical cases), the protection of the non-resident class members' procedural and substantive rights may be critical, given

---

54 See also the discussion of this point in G. Miller's paper in this collection.

55 28 U.S.C.A. §1332(d) (2), (5)(B), (6) (2006). See generally Edward F. Sherman, "Class Actions After the Class Action Fairness Act of 2005" (2006) 90 *Tul. L. Rev.* 1593; for a commentary on the impact of this statute on the multi-state or transborder actions, see T.B. Wolff, "Federal Jurisdiction and Due Process in the Era of the Nationwide Class Action" 156 *University of Pennsylvania Law Review* 2035.

the potentially binding effect of any eventual judgment or settlement. Again, recent experience in Canada suggests that judges are taking seriously their role in preserving rights for local claimants against attempts by legal counsel in other provinces seeking to certify a class that would extend across provincial borders. This landscape of competing and overlapping class actions has given rise to proposals for judicial coordination in the absence of any available federal or binding solution. While these proposals are promising, their actual effect remains to be seen.

This brief portrait of the Canadian experience with class actions runs parallel to the American one, albeit on a much smaller scale and with only a few decades of history. Some important distinctions remain with regard to the transborder dimensions of class actions, such as the absence of a predominance criterion for certification in Canada which can reduce the effect of the conflict of laws element of a transborder action and the absence in Canada of an established system for consolidating multi-province claims in the nature of the American Panel on Multi-district Litigation. The two countries do have in common the federal structure and the constitutional obligation to recognise inter-state/province judgments and to safeguard procedural justice, three elements which are not foreign to the European Union. Still, experience in Canada has shown that in the transborder class action context, procedural justice may take on a more parochial tone than in other types of cases, possibly suggestive of an emerging judicial unease no doubt fuelled to some extent by stories of collusion and abuse in private collective enforcement coming from south of the border. Should that be the case, Canadian judges would perhaps be viewed as more European than North American!

CROSS-BORDER COLLECTIVE DAMAGE ACTIONS IN THE EU

Prof. Dr. Peter Rott*
University of Bremen

1. INTRODUCTION

An American type of class action has not been introduced until now by any of the EU Member States and no such legislation is likely to be introduced in the near future,[1] although there have already been calls for opt-out procedures in cases of large-scale low-value claims, in particular by consumer associations, as reactions to very low opt-in numbers in such cases. One of the reasons given against the introduction of opt-out procedures, even at the national level, is of a constitutional law nature. For example, Article 103 par. 1 of the German Basic Law (Grundgesetz) on the right to be heard has been interpreted by most German authors to render a rule impossible under which a non-party to litigation would be bound to a negative result[2] and the German legislator has excluded a *res judicata* effect on non-parties expressly for this reason in the Capital Market Model Claims Act.[3]

However, a great variety of types of collective actions have developed in recent years. They can be broadly put under the headings of group actions, representative actions, test case procedures and (usually representative) procedures for skimming-off profits. Group actions can be further distinguished as follows: a) group actions, where individual actions are literally grouped into one procedure, as is the case with the English Group Litigation Order and the collective

* Junior Professor for Private Law, in particular European Private Law. Some of the practical information stems from my work for the expert study "Evaluation of the effectiveness and efficiency of collective redress mechanisms in the European Union", organised by Civic Consulting and Oxford Economics, available at http://ec.europa.eu/consumers/redress_cons/collective_redress_en.htm. This study was used to prepare the Commission's Green Paper on Consumer Collective Redress, COM (2008) 794 final.

1 See, for example, the White Paper on Damages actions for the breach of EC antitrust rules, COM(2008) 165 final, that does not even consider the possibility of an opt-out procedure that is the most typical feature of the American style class action.

2 See, for example, A. Stadler, Musterverbandsklagen nach künftigem deutschen Recht, in: P. Gottwald and H. Roth (eds.), *Festschrift für Ekkehard Schumann zum 70. Geburtstag* (Mohr Siebeck, 2002), 465, at 480.

3 See the explanations in Bundestags-Drucksache (BT-DrS.) 15/5091, at 17.

proceedings under the German Capital Market Model Claims Act; b) actions that are brought by groups of claimants, which is possible, for example, under Spanish and Portuguese law; and c) group actions as described by the Glossary of the Consumer Law Enforcement Forum (CLEF)[4] as systems where one claimant, either an individual consumer or a consumer organisation, can seek redress and ask for a decision on behalf of a group with equal or similar problems, giving the members of the group the right to enforce their rights in accordance with the decision. The latter system exists, for example, in Sweden and in Finland, with different rules on legal standing. Representative actions are actions where the representative obtains a judgment that the representative can enforce him or herself. The CLEF Glossary distinguishes a) traditional representative actions where the representative can bring the action on behalf of consumers who will receive the damages themselves, such as the action under the German Legal Advice Act,[5] and b) collective representative actions where the representative receives the damages, a system that is particularly prominent in France. A very special procedure for skimming off the profits gained from unlawful conduct in the field of the law of unfair competition has been introduced in Germany. Unlike the other collective redress mechanisms mentioned in this chapter, it does not aim at compensating consumers that have been the victims of such unlawful conduct but instead tries to re-establish fairness in competition by taking illegal profits off the wrongdoers. This procedure can be initiated by consumer associations but the skimmed-off profits will go into the public purse.

This chapter aims at exploring whether or not, or to what extent, these different procedures can be brought in cross-border cases. Cross-border cases are, first of all, those cases where the claimant and the defendant reside in different countries. The situation is further complicated in cases where there are claimants from different countries, or where, in a type c) group action, victims from different countries could be represented. The legal situation in all these circumstances is analysed under Regulation (EC) No. 44/2001 on jurisdiction and the recognition and enforcement of judgments in civil and commercial matters,[6] which has harmonised within the EC the rules on jurisdiction, and under the new harmonised private international law regime of Regulation (EC) No. 864/2007 on the law applicable to non-contractual obligations (Rome II)[7] and the regime of the new Regulation (EC) No 593/2008 on the law applicable to contractual obligations

4 Available at www.clef-project.eu/cms/project.php.

5 The Legal Advice Act was replaced by the Legal Services Act with effect from July 2008. Under the new §79 par. 2 No 3 of the Civil Procedural Act (Zivilprozessordnung, ZPO), the eligible consumer associations can bring representative actions "within their field of activity and responsibility". Assignment of claims is no longer necessary.

6 OJ 2001, L 12/1.

7 OJ 2007, L 199/40.

(Rome I),[8] although neither has entered into force yet. In a final section, the chapter will consider the working around EC law by bringing or joining a class action in the US and enforcing a US judgment or in-court settlement within the EC.

2. JURISDICTION

Not all EC Member States offer the procedural framework for collective actions, and the available collective actions vary greatly as to their practicability. Therefore, it is crucial to have jurisdiction in a Member State with a practicable legal framework and where several jurisdictions are available, *forum shopping* is the most sensible thing to do. The EC has established a harmonised framework for matters of jurisdiction with Regulation (EC) No. 44/2001 that covers "civil and commercial matters whatever the nature of the court or tribunal". This regulation mainly aims at creating legal certainty.[9] Indeed, the following section demonstrates that it limits the possibility of multinational collective actions, falling behind the more generous jurisdiction rules in the US and Canada.

2.1. SCOPE OF APPLICATION OF THE REGULATION

Those types of collective actions that are brought by individual claimants or by groups of claimants fall into the category of "civil and commercial matters". This had occasionally been doubted by academics in the case of punitive damages actions[10] and recently the German OLG Koblenz has, in the context of the service of a law suit under the Hague Convention on the Service Abroad of Judicial and Extrajudicial Documents in Civil or Commercial Matters, classified a US competition law action for treble damages as being a public law instrument, due to its regulatory function.[11] This approach, however, has been rejected by other

8 OJ 2008, L 177/6.

9 See recital (11) of the Regulation.

10 See, for example, H.H. Hollmann, Auslandszustellungen in US-amerikanischen Zivilsachen und Verwaltungssachen, *Recht der Internationalen Wirtschaft* (RIW) 1982, 784, at 786; C. Wölki, Das Haager Zustellungsabkommen und die USA, *Recht der Internationalen Wirtschaft (RIW)* 1985, 530, at 531 and more recently J. Mörsdorf-Schulte, Spezielle Vorbehaltsklausel im Europäischen Internationalen Deliktsrecht?, *Zeitschrift für vergleichende Rechtswissenschaft (ZVglRWiss)* 104 (2005), 192, at 226 ff.

11 See OLG Koblenz, *Praxis des Internationalen Privat- und Verfahrensrechts (IPRax)* 2006, 25, at 33.

courts[12] and also by the majority of academics,[13] the decisive reason being that such a claim is pursued in a civil law procedure in which the parties are on equal footing and that the award is paid out to private parties.

Also, signing up to a group action that was brought by a representative, for example, a consumer ombudsman or a consumer organisation, certainly comes under Regulation (EC) No. 44/2001, the reason being that those who sign up to collective litigation are bound by the decision of the court.

In contrast, it has always been discussed controversially, in the context of cross-border injunctions, whether or not this also applies to law suits brought by public authorities or ombudsmen. Whilst the ECJ has already, in the case of *Henkel*,[14] confirmed that an injunction in the field of unfair contract terms, brought by the Austrian consumer organisation Verein für Konsumenten-organisation (VKI) comes under the Regulation, or its predecessor respectively, there has been no opportunity yet to decide on actions brought by public authorities or ombudsmen. Some authors have argued that such actions are not "civil and commercial matters".[15] This is, however, unconvincing. At least in cross-border cases, public authorities or ombudsmen do not exercise public power but they act just like any other party to a civil court action. In that respect, they are in no way distinguishable from, for example, consumer associations. Therefore, cross-border collective actions brought by public authorities and ombudsmen should also be covered by Regulation (EC) No. 44/2001.[16]

---

12 See OLG München, *Neue Juristische Wochenschrift (NJW)* 1989, 3102; OLG München, *Neue Juristische Wochenschrift (NJW)* 1992, 3113; OLG Celle, *Niedersächsische Rechtspflege (NdsRpfl)* 2006, 275; OLG Naumburg, *Wirtschaft und Wettbewerb (WuW)* 2006, 932; OLG München, *OLG-Report München* 2006, 801.

13 See H. Koch and F. Diedrich, Grundrechte als Maßstab für Zustellungen nach dem Haager Zustellungsübereinkommen?, *Zeitschrift für Wirtschaftsrecht (ZIP)* 1994, 1830, at 1831; H. Nagel and P. Gottwald, *Internationales Zivilprozessrecht*, 6th ed. (Otto Schmidt, 2007), §7 n. 76; J. von Hein, BVerfG gestattet Zustellung einer US-amerikanischen Klage auf Punitive Damages, *RIW* 2007, 249, at 255.

14 ECJ, judgment of 1 October 2002, case C-167/00 *Verein für Konsumenteninformation v. Karl Heinz Henkel*, [2002] ECR I-8111.

15 See, for example, K. Maurer, Grenzüberschreitende Unterlassungsklagen von Verbraucherschutzverbänden (Lit-Verlag, 2001), at 9; N. Reich, Rechtsprobleme grenzüberschreitender irreführender Werbung im Binnenmarkt, *Rabels Zeitschrift für ausländisches und internationales Privatrecht (RabelsZ)* 56 (1992), 444, at 457 f.; see also the doubts expressed by E. Jayme and C. Kohler, Europäisches Kollisionsrecht 1997 – Vergemeinschaftung durch "Säulenwechsel"?, *Praxis des Internationalen Privat- und Verfahrensrechts (IPRax)* 1997, 385, at 392.

16 For more details, see P. Rott, Das Internationale Privatrecht der Unterlassungsklage qualifizierter Einrichtungen, in: H.-W. Micklitz, P. Rott, U. Docekal and P. Kolba, *Verbraucherschutz durch Unterlassungsklagen* (Nomos, 2006), 265, at 277 ff. See also C. Michailidou, Internationale Zuständigkeit bei vorbeugenden Verbandsklagen, *Praxis des Internationalen Privat- und Verfahrensrechts (IPRax)* 2003, 223, at 224, and the Green Paper on Consumer Collective Redress, COM(2008) 794 final, at para. 58.

Doubts as to the application of Regulation (EC) No. 44/2001 merely remain with regard to the German skimming-off procedure under §10 UWG, the reason being that the skimmed off profits go neither to the victims of the unlawful conduct nor to the representative but to the public purse.[17] On the other hand, the procedure itself follows the normal rule of an adversarial civil law procedure and can therefore not be classified as a public law procedure.[18]

2.2. AVAILABLE COURTS

A. *The Member State Where the Defendant is Domiciled*

No problem arises where the defendant is domiciled in a Member State where collective procedures are available, even where the victims reside in different countries. Under Article 2 of the Regulation, courts of the Member States where the defendant is domiciled[19] always have jurisdiction.

B. *The Special Jurisdiction for Consumer Contracts*

In the case of mass breach of consumer contracts, consumers could also sue in the courts of their own jurisdiction, under Article 15. In contrast, this provision does not apply where a representative, for example, a consumer association or an ombudsman, brings a collective action in favour of consumers. In *Shearson Lehmann Hutton,* the ECJ held that a claimant that is acting in pursuance of his trade or professional activity, as the assignee of the rights of a private individual, does not enjoy the protection provided to consumers.[20]

---

17 On the relevance of the recipient of payment see above.

18 Finally, it has no relation to criminal law, which has occasionally been submitted by German authors; see, for example, R. Sack, Der Gewinnabschöpfungsanspruch von Verbänden in der geplanten UWG-Novelle, *Wettbewerb in Recht und Praxis (WRP)* 2003, 549, at 552; S. Wimmer-Leonhard, UWG-Reform und Gewinnabschöpfungsanspruch oder: Die Wiederkehr der Drachen, *Gewerblicher Rechtsschutz und Urheberrecht (GRUR)* 2004, 12, at 16; S. Engels and T. H. Salomon, Vom Lauterkeitsrecht zum Verbraucherschutz – UWG-Reform, *Wettbewerb in Recht und Praxis (WRP)* 2004, 32, at 42. In contrast, fines will even be considered when calculating the unlawful profits, see §10 par. 2 s. 1 of the Unfair Competition Act. See also H. Köhler, in: W. Hefermehl, H. Köhler and J. Bornkamm (eds.), *Gesetz gegen den unlauteren Wettbewerb*, 26th ed. (Beck, 2008), §10 n. 3.

19 The domicile of a company or other legal person or association of natural or legal persons is further described in Article 60.

20 ECJ, judgment of 19 January 1993, case C-89/91 *Shearson Lehmann Hutton Inc. v TVB Treuhandgesellschaft für Vermögensverwaltung und Beteiligungen mbH*, [1993] ECR I-139. See also H. Koch, Die Verbandsklage in Europa, *Zeitschrift für Zivilprozeß* (ZZP) 113 (2000), 413, at 437.

C. *Special Jurisdictions in Contract and Tort Law Cases*

Alternatively, victims of a mass breach of contract could sue, under Article 5 No 1, in the courts for the place of performance of the obligation in question and tort victims, including victims in product liability cases, could sue, under Article 5 No 3, in the courts for the place where the harmful event occurred or may occur.[21] These options may be attractive in cases where the Member State in which the defendant is domiciled has no collective procedures available or where the procedures in other Member States appear to be better suited to bring the claim. The special jurisdiction for tort litigation may also work for representatives in collective actions. In the above-mentioned case of *Henkel*,[22] the ECJ considered the action for an injunction concerning the use of unfair contract terms, that was brought by the VKI, to fall under Article 5 No 3 of the Brussels Convention, which was the predecessor of Regulation (EC) No 44/2001.

D. *An Additional Jurisdiction by Way of Joining?*

Where no collective procedures are available in the Member State in which the producer is domiciled, or where they are unattractive, the question arises as to whether or not claims of victims from different countries whose individual claims would come under different jurisdictions can be joined in the court of one Member State. For example, products of a Dutch producer may have harmed consumers in Sweden and in Belgium. The Swedish consumers can sue in Sweden and they will be able to bring a Swedish group action. Could the Belgian consumers join in?

First of all, the parties may wish to enter into a choice of court agreement, which is in all circumstances possible, even in the case of consumer contracts.[23] Even the defendant trader or producer may be interested in having all litigation concentrated in one court in order to save expenses for lawyers' fees and so on.

Where no choice of court agreement can be achieved, the only provision that allows the joining of proceedings that would not otherwise come under the same jurisdiction is Article 6 of the Regulation. Article 6 reads:

> A person domiciled in a Member State may also be sued:
> 1. where he is one of a number of defendants, in the courts for the place where any one of them is domiciled, provided the claims are so closely connected that it is expedient to hear and determine them together to avoid the risk of irreconcilable judgments resulting from separate proceedings;

---

21 On the additional jurisdiction in tort cases see ECJ, judgment of 30 November 1976, case 21/76 *Handelskwerkrij G.J. Bier v. Mines de Potasse d'Alsace*, [1976] ECR I-1735.

22 ECJ, judgment of 1 October 2002, case C-167/00 *Verein für Konsumenteninformation v. Karl Heinz Henkel*, [2002] ECR I-8111.

23 See Article 17 of the Regulation. Restrictions apply but choice of court agreements are valid if concluded after the event giving rise to the litigation occurred.

2. as a third party in an action on a warranty or guarantee or in any other third party proceedings, in the court seised of the original proceedings, unless these were instituted solely with the object of removing him from the jurisdiction of the court which would be competent in his case;
3. on a counter-claim arising from the same contract or facts on which the original claim was based, in the court in which the original claim is pending;
4. in matters relating to a contract, if the action may be combined with an action against the same defendant in matters relating to rights in rem in immovable property, in the court of the Member State in which the property is situated.

Based on the wording of this provision, there is no way of having persons from one Member State participate in a group action in a Member State that has only jurisdiction over other members of the group. Nor could a victim sign up to a group action that has been initiated by an ombudsman in a Member State that has no jurisdiction for the individual claim of that victim. The only case that comes anywhere near is Article 6 No 1, which however explicitly relates to a multitude of defendants but not of claimants. Thus, a cross-border action with claimants or participants from different countries can only be brought in a Member State that has jurisdiction for all the relevant individual claims; and this will only be the Member State in which the defendant company is domiciled. This is underlined by the ECJ decision in *Shevill* where the ECJ held that the victim of a libel by a newspaper article distributed in several Member States may bring an action for damages against the publisher before the courts of each Member State in which the publication was distributed and where the victim claims to have suffered injury to his reputation. The courts, however, have jurisdiction to rule solely in respect of the harm caused in the State of the court seised.[24]

Of course, this limitation does not exist in the case of a representative action where only the representative is a party to the law suit, as in the case of the German Legal Services Act. Such representative actions, however, pose different problems, as will be demonstrated in the following sections.

3. PROCEDURAL AND SUBSTANTIVE LIMITATIONS OF THE VARIOUS COLLECTIVE ACTIONS

Even if jurisdiction can be established under Regulation (EC) No. 44/2001, the national remedies or procedures have their serious limitations that may impede cross-border actions. Generally speaking, under the rules of private international

24 ECJ, judgment of 7 March 1995, case C-58/93 *Fiona Shevill and others v. Presse Alliance SA*, [1995] ECR I-415.

law, the courts apply their own domestic procedural law (*lex fori*). Thus, as far as the requirements to be met for a collective action are of a procedural nature, the civil procedural laws or special laws on collective actions of the Member State in which the court is situated apply. In many cases, restrictions mirror a general reluctance towards collective claims for damages, fuelled by the fear to open the gates for US-type litigation. This reluctance is, in particular, expressed in limitations to legal standing but also in unfavourable cost rules that are meant to act as a disincentive to abuse.

3.1. LEGAL STANDING

A. *Collective Actions Brought by Representatives*

First of all, there is a tendency in the Member States to grant legal standing to bring collective actions only to national organisations or bodies.[25] For example, under the Finnish Group Action Act, only the Finnish consumer ombudsman has legal standing, and under the procedure of sec. 47B of the UK Competition Act 1998, only the British consumer association *Which?* is entitled to bring an action. The French collective representative action under Article L 421–1 of the Code de la consommation can only be brought by a consumer organisation that is registered in France and the same applies to claims for collective damages in Greek law.[26] The German collective action under the Legal Advice Act is only available to the German regional consumer centres and consumer organisations that receive public support (meaning support out of the German public purse).[27] In contrast, the skimming-off procedure under the German Unfair Competition Act is available to all foreign qualified entities that are listed in the Commission's register under Article 4(3) of the Injunctions Directive 98/27/EC.[28] This procedure, however, would be fairly uninteresting to foreign qualified entities since the skimmed off profits always go the German public purse.

The issue as to whether or not limitations that exclude foreign consumer representatives from initiating collective action are in line with EC law has already been raised by *Norbert Reich* in 1992, with a view to cross-border injunctions. He argued at the time, that the non-discrimination rule of Article 12 EC required

[25] See generally H.-W. Micklitz, Rechtsvergleich, in: H.-W. Micklitz, P. Rott, U. Docekal and P. Kolba, *Verbraucherschutz durch Unterlassungsklagen* (Nomos, 2006), 219, at 228 ff.

[26] See H. Beuchler, Griechenland, in: H.-W. Micklitz and A. Stadler (eds.), *Das Verbandsklagerecht in der Informations- und Dienstleistungsgesellschaft* (Landwirtschaftsverlag, 2005), 169, at 193 ff.

[27] On the latter see also M. Burckhardt, *Auf dem Weg zu einer class action in Deutschland?* (Nomos, 2005), at 150 f.; Stadler, n. 2 above, at 487 ff.

[28] Last update published in OJ 2008, C 63/5.

Member States to grant facilitated access of foreign consumer association to the domestic courts.[29] He added later on that the then new Article 153 EC confirmed the role of consumer associations.[30] However, no court has ever followed this line of argument. Instead, it was the EC legislator that finally stepped in and adopted the Injunctions Directive 98/27/EC that makes sure that foreign "qualified entities" that may be consumer organisations, public authorities or ombudsmen have legal standing in cases of cross-border violations of consumer law.[31]

The only possible cross-border issue related to such types of collective action is whether foreign consumers could sign up to a claim brought by the Finnish ombudsman or *Which?*, whether the French consumer organisation can sue for the collective damage done not only to French but also to foreign consumers and whether the German consumer organisations can have claims from foreign consumers assigned.

B. *Collective Actions Brought by Consumers Themselves*

No issues of legal standing arise where consumers or victims in general sue individually and then apply to have their claims joined into a collective procedure since individuals always have legal standing when they wish to defend their interests. Any restriction for residents of other Member States would be a blatant breach of the non-discrimination rules of Article 12 EC.[32]

3.2. SUBSTANTIVE LEGITIMACY TO BRING THE CLAIM (*AKTIVLEGITIMATION*)

One issue that is specific to only few legal orders, including in particular Germany and Austria, is the substantive legitimacy of consumer representatives to bring a claim. In these legal orders, consumer associations have their own claims against

29 N. Reich, *RabelsZ* 1992, 444, at 501.

30 N. Reich, Verbraucherpolitik und Verbraucherschutz im Vertrag von Amsterdam, Verbraucher und Recht (VuR) 1999, 3 ff.

31 On the historical background of this directive see H.-W. Micklitz, Cross-Border Consumer Conflicts – A French-German Experience, *Journal of Consumer Policy (JCP)*, vol. 16, 411 ff. (1993); H.-W. Micklitz and P. Rott, Unterlassungsklage, in: E. Grabitz, M. Hilf and M. Wolf (eds.), *Das Recht der Europäischen Union*, vol. III (Beck, 2006), vor Art. 25 n. 2 ff.

32 Concerning the application of Article 12 EC to national civil procedural law, see ECJ, judgment of 1 July 1993, case C-20/92 *Anthony Hubbard (Testamentsvollstrecker) v. Peter Hamburger*, [1993] ECR I-3777; judgment of 10 February 1994, case C-398/92 *Mund & Fester v. Hatrex Internationaal Transport*, [1994] ECR I-467; judgment of 26 September 1996, case C-43/95 *Data Delecta Aktiebolag and Ronny Forsberg v. MSL Dynamics Ltd.*, [1996] ECR I-4661; judgment of 20 March 1997, case C-323/95 *David Charles Hayes and Jeannette Karen Hayes v. Kronenberger GmbH*, [1997] ECR I-1711; judgment of 2 October 1997, case C-122/96 *Stephen Austin Saldanha and MTS Securities Corporation v. Hiross Holding AG*, [1997] ECR I-5325.

traders, independent from the existence of consumers' claims. This applies, in particular, to the skimming-off action under §10 of the Unfair Competition Act.[33] The German concept to require, next to the procedural legal standing, an additional substantive claim, posed major problems prior to the implementation of the Injunctions Directive 98/27/EC, when German courts denied German consumer associations the right to defend the rights of French consumers.[34] A similar restriction is that the *Aktivlegitimation* of consumer associations only relates to the breach of the *lex fori*. Earlier case law of the German Bundesgerichtshof only allowed a breach of German unfair competition law to be brought in the collective proceedings under the German Unfair Competition Act. Where a German trader had used unlawful marketing practices in France, French law applied. Thus, the German Unfair Competition Act was held not to apply at all.[35]

Whilst the Injunctions Directive has solved the problem for injunctions in the consumers' interest,[36] this directive does not apply to cross-border damage claims. The German legislator recently, in 2006, introduced the new §4a into the Injunctions Act, that explicitly allows German qualified entities to bring injunctions against the breach of consumer law that takes effect in other Member States. Nevertheless, nothing seems to prevent the German legislator, or the German courts respectively, from applying the concept of *Aktivlegitimation* again in cases where no injunctions are sought, and therefore to restrict the effect of the skimming-off action to profits made from unlawful conduct vis-à-vis German consumers only.

3.3. A LIMITED "COLLECTIVE INTEREST OF CONSUMERS" AND OTHER DISINCENTIVES

A similar issue arises in the context of representative collective actions, where the representative receives compensation for damage done to the collective interest of consumers. Can, for example, a French consumer association claim damages for all the damage done by a French trader to consumers all over the EC? This appears highly unlikely, the first and foremost reason being that such a trader may face litigation in a number of countries, some individual litigation, some collective actions, for the same breach of the law.

---

33 Long established case law, which was then even codified, see R. Greger, Neue Regeln für die Verbandsklage im Verbraucherschutz- und Wettbewerbsrecht, *Neue Juristische Wochenschrift (NJW)* 2000, 2462. For critical comments, see E. Schmidt, Verbraucherschützende Verbandsklagen, *Neue Juristische Wochenschrift (NJW)* 2002, 25, at 27 ff.

34 See, in particular, OLG Köln, *Verbraucher und Recht (VuR)* 1995, 292 f.

35 See BGH, *Verbraucher und Recht (VuR)* 1998, 173.

36 For details on the effect of the Injunctions Directive on the German *Aktivlegitimation* see P. Rott, n. 16 above, at 279 ff.

But why should it be the French consumer organisation and not the Bulgarian consumer association (that could also bring a representative collective action under Article 188 of the Bulgarian Consumer Protection Act of 2006)? Ultimately, it seems safe to assume that a French court would only consider the damage that was done to the collective interest of French consumers when awarding damages to a French consumer organisation under Article L. 421–1 of the Code de la consommation.

Disincentives could also stem from the envisaged tasks of a consumer organisation. *Which?*, for example, is a membership-based consumer organisation, funded by the membership fees of British consumers. Litigation under sec. 47B of the Competition Act 1998 does not only impose the risk of having to bear the litigation fees but it can also be extremely time-consuming to organise and carry through, which means that it involves weeks or even months of staff working time that are not recoverable from the defendant. Consumer organisations could therefore find it difficult to justify the representation of non-members from abroad. The same could apply in cases where consumer representatives obtain funding from their national governments, as was the case with the consumer organisations that could bring collective actions under the German Legal Advice Act.[37]

3.4. LIMITATIONS AS TO THE TYPE OF CLAIMS THAT ARE ELIGIBLE FOR COLLECTIVE ACTIONS

A number of collective procedures are restricted to certain subjects of the claim. For example, the German Capital Market Model Claims Act only covers claims resulting from false or misleading capital market information. The Act is some kind of experiment that might be extended to other fields of law if it proves to be successful.[38] Also, the collective action under the UK Competition Act 1998 only comes into play once the competition authorities have established anti-competitive behaviour of a trader.

---

37 For these consumer organisations, it would be, in principle, possible to represent foreign consumers. See also Stadler, n. 2 above, at 488 f.

38 See, for example, B. Hess and C. Michailidou, Das Gesetz über Musterverfahren zu Schadensersatzklagen von Kapitalanlegern, *Zeitschrift für Wirtschaftsrecht (ZIP)* 2004, 1381, at 1386 f.

3.5. DISCRETION AS TO THE JOINING OR ADMITTANCE OF INDIVIDUAL CLAIMS

Finally, even in the case of group actions or traditional representative actions that are, in principle, open to foreign claimants, practical considerations may prevent multi-national collective actions. In most legal systems the courts have a certain amount of discretion as to whether or not individual litigation should be joined into one collective procedure (for example, in the case of the UK Group Litigation Order or the German Capital Market Model Act), or whether or not to admit the opting in of victims to a group action and it may well be that foreign claims are regarded unsuited for the collective action. This may, in particular, occur where the common feature of the claim is a question of law rather than a question of fact and where the claims of foreign victims come under a different national legal order than the domestic claims, under the rules of private international law that are discussed in the next section.

4. PRIVATE INTERNATIONAL LAW

Compared to the laws of the US states, the legal landscape in the EC is much more diverse, and it may make a big difference in contract law cases as well as in tort law cases as to which one of the national legal orders applies. This is even true where EC directives are in place since they used to be minimum harmonisation directives that allowed the Member States to adopt or maintain more stringent rules for the protection of consumers. Even with the recent tendency towards full harmonisation in EC consumer law, many issues remain outside the scope of harmonisation and within the national competence.[39] Thus, the determination of the applicable legal order, or orders, in multinational cross-border collective actions, is and will remain an issue.

Collective action may relate to contractual claims or to non-contractual claims (or to both). Cross-border contractual claims will come, in the near future, under the regime of the new Rome I Regulation (EC) No. 593/2008 that replaces the Rome Convention on the law applicable to contractual obligations of 1980, whereas cross-border non-contractual claims will come, from November 2009, under the Rome II Regulation (EC) No. 864/2007.

---

[39] See, for example, the analysis of the scope of application of the new Consumer Credit Directive 2008/48/EC by P. Rott, Die neue Verbraucherkredit-Richtlinie 2008/48/EG und ihre Auswirkungen auf das deutsche Recht, *Wertpapier-Mitteilungen (WM)* 2008, 1104 ff.

4.1. CONTRACT LAW CASES

Contract law cases may relate, for example, to overcharging in contracts on continued performance, such as telecommunications or energy supply contracts. Here, a distinction must be made between consumer contracts and other contracts, since Article 6 of the Rome I Regulation provides for a special regime for consumer contracts.

A. *Consumer Contracts*

Without having to go into detail for the purpose of this chapter, the general rule is that Article 6 of the Rome I Regulation does not prohibit a choice of law agreement but such choice of law cannot deprive the consumer of the mandatory protection offered by his own national consumer law. In the absence of a choice of law, the law of the Member State in which the consumer is domiciled applies.[40]

In essence, this means that in cases where consumers from different Member States are concerned, different national laws apply, either exclusively or their mandatory rules inasmuch they are more favourable to the consumer than the law that the parties have agreed upon. Thus, the different claims within a group action would have to be considered under different legal orders.[40bis] This is also the case if claims have been assigned to a representative, for example, under the German Legal Services Act, since the assignment as such does not change the character of the claim.

The diversity of laws to be applied may not be an absolute impediment to collective actions that include claims of consumers from different jurisdictions but it may be an argument for courts when exercising their discretion. Whether or not a court would accept the aggregation of claims to which different legal orders apply would probably depend on the issue at stake. For example, if the common issue is a matter of fact that is relevant for each of the claims, this should not be a major problem. Also, if the claims ultimately stem from an EC directive, for example, the Package Travel Directive 90/314/EEC that was at stake in some of the cases in which the UK Group Litigation Order was used, the national legal rules may even be identical or very similar so that it makes sense to decide upon them in one collective procedure.

---

40 For a full account, see, for example, K. Bitterich, Kollisionsrechtliche Absicherung gemeinschaftsrechtlicher Standards im Bereich des Verbraucherschutzes: Der Vorschlag für eine Rom I-Verordnung, *Recht der Internationalen Wirtschaft (RIW)* 2006, 262 ff.

40bis See also the Green Paper on Consumer Collective Redress, COM(2008) 794 final, at para. 59.

B. Other Contracts

Not all contracts to which consumers are parties are covered by Article 6 of the Rome I Regulation. Contracts of carriage (other than package travel contracts in the terms of Directive 90/314/EEC) are for example excluded from the above mentioned rules, under Article 6(4) lit. b). In such cases, more flexibility as to the choice of law exists and the choice of law may also be exercised after the conclusion of the contract, even in court. Thus, the parties could bring all the claims under the same legal regime if they wished to do so.

C. Representative Actions

It should be noted that representative actions may only fall under the regime of consumer contracts when the representative is assigned the consumers' claims in order to bring them into one collective action, as was the case under the German Legal Advice Act. Otherwise, particular representative collective actions cannot be considered to be contract law cases even if the incremented conduct relates to contractual relationships. The reasoning is basically the same as in the jurisdiction case of *Henkel* where the ECJ held that the representative consumer organisation itself was in no contractual relationship whatsoever with the trader.[41]

4.2. TORT LAW CASES

Similarly, in tort law cases the normal rules of private international law of the Rome II Regulation point at different legal orders for consumers that reside in different Member States. Under Article 4(1), the law of the country applies in which the damage occurs irrespective of the country in which the event giving rise to the damage occurred and irrespective of the country or countries in which the indirect consequences of that event occur. For product liability cases, Article 5 offers a special rule under which primarily the law of the country applies in which the person sustaining the damage had his or her habitual residence when the damage occurred, if the product was marketed in that country.[42] Assume, for example, a product that was sold all over the EC and has caused damage due to a defect giving rise to product liability. The applicable law will be for each victim the law of the Member State of his residence, provided that the product has been marketed in his country.

---

41 See ECJ, judgment of 1 October 2002, case C-167/00 *Verein für Konsumenteninformation v. Karl Heinz Henkel*, [2002] ECR I-8111.

42 For more details see, for example, G. Wagner, Die neue Rom II-Verordnung, *Praxis des Internationalen Privat- und Verfahrensrechts (IPRax)* 2008, 1, at 7 f.

However, the Rome II Regulation offers more flexibility in consumer cases than the Rome I Regulation. In particular, Article 14(1) allows a choice of law agreement even in consumer cases after the event giving rise to the damage occurred. Thus, the parties to a law suit can remove obstacles to the collective treatment of claims if they wish to do so. In contrast, it would seem that no other mechanism is in place to find a unitary solution for claims of victims from different countries. Although both Article 4 and Article 5 take into account that it may be clear from all the circumstances of the case that the tort is manifestly more closely connected with a different country and in such a case this other country's law applies, it would seem highly unlikely that a number of victims from the same type of product that are residents of another Member State might constitute a close connection to that Member State's law. What the legislator primarily thought of is a closer connection through a contractual relationship in the individual case.

4.3. CONCLUSION

In conclusion, harmonised EC private international law has few or no mechanisms in place to find a common legal order to apply in cases where one particular product or conduct infringed the rights of consumers in different countries. This means in essence that claims from consumers from different countries are likely not to be joined in a collective procedure where a court has the discretion not to join unsuitable claims or to deny claims coming under different legal orders to be joined in one representative collective action, for example, under the German Legal Advice Act.

5. SUMMING UP – THE SITUATION IN THE EC

In a number of representative actions, legal standing is restricted to domestic consumer representatives only or even to one designated body only. This is the case in Finland, in Sweden and in France, and also with the collective action under s. 47B of the UK Competition Act 1998. In these cases, the only cross-border element could be the representation of victims from different countries, which is unlikely to happen, at least in consumer contract law cases, since different national contract laws would apply. This might be different in cross-border tort cases if the parties enter into a choice of law agreement after the damage has occurred.

True collective representative actions, where consumer associations claim damages for the violation of the collective interest of consumers into their own purse, also appear limited to the collective domestic interest since the trader might otherwise face multiple litigation in different countries.

As far as I can see, the only collective action that a foreign representative could bring is the skimming-off action under §10 of the German Unfair Competition Act. This action, however, is most unattractive to foreign entities since the money goes to the German public purse.

Thus, the types of cross-border collective actions that could most likely be brought are actions brought by a group of consumers or individual actions that are joined after they have been brought. Such actions, however, require each individual claim to come under the jurisdiction of the (collective) court. Furthermore, courts would probably not accept the joining of claims that have to be dealt with under different legal orders, according to the rules of private international law.

In practice, no cross-border collective actions have become known in the EC yet. Rather, consumer representatives from different EC Member States take co-ordinated action against the same trader and parallelise their strategies. It should, however, be noted as well that a number of collective procedures have only been introduced very recently in EC Member States and no experience of these procedures exists as of yet.

6. LOOKING BEYOND THE EC BORDERS

The most interesting question related to cross-border cases related to third countries is certainly if and to what extent the US or Canadian class actions can be used in order to obtain a judgment that can then be enforced within the EC. This is a constant fear of industry,[43] and it has already led to numerous and sometimes irritating litigation. Negotiations for an international Convention on Jurisdiction and Foreign Judgments in Civil and Commercial Matters[44] in The Hague have ultimately failed.[45] Thus, the Member States of the EC are free to decide how to deal with North American class actions. At the same time, their attitude towards class actions demonstrates the unlikelihood of this instrument to be introduced in the EC in the near future. This shall be illustrated by a look into German law and practice.

---

43 See the references in Mörsdorf-Schulte, *ZVglRWiss* 104 (2005), 192, at 195 ff.

44 On which see, for example, S. P. Baumgartner, *The Proposed Hague Convention on Jurisdiction and Foreign Judgments* (Mohr Siebeck, 2003).

45 See J. von Hein, Der ausschließliche Gerichtsstand für Kapitalanleger-Musterverfahren – eine Lex Anti-Americana?, *Recht der Internationalen Wirtschaft (RIW)* 2004, 602, at 609 fn. 81.

6.1. SERVICE OF THE CLAIM

As mentioned earlier in this chapter, German courts have occasionally refused to even service US class actions to the German defendant.[46] In 1994, the German Constitutional Court surprised the legal community with an interim order that prohibited the service of a claim by which the claimant claimed punitive damages.[47] The decision was heavily criticised in academic writing [48] and in the main proceedings the Constitutional Court allowed the claim to be served.[49] However, in the *Bertelsmann* case, the Constitutional Court again held the service of a claim (over USD17 billion) to be unconstitutional. The court argued that the claimants merely intended to pressure the defendant into a settlement by threatening the defendant with the litigation costs and with the risk of facing unpredictable proceedings.[50] The OLG Koblenz[51] took this up and asked the Supreme Court (Bundesgerichtshof) to solve the differences between the Regional Courts most of which follow a more liberal line, allowing the service of class actions in Germany. Only recently, however, the German Constitutional Court had again the opportunity to deal with this issue in a case where an employee of the Puerto Rican subsidiary of a German company claimed USD11,114,500 in damages due from alleged discrimination since he had not obtained a leading position in that subsidiary. In that particular case, the Constitutional Court argued that the claim did not threaten the existence of the German company and its service would not damage the company's reputation significantly. However, the Constitutional Court did not overrule the earlier decision in the *Bertelsmann* case but distinguished both cases.[52] Thus, in extreme cases service of a class action may still be denied.

---

46 For a detailed analysis and discussion, see von Hein, supra note 13 at 249 ff.

47 Constitutional Court, *Entscheidungssammlung des Bundesverfassungsgerichtshofs (BVerfGE)* 91, 140.

48 See, for example, E. Juenger and M. Reimann, Zustellung von Klagen auf punitive damages nach dem Haager Zustellungsübereinkommen, *Neue Juristische Wochenschrift (NJW)* 1994, 3274 f.; Koch and Diedrich, supra note 13 at 1830 ff.

49 Constitutional Court, *Entscheidungssammlung des Bundesverfassungsgerichtshofs (BVerfGE)* 91, 335.

50 See Constitutional Court, *Entscheidungssammlung des Bundesverfassungsgerichtshofs (BVerfGE)* 108, 238. For a detailed analysis of the relevant legal issues see K. Hopt, R. Kulms and J. von Hein, *Rechtshilfe und Rechtsstaat: Die Zustellung einer US-amerikanischen class action in Deutschland* (Mohr Siebeck, 2006).

51 OLG Koblenz, *IPRax* 2006, 25.

52 Constitutional Court, *Recht der Internationalen Wirtschaft (RIW)* 2007, 211, at 212.

6.2. RECOGNITION AND ENFORCEMENT OF CLASS ACTION JUDGMENTS

The recognition and enforcement of decisions of courts outside the EC are not subject to Regulation (EC) No. 44/2001, but to the national laws of the Member States. German Courts appear to have difficulties to accept US class action judgments as such.[53] Of course, US judgments are, in principle, recognisable and enforceable in Germany. In a landmark decision of 1992, the Bundesgerichtshof held that neither the pre-discovery trial nor the American rule of costs nor the agreement on contingency fees prevented the recognition of US judgments in Germany.[54] However, difficulties arise once punitive damages or treble damages (in competition law cases) shall be executed. In addition to this, the legislator tries – in a subtle way – to avoid US class actions against German companies.

A. *Punitive Damages and Treble Damages*

Even though the problems around the service of a foreign class action appear to be solved, the issue returns in the guise of a recognition problem. The protection of German or European companies from punitive damages has been discussed repeatedly, under different headings. For example, in the legislative process of the Rome II Regulation, a provision had been included according to which the application of a provision of the law designated by this Regulation which had the effect of causing non-compensatory damages, such as exemplary or punitive damages, to be awarded should be contrary to Community public policy.[55] Although this provision has not lasted very long because it would not only have caught US punitive damages but also English exemplary and restitutionary damages,[56] a general *ordre public* clause still exists in Article 26 of the Rome II Regulation and it is clear that courts will invoke the general *ordre public* clause in order not to award punitive damages even if US law (resp. US state law) is applicable to the case at hand. German courts have consistently rejected the enforcement of their punitive damages parts.[57] The same may happen to a judgment in which

---

53 See for example the German Constitutional Court, *RIW* 2007, 211.

54 See BGH, *Entscheidungen des Bundesgerichtshofs in Zivilsachen (BGHZ)* 118, 312, with references to the academic debate.

55 Article 24 of the Commission's first proposal of 2003, COM(2003), 427 final. German private international law provides for an equivalent provision in Article 40(3) EGBGB, whilst most other EC Member States' private international laws do not, see J. Kropholler and J. von Hein, Spezielle Vorbehaltsklauseln im Internationalen Privat- und Verfahrensrecht der unerlaubten Handlungen – Weniger ist mehr, in: G. Hohloch (ed.), *Festschrift für Hans Stoll zum 75. Geburtstag* (Mohr Siebeck, 2001), 553, at 557 ff.

56 See Mörsdorf-Schulte, supra note 10 at 209 ff.

57 See again BGH, BGHZ 118, 312.

treble damages are awarded under US competition law.[58] A similar approach has been reported from Greece.[59]

B. Legislative Activities

One recent legislative attempt to avoid US class actions against German companies occurred in the field of capital market legislation. The background is that US law is stricter than European or German legislation in this field. The German legislator introduced the exclusive competence of the court of the trader's residence, in §32b of the Civil Procedural Act. Since the (international) jurisdiction of the foreign court is a prerequisite for the recognition of its judgment, the exclusive jurisdiction of the German court renders the recognition of US judgments in the field of capital market law impossible[60] and this is exactly what it was meant to do.[61] This approach was heavily criticised in academic writing since it does not only bar excessive judgments but also judgments that are equivalent to those that could be obtained in Germany.[62]

7. OUTLOOK

This chapter demonstrates the various difficulties in bringing cross-border actions on collective damages. First of all, there is a deeply rooted distrust in class actions, and the EC and its Member States will only move slowly into the field of collective enforcement of damages. Secondly, the players are different from those that dominate US class actions. In order to prevent abusive law suits, most Member States have only entrusted public authorities, ombudsmen or well-reputed consumer organisations with collective enforcement mechanisms. Cost rules and in particular the general prohibition on conditional fees have prevented a litigation industry to develop until now. With so many obstacles in place at national level,

58 See the above-mentioned decision of OLG Koblenz, *IPRax* 2006, 25, to not even allow the service of a treble damage claim. This approach was explicitly rejected by OLG Naumburg, *OLG-Report Naumburg* 2006, 403.

59 See C. D. Triadafillidis, Anerkennung und Vollstreckung von punitive damages-Urteilen nach kontinentalem und insbesondere nach griechischem Recht, *Praxis des Internationalen Privat- und Verfahrensrechts (IPRax)* 2002, 236, at 238.

60 See A. Stadler, Empfehlen sich gesetzgeberische Maßnahmen zur rechtlichen Bewältigung der Haftung bei Massenschäden?, in: *Verhandlungen des 62. DJT Bremen*, vol. II/1 (C.H. Beck, 1998), I 35, at 60; von Hein, *RIW* 2004, 602, at 607 f.; G. Bachmann, Die internationale Zuständigkeit für Klagen wegen fehlerhafter Kapitalmarktinformation, *Praxis des Internationalen Privat- und Verfahrensrechts (IPRax)* 2007, 77, at 84.

61 See F. Reuschle, Möglichkeiten und Grenzen kollektiver Rechtsverfolgung, *Wertpapier - Mitteilungen (WM)* 2004, 966, at 973.

62 See von Hein, supra note 45 at 609.

the cross-border dimension of collective redress has not even been looked at more closely by the EC. Quite likely, harmonisation of collective redress mechanisms or the introduction of a stock of minimum rules on collective actions will have to take place in the Member States and this will have to be initiated by EC law, before even the mutual recognition of legal standing of foreign players in the line of the Injunctions Directive 98/27/EC is achieved. If EC-wide minimum standards can be achieved through EC legislation, jurisdiction issues and the current need for finding a suitable forum should lose their importance.

PART V.
CONCLUSION

ADMINISTRATIVE AND JUDICIAL ENFORCEMENT IN CONSUMER PROTECTION: THE WAY FORWARD

Fabrizio Cafaggi and Hans-W. Micklitz

1. THE RELATIONSHIP BETWEEN ADMINISTRATIVE AND JUDICIAL ENFORCEMENT IN CONSUMER PROTECTION: THE WAY AHEAD

Consumer protection law is in great transformation. Global market integration requires new modes of governance to tackle new forms of risk interdependencies affecting consumer safety and, more broadly, consumer choices. While emerging markets are posing serious problems concerning risks and safety, trilateral or multilateral agreements are far from being frequently used. The main legal instruments are still bilateral agreements concerning co-operation about risk management in product safety.[1]

Consumer protection strategies need to be defined in relation to the broader framework, linking the different regulatory policies, including competition and environment. The relationship between consumer regulation and the level of market competitiveness has become a milestone of enforcement policies. This is not to say that competitive markets need less consumer protection and enforcement; more simply they need different devices and institutions. Competition and consumer law interplay in different ways in highly competitive and non-competitive markets.[2] Thus consumer protection policies need to internalise the current and future level of competitiveness in their design.

Policies interdependencies require coordination among the different actors but how are the main players developing their regulatory strategies?

The US, Canada and Europe still differ quite significantly in relation to enforcement policies although some signs of convergence are stronger than in the

---

1 See the EU/US agreements but see also the MoU between China and EU, both available at http://ec.europa.eu/consumers/safety/int_coop/index_en.htm.

2 See M. Trebilcock, 'Rethinking consumer protection policy', in C. Rickett and T. Telfer (eds.) *International Perspectives on Consumers' access to justice*, Cambridge University Press, 2003, p. 68 ff. at 72 ff.

past.[3] In South America, recent legal reforms have introduced or reinforced class actions and astreintes.[4] In Europe a new stream of legislation concerning group actions has been enacted. In the US CAFA has changed the balance between states and federal level impacting also on substantive law. The key questions concern modes of regulation and combinations of different actors at the stage of enforcement: in particular agencies and courts.[5] In both the US and EC these two dimensions have to be framed within a multilevel system, encompassing both federal and state levels. The main differences are related to the levels of market integration: while in the US the market is fully integrated, in Europe integration has only been partially achieved. These differences are also reflected on the legal frameworks. In the US it is more uniform, while in Europe it is characterised by a higher degree of differentiation at Member State (MS) level.

Conventionally the analysis presents a contrasting picture: the US is characterised by a model grounded on regulation through litigation and organised around the paradigm of private attorney general,[6] the result being adversarial legalism;[7] public regulation plays a less relevant role ever more 'protected' from judicial interference.[8] For pre-emption to occur, the superiority of federal regulatory law over state common law in contract or tort has to be expressly

---

3 For a comparative analysis see F. Cafaggi and H. Micklitz, 'Collective enforcement of consumer law: a framework for a comparative assessment', *ERPL*, 2008, p. 391; S. Issacharoff and G. Miller, 'Will aggregate litigation come to Europe?', *Vanderbilt L. R.*, vol. 62, p. 179 (2009) I. Ramsay, 'Consumer redress and access to justice', in C.E.F. Rickett and T.G.W. Telfer (eds.), *International perspectives on consumers' access to justice*, New York – Cambridge, 2003, p. 42 ff. part. 50 ff.; R. Kagan, 'Should Europe Worry About Adversarial Legalism?', *Oxford Journal of Legal Studies*, 2007, 17, 165, where the author speaks of 'institutional convergence at least with regard to some policy fields'.

4 See in Argentina Law n. 26.361 which has modified law n. 24240 Normas de proteccion y defensa de los Consumidores. Autoridad de Aplicacion. Procedimiento y sanciones. Disposiciones finales. In particular Article 54 concerning a form of opt-out class action and Article 52 bis introducing a form of astreinte named daño puntiivo. For a synthesis see A: Pellegrini Grinover, 'New trends in standing and res judicata in collective suits, General report Civil law' and L. Mullenix, 'New trends in standing and res judicata General report, common law countries', in *Direito processual comparado* (eds) A. Pellegrini Grinover and P. Calmon, Brasilia, 2007.

5 See H. Micklitz, 'Collective private enforcement of consumer law: the key questions', in W. van Boom/M. Loos (eds.), *Collective Enforcement of Consumer Law, Securing Compliance in Europe through Private Group Action and Public Authority Intervention*, Europa Law Publ., 2007, p. 13.

6 On the private attorney general model see J. C. Coffee, 'Understanding the plaintiff's attorney: the implications of economic theory for private enforcement of law through class and derivative actions', *Col. L.R.* vol. 86 p. 669 (1986); Id., 'Rescuing the private attorney general: why the model of the lawyer as a bounty hunter is not working', *MDLR*, vol. 42, p. 215 (1983); W. Rubenstein, 'On what a private attorney general is and why it matters', *Vanderbilt L.R.*, Vol. 57, p. 2130 ff.

7 R. A. Kagan, *Adversarial Legalism. The American Way*, Harward University Press, 2001.

8 See *Riegel v. Medtronic, Inc.*, 552 US (2008), C. Sharkey, 'Products liability pre-emption: an institutional approach', *The George Washington L. R.* vol. 76, p. 449 ff. (2008).

legislated.[9] Regulatory agencies in the US are substantially immune from tort liability and are based on accountability systems grounded on participatory rights, transparency and judicial review.

In Europe MSs have been displaying a much stronger level of public regulation, featuring a collective judicial enforcement model, predominantly based on public institutions (ombudsmen, consumer agencies) or private organisations (consumer associations). European legislation on consumer protection has focused primarily on substantive law, leaving MSs the task to provide for effective enforcement. This choice has been partly influenced by lack of competence and by the principle of procedural autonomy.[10] The separation between substantive and remedial law is causing uneven effectiveness in MS and potentially undermines the goals pursued by the legislative reforms of the last 20 years. For this reason collective redress has recently become a priority in the European and MS agenda.[11] Interestingly enough, implementation of European legislation at MS level reveals a relative preference for private over public enforcement. When MSs have been left with the option, they have chosen more judicial than administrative enforcement (AE), although choices vary from field to field, i.e. between unfair contract terms where private enforcement prevails and unfair trade practices where there is more balance.[12]

Viewed from the consumers' perspective, the two systems, US and EC, present different accountability mechanisms to promote access to justice for consumers and compliance with consumer legislation.

The US system relies primarily on market mechanisms, based on a relatively mature competitive market for legal services that ensures incentives to select the relevant claims and to grant compensation for injured parties.[13]

Europe relies more on social and political mechanisms, associated with liability devices. Effectiveness of public and private institutions to bring claims is

---

9 Justice Scalia writing the opinion for the Court stated "State requirements are pre-empted under the MDA only to the extent that they are "different from or in addition to" the requirements imposed by federal law". See *Riegel v. Medtronic*, cit.

10 See on a US/EC comparison, J. Lindholm, *State Procedure and Union Rights, A Comparison of the European Union and the United States*, Umea University, 2007, p. 386, available at http://ssrn.com/abstract=985885. See also Commissioner Kuneva Speech at the Leuven Brainstorming Meeting on Collective Redress, 29th June 2007, http://ec.europa.eu/consumers/redress_cons/docs/kuneva_leuven_speech290607.pdf; and the New Consumer strategy 2007/2013, SEC (2007) 321, 13th March 2007.

11 See Green Paper on Collective Redress.

12 See with regard to unfair terms and unfair commercial practices the analysis of 25 Member States, H.-W. Micklitz, P. Rott, U. Docekal and P. Kolba, *Verbraucherschutz durch Unterlassungsklagen, Rechtliche und Praktische Umsetzung der Richtlinie Unterlassungsklagen 98/27/EG in den Mitgliedstaaten*, VIEW Schriftenreihe, Band 17, 2007.

13 Consensus over the effectiveness of this system is far from being unanimous. There is a strong debate over the level of consumer protection and the rents generated by the litigation system in the US. Hotly debated is also the level of competitiveness of the market for legal services see below.

predominantly ensured by exerting political pressure and channelling public resources to private organisations and, to an increasing extent, to liability systems. Public entities are held liable for lack of control and even for not enacting proper regulation.[14] Private entities have been held liable for mismanagement of cases.[15]

If we locate the US and EC in the broader global perspective we discover firstly that the models of enforcement of consumer law vary across a wider range of alternatives and that internal differences in Europe, despite the increasing role of European legislation, make it very difficult to speak yet of an integrated European strategy.[16]

Changes are taking place in both environments. In the US there is an increasing deference towards regulatory agencies, limiting the role of state common law in the area of consumer protection, coupled with the introduction of a stricter federal legislation on class actions.[17] In Europe the more recent trend shows an increasing effort to create public regulators in charge of coordinating transborder monitoring and enforcement issues with a volume of MS legislation introducing judicial collective enforcement. The former change is complemented by the increasing role of co-regulation in consumer matters, taking the form of bilateral (public and

---

14 See with regard to product safety control, H.-W. Micklitz and Th. Roethe, *Produktsicherheit und Marktüberwachung im Ostseeraum*, Nomos, 2008; particularly telling ECJ, 17 April 2007, Case C-470/03 COS.MET 2007 (ECR) I-2749; N. Reich, 'A.G.M. COS.MET oder: Wem dient das EU-Produktsicherheitsrecht?', in *Verbraucher und Recht*, 2007, 410.

15 In Germany, a regional consumer advice centre organised in the form of an association went bankrupt after mismanagement. The German Supreme Court indirectly recognised the liability of tenant advice centres for misleading advice, BGH 25.10.2006 VIII ZR 102/06, *NJW* 2007, 428.

16 According to an OECD study, published at the end of 2006, there are five principal models of enforcement:
" *i) those relying on the criminal justice system for penalties*
ii) those in which administrative agencies have power themselves to impose financial penalties
iii) those in which the administrative agencies have power themselves to impose financial penalties
iv) those relying primarily on consumer complaints to an Ombudsman
v) those relying primarily on self-regulatory arrangements and on the enforcement of private rights".
See OECD, Best Practices for consumer policy: report on effectiveness of enforcement regimes, p. 12, available at www.oecd.org.

17 On the regulatory changes see R. Epstein and M. Greeve (eds.), *Federal pre-emption: States' Powers, National interests*, AEI Press, 2007, D. Hensler, 'Has the Fat Lady Sung? The Future of Mass Toxic Torts', *Review of litigation*, 2007 p. 883.
On the role of CAFA (Class action Federal Act), see R. Nagareda, 'Aggregation and its Discontents: Class Settlement Pressure, Class-Wide Arbitration, and CAFA', *Vanderbilt Law and Economics Research Paper*, No. 06-14, available at http://ssrn.com/abstract=920833; C. Sharkey, 'CAFA Settlement Notice Provision: Optimal Regulatory Policy?', *U. Pa. L. Rev.*, Vol. 156, 2008, available at http://ssrn.com/abstract=1133137; H. Erichson, 'CAFA's Impact on Class Action Lawyers', *U. Pa. L. Rev.*, Vol. 156, 2008, available at SSRN: http://ssrn.com/abstract=1083819.

industry) or trilateral (public, industry, consumer associations) agreements.[18] The latter contribute to creating a multilevel structure where injunctive reliefs are primarily legislated at EU level but display only relative uniformity, while damages are regulated at MS level and reflect a higher level of differentiation partly due to an experimental phase.

Another important development in Europe is related to consumer protection for infringements of competition law. Here there is a strong push towards judicial private enforcement driven by European institutions, with sometimes strong resistance from MSs.[19] While the traditional consumer protection seems to be characterised by the increasing importance of public regulation, mainly in the form of co-regulation, consumer protection, related to infringements of competition law, has witnessed a fast growing trend towards private enforcement.[20] The proposal in the White paper by the European Commission is to combine representative actions and opt-in collective actions.[21] The open question is whether the choices to be made in relation to competition infringements about collective redress may be applied to consumer protection law in general. It shall be recalled that the driving force behind private enforcement in competition law has been the ECJ, pushing the European Commission into action.[22] Certainly, at least when consumers are the claimants, coordination between collective redress for violations of consumer law and violations of competition law should take place.

The direction of the changes drives towards complementarity between administrative and judicial enforcement and induces a focus on the variables affecting this combination. But first we need to identify the meanings of public and private enforcement.

Public enforcement includes criminal and administrative regulation which can have different institutional implications: the former is administered primarily

---

18 See F. Cafaggi (ed.), *Reframing self-regulation in European private law*, Kluwer, 2006.

19 See White paper on Damages actions for breach of the EC antitrust rules, COM(2008) 165 final, (hereinafter White paper on damages in antitrust) and Commission staff working paper accompanying the White Paper on Damages actions for breach of EC antitrust rules SEC (2008) 404, and H.-P. Mansel, B. Dauner-Lieb and M. Henssler (Eds.), *Zugang zum Recht: Europäische und US-Amerikanische Wege zur privaten Rechtsdurchsetzung*, Europarecht, 2008.

20 Fostering the legal framework for greater effectiveness in antitrust private enforcement is not only aimed at providing full compensation for victims of violations but also at enhancing deterrence. The approach in the White paper is that of complementarity between public and private enforcement; see White paper on damages in antitrust at p. 3: "the measures put forward in this White Paper are designed to create an effective system of private enforcement by means of damages actions that complements, but does not replace or jeopardise, public enforcement".

21 According to the White paper the two instruments should complement each other.

22 The seminal Courage and Manfredi judgments: ECJ 20 September 2001, Case C-453/99 Courage 2001 (ECR) I-6297; ECJ 12 July 2006, Case C-295/04 Manfredi 2006 (ECR) I-6619.

by Courts, the latter primarily employed by agencies or governmental entities with an increasing involvement of private actors.

Private collective judicial enforcement, in theory, includes injunctions, compensatory damages, profit disgorgement, pecuniary penalties, publicity orders and compliance programmes. A central role in administering these remedies is played by Courts through different forms of aggregate (collective) litigation.[23] In the US the ALI project on the law of aggregate litigation is making an attempt to introduce a functional differentiation among aggregate proceedings and to provide a more structured set of principles concerning settlements.[24] To these proceedings, ADR should be added, given the increasing importance that it is gaining in consumer disputes.[25]

In this framework, monitoring within public enforcement is done by agencies, while in private enforcement the burden is primarily on private actors, the potentially injured parties and, where existing, by private organisations representing them. Monitoring in private enforcement is thus highly context-dependent on the incentives of private parties to detect injuries and bring legal claims to Court. The marketability of the potential legal claim provides incentives to monitor which claims are brought to Court but it may bring about inefficient results. It can help to select which unlawful conducts have to be detected and eventually deterred. Not always the incentives of private parties to monitor correspond to social welfare. For this reason complementarity between public and private actors is necessary.

Important differences occur if the public entity can monitor and enforce directly or can monitor but not enforce, and has to use the Court system to enforce the sanctions. In theory the use of public agencies to monitor and directly sanction would seem to be more effective than separating administrative monitoring from judicial enforcement. But especially in relation to cooperative enforcement, when the enforcer has to conclude agreements with the infringer, the resort to an

---

23 Aggregate or collective litigation includes different forms of aggregation: mass joinder, mass consolidation, model cases, and test or bellwhether cases, assignment of rights, group actions and class actions. These different forms of aggregation presuppose different rules and roles for judges and counsel. See also ALI Principles of the law of aggregate litigation, tentative draft, April 2008 book 1 on general principles.

24 §1.02 Of ALI Principles of the law of aggregate litigation defines 3 types of aggregate proceedings

(a) An aggregate lawsuit is a single lawsuit that encompasses claims or defences held by multiple parties or represented persons

(b) An administrative aggregation is a collection of related lawsuits, which may or may not be aggregate lawsuits, proceeding under common judicial supervision or control

(c) A private aggregation is an informal collection of the claims or defences of multiple parties, represented persons, claimants or respondents proceeding under common non-judicial supervision or control."

Principles of the law of aggregate litigation p. 14 ff.

25 J. M. Scherpe, *Außergerichtliche Streitbeilegung in Verbrauchersachen*, Mohr Siebeck, 2002.

independent judiciary may ensure transparency and reduce capture. Thus the higher the use of cooperative enforcement the more necessary it is to resort to separation between monitoring and enforcement.[26]

Important differences between administrative and judicial enforcement are related also to the players. While in relation to Administrative enforcement (AE) the main players are agencies and enterprises, in litigation consumers play a much more active role. Recent changes at MSs level[27] in participatory rights and standing have expanded the voice of consumers, both individually and collectively in AE but still the main responsibility and discretionary power is on the public entity.

However some qualifications to the above described picture are needed. Many European legal systems use a mix: monitoring is passed to public entities, being them agencies, ombudsmen or governmental entities, while enforcement is delegated to the Courts. Often monitoring is the result of cooperative efforts between public and private entities. Private individuals and organisations report to the public entity which is empowered, *de jure* or *de facto*, to bring the legal claim before the Court. While reporting by private entities does usually not imply a duty to act, in many legal systems public authorities would have to give reasons for inaction if a serious and well structured complaint has been produced. Public authorities differ as to their monitoring policies, giving more or less weight to their own internal systems of control or to external reporting.[28]

Even when there is no legal monopoly of standing on the public entity, as is the case in the UK or in the Scandinavian countries, the OFT and the Ombudsmen have *de facto* the most relevant role to decide whether or not a certain case should be litigated. The development of cooperative ventures between public and private entities suggest that there is no coincidence between judicial and private enforcement because often judicial enforcement is triggered by public entities on the basis of information gathered through a complex network composed of private and public actors.

For these reasons we prefer to speak of administrative versus judicial enforcement rather than juxtaposing public and private enforcement.

---

26 See F. Cafaggi, '*Cooperative enforcement*', paper presented at NYU/ALI/EUI conference on 13th June, 2008.

27 The European Community has done little in secondary consumer legislation to strengthen participatory rights of consumers in product regulation. Two prominent examples are the Product Safety Directive 2001/95/EC and the Regulation on Transborder Enforcement 2006/2004 where MSs rejected respective proposals during the law-making process. That is why participation depends on the MSs; see with regard to energy, telecommunications and transport, J. Keßler and H.-W. Micklitz, *Kundenschutz in liberalisierten Märkten*, Nomos, 2008.

28 The most developed system seems to be the super-complaint procedure under which consumer organisations may address the OFT in the UK which then is obliged to investigate the complaint within 90 days, EA Section 11 and 205 2002.

In this contribution we consider administrative regulation more than criminal penalties although some MS have so far heavily relied on the use of criminal penalties to enforce consumer protection law.

The provision of adequate and effective collective redress to European consumers should be based on the combined use of administrative regulation and collective judicial enforcement. While rule-making has become increasingly European, enforcement remains strongly in the hands of national authorities, be they administrative agencies or Courts. This separation, partly justified by the principle of procedural autonomy, makes it necessary to engineer coordination in enforcement policies at State level. Such coordination has to occur at national level between administrative authorities and courts, and at European level among the judiciaries and the administrative agencies. The recent case law on damages in competition infringement shows perfectly this point. Common rules, in primary legislation, translate into very different outcomes when enforced at national level.[29]

2. ADMINISTRATIVE AND/OR JUDICIAL CO-OPERATION IN EUROPE

Setting the US aside where there exists a Federal Rule on class actions and a procedure to overcome competing multi-state jurisdictions, Canada and the EU seem to face similar challenges: the absence of common rules on class actions/group actions at the 'federal' level and therefore the absence of a court with exclusive jurisdiction in transborder cases.

2.1. ACTIONS FOR INJUNCTION

A. *Shift from Judicial Collective Enforcement to Administrative Co-Operation?*

The Regulation 2006/2004[30] on transborder co-operation in consumer law aimed at shifting the balance from judicial to administrative enforcement. Although Directive 98/27/EC left it to the MSs to determine whether an administrative authority or a consumer organisation may be the competent entity, it was guided by the overall spirit to foster private judicial enforcement via consumer

[29] See White paper, Commission staff working document and Impact assessment available at http://ec.europa.eu/comm/competition/antitrust/actionsdamages/documents.html. See on these questions J. Basedow (ed.) *Private enforcement of EC competition law*, Kluwer Law International, 2007.

[30] OJ L 364, 9 December 2004, 1.

organisations.[31] This attempt more or less failed, since very few transborder cases have been brought to court. This might be largely due to the still underdeveloped, understaffed and underfinanced consumer organisations all over Europe. The Directive has produced partially satisfactory results in regions where the cross-border trade is constantly high and where consumers are used to shop across the borders, such as in Austria/Germany, the triangle Belgium/Netherlands/Germany and in the Scandinavian countries.[32]

Whilst Directive 98/27 was clearly adopted in the aftermath of the *Homeshopping* case,[33] which blatantly demonstrated the deficiencies in getting to grips with transborder litigation, the history of Regulation 2006/2004 is more complex. It is closely linked to the elaboration of Directive 2005/29/EC[34] on unfair commercial practices. Although Directive 2005/29/EC did in no way change the enforcement mechanism, which was literally taken over from Directive 84/450/EEC[35] on misleading advertising, the European Commission was convinced that there was a need to strengthen transborder enforcement in the advertising law and more broadly in consumer law. As it is well-known, the Regulation obliges MSs to establish or to designate a public body to serve as co-operation partner in the network.[36] Passing the overall difficulties of dealing with transborder litigation in review, it seems plausible to try to find solutions to transborder consumer conflicts by way of co-operation. However, the scope of the Regulation is bound by a set of directives and the type of infringement is typically one which results either from unfair contract terms or from unfair commercial practices.

In the following part we address separately different remedies and then suggest that coordination problems between injunctions and pecuniary remedies have arisen in the EU. We provide some examples and then suggest that at least for transborder litigation, a rapid intervention is needed.

B. *The European Minimum Standard – Action of Injunctions*

Since the adoption of Directive 84/450/EEC on misleading advertising, the action of injunction belongs to the core of consumer law remedies. It is enshrined in two

---

31 See in particular recital 2 of the Regulation and preparatory documents.

32 See for a full account of the empirical analysis, H.-W. Micklitz/P. Rott/U. Docekal/P. Kolba, cit. supra at n. 12.

33 H.-W. Micklitz, 'Cross-Border Consumer Conflicts – A French-German Experience', *JCP Special Issue, European Consumer Policy After Maastricht*, 1993, p. 411; Id., 'Transborder Law Enforcement – Does it exist?', in U. Bernitz and S. Weatherill (eds.), *The Regulation of Unfair Commercial Practices under EC Directive 2005/29: new rules and new techniques*, Hart Publishing, 2007, p. 235.

34 OJ L 149, 121 June 2005, 22.

35 OJ L 250, 19 September 1984, 17.

36 On this shift already, F. Cafaggi and H.-W. Micklitz, 'Collective enforcement of consumer law: a framework for a comparative assessment', *European Review of Private Law*, 2008, p. 391.

major fields of consumer law, unfair trade practices law, now condensed in Directive 2005/29/EC, and unfair terms law, Directive 93/13/EC[37] currently under review.[38] The European Commission could rely on a longstanding regulatory strategy in Austria, Germany and some other old MSs. This solid background allowed the European Community to harmonise the regime for injunctions, a development which nevertheless stimulated changes in quite a number of MSs. Directive 98/27/EC on injunctions is meant to give shape to the remedy in national *and* in transborder litigation. Injunctions are aiming at setting an end to unfair or misleading advertising or the use and recommendation of unfair standard contract terms. It is a stop order mechanism that can prohibit future infringements but also include cease and desist orders.[39] The Directive has also promoted the introduction of penalties for lack of compliance with injunctions.[40] In case of default, MS legislation can choose between payment to the public purse or to the claimant.[41] These resources are generally devoted to promote further litigation.

The Directive provides for a mechanism which MS may implement whereby the claimant has to seek an agreement concerning the injunction before the legal claim is brought before the Court.[42] Prior consultation is required but no reference to the legal value of the agreement reached by the parties is made especially in relation to preclusion issues.[43] This provision shows the importance of the bargaining model in Europe and the attempt to reduce the level of litigation that might arise.[44]

---

37 OJ L 95, 21 April 1993, 29.

38 Green Paper on the Revision of the Consumer *Acquis*, COM (2006) 744 final, for a deeper analysis see M.B.M. Loos, *Review of the European Consumer Acquis*, Sellier, 2008, p. 40.

39 See Article 2.2(a) EC Directive 98/27.

40 See Article 2.1(c) " insofar as the legal systems of the MS concerned so permits an order against the losing defendant for payments into the public purse or to any beneficiary designated in or under national legislation, in the event that a failure to comply with the decision within the a time limit specified by the courts to administrative authorities, of a fixed amount for each day' s delay or any other amount provided for in national legislation, with a view to ensuring compliance with the decisions.".

41 See Article 2.1(c) EC Directive 98/27.

42 See for example Article 4 of the Cooperation agreement between the Nordic Consumer Ombudsmen available at www.forbrug.dk/english/dco/icpen0/nordic-cooperation/ncoagreement/; see on the degree to which MSs have introduced this obligation, H.-W. Micklitz, P. Rott, U. Docekal and P. Kolba, *Verbraucherschutz durch Unterlassungsklagen, Umsetzung und Anwendung der Richtlinie 98/27/EG*, Nomos 2007, at page 234.

43 See for references concerning the differences between agreements concerning injuntive relieves and those concerning compensatory damages Cafaggi/Micklitz, supra at n. 3, p. 391 ff.

44 For the different models of adjudication developed in Europe and the US, see Cafaggi/Micklitz, supra at n. 3, p. 391 ff.

The draft Directive on injunctions went further.[45] The original draft did not even mention injunctions[46] and the European Parliament[47] did not even discuss the purpose of the action, whereas the Social and Economic Committee[48] advocated for the integration of liability claims. This is worth recalling as the European Commission intends to publish a proposal for the revision of Directive 1998/27/EC.[49] It would not be the first time that the European Commission goes back to its earlier proposals. Harmonisation of EC remedies could then be extended beyond injunctions. As EC law stands, it is fair to conclude that injunctions constitute the sole harmonised remedy all over Europe.

Directive 98/27/EC regulated standing, identifying two groups of potential claimants that MSs could choose: independent public bodies and consumer organisations. They can select one or both. The Directive set up a notification procedure under which MSs notify the European Commission of 'qualified entities' which defend the collective interests of consumers. A principle of mutual recognition has been established by the Directive in order to empower foreign entities to act.[50] MSs benefit from considerable leeway in choosing not only between administrative or judicial enforcement via consumer organisations, but they are also relatively free in setting their own standards on what they define as a consumer organisation. The Commission publishes regularly a list of qualified entities which are granted standing in their home countries and to which national courts of other MSs are legally bound.[51]

2.2. EUROPEAN GROUP ACTIONS AND AMERICAN CLASS ACTIONS

In the late 70s and early 80s a debate in some European MSs took place on the feasibility and transferability of the US class action to Europe. This discussion blossomed when consumer policy in Europe was at its peak. However, it seems as if the time was not yet ripe for going beyond individual litigation. France failed

---

45 Article 1(1) of the Draft ran as follows: The purpose of this Directive is to coordinate the laws, regulations and administrative provisions of MSs relating to certain remedies designed to protect consumers' interests, so as to ensure the smooth functioning of the internal market. The 'action for injunction' was only mentioned in recital 3 and reappeared in the heading of Article 2, OJ C 1007, 13 April 1996, 3.

46 OJ C 107, 13 April 1996, 3.

47 OJ C 362, 2 December 1996, 236.

48 OJ C 30, 30 January 1997, 312 under 2.4, see in more detail Micklitz/Rott in E. Grabitz/M. Hilf II, *Das Recht der Europäischen Union*, Beck, 2003, Band 2, A 25, paragraph number 6–9.

49 See EC Commission.

50 See recital 11 and Article 4.1 of EC Directive 98/27.
For the implementation of the mutual recognition principle through specific agreements see, for example Article 3 of the Cooperation agreement between the Nordic Consumer Ombudsmen, cit.

51 OJ 63, 8 March 2008, 5.

after lengthy discussions around the codification of consumer law as well as Germany, where collective actions were debated in the field of unfair commercial practices for many years.[52] Both projects were however of paradigmatic importance.

In France the ambitious project of the Commission de la Refonte aimed at developing a fully fledged consumer code standing side-by-side to the Code Civil and setting standards for the development in Europe. In the end, a Code de la consommation was adopted but it was more a compilation of laws than a codification in the proper sense. The rather ineffective 'action des la représentation conjointe', regulated in Article L-422, could hardly substitute a class action type of regulation.[53]

In Germany the ground was well prepared with comprehensive empirical studies meant to analyse the potential damage of unfair and misleading advertising in relation to consumers.[54] The outcome was a right of withdrawal if the consumer had been driven by misleading advertising. It never gained any importance. Similar experience could be reported from the Scandinavian countries.

Directive 98/27 on injunctions was enacted in 1998. In less than 10 years the scene has dramatically changed. Again MSs have taken the lead. Today it seems that MSs are convinced that they need some sort of a collective redress mechanism to reach beyond mere injunctions and aim at collective compensation. Why is that so? And why now? As mentioned we locate the change in the separation between substantive vs. procedural remedies and in the development of a proper common community interest.[55]

This does not mean that the common incentives have led to similar solutions. MSs' legislative attempts to get to grips with collective private enforcement may serve as a perfect example for making the overall formula 'united in diversity'[56] a leading principle. Each MS follows its proper legal culture and tradition. The result is an enormous variety of solutions, each grounded in national particularities and in

---

52 See for Germany H.-W. Micklitz, 'Kollektiver Schadensersatz im UWG – Scheitern oder Neubeginn', in. H.-W. Micklitz (ed.), *Rechtseinheit oder Rechtsvielfalt in Europa*, Zur Rolle und Funktion des Verbraucherrechts in den MOE-Staaten und in der EG, Band 1 der VIEW Schriftenreihe, 1996, p. 383. For France J. Calais-Auloy, *Proposition pour un nouveau droit de la consommation*, rapport de la Commission de la Refonte du droit de la consommation au secrétaire d'État auprés du ministre de l'Économie, des Finances et du Budget chargé du Budget et de la Consommation, 1985.

53 See J. Franck, *Collective enforcement of the consumer rights – the French perspective*, Dokumentation der Bamberger Verbraucherrechtstage, herausgegeben vom Bundesministerium für Landwirtschaft, Ernährung und Verbraucherschutz, 2006, p. 153.

54 R. von Falckenstein, *Die Bekämpfung unlauterer Geschäftspraktiken durch Verbraucherverbände, Bundesanzeiger*, 1977.

55 See for an account H.-W. Micklitz, 'The Interest in Public Interest Litigation', in N. Reich/ H.-W. Micklitz (eds.), *Public Interest Litigation before European Courts*, Band 2 der VIEW Schriftenreihe, 1996, 21 ff at 29.

56 Taken from the Treaty, http://europa.eu/abc/symbols/motto/index_en.htm.

a bewildering confusion in terminology which renders difficult a deeper comparison of the models. Furthermore it may also constitute more a barrier to European justice than an incentive for competition between legal orders. The development is so fast that research is outdated before it is published. The 2006 Stuyck study does no longer represent the state of art in Europe.[57] Stanford and Oxford University have taken the initiative to install a stable network of researchers aiming at keeping pace with the ongoing development not only in Europe but worldwide.[58]

However, this does not mean that there are no common denominators at all. The benchmark of the European debate has been the US class action regulation. In the European political debate the US class action is characterised by three constitutive elements: opt-out, jury trial and contingency fee.[59] As the jury trial is rather alien at least to continental procedural systems, the debate has focused on opt-out vs. opt-in and on contingency fee vs. the loser pays principle. There is no public hearing or no political conference where the US class action does not show up, either favoured as the sole solution to protect effectively consumers or as a '*horror juris*' which is blamed for destroying the much more balanced European legal systems. Such a rough dichotomy clearly overlooks the mutual convergence tendencies. In the US, there are constant and ongoing efforts to cut back the misuses of the class action, to introduce a second opt-out option after the settlement has taken place and to intensify the judicial control of contingency fees.[60]

In Europe, there is a strong move towards a group action, based on opt-in. Sweden has set the standard after long-lasting debates and a last minute shift in Parliament from opt-out to opt-in. However, not only Portugal, Spain, and to some extent Denmark and Norway have introduced an opt-out solution, but also the UK and Germany, at least with regard to unfair commercial practices allow for opt-out type actions.[61] The liberalisation of the verdict of contingency fees at

---

57 *An analysis and evaluation of alternative means of consumer redress other than redress through ordinary judicial proceedings – Final Report*, Study for the European Commission, (hereinafter Stuyck Report), available at http://ec.europa.eu/consumers/ redress/reports_studies/index_en.htm.

58 See www.globalclassactions.stanford.edu. 26 country reports are available on the internet as well as some of the national legislation.

59 See the already paradigmatic documentation of H.-P. Mansel/B.Dauner-Lieb/M. Henssler (eds), *Zugang zum Recht: Europäische und US-Amerikanische Wege zur privaten Rechtsdurchsetzung*, 2008, where representatives from industry and the academia discussed the pros and cons of group actions; A. Stadler in this volume.

60 See H. Beuchler, *Class Actions und Securities class actions in den Vereinigten Staaten von Amerika*, Nomos, 2007.

61 Countries reports in www.globalclassactions.stanford.edu: Denmark, E. Werlauff, Germany, D. Baetge, Finland, K. Viitanen, Norway, C. Bernt-Hamre, Portugal, Henrique Sousa Antunes, Spain, Pablo Gutiérrez de Cabiedes Hidalgo, Sweden, H. Lindblom as well as the more comprehensive national reports on Germany, the United Kingdom, Sweden in H.-W. Micklitz and A. Stadler, *Das Verbandsklagerecht in der Informations- und Dienstleistungsgesellschaft*, Landwirtschaftsverlag, 2005.

least in some MSs, documents the growing preparedness to take into consideration the fact that the success or failure of group actions in the European sense depends to a large extent on lawyers who have to be remunerated for the higher intensity of work and the higher risk.[62]

We will not try to compare the different solutions adopted in the MSs. Application of the new laws is still rather limited. The experience is even more circumscribed with regard to collective judicial enforcement of consumer law. At this stage we can analyse the law in the books and identify the regulatory strategies lying behind the diversity.

2.3. THREE MODELS OF GROUP ACTIONS IN 27 MEMBER STATES

Some clarifications on the terminology are needed. Collective action is used as the overarching category in contrast to individual action. This complies to a large extent with the US terminology of aggregate litigation.[63] However, subcategories have to be built to reflect the European approach. We distinguish between representative action, group action (opt-in or opt-out), model cases or test case and US class actions.[64]

A. *The Search for the Perfect European Model*

The search for a European approach to aggregate litigation is largely determined by the strong desire to develop a legal model which avoids the so-called deficiencies of the US class actions in response to the separation between substantive and remedial law in a multi-layered Europe. The European Commission is, at least in theory, not bound to the US agenda. It could and it does to some extent more openly and less ideologically address the question whether and why collective actions, to put it in neutral terms, are needed. This comes clear in the White Paper on Private Enforcement in Competition law. The shift to private enforcement is fostered by European institutions, the ECJ with *Courage*[65] and *Manfredi*[66] and the European Commission with the Green and White Paper on private enforcement following suit.

---

62 Sweden has introduced risk agreements; Italy has got rid of the prohibition concerning fee agreements between lawyers and clients, see for a fuller presentation of the laws of the MSs, M. Ros, Féderation des Barreaux d'Europe (FBE) *Der Erfolg und das Honorar des Anwalts – Entwicklungen zu erfolgsorientierter Vergütung des Anwalts Tagungsbericht*, Form Anwalts Revue de l'Avocat, 8/2006, 299.

63 See ALI project on the law of aggregate litigation Chapter 1.

64 See already, Cafaggi/Micklitz, supra n. 3, p. 391 ff.; J. Stuyck in this volume p. 63 ff.

65 ECJ 20 September 2001, Case C-453/99 Courage 2001 (ECR) I-6297.

66 ECJ 12 July 2006, Case C-295/04 Manfredi 2006 (ECR) I-6619.

Outside and beyond competition law that is in consumer law, the position of the European Commission is weaker, not least because of its reduced legislative competence. One may wonder, however, whether the rather weak position of the European Commission in consumer law would not enable the arguments in favour of private collective enforcement strategies to be openly addressed. The envisaged green paper of DG Sanco, to be expected in 2008/2009, will have to demonstrate whether the European Commission is willing to discuss and rethink the principle of the procedural autonomy of the MSs in a European Community.

Be that as it may, Sweden has set the agenda not only for the Scandinavian countries in the long established spirit of Nordic legislative co-operation[67] but for most of the old MSs in its long and intensive political debate over the pros and cons of transferring the US class action model to Europe. The result has been an opt-in solution, which was lately based on the need to respect the right to be heard of all those who are involved in mass actions but are not leading the case.[68] None of the MSs, perhaps with the exception of the UK, undertook such a serious effort to do justice to the US experience beyond oversimplification and the horror of an open political debate. In Germany the then competent Ministry of Consumer Protection launched a research project which led to the development of an academic draft.[69] A public hearing in France in June 2006 did not go beyond the rather simplified debate over the pros and cons of opt-in and opt-out.[70] In Germany and in the Netherlands the respective legislation is not so much the result of public debate of the pros and cons of a group actions and its possible outlook, but of social events which pushed the legislature into action. The German Capital Markets Model Case Act is the result of the so-called Telecom case.[71] The Dutch Law on mass damages is very much going back to huge litigation over the disastrous effects of hormones.[72]

The Swedish law on Group Actions[73] takes up all issues which are discussed in the US class action. However, the overall aim is to set up a perfect legal model

67 See U. Bernitz, *European Law in Sweden*, Jure Bokhandel, 2002, Chapter 6, p. 95.

68 See H.-W. Micklitz/A. Stadler, Das Verbandsklagerecht in der Informations- und Dienstleistungsgesellschaft, Landwirtschaftsverlag, 2005, p. 497.

69 See H.-W. Micklitz/A. Stadler, supra n. 68, p. 497. However, neither the research nor the draft ever reached the political level. This might be due to the fact that the study had been undertaken by the 'wrong' ministry. For legislative matters the Ministry of Justice claims competence.

70 See www.globalclassactions.stanford.edu the French report written by V. Magnier. The new French government has not yet decided whether to take up Chirac's initiative again which led to a proposal in Parliament which might be regarded as a developed form of the l'action de la representation conjointe.

71 Nearly 16,000 private investors sued German Telecom at the Court of First Instance in Frankfurt for having published relevant information too late which would have affected the emission of the second tranche of telecom shares.

72 See An. Mom in H.-W. Micklitz/A. Stadler, supra n. 68, p. 435; E. Hondius in this volume and I. Tzankova, Country report Netherlands www.globalclassactions.stanford.edu.

73 Reprinted in H.-W. Micklitz/A. Stadler, p. 628, translated by the Government Office, Office for Administrative Affairs, Stockholm Sweden.

which avoids the incriminated pitfalls of the US solution and embeds the European version of the group action into a tight legally formalised legal jacket. The act devotes careful attention to the determinants of what constitutes a group action, to the commencement of the procedure, to the choice of the appropriate group representative, his or her control by the judges, the tasks and duties of lawyers and judges during the litigation to carefully manage the litigation, to settlement in courts and its possible legal effects.[74] The respective legislative acts adopted in Denmark, Finland and Norway follow the Swedish opt-in model though allowing opt-out claims in particular circumstances.[75] The German 'Academic' Draft Act was inspired by the Swedish model as well.[76]

The UK Group Litigation Order[77] does not copy the US class action, but it fits nevertheless into the overall search for an appropriate European model. In essence it maintains the individual character of the litigation and reduces the collective elements to the strict minimum.[78] The beginning and end of the procedure are and remain individual claims. However, the GLO recognises the need for the judge to shape the procedure and even explicitly refers to the 'managing judge'.[79]

B. *The Key Role of Consumer Associations*

The role and function of consumer organisations varies considerably in Europe. It is tempting to use the distinction between pluralistic and corporatist societies as a paradigm to assess and to define the role of associations. In such a rough pattern the US appears as a pluralistic society, whereas in particular the Scandinavian countries, Austria, Germany and the Netherlands are generally roughly associated with corporatist societies. This might suggest that consumer organisations are strong in corporatist countries. This, however, is only partly true. It might fit with regard to Austria, Germany and the Netherlands, but it is less true with regard to the Scandinavian countries where public agencies are the key players in collective enforcement. However it must equally be admitted that the distinction is superficial and might vary with regard to different policy fields even among

74 See H.-W. Micklitz, 'Collective private enforcement of consumer law: the key questions', in W. van Boom/M. Loos (eds.), *Collective Enforcement of Consumer Law, Securing Compliance in Europe through Private Group Action and Public Authority Intervention*, supra n. 74, 2007, 3; from a Swedish perspective, country report Sweden, written by E. Lindblom www.globalclassactions.stanford.edu.

75 See K. Viitanen, in W. van Boom/M. Loos (eds.), European Law Publishing, p. 83, as well as the respective country reports for Denmark, Finland and Norway in www.globalclassactions.stanford.edu.

76 A. Stadler/H.-W. Micklitz, supra n. 68, p. 1471.

77 A. Stadler/H.-W. Micklitz, supra n. 68, p. 795 at 891.

78 See R. Mulheron, *The class action in common legal systems. A comparative perspective*, Hart, 2004.

79 See GLO Rule 19.13 and Hodges, 'Multi-Party Actions – A European Approach', 11 *Duke J. of Comp & Int'l L* (2001), 321.

MSs.[80] This seems to be true even within the same policy field. Consumer organisations are playing an ever increasing role even in countries which are not regarded as prototypes of corporatist states such as France and Italy. In France, for example, the state is traditionally regarded as representing the public interests which include consumer policy.[81]

So alternative explanations to the role of consumer organisations in enforcement policies are needed which reach beyond the dichotomy of pluralistic vs. corporatist societies. They may be found in the interplay between public government and consumer organisations. We may observe MSs with strong public and private institutions (Germany and France), countries with strong private and weak public institutions (Italy) or countries with weak public and weak private institutions (the new MSs). Such a distinction might provide for new insights, but is again of limited value. Germany has strong public institutions, but not in the field of consumer law, not even with regard to product safety. More or less the same applies to France, where consumer organisations are the key players as public institutions have no or limited regulatory power in the field of consumer law enforcement. More research is needed to explain the role and function of consumer organisations. However, in contrast to the US it is obvious that consumer organisations have a role to play in the shaping and in the implementation of consumer law via collective actions. The introduction of the action for injunction and the MSs preparedness to give exclusive standing to consumer organisations has certainly contributed to the current situation in Europe.

The prototype is the representative action 'invented' in Austria and then co-opted for by Germany. Both countries rely heavily on consumer organisations in private collective enforcement. This is largely due to a common history under which private organisations rather than administrative bodies were regarded as the appropriate enforcers of unfair commercial practices legislation.[82] When the pressure grew to extend the available remedies beyond injunction, the Austrian consumer organisations managed to get confirmation in the Supreme Court for their strategy, to litigate on behalf of consumers who had individually transferred their rights to claim compensation to the organisation.[83] Since then the Austrian

---

80 See. Ch. Strünck, *Die Macht des Risikos, Interessenvermittlung in der amerikanischen und europäischen Verbraucherpolitik*, Nomos, 2006, p. 18 and 44.

81 F. Baumgartner, 'Public Interests Groups in France and in the United States', 9 Governance, 1.

82 A. Bakardjieva Engelbrekt, *Fair Trading in Flux, National Legacies, Institutional Code and The Process of Europeanisation*, PhD Thesis, University of Stockholm, 2003.

83 See A. Klauer, 'Massenschäden erfordern Sammelklagen – Praxisprobleme aus der Sicht von Verbraucher/innen', in T. Gabriel/B. Priker-Hörmann, *Massenverfahren Reformbedarf für die ZPO? Verbraucherrecht, Verbraucherpolitik*, Band 33, 2005, 79, where the development of the Austrian Sammelklage is presented in full, from a German perspective A. Stadler/A. Mom, *Tu felix Austria? – Neue Entwicklungen im kollektiven Rechtsschutz im Zivilprozess in Österreich*, Recht der Internationalen Wirtschaft, 2006, 199.

consumer organisations improved their management skills and developed a fine-tuned strategy to collect claims in appropriate cases and to claim compensation.[84] They have filed more than twenty cases and successfully managed them.[85] The key to the success has been the role of the so-called process insurer, an insurance company which bears the risk, but claims 30% of the profit. Consumers who transfer their rights to the organisation have to sign a document that they agree with this form of 'contingency fee'.

The parallel German rule has been the result of a 'clandestine' co-operation between German consumer organisations and the competent Ministry of Justice.[86] Both managed to smuggle the new power into the much debated law on the reform of the German Civil Code. German consumer organisations started a test case and had to learn how reluctant German Courts react against any attempt to stretch the civil procedural law beyond the boundaries of individual litigation. In the end the legislator had to intervene to correct the imperfections.[87] German consumer organisations seem now to be prepared to go down the Austrian way in seeking support from so-called process insurers.[88]

The French action en représentation conjointe comes near to the Austrian/German approach, but never played a role in practice, mainly because of the high risk consumer organisations run in financing the litigation. The French Draft Act which was officially withdrawn, pointed in the same direction.[89]

The Dutch and the Italian laws rely heavily on consumer organisations. The Dutch law requires collective litigants, consumer organisations as well as associations or foundations established just for that very purpose, to conclude a settlement, which is then approved by the courts and extended to the whole class. It is an opt-out mechanism based on the assumption that litigants are able to find a compromise which is not only acceptable for both sides but also for the court. It is quite a unique procedure which has been applied twice.[90] The Italian law on group actions, which shall enter into force on the 1 January 2009, grants standing to consumer organisations.[91] Those consumers and users who intend to benefit

84 Which does not mean that the representative action is the appropriate means in all constellations where consumers suffer damages; see the different contributions in T. Gabriel/B. Pirker-Hörmann, supra n. 83.

85 A. Klauer, supra note 83, at p. 79.

86 See T. Brönneke (Hrsg.), *Kollektiver Rechtsschutz im Zivilprozess, Gruppenklagen, Verbandsmusterklagen, Verbandsklagebefugnis und Kosten des kollektiven Rechtsschutzes*, Nomos, 2001.

87 See BGHZ 170, 18 and then the amendment in §8 Abs. 2 Rechtsdienstleistungsgesetz, BGBl. 2007, 2840.

88 This is the case in the pending litigation initiated by the Hamburg consumer advice centre against a telecom company.

89 See www.globalclassactions.stanford.edu the French report written by V. Magnier.

90 See A. Stadler/H. Micklitz, supra n. 68, p. 343.

91 Article 140-bis of the Italian Consumer Code; see for details www.globalclassactions.stanford.edu, E. Silvestri, Italian report.

from the protection afforded by Article 140-bis must notify the association in writing and their intention to join the collective action. Just in line with the dominating philosophy in Europe, Italy has introduced an opt-in procedure.

C. *Collective Consumer Actions in New Democracies*

The southern new Member States of Portugal, Spain and Greece introduced collective consumer actions shortly after their transformation into democracies. It is a major characteristic of these countries that consumer law and consumer policy formed an integral part of the democratisation process. This is overtly documented in the respective consumer legislations.[92] The historical background might explain why the respective rules on collective action in these countries are rather broad and policy oriented. They sometimes look more like policy programmes needing further fine-tuning by the legislator than fully fledged laws.[93] However, the rules on collective actions in the consumer protection acts have gradually been supplemented by more detailed rules in regulations enshrined in the civil procedure or in separate legislative acts.[94]

The original versions tend to refer in a large sense to the collective or diffuse interests somewhat inspired by the French concept of the 'intérêt collectif'.[95]Article 20 of the Spanish Law on Consumer Protection 26/1984 and Article 11 of the Civil Procedure Act refer to the diffuse and collective interests that consumer organisations have to defend.[96] Article 12(4) and (5) of the Portuguese Law 24/96 refers to liability claims and regulates standing in Article 13 *inter alia* of the Public Prosecutor who may intervene to protect the collective and diffuse interests of consumers.[97] However, Portugal has introduced new legislation to be added to that introducing popular action enacted in 1995.[98] The system of aggregation established by the legislator in Decree-Law 108/2006, of 8 June, pursuant to Council of Ministers Resolution 100/2005, of 30 May, is of substantially more limited reach. The measure allows the judge to operate through "mass acts" so long as there is an element of connection between the actions and the combined performance of a procedural act or diligence simplifies the court's task. The

92 See J.W. Gerlach, 'Die moderne Entwicklung der Privatrechtsordnung in Spanien', ZVglRWiss 85 (1986), 247; H.-W. Micklitz/Th. Roethe/St. Weatherill (eds.), *Federalism and Responsibility*, Graham & Trolmann, 1994.

93 See A. Stadler/H. Micklitz, supra n. 68, p. 169 (Greece), p. 655 (Spain).

94 Www.globalclassactions.stanford.edu Portugal, Henrique Sousa Antunes, country report, Spain Pablo Gutiérrez de Cabiedes Hidalgo.

95 See on this concept, H.-W. Micklitz/A.Stadler, p. 115.

96 Www.globalclassactions.stanford.edu Spain Pablo Gutiérrez de Cabiedes Hidalgo with an English translation of the respective Acts.

97 Www.globalclassactions.stanford.edu Portugal, Henrique Sousa Antunes with English translations.

98 Law 83/95 and Decree-Law 108/2006.

intervention of the legislator was the result of an increase of mass non-compliance, in particular with regard to "small debts of communications companies, consumer credit, car leasing and, in general, all the natural litigation of a consumer society".[99]

It seems as if the Middle and Eastern European countries have chosen a different path. Early hopes that the transformation process will equally yield strong civil societies with active consumer organisations that collaborate with public agencies has not become true or if any to a much more limited extent.[100] Whilst market building was certainly fostered in particular in the pre-accession period, last but not least under pressure from the European Community, the middle and Eastern European countries were reluctant to integrate collective actions into their respective consumer laws, meant to implement the various EC directives. The action for injunction constituted the bottom-line of reform, sometimes undertaken much more to pay lip service to the EC law requirements than to vitalise a new remedy in a changed economic and political environment.[101] However, the wave of law making has now reached the new MSs as well. Nearly twenty years after the breakdown of communism, the middle and Eastern European countries are undertaking major efforts to keep up with the development in the old MSs.[102] It is suggested, however, that not all new MSs are prepared to introduce collective remedies beyond injunctions. Poland[103] and the Czech Republic[104] belong to countries where there are not even concrete plans.

2.4. REGULATING ENTRY AND EXIT. COMPARING *EX ANTE* AND *EX POST* INTERVENTION

Regulation in collective judicial enforcement relates to various aspects of standing, financing and entry and exit options. Legally speaking MSs are free to regulate *ex*

---

99 Www.globalclassactions.stanford.edu Portugal, Henrique Sousa Antunes, with English translations.

100 H.-W. Micklitz, 'Verbraucherschutz West versus Ost – Kompatibilisierungsmöglichkeiten in der Europäischen Gemeinschaft – Einige Vorüberlegungen', in: H. Heiss (ed.) *Brückenschlag zwischen den Rechtskulturen des Ostseeraums*, Tübingen, 2001, 137–182.

101 This is the overall finding of empirical investigation in 25, not 27 MSs, H.-W. Micklitz/P. Rott/U. Docekal/P. Kolba, see also A. Bakardjeva, "Grey Zones, Legitimacy Deficits and Boomerang Effects: On the Implications of Extending the *Acquis* to Central and Eastern Europe", in: Wahl/Cramér (eds.), *Swedish Yearbook of European Law* (Oxford: Hart Publishing, 2006), 1–36 and Ead. in this book, p. 91 ff.

102 See A. Bakardjieva, in this volume, p. 91 ff.

103 But see Safjan, Gorywoda and Jańczuk in this volume p. 175, fn. 17, who mention that a draft law on group claims is currently being discussed at governmental level; www.globalclassactions.stanford.edu Poland: M. Tulibacka.

104 See Tychý/J. Balarin, in this volume p. 207; L. Tichý (ed.), *Procesni Ochrana Kolektivnich Zajamü/Schutz der kollektiven Interessen im Zivilprozess*, 2008.

post or *ex ante*. Directive 98/27/EC, which adopts an *ex ante* approach with highly regulated entry, applies only to injunctions.[105]

Standing differs quite significantly across countries in group litigation. In some MS, standing is open to private, both individual representative and collective organisations, and public;[106] in others only to individual representatives and *ad hoc* organisations;[107] in others only to private organisations.[108]

Ex ante governmental intervention occurs when States organise civil society by limiting standing to consumer organisations and/or public agencies, by excluding self-organisations from acting as claimants and in providing funding from the public purse. The practical effect of *ex ante* intervention is control over access to justice. According to this perspective, collective judicial enforcement shall not be driven by market forces, but shall develop and grow, if at all, under the auspices of state control. European business arguing against US class action directly or indirectly supports *ex ante* intervention. The flood gates to the judiciary should not be opened.

Ex post intervention refers to a regulatory model where states leave the organisation and the funding of collective actions to civil society or even beyond where the state sets incentives to promote that goal. It relies on self-organisation, be it on an *ad hoc* basis or on lawyers which organise claimants and bundle consumer complaints. Such a regulatory model requires room for competition between potential plaintiffs; it implies more leeway for civil society, more economic incentives for lawyers and more powers for the managing judge.

One may wonder whether there is a silent but steady shift in Europe from the *ex ante* state control to the market based *ex post* US control of access to the judiciary in collective actions. Although Europe is in a test phase, our tentative answer to a paradigm shift is a cautious yes. Collective actions might then become a regulatory device to rebalance matters of (social) justice.[109]

Prominent candidates for such a move are the UK Group litigation order, the Dutch settlement approval concept and the German Capital Market Model Case Act. The UK model allows for self-organisations and fosters the concept of the

105 See Cafaggi/Micklitz, supra at n. 3, p. 391 ff.

106 See the Swedish Act of 2002, more generally in the Scandinavian countries, see K. Viitanen, in W. van Boom/M. Loos, p. 83, as well as the respective country reports for Denmark, Finland and Norway in www.globalclassactions.stanford.edu.

107 This is the case in the German Capital Markets Model Case Law.

108 See the Italian model in Article 140bis codice del consumo and the Dutch group actions, Hondius in this volume.

109 A. Gidi, 'The Class Action Code: A Model for Civil Law Countries', *Ariz. J. Int'l and Comp. Law*, vol. 32, p. 37 (2005); C. Meller-Hannich, 'Einführung auf dem Weg zu einem effektiven und gerechten System des kollketiven Rechtsschutzes', in Id. (ed), *Kollektiver Rechtsschutz im Zivilprozess*, 2008, 13; sceptical on this issue, R. Stürner, 'Rechtsdurchsetzung durch Gewährung von Klaganreihen?', in H.-P. Mansel, B. Dauner-Lieb, M. Henssler (eds.), *Zugang zum Recht: Europäische und US-Amerikanische Wege zur privaten Rechtsdurchsetzung*, 2008, 113, 118.

managing judge.[110] The societal Dutch model puts moral pressure on the conflicting parties to settle the conflict. The feasibility of this concept seems to be linked to particularities of Dutch society.[111] The standard method in aggregate litigation works exactly the other way around. Litigation in court ends up in a settlement.[112] The German model shows promising tendencies since the Capital Markets Model Case Act favours enforcement via lawyers and lead plaintiffs and no longer relies only on consumer organisations. Typically for Germany, however, it is a rather mixed scene. Representative actions lie in the hands of registered public consumer organisations alone.

We will describe to the *ex ante* and *ex post* regulation of entry with regard to the four potential sets of plaintiffs: consumer organisations, *ad hoc* organisations, statutory agencies and lead plaintiffs in tandem with lawyers.

A. *Consumer Organisations*

Consumer organisations exist in all MSs with different weight, legitimacy and accountability.[113] The policy question is whether and why consumer organisations should have standing in group actions.

Their organisation and performance requires skills and resources. It is useless to grant standing to consumer organisations if they are unable to monitor effectively violations and to select claims to be brought before courts. This, however, happens in nearly all MSs. The long list of notified consumer organisations does in no way correlate with their practical importance.[114] In Europe only a few consumer organisations are effective litigants. As long as the question of funding is not solved, it remains somewhat artificial to discuss the pros and cons of standing for consumer organisations in group actions.

None of the MSs has adopted particular laws on consumer organisations to regulate solely and particularly the status and the potential funding of consumer organisations to promote litigation. Their regulatory status is generally based on the law of associations and on constitutional freedoms of speech and self-organisation. Funding does not play a role here.

Particular requirements related to standing might be found in the respective EC rules on actions for injunctions.[115] These requirements, however, define only a minimum and are rather vague. The European Commission does not have the

110 See H.-W. Micklitz/A. Stadler, p. 857; Ch. Hodges, country report, www.globalclassactions.stanford.edu.

111 See A. Mom, Diss. 2007 and E. Hondius in this volume, p. 235 ff.

112 See A. Klauer and A. Stadler/A. Mom.

113 See Article 3 EC Dir. 98/27 on which Cafaggi and Micklitz, Collective enforcement of consumer law: a framework for a comparative assessment, supra at n. 3, p. 391 ff.

114 See Micklitz/Rott/Docekal/Kolba, Verbraucherschutz durch Unterlassungsklagen, Nomos, 2007.

115 See Article 3 EC Directive 98/27.

power to impose on MSs an obligation to provide adequate funding.[116] It is for the MSs to decide funding.

In the laws implementing Directive 98/27/EC and some of the Consumer Codes they have laid down criteria on the characteristics of consumer organisations.[117] There are no commonly agreed criteria on consumer organisations. It is obvious, however, that consumer organisations are submitted to much more stringent criteria in the new MSs than in the old MSs.[118]

The role of consumer organisations in group actions varies across MS, lacking a European directive. Although consumer organisations are particularly strong in Austria and Germany, last but not least because these states provide nearly 100% of the funds, it can by no means be taken for granted that they will be entrusted with group actions in the here defined terminology.[119] Germany has excluded consumer organisations from the Capital Market Model Case Act, but granted them a monopoly in test cases. The distinction should not be overestimated, however, as the adoption of the respective law is more erratic than systematic. Which way Austria will go is by no means clear. The Netherlands and in particular Italy have granted consumer organisations alone standing, thereby excluding all other potential players.[120] In countries with strong public authorities, consumer organisations are often relatively weak. This is true with regard to the UK and the Scandinavian countries. In the UK and in the Scandinavian countries strong agencies form an integral part of the respective form of capitalism.[121] Denmark, Finland, Norway and Sweden have granted standing to both; in practice, however, the Ombudsmen are the key players.[122]

In the new MSs weak public authorities and weak consumer organisations go hand in hand. Public institutions in socialist times were weak because the party was the running leader. To limit private constituencies' power the new MSs have chosen primarily to rely on public institutions. This leads to the problematic effect that weak state authorities tend to control the access of consumer organisations to the judiciary beyond mere minimum standards. It seems as if consumer organisations and public authorities are competing in the enforcement of consumer law. The constant need for public funding provides a prominent ground

---

116 However, the European Commission may ask MSs to provide for adequate funding, which it has done in the consumer strategy 2007–2013.

117 See for example the Italian Consumer Code Article 137.

118 The old MSs leave the organisation of consumers to civil society and limit the regulatory requirements to the strict minimum. Often these criteria are not even enshrined in mandatory legislation but are the result of diverse court rulings. See H.-W. Micklitz/P. Rott/U. Docekal/P. Kolba, 47, supra n. 114. In this volume, see Bakardjeva p. 91 ff.

119 Taken from CLEF.

120 See Article 140*bis* of the Italian consumer code.

121 See Hall and Soskic, *Varieties of Capitalism*, 2001.

122 P. H. Lindblom, National Report: Group litigation in Sweden, in the framework of the Globalization of class action project, available at www.globalclassactions.stanford.edu.

for playing off consumer organisations against each other by providing limited funding to a large number of organisations. Such a strategy keeps the influence of consumer organisations low and enhances the position of the statutory authorities.[123]

B. *Self or Ad Hoc Organisations*

Under the framework of Directive 98/27 organisations need to be registered to be granted standing.[124] Only organisations with a stable infrastructure and longstanding experience should be regarded as qualified entities having standing to sue. The Directive sets precedents which run counter to the idea of self-organisations, where these elements are missing or only available in rudimentary form.

Ad hoc organisations are the result of incidents and accidents. Self-organisations emerge on an *ad hoc* basis as the result of homogenous interests in collective litigation.[125] The victims or better the parents of the thalidomide catastrophe or of the hormone case in the Netherlands have organised themselves into the form of associations.[126] In Germany the companies which suffered from a cement cartel have established a BGB-Gesellschaft Partnership under the German Civil Code).[127] In Belgium a company has been created to defend injured parties in competition law infringements.[128]

The question then is whether self-organisations should have standing. There are policy arguments for and against penalising *ad hoc* organisations while privileging rooted and stable organisations.

The main reasons why longstanding, representative organisations are given standing in those countries where *ad hoc* organisations are not granted standing are twofold: a) to prevent opportunism[129] and b) to empower existing organisations and avoid competition and to some extent the emergence of strong civil society.

---

123 A. Bakardjieva, in this volume.

124 OJ L 166, 11 June 1998, 51.

125 Such self-organisations may be reported in particular from the field of product safety, where the victims of an accident gather together to better defend their interests. Then a stable organisation is needed which may be organised according to the law of associations or company law as far as this applies also to non-profit making institutions.

126 See Hondius in this volume.

127 B. Hess, 'Verbesserung des Rechtsschutzes durch kollektive Rechtsbehelfe', in H.-P. Mansel/B. Dauner-Lieb/M. Henssler (Hrsg.), *Zugang zum Recht: Europäische und US-Amerikanische Wege zur privaten Rechtsdurchsetzung*, Nomos, 2008, 61, 70–71 with references to the diverse forms of self-organisation.

128 Whose name is Cartel Damages Claims (CDC) www.carteldamageclaims.com/english/press.htm, similar developments are reported from the Netherlands.

129 An *ad hoc* organisation can be created to exploit specific opportunities without being grounded in civil society.

The arguments to grant standing to *ad hoc* organisations are a) to favour the creation of groups of victims in order to generate economies of scale and b) to put pressure on existing organisations, promote social and legal pluralism and to avoid rent-seeking.

In Europe the picture is rather scattered which reflects to some extent the distinction between liberal and corporatist societies. Corporatist societies, such as Germany, prevent the formation of new and *ad hoc* organisations to negotiate with existing and well recognised organisations or make them even mandatory, like the Dutch law on group actions.[130] Liberal societies, such as the UK, favour the formation of new organisations and try to prevent rent-seeking of the existing ones. However, the picture becomes blurred once the comparison is extended. In Austria, a classical corporatist country, self-organisations have been granted standing by the highest court in the country.[131] As to group actions in Sweden self-organisations are allowed.[132]

C. *Administrative Agencies*

Consumer agencies in Europe take very different forms. They may be (1) independent regulators, (2) they may be part of the government or (3) something in between. It has to be recalled that the policy of the European Commission is bound so far to the establishment of public enforcement bodies with regard to transborder litigation only.[133] There is no (not yet) EC policy similar to the services of general economic interests to advocate for the setting up of independent consumer agencies dealing also with internal national matters. But even the ideal type of consumer agency, the independent and separate public body with proper competences and well equipped, runs similar risks as those of consumer organisations. If the public body launches a collective action, it runs the same financial risk. It cannot go bankrupt, but it can be held liable for improper judicial advice.[134] What matters even more is that consumer agencies differently from other national regulators such as cartel offices or the network regulators (energy,

130 However, the former relatively strict approach of the German Federal Supreme Court which prohibited the transfer of rights to an association which then could sue on behalf of the assignees is going to be softened now; see references in B. Hess, supra n. 127, fn. 99.

131 See the documentation of the case law in A. Klauer, supra n. 83, in T. Gabriel/B. Pirker-Hörmann, p. 79.

132 Compare Sweden where *ad hoc* organisations can be created, see P. H. Lindblom, National Report: Group litigation in Sweden, in the framework of the Globalization of class action project, available at www.globalclassactions.standford.edu.

133 See Regulation 2006/2004 Article 1.

134 There are two famous examples both from the area of product safety and both concern the public warning against health risks. See OLH Stuttgart *NJW* 1990, 2690 – Birkel, and ECJ, 17 April 2007, Case C-470/03 COS.MET 2007 (ECR) I-2749; N. Reich, 'A.G.M. COS.MET oder: Wem dient das EU-Produktsicherheitsrecht?', *Verbraucher und Recht*, 2007, 410.

telecom) often do not have their own sources of income and depend entirely on transfers from the government. Only when competition agencies have been given enforcement tasks in the field of consumer protection can they use the resources generated by infringements of competition law.

In MSs with strong public enforcement structures in the field of consumer law and weak consumer organisations, the former often play a relevant role in collective judicial enforcement. In the Scandinavian countries, consumer law judicial enforcement lies in the hands of the Ombudsmen, entitled to file collective compensation claims. Similar tendencies are to be reported from the UK where the enforcement lies primarily in the hands of the Office of Fair Trading and from the new MSs, where often separate units of the competent Ministries are in charge of the enforcement.[135] The EC move towards the establishment of consumer agencies in each MS may even strengthen this development. Consumer organisations are then reduced to mere watchdogs which might file motions to the consumer agency, at the best establishing co-operation mechanisms.

D. *Lead plaintiffs and lawyers in tandem*

Lead plaintiffs are relatively new actors in European collective judicial enforcement. The terminology and the category are definitely borrowed from the US class action. There is overall agreement that group actions of several, maybe hundreds, of claimants need a plaintiff to lead the case. In Europe this is predominantly the claimant who has the strongest economic interest in the outcome. MSs do not apply the first come first serve principle.[136] This might be due to the fact that there is less fear in the MSs that lawyers are competing against each other with their respective claimants on the basis of ill-founded and less-settled claims. So far, this has not happened or where there are tendencies like in financial services litigation, these seem to be under the control of the competent judges.

The true problem for the EU MSs is the definition of the role and function of the lawyer. In the US, lawyers are the driving force behind the class action, due primarily to the contingency fee structure. Collective judicial enforcement, in the field of consumer protection, is regarded as business which needs investment. Europe, at least European governments, are far away from such approach. Whilst there is a strong move to look at lawyers as service providers, they are still regarded as being part of the judicature, thereby fulfilling quasi statutory tasks.[137] EC law too remains ambivalent. Whereas lawyers are regarded in competition law as enterprises, the ECJ exempted the chambers of advocates from the scope of

135 On the enforcement powers of OFT see I. Ramsay, *Consumer law and policy*, Hart, 2007; G. Howells and S Weatherill, *EU consumer law & policy*, EE, 2005.

136 See references in a comparative perspective, A. Stadler/H.-W. Micklitz, p. 1390.

137 M. Ros, Fédération des Barreaux d'Europe (FBE), p. 299.

application of EC law.[138] Europe is not willing to go down the American road which means in essence that new forms of funding should be considered. This, however, is not really the case.

3. REFRAMING THE EUROPEAN DEBATE IN THE LIGHT OF THE US AND CANADIAN EXPERIENCES

Two different yet related questions concerning consumer enforcement policies are before Europe: (1) the definition of a consistent multilevel system with strong coordination between European and MS legislation, (2) the relationship between administrative and judicial enforcement and within the latter between injunctive reliefs and pecuniary remedies. Furthermore, should the strategy distinguish between transborder and domestic litigation? Should specific rules and policies be devised to promote European aggregate litigation?

We try to address these points by breaking them down into 5 issues:

(1) the constitutional dimension of collective redress, (2) the relationship between administrative and judicial enforcement, (3) the role of hybrid class actions and the interplay between injunctions and pecuniary remedies, (4) the effects of remedial strategies on consumer substantive laws and (5) the players.

We end with a brief analysis of what European institutions should do next (6).

3.1. THE CONSTITUTIONAL BALANCE BETWEEN COLLECTIVE AND INDIVIDUAL REDRESS IN LIGHT OF THE DEBATE BETWEEN PUBLIC AND PRIVATE ENFORCEMENT

Aggregate litigation often involves separation between ownership of the claims and control over litigation. This separation raises agency problems with constitutional relevance. The degree of separation and the rights of principals (consumers) to monitor the agents (public entities, private consumer organisations, lead plaintiffs, law firms, etc.) are limited by constitutional principles.

The right to access the class, the definition of the class, the limits of res-judicata, preclusion of subsequent litigation, the effects of settlements and the right to opt out all bear constitutional relevance both in the US and EU.[139]

---

138 ECJ 19 February 2002 C-303/99, 2002 (ECR) I-1577.

139 See G. Hazard, 'Erie doctrine repealed by Congress', *U. Pa. L. R.*, 2008, forthcoming Burbank, 'The class action fairness Act in historical context: a preliminary view', 2008, research paper

In the US the focus has been on due process rights to individualised treatment and a right to trial by the same jury of non-separable issues. The tension between aggregate litigation and individual rights has been at the core of judicial and scholarly attention. The principles are differentiated in relation to the type of remedy.[140] Due process requires broad opt out opportunities in divisible remedies while it does not require the same for indivisible remedies.[141] In the former case, rights of individual claimants are generally characterised by exit, voice and loyalty.[142] The right to opt out and escape the preclusive effect of the judgement (exit), the right to participate and be heard (voice) and the right to adequate representation constitute the pillars of individual protection and define the boundaries of aggregate litigation.[143] Lately a shift towards opt-out policy has been explicitly advocated in the field of securities litigation to improve accountability.[144]

In Europe the general principles focus on the individual rights to limit modes of collective enforcement, sometimes even in a human rights dimension.[145] Differences exist at MS level not only between old and new MS but within Western

---

08/03, available at SSRN: http://ssrn.com/abstract=1083785.

140 Significant differences exist between aggregate litigation seeking injunctive reliefs and that seeking pecuniary rewards. Individual rights are not considered insuperable obstacles to collective redress. In the area of injunctions opt-out rights are often reduced or eliminated, in that of damages individual rights are given greater importance but limitations to opt out are still held admissible. See *Ortiz v. Fibreboard Corp.* 527 U.S. 815 (1999, *Molski v. Gleich* 318 F3d 937, 948–9 (9th Cir 2003), for a review, see R. Daniels, 'Monetary damages in mandatory classes: when should opt-out rights be allowed', *Ala L.R.*, 57 p. 499 ff. (2005).

141 See ALI Principles §2.08 comment c:
"Aggregate treatment of related claims need not afford claimants an opportunity to avoid the preclusive effect of any determination of those claims if the court finds that the aggregate proceeding should be mandatory in order
(1) to manage fairly and efficiently indivisible relief
(2) to allocate equitably a pre-existing limited fund among claimants; or
(3) to facilitate the fair and efficient adjudication of claims asserted in individual lawsuits subject to court-ordered consolidation.".

142 See S. Issacharoff, 'Governance and legitimacy in the law of class actions', *Sup. Ct. rev.* (1999) 999, p. 337 and J. Coffee, 'Class action accountability: Reconciling exit, voice and loyalty in representative litigation', *Col. L. R. 100*, 2000, p. 370 ff. at 376–7.

143 See ALI Principles §2.08 comment c: "In the context of aggregate litigation the right of exit in subsection (a)(1) consists of the opportunity to escape the preclusive effect of the aggregate proceeding. The right of voice in subsection (a)(2) consists of the opportunity to participate in the aggregate proceeding and, as its antecedent, notice of that proceeding. The right of loyalty in subsection (a)(3) consists of judicial review, as a precondition for aggregate treatment, to ascertain whether any structural conflicts of interest exist in representation of claimants.".

144 See J. Coffee, Jr., 'Accountability and competition in securities class actions: why exit works better than voice', w.p. 329 available at http://papers.ssrn.com/abstract 1113845 suggesting, in relation to securities class actions, that Courts should: "not certify the class action before the settlement's terms have been publicly disclosed... reject proposes settlements that have disproprortionate reductions for opt outs. But Courts should not reject setllements that give the class the benefit of any hygher payment made to an opt out..." (p. 52).

145 See A. Stadler in this volume.

Europe. The new generation of Constitutions, introducing consumer protection clauses, have balanced the individual and collective dimensions, often providing constitutional basis for collective redress.[146] Thus they strike a different balance from the framework defined in the first half of the XX century in western democracies. These differences may require some balancing at EU level.

European legal systems seem to give greater importance to individual rights and limit the possibility to introduce opt-out systems in national legislation due to constitutional principles concerning access to justice.[147] New legislation in the Scandinavian countries has introduced some forms of aggregate litigation with the possibility to opt out where standing is attributed exclusively or primarily to Public organisations.[148] The debate is not entirely consistent. There is some tension between the emphasis on individual rights in the group action debate and the legislation on injunctions granting, *de jure* or *de facto*, monopoly of standing to consumer organisations and public organisations, without providing strong accountability mechanisms, especially towards non-members and the public.

A more balanced set of solutions is needed. On the one hand some trade-off between benefits and costs of aggregate litigation needs to be made with some detriment to individual consumer rights. The necessity to ensure stable solutions reached either through judgements or settlements may preclude individual claimants to litigate the matters over and over in different jurisdictions. On the other hand, higher protection of individual rights in systems may be ensured by increasing accountability mechanisms associated with public and private organisations to which standing is granted. Delegation to private organisations of consumer protection should be combined with specific rules protecting non-members who may be affected by the binding effects of the judgement or the settlement concluded by private organisations.

---

146 This is the case in Portugal where Article 52(3) of the Constitution as amended in 1989 states "Everyone shall be granted the right of popular action, either personally or via associations that purport to defend the interests in question, including the right of an aggrieved party or parties to apply for compensation" and in Spain Constitution 1978, Section 125 of the Constitution 'Citizen' may engage in popular action and take part in the administration of justice through the institution of the jury, in manners and respect to those criminal trials as may be determined by law, as well as in customary and traditional courts.

147 See for example the debate on the constitutional right to be heard which has taken place in Germany with the introduction of KapMuG. Constitutional arguments imposed the right to be heard on interested parties other than the chosen plaintiffs and limits to the binding effects only on those who were able to 'influence' the outcome of the proceedings. See D. Baetge, Class actions, group actions and other forms of collective litigation, available at www.law.stanford.edu/display/images/dynamic/events_media/Germany_National_Report.pdf. Similar issues have arisen in Italy in relation to the introduction of the new regime.

148 See Denmark and Norway which for many other issues have followed the opt-in Swedish model, www.globalclassactions.stanford.edu, (see for Denmark, E. Werlauff and for Norway C. Bernt-Hamre).

3.2. ADMINISTRATIVE AND JUDICIAL ENFORCEMENT

The interplay between administrative and judicial enforcement works differently across the Atlantic both for institutional and cultural reasons.[149] The operations of the two basic institutions, Courts and Agencies, still widely differ and the main players, on both the plaintiff's and defendant's sides, are provided with very different incentive systems.

Given that both enforcement mechanisms are aimed at regulating conducts and deterring unlawful behaviour it is necessary to differentiate sanctions and penalties to achieve the desired level of deterrence. In theory both enforcement mechanisms concern relative homogeneous risks and conducts, however they may differ as to temporal and spatial dimensions and to the ways conflicting interests of those negatively affected are balanced. When risks and injuries are highly specific clearly judicial should be preferred over AE.

Two important conclusions may be drawn on the relationship between judicial and administrative enforcement:

a) While it is acceptable and sometimes even desirable to combine administrative and judicial enforcement in relation to different remedies, institutional overlap for the same remedy should be avoided. Conferring power to delete an unfair term, to enjoin an unfair trade practice or to recall a defective product at the same time on administrative and judicial authority may bring about inconsistent results, increasing social costs without adding any substantial benefit.[150] The case of different institutions employing identical remedies should be avoided. Institutional complementarity should operate between remedies not within the same remedy unless the requirements to administer the remedy are so different to pursue different goals.
b) The coordination between enforcers does not necessarily imply the definition of hierarchy between the two types of enforcement when they concern the same subject matter. Coordination imposes prioritisation. Combined use of administrative and judicial collective enforcement in consumer protection poses questions of priority/pre-emption. Should administrative have priority over judicial enforcement? To what extent may divergent conclusions between agencies and courts be allowed about infringements, i.e. can the same conduct be considered lawful by an administrative agency and unlawful by a court?

---

149 See F. Cafaggi/H. Micklitz, supra n. 3, p. 391.

150 This does not mean, however, that private collective judicial enforcement should and could be played off against administrative enforcement, but see for such an argument, F.J. Säcker, *Die Einordnung der Verbandsklage in das System des Privatrechts*, C.H. Beck, 2006; J. Jahn, 'Der Klage-Druck auf die Industrie wird weiter steigen', in H.-P. Mansel/B. Dauner-Lieb/M. Henssler (eds), *Zugang zum Recht: Europäische und US-Amerikanische Wege zur privaten Rechtsdurchsetzung*, 2008, 19, 24.

The institutional complementarity approach suggests that divergences are not problematic if and when the two modes of enforcement perform complementary goals.[151] They only become an issue if the same standards and goals lead to different and conflicting outcomes.

It is important to decide rules about sequencing between administrative and judicial enforcement, especially if information costs are taken seriously.[152] Most of the debate in the US about cost-effectiveness of administrative versus judicial enforcement gravitates around cost-effectiveness in information acquisition.[153] Often, however, as the case of competition clearly shows, private enforcement follows public enforcement and adds little information to that generated by public enforcers. Thus appropriate sequencing and the possibility of allocation of tasks between administrative and judicial enforcers, making available the evidence already produced may translate into welfare enhancing policies. Some form of participation of public enforcers to private enforcement may therefore be desirable.[154]

An open question concerns the different methods to define penalties and damages in relation to the deterrence effect and how the power to use penalties should be allocated between Courts and Agencies.[155] How should they be coordinated when both a fine and damages can be inflicted upon the infringer as the cases of unsafe product or competition infringements show?

3.3 INJUNCTIONS AND PECUNIARY REMEDIES

Judicial collective enforcement can ensure deterrence, provide redress and contribute to risk management in case of latent injuries. The gap being filled by

---

151 See F. Cafaggi, 'A coordinate Approach to Regulation and Civil Liability in European Law: Rethinking Institutional Complementarities', in F. Cafaggi, *The institutional framework of European private law*, Oxford University Press, 2006, p. 191.

152 In the field of damages for breach of competition law the White Paper recalls that once the European Commission finds a breach of Article 81 and/or 82 victims can rely on this decision as binding proof in civil proceedings for damages. Different rules apply in MS as to the relationship between Competition authorities and Courts. To enhance coordination and avoid different results, the Commission has proposed the following rule: "national courts that have to rule in actions for damages on practices under Articles 81 or 82 on which and NCA (National competition authority) in the ECN (European competition network) has already given a final decision finding an infringement of those Articles, or on which a review court has given a final judgment upholding the NCA decision or itself finding an infringement, cannot take decisions running counter to any such decision or ruling." White paper on damages in antitrust, at p. 6.

153 See D. Rosenberg and J. Sullivan, 'Coordinating private class action and public agency enforcement of antitrust law', *Journal of competition law and economics*, 2, (2006), p. 159 ff.

154 See J. Fisch, 'Class action reform, qui tam and the role of plaintiff', *Law and contemporary problems*, vol. 60, (1997), p. 167 ff.

155 See OECD, Best Practices for consumer policy: report on effectiveness of enforcement regimes, available at www.oecd.org.

the introduction of group actions at MS level not only refers to compensation but also to deterrence and to a lesser extent, so far, to risk management.[156] Effective aggregate litigation will ensure that small individual claims will be brought before Courts. But it will also ensure that claims that would hardly justify huge investments to generate evidence at the individual level can be brought at a collective level given the possibility to spread the costs across a large number of claimants.

The combined use of injunctions and pecuniary remedies will thus enhance deterrence and perhaps reduce or better qualify the role of administrative regulation. It is beyond the scope of this essay to deal in depth with the optimal combination but it is clear that no uniform principles can be drafted in Europe across different consumer fields. A different balance between the two remedies is needed in unfair contract terms, trade practices, product safety, etc. The role of damages in unfair contract term litigation is different from that in unfair trade practices and product liability. Each sub-sector of consumer law will have to strike its own balance, partly drawn from legislation partly on procedural strategies that claimants will choose case by case.

In the US, the possibility to combine remedies in class actions is ensured when monetary reliefs concern the whole class. These are hybrid class actions.[157]

In Europe, in addition to compensatory damages other types of pecuniary remedies exist or have recently been introduced: in particular, restitutionary damages, unjust enrichment and penalties. The new legislation on group actions is generally not limited to compensatory damages but it refers to disgorgement of profits or the so-called skimming off.[158] While now it is possible to seek injunctive reliefs and different forms of pecuniary remedies, the prerequisites are still different; thus an unfair term may be subject to injunctive relief and restitutionary damages but not qualify for compensatory damages. An unfair commercial practice may be stopped by injunction without giving rise to compensatory damages unless negligence is proved.[159]

---

156 In Europe the level of deterrence seems still lower than desirable, given the lower than expected effectiveness of injunctions, especially in transborder litigation, and the compelling necessity to combine it with pecuniary remedies. In relation to the latter it is evident that purely compensatory damages may often be insufficient and need to be combined with restitutionary damages when the level of profit gained by the unlawful term or practice is much higher than the amount of compensation the injured consumers can claim.

157 Solutions among circuit Courts are not convergent. See E. Sherman, 'Segmenting aggregate litigation: Initiatives and Impediments for reshaping the trial process', *The Review of litigation*, 2006, vol. 25 p. 707 ff.

158 H.-W. Micklitz/A. Stadler, *Unrechtsgewinnabschöpfung – Möglichkeiten und Perspektiven eines kollektiven Schadensersatzanspruches im UWG*, Band 11 der VIEW Schriftenreihe, 2003.

159 This might be the case if intention is required for restitution or skimming off while it is not for the injunctive relief.
In Germany, skimming off requires intention unlike injunctive relief where not even negligence is required, A. Stadler/H.W. Micklitz, 'Der Reformvorschlag der UWG-Novelle für eine

Two issues stand out for legislative intervention: the regulation of entry to litigation, including but not limited to standing; (2) the conclusion of the litigation either with a judgment or settlement, both in relation to injunctions and damages and their binding effects on 'third parties'.[160]

(1) We have extensively discussed the differences in standing between injunctions and damages.[161] While in relation to the former consumer associations and public entities have the monopoly, a wider range of claimants can bring claims for pecuniary remedies. The ex ante model for injunctions is complemented by a mixed model for pecuniary remedies. This difference partly reflects the different preferences and models at national level and partly the different incentives especially in the private realm. Injunctions are more appealing for consumer organisations than for lawyers, at least for profit driven ones. A different balance may be struck in relation to public interest litigation in the field of fundamental rights.

(2) Both in relation to injunctions and to pecuniary remedies, settlement is a likely, at times even desirable, outcome. However the incentives to settle differ quite significantly whether the leading claimant is a public entity, a consumer organisation or a lawyer representing a group of consumers and whether the 'dominant' remedy sought is an injunction or damages. The nature of repeat player and the extent to which litigants are also involved in negotiations over rule-making play a substantial role in defining the incentive structure.

The extent to which consumers' ability to reduce risks, individually and collectively, may affect the choice between individual and collective litigation and that between injunctions and pecuniary remedies is not sufficiently debated.[162] It is an underinvestigated question which deserves much more attention by legislators and judges.[163]

Verbandsklage auf Gewinnabschöpfung', *wrp* 2003, 559–562, now OLG Stuttgart, 24.03.2006, 2 U 58/6 *Lidl v. Verbraucherzentrale Bundesverband.* Pending before the German Supreme Court. The conflict deals exactly around the question of intention and what is meant and needed to provide evidence.

160 See G. Hazard Jr., J.L. Gedid and S. Sowle, 'An historical analysis of the binding effects of class suits', *U. Pa. L. R.* 146, p. 1849 ff. (1998).

161 See above text and footnotes, p. 377 ff.

162 See F. Cafaggi, 'Responsabilità del produttore', *Trattato di diritto privato europeo*, N. Lipari (ed.), Padova, 2003, p. 393; Id., 'A Coordinated Approach to Regulation and Civil Liability in European Law: Rethinking Institutional Complementarities', in F. Cafaggi (ed.), The Institutional Framework of European Private Law, Oxford University Press, 2006, p. 191.

163 But see in the US context a thoughtful yet not necessarily convincing analysis Judge Posner opinion in In re Rhone Poulenc Rorer, INC 51 F3d 1293 (7th Cir. 1995); *Castano v. American Tobacco Co.* 84 F.3d 734 (5th Cir. 1996).

3.4. THE 'INDIRECT' EFFECTS OF NATIONAL LEGISLATION CONCERNING GROUP ACTIONS ON SUBSTANTIVE CONSUMER LAW

Divergences in procedural rules concerning group actions should affect substantive rules which are already harmonised. European consumer legislation was enacted without specific references to mass litigation. The implicit reference was to individual litigation but the procedural and remedial part was just outlined. In fact due to the principle of procedural autonomy, often references to remedies was generic or incomplete, leaving MS the power to complete the legislation either in the implementing Act or by reference to existing law.

The enactment of national legislation concerning mass litigation poses numerous challenges to substantive consumer legislation. On the one hand it will certainly improve effectiveness and discourage unlawful conduct when infringements cause a large amount of small size claims. On the other hand it will underline the necessity to distinguish between substantive rules applied to individual and to mass litigation. Questions concerning causation, harms and damages have to be treated differently in aggregate litigation as the US experience clearly shows. In particular, damages in aggregate litigation have a fairness dimension[164] which is foreign to individual litigation. The compensation has to be defined according to the general principle of full compensation but within the constraints of a fairness criterion related to the distribution among the injured parties given the level of available resources often below the level of full compensation that should in principle be satisfied. The challenges may be solved by judicial discretion, through a process of adaptation. Potential divergences in national solutions may however require coordination among judiciaries to reach consistent solutions. It would be desirable that both the review of the Consumer *Acquis* and the DCFR will take due consideration of aggregate litigation in drafting the new rules.

3.5. THE PLAYERS

Who are or should be the litigants? The creation of an integrated European market suggests that the institutional framework should favour transborder litigation. On the defendant side this does not represent a contested issue. On the claimant side, major differences exist, depending on the nature of the claimant.

164 C. Meller-Hannich, 'Einführung auf dem Weg zu einem effektiven und gerechten System des kollketiven Rechtsschutzes', in Ead. (ed.), *Kollektiver Rechtsschutz im Zivilprozess*, Nomos, 2008, p. 13; A. Stadler, 'Rechtspolitischer Ausblick zum kollektiven Rechtsschutz', ibidem, p. 93.

We have contrasted different standing regulations concerning injunctions and pecuniary remedies to highlight the different models of centralised and decentralised control over access to litigation.

Ex ante regulation may be understood as a device to exercise state control over those who may file collective actions in courts. The market for mass litigation is thus limited by entry regulation. These systems empower the State to choose among organisations with a top-down centralised decision-making process. They often may reduce legal pluralism and hinder legal innovation.

Ex post intervention leaves much room for market forces and self-organisation in civil societies to decide who emerge as litigants. It is a decentralised system that may increase competition and to some extent accountability if well governed. Lack of rules in *ex post* systems may however also produce *de facto* monopolies and thus reduce accountability and legal innovation.

Engineering effective aggregate litigation requires both public policies and new rules concerning the major players and their agency relationships with claimants. These interventions may vary according to the specific strategy, whether based on consumer organisations or more 'market' oriented but the current state is not satisfactory in both cases. Whichever preference will be expressed by each MS, it is clear that both groups will be involved and that some degree of competition between law firms and consumer organisations will arise. But this competition, if limited, can be beneficial.

The relationship between the claimant and the represented consumers is regulated by national laws, very different both between public and private organisations and within the latter between consumer organisations and plaintiff lawyers.

The typical duty of loyalty, characterising the lawyer/client relationship, differs significantly from the duties owed by the private organisations to the class members where the law of association generally applies, and from those related to public bodies, where administrative law applies.[165]

Funding affects incentives but also rules concerning aggregate litigation. The differences within Europe are conspicuous. Consumer organisations, which receive financial subsidies out of the public purse are financed on a yearly basis. If they are well equipped like in Austria or Germany, France and Italy, they have an annual budget for filing law suits. This means that they have to make a choice and to invest where the return rate – in particular in public reputation – is high. When a collective action, an action for injunction or a representative action, ends up in a high cost risk due to the loser pays principle, the consumer organisation has to

165 See F. Cafaggi, 'Adequate representation of consumer in public and private collective enforcement', unpublished manuscript. In relation to the US, see G. Hazard Jr., 'Modeling class counsel', *Nebraska L.R.* vol. 81, p. 1397 ff. (2003).

seek approval from the Ministry.[166] They may be held liable by consumers who may argue that the organisation has not properly led the case.[167] The result is a bargaining process over the question whether the organisation shall file the law suit and more generally how many collective actions should be brought to court. In essence the state exercises control of collective judicial enforcement by restricting standing and channelling funding. Notice however that even those MS known as being more market oriented like the UK, select consumer organisations quite strictly which can play regulatory or enforcement functions. For example in the UK only one organisation has been recognised in the field of unfair contract terms.[168]

The specificity of transnational litigation requires *ad hoc* interventions. Strategies will vary depending on the nature of the claimants. The different forms of coordination should mainly refer to homogeneous parties. Separate coordinating strategies are required for public organisations (e.g. ombudsmen or OFT), for private consumer organisations or law firms to bring legal claims before national Courts on behalf of consumers coming from different jurisdictions.

Promoting a market for European legal services to individual consumers and their organisations should become an institutional priority. Public policy requires rules that can promote the birth of an efficient market. This implies not only funding pilot litigation at EU level but also introducing stricter regulation to avoid opportunistic behaviour and to ensure that lawyers act as loyal agents of consumer-principals.[169] Major reforms concerning law of lawyer-client relationships are thus needed. The principles should be defined in a European legislative act. Alternatively soft law should be drafted, concerning lawyer-client relationships and association-claimant relationships. These principles should operate in relation to judicial collective enforcement, including both injunctions and damages, and then be implemented through national legislation or co-regulation.

Different arrangements can be devised among private organisations to bring claims. Cooperation can have different forms or degree. It may be centre-driven or based on decentralised market driven patterns. In the first case the role of the BEUC can become extremely important.[170] Coordination among national consumer organisations is far from being satisfactory. It is, however, bound to the

166 There are no rules in Austria and Germany, but it is current practice which results out of the public financing.

167 In Germany, BGH 25 October 2006 VIII ZR 102/06, *NJW* 2007, 428.

168 C. Hodges, 'Collectivism: evaluating the effectiveness of public and private models for regulating consumer protection', in W. van Boom/M. Loos, *cit.* p. 207.

169 This has already happened in the home-shopping case which forestalled Directive 98/27/EC, see H.-W. Micklitz, *Cross-Border Consumer Conflicts, A French-German Experience*, JCP special issue, 1993.

170 The BEUC has among its institutional tasks that of co-ordinating the activities of the national consumer organisations. This is however a touchy issue, as Member State organisations

availability of the necessary resources and skills. Funding, if any, is provided on a national basis. Ministries might face problems in funding, e.g. transborder litigation, where not only nationals benefit.

The same need for coordination has to occur among law firms.[171] In the US the effort to aggregate claims has pushed towards cooperation among law firms.[172] Often this cooperation has reduced competition at the expense of consumers who have been proposed settlements at an early stage and for lower amounts they would have been able to obtain.[173] More recently the use of opt-out options, in the field of securities where big institutional investors play a major role, has triggered more competition and it is reshaping the relationship among plaintiffs and defendants' lawyers.[174] In the field of consumer protection, where no reasons to opt out exist, the level of competition is low and often there is collusion to define the lead plaintiff.

Differences in Europe concerning legal systems make these developments necessary and urgent. But learning from the US experience, private contractual arrangements among law firms located in different MS may not be sufficient. The role of national judiciaries to promote the creation of European litigants must increase. Here again the powers given to judges by national legal systems may differ significantly. This may engender judicial activism in some legal systems, higher than in others. But to avoid the formation of jurisdictional monopoly, judicial cooperation in consumer collective litigation is necessary.

The increasing role of aggregate litigation in Europe will empower national judiciaries. Judges will have to select meritorious claims and avoid frivolous litigation. They will have to ensure adequate representation of consumer interests in litigation; they will have to ensure fair distribution at the end of the proceedings, be it a judgment or a settlement.

For these reasons it is of strategic importance to devise coordination mechanisms among national judiciaries, similar to the Multidistrict litigation Panel in the US that can contribute to coordinating transboundary litigation. Absent a federal judiciary, a European coordinating body will not be able to

enviously defend their autonomy. The BEUC is nevertheless in the CLEF which is sponsored by the European Commission.

171 Ingenious franchise agreements to generate evidence have been devised in the US in order to promote cost-sharing and economies of scale. With regard to Germany, see the references in B. Hess, 'Verbesserung des Rechtsschutzes durch kollektive Rechtsbehelfe', in H.-P. Mansel, B.Dauner-Lieb and M. Henssler (eds.), *Zugang zum Recht: Europäische und US-Amerikanische Wege zur privaten Rechtsdurchsetzung*, Nomos, 2008, p. 61, 70–71.

172 See for an historical analysis S. Burbank, the class action fairness Act in historical context:a preliminary view, research paper 08/03, available at http.papers.ssrn.com/abstract 1083785.

173 See T. Eisemberg and G. Miller, 'Attorneys fees in class action settlements: an empirical study', *J. Empirical studies* 1, p. 27 ff. (2004).

174 See J. Coffee, Jr., Accountability and competition in securities class actions: why exit works better than voice, supra n. 144.

exercise the same powers but certainly can provide information to the national Courts involved in litigation and try to ensure some consistency in outcomes.

The litigation will also depend on agencies. They are generally empowered to bring legal claims concerning injunctions and in some MS also group actions. In this perspective they are part of the judicial enforcement system not of the administrative one. As a potential claimant has to select the claims to be litigated and the remedies to be sought, to perform this task, two requirements should occur: a) independence from political power and (b) accountability to the injured parties whose interests will be involved in litigation

It is hard to imagine that a consumer agency is totally freed from political influence when it does not have financial independence. The solution is that consumer agencies are guaranteed and given independency, last but not least by allowing them to raise their proper funds, e.g. via fines. The question whether individual consumers or consumer organisations may sue the inactive public agency for not taking action, may then loose importance. This remedy seems to play a certain role in the new MSs.[175]

3.6 THE ROLE FOR EUROPEAN GOVERNANCE TO FOSTER EFFECTIVE AGGREGATE LITIGATION IN CONSUMER LAW

Europe is facing a period of intense change. Several MS have enacted or are about to enact national legislation concerning group actions.[176] These statutes will have to be combined with those on injunctions and to administrative regulation to define an integrated and coordinated design of effective consumer protection.[177]

Differences concern not only institutional engineering but the basic options and the scope of litigation. The different weight attributed to settlements, the different relationships with individual litigation reveal that not only the rules but also the scope of the game varies extensively.

Europe should promote experimentalism in the future. MS should continue to produce legislation according to their constitutional principles, preferences and traditions. These developments should however internalise the necessity to build appropriate institutions for coordination. For example the lack of a competitive market for legal services on the claimants' side may suggest the adoption of opt-in mechanisms in the first stage while shifting towards some form of opt-out only

175 A. Bakardjieva, in this volume.

176 See above, at p. 434.

177 Some level of coordination has been introduced only in a few states. For example the group action Swedish Act allows the seeking both injunctions and damages.

when sufficient competition in the market for legal services will generate incentives to produce information to enable informed choices by potentially injured plaintiffs.[178]

MS will learn from each other but this process will have costs. Legislative differentiation may, to some extent, prevent effectiveness of transnational consumer litigation if it is not well coordinated. To the extent that the predominance requirement operates, it will be difficult to find common questions of law in such a differentiated legal landscape.[179] This differentiation can even be instrumentally promoted by introducing apparently consumer-friendly and legally binding jurisdictional clauses in contractual relationships which would bind parties to apply consumer-based jurisdiction to the potential class action.[180] In this case, aggregating consumers coming from different jurisdictions may become difficult because applicable rules to the disputes are different according to consumer nationalities and it would be hard, if not impossible, for the same judge to apply as many rules as the jurisdictions involved by way of aggregation. Transborder litigation concerning consumers coming from different jurisdictions should permit the choice of one single substantive law or a limited number. The alternative, quite costly, is the subdivision in class according to nationalities.

At the same time a European solution might be needed to handle arbitration clauses. The US and Canadian courts have taken a liberal approach to the detriment of consumers. In Europe the landscape is highly segmented, in

178 Different arguments have been provided to suggest that scarce participation of consumers suggest the desirability of opt-in systems. See R. Mulheron, 'Reform of collective redress in England and Wales: a perspective of need', available at www.civiljusticecouncil.gov.uk. These arguments focus on the current institutional setting and do not place particular importance on institution building. We suggest that the long-term goal of building appropriate institutions for aggregate litigation may justify lower rates of participation in litigation. Furthermore a distinction between effective participation and coverage should be made. Opt-in solutions may ensure broader coverage and thus have strong deterrence effect but certainly they do not 'promote' consumer active participation. On the contrary they favour consumer apathy.

179 The predominance requirement is very relevant in the US. According to rule 23(b)(3) Rules of Civil Procedure questions of law or fact to the members of the class predominate over any questions affecting the individual members, and that a class action is superior to other available methods for the fair and efficient adjudication of the controversy. The matters pertinent to the findings include (A) the interest of members of the class in individually controlling the prosecution or defence of separate actions (B) the extent and nature of any litigation concerning the controversy already commenced by or against any members of the class; (C) the desirability or undesirability of concentrating the litigation of the claims in the particular forum (D) the difficulties likely to be encountered in the management of the action. On the issue of predominance in the US context see R. Nagareda, 'Administering adequacy in class representation', 82 *Tex.L.R.* 287 (2003).

180 The ECJ decided in favour of consumers, Judgment 27 June 2000, Case C-281/98 2000 (ECR) I-4139.

particular since the ECJ refused to set common standards under Directive 93/13/EC.[181]

The effects of aggregate litigation on substantive law should thus be monitored and changes should occur to ensure consistency between consumer protection laws and aggregate litigation at EU level.

For the time being, the role of European institutions should be limited to ensure that national legislation promotes transnational litigation by offering a framework for:

a) coordinating collective redress for violations in consumer and competition laws;
b) allowing the creation of claimants' groups beyond national areas; this may require different strategies when MSs adopt opt-out legislation by permitting opt-in by non-residents;
c) devising public policies, including funding and information, to promote aggregate litigation.

1) The funding policy in particular should be inspired by two concurring principles: contributing to the creation of a solid market for legal services and promoting pilot transboundary litigation.[182] Rules at EU level should also regulate the lawyer-client relationship in aggregate litigation and accountability of consumer organisations to non-members when they act on their behalf, to ensure loyalty and adequate representation. Liberalising agreements concerning fees in aggregate litigation can contribute to increase incentives to engage in selective litigation.[183] The role and function of process insurers which play an increasing role in collective litigation should be openly addressed.[184]

---

181 It reminds one to recall Claro to highlight the differences, ECJ, 26 October 2006, Case C-238/05 2006 (ECR) I-11125 and N. Reich in this volume.

182 Interesting proposals concerning costs allocation rules have been made in the White paper on damages in antitrust pp. 9 and 10 " The Commission encourages Member States:
- to design procedural rules fostering settlements as a way to reduce costs
- to set court fees in an appropriate manner so that they do not become a disproportionate disincentive to antitrust damages claims
- to give national Courts the possibility of issuing cost orders derogating in certain justified cases from the normal cost rules, preferably upfront in the proceedings".

183 Especially when the English rule applies, the possibility to share part of the financial risks of litigation between clients and lawyers is of the outmost importance. This liberalisation would also encourage law firms to be accurate in selecting claims and to devise financial instruments that may reduce the risks. See for recent law reforms Sweden, within the Group litigation Act, regulating risk agreement among lawyers and clients (sec. 38, 39, 40, 41).

184 They are the key to the success of the Austrian representative action and they can be found in Germany too, B. Hess, 'Verbesserung des Rechtsschutzes durch kollektive Rechtsbehelfe', supra n. 127, p. 72 with references to the debate and the case law, pleading for statutory rules.

2) Setting up a European notification scheme where all pending cases are made publicly available European-wide; likewise creating a data-file and making all national legislations on collective actions available in English.

d) Promoting judicial coordination in transborder litigation. European institutions should promote coordination among MS' Courts before which are tried cases including consumer claimants coming from other MS. Procedural economies would be required to choose one court and thus one MS, but the differences in substantive and procedural law may not make the choice costless.[185] Subclassing, according to different applicable state laws, may also be a solution that can favour aggregation without being subordinated to the existence of a uniform body of laws across MS;[186]
e) providing the ground for mutual references to the facts as determined by a court or by a public authority in transboundary litigation;[187]
f) fostering mutual recognition of judgments to a higher extent than it has so far been achieved;[188]
g) regulating uniformly Courts' approval of settlements with particular concern for fair distribution of proceedings and preclusion effects, also in order to avoid replicating litigation for the same case in different MS.[189] In particular for settlements involving consumers, coming from different jurisdictions, trying cases before different courts, it would be useful to draft common rules given the differences in national regimes of contract law, predominantly regulating settlement arrangements;
h) modifying the consumer *acquis* to adjust substantive law to aggregate litigation;

185 Similar issues have arisen in the Canadian experience where the Uniform Law Commission of Canada has produced a set of proposals available at www.chlc.ca.

186 This path is chosen sometimes in the US. See In re Welding Fume Products Liability Litig. 245 *F.R.D.* 279 (N.D. Ohio 2007): "*A Court could manage the differences in medical monitoring law among the eight states chosen by the plaintiffs by holding separate separate trials for each state-wide sub class, or perhaps a combined trial for a few statewide subclasses, where the law in those states is similar enough to allow the creation of jury instructions and a verdict form that is not too complex.*", cited by the Reporters note in the ALI Principles, p. 162.

187 R. Stürner, 'Rechtsdurchsetzung durch Gewährung von Klaganreihen?', supra n. 127, p. 113, 127.

188 Rott, in this volume demonstrates that the Brussels Convention, as well as the Brussels Regulation does not face the phenomenon on the mutual recognition of group action judgments and/or settlements.

189 In the US, state court settlements are much less stable than federal court settlements, where the approving Court can provide better preclusion safeguards, see R. Nagareda, 'Class actions in the administrative state: Kalven and Rosenfield Revisited', *U. Chi L.R.* 75, 2008, available at SSRN: http://ssrn.com/abstract=1014659.

i) improving private international law rules in both Rome I and Rome II to adjust substantive law of tort and contracts to mass litigation in a uniform way;[190]
j) coordinating with the review process of Injunctions Directive 98/27;[191]
k) coordinating with the strategy concerning disputes on small claims defined by Regulation 861/2007.[192]

The overall question will nevertheless be to what extent it is possible to elaborate guidelines or recommendations on how jurisdictional conflicts between multiple competent courts might be solved. Ideally the above mentioned actors of civil society should participate. However, the four parties do not share common interests. Judges might be interested in avoiding duplication of work and favour a single court solution. Lawyers are squeezed between efficiency considerations which speak in favour of a single court solution, and profit interests which might be better served in regionalised judicial markets. Only consumer organisations are structurally bound to a single court solution at least as long as the interest of 'their' consumers are taken into account. The role and function of the MSs and the European Commission needs to be redesigned. MSs are reluctant to grant powers to the EU to adopt a European group action. They might be less reluctant in supporting the search for appropriate solutions of multiple competent courts. However, the born leader in such an initiative is certainly the European Commission.

4. CONCLUDING REMARKS

Consumer law enforcement laws have been subject to important changes both in Europe and the US. The meaning of enforcement and its modes have changed. The public/private divide does not overlap with administrative versus judicial

190 In case of aggregate litigation where consumers come from different jurisdictions regulated by different substantive laws it is necessary to engage in a choice of law analysis and verify whether common legal issues arise. The ALI Principles §2.05 suggest this.
(b) The Court may authorise aggregate treatment of multiple claims, or of a common issue therein, when the Court determines that:
(1) a single body of laws applies to all such claims or issues;
(2) different claims or issues are subject to different bodies of law that are the same in functional content; or
(3) different claims or issues are subject to different bodies of law that are not the same in functional content but do present a limited number of patterns that the Court, for reasons articulated pursuant to §2.12, can manage means of identified procedures at trial.

191 See Report from the Commission concerning the application of Directive 98/27 of the European Parliament and of the Council on injunctions for the protection of consumers, Brussels, 18 November 2008 COM (2008) 756.

192 OJ L 199, 31 July 2007, 1.

enforcement. Judicial enforcement encompasses both administrative and market-based regulatory devices (contract and extra-contractual liability).

Both in relation to administrative and judicial enforcement the adversarial approach is losing its appeal due to an increasing number of settlements and more broad contracting.

The use of contracting affects not only rule-making but also enforcement. It may increase compliance especially when repeat players are the infringers. The role of negotiation and settlement is expanding, both in administrative regulation and in adjudication. The differences cannot be located in the process of contractualization, affecting both types of enforcement, but in the modes of contractualization which still widely differ.

We have developed the analysis along the relationship between administrative and judicial enforcement, focusing predominantly on the remedial alternatives provided by the latter. The premise is that subfields of consumer legislation diverge significantly and often require different enforcement strategies, especially as to the combination between injunctions and pecuniary remedies. The goal of expanding consumer choices has an impact not only on rule-making and on the regulatory choices but also on the selection of enforcement strategies.

In Europe from the second half of the nineties of the last century law reforms have been enacted introducing first injunctions and then, at the national level, group actions; these changes have not materialised in a floodgate of litigation. On the contrary the first analyses reveal a certain degree of ineffectiveness if measured only by the rate of litigation.[193] Even from a theoretical standpoint, however, it is debatable that the success of the new statutes should be measured by the increase of litigation. The deterrence effect may play in the opposite direction; the best laws are those that ensure a higher level of safety and lower levels of litigation.

The main goal of the law reforms was not, of course the quantitative increase of litigation, but its qualitative improvement, certainly coupled with a higher degree of justice accessibility. But it is clear that a higher level of litigation than before is expected and socially desirable. Costs and time effective litigation is an important public good for modern democracies. Some efforts should be made, especially by political scientists and economists to improve methodologies in measuring effectiveness and impact so that more rapid readjustments concerning collective enforcement can be adopted at EU level. Which combinations of

---

193 See for example the analysis of Lindblom concerning the low level of litigation in Sweden. He identifies numerous potential factors: "the plaintiff's cost liability- which also applies to public organisation actions – the absence of state funds that support litigation, the absolute opt-in requirement, the lack of pre-trial discovery, the lack of a post-trial calculation mechanism and standardized computation of damages ... the negative attitude among insurance companies, and the negative stance of the Swedish bar association as well as the general problems – primarily slowness, costs and lack of expertise – which make it hard for even ordinary litigation to compete against arbitration and other forms of alternative dispute resolution in a free market.".

judgments and settlements are socially desirable is hard to predict but certainly some regulation of settlements and a higher level of transparency will contribute to consumer protection.

A European path towards aggregate litigation is developing but the differences with the US regime are still very significant. This is certainly due to the different institutional frameworks but it is also related to the high level of knowledge that Europeans have about the advantages and disadvantages of the US systems. The learning process has involved other common law experiences, particularly those of mixed jurisdictions like Canada, but also Australia, where effective law reform have taken place. South American countries have developed interesting law reforms that deserve more attention than it has been so far devoted.

Europeans will proceed towards an integrated path to combine administrative and judicial enforcement. This combination will partly depend on how effective administrative and judicial coordination will be within and between them. The opt-in/opt-out alternative is losing policy attraction. It has become clear that integrating the two might be the most desirable solution. The opt-in, at least for the time being, seems the most desirable when private claimants act; the opt-out may be a viable alternative when public bodies act, since they are bound by stricter rules of compliance with the rule of law, accountability, transparency and openness. Due process rights would thus still be guaranteed in an opt-out system when public entities bring the claims before the Courts.

In the US, important changes have also been taking place. On the one hand, the use of litigation as a regulatory device has been limited and channelled to be complemented by administrative regulation. The transformation moves in two directions from the State to the federal level and from the judicial to the administration. CAFA and the recent Supreme Court case law show a movement towards federalisation of judicial collective enforcement.[194] Supreme Court case law has also rebalanced federal statutory regulation and state common law of torts, strengthening administrative regulation.

The move towards a stronger role for administrative regulation has different meanings across the Atlantic. Different accountability systems have been associated with this development in the US and Europe. While in the US stronger procedural rights have been associated with tort immunity, in Europe weaker procedural rights are combined with a fast growing expansion of tort liability of public regulators. Other differences are related to the internal changes of the regulatory process and the shift from *ex ante* to *ex post* within public regulation.[195]

194 C. Hazard, Jr., Has the Erie Doctrine Been Replaced By Congress?, 156 U. Pa. L. Rev. 1629 (2008), S. Issacharoff, 'Governance and legitimacy in the law of class actions', S. Ct. Rev. 337 (1999).

195 For references see Cafaggi/Micklitz, supra n. 3; R. Nagareda, Aggregate Litigation Across the Atlantic and the Future of American Exceptionalism, Vanderbilt L.R. Vol. 62, p. 1 (2009).

To what extent the comparative scenario just described will affect the modes of consumer international litigation? The new challenge ahead is consumer international litigation, where different models will be compared not as a purely academic exercise but as a matter of concrete litigation strategy for litigating consumer matters.[196] Today, unlike thirty or forty years ago, it is possible to respond to worldwide consumer violations with an international strategy where choice of forum but also the best available means can be chosen by consumer advocates. While AE both at EU and US level is not only a viable complement to judicial enforcement but at times the most effective path, at the international level, judicial enforcement seems to represent the way ahead for the years to come until hybrid effective and accountable institutions emerge.

196 See R. Nagareda, supra n. 195.

INDEX

G

I

L

M

P

U

www.ingramcontent.com/pod-product-compliance
Ingram Content Group UK Ltd.
Pitfield, Milton Keynes, MK11 3LW, UK
UKHW051918100926
8556IPUK00021B/1248

9 789050 957786